重　要

付属音声は、パソコンや携帯音楽プレーヤーで利用できる **MP3 ファイル形式** です。一般的なラジカセや音楽 CD プレーヤーでは再生できませんので、ご注意ください。

●音声ファイル（MP3 形式）の利用方法

1 CD-ROM の中身を表示

CD-ROM をパソコンに挿入したあと、左のような画面が出る場合は **〈フォルダを開いてファイルを表示〉** をクリック。CD-ROM の中身を表示させます。

※左の画面が出ない場合は、〈スタート〉⇒〈コンピュータ〉⇒〈CD/DVD/BD ドライブ（でる模試 600 問）〉をダブルクリック。

コレをクリック。

2 フォルダーをパソコン上にコピー

CD-ROM の中身が表示されたら、TEST 1、TEST 2 などの 6 つのフォルダーをパソコン上にコピーします。**フォルダを選択し、希望する場所にドラッグ & ドロップ** すれば、コピーが始まります。

この 6 つのフォルダーをコピーしたい場所にドラッグ & ドロップ。

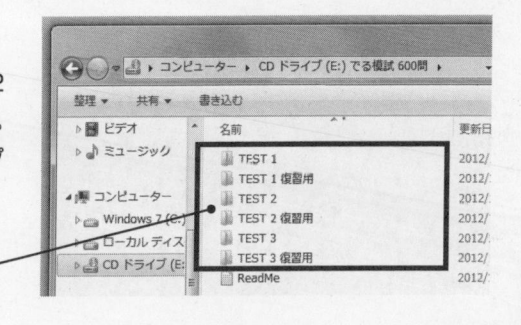

3 iTunes への読み込み

iTunes を起動したら、ライブラリの〈ミュージック〉を開きます。次に、手順 2 で保存した場所から **6 つのフォルダを iTunes の画面上にドラッグ & ドロップ** すると、iTunes に音声ファイルが読み込まれ、利用できるようになります。

① ここで〈ミュージック〉を選ぶ。

② iTunes の画面上にドラッグ & ドロップ。

※ 2013 年 4 月現在の最新のソフトウェアをもとに解説しています。アップデートにより操作方法が変更される場合があります。
※ Windows Media Player での利用方法、Mac での利用方法は CD-ROM 内の〔ReadMe.txt〕ファイルをご参照ください。

新TOEIC® テスト
でる模試 600問

ハッカーズ語学研究所 著

ask PUBLISHING

Copyright © 2012 Hackers Language Research Institute Co., Ltd.
Published in Japan, 2012

This edition is published in Japan under a License Agreement between Hackers Language Research Institute Co., Ltd. and ASK Publishing Co., Ltd. through Eric Yang Agency, Inc.

All rights reserved. NO part of this Publication may be reproduced, stored in a retrieval system, or transmitted, in any form or by any means, electronic or mechanical, including photocopying, recording, or otherwise, without the prior written permission of the copyright owner, Hackers Language Research Institute Co., Ltd.

Japanese edition copyright © 2012 ASK Publishing Co., Ltd.

Copyright © 2012 Educational Testing Service. www.ets.org

The TOEIC® Test Directions are reprinted by permission of Educational Testing Service, the copyright owner. All other information contained within this publication is provided by Hackers Language Research Institute Co., Ltd. and Ask Publishing Co., Ltd. No endorsement of any kind by Educational Testing Service should be inferred.

日本版英語翻訳 ── 天満 嗣雄
　　　　　　　　　山口 晴代
　　　　　　　　　遠藤 功樹
　　　　　　　　　株式会社 CPI Japan

日本版韓国語翻訳 ── 博文国際株式会社
　　　　　　　　　　有限会社 コーディネートワン・インターナショナル

コラム執筆 ─── 濵﨑潤之輔
　　　　　　　　porpor
　　　　　　　　50歳のおじさん

編集協力 ─── 株式会社 メディアビーコン
　　　　　　　株式会社 鷗来堂

音声編集 ─── 株式会社 巧芸創作

はじめに

2011年初夏、ソウル。

　はじめてハッカーズのオフィス兼学校を訪問したときのことです。朝9時ごろだったでしょうか。タクシーを降りた私の目の前にある正面玄関は、学生でごったがえしていました。
　感心した私は、「朝早くからみなさん熱心ですね」と、案内をしてくれた担当者に声をかけました。しかし、彼女は、けげんな顔をしています。一瞬考えてから「あぁ、夏休み中は、みんな6時半から自習してますから」との返答が！　驚きました。彼らにしてみれば、9時というのは、ちっとも朝早くなんかなかったのですね。
　これが、ハッカーズ・ショックの始まりでした。

●OPEN HOURS：上から3つ目が「自習室」が開いている時間を示している

　学内でも驚きの連続です。100名以上入る教室が、どれもすし詰め状態。休み時間には、ドアの前に長蛇の列ができています。少しでもよい席に座りたくて、並んで待っているのです。
　自習室をのぞいてみれば、学生同士で教え合うチームラーニングに取り組んだり、黙々とひとりテキストに向かったり。学習スタイルはさまざまですが、真剣な学生であふれ返っていました。
　私は、ただ、ただ、彼らのTOEICに対する熱意に圧倒されました。

●教室が空くのを待つ学生たち：少しでもよい席に座ろうと並んでいる

　韓国の代表的な書店であるKyobo文庫本店に場を移しても、ショッキングな光景は続きます。TOEICコーナーが賑わっているのは、日本と変わりませんが、並んでいる参考書の大きくて分厚いこと。電話帳かと見まがうばかりです。しかも、手に取ってみると、それはリスニング対策で、リーディング対策はさらに別にあるのです。
　そして、そんなTOEICコーナーで、もっとも強烈な存在感を示していたのがハッカーズでした。日本で人気の『公式問題集』よりもはるかに目立っています。ランキングを見れば、語学ジャンルだけでなく、総合トップ20にまでランクインしているではありませんか。
　日本では、いくら売れているといっても、TOEICテキストが文芸書やビジネス書と並んで、ベストセラーリストにのぼるなんてことは、考えられません。

カフェで気持ちを落ち着けたあと、自然と頭に浮かんできたのは「なぜハッカーズはこんなに支持されるのか？」という疑問です。
　この謎を解くべく、ハッカーズのテキストを大量に買い込んだ私は、帰国後、片っ端から問題を解いていきました。ちょうど、990点獲得を目指して受験をくり返していた時期だったので、自分のスコア結果そのものがテキストの評価につながるだろうと考えました。

　仕事を終えたあと、連日深夜まで、マクドナルドで"電話帳"と格闘です。100円コーヒーを何度おかわりしたことか。
　当時、公開テストにおけるPart 7の難問化が進行していました。私も苦労をしていたので、たくさん読解問題を解きたいと思い、『HACKERS TOEIC 実戦1000題 LISTENING 2』、『HACKERS TOEIC 実戦1000題 READING 2』という模試本を重点的に取り組みました。
　読解素材の長さや難しさ、巧妙に仕掛けられたトリック。さすが、韓国を席巻するだけはある、と納得できるクオリティでした。ただ、その反面、Part 5などで「こんな難しい単語でないよ！」と感じる問題があり、小さな疑念も感じていました。

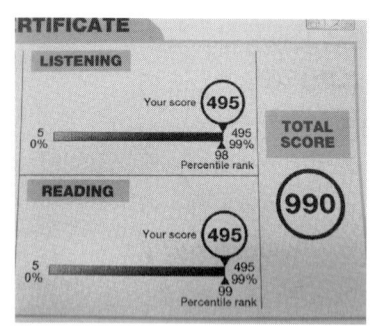

●ハッカーズのテキスト研究のおかげ

　しかし、それは、私の知ったかぶりに過ぎませんでした。というのも、私がバカにしたまさに、その単語が公開テストで出題されたのです（このときの「でた！」という驚きが本書のタイトルにつながっています）。おかげで私は、その問題に正解できましたし、2011年9月の公開テストでは、はじめての990点満点を獲得することもできました。
　ハッカーズのテキスト研究以外、とくにこれといった対策はしていません。原動力となったのは、間違いなくハッカーズでした。

　この模試本はすごい！　そう確信した私は、以降、この2冊を日本に紹介すべく、まっしぐらに努力をしてきました。今回、日本の事情に合せた内容を加味しつつ※、『新 TOEIC® テスト でる模試 600問』として、ハッカーズのテキストを提供できるのを、ほんとうにうれしく思います。必ずや、みなさんの学習を助ける1冊になります。ぜひ、ご活用ください。

アスク出版　編集担当 T

※本書は、日本の学習者のスタイルに合せ、原書『HACKERS TOEIC 実戦1000題 LISTENING 2』と『HACKERS TOEIC 実戦1000題 READING 2』の2,000問から600問を抜粋して掲載。また、「はじめに」「本書の使い方」「TOEIC® テスト 受験ガイド」「パート別の基本戦略」、および別冊の「TOEIC豆知識」「語註」は日本版のために加筆したものです。

目次 ● Contents

はじめに …… 3
目次 …… 5
マークシート …… 169

本書の使い方 —————————————— 6
本書の構成 …… 6
「本体」の使い方／模試への取り組み方 …… 7
「別冊 解答・解説」の使い方／答え合わせ・復習のやり方 …… 8
音声ファイルの使い方 …… 12
学習の進め方 …… 13

TOEIC® テスト 受験ガイド —————————— 15
TOEIC® テストって何だ？ …… 15
受験当日のシミュレーション …… 18

パート別の基本戦略 —————————————— 20

でる模試 TEST 1 ——————————————— 35

でる模試 TEST 2 ——————————————— 79

でる模試 TEST 3 ——————————————— 123

別 冊

別冊 解答・解説 TEST 1
別冊 解答・解説 TEST 2
別冊 解答・解説 TEST 3

本書の使い方

● ● ● 本書の構成

▌本 体

- 模試3回分（TEST 1／TEST 2／TEST 3）の問題
- スコア換算表
- TOEIC® テスト 受験ガイド
- パート別の基本戦略
- マークシート

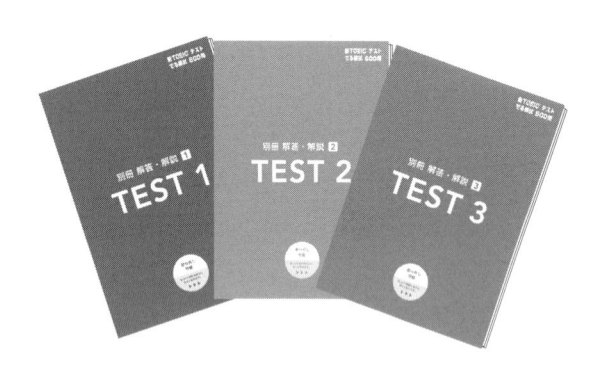

▌別冊 解答・解説（3分冊）

- 携帯しやすいように3分冊した、解答・解説
- 問題英文もすべて掲載

▌CD-ROM

MP3形式で音声データを収録

- 模試3回分の音声
- リーディング Part 5 の音声（※復習用）

☞ 詳細は、p.12の「音声ファイルの使い方」を参照

重要

本書に付属する音声は、パソコンや携帯音楽プレーヤーで利用できる **MP3** ファイル形式です。一般的なラジカセや音楽 CD プレーヤーでは再生できませんので、ご注意ください。

「本体」の使い方／模試への取り組み方

「本体」には、模試3回分を収録していますが、必ず以下の方法で解いてください！

本番と同じように解く！

TOEICでは、その"**特徴に慣れる**"というのが第一の受験対策。TOEIC独自のスタイルを体感すべく、必ず次の4点を守って、本番さながらに取り組んでください。

> ✓ ① 全200問を通して受験する
> ✓ ② 時間をキッチリ計り、2時間以内に解くことを強く意識する
> ✓ ③ マークシートに解答する
> ✓ ④ 受験中のメモや下線を禁止する

制限時間をオーバーしても最後まで

2時間以内に、解ききれなかった場合は、時計を止めずに、そのまま最後まで解答を続けます。そして、何分オーバーしたのかを記録してください。今後、短縮すべき時間の目安になります。

ただし、制限時間外に解いた問題については、たとえ正解しても、正答数にはカウントしません。

● 本体の巻末に収録しているマークシート。学習日・解答時間・正答数・予想スコアを記録する欄もあり。

「別冊 解答・解説」の使い方／答え合わせ・復習のやり方

模試を解いたあとは、「別冊 解答・解説」で答え合わせをし、右の〈スコア換算表〉で、予想スコアを算出してください。あなたのスコアレベルを知ることができます。

そして、もっとも重要なことですが、間違った問題については、**解説の読み込み**と**復習**が必須です。なぜなら、人は同じような問題をくり返し間違うからです。TOEIC本番で、誤りをくり返さないために、なぜ間違ったのか、その理由を認識しなければいけません。

そのために、次に紹介するふたつの機能を、ぜひ活用してください。

間違いメモ

解説を読むだけでは、知識は定着しません。そのときは、わかった気がしていても、翌日には忘れてしまうこともしばしば。そうならないために、間違った理由を自分のことばでメモしましょう。**自分で自分に、なぜ間違ったのかを説明してみる**のです。そのためのスペースがこの〈間違いメモ〉です。

☞ 使用例は、p.10〜11を参照

携帯用問題集

知識の定着には、**くり返し問題を解く**ことも効果的。間違った問題は、少し時間をあけて復習してください。

そのために、「別冊 解答・解説」を常に携帯し、問題集として活用してください。問題英文を掲載し、これだけで復習できるようになっています。

復習については、本番同様に受験する必要はありません。5分でも10分でも、**手があいた隙に数問ずつチャレンジ**しましょう。

カバーのソデを切り離して、目隠しとして利用できる！

●復習時に、訳や正解が見えにくいようレイアウトも工夫。本体カバーのソデを切り取って、目隠しとすれば、さらに使いやすくなります。

スコア換算表

答え合わせが終わったら、リスニングとリーディングの正答数を元に予想スコアを算出しましょう。ただし、この予想スコアはあくまで参考値とお考えください。

LISTENING							READING					
正答数	予想スコア	正答数	予想スコア	正答数	予想スコア	正答数	予想スコア	正答数	予想スコア	正答数	予想スコア
100	495	66	330	32	160	100	495	66	325	32	155
99	495	65	325	31	155	99	490	65	320	31	150
98	490	64	320	30	150	98	485	64	315	30	145
97	485	63	315	29	145	97	480	63	310	29	140
96	480	62	310	28	140	96	475	62	305	28	135
95	475	61	305	27	135	95	470	61	300	27	130
94	470	60	300	26	130	94	465	60	295	26	125
93	465	59	295	25	125	93	460	59	290	25	120
92	460	58	290	24	120	92	455	58	285	24	115
91	455	57	285	23	115	91	450	57	280	23	110
90	450	56	280	22	110	90	445	56	275	22	105
89	445	55	275	21	105	89	440	55	270	21	100
88	440	54	270	20	100	88	435	54	265	20	95
87	435	53	265	19	95	87	430	53	260	19	90
86	430	52	260	18	90	86	425	52	255	18	85
85	425	51	255	17	85	85	420	51	250	17	80
84	420	50	250	16	80	84	415	50	245	16	75
83	415	49	245	15	75	83	410	49	240	15	70
82	410	48	240	14	70	82	405	48	235	14	65
81	405	47	235	13	65	81	400	47	230	13	60
80	400	46	230	12	60	80	395	46	225	12	55
79	395	45	225	11	55	79	390	45	220	11	50
78	390	44	220	10	50	78	385	44	215	10	45
77	385	43	215	9	45	77	380	43	210	9	40
76	380	42	210	8	40	76	375	42	205	8	35
75	375	41	205	7	35	75	370	41	200	7	30
74	370	40	200	6	30	74	365	40	195	6	25
73	365	39	195	5	25	73	360	39	190	5	20
72	360	38	190	4	20	72	355	38	185	4	15
71	355	37	185	3	15	71	350	37	180	3	10
70	350	36	180	2	10	70	345	36	175	2	10
69	345	35	175	1	5	69	340	35	170	1	10
68	340	34	170			68	335	34	165		
67	335	33	165			67	330	33	160		

別冊の使い方《図解》

1 音声ファイル
見開きで利用する音声のトラック名（曲名）をまとめて表示。
☞ 音声ファイルについてはp.12を参照

2 訳
すべての英文（選択肢を含む）に訳を用意。

※内容はダミーです。

TEST 1 PART 1　音声ファイル 🔊 T1_P1_Q01 ▶ T1_P1_Q05
問題&訳

1.
(A) She is boarding a bus.
(B) She is reading a book.
(C) She is using an office equipment.
(D) She is going outside.

(A) 彼女はバスに乗り込もうとしている。
(B) 彼女は本を読んでいる。
(C) 彼女はオフィス機器を使用している。
(D) 彼女は外に出ようとしている。

6 問題英文・写真
別冊だけで問題を解けるように、写真や問題英文も掲載。

7 ナレーターの国籍表示
英文を読み上げているナレーターの国籍を表示。
🇺🇸 アメリカ
🇬🇧 イギリス
🇦🇺 オーストラリア

③ 正解・解説・難易度
可能な限り詳しい解説を掲載。
5段階での難易度表示もあり。
Part 7では ⇄ で表現の言い換え（パラフレーズ）を明示。

④ TOEIC豆知識
知っているときっと役に立つ(!?)
TOEICトリビアを紹介。

⑤ 重要語句
重要な単語や熟語を紹介。
別冊巻末には索引もあり。

TOEIC豆知識 公開テストのスコアがインターネットで公開される日は、回線が混雑してTOEIC SQUAREサイトにつながらないことも多い。そんなときは、携帯用のサイト(http://m.toeic.or.jp)をチェックしてみて。すんなりスコアを確認できることが多い。

正解＆解説

1. 正解 (C)　　　難易度 ■■■□□ 難

女性がコピー機を操作している様子を is using an office equipment（オフィス機器を使用している）と描写した (C) がもっとも適切。(A) のバスは見当たらない。(B) の a book は写っているが、女性は読んでいない。女性は外に出ようとしていないので、(D) の描写も写真に一致しない。

間違いメモ＆単語

あなたの解答　A B C D
メモ
_____
_____
_____

☐ board 〜に乗り込む
☐ outside 外で、屋外へ

〈間違いメモ〉の使い方

① 誤答を記録
A ✗ C D：はじめて模試を解いたときに、間違った選択肢にチェックを入れておきます。復習時に再度間違えば ✗。3回目は ✗ というように記録。こうすれば、あなたが苦手とするポイントがひと目でわかります。

② メモ
間違った理由を、自分で自分に説明するつもりで、書き留めておきましょう。解説の要点を書き換えるだけでも構いません。

③ テスト直前に見直し
受験当日、会場入りしてから、自分のメモを見直しましょう。最高の直前対策になります！

あなたの解答　A ✗ C D
メモ
動作を表す is putting on に
ひっかかった！

音声ファイルの使い方

　CD-ROMに収録している音声は、パソコンや携帯音楽プレーヤーで再生が可能なMP3ファイル形式です。一般的なラジカセや音楽CDプレーヤーでは再生できないので、ご注意ください。

CD-ROMの中身

　模試ごとに、音声が収録されています。また、復習用のPart 5の音声もフォルダを分けて収録。これらを、iTunesやWindows Media Playerなどの、再生アプリケーションに取り込んでご利用ください。その手順は〔ReadMe.txt〕に記しています。

　携帯音楽プレーヤーへの取り込み方法については、各プレーヤーの説明書をご覧ください。

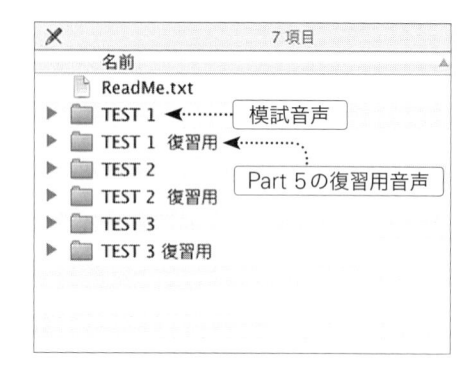

　音声ファイルにはすべて**書名**（アルバム名）、**出版社名**（アーティスト名）、**トラック名**（曲名）を設定済み。

① **書名（アルバム名）**：模試ごとに、『新TOEICテスト でる模試600問〈TEST 1〉』、『同〈TEST 2〉』、『同〈TEST 3〉』に設定。また、復習用音声については、『同〈TEST 1〉復習』と設定しています。

② **出版社名（アーティスト名）**：すべて「アスク出版」と設定。

③ **トラック名（曲名）**：どの問題の音声かがすぐにわかるよう、次のルールで曲名を設定しています。

T［模試回］**_P**［パート番号］**_Q**［問題番号］

例）　**T1_P2_Q23** ……〈TEST 1〉のPart 2、問題番号No.23の音声
　　　T2_P4_74-76 ……〈TEST 2〉のPart 4、No.74～76の説明文音声
　　　T2_P4_Q74-76 …〈TEST 2〉のPart 4、No.74～76の設問音声

　　　　　　　※ Part 3と4では、会話・説明文と設問を別ファイルにしています。
　　　　　　　　設問音声のほうに、「Q」が付いています。

　例外的にディレクションは〈T1_P1_Dir〉、リスニングの終わりを知らせる音声は〈T1_P4_End〉と設定。

学習の進め方

「模試への取り組み方」と「答え合わせ・復習のやり方」(p.7～8)を最低限守って、あとは、自分にあった学習を進めてください。

ただ、「勉強のやり方がわからない！」という方のために、次の2つの学習モデルをオススメします。

1週間モデル

受験まで間がない場合に、**① TOEICへの慣れ**、**②間違いやすいポイントの削減**、に重点をおいたモデル。

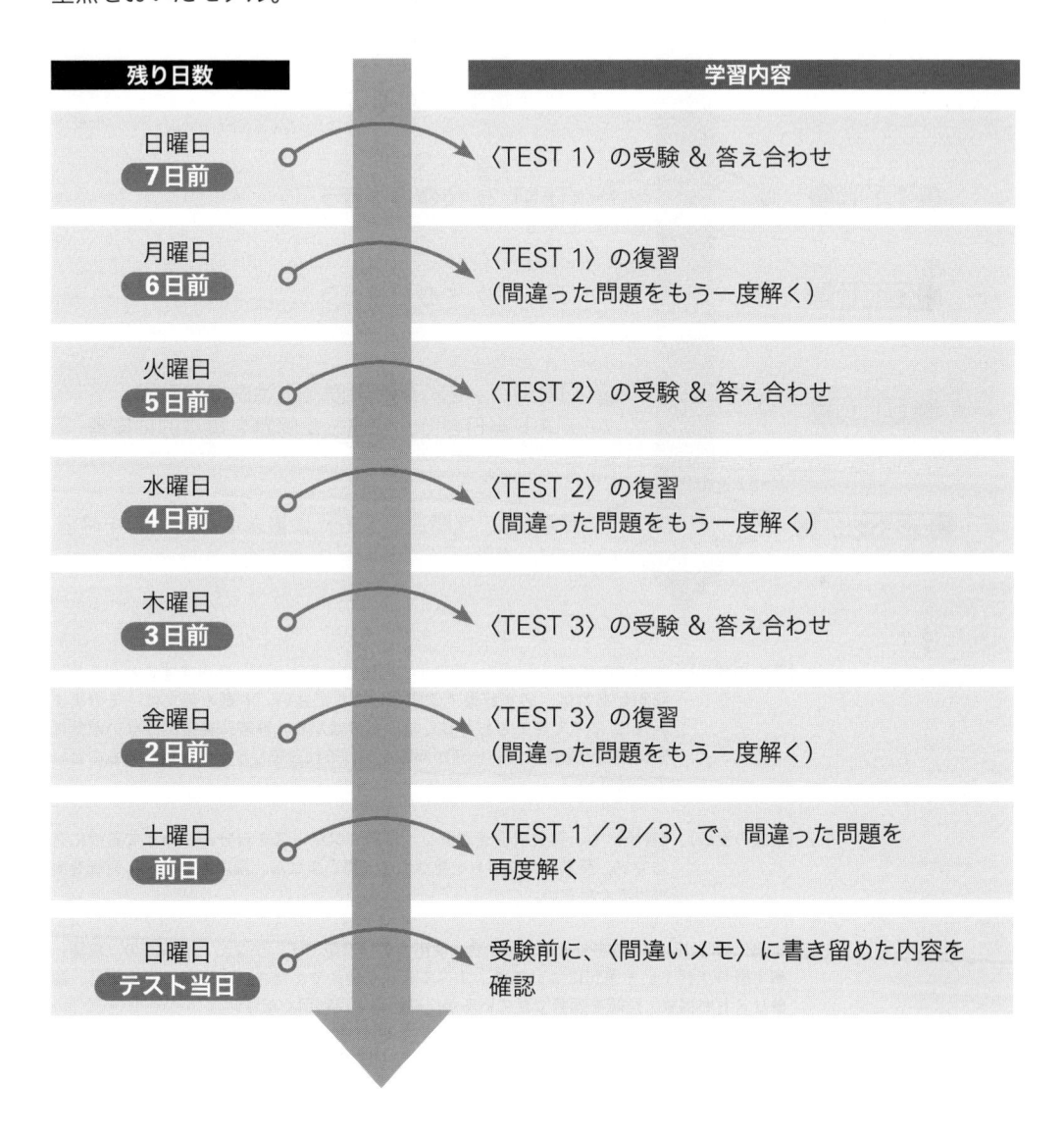

残り日数	学習内容
日曜日 7日前	〈TEST 1〉の受験 & 答え合わせ
月曜日 6日前	〈TEST 1〉の復習 （間違った問題をもう一度解く）
火曜日 5日前	〈TEST 2〉の受験 & 答え合わせ
水曜日 4日前	〈TEST 2〉の復習 （間違った問題をもう一度解く）
木曜日 3日前	〈TEST 3〉の受験 & 答え合わせ
金曜日 2日前	〈TEST 3〉の復習 （間違った問題をもう一度解く）
土曜日 前日	〈TEST 1／2／3〉で、間違った問題を再度解く
日曜日 テスト当日	受験前に、〈間違いメモ〉に書き留めた内容を確認

1カ月モデル

十分な準備期間がある場合の学習法。このモデルでは、〈1週間モデル〉の2点に加え、③ **英文をしっかり理解すること**、④ **頻出表現や単語を身につけること**、に重点をおきます。

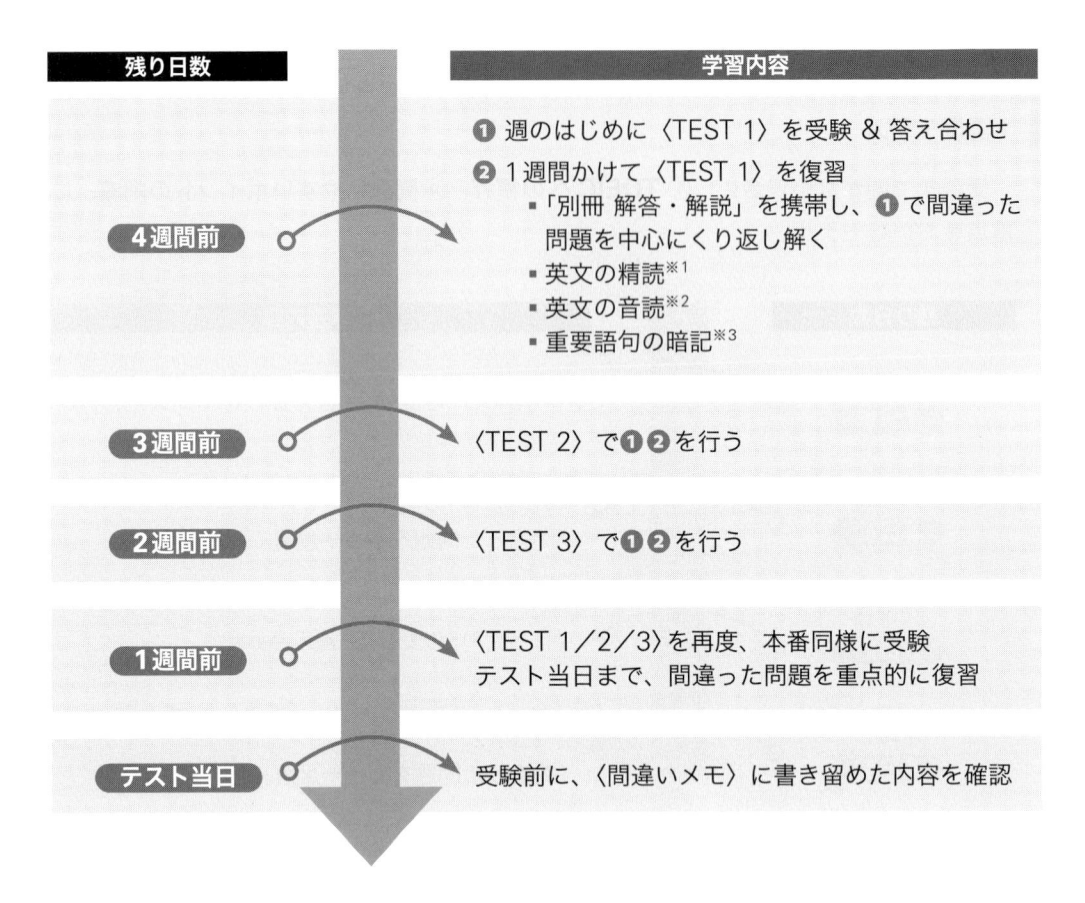

残り日数	学習内容
4週間前	❶ 週のはじめに〈TEST 1〉を受験 & 答え合わせ ❷ 1週間かけて〈TEST 1〉を復習 ・「別冊 解答・解説」を携帯し、❶で間違った問題を中心にくり返し解く ・英文の精読[※1] ・英文の音読[※2] ・重要語句の暗記[※3]
3週間前	〈TEST 2〉で❶❷を行う
2週間前	〈TEST 3〉で❶❷を行う
1週間前	〈TEST 1／2／3〉を再度、本番同様に受験 テスト当日まで、間違った問題を重点的に復習
テスト当日	受験前に、〈間違いメモ〉に書き留めた内容を確認

※1【英文の精読】 すべての英文について、細部まで理解できるよう読み込みます。わからない語句があれば、必ず辞書で確認をしてください。本書の英文は、そのままTOEICにでてきてもおかしくないものばかり。解答に直接関係ない部分にも、頻出の単語やフレーズが満載です。それらをしっかり、自分のものとしてください。

※2【英文の音読】 〈音読〉も、英文構造を理解し、単語やフレーズを自分のものとするのに有効です。英文スクリプトを見ながらで構いません。音声を参考に、音読を実践してください。

※3 本書にはTOEICに必ずでる単語・熟語・慣用表現が満載です。少なくとも解説の「単語」欄で取り上げている語句については、すべて意味を覚えてください。別冊の巻末には、語彙リストも掲載。意味を理解できているか、確認用にご利用ください。

TOEIC® テスト 受験ガイド

TOEIC® テストって何だ？

Q1 • TOEIC® って、どんなテスト？

A • TOEIC（トイック／トーイック）は、アメリカにある世界最大の教育研究機関 Educational Testing Service が制作したテストで、日本では国際ビジネスコミュニケーション協会がライセンスを受けて実施しています。日本での受験者数は右肩上がりで、2012年度に過去最高の**年間230万人**を突破！

楽天株式会社やユニクロ（株式会社ファーストリテイリング）が、全社員に一定スコアの獲得を義務づけるなど、**ビジネス英語運用能力を測る基準**として定着しています。

> ちなみに、韓国の受験者は年間211万人。人口が日本の半分以下であることを考えると、すごい数ですね。さらに、大卒新入社員に900点以上のスコアを求める企業もたくさんあります。韓国がTOEIC大国と言われる由縁は、こうした数値からもうかがえます。

Q2 • 合格点はいくつ？

A • TOEIC に、合格点はありません！ 評価は、**10〜990点のスコア**で行われます。従って、受験級というのもありません。

そのスコアですが、試験日から30日以内に郵送される、「公式認定証」に記載されています。もし、インターネットで受験申込をし、「テスト結果インターネット表示」を「利用する」を選んでいれば、公式認定証よりも早く、スコアを確認することが可能です。

日本の平均点は、2013年6月のテストで、**583.0点**。なので、はじめて受験する人にとっては、600点突破がひとつの目標になるでしょうね。

> 韓国の直近の平均点は640.83点！（※2013年6月実施回）

Q3 • どんな問題がでるの？

A • リスニングとリーディングふたつのセクションに分かれており、解答はすべてマークシートで行います。スピーキングやライティングの能力は問われません。

所要時間は2時間で、問題数は200問！ 浴びるように英語を聞いて、読んで、問題に答えなければいけません。英語を理解する力に加え、情報を素早く、的確に処理する能力が問われます。

> スピーキングとライティングについては、別にTOEIC Speaking and Writing Testsというものがあります。

15

パート	リスニング				リーディング		
	Part 1	Part 2	Part 3	Part 4	Part 5	Part 6	Part 7
問題のタイプ	写真描写問題	応答問題	会話問題	説明文問題	短文穴埋め問題	長文穴埋め問題	読解問題
問題数	10	30	30	30	40	12	48
所要時間	約45分				75分		

Q4. いつ受けられる？

A. 2013年から1・3・4・5・6・7・9・10・11・12月の**年10回実施**。ただし、地方都市では毎回実施されるわけではないので注意してください（下のQ5 参照）。

> 韓国は、2011年は年14回実施（毎月1回に加え、2・8月に2回実施）。

Q5. どこで受けられる？

A. 全国80都市での受験が可能です。しかし、受験地ごとに実施回が異なるため、特に地方在住の方は注意が必要です。詳細は公式Webサイト（http://www.toeic.or.jp/）に案内があります。

指定できるのは、「東京」「福岡」といった都市だけで、受験会場は指定できません。会場は、受験票（試験の2週間前に郵送）が届いてはじめてわかります。

Q6. いくらで受けられる？

A. 受験料は**5,565円**（税込）。ただし、〈インターネット申込〉を行うと、1年後の同月に実施される回の受験料が4,950円（税込）になる「リピート受験割引サービス」があります。

> 韓国の受験料は42,000ウォン。2012年10月1日の為替レートで、約2,940円です。安い!!

Q7. 申込方法

A. 申込方法は、①〈インターネット申込〉と②〈コンビニ端末申込〉の2種類。

①〈インターネット申込〉

TOEIC SQUARE（http://square.toeic.or.jp/）で会員登録（無料）をし、ネット上で申込みます。支払い方法は「クレジットカード」、「コンビニ支払い」、「楽天あんしん支払いサービス」の3種類。

> サイト上でのスコア確認や、「リピート受験割引サービス」、「楽天あんしん支払いサービス」（楽天のポイントを利用可能）など、特典が多い①の申込方法がオススメです。

② 〈コンビニ端末申込〉

　　セブン-イレブン、ローソン、ファミリーマート、ミニストップに設置されている、情報端末を使って申し込む方法。

Q8. やってはいけないことってある？

A. カンニングはもちろん許されませんが、そのほか、次のようなことも禁止。

① 試験中のメモや、下線を引くこと。

② リスニング中にリーディングセクションの問題を見る・解くこと。また、その逆。

③ 携帯電話やスマートフォンを時計代わりに使うこと。もちろんアラームや受信音を鳴らすことは厳禁。この点は、非常に厳しくて試験前に電源を落としているか確認があり、かばんにしまうよう指示されます。

④ 問題冊子と解答用紙の持ち出し。TOEICの問題は完全非公開です。解答用紙はもちろん、問題冊子も試験後回収され、全数揃っていることが確認できるまで、退出できません。

● Webサイト／問い合わせ先

```
TOEIC 公式サイト    ☞  http://www.toeic.or.jp/
TOEIC SQUARE       ☞  http://square.toeic.or.jp/
```

（一財）国際ビジネスコミュニケーション協会

- **IIBC試験運営センター**　〒100-0014　東京都千代田区永田町2-14-2　山王グランドビル
  　TEL：03-5521-6033　FAX：03-3581-4783
  　（土・日・祝日・年末年始を除く 10:00〜17:00）

- **名古屋事業所**　〒460-0003　名古屋市中区錦2-4-3　錦パークビル
  　TEL：052-220-0286
  　（土・日・祝日・年末年始を除く 10:00〜17:00）

- **大阪事業所**　〒541-0059　大阪府大阪市中央区博労町3-6-1　御堂筋エスジービル
  　TEL：06-6258-0224
  　（土・日・祝日・年末年始を除く 10:00〜17:00）

受験当日のシミュレーション

テスト当日の流れを整理しておきましょう。特に、**前日〜会場入り**までの流れをよく確認しておいてください。この部分をおろそかにすると、万全の体制で試験に臨めません。

日 時	流 れ
前日	・受験票への写真の貼付 ・必要なものを用意　※右ページのリストを参照 ・受験会場までの移動手段と所要時間を確認。そこから逆算して、当日の出発時間を決めておく
当日朝	**朝食と昼食のタイミングに注意が必要** ・テストはちょうど昼どきにスタート。満腹すぎても、空腹すぎても、実力を発揮できないので、早めの昼食（もしくは、遅めの朝食）を取るように！
11:45〜12:30	**入場** ・身分証明証と受験票を受付に提示して入場。 ・指定された席につき、解答用紙（マークシート）のA面に受験番号や氏名など必要事項を記入する。
12:35頃	**ガイダンスの開始** ・受験の手引きが日本語で放送される。 **音テスト** ・音量・音質の確認。聞こえ難ければ、遠慮なく係員に伝えて、座席を変更してもらう。
12:45	**受験票Bの回収** ・身分証明書の確認も同時に行われる。 ・携帯電話の電源が切れているかも確認され、かばんにしまうよう指示。 ・これ以降、机上に置けるのは、筆記用具、時計、解答用紙のみ。 ※2013年9月のテストより、受付後のトイレ休憩がなくなったので要注意。 **問題冊子の配布** ・問題冊子にも、受験番号と氏名を記入。 （5分ほど待ち時間）

> 手慣れた受験者のなかには、試験直前に栄養ドリンクを飲む人も多いようです。

> 要望があれば、遠慮なく係員に言ってみましょう。親切に対応してくれます。

日 時	流 れ
13:00	**テスト開始！** ・「間もなくリスニングテストを開始します」のアナウンス後、リスニングセクションがスタート。 （Part 1～4と音声に従って解答を進める）
13:45頃	**リスニング終了、リーディングスタート** ・指示は特にないので、すぐに Part 5 に取りかかる。
14:05	**Part 5を終了** （※目標時刻：☞詳細は pp.30～31を参照）
14:11	**Part 6を終了** （※目標時刻：☞詳細は p.32を参照）
15:00頃	**テスト終了！** **解答用紙、問題冊子の回収** ・全数あるかの確認。
15:05頃	退場

● 必要なものリスト

☐ 受験票	・写真の貼付と署名欄への記入を忘れないこと。 ・写真の大きさは、4×3 cm。白黒でも可。
☐ 本人確認書類	・写真付きの身分証明書。運転免許証、パスポート、社員証、学生証、住民基本台帳カードなど。
☐ 時計	・会場には時計がない場合も多いので必ず用意。携帯電話を時計代わりに使うことはできません。
☐ 鉛筆2～3本 （シャープペン）	・マークのしやすさから、鉛筆のほうがオススメ。必ず複数本持参すること。 ・シャープペンの場合は、替え芯を忘れずに！
☐ 消しゴム	

パート別基本戦略

全体戦略

　ここからは、少しでも高スコアを獲得するための基本戦略を説明していきます。まずは、全体的な戦略から。

あきらめる勇気！

　TOEICのスコアは正答数をもとに算出されます。各問題の**配点は均一**なので、単純に正答数が多ければ、スコアも高くなります。ということは、難しい問題を1問捨ててでも、やさしい問題を2問正解したほうが、高スコアがでるわけです。

　800点以上のハイスコアを目指すのでない限り、わからない問題に固執しないことです。あきらめる勇気を持って、「**取れる問題から取っていく**」。それが、基本中の基本戦略なのです。

ディレクションは無視！

　各パートの冒頭には、〈**ディレクション**〉と呼ばれる指示文が印刷されています（リスニングセクションでは、音声もあり）。これは、各パートの問題形式を説明するもので、特に重要なことは述べられていません。

　本書の模試に同一のものを掲載しています。事前に内容を把握しておき、本番ではおもいっきり無視しましょう。そのぶんの時間を解答にあてます。

　日本語訳は、p.22からのパート別解説に掲載。

●Part 1のディレクション

自分なりのマーキング方法の確立

　ていねいにマークしようとするあまり、必要以上に時間がかかっていないか、意識してみましょう。そんな細かいこと、とバカにするなかれ。200問を矢継ぎ早に解かなければならないTOEICでは、**コンマ何秒の時間も貴重**です。

　やはりシャープペンよりも、すこし先の丸くなった**鉛筆**の方が効率的にマークできると思います。あるいは、マークシート専用のシャープペンというものも販売されているので、活用してみるのもいいでしょう。

　また、リスニング中は解答欄に、**小さな印**だけをつけておき、リーディングに入った瞬間、まとめて塗りつぶす、というテクニックもあります。

　いずれにしろ、本書を通して、**自分にあったマーキング方法**を確立してから、TOEIC本番に臨みましょう。

●リスニング中は音に集中するため、印だけつけるテクニックもあり

ペン先ずらしマーキング

　リスニングのPart 1と2では、選択肢は印刷されていません。そのために起きるミスがあります。

　例えば、(A)を聞いて、「**"コレ"**正解っぽいけど、自信ない。最後まで聞いてから決めよう」というケースが多々あります。そうして、(D)まで聞き終えて、「よし、やっぱり**"コレ"**が正解だ！」と確信できても、肝心の**"コレ"**が(A)だったのか、(B)だったのか、わからなくなることがあるのです。

　このミスを防ぐために、鉛筆の先を、マークシートの(A)(B)(C)(D)欄に向けておきます。そうして、音声にあわせてペン先をずらし、「コレ正解かも」と思う選択肢があれば、**そこで止めておく**のです。

　例えば、(A)の音声を聞いて間違いと判断できれば、ペン先を(B)に移動。その(B)が「コレ正解っぽい」となれば、そこでペン先を止めたまま、(C)(D)の音声を聞きます。こうしておけば、最後まで聞いて、やはり"コレ"が正解だと確信できた場合に、迷うことなく(B)を塗りつぶすことができます。

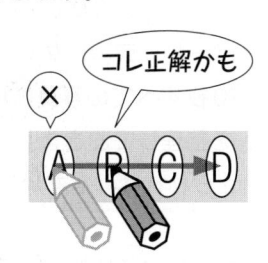

●音声に合わせて、ペン先をずらしていき、正解かなと思う選択肢で止めておく

　次ページからは、パートごとの戦略です。

Part 1 〈写真描写問題〉の基本戦略

問題形式

写真を描写する4つの英文 (A) (B) (C) (D) が読まれ、そのなかから、写真をもっとも適切に描写したものを選ぶ問題。問題冊子には、写真のみが印刷されていて、英文は音声で1度読まれるだけ。

基本データ

- 問題数………10問（No. 1～10）
- 解答時間……5秒間
- 所要時間……約6分

特 徴

1. **写真は2パターン**：写真内容は〈人物写真〉と〈モノ・風景写真〉に大別できます。

2. **〈人物写真〉**：人物写真は、さらに〈1人〉と〈複数〉に分類可。どちらも、〈動作〉に加え、「帽子をかぶっている」、「半袖シャツを着ている」といった〈状態〉にも注目します。
   さらに、〈複数〉の場合には、登場人物に共通の〈動作〉、〈状態〉が描写されることも多いので、何か同じことをしていないか、目を光らせます。

3. **〈モノ・風景写真〉**：モノや風景を写した写真。どこに何があるのか、**モノの位置関係**を把握しましょう。「椅子が空席だ」というように、〈状態〉の描写も出題されるので、要注意。

基本戦略

1. **すべての写真に目を通す**：全パート、ディレクションは無視です（☞p.20参照）。Part 1 では、その約90秒の間に、**10枚すべての写真に目を通し**、人物の〈動作〉、〈状態〉、モノの〈位置関係〉、〈状態〉を整理しておきましょう。こんな英文が読まれるかも、と予想して、正解を待ち伏せられれば、なおいいですね。

2. **〈状態〉と〈動作〉の混同に注意**：Part 1の典型的なひっかけに、〈状態〉と〈動作〉の混同があります。例えば、写真の人物が**眼鏡をすでにかけた〈状態〉**であるのに対し、He's putting on glasses.（眼鏡を今かけようとしている）という〈動作〉の英文でひっかけをねらってくるので、要注意です。

③ **抽象的な言い換えにも要注意**：car を vehicle（車→乗り物）、printer を machine（プリンター→機械）というように、写真中のモノをより抽象的な表現に言い換えることがあります。車が写っているからといって、car ばかりを意識していると、vehicle を使った正解選択肢を聞き逃してしまうことも。要注意です。

> **ワンモア Point**
> Part 1はもっともやさしい、とよく言われます。なので、わからない問題があると、「やってしまったぁ～」という気持ちになるものです。しかし、最近は、上級者をも唸らせる難問が1～2問出題されています。
> ですから、思うように解答できなかったとしても、くよくよしないことです。次は、反射神経を必要とする Part 2 です。終わった問題のことを引きずるのは、命取りになります。
> 気持ちをサッと切り替えることも、重要なテクニックです。

ディレクション訳

本書は本番と同じディレクションを使用しています。ここでは、その訳文を紹介（※グレーに網掛けしている個所は音声のみ）。英文は、各模試を参照してください。

リスニング・テスト
リスニング・テストでは、話し言葉の英語の理解度が問われます。リスニング・テストはおよそ45分間。4つのパートにわかれ、各パートで指示が与えられます。解答は、別紙の解答用紙に行ってください。問題冊子に解答を書き込んではいけません。

パート1
指示：このパートでは、問題冊子の写真について、それぞれ4つの英文を聞きます。英文を聞いたのち、写真をもっとも的確に描写しているものをひとつ選んでください。それから、解答用紙の該当する個所に答えをマークしてください。読まれる英文は問題冊子に印刷されておらず、また1度しか読まれません。

次の例題を見てください。　　　　　　　　　　　　　　　　　　　　　　　解答例
例題　　　　　　　　　　（※ここに写真が掲載されています）　　　　　Ⓐ Ⓑ ● Ⓓ

では、4つの英文を聞きましょう。
(A) 彼らは部屋を出ていくところです。
(B) 彼らはその機械のスイッチを入れているところです。
(C) 彼らはテーブルのそばに立っています。
(D) 彼らは新聞を読んでいます。

(C) の英文、「彼らはテーブルのそばに立っています」が写真をもっとも的確に描写しているので、(C) を選んで解答用紙にマークしてください。
それでは、パート1を始めます。

Part 2 〈応答問題〉の基本戦略

問題形式

まず問い掛けが読まれます。続けて (A) (B) (C)、3つの応答が読まれるので、もっとも適切なものをひとつ選ぶ問題です。英文はすべて音声で1度読まれるだけ。問題冊子には何も印刷されていません。

基本データ

- 問題数………30問（No. 11 〜 40）
- 解答時間……5秒間
- 所要時間……約10分

特　徴

1. **Wh疑問文**：30問中、多いときで **12 〜 13問** は、問い掛けが **Wh 疑問文** です。5W1H（Who、What、When、Where、Why、How）の聞き取りが正答に直結します。

2. **Wh疑問文以外**：残りは、Yes / No 疑問文、付加疑問文、選択疑問文に加え、平叙文、命令文が出題。

基本戦略

1. **即断即決！**：Part 2 は、**もっともテンポが速い**パートです。次々に英文が読まれるので、思い悩んでいては、次の問題に差し支えます。迷った場合でも、必ず5秒以内にどれかひとつを選びマークします。

2. **はじめの1〜2語に集中！**：半数近くが Wh 疑問文になるので、もっとも大切なのは、**問い掛けの最初の1〜3語を聞き逃さない**ことです。5W1H（Who、What、When、Where、Why、How）さえ聞き取れれば、正答できる問題がたくさんあります。1〜3語としているのは、How long 〜？や Why don't you 〜？という形もでるため。

3. **自然な応答を意識する！**：日本人は、Do you 〜？には Yes / No、Why 〜？には Because で答える、と習ってきました。しかし、実際の会話は、そうした教科書的やりとりばかりではありません。Part 2 を解く際も、教科書的ルールよりも、問い掛けと応答が**自然につながるかどうか**、を強く意識します。それが、正解への近道です。

④ **音のくり返しに注意！**：問い掛けに登場する語句（あるいはそれに発音が類似した語句）を、間違い選択肢に含めたひっかけが頻出です。答えがわからないとき、聞き覚えのある語句がくり返されただけで、ついその選択肢を選びたくなるもの。その心理を突いたひっかけです。注意してください。

⑤ **連想のひっかけ**：問い掛けの語句から連想される内容でひっかけをねらってきます。

　例） When are you going to lunch?（いつ昼食にでかける？）
　　　(A) I like sandwiches.（サンドイッチが好きです）

　(A) には lunch から連想される sandwiches が含まれていますが、内容的にはちぐはぐな応答です。④ と同じで、なんとなくつながりのある内容を選びたくなる心理を突いた、ひっかけです。

> **ワンモア Point**　Part 2 のディレクション中は、特にやることはありません。基本はリラックスする時間にあてますが、となりのページにある Part 3 の設問を先読みするというテクニックもあります（☞〈設問先読み〉については、次ページ参照）。余裕がある場合は、挑戦してみるのもいいかも。

ディレクション訳

※グレーに網掛けしている個所は音声のみ

パート 2
指示：英語の質問または発言と、3つの応答を聞きます。これらは問題冊子に印刷されておらず、1度しか放送されません。質問または発言へのもっとも適切な応答を選び、解答用紙の (A)、(B)、または (C) にマークしてください。

例題　　　　　　　　　　　　　　　　　　　　　　　　　　　　　　　解答例
まず、次のように放送されます：　　会議室はどこですか　　　　　　　Ⓐ ● Ⓒ
さらに、次のように放送されます：　(A) 新しい部長に会うためです。
　　　　　　　　　　　　　　　　　(B) 右側のいちばん手前の部屋です。
　　　　　　　　　　　　　　　　　(C) ええ、2時です。

「会議室はどこですか」という質問への最適な応答は、選択肢 (B)「右側のいちばん手前の部屋です」なので、(B) が正解。解答用紙の (B) にマークしてください。
それでは、問題 No. 11 から始めましょう。

Part 3 〈会話問題〉の基本戦略

問題形式

まず、2人の人物による会話が放送されます。続けて、その内容に関する設問が3つ読まれるので、それぞれ (A) (B) (C) (D)、4つの選択肢から正しい答えを選ぶ問題。問題冊子に印刷されているのは、設問と選択肢で、会話は音声のみです。

基本は男女のペアでA→B→A→Bの2往復の会話ですが、A→B→Aの1往復半のものも1～2題含まれます。また、同性同士の会話もまれに出題されます。

基本データ

- 問題数………30問（No. 41～70）、会話10題に、それぞれ3つの設問
- 解答時間……8秒間（ひとつの設問につき）
- 所要時間……13～14分

特 徴

1. **2タイプの設問**：設問は、会話の主題に関わる**〈全体を問う設問〉**と、細部を尋ねる**〈詳細を問う設問〉**に大別。

2. **〈全体を問う設問〉は冒頭に注意！**：①〈テーマ〉、②〈目的〉、③〈場所〉など、会話の主題に関わる設問。

    例） ① What are the speakers discussing?（話し手たちは何について議論しているのか）
    ② Why is the woman calling?（なぜ女性は電話しているのか）
    ③ Where does the conversation most likely take place?
    　（この会話はおそらくどこで行われているか）

    特徴として、3つの設問のうち**1問目**にきます。また、多くの場合、会話のはじめにヒントが述べられるので、**冒頭に意識を集中**させます。

3. **〈詳細を問う設問〉は主語に注目！**：多様な質問がありますが、典型的なものとして、話者の①〈依頼内容〉、②〈提案内容〉、③〈問題点〉、そして④〈次の行動〉を問うものがあります。

    例） ① What does **the man** ask the woman to do?
    　（男性は女性に何をするよう頼んでいるか）
    ② What does **the woman** offer?（女性は何を申し出ているか）
    ③ What is the problem?（問題点は何か）
    ④ What will **the man** probably do next?（男性はおそらく次に何をするか）

主語によって、話者のうち、**どちらの発言に注目すればよいのか目星をつける**ことができます。例えば、例の①であれば、男性の発言に注目、②であれば、女性の発言に注目、というように的を絞ることが可能です。

④ **答えは設問順！**：3つの設問の**答えは、設問順に登場**します。つまり、No. 41の答えは会話の冒頭、No. 42は中盤、No. 43は後半という具合です。順番が入れ替わることもありますが、目安として知っておくと解答しやすくなります。

基本戦略

〈設問先読み〉：Part 3と4の基本戦略は、何よりもまず〈設問先読み〉です。会話（説明文）が読まれる前に、3つの設問に目を通し、質問内容を把握しておく戦略です。そうすることで、**答えを待ち伏せながら会話（説明文）を聞く**ことができ、正答率が高まります。

ただし、時間的余裕はいっさいないので、基本的に〈設問〉だけを先読みし、余裕がある場合に〈選択肢〉にまで目を通すようにしましょう。

☞詳しい手順はp.29の「設問先読みの手順」を参照

> **ワンモアPoint**
> 設問先読みは、〈設問〉だけを先読みというのが基本方針ですが、余裕がある方には、〈設問〉＋〈選択肢(A)〉の先読みをオススメします。
> 設問だけだと、質問のポイントがぼやけてしまう場合があるのですが、ひとつだけでも、選択肢に目を通すことで、何を尋ねているのかがクリアになります。

ディレクション訳

パート3
指示：2人の人物の会話を聞きます。各会話で2人が話す内容について、3つの質問がなされます。それぞれの質問に対して、もっとも適切な答えを1つ選び、解答用紙の(A)、(B)、(C)、(D)のどれかにマークしてください。会話は問題冊子に印刷されておらず、また放送は1度だけです。

Part 4 〈説明文問題〉の基本戦略

問題形式

まず、ひとりの話し手による英文（TOEICでは、これを〈説明文〉と呼ぶ）が読まれます。続けて、その内容に関する設問が3つ放送されるので、それぞれ (A) (B) (C) (D)、4つの選択肢の中から正しい答えを選びます。問題冊子に印刷されているのは、設問と選択肢で、説明文は音声のみ。リスニング最後のパートです。

基本データ

- 問題数………30問（No. 71〜100）、説明文10題に、それぞれ3つの設問
- 解答時間……8秒間（ひとつの設問につき）
- 所要時間……14〜15分

特徴

説明文の種類：次のようなタイプの説明文がよく出題されます。

① 留守電メッセージ…………旅行やチケットの予約状況の確認、アポイントの変更など
② 自動応答メッセージ………休業日に、病院や企業に電話した際に流れるメッセージなど
③ ラジオ放送・ニュース………コマーシャル、交通ニュースやビジネスニュースなど
④ 公共施設でのアナウンス……飛行機や電車の遅延案内など
⑤ 会議の抜粋・社内案内………経営状況の報告や、新入社員、退職者の紹介など
⑥ 講演者の紹介………………ワークショップや学会で発表をする演者の紹介など

基本戦略

1 **設問先読み**：最重要は、Part 3と同じく設問の先読み！

2 **following〜をヒントに！**：毎回、説明文の前に、以下のような導入文が読まれます。

> Questions 71 through 73 refer to the following **telephone message**.
> （設問71から73は次の**留守電メッセージ**に関する質問です。）

following 以下で、これから読まれる**説明文のタイプ**が明らかにされています。たったこれだけの情報ですが、状況をイメージできることで、聞き取りはずいぶん楽になります。following〜を聞き逃さないように！

設問先読みの手順（Part 3を例に）

テストの流れ		やること	ポイント
① ディレクション 約30秒		No. 41〜43 の先読み	欲ばりすぎても混乱するので、多くても No. 44〜46 までにする。先読みは基本的に設問のみ。余裕があれば、選択肢にまで目を通す。
② 会話の放送		会話の聞き取りに集中	
③ 設問 No. 41 の放送 約5秒		設問の放送は無視して、No. 41〜43 の解答を一気に行う	
無音（解答時間） 8秒			
設問 No. 42 の放送 約5秒			
④ 無音（解答時間） 8秒		設問 No.46〜48 の先読み開始	3つ目の設問が読みあげられる前（18〜22秒の間）に、先読みに移る。
設問 No. 43 の放送 約5秒			
無音（解答時間） 8秒			
⑤ ふたつ目の会話の放送		会話の聞き取りに集中	

③〜⑤の流れをくり返す

ディレクション訳

パート4

指示：1人の人物によるトークを聞きます。各トークで話される内容について、3つの質問がなされます。それぞれの質問に対して、もっとも適切な答えを1つ選び、解答用紙の (A)、(B)、(C)、(D) のどれかにマークしてください。トークは問題冊子に印刷されておらず、また放送は1度だけです。

Part 5 〈短文穴埋め問題〉の基本戦略

問題形式

ここからリーディング・セクションがスタートです。Part 5 は短い英文に空所（-------）があり、そこに入る適切な語句を (A) (B) (C) (D)、4つの選択肢から選ぶ問題。問われるのは、文法知識と語彙力です。

基本データ

- 問題数……………40問（No. 101～140）
- 目標解答時間……全体20分、1問につき30秒

特　徴

1. **選択肢でタイプを見極め**：Part 5 は〈文法問題〉と〈語彙問題〉の2タイプに大別可。選択肢を見て、ある単語の派生形や変化形が並んでいる場合は〈文法問題〉、バラバラの単語が並んでいる場合は〈語彙問題〉と識別できます。

2. **〈文法問題〉**：(A) increased／(B) increasing／(C) increase／(D) increasingly というように、**似通った選択肢が並んでいる場合**は、〈文法問題〉タイプ。空所に適した品詞や、動詞の時制など文法的知識を動員して解く問題です。空所前後を見るだけで答えられる場合もあり、時間短縮をねらえます。

3. **〈語彙問題〉**：(A) concentrate／(B) separate／(C) construct／(D) reimburse というように、**品詞は同じ（ここでは動詞）で、意味が異なる選択肢が並んでいる場合**は、〈語彙問題〉タイプ。問題文の文脈をとらえて、意味的に正しい語句を選ばなければいけません。
   語句の意味を知らなければ答えられない問題なので、答えに迷った場合は時間をかけすぎないのがポイント。もっとも可能性が高いと思われるものを即決し、次の問題に移ろう。

基本戦略

1. **何よりも時間配分！**：音声に追われるリスニング・セクションに対し、**時間に追われるのがリーディング・セクション**。990点取得者でも、ギリギリ解き終えられるかどうか、という厳しいセクションです。特に、Part 7 の負担が大きく、そこにどれだけ多くの時間を割けるかが、勝負の分かれ目です。
   そこで、重要となるのが、**パート毎の時間配分**。「Part 5 は○○分」というように、スケジュールを設定して、それに沿ってテキパキ解答していく必要があります。

Listening 45分 + Reading 75分

　　Part 5の配分は、最低でも**20分（1問あたり30秒）**が目安です。これを死守してください。

2 **選択肢から解く！**：問題文をひとつひとつ頭から訳していったのでは、1問30秒は守れません。以下の手順で解答しましょう。

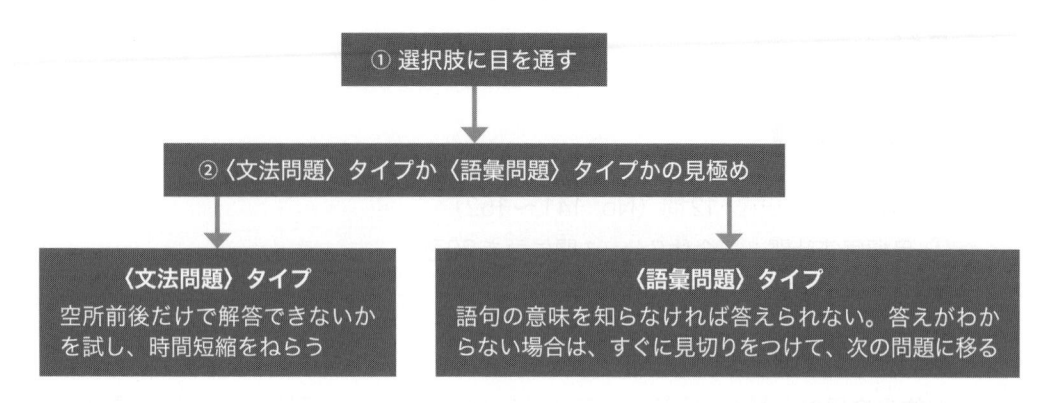

```
① 選択肢に目を通す
          ↓
② 〈文法問題〉タイプか〈語彙問題〉タイプかの見極め
     ↓                              ↓
〈文法問題〉タイプ                〈語彙問題〉タイプ
空所前後だけで解答できないか      語句の意味を知らなければ答えられない。答えがわか
を試し、時間短縮をねらう          らない場合は、すぐに見切りをつけて、次の問題に移る
```

ワンモア Point

　　1問30秒といっても、チラチラ時計を気にしていては、逆に時間の無駄です。それに、10秒で解ける問題もあれば、40秒かかる問題もあります。なので、5分までに10問、10分までに20問と、まとまった単位で時間を意識するといいですね。
　　また、TOEICは、いつも同時刻に開始されます。リーディング・セクションのスタートは1時45分。1時50分までに No. 110、1時55分までに No. 120というように、時刻で管理するほうが、無駄がありません。2時5分までに Part 5 を終えられれば、スケジュール通りということです。

ディレクション訳

リーディング・テスト

リーディング・テストでは、さまざまな文章を読み、数種類の読解問題に答えます。リーディング・テストは全体で75分。3つのパートにわかれ、パートごとに指示があります。75分間という限られた時間内に、できるだけ多くの問題に答えましょう。

答えは別紙の解答用紙にマークします。問題冊子には書き込まないでください。

パート5

指示：以下の文はそれぞれ、単語やフレーズが欠けています。各文の下に、4つの選択肢があるので、もっとも適切なものを選び、文を完成させましょう。そして、解答用紙の (A)、(B)、(C)、(D) のどれかにマークしてください。

Part 6 〈長文穴埋め問題〉の基本戦略

問題形式

Eメールや手紙など、4つの長文が提示され、それぞれに3つの空所（-------）が設けられています。それらに入る適切な語句を (A) (B) (C) (D)、4つの選択肢から選んで答えます。

基本データ

- 問題数……………12問（No. 141～152）
- 目標解答時間……全体6分、1問につき30秒

特　徴

全体の文脈から解く：各設問の基本的特徴は、Part 5 と同じ。ただし、問題によっては、空所を含むセンテンスだけは、答えられないものもあります。その場合は、**文意の流れをとらえて**、答えなければいけません。

この手の問題になりやすいのが、〈文法問題〉としては、時制を判断するもの、〈語彙問題〉としては、前後の文をつなぐ語句を選ぶものです。

基本戦略

時間配分：Part 5 に引き続き、タイムマネジメントが最重要戦略となります。Part 6 は、**12問を6分（1問30秒）**で解き終えることを強く意識してください。

ディレクション訳

パート6
指示：次の文書を読んでください。いくつかの文で、単語やフレーズが欠けています。その文の下に、4つの選択肢があるので、もっとも適切なものを選び、文を完成させましょう。そして、解答用紙の (A)、(B)、(C)、(D) のどれかにマークしてください。

Part 7 〈読解問題〉の基本戦略

問題形式

　Eメールや手紙、広告や新聞・雑誌記事など、13の文書（TOEICではパッセージと呼ぶ）が提示され、それぞれに2～5問の設問が設定されています。各設問、4つの選択肢 (A) (B) (C) (D) から、正しい答えを選びます。
　13の文書には、〈シングル・パッセージ〉と〈ダブル・パッセージ〉があります。

〈シングル・パッセージ〉：前半の9文書。それぞれ、ひとつの文書で構成され、2～5問の設問が設定。

〈ダブル・パッセージ〉：後半の4文書。それぞれ、ふたつの文書で構成され、5問ずつの設問が設定。

基本データ

- 問題数……………48問（No. 153～200）
  〈シングル・パッセージ〉：9文書（設問数28問）
  〈ダブル・パッセージ〉　：4文書（設問数20問）
- 目標解答時間……全体49分、1問につき約1分

特徴

① **パッセージの種類**：次のようなタイプがよく出題されます。

　① Eメール・手紙……内容はさまざま
　② 宣伝・求人広告……商品やサービスの宣伝に加え、求人広告が頻出
　③ 記事………………企業の合併や移転を伝えるビジネス記事、本や演劇の批評記事が頻出
　④ 告知・メモ………社内での業務連絡のほか、お店や公共施設における客への注意事項など
　⑤ Webサイト ………企業の業務内容を伝えるものなど多岐にわたる
　⑥ 招待状……………イベントへの招待状
　⑦ 旅行日程表・イベントプログラム
　　　………………出張の日程表や、イベントの予定表など、スケジュールを伝えるもの

② **設問の分類**：設問は、Part 3 & 4と同じく、〈**全体を問う設問**〉と〈**詳細を問う設問**〉に分類できます。ただ、以下で紹介する、より細かい分類を理解できていると、時間短縮に役立ちます。

③ **Not 問題**：「～していない」ものを問う設問。

　例）What is NOT mentioned about the book?（本について言及されていないことは何か）

このタイプは、**選択肢をひとつひとつ文書と照らし合わせ、一致しないもの**を選ばなければいけません。その分、時間がかかる問題。

4 **「ほのめかし」問題**：ヒントが暗にほのめかしてあるだけで、文書中に明確な答えがない設問。いくつかの情報をつなぎ合わせたり、**推測を働かせ**たりして答えなければならないので、非常に難しく、時間もかかります。

　　例）What can be **inferred** about 〜 ？ （〜について推論できることは何か）
　　　　What is **implied** about 〜 ？ （〜について示唆されていることは何か）
　　　　Who will **most likely** use the shuttle bus?
　　　　（シャトルバスを利用するのは、おそらく誰か）

5 **クロスリファレンス問題**：〈ダブル・パッセージ〉に特有の設問。ふたつの文書にヒントが分散しており、**両方を交互に参照**しなければ解答できません。その分、時間もかかります。

基本戦略

1 **1問1分！**：ひきつづき、時間配分が最重要戦略です。**ひとつの設問につき約1分、全体を49分**で答えきることを強く意識してください。

2 **難問の見極め！**：くり返しになりますが、Part 7を最後まで解ききるというのは、時間的に非常に厳しいタスクです。難しい問題もやさしい問題も配点は同じなので、場合によっては、**難問をあきらめて、簡単な問題に注力**するという決断も必要です。
　　その際、**難問の見極め基準**となるのが、[特徴]の項目3 4 5の設問です。時間が足りなければ、これらをあきらめ、1問でも多くの問題を解くようにしましょう。

> **ワンモア Point**
> Part 7は、後半になるに従って、文章が長く、複雑になります。そのため、先に後半の問題を解いてから、前半に移るというテクニックもあります。時間的・気分的に余裕があるうちに、複雑な問題を解いたほうが正答率が高まるためです。
> このテクニックを採用する場合は、〈ダブル・パッセージ〉、もしくは〈シングル・パッセージ〉の最後の2文書から始めるとよいでしょう。
> ただし、解答欄がズレないよう、よくよく注意してください。

ディレクション訳

パート7
指示：このパートでは、雑誌や新聞記事、手紙、広告などの文書を読みます。各文書に複数の設問があります。設問には、もっとも適切な答えを選び、解答用紙の(A)、(B)、(C)、(D)のどれかにマークしてください。

でる模試 本番のTOEICと同じように取り組もう！

TEST 1

所要時間	2時間

音声ファイル

書名（アルバム名）
新TOEICテスト でる模試 600問 〈TEST 1〉

トラック名（曲名）
- Part 1: T1_P1_Dir ▶ T1_P1_Q10
- Part 2: T1_P2_Dir ▶ T1_P2_Q40
- Part 3: T1_P3_Dir ▶ T1_P3_Q68-70
- Part 4: T1_P4_Dir ▶ T1_P4_End

用意するもの
えんぴつ（シャープペン）
消しゴム
時計
マークシート（巻末に収録）

解答解説　別冊 解答・解説❶ TEST 1

MP3 T1_P1_Dir ▶ T1_P1_Q10

LISTENING TEST

In the Listening test, you will be asked to demonstrate how well you understand spoken English. The entire Listening test will last approximately 45 minutes. There are four parts, and directions are given for each part. You must mark your answers on the separate answer sheet. Do not write your answers in your test book.

PART 1

Directions: For each question in this part, you will hear four statements about a picture in your test book. When you hear the statements, you must select the one statement that best describes what you see in the picture. Then find the number of the question on your answer sheet and mark your answer. The statements will not be printed in your test book and will be spoken only one time.

Example

Sample Answer
Ⓐ Ⓑ ● Ⓓ

Statement (C), "They're standing near the table," is the best description of the picture, so you should select answer (C) and mark it on your answer sheet.

1.

2.

3.

4.

5.

6.

GO ON TO THE NEXT PAGE →

7.

8.

9.

10.

PART 2

Directions: You will hear a question or statement and three responses spoken in English. They will not be printed in your test book and will be spoken only one time. Select the best response to the question or statement and mark the letter (A), (B), or (C) on your answer sheet.

Example

Sample Answer
Ⓐ ● Ⓒ

You will hear: Where is the meeting room?

You will also hear: (A) To meet the new director.
                         (B) It's the first room on the right.
                         (C) Yes, at two o'clock.

The best response to the question "Where is the meeting room?" is choice (B), "It's the first room on the right," so (B) is the correct answer. You should mark answer (B) on your answer sheet.

---

11. Mark your answer on your answer sheet.

12. Mark your answer on your answer sheet.

13. Mark your answer on your answer sheet.

14. Mark your answer on your answer sheet.

15. Mark your answer on your answer sheet.

16. Mark your answer on your answer sheet.

17. Mark your answer on your answer sheet.

18. Mark your answer on your answer sheet.

19. Mark your answer on your answer sheet.

20. Mark your answer on your answer sheet.

21. Mark your answer on your answer sheet.

22. Mark your answer on your answer sheet.

23. Mark your answer on your answer sheet.

24. Mark your answer on your answer sheet.

25. Mark your answer on your answer sheet.

26. Mark your answer on your answer sheet.

27. Mark your answer on your answer sheet.

28. Mark your answer on your answer sheet.

29. Mark your answer on your answer sheet.

30. Mark your answer on your answer sheet.

31. Mark your answer on your answer sheet.

32. Mark your answer on your answer sheet.

33. Mark your answer on your answer sheet.

34. Mark your answer on your answer sheet.

35. Mark your answer on your answer sheet.

36. Mark your answer on your answer sheet.

37. Mark your answer on your answer sheet.

38. Mark your answer on your answer sheet.

39. Mark your answer on your answer sheet.

40. Mark your answer on your answer sheet.

PART 3

Directions: You will hear some conversations between two people. You will be asked to answer three questions about what the speakers say in each conversation. Select the best response to each question and mark the letter (A), (B), (C), or (D) on your answer sheet. The conversations will not be printed in your test book and will be spoken only one time.

41. Why is the woman going to the printing company?

    (A) She wants to apply for a job.
    (B) She has to deliver an order.
    (C) She wants to submit an article.
    (D) She has to get posters made.

42. Why is the woman concerned?

    (A) She is afraid of missing a deadline.
    (B) She cannot locate an office building.
    (C) She may not make it to an office on time.
    (D) She doesn't know how to use the printer.

43. How will the woman most likely get to the printing company?

    (A) By crossing a pathway
    (B) By taking the stairs
    (C) By walking a few blocks
    (D) By switching elevators

44. Why is the woman running late?

    (A) She is stuck in traffic.
    (B) She woke up late.
    (C) Her car broke down.
    (D) She missed her train.

45. At what time will the speakers meet?

    (A) At 7 o'clock
    (B) At 8 o'clock
    (C) At 8:30
    (D) At 10:30

46. What does the man ask the woman to do?

    (A) Meet at his office
    (B) Wait at the train station
    (C) Call when she arrives
    (D) Take an earlier train

47. Where does the conversation most likely take place?

(A) At a performing arts center
(B) At a box office window
(C) At a dining establishment
(D) At a travel agency

48. What is the man's problem?

(A) He's late for the performance.
(B) Wrong tickets were delivered.
(C) He has not received his order.
(D) A product is missing.

49. What does the woman offer?

(A) Upgraded seats
(B) A replacement product
(C) Complimentary meals
(D) A voucher for a future visit

50. What is the problem?

(A) Some participants didn't come.
(B) Some workshop materials haven't been copied.
(C) A seminar was rescheduled.
(D) A speaker will be late for an event.

51. What does the man offer to do?

(A) Prepare the venue
(B) Contact some guests
(C) Return to the office
(D) Distribute questionnaires

52. When will the activity begin?

(A) At 8:30 A.M.
(B) At 9:00 A.M.
(C) At 2:00 P.M.
(D) At 5:00 P.M.

53. What does the man suggest the woman do?

(A) Take a different route
(B) Use a different method of transportation
(C) Listen to the weather report
(D) Leave her car in the parking lot

54. What does the woman say about her apartment?

(A) It is near her workplace.
(B) It is not in the city center.
(C) It is not close to a station.
(D) It does not have parking spaces.

55. What does the man say he will do for the woman?

(A) Give her a map
(B) Drive her to the office
(C) Forward her a link
(D) Make a reservation

56. What are the speakers mainly discussing?

(A) Project deadlines
(B) Production changes
(C) The company relocation
(D) The factory production

57. What does the woman inquire about?

(A) The purchase of new equipment
(B) Extended work hours
(C) The hiring of employees
(D) Technical training courses

58. What does the manager plan to do?

(A) Assign some tasks to workers
(B) Develop a new manufacturing manual
(C) Ask supervisors to organize an employee seminar
(D) Evaluate current operating procedures

59. What is the conversation mainly about?

(A) A comedy show
(B) A new movie
(C) A TV program
(D) A theater play

60. What does the man think of the plot?

(A) It wasn't humorous enough.
(B) It was highly entertaining.
(C) It was not very original.
(D) It didn't seem realistic.

61. What does the woman need to do this week?

(A) Hand in some documents
(B) Make a monthly presentation
(C) Purchase a movie ticket
(D) Attend a writing seminar

62. What most likely is the topic of the workshop?

(A) Production techniques
(B) International investment
(C) Office equipment development
(D) Marketing strategies

63. What is mentioned about Lilian Kraft?

(A) She works for an advertising firm.
(B) She helped organize the workshop.
(C) She offered some useful ideas.
(D) She will make a presentation later that day.

64. According to the woman, what will happen after today's workshop?

(A) Ms. Kraft's book will be offered for sale.
(B) There will be a complimentary dinner.
(C) Attendees will receive a certificate of completion.
(D) A short film presentation will be shown.

65. What is the man looking for?

(A) Some toys for his children
(B) Presents for some corporate investors
(C) Floral arrangements for an event
(D) Someone to plan a party

66. What does the man ask the woman about?

(A) The purpose of the celebration
(B) An advertisement he read in a newspaper
(C) The availability of items under a certain price
(D) Some merchandise he saw in a catalog

67. According to the woman, why is there an extra charge?

(A) The products must be wrapped in paper.
(B) There are state and national taxes.
(C) The man needs the order immediately.
(D) The purchases must be delivered.

68. Why are the speakers going to Madrid?

(A) To meet potential clients
(B) To sign a trade agreement
(C) To attend a business event
(D) To conduct a seminar

69. What does the man mention about the flight?

(A) It leaves in the afternoon.
(B) It has no available seats.
(C) It lasts for more than nine hours.
(D) It makes no stops along the way.

70. What do the speakers agree to do?

(A) Take a taxi to the airport
(B) Leave on a later date
(C) Use long-term parking
(D) Stay at the same hotel

GO ON TO THE NEXT PAGE

PART 4

Directions: You will hear some talks given by a single speaker. You will be asked to answer three questions about what the speaker says in each talk. Select the best response to each question and mark the letter (A), (B), (C), or (D) on your answer sheet. The talks will not be printed in your test book and will be spoken only one time.

71. Where does the speaker work?

    (A) At a computer company
    (B) At a department store
    (C) At a market research firm
    (D) At a banking establishment

72. How can the listener receive a free gift?

    (A) By signing up for a credit card
    (B) By answering a few questions
    (C) By opening a charge account
    (D) By making a purchase

73. What does Ms. Richards ask the listener to do?

    (A) Return a call
    (B) Fill out a survey
    (C) Visit the office
    (D) Pay a bill

74. Why is there a delay on Highway 21?

    (A) There was a car accident.
    (B) There is ongoing roadwork.
    (C) Weather conditions are poor.
    (D) Some streets are flooded.

75. What are motorists advised to do?

    (A) Leave their homes early
    (B) Listen to hourly reports
    (C) Bring a city street map
    (D) Take alternate routes

76. What will listeners most likely hear next?

    (A) A business report
    (B) A weather forecast
    (C) Product advertisements
    (D) Local news

77. What is the announcement mainly about?

(A) A schedule of events for a science fair
(B) Information on exhibited photographs
(C) Guidelines for visitors on a tour
(D) Instructions for usage of photography equipment

78. What does the speaker ask listeners to do?

(A) Leave their cameras at the entrance
(B) Meet at the snack bar
(C) Board the shuttle bus
(D) Stay in the shuttle until told to do otherwise

79. According to the speaker, what can listeners do during the break?

(A) Purchase something to eat
(B) Browse through a selection of souvenirs
(C) Fill out a registration form for a course
(D) Participate in a wildlife presentation

80. What is the purpose of the message?

(A) To reply to an inquiry
(B) To promote a service
(C) To confirm an appointment
(D) To request some information

81. What does the speaker say Mr. Carlos needs to do?

(A) Prepare an itinerary for his upcoming trip
(B) Submit some required documentation
(C) Contact a hotel for reservations
(D) Pay a fee with his credit card

82. What service does Ms. Meyers offer?

(A) Legal advice for a contract
(B) Authentication of certificates
(C) Assistance with visa applications
(D) Booking international flights

83. Who is Justin Smith?

(A) A cross-country runner
(B) An athletic coach
(C) A radio announcer
(D) An organization leader

84. What does United Surgeons mainly do?

(A) Supply health care to those in need
(B) Establish medical clinics across the country
(C) Provide exercise programs for schools
(D) Sponsor professional sports competitions

85. What will the money raised from the fun run be used for?

(A) To pay for athletic equipment
(B) To educate children
(C) To construct a new facility
(D) To cover costs of the sporting event

86. Where does the speaker most likely work?

(A) At a reservations desk
(B) At a convention center
(C) At a real estate firm
(D) At an electronics company

87. Why have the travel plans been changed?

(A) A flight has been suddenly cancelled.
(B) Accommodations are not available.
(C) A work emergency has occurred.
(D) Staff members are too busy.

88. What are some of the listeners asked to do?

(A) Come to a joint decision
(B) Volunteer for a special project
(C) Prepare a detailed report
(D) Develop some marketing ideas

GO ON TO THE NEXT PAGE

89. Where does the speaker most likely work?

    (A) At a sports club
    (B) At a publishing company
    (C) At a photo studio
    (D) At a textile manufacturer

90. What should Kathryn do before she leaves the office for vacation?

    (A) Interview an athlete
    (B) Submit a proposal
    (C) Attend a workshop
    (D) Organize her schedule

91. What most likely will Joanne do while Kathryn is away?

    (A) Write a story for a publication
    (B) Interview a subject for an article
    (C) Take some pictures of a sports event
    (D) Work on the layout of a magazine

92. What has Professor Montgomery done recently?

    (A) Written a book
    (B) Conducted a study
    (C) Started a research project
    (D) Made arrangements for a lecture series

93. What subject will Professor Montgomery speak about?

    (A) Links between DNA and human personality
    (B) Findings in the field of genetic mutation
    (C) Future plans for the university
    (D) The history of medical research

94. What does the speaker say will happen after the lecture?

    (A) Schedules will be distributed.
    (B) Copies of books will be signed.
    (C) Audience questions will be answered.
    (D) Refreshments will be served.

95. Who most likely is listening to the talk?

    (A) Packaging experts
    (B) Graphic designers
    (C) Company executives
    (D) Corporate accountants

96. Why have sales of Crash-Cola decreased?

    (A) Customers are not familiar with the product's new packaging.
    (B) There has been increased competition.
    (C) They have had to raise their prices.
    (D) Consumers don't like the flavors.

97. What does the speaker ask listeners to do?

    (A) Test some new products
    (B) Submit sales reports
    (C) Redesign a logo
    (D) Make some suggestions

98. Who will be giving talks during the event?

    (A) Faculty members from Keller University
    (B) Professionals from across the country
    (C) Science writers from a journal
    (D) Producers of educational programs

99. What does the speaker ask listeners to do?

    (A) Refrain from using video cameras
    (B) Stay in their seats until the conclusion
    (C) Register by filling out forms at the entrance
    (D) Take notes during the presentation

100. How can listeners learn more about other events?

    (A) By calling the department of science
    (B) By viewing a posted schedule
    (C) By listening to a recorded message
    (D) By looking at a brochure

This is the end of the Listening test. Turn to Part 5 in your test book.

NO TEST MATERIAL ON THIS PAGE

GO ON TO THE NEXT PAGE

READING TEST

In the Reading test, you will read a variety of texts and answer several different types of reading comprehension questions. The entire Reading test will last 75 minutes. There are three parts, and directions are given for each part. You are encouraged to answer as many questions as possible within the time allowed.

You must mark your answers on the separate answer sheet. Do not write your answers in your test book.

PART 5

Directions: A word or phrase is missing in each of the sentences below. Four answer choices are given below each sentence. Select the best answer to complete the sentence. Then mark the letter (A), (B), (C), or (D) on your answer sheet.

101. The art class meets ------- every week at the community center on Vine Avenue.

    (A) each
    (B) one
    (C) another
    (D) once

102. In an effort to attract more customers, Hanford Jewellers now offers ------- cleaning services for gold or silver items at any of its five branches.

    (A) liberated
    (B) compensated
    (C) unbound
    (D) complimentary

103. Passengers are required to follow the Ministry of Transport's security policies listed on signs ------- the international terminal.

    (A) among
    (B) into
    (C) between
    (D) throughout

104. Due to financial constraints, there will be a ten-day ------- in the release of the employees' annual bonuses.

    (A) delay
    (B) tardy
    (C) long
    (D) out

105. Southland Manufacturing is ------- looking for a replacement for Roger Hanson, the vice president of finance, who is retiring at the end of the month.

    (A) critically
    (B) imperatively
    (C) necessarily
    (D) urgently

106. Mr. Ing chose to fly to the conference in Los Angeles earlier than scheduled ------- he would have extra time to visit some potential clients.

    (A) so that
    (B) in order
    (C) even if
    (D) ahead of

107. Exhausted by her weeklong search for a suitable apartment, Ms. Stein decided to rent the one on Albright Avenue, as it was the least ------- among those she had seen.

    (A) expend
    (B) expenses
    (C) expensively
    (D) expensive

108. Investors are quite pleased that profits for the new hotel chain are rising steadily and will likely go ------- the company's target for this year.

    (A) further
    (B) ahead
    (C) beyond
    (D) cautiously

109. Nurses who work in the emergency room must not only assist doctors in procedures, ------- keep patients calm during stressful situations.

    (A) in addition
    (B) but also
    (C) let alone
    (D) because of

110. Jack Elliot submitted his resignation to Gulliver's Café last year because he decided to establish a coffee shop of ------- own in the downtown area.

    (A) him
    (B) his
    (C) he
    (D) himself

111. Joanna Saunders ------- working as a ticketing agent for Starlight Travel and Tours ever since she relocated to San Francisco ten years ago.

    (A) was
    (B) could be
    (C) has been
    (D) is

112. All budget proposals should include ------- figures from the last fiscal year and concise spending projections for next year.

    (A) obvious
    (B) permanent
    (C) sheer
    (D) accurate

113. ------- frequent reminders about efficient energy consumption, more households are starting to buy eco-friendly appliances that use less electricity.

    (A) In response to
    (B) Apart from
    (C) In spite of
    (D) Except for

114. Trade officials estimate that food exports ------- by 25 percent in the next three quarters because of increasing demand.

    (A) will grow
    (B) grow
    (C) grew
    (D) had grown

115. Invited guests were informed that the awards ceremony for the sales department will start ------- at 7 P.M. at the Ogilvy Hotel.

    (A) normally
    (B) promptly
    (C) lately
    (D) mostly

116. The president of the bank was interviewed by Melinda Carlson, a well-known ------- for an international news magazine.

    (A) journalism
    (B) journalistically
    (C) journal
    (D) journalist

117. Supporters of the plan to deregulate the power industry say that ------- competition will force suppliers to better serve consumers.

    (A) narrow
    (B) open
    (C) rolling
    (D) failed

118. An increase in the national population will ------- result in a much greater demand for social services, food, and housing.

    (A) conditionally
    (B) materially
    (C) inevitably
    (D) sparingly

119. The brochures released by Towler Prudential provide additional information on ------- plans offered by the insurance provider.

    (A) prevailed
    (B) various
    (C) conquered
    (D) allowing

GO ON TO THE NEXT PAGE

120. It is critical during these difficult economic times for companies to ------- their most self-motivated and productive employees.

(A) attempt
(B) retain
(C) observe
(D) impress

121. The university's annual graduation ------- is slated to take place on Saturday morning at ten o'clock at the campus's main auditorium.

(A) course
(B) convention
(C) ceremony
(D) registration

122. The Department of Labor has launched a Web site designed to help companies interact with people seeking -------.

(A) employing
(B) employee
(C) employment
(D) employed

123. The family-owned company maintains a policy of promoting members to senior positions only ------- they have earned graduate degrees in business.

(A) where
(B) than
(C) whereas
(D) after

124. In addition to clothing production, KL Textiles is involved in ------- raw materials into high-quality cotton, silk, and wool cloth.

(A) packaging
(B) processing
(C) handling
(D) exchanging

125. In some parts of the world, sophisticated forgeries make it difficult even for experts to detect whether a product is ------- or not.

(A) factual
(B) authentic
(C) customary
(D) conclusive

126. Management at the new shopping center on Broad Street expects to draw large crowds on its first day, as the opening ------- with a national holiday.

(A) escorts
(B) coincides
(C) contains
(D) substitutes

127. The Hammersmith Business Association will subsidize a new ------- of lectures to promote entrepreneurship in the country.

(A) series
(B) trade
(C) ground
(D) advance

128. We ask that all passengers please let the flight attendants know ------- you will need immigration forms or if you are just in transit.

(A) whereas
(B) than
(C) whether
(D) rather

129. The manager of the restaurant is considering hiring two more waiters after receiving numerous complaints from diners ------- slow service.

(A) regarded
(B) regarding
(C) regards
(D) to regard

130. Customers are urged to read through all the ------- carefully before installing the software on their computers.

(A) confirmations
(B) schedules
(C) instructions
(D) corrections

131. Claris Trading chairperson Denise Lim sent the largest ------- to the Red Crusade's dental mission in Africa.

    (A) donor
    (B) donating
    (C) donate
    (D) donation

132. Guests are entitled to a number of benefits, ------- discounted spa services and unlimited use of the resort's water sports equipment.

    (A) some of
    (B) as of
    (C) such as
    (D) similar to

133. Following the completion of their six-month study on office efficiency, Bartholomew and Associates ------- a new management system to better improve productivity in the company.

    (A) was creating
    (B) will create
    (C) was created
    (D) is created

134. Volunteers have been instructed to wear brightly colored vests so that they might be more easily ------- among the crowds of people expected to attend this weekend's parade on Main Street.

    (A) shown
    (B) admitted
    (C) decided
    (D) distinguished

135. Although the board has given the proposed service package submitted by a local firm its final -------, the parties will not enter into a contract until the price is agreed upon.

    (A) achievement
    (B) contemplation
    (C) approval
    (D) determination

136. Having reviewed the proposal, the clients indicated that they were quite satisfied with the overall plan and requested ------- major changes.

    (A) lot
    (B) any
    (C) many
    (D) few

137. A brief ------- from the anthology of acclaimed essayist Nigel Murphy was featured in a major daily newspaper along with a book review written by one of the paper's columnists.

    (A) extractor
    (B) extract
    (C) extractive
    (D) extracting

138. ------- by a group of advertising professionals, Speedline Creative Concepts quickly achieved the distinction of being a leading firm in branding and logo-making.

    (A) Identified
    (B) Established
    (C) Classified
    (D) Manufactured

139. A 20 percent discount on annual fees will be given to patrons ------- renew their gym membership before the end of the year.

    (A) whose
    (B) who
    (C) those
    (D) when

140. The purpose of planning ------- is to ensure that the company can respond adequately to anticipated threats and to unforeseen opportunities.

    (A) comparably
    (B) redundantly
    (C) strategically
    (D) predictably

GO ON TO THE NEXT PAGE

PART 6

Directions: Read the texts that follow. A word or phrase is missing in some of the sentences. Four answer choices are given below each of the sentences. Select the best answer to complete the text. Then mark the letter (A), (B), (C), or (D) on your answer sheet.

Questions 141-143 refer to the following press release.

Fireflies Set for First Concert

The Fireflies is ready to light up the Truffle Coliseum at its first major concert on June 5 at 8 P.M. The performance, which will also feature guest appearances from rock stars Lincoln Browning and Meagan Page, is ------- to be the grandest musical event of the season.

    141. (A) required
          (B) subjected
          (C) outlined
          (D) projected

Thousands of fans from all over the UK and nearby countries are expected to attend the concert. -------, VIP and general admission tickets to the show were sold out five days

  142. (A) Provided that
       (B) Instead
       (C) In fact
       (D) Nevertheless

after the event was announced on the band's Web site. The Fireflies' lead singer Alfred Morgan welcomed the public's ------- response to the announced concert.

    143. (A) persuasive
          (B) intimidated
          (C) enthusiastic
          (D) obsessed

"We are grateful for the massive support we are receiving now, and it has inspired us to work doubly hard for this upcoming show," Morgan said.

Questions 144-146 refer to the following article.

A New Approach to Gift Shopping

For the last four years, Alyssa Russell has helped people remember the important dates on their calendars. Her company Gift Shoppers is an online business that sells gifts for all types of events, which in ------- would make it a rather traditional company.

    144. (A) it
         (B) their
         (C) them
         (D) itself

What separates Gift Shoppers from other companies is that it automatically sends reminders to its clients about important events, including anniversaries and holidays.

"Although lots of companies sell their merchandise online, I think we ------- a novel way

    145. (A) develop
         (B) have developed
         (C) were developed
         (D) are developing

of shopping," says Russell. Members of the company's Web site mark special days on a calendar when they apply. Gift Shoppers sends messages to its members five days before each event, helping them ------- to buy a gift. The company also provides a list of

    146. (A) remember
         (B) record
         (C) renew
         (D) review

gift suggestions. "I am surprised at how successful the idea has been," explains Russell. "We have many clients who are just too busy to remember these types of things. Our service guarantees they never miss important dates again."

GO ON TO THE NEXT PAGE

Questions 147-149 refer to the following announcement.

MxGuard Released

Greyton Labs has finally made its new software, MxGuard 2.0, available on the market this week. It provides maximum ------- against malicious programs that can harm your

147. (A) protector
(B) protection
(C) protectable
(D) protective

computer system while you surf the Internet.

Features ------- identity security when banking and making online purchases, an

148. (A) indicate
(B) enclose
(C) redirect
(D) include

integrated virus and spyware scanner, an e-mail monitor for blocking unsolicited messages, and an enhanced firewall to prevent unwanted access to your system.

MxGuard 2.0 is ------- distributed by Greyton Labs and costs $55 for a one-year

149. (A) expressively
(B) attentively
(C) exclusively
(D) graciously

subscription for home users and $250 for business users. Both come with 24-hour customer support. The software is now available for download at www.greytonlabs.com/mxguard.

Questions 150-152 refer to the following e-mail.

TO: Ethan Reid <ethan12@geallmail.uk>
FROM: Olivia Griffith <livgriffith@nymphmail.uk>
DATE: June 8
SUBJECT: Hello

Hi Ethan,

How are you doing? I hope you're adjusting well to your new life in Birmingham. It's already been a month since you moved from Liverpool and not much has changed around here. Everybody in the office ------- you a lot.

      150. (A) was missed
           (B) missing
           (C) had missed
           (D) misses

By the way, I remember how you ------- talked about your experience as a physical education

      151. (A) very
           (B) often
           (C) fairly
           (D) apparently

teacher before you came here. I'm thinking of enrolling my seven-year-old son, Dylan, in a tennis class in the summer. I want him to engage in an activity that will help him develop his strength and coordination skills. Do you think the sport will be too ------- for him? I haven't

      152. (A) eager
           (B) crucial
           (C) strenuous
           (D) determined

played tennis myself, so I thought I'd ask your expert opinion on the matter.

I'd really appreciate your advice and look forward to hearing from you.

Regards,

Olivia

GO ON TO THE NEXT PAGE

PART 7

Directions: In this part your will read a selection of texts, such as magazine and newspaper articles, letters, and advertisements. Each text is followed by several questions. Select the best answer for each question and mark the letter (A), (B), (C), or (D) on your answer sheet.

Questions 153-154 refer to the following card.

City Explorer 3

Thank you for purchasing the City Explorer card.
This card gives you access to major attractions throughout the city for three days, and it will be activated on your first use. This card also serves as a pass to various city tours and admission to museums in different locations.

Present this card at participating restaurants and souvenir shops and get 10 percent off food and merchandise.

We hope that you enjoy your trip!
Trapezon City Travel Board

For information on major attractions, see the reverse side of the card.

153. What is indicated on the card?

(A) It entitles the holder to free meals.
(B) It acts as a ticket to popular destinations.
(C) It allows holders to make charges at local establishments.
(D) It gives access to public transportation for three days.

154. What information is included on the card?

(A) The locations of where it is available for purchase
(B) The admission fees for museums
(C) A list of establishments offering discounts
(D) Details about tourist sites

Questions 155-156 refer to the following advertisement.

EVERIDGE CERTIFIED ACCOUNTANTS
825 Burrard, Suite 19-A, Vancouver BC

Having trouble with your tax forms? Are the finances of your small business more than you can handle? Let ECA, the fastest-growing accounting firm in Canada, take care of all your accounting worries!

We offer:
▷ Personal income tax returns
▷ Setup and maintenance of a bookkeeping system
▷ Preparation of financial statements
▷ Contract assistance

For a full list of our services and accountants, visit www.everidgeacc.co.ca. To make an appointment, call us at (604) 555-8872 to speak to one of our representatives, or send an e-mail to everidgeacc@coolmail.com.

155. What is NOT a service offered by ECA?

(A) Assistance with income tax forms
(B) Help with creating a contract
(C) Investment consultation
(D) Developing accounting systems

156. Why would a customer visit the ECA Web site?

(A) To arrange a personal tax consultation
(B) To find out the fees for an accounting service
(C) To view online samples of business contracts
(D) To get information about ECA employees

Questions 157-159 refer to the following invitation.

The New Hampton Professionals Society
would like to invite you to attend our

12th Annual Melody for Charity Night

on Saturday, July 24, at 6:00 P.M.
at the Greenfield Theater

Six classical compositions by world-renowned composers
Johannes Linden and Vladimir Tepanor of the Salzburg Conservatory

will be performed by the
Smithson Philharmonic Orchestra

Cost per person: $80   Attire: Formal

Proceeds from the evening are set to benefit welfare institutions in the northern city of Henlin, namely St. Peter's Orphanage and the Rainbow House for Children. Please RSVP by July 1. For more information, visit www.stpetersorphanage.com and www.rainbowhouse.com.

157. What will take place on July 24?

(A) An organizational meeting
(B) A fundraising concert
(C) The introduction of new composers
(D) The opening of a new association

158. Who are Johannes Linden and Vladimir Tepanor?

(A) They are famous conductors of an orchestra.
(B) They are representatives of a charitable organization.
(C) They are respected artists from a music school.
(D) They are well-known producers in the entertainment industry.

159. What is NOT indicated about the event?

(A) It is sponsored by a group of professionals.
(B) Individuals are required to dress formally.
(C) It will be held on the weekend.
(D) Refreshments will be served to all guests.

Questions 160-162 refer to the following advertisement.

Time Out Vendors

Refresh D-02
Cold Drink Vending Machine

The all-new Refresh D-02 Vendor will give your customers wider drink selections in bottles and cans. The Refresh D-02 Vendor can now load ten types of drinks ranging from sodas and fruit juices to bottled water. This machine is an update of our D-01 model, but still includes a removable back-lighted display, which makes branding and pricing convenient. Loading drinks is also very simple with the machine's easy-loading product shelves.

Specifications	
Dimensions	Height 1.8m Width 0.8m Depth 0.8m
Weight	261kg
Number of Drink Selections	10
Standard Capacity	20 oz. Bottle (200 pieces)
Payment Mechanism	Dollar Bill Acceptor Coin Acceptor

For more details on Refresh D-02 Vendor, call 555-8591 or visit www.timeoutvendors.com.

---

160. What is indicated about Refresh D-02?

(A) It should be kept in cool areas.
(B) It is a modified version of a previous model.
(C) It is available for rent.
(D) It has a security sensor.

161. What information is NOT included in the advertisement about the machine?

(A) Specifications about its size
(B) Its storage capacity
(C) Details about rental rates
(D) A list of items that it is capable of selling

162. What is stated about the machine's payment device?

(A) It accepts paper money.
(B) It identifies foreign currency.
(C) It holds different types of containers.
(D) It does not recognize coins.

Questions 163-165 refer to the following notice.

The Tenth Annual Portland Holiday Gift Fair!

The City of Portland and the Willamette Convention Center are pleased to announce the opening of our Tenth Annual Holiday Gift Fair, running from November 25 to December 8. Open daily from 10 A.M. to 9 P.M. at the convention center on Naito Parkway, the fair will feature products from more than 600 vendors this year. The fair will be held in the center's largest exhibit area, Riverside Hall.

Entrance to the fair is $5 for adults and $3 for children under twelve and senior citizens. There is no admission charge for children under five years of age. Attendees can also take part in hourly draws with more than $18,000 of merchandise to be given away over the course of two weeks! Booths include holiday gifts, decorations, cards, toys, food, and so much more! Get all your holiday supplies ahead of time by visiting this amazing event.

For a list of vendors, please visit www.willamettecon.com/events. Tickets for the fair can be purchased on the Web site beginning November 10.

163. For whom is the notice most likely intended?

(A) City officials
(B) Senior citizens
(C) Holiday shoppers
(D) Local gift shop owners

164. What is indicated about the convention center?

(A) It was recently constructed.
(B) It has a seating capacity of 600.
(C) It sells tickets at the door.
(D) It has several exhibit halls.

165. What is NOT mentioned about the event?

(A) It will include free prizes.
(B) It will exhibit a variety of products.
(C) It is free for 10-year-old children.
(D) It is scheduled to last for two weeks.

Questions 166-167 refer to the following e-mail.

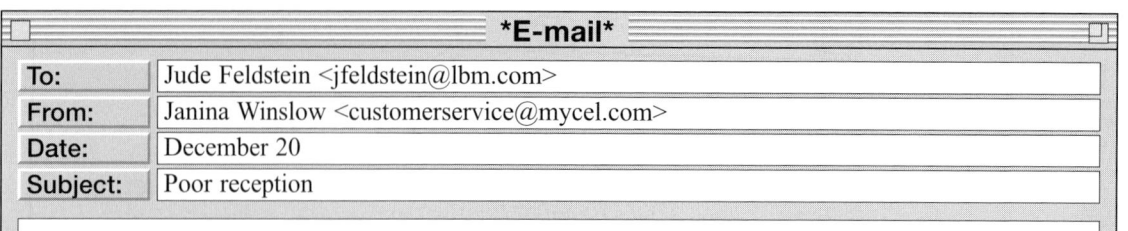

E-mail

To:	Jude Feldstein <jfeldstein@lbm.com>
From:	Janina Winslow <customerservice@mycel.com>
Date:	December 20
Subject:	Poor reception

Dear Mr. Feldstein,

Thank you for informing us about the intermittent reception that you have been experiencing with our wireless phone service for the past few days. You wanted us to explain what the problem was and also asked for a discount on your service fee for this month.

First, we believe that this problem is due to the ongoing repair work on our cell phone towers in the Mountainview area, which were severely damaged during the recent snowstorm. Our maintenance crew is already working around the clock in order to fix the problem. Rest assured that normal service will resume at the soonest possible time.

And in regard to your second inquiry, I would first like to apologize for the inconvenience. Because you are a valued customer, we are deducting $15 from your next billing statement. We hope that this addresses the amount of trouble our service has caused you.

We hope that you continue using MyCel as your wireless service provider.

Sincerely,

Janina Winslow
MyCel Customer Service

---

166. What is the purpose of the e-mail?

(A) To inform a customer of a work date
(B) To report an Internet connection problem
(C) To respond to a customer's request
(D) To persuade a customer to renew a subscription

167. What did Ms. Winslow offer to provide Mr. Feldstein?

(A) An extended service contract
(B) A day's worth of free phone calls
(C) A revised line of credit
(D) A reduction on a monthly charge

Questions 168-171 refer to the following article.

TV Station to Air New Shows

LBN Channel 5, the country's largest media corporation and most popular broadcast network, hopes to revive its flagging prime time ratings next season with the airing of two new television series, *Vanished* and *Casual Living*.

Vanished revolves around a law enforcement unit in Chicago that specializes in cases of missing persons. However, unlike other crime dramas, each episode of the program is based on real-life events. Lead character Johnny Slack (played by actor Dennis Javier) and his team of detectives struggle to solve mysterious disappearances in a short amount of time. *Vanished* will air every Thursday at 9:30 P.M.

Meanwhile, on the reality program *Casual Living*, actor and restaurant chain heir Brent Masterson gives up his privileged lifestyle and travels to a remote ranch in the small town of Banchetta. There he must take up residence with the Holsten family and learn to adjust to simple life on a farm. His experience leads him to realize that nothing is ever as easy as it looks. *Casual Living* airs every Sunday at 8:00 P.M.

168. What is the article about?

(A) A local law enforcement unit
(B) Information about a famous actor
(C) The reorganization of a media network
(D) Future television programs

169. What is indicated about *Vanished*?

(A) It will be aired at 8 P.M.
(B) It will be hosted by Brent Masterson.
(C) It is based on authentic cases.
(D) It is about life in a small town.

170. What is NOT mentioned about LBN?

(A) Its prime time ratings have been low.
(B) It produces critically acclaimed TV programs.
(C) It is a popular channel among viewers.
(D) Its media business is the biggest in the nation.

171. What does the article indicate about *Casual Living*?

(A) The first season will be filmed in Chicago.
(B) It will depict a person's real-life experiences.
(C) Each episode is about one hour long.
(D) It shows how the Holsten family run a restaurant.

GO ON TO THE NEXT PAGE

Questions 172-175 refer to the following article.

Business Icon Tells of Journey Up the Ladder
By Ruby Wang

BEIJING—Behind the success of the Shanghai Marketing Association is a tough man of humble beginnings. President Gino Chen's valued professional advice, which has helped hundreds of businesses, did not come from books, but from his experience as an employee at a multinational firm.

Chen began his career at Keaston Corporation, a US food manufacturer. During that time, China was in the process of opening up its economy to foreign investors, and Keaston was one of the first multinational firms to expand into the mainland. Chen believed that Keaston used unconventional methods of employee training and work processes and that landing a job at the firm would give him the experience crucial to his career growth.

Chen's first job as a sales representative for Keaston had him driving a van around Beijing delivering meat products to groceries and small retailers.

"The job was difficult, but I was never disheartened. In fact, it helped me appreciate the importance of hard work as well as good communication and people skills," Chen said. "The job prepared me to handle greater responsibilities in the company."

After ten years of fieldwork, Chen was promoted to provincial sales director, managing several branches of the company. In 1998, he became the regional sales chief for East Asia, and by the time he retired, he was the general manager for South Pacific Asia with twenty-five years of experience in the retail industry.

Now the sixty-seven-year-old devotes a lot of his time to speaking to leading groups of entrepreneurs and sales executives around the globe, in an effort to enhance the marketing techniques of their businesses.

172. Why was the article written?

(A) To discuss marketing trends
(B) To give information about an executive
(C) To provide details about an association
(D) To describe award-winning companies

173. What is stated about Keaston in the article?

(A) It used management systems different from other companies.
(B) It created useful marketing strategies for new businesses.
(C) It merged with a Chinese firm.
(D) It primarily sold fresh produce.

174. What is NOT indicated about Gino Chen in the article?

(A) He started his career as a deliveryman.
(B) He has a lot of experience in the retail sector.
(C) He provides expert advice to businesses.
(D) He often gives lectures to university students.

175. The word "appreciate" in paragraph 4, line 3 is closest in meaning to

(A) upgrade
(B) understand
(C) add
(D) thank

Questions 176-180 refer to the following Web site.

🐴 Childsplay Incorporated

| NOTICE | ATTENDANCE | PERSONAL BOARD | SCHEDULE |

Training Materials

- Manuals
- Policies
- **Travel Information**

Holidays

Open Forum

Part of your duties at Childsplay Inc. will include attending trade fairs not only in the US, but around the world. When planning such trips and participating in these events, it is important to follow this checklist:

- Confirm with the travel and legal departments that you have all the necessary documents to attend or participate in the event. This includes visas, passports, licenses, and any other required documentation.
- Make sure to put in detailed requests for transport and hotels to our travel department at least a month in advance.
- Provide a list of contact information for the colleagues in your departments prior to departure.
- Keep all original receipts for any expenses during your travel. Without the receipts, you will not be eligible for reimbursement.
- When attending trade fairs in countries where English is not the first language, make sure at least one member of your team speaks the local language, or make arrangements to hire an interpreter. Business can be easily lost if we are unable to communicate with potential clients.
- Read up on local culture and customs. Take some time and search the Internet for information on the cuisine, history, and geography. Impress potential clients with your knowledge and respect for their culture and heritage.

Email:

Inbox: 2

Links:

- Headquarters
- Accounts
- Marketing
- Production
- Design

176. For whom was the checklist probably written?

(A) Event organizers
(B) New members of staff
(C) Potential clients
(D) Training manager

177. What are readers NOT told to research before traveling abroad?

(A) Local foods
(B) Landscape features
(C) Current governments
(D) Traditional customs

178. Why would an employee contact the legal department?

(A) To get help registering a business
(B) To receive assistance with a contract
(C) To learn about laws in foreign countries
(D) To verify necessary information

179. What is mentioned in the checklist about accommodations?

(A) It is arranged by a travel agent.
(B) It should be located near the trade fair facility.
(C) It must be requested ahead of time.
(D) It does not have to be paid for until the date of arrival.

180. What are international trade fair participants advised to do?

(A) Register at least a month in advance
(B) Make certain they speak the local language
(C) Conduct research on market trends
(D) Hire additional sales staff locally

GO ON TO THE NEXT PAGE

Questions 181-185 refer to the following e-mail and list.

E-mail

To:	dee_stewart@highlandsmail.com
From:	custserv@fionnantiques.com
Date:	February 8
Subject:	Fionn's latest acquisitions

Dear Ms. Stewart,

We are pleased to inform you that Fionn Antiques has recently acquired some valuable items that date from the 17th through the 19th centuries. As one of our most valued clients, you have the privilege to purchase any of the items before we put them on display in our store.

Attached you will find the descriptions and prices of our newest acquisitions. Please note that the item made in France is discounted by 10 percent. As always, you can place your order either by filling out our online form or by calling us at 555-7311. Domestic delivery takes five business days, while international orders are shipped in seven to fourteen days.

We look forward to your continued patronage.

Fionn Antiques
February Acquisitions

Estrela Ceramic Vase
This exquisite work of art was handmade in Portugal in 1845. The vase has the look of a woven basket skilfully rendered by the artist. The flowers at the center are colorful and highly detailed, with flowing and overlapping petals that are very difficult to mold. Price: $420

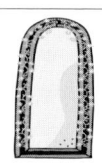

Quadri Rosewood Mirror
This deeply carved 18th-century Italian mirror has retained its warm, bleached wood tone. The sturdy rosewood edges depict luscious leaves, and the glass mirror is antiqued with fine specks. Price: $2,250

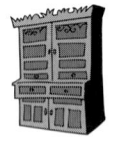

Werdenstil Oak Cabinet
This 17th-century cabinet from Austria is made of oak, with a crosshatched see-through panel at the top and a carved sun at the bottom of the door. The interior is fitted with two shelves. Price: $1,845

Anduze Crystal Candleholder
This beautifully crafted piece is considered one of the finest examples of 19th-century French glasswork. The candleholder stands 10.25 inches high and has a base of 4.75 inches in diameter. Its simple yet elegant design makes it a perfect accent piece for any room. Price: $575

181. What is the purpose of the e-mail?

(A) To promote an auction
(B) To announce a new delivery service
(C) To advertise several products
(D) To verify purchase information

182. What is indicated about Fionn Antiques?

(A) It offers a selection of contemporary furnishings.
(B) It operates several international retail outlets.
(C) It conducts some of its business on the Internet.
(D) It specializes in items from the 19th-century.

183. What is true about Ms. Stewart?

(A) She will place her order online.
(B) She is organizing an antiques auction.
(C) She has purchased from Fionn Antiques before.
(D) She recently inquired about the status of her order.

184. What is stated about the vase?

(A) It was hand-carved from rosewood.
(B) It was not easy to produce.
(C) It will require special shipping services.
(D) It was manufactured in a Portuguese factory.

185. What item is available at a reduced price?

(A) The vase
(B) The mirror
(C) The cabinet
(D) The candleholder

GO ON TO THE NEXT PAGE

Questions 186-190 refer to the following e-mail and advertisement.

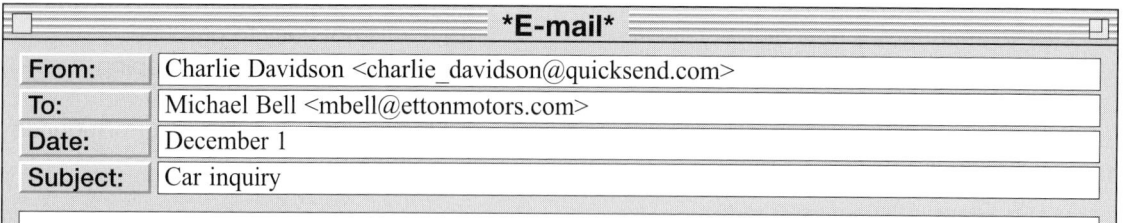

E-mail

From:	Charlie Davidson <charlie_davidson@quicksend.com>
To:	Michael Bell <mbell@ettonmotors.com>
Date:	December 1
Subject:	Car inquiry

Dear Mr. Bell,

I recently saw an advertisement for some of your vehicles in a newspaper. I am currently based in Qatar, and will be coming to London for the holidays. During my vacation, I plan to buy a new car for my family. I'm looking for one that has reliable safety features and requires little maintenance. As I live in Qatar, I also need a vehicle that can handle extreme heat and has a strong air conditioning system.

I actually tried checking your Web site to get some additional details on your sports utility vehicles, but unfortunately I was unable to download the description pages. I was wondering if you could send me information about the vehicles you carry to my e-mail, as I would like to study my options before I leave.

I will arrive on December 20 and stay in London for two weeks only. Please send me the information as soon as possible so that I may select which vehicles I would like to schedule for a test drive in advance. I would also be pleased to receive a list of requirements and options about payment terms.

Thank you and I hope to hear from you soon.

Sincerely,

Charlie Davidson
Contract Manager
Hani Rashid Corporation
Office phone: (00947) 555-2941

ETTON MOTORS

www.ettonmotors.com

Imagine a car that has everything you need for safe and convenient driving. A new addition to Etton Motors' sports utility vehicles, Nervo 200 was especially designed for outstanding off-road performance. Its fuel-efficient and low-emission 2.5-liter diesel engine has the capacity to produce ample power and torque for high-speed cruising.

Nervo 200 also boasts superior security features. The car's body has front and side impact beams that protect the interior from collisions. Rated five stars by the International Transport Safety Laboratory, the car is equipped with antilock brakes and an electronic stability control that detects and minimizes skids, preventing accidents on slippery surfaces.

Nervo 200 perfectly suits individuals with simple and practical tastes, as it includes all the features of a standard sports utility vehicle-automatic windows, a door lock system, power steering, fold-down rear seats, and a digital stereo, among others. Take a ride in a Nervo 200 at the Etton Motors dealer nearest you. To schedule a test drive, please call our customer hotline at 555-0999.

186. Why did Mr. Davidson write to Mr. Bell?

(A) To postpone an upcoming test drive
(B) To submit some required information
(C) To explain what type of product he is looking for
(D) To file a complaint about a vehicle

187. What is implied about Mr. Davidson?

(A) He is relocating to London in two weeks.
(B) He is paying in monthly installments.
(C) He has insufficient funds for the Nervo 200.
(D) He has limited time to purchase a vehicle.

188. What feature of the Nervo 200 meets Mr. Davidson's standards?

(A) It requires little upkeep.
(B) It consumes a small amount of fuel.
(C) It is highly rated for safety.
(D) It comes with a stereo system.

189. What is NOT indicated about Etton Motors?

(A) It offers vehicle test drives to customers.
(B) It operates several different dealerships.
(C) It has additional product information on a Web site.
(D) It is opening a repair and maintenance center.

190. In the advertisement, the word "boasts" in paragraph 2, line 1 is closest in meaning to

(A) improves
(B) possesses
(C) widens
(D) adds

GO ON TO THE NEXT PAGE

Questions 191-195 refer to the following Web page and product brochure.

Stop and Sew
For all your dressmaking and tailoring needs

Home | About Us | Locations | **Customer's Page** | Contact Us

Great finds at Stop and Sew
- Fabric
- Ribbons
- Laces
- Accessories
- Notions

Find a product

Dear Stop and Sew,

Congratulations on the opening of your new store!

I have always been a fan of Stop and Sew. My three years of experience as a fashion designer wouldn't have been so successful if it weren't for the unique sewing products available at your store. Your wide selection of textiles for every taste and occasion has always allowed me to be as imaginative and creative as I want.

As always, your store is very well organized with fabrics arranged by purpose and material. On top of that, your knowledgeable salespeople are helpful and provide exceptional assistance. They made some fine recommendations recently as I was picking out textiles for my swimwear collection.

As your business thrives, more customers are bound to hear about your excellent products. I have often observed that your fabric collections quickly sell out at many of your stores. Now that the wedding season is here, many dressmakers and designers like me would be happy if you ensured that all your outlets had sufficient supplies of the fabrics we need for our production.

Thank you and I wish you continued success!

Cheers,

Jenna Palmer

Stop and Sew

Basic Fabric

Cotton
- One hundred percent natural
- Breathable and comfortable to wear
- Machine washable
- Recommended for making shirts

Merino Wool
- Made of the finest and softest wool from Merino sheep
- Breathable and insulating, this will keep people warm in the winter and cool in the summer
- Machine washable
- Recommended for making infant garments, high fashion clothing, and sportswear
- Available in different colors

Silk
- One hundred percent natural
- Lustrous, easy-to-dye fabric with exceptional flow
- Recommended for making night gowns and wedding gowns

Linen
- One hundred percent natural
- Stronger than cotton
- Recommended for making jackets and trousers as well as bed sheets, tablecloths, and curtains

Bamboo
- Made from bamboo fibers
- Environment-friendly
- Has antibacterial properties
- Recommended for making infant clothing and undergarments

Spandex
- Lightweight and highly stretchable
- Resistant to flexing, heat, sunlight, detergent, and perspiration
- Recommended for making foundation garments, swimsuits, skiwear, dance apparel, and skating costumes

191. What does Ms. Palmer like about Stop and Sew?

(A) It arranges textiles by color.
(B) It has exceptional customer service.
(C) It has a wide selection of sewing machines.
(D) It offers helpful dressmaking tutorials.

192. On the Web page, the word "taste" in paragraph 2, line 3 is closest in meaning to

(A) preference
(B) flavor
(C) decision
(D) feeling

193. What kind of textiles did Ms. Palmer buy at Stop and Sew before?

(A) Linen
(B) Bamboo
(C) Silk
(D) Spandex

194. What is indicated about Ms. Palmer?

(A) She needs samples of fabrics.
(B) She is a first-time customer of Stop and Sew.
(C) She is eligible for a bulk order rate.
(D) She may require silk for her work.

195. What is NOT mentioned about Merino wool?

(A) It can be cleaned in a washing machine.
(B) It can be used in clothing for different seasons.
(C) It has antibacterial properties.
(D) It can be used for making athletic clothing.

GO ON TO THE NEXT PAGE

Questions 196-200 refer to the following program and e-mail.

Reconstructing the Past: Traditions and Transformations
A symposium organized by the
National Consortium of Archaeologists (NCA)

Date: April 29, Wednesday
Venue: Demesne Convention Center

P R O G R A M		
8:00-8:30	Breakfast	
8:30-8:45	Opening Remarks	Saisha Gershon, President, NCA
8:45-10:15	Cultural Heritage and Awareness	Tobias Epstein
10:15-10:30	Intermission	
10:30-12:00	Artifacts and Material Culture	Dinah Adaskin
12:00-1:00	Lunch	
1:00-2:30	Indigenous Landscapes and Seascapes	Gabriel Cramer
2:30-2:45	Intermission	
2:45-4:15	Subsistence and Social Organization	Chantelle Steward
4:15-5:00	Panel Discussion	
5:00-7:00	Cocktail Party	

The deadline for registration is on the first day of April. The registration fee of $175 is inclusive of conference materials and beverages served during breaks. Meal charges for lunch and the cocktail party are not included in the fee and must be paid separately. Accepted payment methods are cash, check, and credit card.

E-mail

To:	allmembers@archaeologyconsortium.org
From:	frenkel@archaeologyconsortium.org
Subject:	NCA Symposium
Date:	March 30

Hi everyone,

Thank you to everyone for your support and assistance in organizing our upcoming symposium. I wanted to inform you all of a few changes to the program.

First, the times of Ms. Adaskin's and Mr. Cramer's presentations have been switched because Ms. Adaskin has an urgent business meeting that will run until noon that day. Second, the presentation scheduled to be given by Ms. Steward has been changed. Ms. Steward has been called to report to the Geneva Archaeological Institute to oversee a new project, so she won't be able to attend the event. Her research associate Eden Bettelheim will take her place.

Lastly, those who have not yet registered to the symposium are encouraged to do so as soon as possible. As you all know, this is the first event that our organization has ever coordinated, so we would strongly appreciate the support of all our members.

Sincerely,
Reuben Frenkel

196. What is indicated in the program?

(A) All guest speakers are members of the NCA.
(B) Attendees must pay extra for materials.
(C) Drinks will be offered to guests during intermissions.
(D) There will be a closing speech by the president.

197. What is suggested about Gabriel Cramer's presentation?

(A) It has been removed from the program.
(B) It will be given before the morning break.
(C) It has been rescheduled to an earlier time.
(D) It will be led by a research group.

198. What is the purpose of the e-mail?

(A) To give information on new consortium leaders
(B) To ask for feedback on an activity schedule
(C) To provide updates on an upcoming event
(D) To confirm attendance to a society meeting

199. What time will Ms. Bettelheim most likely start her presentation?

(A) At 8:45 A.M.
(B) At 10:30 A.M.
(C) At 1:00 P.M.
(D) At 2:45 P.M.

200. What is NOT true about the symposium?

(A) It will only charge admission to nonmembers of the consortium.
(B) It requires advance registration.
(C) It does not include a complimentary lunch.
(D) It is the first event to be hosted by the NCA.

Stop! This is the end of the test. If you finish before time is called, you may go back to Part 5, 6, and 7 and check your work.

COLUMN ①

TOEICの達人に聞く

濵﨑 潤之輔 さん

- TOEICスコア：990点
- TOEIC歴：2006年10月に初受験～現在に至る
- ブログ：独学でTOEIC 990点を目指す！
  (http://independentstudy.blog118.fc2.com/)
- twitter：@HUMMER_TOEIC　● Facebook：「濵﨑潤之輔」

　ここ数年、僕はTOEIC公開テストを休まず受験し、その分析を続けています。また、TOEIC書籍の編集や、企業・大学での講義を通じて得たものを、最大限学習者に還元するよう努めてきました。何度か韓国にも渡り、キム・デギュン先生やイ・イクフン語学院などの大御所と仕事をする一方で、韓国で出版されたTOEIC関連書籍の研究も続けています。その過程で、TOEIC大国・韓国のすごさを肌で感じてきたので、ここでは、その一端をご紹介したいと思います。

● 研究のために50人が受験！

　韓国では「既出問題の再構成」という触れ込みで、公開テストを入念に分析した問題集が人気です。そのため、大きな語学学校では毎回、公開テストに40～50人規模の人員（ネイティブを含む）を送り込んで受験させています。そして、即日ディスカッションをし、最新傾向を徹底的に調べ上げた上で、データベース化する、という作業を行っています。

　韓国では年14回もの公開テストが実施されていますが、彼らは地道にこのルーティンをくり返しています。少しでも精度の高いテキストを作るための努力を決して惜しまないのです。

　書店ではTOEIC関連のイベントも多く、大手書店のKyobo文庫では、有名講師のTOEIC講座を毎月開催している店舗もあります。夏休みになれば、1週間連続のイベントもあって、連日大盛況。韓国のTOEIC熱の高さを物語っています。

● 目の肥えた学習者

　そこまで熱心なのには、理由があります。韓国のTOEIC受験者は、半数以上が学生という特徴があるのですが、卒業要件として730点以上を求める大学も多く、数年来の就職難とあいまって「何がなんでもTOEICで高得点を取得しなければならない」という危機感が彼らにはあるのです。毎日10時間以上、TOEICの学習を続けている大学生も決して珍しくありません。

　みな必死ですから、TOEICを教える講師や学校、参考書に対する目は非常にシビアです。いい加減な内容のものは見向きもされません。

　教える側の努力と学ぶ側の熱意。このぶつかり合いによって、「最新傾向を反映した質の高いテキストが必然的にたくさん売れる」という環境が、韓国では確実に築き上げられているのです。

　そうした土壌から生まれた参考書の中でも、ここ7～8年にわたって不動の人気を保ち続けているのが、ハッカーズのTOEIC対策本です。

　私も韓国から取り寄せて実際に使ってみましたが、数ある類書の中でも「もっとも信頼度が高い」と自信を持ってお薦めできるクオリティです。日本版の出版により、手軽にハッカーズのテキストが入手できるようになったことを、いち学習者としてとても嬉しく思います。みなさんがこの模試を信じて学習を続け、目標スコアを獲得されることを心より願っています。

でる模試 本番のTOEICと同じように取り組もう！

TEST 2

| 所要時間 | 2時間 |

| 音声ファイル | 書名（アルバム名） |

新TOEICテスト でる模試 600問 〈TEST 2〉

トラック名（曲名）
- Part 1: T2_P1_Dir ▶ T2_P1_Q10
- Part 2: T2_P2_Dir ▶ T2_P2_Q40
- Part 3: T2_P3_Dir ▶ T2_P3_Q68-70
- Part 4: T2_P4_Dir ▶ T2_P4_End

| 用意するもの | えんぴつ（シャープペン） |

消しゴム
時計
マークシート（巻末に収録）

| 解答解説 | 別冊 解答・解説❷ TEST 2 |

LISTENING TEST

In the Listening test, you will be asked to demonstrate how well you understand spoken English. The entire Listening test will last approximately 45 minutes. There are four parts, and directions are given for each part. You must mark your answers on the separate answer sheet. Do not write your answers in your test book.

PART 1

Directions: For each question in this part, you will hear four statements about a picture in your test book. When you hear the statements, you must select the one statement that best describes what you see in the picture. Then find the number of the question on your answer sheet and mark your answer. The statements will not be printed in your test book and will be spoken only one time.

Example

Sample Answer
Ⓐ Ⓑ ● Ⓓ

Statement (C), "They're standing near the table," is the best description of the picture, so you should select answer (C) and mark it on your answer sheet.

1.

2.

3.

4.

5.

6.

7.

8.

9.

10.

PART 2

Directions: You will hear a question or statement and three responses spoken in English. They will not be printed in your test book and will be spoken only one time. Select the best response to the question or statement and mark the letter (A), (B), or (C) on your answer sheet.

Example

Sample Answer
Ⓐ ● Ⓒ

You will hear: Where is the meeting room?

You will also hear: (A) To meet the new director.
(B) It's the first room on the right.
(C) Yes, at two o'clock.

The best response to the question "Where is the meeting room?" is choice (B), "It's the first room on the right," so (B) is the correct answer. You should mark answer (B) on your answer sheet.

11. Mark your answer on your answer sheet.
12. Mark your answer on your answer sheet.
13. Mark your answer on your answer sheet.
14. Mark your answer on your answer sheet.
15. Mark your answer on your answer sheet.
16. Mark your answer on your answer sheet.
17. Mark your answer on your answer sheet.
18. Mark your answer on your answer sheet.
19. Mark your answer on your answer sheet.
20. Mark your answer on your answer sheet.
21. Mark your answer on your answer sheet.
22. Mark your answer on your answer sheet.
23. Mark your answer on your answer sheet.
24. Mark your answer on your answer sheet.
25. Mark your answer on your answer sheet.
26. Mark your answer on your answer sheet.
27. Mark your answer on your answer sheet.
28. Mark your answer on your answer sheet.
29. Mark your answer on your answer sheet.
30. Mark your answer on your answer sheet.
31. Mark your answer on your answer sheet.
32. Mark your answer on your answer sheet.
33. Mark your answer on your answer sheet.
34. Mark your answer on your answer sheet.
35. Mark your answer on your answer sheet.
36. Mark your answer on your answer sheet.
37. Mark your answer on your answer sheet.
38. Mark your answer on your answer sheet.
39. Mark your answer on your answer sheet.
40. Mark your answer on your answer sheet.

MP3 T2_P3_Dir ▶ T2_P3_Q68-70

PART 3

Directions: You will hear some conversations between two people. You will be asked to answer three questions about what the speakers say in each conversation. Select the best response to each question and mark the letter (A), (B), (C), or (D) on your answer sheet. The conversations will not be printed in your test book and will be spoken only one time.

41. What is the man working on?

    (A) A budget report
    (B) An analysis of production
    (C) An agenda for a meeting
    (D) A manufacturing schedule

42. What does the man say he will do?

    (A) Contact the board chairman
    (B) Make copies of a report
    (C) Calculate production costs
    (D) Update the woman on his work progress

43. What does the woman ask the man to do?

    (A) Meet for lunch
    (B) Schedule an appointment
    (C) Forward some documents
    (D) Speak to a client

44. Where most likely are the speakers?

    (A) At a repair shop
    (B) In a factory
    (C) In a store
    (D) In an office

45. What does the woman say about the new products?

    (A) They are imported.
    (B) They are colorful.
    (C) They are discounted.
    (D) They are comfortable.

46. What problem does the man mention?

    (A) An item has been sold out.
    (B) He is suffering from a medical problem.
    (C) The color he wants is not available.
    (D) He doesn't have enough support staff.

GO ON TO THE NEXT PAGE

87

47. What are the speakers discussing?

(A) A university class
(B) A language course
(C) A travel package
(D) A work schedule

48. What does the woman mention about the hotel?

(A) It will raise its charges.
(B) It is located in South America.
(C) It often accommodates foreign guests.
(D) It provides student rates.

49. When will the classes most likely start?

(A) On Monday
(B) On Tuesday
(C) Next Wednesday
(D) Next Friday

50. What type of business do the speakers work for?

(A) A recruitment company
(B) A public relations firm
(C) A legal office
(D) A banking institution

51. What does the woman require for an assistant?

(A) College education
(B) Willingness to relocate
(C) Flexible schedule
(D) Relevant experience

52. What does the man say about Sam Washington?

(A) He currently works in Baltimore.
(B) He has an educational background in law.
(C) He resides near the office.
(D) He recently relocated.

53. Who does the woman say she just spoke to?

(A) A trade fair representative
(B) A clerk from a rental agency
(C) An employee from a printing business
(D) A layout designer

54. What does Mr. Fredrick recommend the woman do?

(A) Ask a colleague to accompany her
(B) Contact the print shop
(C) Attend the trade fair
(D) Distribute some catalogs

55. What does the woman offer to do?

(A) Send a billing statement
(B) Check for errors in a catalog
(C) Arrange a meeting with Mohinder
(D) Deliver a payment to the printer

56. Where most likely do the speakers work?

(A) At a convention center
(B) At a travel agency
(C) At a financial firm
(D) At a hotel

57. Why is Greystone Financial calling?

(A) To schedule a conference
(B) To ask about ticket availability
(C) To inquire about vacancies
(D) To request a deposit payment

58. What will the woman probably do next?

(A) Call Greystone Financial
(B) Reschedule a conference event
(C) Contact another department
(D) Fill out a reservation form

59. What type of business do the speakers probably work at?

(A) A local newspaper
(B) A supermarket
(C) A culinary school
(D) A restaurant

60. What did the critic mention in the review?

(A) Items are reasonably priced.
(B) A book will soon be available.
(C) Service was excellent.
(D) A product will help business owners.

61. What does the man say he will do?

(A) Advertise a job position
(B) Try a new product
(C) Post an article
(D) Write to a publication

62. Who is Ellen Grey?

(A) A security officer
(B) A personal assistant
(C) A workshop instructor
(D) A new employee

63. Why is the woman meeting Mr. Chambers?

(A) She is interviewing for a job.
(B) She needs to get a security pass.
(C) She is scheduled to receive training.
(D) She wants to discuss a building project.

64. According to James Walsh, what is the security pass for?

(A) Going through the main office entrance
(B) Usage of the elevators
(C) Accessing a parking facility
(D) Entering a private office

65. Where most likely does the woman work?

(A) At a food factory
(B) At a newspaper company
(C) At a consultancy firm
(D) At an advertising agency

66. According to the man, why was the merger delayed?

(A) Employees are refusing to follow some policies.
(B) Production equipment had to be improved.
(C) Executives are still working on the contract.
(D) Financial issues had to be settled.

67. What does the man say will happen on May 1?

(A) The companies will announce some information.
(B) The current contracts will expire.
(C) An official offer will be made.
(D) A corporate purchase will be completed.

68. What are the speakers talking about?

(A) A shipment of supplies
(B) Bill payment options
(C) Changes to a purchase
(D) Home renovation plans

69. What does the woman offer to do for the man?

(A) Send his purchase through expedited delivery
(B) Give him a price reduction on some products
(C) Mail him a catalog of merchandise
(D) Provide him with a full refund

70. What does the man ask the woman to do?

(A) Use the same method of payment
(B) Forward a price list
(C) Send him a bill
(D) Exchange an item

GO ON TO THE NEXT PAGE

PART 4

Directions: You will hear some talks given by a single speaker. You will be asked to answer three questions about what the speaker says in each talk. Select the best response to each question and mark the letter (A), (B), (C), or (D) on your answer sheet. The talks will not be printed in your test book and will be spoken only one time.

71. What is the organization raising money for?

    (A) An association of teachers
    (B) A planned renovation
    (C) Regional parks
    (D) School libraries

72. What type of event will the association hold?

    (A) A benefit concert
    (B) An athletic competition
    (C) A family picnic
    (D) A seasonal celebration

73. What does the speaker ask listeners to do?

    (A) Volunteer to work with a committee
    (B) Donate books to the school
    (C) Help clean up city parks
    (D) Sell tickets for an event

74. What is the purpose of the message?

    (A) To offer a discounted subscription plan
    (B) To announce a regular maintenance schedule
    (C) To assist customers outside of office hours
    (D) To promote a new selection of products

75. What should listeners do if they have Internet problems?

    (A) Scan their computers
    (B) Reset their machines
    (C) Visit a repair center
    (D) Call another number

76. Who would most likely leave a message?

    (A) A subscriber experiencing slow connectivity
    (B) A customer questioning some charges
    (C) A field technician submitting a report
    (D) A business client making a proposal

77. Why is the speaker contacting Ms. Lee?

    (A) To ask for an application form
    (B) To inform her of a company event
    (C) To arrange a job interview
    (D) To request a deadline extension

78. What is the speaker's occupation?

    (A) Production manager
    (B) Merchandise developer
    (C) Educational instructor
    (D) Human resource director

79. What is Ms. Lee asked to do?

    (A) Bring copies of documents
    (B) Mail a registration form
    (C) Submit a production report
    (D) Attend an employee meeting

80. Why was the announcement made?

    (A) To inform passengers of a change in schedule
    (B) To announce a train's delayed departure
    (C) To ask listeners to submit travel documents
    (D) To recommend places of interest to visitors

81. What does the speaker recommend?

    (A) Waiting at Port Edgerton
    (B) Taking a taxi into Manhattan
    (C) Boarding a bus to River Road
    (D) Catching a train at Midtown

82. What should listeners do if they want more information?

    (A) Check a schedule posted on the wall
    (B) View a monitor in the waiting area
    (C) Telephone a ticket counter at the station
    (D) Speak to a company representative

83. What type of products are being tested?

    (A) Freshly baked goods
    (B) Fast-food sandwiches
    (C) Dietary supplements
    (D) Instant meals

84. What does the speaker ask listeners to provide?

    (A) Identification cards
    (B) Reactions to a product design
    (C) Personal details
    (D) A list of qualifications

85. What can listeners expect to receive?

    (A) Discounts on merchandise
    (B) Monetary compensation
    (C) A free ticket to an event
    (D) A complimentary gift basket

86. Where most likely does the speaker work?

    (A) At an academic institution
    (B) At a research facility
    (C) In a science laboratory
    (D) In the admissions office

87. What problem does the speaker mention?

    (A) A lack of faculty members
    (B) Increased enrollment
    (C) Shortage of classrooms
    (D) Expensive tuition fees

88. What will most likely happen next semester?

    (A) Professors will get a salary raise.
    (B) The science club will accept more members.
    (C) Some students can choose to study at night.
    (D) Some classes may be cancelled due to overcrowding.

GO ON TO THE NEXT PAGE

89. Where most likely did Ms. Kim meet Ms. Santino?

    (A) At a fashion event
    (B) At a trade fair
    (C) At a business conference
    (D) At a human resources office

90. Why did Ms. Santino leave the message?

    (A) To ask about some products
    (B) To inquire about a job position
    (C) To schedule an interview
    (D) To provide information on an event

91. What will Ms. Santino probably do this morning?

    (A) Return from a trip
    (B) Call again later
    (C) Complete a design sample
    (D) Send some documents

92. What is the main purpose of the announcement?

    (A) To inform listeners about a service
    (B) To report changes in public policy
    (C) To promote the services of a bank
    (D) To remind citizens to pay their taxes

93. According to the announcement, who is qualified to apply for a loan?

    (A) Those who have some type of employment
    (B) Those who have an income in excess of $24,000
    (C) Those who reside within the state
    (D) Those who have no outstanding debt

94. According to the speaker, what can be found on a Web site?

    (A) A list of pension benefits
    (B) The complete details of a program
    (C) An application form for housing relief
    (D) The terms and conditions of a contract

95. What does the message mainly concern?

    (A) A travel itinerary
    (B) Payment options
    (C) Requested information
    (D) A lease agreement

96. According to the message, what will Ms. Forbes need to do?

    (A) Transmit a photocopied document
    (B) Send her credit card information
    (C) Apply to renew her passport
    (D) Fill out an application form

97. What is mentioned about Brent Stewart?

    (A) He works out of the Hong Kong branch.
    (B) He will address Ms. Forbes's further concerns.
    (C) He will be arriving at the airport on August 4.
    (D) He received the payment for a deposit.

98. What is the report about?

    (A) A health beverage
    (B) A restaurant chain
    (C) A business merger
    (D) A marketing project

99. What may Hagley-Weldon be planning to do in the future?

    (A) Develop new items to sell
    (B) Expand its operations into North America
    (C) Form a partnership with Gridleys Corporation
    (D) Hire a new board chairman

100. According to the report, why was Hagley-Weldon formed?

    (A) To decrease the cost of manufacturing
    (B) To broaden operations internationally
    (C) To increase the amount of production
    (D) To deal with a competitor in the market

This is the end of the Listening test. Turn to Part 5 in your test book.

NO TEST MATERIAL ON THIS PAGE

READING TEST

In the Reading test, you will read a variety of texts and answer several different types of reading comprehension questions. The entire Reading test will last 75 minutes. There are three parts, and directions are given for each part. You are encouraged to answer as many questions as possible within the time allowed.

You must mark your answers on the separate answer sheet. Do not write your answers in your test book.

PART 5

Directions: A word or phrase is missing in each of the sentences below. Four answer choices are given below each sentence. Select the best answer to complete the sentence. Then mark the letter (A), (B), (C), or (D) on your answer sheet.

---

101. Please call me once Mr. Bates confirms our appointment with ------- regarding preparations for the art exhibit.

(A) he
(B) him
(C) his
(D) himself

102. The new kitchen appliances from Eaton Electronics are ------- easy to use and affordable.

(A) every
(B) both
(C) while
(D) such

103. Avion Air ------- the right to add a fuel surcharge to any tickets purchased up to 24 hours before the scheduled time of departure.

(A) reserves
(B) relates
(C) collects
(D) allows

104. The studio must quickly find a ------- for the director before production begins next month.

(A) member
(B) predecessor
(C) equivalent
(D) replacement

105. To enter the literary contest, write a one-page essay about a travel destination and send it ------- the specified envelope.

(A) of
(B) in
(C) at
(D) by

106. Environmental groups campaigned ------- against the construction of a cement factory near the national park.

(A) persistence
(B) persistent
(C) persistently
(D) persisting

107. All office employees were asked to make sure to turn ------- all the lights in the office before leaving for the day.

(A) over
(B) off
(C) around
(D) along

108. Mr. Lynch asked to see several samples of products before ------- to sign the contract with the supply company.

(A) agreement
(B) agreed
(C) agrees
(D) agreeing

109. The vintage paintings to be auctioned off by the Heritage Foundation are kept ------- in a well-ventilated location.

    (A) certain
    (B) realistic
    (C) secure
    (D) confident

110. Mr. Wilkins would like some ------- setting up the audio-visual equipment in the conference room before the seminar on Thursday.

    (A) assisted
    (B) assistance
    (C) assist
    (D) assisting

111. Every $200 purchase of Billow Swimwear entitles shoppers to receive ------- a towel or a pair of slippers.

    (A) also
    (B) either
    (C) until
    (D) neither

112. If the building owner ------- the proposed lobby renovation tomorrow, work will begin as soon as next week.

    (A) approval
    (B) approving
    (C) will approve
    (D) approves

113. ------- of purchases made on our Web site will be sent to customers' e-mail accounts within one day of the transactions.

    (A) Confirmation
    (B) Observation
    (C) Delegation
    (D) Admission

114. The renowned author ------- his award-winning autobiography with a short quote from a Japanese poet which summarized the theme of the book.

    (A) conclude
    (B) was concluded
    (C) to conclude
    (D) concluded

115. Ms. Desi has been operating ------- fast food franchise for the past ten years and is hoping to open another branch in the near future.

    (A) her own
    (B) hers
    (C) she
    (D) herself

116. Sullivan Properties has requested an official ------- from a licensed realtor to find out the current value of its commercial building in Portland.

    (A) level
    (B) total
    (C) appraisal
    (D) capital

117. Arayat Tours is offering summer cruise packages to customers ------- in exploring the Caribbean Islands.

    (A) interesting
    (B) interest
    (C) interested
    (D) interestingly

118. Since the donation contained perishable food items, volunteers were concerned it might ------- have expired when it reached its final destination.

    (A) never
    (B) already
    (C) more
    (D) occasionally

119. Young painters are encouraged to attend workshops ------- to learn new techniques that will improve their skills.

    (A) frequented
    (B) frequently
    (C) frequency
    (D) frequenting

GO ON TO THE NEXT PAGE

120. The report ------- mentioned an upcoming merger between a textile company in the United States and a prominent fashion boutique in France.

(A) intensely
(B) briefly
(C) rarely
(D) anymore

121. Business class passengers on Trans-Con Air receive several benefits ------- access to the lounge, larger seats, and gourmet meals.

(A) inclusive
(B) including
(C) inclusively
(D) included

122. To promote its ecologically friendly technology, Kazka Motors will ------- a hybrid car model by the end of the year.

(A) store
(B) spend
(C) submit
(D) launch

123. The financial consultant ------- Ms. Broderick to downsize the staff at the Denver branch to lower operational expenses.

(A) suggested
(B) advised
(C) commented
(D) argued

124. ------- intense competition in the market, HiMobile continues to be the top cellular phone manufacturer in Asia.

(A) Concerning
(B) Except
(C) Around
(D) Despite

125. ------- are nearly finished for Oakville's centennial anniversary parade to be held along Main Street this coming Sunday.

(A) Preparers
(B) Preparations
(C) Prepared
(D) Preparing

126. Scientists have been saying for years that solar energy has incredible ------- to become the world's leading power source in place of fossil fuels.

(A) insight
(B) potential
(C) relevance
(D) suggestion

127. Somerset Airlines provides special boarding services at the departure gates for ------- requiring extra help or traveling with small children.

(A) that
(B) whose
(C) those
(D) they

128. Because of her new position as financial vice president at the company's European headquarters, Marina Latke ------- to London in October.

(A) relocate
(B) relocating
(C) is relocated
(D) will relocate

129. Chemical materials such as detergents and other cleaning agents should be kept in locked locations which are not ------- to small children.

(A) access
(B) accessing
(C) accessed
(D) accessible

130. At a meeting of finance ministers in June, Mr. Yao Jie Bin will give a brief ------- on the benefits of China's efforts to control its currency.

(A) situation
(B) revelation
(C) presentation
(D) perception

131. For this year's annual company conference, the planning committee is putting together an ------- trip to Hawaii that will last for three days.

(A) exciting
(B) excited
(C) excites
(D) excitement

132. Please note that all publications on sale at the West-End Book Store are categorized and arranged on shelves ------- subject and genre.

(A) in order to
(B) permitting
(C) according to
(D) alike

133. For train passengers with excess baggage, FineTrak Railways will impose a fee of $13 for every ------- bag.

(A) promising
(B) supplementary
(C) additional
(D) unprepared

134. Because of the ------- working conditions and the low salaries offered by Benton Manufacturing, many employees handed in their resignations.

(A) practical
(B) unfavorable
(C) combined
(D) functional

135. Refunds or exchanges for any of Dunway Electronics' products may be requested at all ------- dealers.

(A) authorization
(B) authority
(C) authorize
(D) authorized

136. The company judiciously added a popular item to an existing product bundle with the expectation that sales of the new combination would ------- the targeted goal for the quarter.

(A) exceed
(B) react
(C) declare
(D) apprise

137. ------- the author satisfies the publishing company's requirements for a new edition of the book Art Through the Ages, publication will have to be postponed.

(A) Unless
(B) Rather than
(C) Whenever
(D) As long as

138. Staff members attending the picnic should bring ------- food they would like to share with the group, apart from burgers and beverages, which will be provided by the company.

(A) whenever
(B) whomever
(C) whatever
(D) wherever

139. The tour leader is making arrangements to accommodate a group of visitors who have requested an ------- to a small island near their location.

(A) itinerary
(B) excursion
(C) option
(D) approach

140. In ------- with the health department's stipulations, restaurant owners must conduct sessions with kitchen service operators to familiarize them with food safety regulations.

(A) participating
(B) pursuing
(C) according
(D) keeping

GO ON TO THE NEXT PAGE

PART 6

Directions: Read the texts that follow. A word or phrase is missing in some of the sentences. Four answer choices are given below each of the sentences. Select the best answer to complete the text. Then mark the letter (A), (B), (C), or (D) on your answer sheet.

Questions 141-143 refer to the following article.

Napping is Healthy, Not a Sign of Laziness!

Young children often get away with taking naps in the afternoon, but any adult who tries to do the same will usually be called "lazy". -------, new studies show that such brief

141. (A) However
(B) Since
(C) Besides
(D) Otherwise

afternoon naps, or "power naps", may actually be good for health, regardless of age.

Naps lasting between 20 and 60 minutes in the afternoon have numerous -------,

142. (A) evidence
(B) attempts
(C) benefits
(D) improvements

including stress reduction and heightening learning abilities and reaction times. In addition, naps can even help with people's vision and upgrade their work performance.

Studies show that 20 minutes of sleep in the second half of the day is actually more helpful to our bodies than 20 minutes of extra sleep in the morning. People who take naps wake up feeling more ------- and motivated than those who sleep in during the

143. (A) energize
(B) energetically
(C) energy
(D) energetic

morning. So the next time your boss catches you napping on the job, just say, "I'm only having a nap because it will help me be more productive," and see if the excuse works!

Questions 144-146 refer to the following letter.

Tina Louis
1877 Birchwood Street
Summerland, BC, Canada

Dear Ms. Louis,

It is my pleasure on behalf of the company to ------- offer you a summer internship at HBC-

    144. (A) honorably
        (B) exceptionally
        (C) temporally
        (D) officially

TV. The internship will begin on June 2 and end on August 31. You will work together with our reporters, producers, and technical staff during this period to learn about the operations and production of a TV news program.

As was explained at your interview, all interns work on a ------- basis for the first two weeks.

    145. (A) provisional
        (B) undecided
        (C) permanent
        (D) persistent

At this point, the staff you work with will evaluate your performance. Following that, a decision ------- about which particular department would be best suited for you. And though

    146. (A) has been making
        (B) was made
        (C) will be made
        (D) is making

we do not offer salaries for any intern positions, we do provide a modest allowance of $100 per week to cover the cost of your meals and transportation.

I hope you will find the internship useful and educational. Please let me know by Friday, May 25, whether you are interested.

Sincerely,

Robert Denver
Programming Director, HBC-TV

GO ON TO THE NEXT PAGE

Questions 147-149 refer to the following letter.

Dear Editor,

I am writing in response to an article that appeared in your June 16 issue, entitled "The Real Cost of Business," in which you assert that Leyton Teas CEO Dana Brubeck is being pushed out of the company by management. That statement is simply false. In fact, our company ------- involved in merger negotiations with a competitor and Mr. Brubeck will most likely be

147. (A) has been
(B) have had
(C) will have been
(D) will have

serving on the board of directors.

While it is ------- that Leyton Teas has suffered decreasing profitability under Mr. Brubeck,
    148. (A) inevitable
       (B) true
       (C) particular
       (D) complex

this is not a reflection of his leadership abilities and we feel any suggestions to that effect are damaging to his reputation. Therefore, we ask that you print a ------- of the article in an
                                            149. (A) version
                                                 (B) definition
                                                 (C) retraction
                                                 (D) caption

appropriate and timely manner.

In the future, should you need any further information about our affairs, I will be happy to assist you. Please feel free to contact me at lizbyron@leyton.com.

Thank you.

Elizabeth Byron
Public Relations
Leyton Teas

Questions 150-152 refer to the following e-mail.

From: Laura Masterson <lauram@bizpeople.org>
To: Zachary Wilson <zwilson@cybermail.net>
Date: July 7
Subject: Schedule

Dear Mr. Wilson,

You have registered to participate in Biz People's leadership skills course.

Because of the sudden increase in ------- this year, our organization has decided to

150. (A) enlistment
(B) attention
(C) enrollment
(D) occupancy

divide the course into two separate sessions. Instead of just Wednesdays from 9:00 A.M. to 11:00 A.M., we will now offer the same course on Fridays, which will meet from 7:00 P.M. to 9:00 P.M. Both sessions will be taught by Ms. Christina Lopez, a former chief executive officer ------- over 30 years of experience in corporate management.

151. (A) plus
(B) with
(C) about
(D) from

Due to the change, we are asking all those who have already signed up to register again by visiting our Web site at http://www.bizpeople.com/seminars.

We are sorry for the inconvenience and for more information, kindly respond to this e-mail or call our office at (809) 555-9238 during ------- business hours.

152. (A) frequent
(B) normal
(C) opened
(D) average

Truly yours,

Laura Masterson
Biz People Career Development Services

PART 7

Directions: In this part your will read a selection of texts, such as magazine and newspaper articles, letters, and advertisements. Each text is followed by several questions. Select the best answer for each question and mark the letter (A), (B), (C), or (D) on your answer sheet.

Questions 153-154 refer to the following notice.

Milton Furnishings

To our valued customers,

Beginning September 1, you will be required to present a valid identification card every time you make a credit card purchase at Milton Furnishings. This is in connection with the increasing incidence of credit card fraud at retail stores across the country. Please show any of the following proofs of identification at the checkout counter:

Passport
Driver's license
Voter's ID
Company ID

Thank you for your cooperation.

Management

153. Why was the notice written?

(A) To announce the closure of a business
(B) To inform clients of a new store policy
(C) To recommend a payment option
(D) To publicize a sale

154. What will the store do to protect itself from fraud?

(A) Limit the number of accepted credit cards
(B) Call banks before accepting credit payments
(C) Ask customers to show personal documents
(D) Request shoppers to make purchases with cash

GO ON TO THE NEXT PAGE

Questions 155-157 refer to the following e-mail.

E-mail

To: All bank staff
From: Donald Manzo
Subject: Welcome reception
Date: August 5

We are holding a reception to welcome our new regional vice president, Gertrude Crowley. Ms. Crowley previously worked as branch manager of Knightland Bank's affiliate in Charleston. After five years there, she led our branch in Atlanta for two years and then transferred to New Orleans, where she has been since working as their district manager. She will now head the southeast district from our regional office here in Nashville.

The reception will be held at the Bluegrass Hotel on Friday, Aug.9, at 7:30 P.M. If you plan on coming, please notify my secretary at extension #44. Also, please let him know if you will be bringing a guest.

Thank you.

---

155. What is the main purpose of the e-mail?

(A) To invite employees to an event
(B) To inform staff of a work schedule
(C) To request attendance to a branch meeting
(D) To ask for help setting up a reception

156. Where has Ms. Crowley NOT previously worked?

(A) Charleston
(B) Atlanta
(C) New Orleans
(D) Nashville

157. How can employees confirm their attendance?

(A) By sending a reply e-mail
(B) By contacting Mr. Manzo's assistant
(C) By calling the hotel
(D) By speaking to Mr. Manzo

Questions 158-159 refer to the following information.

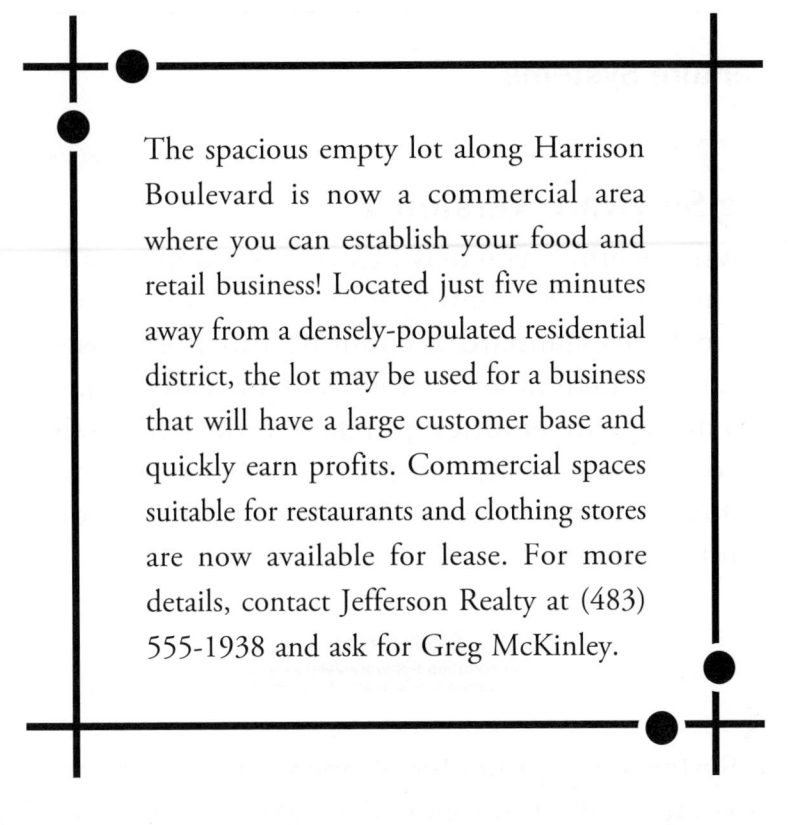

The spacious empty lot along Harrison Boulevard is now a commercial area where you can establish your food and retail business! Located just five minutes away from a densely-populated residential district, the lot may be used for a business that will have a large customer base and quickly earn profits. Commercial spaces suitable for restaurants and clothing stores are now available for lease. For more details, contact Jefferson Realty at (483) 555-1938 and ask for Greg McKinley.

158. For whom is the information most likely intended?

(A) Prospective tenants
(B) Real estate agents
(C) Residents near the commercial area
(D) Retailing experts

159. What is stated about the commercial spaces?

(A) They are located near an area inhabited by many people.
(B) They are five minutes away from Harrison Boulevard.
(C) They are available for residential use.
(D) They are suitable for food establishments only.

Questions 160-161 refer to the following information.

Ace Venture Systems

Home   Products   News   Contact Us

Accounting Software Version 1

Ace Venture Systems brings you new business accounting software for small and medium enterprises. Accounting Software Version 1 is a FREE software package that includes standard accounting functions essential to small business operations. Like other customized software, it has features that allow users to manage inventories, purchase orders, and sales data. It can also be used to organize financial reports and bank account information. Discover what Accounting Software Version 1 can do for your business by clicking the button below:

Download
Accounting Software Version 1

Ace Venture Systems is a promoter of open source software. It develops reliable business applications for more than 200,000 users free of charge. For comments and suggestions on Accounting Software Version 1, please complete our user feedback sheet by clicking <u>here</u>.

160. Why was the information published?

(A) To introduce accounting methods
(B) To promote a computer program
(C) To form a network of small companies
(D) To gather suggestions for a new project

161. What is NOT true about Ace Venture Systems?

(A) It supports the use of open source computer programs.
(B) It asks for clients to give them feedback.
(C) It offers software on a trial basis.
(D) It provides direct downloads on its Web site.

Questions 162-164 refer to the following article.

CEO of Nature's Wonders Pens Insightful Autobiography

Anna Broderick decided it was time for a change. After working for over fifteen years in the cosmetics industry, she handed in her resignation at Landon Cosmetics and embarked on forming her own beauty product empire. Ten years later, Nature's Wonders is now one of the most prominent cosmetics companies on the globe. With stores in more than 30 countries, Broderick credits her success to creating products that are natural, affordable, and environmentally friendly.

In her autobiography released this week entitled *The Search for the Fountain of Youth*, Broderick tells her story. She proves herself to be not only a brilliant businesswoman, but also a talented writer. She describes her struggle to create a company that focuses more on social issues rather than profit. The book is already number eight on the best-seller list and is a great read for struggling entrepreneurs or those looking for inspiration in the often brutal world of business.

162. In what type of publication would this article most likely appear?

(A) A company manual
(B) A travel guide
(C) A business journal
(D) A product brochure

163. Why did Ms. Broderick quit her job at Landon Cosmetics?

(A) A competitor offered her a better position.
(B) She wanted to pursue a graduate degree.
(C) There wasn't enough opportunity for advancement.
(D) She decided to open her own business.

164. What is indicated about *The Search for the Fountain of Youth*?

(A) It hasn't yet been released.
(B) It has sold many copies.
(C) It won an award.
(D) It is part of a series.

GO ON TO THE NEXT PAGE

Questions 165-167 refer to the following Web site.

The Knowledge Encyclopedia
Seek. Read. Discover.

About us | **Daily Trivia** | Site Map | Contact Us

Today's Trivia

Did you know that the traffic light was originally invented for railways?

In the nineteenth century, railroad engineers invented the traffic light to prevent train collisions and, most importantly, pedestrian accidents. However, it took much trial and error before the first railway traffic light was formally used. Railroad engineers had a problem selecting colors that would effectively communicate warnings to people. In the 1830s, they tried using red for "stop" and green for "caution". For "go", they used a white light that signaled "all clear". This combination of lights did not work since the green light was often mistaken for "go". Because of this, they settled on green for "go" and introduced a yellow light to signal "caution".

The device was used for road traffic as early as 1868 in London, England. Outside the Parliament building stood a gas-powered traffic light that was manually controlled to shift from red to green. It was intended to facilitate steam automobiles and wagon traffic.

The first electric traffic light was created by James Hoge of Ohio in 1918. Two years later, a Detroit policeman named William Potts came up with the three-colored traffic light we use today. The device evolved as it spread across the world, with varying functions depending on the needs of specific locations.

Go
Search

The Knowledge Encyclopedia
©Copyright 2010
All rights reserved

---

165. Why was the traffic light invented?

(A) To increase the speed of train travel
(B) To protect people traveling on foot
(C) To allow cars to cross railway tracks safely
(D) To replace gas-powered lamps

166. What is mentioned about the traffic light made by railway engineers?

(A) It could not be modified for road use.
(B) It could not be seen from far distances.
(C) It had confusing colors.
(D) It was operated manually.

167. According to the information, when was the modern traffic light first put into use?

(A) In 1830
(B) In 1868
(C) In 1918
(D) In 1920

Questions 168-171 refer to the following flyer.

The Night
A concert

On December 5, French balladeers Roy Easton and Melissa Amber will be at the Maroon Theatre for their second concert in Los Angeles, California. The event will also feature French pianist Amanda Ewell as well as American soul singers Andy Red and Cindy Dawson, who will accompany Mr. Easton and Ms. Amber during their performance. During the concert, Ms. Amber will also be introducing her inspirational album, *Crossroads*, which was launched in Paris last week.

Witness an extraordinary fusion of French and American artists. Buy three tickets and get a backstage pass absolutely free. This promotion is good until November 20 and is not valid for general admission ticket purchases. Tickets are available at any Gatewing outlet nationwide. They may also be purchased online at www.gatewing.com. A flat rate shipping fee of $8 applies. Recordings from both Mr. Easton and Ms. Amber will be available for purchase.

GATEWING
555-2541

168. Why was the flyer written?

(A) To introduce a new artist
(B) To promote an event
(C) To advertise an upcoming album
(D) To launch a Web site

169. In paragraph 2, line 4 the word "flat" is closest in meaning to

(A) bland
(B) marginal
(C) smooth
(D) fixed

170. What is suggested about the general admission tickets?

(A) They will be given free to French nationals.
(B) They do not come with backstage passes.
(C) They will be sold at a discount.
(D) They cannot be purchased in other states.

171. What is NOT mentioned about the concert?

(A) Several singers will perform with Mr. Easton and Ms. Amber.
(B) Items will be available for sale.
(C) A new recording will be promoted.
(D) Performers will sign autographs.

GO ON TO THE NEXT PAGE

Questions 172-175 refer to the following advertisement.

Carlton Motors CLEARANCE SALE ON NOW!

Prices on all cars, trucks, and minivans have been slashed at Carlton Motors at 219 Birch Avenue! In preparation for our move to a new location, all current stock must go. Take advantage of incredible savings of up to 40 percent on vehicles from Carson, Miyaki Automotive, DMC, and Ridgemont Motors! We also carry a full range of scooters and motorbikes. We are sure to have the perfect vehicle for all of your needs!

Carlton Motors ensures the reliability of its vehicles by offering full warranties, biannual car tune-ups, and comprehensive repair services. All vehicles sold come with a full one-year warranty, with reasonable rates offered for additional coverage. Also, we will change your oil every four months for two years, free of charge!

So come on down to Carlton Motors for a test drive of one of our many quality vehicles today! But hurry, as this sale lasts only until January 2! Our showroom is open from 10 A.M. to 8 P.M. For further information, call us at 555-7798, or visit our Web site at www.carltonmotors.co.au for descriptions of the vehicles we have on offer.

172. Why is Carlton Motors having a sale?

(A) It is closing one of its stores.
(B) It needs to make space for new stock.
(C) It is relocating the showroom to another area.
(D) It did not meet its sales target for the year.

173. What is indicated about Carlton Motors?

(A) It stocks a wide range of car accessories.
(B) It is open seven days a week.
(C) It also sells used automobiles.
(D) It has several brands of vehicles available.

174. According to the advertisement, what does the business encourage people to do?

(A) Try out any of their vehicles
(B) Sign up for car insurance
(C) Pay for vehicles in installments
(D) Compare their prices with competitors'

175. What service is NOT mentioned in the advertisement?

(A) Vehicular repairs
(B) Complete warranties
(C) Oil change
(D) Car registration

GO ON TO THE NEXT PAGE

Questions 176-180 refer to the following newsletter.

August Highlights Union of Nations
Sanjay Raghavan

Sanjay Raghavan has been working for the Union of Nations for twelve years. He began working as a volunteer at the children's welfare division in our South Asia headquarters in Calcutta, India. Since then, he has participated in numerous missions to help carry out development goals of the organization in developing countries. He also worked as one of our fundraising officers in London and director for relief operations in Haiti. A year ago, he transferred to our main headquarters in New York, where he is now the executive director at the World Children's Fund.

Mr. Raghavan has always given priority to helping the world's children, for he believes that they hold the key to improving the future. He believes that children should be nurtured and encouraged to obtain an education to become successful later in their lives. He recalls meeting a peacekeeper when he was just ten years old, who helped evacuate his family after a tsunami wiped out their makeshift home in Chennai. "Since that day, I've always wanted to make a difference by helping others, and that's what inspired me to follow this career path."

Christa Ramstein, a current member of Mr. Raghavan's staff, describes him as a responsive person who is always ready to provide assistance to those in need. "He has even set up his own foundation to give scholarships to underprivileged children in his hometown."

Prior to becoming a volunteer for the Union of Nations, Mr. Raghavan earned his bachelor's degree in development studies from Cochin State College and his master's degree in international affairs at the University of East Calcutta.

176. What is the purpose of the article?

(A) To give information about outreach programs
(B) To outline the achievements of an employee
(C) To announce a yearly fundraising event
(D) To describe living conditions in foreign countries

177. Where did Mr. Raghavan start his career?

(A) Chennai
(B) New York
(C) Calcutta
(D) London

178. The word "responsive" in paragraph 3, line 2 is closest in meaning to

(A) adventurous
(B) communicative
(C) persuadable
(D) grateful

179. What is suggested about Ms. Ramstein?

(A) She began her own foundation.
(B) She participated in relief operations.
(C) She is giving away scholarships.
(D) She is working in New York.

180. What is NOT mentioned about Mr. Raghavan?

(A) He donated money to charity institutions.
(B) He experienced hardship at a young age.
(C) He worked in different parts of the world.
(D) He obtained his education in India.

GO ON TO THE NEXT PAGE

Questions 181-185 refer to the following e-mails.

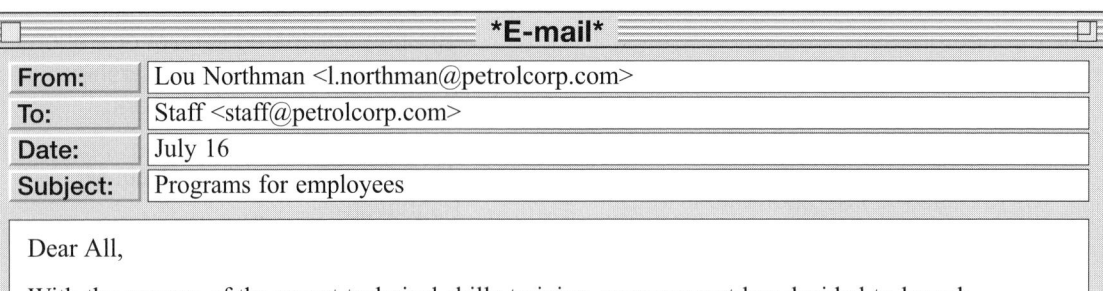

E-mail

From: Lou Northman <l.northman@petrolcorp.com>
To: Staff <staff@petrolcorp.com>
Date: July 16
Subject: Programs for employees

Dear All,

With the success of the recent technical skills training, management has decided to launch personality development programs to help employees become better team players. Our human resources consultant, Mr. Christian Olsen, will be conducting a series of classes next month. The sessions will primarily be about stress management and interpersonal skills enhancement. Classes in interpersonal skills enhancement will be held on Thursdays from 6 P.M. to 8 P.M., while stress management classes will be conducted on Fridays, at the same time slot. Since the conference room can accommodate up to fifty persons only, the classes will be filled on a first-come-first-served basis.

If you are interested, please e-mail Mr. Olsen (c.olsen@corpway.com) with your chosen program. He and his team are finalizing the training, and they wish to know which departments most of the participants will come from. In addition, we have attached Mr. Olsen's new e-book, *The Game of Work*, which was launched last week. This free e-book about the benefits of efficient communication at work is exclusive to employees of the company. We hope that the book will be useful to all of you.

Please respond to acknowledge receipt of this e-mail. We will be happy to address your questions regarding the program. Thank you.

Lou Northman
Assistant Director
Human Resources Department

E-mail

From: Ashley Gibson <a.gibson@petrolcorp.com>
To: Christian Olsen <c.olsen@corpway.com>
Date: July 23
Subject: Personality Development Programs

Dear Mr. Olsen,

I was pleased when I received an e-mail from the human resources department, saying that you would be offering personality development programs for the staff. I want to sign up for your Friday class. I've learned a lot from reading your books on career enhancement and leadership, and I believe attending the program will improve my efficiency at work.

Thank you very much, and I look forward to meeting you in person.

Sincerely,

Ashley Gibson
Junior Accountant
Finance Department

181. Why was the first e-mail written?

(A) To recommend a book about work productivity
(B) To announce upcoming company activities
(C) To gather feedback on a recently offered program
(D) To provide teamwork enhancement tips

182. What did Mr. Northman mention about Mr. Olsen?

(A) He will hold classes for the staff.
(B) He organized the technical skills training.
(C) He works as a professor in a business school.
(D) He leads the human resources department.

183. What is indicated about the book?

(A) It is a known reference material.
(B) It is a revised edition.
(C) It was written by a psychologist.
(D) It was recently published.

184. What program will Ms. Gibson attend?

(A) Interpersonal skills enrichment
(B) Leadership skills development
(C) Stress management
(D) Career enhancement

185. What is indicated about Ms. Gibson?

(A) She has met Mr. Olsen before.
(B) She wants to read some of Mr. Olsen's published work.
(C) She works in a managerial position.
(D) She received a message from another department.

Questions 186-190 refer to the following advertisement and e-mail.

Rajasiha Travels
Thailand's Premier Travel Agency

810 Maruek Blvd. Pomprab, Bangkok 10100
(662) 555-9174
www.rajasihatravels.th

Day Tours
Hiking Trips
Luxury Cruises
Safari Adventures

Log on to our Web site to learn more about our affordable tour packages!
Special rates are available to groups of five people or more.

For inquiries, please contact our sales manager,
Sunee Mookjai, at mookjai@rajasihatravels.th.

E-mail

To:	mookjai@rajasihatravels.th
From:	eddy.dakila@yphmail.com
Date:	December 18
Subject:	Safari adventure

Dear Ms. Mookjai,

Your agency was highly recommended by my colleague, Anita Bayani, who went on your Phuket Luxury Cruise last October. She said that your tour packages were reasonably priced and that your agents were very friendly and accommodating. So I visited your Web site to check out your packages and I have to say that the Kanchanaburi Safari Adventure is exactly what my friends and I are looking for. I plan on booking the tour for our group of eight, but I have a few questions that I hope you can answer.

First, I want to know whether you accept payments through bank transfer. Also, I am wondering whether you charge a fee for making changes to a reservation, like if I need to reschedule the tour dates. Lastly, will there be a tour guide to accompany us when we explore the local scenery and wildlife in Kanchanaburi?

I would appreciate it if you could call me on my mobile number, 555-2583, to address these inquiries. I will book the tour at that time and pay by bank transfer, if it is acceptable. Otherwise, I will pay by money order. Thank you and I hope to hear from you soon.

Eduardo Dakila

186. What is NOT mentioned in the advertisement about Rajasiha Travels?

(A) The rates of its packages
(B) The location of its office
(C) The address of its Web site
(D) The name of its sales manager

187. What is indicated about Rajasiha Travels?

(A) It has job openings in sales.
(B) It prefers cash payments.
(C) It upgraded its Web site last October.
(D) It has been used by Ms. Bayani in the past.

188. What does Mr. Dakila NOT ask about?

(A) Whether any free services are included with the package
(B) Whether a tour guide will be present
(C) Whether he can pay by wiring money through a bank
(D) Whether making booking changes is free

189. How does Mr. Dakila intend to make his reservation?

(A) By e-mail
(B) In person
(C) On the phone
(D) On the Rajasiha Web site

190. What can be inferred about Mr. Dakila?

(A) He will travel to Thailand with Ms. Bayani.
(B) He is eligible for a discount on his booking.
(C) He is a long-time client of Rajasiha Travels.
(D) He will reserve more than one tour package.

GO ON TO THE NEXT PAGE

Questions 191-195 refer to the following memo and e-mail.

MEMORANDUM

FROM: Meena Rajpur, public relations associate director, Cassa Bank
TO: Gianna Vinti, regional manager, Cassa Bank
DATE: Oct. 5
SUBJECT: Requested menu changes

Dear Ms. Vinti,

I received the requested menu changes you sent me for our awards dinner on Oct. 12. I contacted the hotel and worked out a few things. First, we have added a bar and cocktail service at the beginning of the evening. Below is the revised menu. The only things that are unchanged are items that will be served during speeches and presentations.

Cocktail hour	6:00-7:00 P.M.	Cocktails, hors d'oeuvres
Dinner	7:00-8:30 P.M.	Cream of asparagus soup Fresh tomato and mozzarella salad Roasted rack of lamb OR Tortellini with spinach and ricotta (vegetarian option) Grilled pepper and zucchini Bread rolls and butter
Speeches and presentations	8:30-9:30 P.M.	Assorted desserts Coffee and tea

I also want to mention that the dining hall is ours to use until 11:00 P.M. However, we may want to inform everyone that valet service will not be available after 10:30 P.M.

I hope these changes will suit your requirements. Please contact me to confirm.

E-mail

To:	Meena Rajpur <mraj@cassabank.com>
From:	Andrew Norton <Norton@nirvanahotel.net>
Subject:	Confirmation of reservation and menu
Date:	Oct. 4

Dear Ms. Rajpur,

This e-mail is confirmation for the reservation of our Ruby Dining Hall for your company's awards ceremony on Oct. 12, from 6:00-11:00 P.M. We are also pleased to provide a coat check room on the second floor of the hotel, near the stairs leading to the Ruby Dining Hall.

I can also confirm that all the changes you requested to the menu will be made. You also asked if our hotel can provide flower arrangements for the tables. We would be more than happy to arrange this for you. You can contact our flower shop at 555-9887 ext. 18, or visit our florist personally at the hotel. Her name is Veronica Darby, and the shop is located on the same floor as the coat check.

If I can be of any further service, please don't hesitate to contact me.

Sincerely yours,

Andrew Norton, Nirvana Hotel event coordinator

191. What is the main purpose of Ms. Rajpur's memo?

(A) To request a menu
(B) To confirm some changes
(C) To provide an invitation
(D) To ask for a guest list

192. What item on the menu has not been changed?

(A) Soup
(B) Cocktails
(C) Salad
(D) Dessert

193. When will the guests have to leave the facility?

(A) By 8:30 P.M.
(B) By 9:30 P.M.
(C) By 10:30 P.M.
(D) By 11:00 P.M.

194. What is NOT provided by the hotel?

(A) Bar service
(B) Coat check
(C) Internet access
(D) Valet service

195. What is indicated about floral arrangements?

(A) They have already been paid for.
(B) They can be provided by an establishment in the hotel.
(C) They will be ordered by the event coordinator.
(D) They can be delivered for an additional charge.

GO ON TO THE NEXT PAGE

Questions 196-200 refer to the following review and e-mail.

Midsummer Bed and Breakfast
Clopton Bridge, Stratford-on-Avon
CV37 7HP, United Kingdom

Located in the historic town of Stratford-on-Avon, Midsummer Bed and Breakfast is in a fascinating location and is surrounded by incredible scenery. The renovated farmhouse is just a five-minute walk from the village center, where visitors can explore numerous shops, attend performances at the Royal Shakespeare Theatre, and tour numerous museums and tourist sites. Only 20 miles from Birmingham, Midsummer Bed and Breakfast is easily reached by rental car. A bus service also runs between Stratford, Birmingham, and Warwick. Midsummer provides a full buffet breakfast and lunch, private suites, parking, telephone and Internet access, and can even arrange tours of Stratford for its guests. Members of the Allied Frequent Flier Plan receive a discounted room rate. For further information or to inquire about reservations, visit www.alliedfliers/UKhotels.co.uk.

E-mail

To:	Kenji Watanabe <wantken@yippee.co.jp>
From:	Ann Reeves <reservations@alliedfliers.co.uk>
Subject:	Confirmation of reservation
Date:	June 24

Dear Mr. Watanabe,

Thank you for your reservation request for the Midsummer Bed and Breakfast located in Stratford-on-Avon. Your booking has been confirmed for the following dates:

Check-in	August 10
Check-out	August 14
Number of guests	2
Reservation number	PC-549613
Cost per night	£45
Allied Frequent Flier number	KW-22872

The following policies apply to your reservation:

1. Cancellations can be made up to 48 hours prior to the date of stay. Cancellations made after 48 hours are subject to a £50 cancellation fee.
2. Guests may check in after 11 A.M. and check out at the same time on their day of departure. There is a charge of £10 for each additional hour after check-out.
3. Credit cards will be charged for half the total amount on the day of check-in. The balance will be paid along with any additional room charges when checking out.

Should you require any further information, or have any questions about your reservation, feel free to send me an e-mail.

Ann Reeves
Allied Fliers Reservations UK

196. What feature of Midsummer Bed and Breakfast is NOT mentioned in the review?

(A) It is located near several tourist attractions.
(B) It provides parking facilities for guests.
(C) It is within walking distance of public transportation.
(D) It serves two meals every day.

197. Where is Midsummer located?

(A) Next door to a museum
(B) A short walk from Warwick
(C) In a scenic area
(D) By the entrance of a historic site

198. What is the main purpose of the e-mail?

(A) To request payment
(B) To ask for credit card information
(C) To provide details of a reservation
(D) To inform customers of a policy change

199. When will Mr. Watanabe probably arrive at Midsummer?

(A) June 10
(B) June 24
(C) August 10
(D) August 14

200. What can be inferred about Mr. Watanabe?

(A) He has stayed at Midsummer before.
(B) He is traveling with his wife.
(C) He will first travel to Birmingham.
(D) He received a discounted rate.

Stop! This is the end of the test. If you finish before time is called, you may go back to Part 5, 6, and 7 and check your work.

COLUMN ②

TOEICの達人に聞く

porpor さん

- TOEICスコア：980点
- TOEIC歴：2006年9月の初受験から、6年以上
- ブログ：TOEIC 990点への道 ──日本から出ずに満点──
  (http://blogs.yahoo.co.jp/porpor35)
- twitter：@porpor35

　みなさん、こんにちは！ porporです。「TOEIC 990点への道 ──日本から出ずに満点──」というブログを書きながら、990点目指して学習を続けるサラリーマンです。TOEIC初受験から、はや6年。年がら年中、TOEICのことを考えています。よく続くものだと、われながら感心しています。

　そんな変人（笑）の私が、なぜここまでTOEICにはまったのか。それは、当たり前ですが、楽しいから。ここでは、私なりのTOEICの「楽しみ方」をお伝えしたいと思います。

●ブログはTOEIC学習のブースター

　TOEICとの出会いは、大学生の時。目的は就職活動の準備と英語力チェックです。インターネットで情報収集してみると、たくさんのTOEIC学習ブログが見つかりました。内容はまちまちでしたが、みなさんの「目標に向かって自分を高める姿」に惹かれ、私もブログを始めることに。

　その日から私の学習は加速しました。

　ブログには、「学習内容」を書くだけでなく、「悩み」を吐露することもあります。そんなときは、TOEICという共通テーマを持つブロガーさんたちから、たくさんのコメントをいただきます。励ましだったり、ヒントだったり。学習仲間との新たなつながりが、私を後押ししてくれたのです。

　もちろん、自分からほかの方のブログを訪問することもあります。教材や学習法のアイデアを発見でき、自分のやり方を見直すいいキッカケになりますから。

　もう一歩進んで、TOEIC本の著者イベントや、ブロガーさん主催の勉強会へも積極的に参加するようになりました。リアルの場で得られる刺激は、さらに力となりました。

　このように、ブログを通じて、多くの学習仲間と出会えたことが、TOEICを続けている最大の要因だろうと思います。学習は孤独との戦いでもありますが、同じように頑張っている仲間の存在を感じられれば、心強いですからね。

●努力は必ず報われる

　ブログと学習のよいサイクルを作ることで、スコアは着実に伸びていきました。あとは、結果を見ては、学習に修正を加え、問題を解いては、記録し、知識を追加・修正していく。トライアンドエラーの繰り返しですね。そうやって、学習を正しく積み重ねていけば、スコアは確実に伸びていきます。

　スコアという目に見える形で成果を得られるのも、楽しいです。TOEICは、こちらの「頑張りにしっかり応えてくれる」試験なんですね。

　6年間試行錯誤をくり返しながら、990まで、もう一歩というところまできました。みなさんも目標達成に向けてがんばってください！ 私も、努力は必ず報われると人生を賭けて証明したいと思います。あと10点。過程や結果は、ブログで公表していきますので、ぜひご覧ください。おたがいに目標を目指して、楽しく走り続けましょう！

でる模試 本番のTOEICと同じように取り組もう！

TEST 3

| 所要時間 | 2時間 |

音声ファイル

書名（アルバム名）
新TOEICテスト でる模試600問〈TEST 3〉

トラック名（曲名）
- Part 1: T3_P1_Dir ▶ T3_P1_Q10
- Part 2: T3_P2_Dir ▶ T3_P2_Q40
- Part 3: T3_P3_Dir ▶ T3_P3_Q68-70
- Part 4: T3_P4_Dir ▶ T3_P4_End

用意するもの

えんぴつ（シャープペン）
消しゴム
時計
マークシート（巻末に収録）

解答解説

別冊 解答・解説 ❸ TEST 3

LISTENING TEST

In the Listening test, you will be asked to demonstrate how well you understand spoken English. The entire Listening test will last approximately 45 minutes. There are four parts, and directions are given for each part. You must mark your answers on the separate answer sheet. Do not write your answers in your test book.

PART 1

Directions: For each question in this part, you will hear four statements about a picture in your test book. When you hear the statements, you must select the one statement that best describes what you see in the picture. Then find the number of the question on your answer sheet and mark your answer. The statements will not be printed in your test book and will be spoken only one time.

Example

Sample Answer
Ⓐ Ⓑ ● Ⓓ

Statement (C), "They're standing near the table," is the best description of the picture, so you should select answer (C) and mark it on your answer sheet.

1.

2.

3.

4.

5.

6.

7.

8.

9.

10.

PART 2

Directions: You will hear a question or statement and three responses spoken in English. They will not be printed in your test book and will be spoken only one time. Select the best response to the question or statement and mark the letter (A), (B), or (C) on your answer sheet.

Example

Sample Answer
Ⓐ ● Ⓒ

You will hear: Where is the meeting room?

You will also hear: (A) To meet the new director.
(B) It's the first room on the right.
(C) Yes, at two o'clock.

The best response to the question "Where is the meeting room?" is choice (B), "It's the first room on the right," so (B) is the correct answer. You should mark answer (B) on your answer sheet.

11. Mark your answer on your answer sheet.
12. Mark your answer on your answer sheet.
13. Mark your answer on your answer sheet.
14. Mark your answer on your answer sheet.
15. Mark your answer on your answer sheet.
16. Mark your answer on your answer sheet.
17. Mark your answer on your answer sheet.
18. Mark your answer on your answer sheet.
19. Mark your answer on your answer sheet.
20. Mark your answer on your answer sheet.
21. Mark your answer on your answer sheet.
22. Mark your answer on your answer sheet.
23. Mark your answer on your answer sheet.
24. Mark your answer on your answer sheet.
25. Mark your answer on your answer sheet.
26. Mark your answer on your answer sheet.
27. Mark your answer on your answer sheet.
28. Mark your answer on your answer sheet.
29. Mark your answer on your answer sheet.
30. Mark your answer on your answer sheet.
31. Mark your answer on your answer sheet.
32. Mark your answer on your answer sheet.
33. Mark your answer on your answer sheet.
34. Mark your answer on your answer sheet.
35. Mark your answer on your answer sheet.
36. Mark your answer on your answer sheet.
37. Mark your answer on your answer sheet.
38. Mark your answer on your answer sheet.
39. Mark your answer on your answer sheet.
40. Mark your answer on your answer sheet.

PART 3

Directions: You will hear some conversations between two people. You will be asked to answer three questions about what the speakers say in each conversation. Select the best response to each question and mark the letter (A), (B), (C), or (D) on your answer sheet. The conversations will not be printed in your test book and will be spoken only one time.

41. What most likely is the woman's job?

    (A) A travel agent
    (B) A restaurant employee
    (C) A hotel receptionist
    (D) A tour guide

42. What is the problem?

    (A) Tickets are sold out.
    (B) A facility is fully booked.
    (C) There are no free tables.
    (D) A tour has been cancelled.

43. What does the woman suggest?

    (A) Trying another establishment
    (B) Making a booking for Monday
    (C) Delaying a trip
    (D) Reserving a room in advance

44. Why is the man calling?

    (A) He has to register for a convention.
    (B) He has to cancel an appointment.
    (C) He wants to get a prescription.
    (D) He needs to see a doctor.

45. What does the woman suggest the man do?

    (A) Visit a nearby pharmacy
    (B) Fill out an application form
    (C) Come back on another day
    (D) Check his schedule

46. What will the man probably do?

    (A) Sign up for insurance
    (B) Meet with a different physician
    (C) Attend a hospital meeting
    (D) Purchase medicines at a pharmacy

GO ON TO THE NEXT PAGE

47. Where is Ms. Garner?

(A) At a client meeting
(B) At an accounting seminar
(C) On vacation
(D) On her lunch break

48. Why does the man want to see Ms. Garner?

(A) To discuss his taxes
(B) To give her some documents
(C) To inquire about a billing statement
(D) To talk about his work schedule

49. What does the woman offer to do?

(A) Deliver a message
(B) Copy the papers
(C) Order lunch for Ms. Garner
(D) Schedule a meeting

---

50. Why is the man going to Montreal?

(A) To attend a conference
(B) To meet an investor
(C) To visit relatives
(D) To purchase merchandise

51. What does the man say will happen while he is away?

(A) An advertising campaign will be launched.
(B) A colleague will take care of his work.
(C) The company directors will meet.
(D) An order of products will arrive.

52. What type of company do the speakers most likely work for?

(A) Product development
(B) Event planning
(C) An advertising agency
(D) An airline

---

53. What does the woman want?

(A) Directions to a convention center
(B) Some new furniture
(C) Information about reservations
(D) Some flowers for an event

54. What does the man suggest?

(A) Creating the same kind of arrangements as before
(B) Checking out the event location
(C) Viewing the products at the shop
(D) Placing a larger order

55. What does the man offer to send the woman?

(A) A price quotation
(B) A coupon for a discount
(C) A schedule of events
(D) A list of items

---

56. What event does the man mention?

(A) A feedback session
(B) A conflict resolution meeting
(C) A workshop for personnel department staff
(D) A seminar for departmental directors

57. What does the man say will be discussed next week?

(A) Executive coaching
(B) Developing teamwork
(C) Evaluating workers
(D) Work productivity

58. What does the woman mention about the skills to be taught at the workshop?

(A) They are needed for building work relationships.
(B) They are helpful in improving customer service.
(C) They are important for solving personnel issues.
(D) They are required for employee promotions.

59. What does the woman want to do?

(A) Schedule an appointment
(B) Have landscaping work done
(C) Pick up a cost estimate
(D) Visit a project site

60. What is the problem?

(A) A landscape project is incomplete.
(B) The man is unable to locate the work site.
(C) An employee is currently unavailable.
(D) The woman is late for an appointment.

61. Why can't the woman return in half an hour?

(A) She has another engagement.
(B) She is late for a meeting.
(C) She is leaving town.
(D) She has to return to her office.

---

62. What are the speakers discussing?

(A) A computer factory
(B) A renovated office building
(C) A convention center
(D) A storage facility

63. According to the man, what is convenient about the building's location?

(A) It is in the country.
(B) It is near the subway station.
(C) It is by an industrial area.
(D) It is situated near the office.

64. Why is the man pleased?

(A) He won't have to travel so far to work.
(B) He will be able to place orders online.
(C) He will save time at work.
(D) He won't have to take public transportation.

---

65. Where does the man most likely work?

(A) At a gift shop
(B) At a recording studio
(C) At a music store
(D) At a print shop

66. What is the woman looking for?

(A) A book for a friend
(B) Some tickets to a concert
(C) A gift for her daughter
(D) Some information about a performer

67. What does the man offer to do for the woman?

(A) Contact her when an item is available
(B) Call another branch
(C) Make a copy
(D) Show other merchandise

---

68. What is the main subject of the show?

(A) The new leader of an organization
(B) The achievements of a local group
(C) The launch of an association
(D) The plans for a restoration project

69. What project has the woman recently worked on?

(A) The construction of a community center
(B) The expansion of a parking site
(C) The renovation of a daycare center
(D) The refurbishment of a recreational area

70. According to Ms. Fontana, what happens on weekends?

(A) People have meals in the park.
(B) Fun activities are organized for families.
(C) People choose to stay indoors.
(D) Sporting events are hosted by the association.

GO ON TO THE NEXT PAGE

PART 4

Directions: You will hear some talks given by a single speaker. You will be asked to answer three questions about what the speaker says in each talk. Select the best response to each question and mark the letter (A), (B), (C), or (D) on your answer sheet. The talks will not be printed in your test book and will be spoken only one time.

71. What is the purpose of the announcement?

(A) To give information about airport services
(B) To notify people about a departure change
(C) To direct passengers to another gate
(D) To advise travelers to be careful

72. What problem is mentioned?

(A) The airport in Madrid has not yet reopened.
(B) The city has bad weather conditions.
(C) The area has heavy air traffic.
(D) The aircraft has mechanical problems.

73. What are passengers asked to do?

(A) Call a travel agent
(B) Wait at the terminal
(C) Take other flights
(D) Request a refund

74. Where does the caller work?

(A) At an island resort
(B) In a bridal store
(C) In a party supply company
(D) At a flower shop

75. According to the speaker, what is the problem?

(A) A product is unavailable.
(B) A price quote is incorrect.
(C) A shipment has been delayed.
(D) A purchase was damaged.

76. What does the speaker want to know from Ms. Johnson?

(A) Which type of product she prefers
(B) How much she'd like to pay for shipping
(C) Where to deliver an item
(D) What her credit card number is

77. Who is Ellen Rossi?

   (A) A graphic designer
   (B) A professional artist
   (C) A language instructor
   (D) A software developer

78. What does the speaker say about the computer program?

   (A) It has features that are difficult to use.
   (B) It will be useful for professional designers.
   (C) It is recently developed software.
   (D) It is available for purchase on a Web site.

79. What will the listeners do this afternoon?

   (A) View a brief demonstration
   (B) Learn how to manage their time
   (C) Experience a product first-hand
   (D) Submit samples of their work

80. When is the report being broadcast?

   (A) In the morning
   (B) At noon
   (C) In the afternoon
   (D) At night

81. What is causing the traffic problems?

   (A) A bridge has been closed for repairs.
   (B) A construction crew is occupying several lanes.
   (C) Some vehicles are slowing down the flow of traffic.
   (D) A snowstorm has severely restricted visibility.

82. What will listeners hear next?

   (A) A weather forecast
   (B) An advertisement
   (C) A talk show
   (D) A news report

83. What field does Ms. Stevens work in?

   (A) Interior decoration
   (B) Construction management
   (C) Event planning
   (D) Landscaping design

84. What does Ms. Stevens recommend?

   (A) Including a seating area
   (B) Holding the event in a park
   (C) Adding a walkway to the plan
   (D) Installing a water fountain

85. What does Ms. Stevens ask Mr. Carranza to do?

   (A) Return a phone call
   (B) Decide on a meeting place
   (C) Look over a planned budget
   (D) Start working on a project

86. Why has there been a change?

   (A) A speaker has announced his resignation.
   (B) A discussion has been extended.
   (C) A lecturer has fallen ill.
   (D) A holiday has been declared.

87. What will Ms. Armstrong speak about?

   (A) Developing economies
   (B) World trade agreements
   (C) Global recession
   (D) Departmental news

88. When will Mr. Cornelius most likely give his talk?

   (A) In a few minutes
   (B) Later that afternoon
   (C) The following morning
   (D) At the next seminar

GO ON TO THE NEXT PAGE

89. What is the main purpose of the talk?

(A) To introduce a new replacement
(B) To provide updates about a program
(C) To ensure the continuity of projects
(D) To motivate underperforming staff

90. What recently happened at the business?

(A) A key employee has resigned.
(B) An office building was damaged.
(C) A product launch was delayed.
(D) A team leader was reassigned.

91. What are listeners asked to expect?

(A) Stricter employee evaluations
(B) A heavier work load
(C) Larger performance bonuses
(D) A flexible schedule

---

92. Who most likely are the listeners?

(A) Market analysts
(B) Restaurant staff
(C) Sales representatives
(D) Consulting firm specialists

93. According to the speaker, why are French Bistro's sales low?

(A) It is located on the outskirts of the city.
(B) Their products are too expensive.
(C) The quality of service has deteriorated.
(D) They are losing business to competitors.

94. What does the speaker suggest?

(A) Providing food samples
(B) Increasing the amount of advertising
(C) Reducing the number of menu items
(D) Extending operating hours

---

95. Who is Tommy Holmes?

(A) A school principal
(B) A pediatrician
(C) A psychologist
(D) A college professor

96. What will be discussed in the program?

(A) A survey about parenting
(B) A new medical breakthrough
(C) The effects of insufficient sleep
(D) The diseases affecting children

97. What did Dr. Holmes do recently?

(A) He wrote a best-selling book about the brain.
(B) He developed a partial cure for insomnia.
(C) He hosted an educational program on TV.
(D) He published his medical findings.

---

98. Who most likely is the talk intended for?

(A) Company shareholders
(B) Publication editors
(C) Web site designers
(D) Security officers

99. What have customers complained about?

(A) High subscription rates
(B) Low level of security
(C) Incorrect billing figures
(D) Complicated payment process

100. How does the company intend to address the problem?

(A) By redesigning a Web site
(B) By hiring a marketing expert
(C) By sending out a mass e-mail
(D) By launching an advertising campaign

This is the end of the Listening test. Turn to Part 5 in your test book.

NO TEST MATERIAL ON THIS PAGE

READING TEST

In the Reading test, you will read a variety of texts and answer several different types of reading comprehension questions. The entire Reading test will last 75 minutes. There are three parts, and directions are given for each part. You are encouraged to answer as many questions as possible within the time allowed.

You must mark your answers on the separate answer sheet. Do not write your answers in your test book.

PART 5

Directions: A word or phrase is missing in each of the sentences below. Four answer choices are given below each sentence. Select the best answer to complete the sentence. Then mark the letter (A), (B), (C), or (D) on your answer sheet.

101. Ms. Jackson just called to ask that ------- meeting be moved to Thursday rather than Friday as scheduled.

    (A) her
    (B) she
    (C) hers
    (D) herself

102. Ambassador Carl Ferrer was ------- the six diplomats who sponsored a medical mission to several countries in Latin America.

    (A) late
    (B) chosen
    (C) apart
    (D) among

103. Customers can upsize beverages at ------- extra expense by presenting their Coffee Tree loyalty cards.

    (A) none
    (B) no
    (C) not
    (D) nor

104. The number of customers requesting refunds or exchanges at the electronics store has decreased ------- since last quarter.

    (A) noticing
    (B) notices
    (C) noticeable
    (D) noticeably

105. The company wanted to build its headquarters in the financial district ------- near the city center.

    (A) so
    (B) or
    (C) to
    (D) either

106. Fairview Hotels has six ------- on the North American mainland and two resorts in Hawaii, and has plans to build one more hotel in Alaska next year.

    (A) amenities
    (B) supplements
    (C) locations
    (D) categories

107. A team of psychologists conducted an ------- study about the negative effects of video games on the thought processes of young children.

    (A) extent
    (B) extensive
    (C) extensively
    (D) extents

108. As ------- as the visiting guests arrive, staff from the personnel office will give them a tour of the factory, then take them to the auditorium for the presentation.

    (A) fast
    (B) long
    (C) soon
    (D) lately

109. There was such high demand for the new mobile phones ------- customers had to sign up on a waiting list.

(A) before
(B) that
(C) unless
(D) still

110. Please be reminded that proper business attire must be worn in the office at ------- times.

(A) much
(B) all
(C) every
(D) almost

111. As a special promotion, customers who sign up for a one-year ------- to Emerald Cable TV by the end of the week can enjoy a month of free service.

(A) contribution
(B) subscription
(C) dealership
(D) partnership

112. During her time working as an editor at the publishing company, Natasha worked quite ------- with most of the staff writers.

(A) closing
(B) close
(C) closely
(D) closed

113. The flowers planted in front of the building did not survive because they do not ------- well in the direct sunlight.

(A) discover
(B) grow
(C) behave
(D) accept

114. Dalton Insurance Company now gives clients more ------- in regard to payments, permitting them to purchase policies in installments.

(A) credibility
(B) research
(C) acceptance
(D) flexibility

115. The local amusement park offers residents a far less ------- option for spending their holidays than traveling overseas.

(A) assumed
(B) remote
(C) expensive
(D) reduced

116. Because the restaurant appliances were damaged during shipment, Mr. Morgan ------- them to the supplier and requested that they be replaced as quickly as possible.

(A) adjusted
(B) returned
(C) refunded
(D) prohibited

117. The construction crew closed Sunset Avenue for several days so they could install a new water pipe system ------- street level.

(A) by
(B) below
(C) near
(D) beside

118. It is advisable to have a dental checkup ------- because only a dentist can identify potential teeth problems before they worsen.

(A) regularize
(B) regularly
(C) regulars
(D) regularization

119. ------- the safety of both drivers and passengers, the Department of Transportation urges everyone not to keep flammable substances in the trunks of vehicles.

(A) Around
(B) About
(C) With
(D) For

GO ON TO THE NEXT PAGE

120. Mrs. Nordstrom seemed very pleased with the planned ------- to the main entrance of her firm's main office, and gave her approval to go ahead with construction.

(A) permissions
(B) adaptations
(C) modifications
(D) regulations

121. The mechanic said he can fix Ms. Ang's car, but that it will soon be ------- for her to replace the engine.

(A) necessary
(B) permissible
(C) prohibited
(D) considerable

122. Clients are required to sign the shipping order that ------- their merchandise to confirm receipt of their purchases.

(A) accompanying
(B) accompanies
(C) accompany
(D) accompaniment

123. Ms. Bana ------- for Richmond Bank for 15 years by the time she was promoted to financial vice president.

(A) has worked
(B) will have worked
(C) is working
(D) had worked

124. After opening the protective cover of the photocopier, remove the empty ink cartridge by pressing the green tabs and ------- lifting it from the machine.

(A) carefully
(B) internally
(C) automatically
(D) vaguely

125. Wentworth TV studios is currently developing a production schedule of upcoming projects for its recently ------- documentary film department.

(A) creating
(B) creator
(C) creates
(D) created

126. Mai-Thai Resort in Phuket ------- right beside the beach and just a 10-minute drive from the international airport.

(A) situates
(B) has situated
(C) is situated
(D) situating

127. The work on the new subway station is ------- complete and the line should be fully operational in less than a month's time.

(A) rapidly
(B) usually
(C) nearly
(D) possibly

128. Only applicants who meet the requirements for the design position will be contacted to arrange ------- for interviews.

(A) methods
(B) appointments
(C) developments
(D) services

129. ------- the problems with the new assembly line equipment have been repaired, the factory's new production schedule will be put into effect.

(A) Meantime
(B) Despite
(C) Moreover
(D) Once

130. Recent reports show that Southeast Asian countries have decreased their ------- on fossil fuels by using alternative energy sources.

(A) reliance
(B) relies
(C) reliable
(D) reliability

131. During the opening remarks, the speaker announced that the first lecture at the workshop was cancelled due to the ------- illness of the guest speaker.

    (A) treated
    (B) stringent
    (C) unexpected
    (D) comprehensive

132. The company president told the union representative that he would increase pay by 2 percent in an ------- to appease the striking workers.

    (A) obligation
    (B) effort
    (C) option
    (D) indication

133. Many of the newspaper's readers wrote in to praise Sunday's short but ------- article explaining everything there is to know about the healthcare debate.

    (A) adversary
    (B) reminding
    (C) compound
    (D) informative

134. The executive officer's memorandum cited the investors' ------- about using investment funds for research into alternative energy sources.

    (A) limitations
    (B) combinations
    (C) reservations
    (D) contractions

135. Museum caretakers have blocked off a section opposite the abstract art exhibit to prevent visitors from wandering into the area where a damaged oil pastel painting -------.

    (A) is restoring
    (B) having been restored
    (C) had restored
    (D) is being restored

136. If one of Tottenham Department Store's products is ------- out of stock, a sales assistant can request an order from another branch for a customer.

    (A) temporarily
    (B) promptly
    (C) normally
    (D) extremely

137. ------- the exercise routine conducted during the morning workout session is tedious, it has proven quite beneficial for reducing excess weight.

    (A) Whenever
    (B) Although
    (C) However
    (D) After

138. ------- donating a sum of money to an area damaged by the flood, the RADG Company has decided that contributing needed services and goods would be more helpful.

    (A) Aside from
    (B) Because of
    (C) Instead of
    (D) In addition

139. Customers who request express delivery of their orders from BookEnd's Web site will have to pay a(n) ------- fee of eight dollars per publication.

    (A) additional
    (B) contrary
    (C) exaggerated
    (D) promotional

140. Peerless Travel has formulated ------- plans to ensure that all travelers who enroll in a tour package have a safe journey.

    (A) immigration
    (B) contingency
    (C) survival
    (D) indication

GO ON TO THE NEXT PAGE

PART 6

Directions: Read the texts that follow. A word or phrase is missing in some of the sentences. Four answer choices are given below each of the sentences. Select the best answer to complete the text. Then mark the letter (A), (B), (C), or (D) on your answer sheet.

Questions 141-143 refer to the following letter.

Barbara Underwood
602 Infinity Lane
Houston, TX 77014

Dear Ms. Underwood,

I am pleased to inform you that we have received your application for the bachelor's program in chemistry for this coming school year. Your ID number is #1209241. Please keep this number for future -------. The school will always try to notify you when a

        141. (A) promotion
            (B) resource
            (C) reference
            (D) consideration

change in your application occurs. However, in the event that you do not receive a notification, it remains your responsibility to ensure you are up-to-date with all application requirements. Therefore, you are encouraged to log on to our Web site at www.hamilton.edu/newapps, using the ID number to gain access and ------- your admission status.

        142. (A) trail
            (B) stalk
            (C) solve
            (D) track

Once logged in, your status page will indicate which documents have been received and which ones still need to be submitted. If you have been approved for admission, several links will appear to pages ------- further details on financial aid and other student services.

        143. (A) provide
            (B) provides
            (C) provided
            (D) providing

Thank you for your interest in Hamilton University and we wish you all the best!

Sincerely,

Jenna Hoffman
Admissions Officer

Questions 144-146 refer to the following memo.

To: All Interested Individuals
From: Natasha Zimmerman
Date: February 20
Subject: Baking Classes

Bake the best cakes and pastries with Chef Phil Lassopo!

Next month, the Culinary Institute of Bourdain (CIB) will be offering baking classes with Chef Phil Lassopo, host of the Cuisine Channel's *The Sweetest Things*. Learn how to make ------- baked goods from cupcakes to éclairs and other signature confections. Listen to

144. (A) inedible
(B) profound
(C) quality
(D) imported

informative lectures and demonstrations made by none other than Chef Phil Lassopo himself! Beginners and professionals in the food industry are welcome.

------- classes will be held on Saturdays from 1:00 P.M. to 3:00 P.M. at the CIB campus in

145. (A) Much
(B) Every
(C) Each
(D) All

Baltimore.

For more information, please contact the institute's registration office at 555-3832.

We are looking forward to ------- you there!

146. (A) joining
(B) viewing
(C) having
(D) getting

Questions 147-149 refer to the following e-mail.

TO: Aldo Hernandez [hernal@dmail.com]
FROM: Heather Heaton [heatheat@service.mtelectric.com]
SUBJECT: Repair update
DATE: May 12

Dear Mr. Hernandez,

Our technician has found the problem with your mobile phone, which you left at the MT Electric service center on May 10. The speaker ------- is damaged, which can happen when

147. (A) invention
(B) element
(C) substance
(D) matter

a phone is dropped or exposed to water.

Unfortunately, I also noticed that your warranty on this particular phone -------. You can

148. (A) expires
(B) expire
(C) has expired
(D) expiring

purchase an additional year of warranty, or we can go ahead with the repairs if you wish. The cost of repair will be $48.50, including labor and replacement parts.

Please let us know if you would like us to proceed. Your phone can be ready by tomorrow at noon. Credit card or cash payments are -------, but we do not take personal checks.

149. (A) acceptable
(B) negotiable
(C) capable
(D) deferred

Thank you, and I hope to hear from you soon.

Questions 150-152 refer to the following announcement.

Southwestern Residences
IMPORTANT ANNOUNCEMENT

The building management ------- maintenance checks on the condominium's electrical

150. (A) has performed
(B) was performing
(C) to perform
(D) will be performing

circuits and switch boxes on Monday, between 10 A.M. and 1 P.M. This is in accordance with the city government's Fire Protection Policy. During the activity, power supply throughout the condominium will be unavailable. If there is no urgent repair work to be done, electricity will be restored immediately following the inspection. -------, the power

151. (A) Otherwise
(B) Above all
(C) Consequently
(D) On the contrary

interruption will last for a few more hours.

For details ------- this and other related matters, please contact the building

152. (A) attending
(B) considering
(C) persisting
(D) regarding

superintendent, Ms. Jena Gordon, at 555-2124, ext. 21.

Thank you for your patience and understanding.

PART 7

Directions: In this part your will read a selection of texts, such as magazine and newspaper articles, letters, and advertisements. Each text is followed by several questions. Select the best answer for each question and mark the letter (A), (B), (C), or (D) on your answer sheet.

Questions 153-154 refer to the following memo.

MEMORANDUM

TO: All staff

We have come to the end of another successful year and would like to thank all our staff members for their hard work. As we do each year, we are organizing a special holiday evening for you all. This year it will be held at the Mansfield Hotel on Lakeview Avenue on Dec. 22 at 7:00 P.M. Staff are free to bring their husbands, wives, or partners.

Reservations need to be made in advance, so please RSVP Lionel Grimm of the personnel department at ligrimm@austel.com and let him know how many guests you will be bringing.

Thank you!

153. What is the memo mainly about?

(A) Work schedules for the upcoming year
(B) Taking time off for holidays
(C) An annual company event
(D) An awards ceremony for hardworking staff

154. What are staff members asked to do?

(A) Come to a company meeting
(B) Send an e-mail to a colleague
(C) Inform the company of vacation plans
(D) Confirm a reservation

Questions 155-156 refer to the following notice.

NOTICE:
Residents of Mayfair Towers

Starting next week on June 5, the main parking garage will be closed for renovations. We apologize for the inconvenience this will cause, but hope that the renovations will be worth it. All surfaces will be repaved and the walls will be painted. Work is expected to take two weeks. In the meantime, provisional parking will be provided for residents across the street in the Orleans Parkade. Please pick up a parking pass for the facility at the administrative office. Parking will also be permitted at the tower's outdoor parking lot and at the rear of the building as well. If you have any questions, please call us at 555-9988.

Thank you for your cooperation in this matter.

155. What is the main purpose of the notice?

(A) To provide information on parking passes
(B) To inform tenants of temporary changes
(C) To announce upcoming roadwork
(D) To ask for volunteers for a project

156. What is NOT an area where residents can park their vehicles?

(A) The back of the tower
(B) The Mayfair garage
(C) The Orleans Parkade
(D) The outdoor parking area

Questions 157-158 refer to the following e-mail.

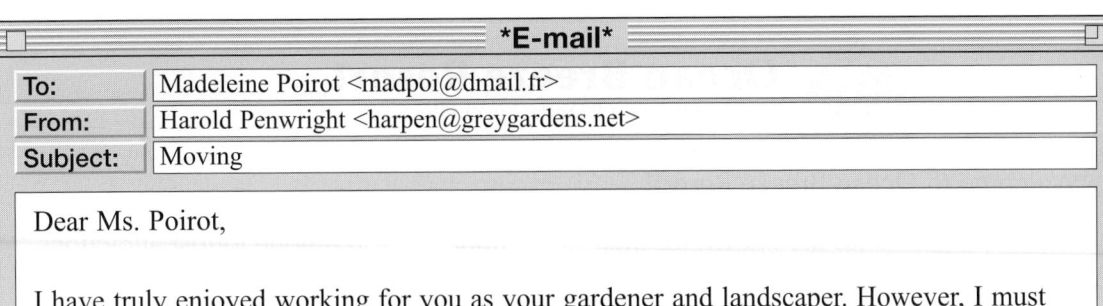

E-mail

To: Madeleine Poirot <madpoi@dmail.fr>
From: Harold Penwright <harpen@greygardens.net>
Subject: Moving

Dear Ms. Poirot,

I have truly enjoyed working for you as your gardener and landscaper. However, I must inform you that I will be retiring from Grey Gardens Landscaping at the end of this month and moving with my wife to Orlando. I just want to thank you for all your kindness and generosity over the past five years.

When I leave, my assistant Geraldine Smith will be taking over my duties. She has worked with you on numerous occasions, so you are probably aware of her professionalism. She will contact you shortly to find out if you would like to continue having Grey Gardens conduct your regular weekly service. I am sure you will be pleased with her quality of work. Thanks once again for your patronage.

Sincerely,

Harold Penwright

---

157. What is the main purpose of the e-mail?

(A) To request payment for services
(B) To show appreciation to a customer
(C) To inform a customer of a staff change
(D) To recommend a new company

158. What is mentioned about Ms. Smith?

(A) She owns the gardening service company.
(B) She is a long-term customer.
(C) She has been employed by Grey Gardens for a long time.
(D) She has worked for Ms. Poirot before.

Questions 159-161 refer to the following notice.

Ocean Breeze Resort
Shipwon Islands, Seychelles

Welcome to Ocean Breeze Resort!

The Shipwon Islands are known for their rich marine life and unique tourist attractions. To enjoy the best of the islands, we recommend that you try these activities:

Island Hopping
Hop onto one of our boats for a day tour among Shipwon's many mangroves and jungles, lagoons, limestone cliffs, and white sand beaches. Snorkeling gear is provided for those who want to explore Shipwon's extensive coral reefs, which are home to thousands of underwater creatures.

Miligan Tour
Located south of Shipwon is Miligan, a wildlife sanctuary where you can interact with monkeys and exotic birds in their natural environment. Miligan is a 30-minute boat ride from Ocean Breeze Resort.

Trekking
Join a guided tour of Mt. Amitan and enjoy splendid views of Engle Bay. Our tour guides and mountaineers will accompany you on this adventure.

To book an activity, please coordinate with the receptionists at the front desk. Discounts will be given to groups of ten or more.

---

159. What is the purpose of the notice?

(A) To describe activities
(B) To provide a travel schedule
(C) To promote special discounts
(D) To explain animal conservation

160. What is indicated in the notice?

(A) All tours will include a guide.
(B) Boats will be used on some tours.
(C) Tourists must pay in advance.
(D) Reduced rates are not available.

161. What will NOT be seen during an Island Hopping trip?

(A) Tropical forests
(B) Underwater wildlife
(C) An animal park
(D) Sandy shores

Questions 162-164 refer to the following advertisement.

BTC 12
An Entertainment Network

Advertise With Us

Make your products and services known by advertising on the prime time shows of the BTC Channel. As the No. 1 entertainment channel in the country, the network reaches more than ten million viewers every day, according to the latest report of MediaLine-UK Survey. Our award-winning shows attract a wide range of viewers, so marketing your product or service on our channel will reach thousands of consumers.

Prime time Package

- One-to-two-minute airtime for advertising spots on all prime time shows
- A button advertisement on the BTC Web site
- Inclusion of your company logo in SMS promotions flashed after the end of each show

For more details about the package, please contact the BTC 12 Advertising Services Department at 555-8888 and ask for an account executive.

Learn more about our ongoing and upcoming prime time shows on www.BTC12.com.

162. What is mentioned about BTC 12?

(A) It is the most profitable TV network in the country.
(B) It is the country's top entertainment network.
(C) It offers only nighttime programming.
(D) It has affiliates around the world.

163. What is NOT included in the Prime time Package?

(A) An online advertisement
(B) Broadcast commercial spots
(C) SMS advertising
(D) A product presentation on a show

164. How can clients find out about the cost of the package?

(A) By calling a network representative
(B) By visiting a Web site
(C) By writing an e-mail
(D) By sending a text message

GO ON TO THE NEXT PAGE

Questions 165-167 refer to the following e-mail.

E-mail

To: Richard Callahan <rcallahan@juno.net>
From: Lorraine Jardine <customercare@hellotel.com>
Date: January 10
Subject: Monthly bill

Dear Mr. Callahan,

We received your e-mail yesterday about the sudden increase in your cell phone bill for the month of December. You mentioned that aside from your usual $50 monthly charge, it indicated additional charges amounting to $20 for service features that are not included in your subscription plan.

We are deeply sorry for this error. I have spoken to our IT department and was informed that there have been problems with our company's automated billing system. We have already taken appropriate steps to prevent this mistake from happening again.

In the meantime, we have credited your account for the overcharge and have given you free unlimited text messaging for the month of January. We hope that this addresses any inconvenience it may have caused you.

We would like to thank you for bringing this to our attention and hope that you will remain a loyal customer.

Sincerely,

Lorraine Jardine
Customer Service Representative
Hello Telecom

---

165. What is the main purpose of the e-mail?

(A) To request additional payment
(B) To cancel a subscription
(C) To apologize for a problem
(D) To report an error

166. What is the reason for the increase in Mr. Callahan's bill?

(A) He signed up for an extra service.
(B) He forgot to make a payment.
(C) There was a computer problem.
(D) There were hidden charges.

167. What does Ms. Jardine offer Mr. Callahan?

(A) A free service for a limited time
(B) A refund check
(C) An updated billing statement
(D) New product discounts

Questions 168-171 refer to the following memo.

TO: Sharon Littleton, branch manager
FROM: Shawn Bell, regional accounting director
SUBJECT: Expense reports
DATE: Sept. 5

Hi Sharon,

I received your quarterly expense report last week and have had some time to look over it. I wanted to write you and say how happy I am that you are managing to follow the budget in the Portland branch, as the expenditures have been quite moderate. I did want to mention that my associate, Brenda Russell, has been doing some research to find out if we can find a better Internet provider for you. You mentioned that your current provider, Oregon-Com has recently raised their rates, and that you haven't been pleased with their service, as the Internet is often down and the staff haven't been helpful. She is looking to see if there's a better package deal for businesses which supplies Internet and a telephone connection together. This might help lower your expenses even further. I will let you know what we find out, and you can also contact me if you have any ideas or preferences.

EXPENSE REPORT: PORTLAND BRANCH

Expenditures	May	June	July	August
Utilities	$489.34	$547.87	$532.29	$496.52
Office supplies	$113.67	$87.54	$76.38	$122.57
Telephone	$429.92	$321.76	$214.96	$378.45
Internet	$280	$280	$280	$280
TOTAL	$1312.93	$1237.17	$1103.63	$1277.54

168. What is the main purpose of the memo?

(A) To inform Ms. Littleton of budget cuts
(B) To request figures on office expenditures
(C) To give feedback on a financial report
(D) To suggest a new Internet service

169. The word "moderate" in paragraph 1, line 3 is closest in meaning to

(A) unimportant
(B) average
(C) negotiable
(D) timid

170. What does the memo indicate about the Internet provider currently used in Portland?

(A) It offers discounted package rates.
(B) Ms. Littleton has been unsatisfied with its service.
(C) It recently contacted Ms. Russell.
(D) Its staff always provides assistance when needed.

171. According to the memo, what is Ms. Russell currently doing?

(A) Creating a budget for the next financial quarter
(B) Sending payments to creditors
(C) Working on a deal with Oregon-Com
(D) Looking for better offers

GO ON TO THE NEXT PAGE

Questions 172-175 refer to the following e-mail.

E-mail

From: Leonard Irvin <l.irvin@ecca.com>
To: Violet Curtis <v_curtis@bestmail.com>
Subject: Admission to Empress Center for Culinary Arts
Date: July 30

Dear Ms. Curtis,

We are pleased to inform you that you have passed the written entrance exam for the Culinary Arts and Technology Management Course at the Empress Center for Culinary Arts (ECCA).

As a standard school policy, we require applicants of academic programs to take our 12-hour Kitchen Discovery Training in order to assess their cooking skills. Training begins on September 2 and will be conducted on every successive Friday of the month from 1 P.M. to 4 P.M. Top ECCA alumni will facilitate classes in Italian pasta, French cuisine, and basic baking. Taster magazine editor in chief Pedro de Luca will hold the Italian pasta class on the first Friday, while Chef's Delight host Allan Spears will be in charge of the French cuisine class on the following Friday. Pastry chef Noreen Baltimore of Oregon Hotel will give baking classes on the last two Fridays of the month. The training fee is $300. Payment includes cooking ingredients, a culinary knife set, and copies of featured recipes.

If you are interested in pursuing the application, please register for training before August 25. For inquiries, reply to this e-mail or call our office hotline at 555-9687.

Thank you.

Sincerely,

Leonard Irvin
Director
Student Admissions Office

172. What is mentioned about Kitchen Discovery Training?

(A) It is a requirement for a job application.
(B) It is offered to professional chefs.
(C) It is a prerequisite to a culinary arts course.
(D) It is organized by ECCA students.

173. What is implied about Ms. Curtis?

(A) She is interested in baking.
(B) She wants to take up an academic program.
(C) She works for a food magazine.
(D) She is applying for a position in the ECCA.

174. Who will NOT teach one of the courses?

(A) Allan Spears
(B) Noreen Baltimore
(C) Pedro de Luca
(D) Leonard Irvin

175. On which Friday of September will the French cuisine class be held?

(A) The first
(B) The second
(C) The third
(D) The fourth

GO ON TO THE NEXT PAGE

Questions 176-180 refer to the following article.

New Museum to Open in the Spring

At a press conference held yesterday, Minister of Antiquity, Fatima Hawas said that the deadline for the completion of the Royal National Museum of History has been delayed until the spring.

Originally scheduled to open in November of this year, the new museum and its facilities will now open on March 1 next year. Hawas said the delay was due to the unexpected challenges of moving the nation's treasures from across the country to the new museum in a safe manner. "We did not expect that the transfer of some larger artifacts and sculptures would be so difficult. But we don't want to rush the process and risk damage to any of our nation's treasures."

Construction of the new museum, located on the outskirts of the capital city, started five years ago. In addition to the public exhibition areas, the facility boasts large warehouses for artifacts not on display, a 500-seat auditorium for special events, an educational center for visiting archaeologists and professors, and dining and shopping establishments.

Mohammad Sharrif was appointed to head up the project by Hawas six years ago. Sharrif said, "This is probably the most challenging project I have ever worked on, but also the most rewarding." Sharrif claims that the current museum facilities in the capital city are in terrible condition and lack the necessary security systems. "My main goal was to make a home for our nation's treasures where they can be kept safely for generations to come. In addition, we hope that the Royal National Museum will benefit the tourism industry. We are predicting a 20 percent increase in tourists next year due primarily to the grand opening of this new facility."

176. What is the purpose of the article?

(A) To announce an upcoming renovation project
(B) To give an update on a facility construction
(C) To promote a museum exhibition
(D) To provide details of a grand opening

177. According to the article, why was the opening rescheduled?

(A) There were problems relocating some items.
(B) There were insufficient funds to complete the building.
(C) There was a problem caused by government policy.
(D) There was a security system malfunction.

178. Who is Mohammad Sharrif?

(A) A government representative
(B) A university professor
(C) A local archaeologist
(D) A leader for a project

179. What is NOT mentioned as being a part of the new facility?

(A) Display spaces
(B) Storage areas
(C) Eating facilities
(D) Library archives

180. What did Mr. Sharrif indicate about the project?

(A) It is costing more than expected.
(B) It will attract more visitors to the country.
(C) It is being promoted internationally.
(D) It was not as difficult as he had expected it to be.

GO ON TO THE NEXT PAGE

Questions 181-185 refer to the following list and e-mail.

Red Lantern Tours

See the ancient wonders of Beijing with Red Lantern Tours! We can provide you with tour guides who are fluent in English, French, Japanese, or Spanish. They are government-licensed guides that will help make your trip to Beijing both exciting and memorable. Included in all tours are transportation, entrance fees to all sites, and brochures and maps for places of interest. Red Lantern Tours offers the following four packages:

Morning Tour 9:00 A.M.–12:30 P.M. $65	Pickup from hotel Tour of Forbidden City Snack and beverage Return to hotel	Day Tour 9:00 A.M.–6:00 P.M. $120	Pickup from hotel Tour of Forbidden City Lunch Buffet Tour of Olympic Village Visit to National Museum of China Return to hotel
Day and Evening Tour 9:00 A.M.–9:00 P.M. $180	Pickup from hotel Tour of Forbidden City Lunch Buffet Visit to Palace Museum Tour of Olympic Village Dinner Buffet Visit to Tiananmen Square Visit to Night Market Return to hotel	Two Day Tour $240	Day one same as Day and Evening Tour Day two Pickup from hotel Tour of Great Wall of China Lunch Buffet Visit to tourist market Tour of Ming Dynasty Tombs Return to hotel

If you have questions, or would like to make a reservation, send us an e-mail at reservations@redlanterntours.net or visit our Web site at www.beijingredlantours.com.

***Groups of four or more visitors are eligible for a 20 percent discount.

E-mail

To: reservations@redlanterntours.net
From: Judie Bond <jbond@spemail.com>
Subject: Change to reservations

I booked a tour of Beijing through your company for four colleagues and myself. I was recently informed that our company has given us an additional day in the city to do some sightseeing. So I would like to change our reservations from the Day Tour to the one that includes a visit to the Great Wall of China. You may charge the additional fee to the credit card number I gave you before.

Also, some of my colleagues and I are vegetarian and I was wondering if there are options for us in the meals you provide. Please let me know. In addition, we will be staying at the Ching Hotel, so please inform me at what time we should be ready for pickup.

Thank you for your patience, and I hope these changes will not be too much trouble.

Sincerely,

Judie Bond

181. What is NOT included in the price of the tours?

(A) A tour guide
(B) Admission charges
(C) Airport transportation
(D) Maps and pamphlets

182. Which tour does Ms. Bond want to go on?

(A) Morning Tour
(B) Day Tour
(C) Day and Evening Tour
(D) Two Day Tour

183. What is suggested about the tours?

(A) Some food and drinks are provided.
(B) They are highly recommended.
(C) They are operated by the government.
(D) Refunds are not provided for cancellations.

184. What can be inferred about Ms. Bond's reservation?

(A) It hasn't been made.
(B) It was discounted.
(C) It is only for one day.
(D) It was paid for by the company.

185. What is mentioned about Ms. Bond's colleagues in the e-mail?

(A) They are visiting a branch in Beijing.
(B) Some of them do not eat meat.
(C) They are staying at different hotels.
(D) Some of them are unable to come on the trip.

GO ON TO THE NEXT PAGE

Questions 186-190 refer to the following e-mails.

E-mail

To:	Lalaine Bryant <l.bryant@fastmail.com>
From:	Touch Shopping <orders@touchshopping.com>
Subject:	Order confirmation
Date:	July 13

Dear Ms. Bryant,

Thank you for purchasing products from Touch Shopping. The details of your order are as follows:

Customer name: Lalaine Bryant
Billing and shipping address: Unit 501 Baritone Gardens, 95 Belair Court, Matawan, NJ 07747

Product #	Description	Unit	Price
KP2053	Baker's Choice loaf pan: Nonstick metal	2	$29.98
KP5125	Childe mixing bowl: Three-piece set of stainless steel mixing bowls	1	$13.25
KP0245	Socorro measuring cups: Four-piece set of dry plastic measuring cups	1	$14.50
KP4800	Feighton pizza wheel: Stainless steel	1	$10.99
Delivery charge			$0
Total			$68.72
Mode of payment: Galaxy Credit Card Card number: 6677 5369 3140 4500			
*All products are inclusive of tax. Free delivery applies to areas within New Jersey only.			

Please allow three days for the shipment of your order. Merchandise may be returned within two weeks following delivery. For questions and other concerns, please send an e-mail to orders@touchshopping.com. Visit www.touchshopping.com to learn more about our new products and promotions.

We hope to serve you again.

Respectfully yours,

Touch Shopping

E-mail

To:	Touch Shopping <orders@touchshopping.com>
From:	Lalaine Bryant <l.bryant@fastmail.com>
Subject:	Product order
Date:	July 19

Dear Touch Shopping,

I received the merchandise I bought from your store yesterday. Although the products were in good condition, I noticed that you sent me the wrong loaf pans. I ordered nonstick metal pans, but you delivered ceramic ones. Since I needed extra pans for baking today, I had no choice but to use the ones you sent me. One thing I liked about the ceramic pans was that I was able to use them for both baking and serving cake. However, I still find it easier to bake using the metal pans as they conduct heat more quickly and evenly. In addition, they are durable and their nonstick surface makes them easy to clean.

Nevertheless, I've decided not to return the ceramic pans. But I do request that you coordinate with my bank and make the necessary deductions to my credit card bill because the ceramic pans are cheaper than the ones I originally ordered. I expect to see the changes reflected in my next billing statement.

I look forward to your immediate action on this matter.

Sincerely,

Lalaine Bryant

186. What information is included in the first e-mail?

(A) A delivery date
(B) A company address
(C) Client details
(D) Product discounts

187. What is implied about Touch Shopping?

(A) It publishes baking recipes.
(B) It operates a shipping firm.
(C) It is located in Matawan.
(D) It sells cooking equipment.

188. What is NOT stated about product KP2053?

(A) It is easy to clean.
(B) It is good for serving cakes.
(C) It is long lasting.
(D) It is designed to distribute heat evenly.

189. What did Ms. Bryant ask Touch Shopping to do?

(A) Deliver new products
(B) Correct the charge to her account
(C) Provide her with a replacement
(D) Send her an order form

190. In the second e-mail, the word "reflected" in paragraph 2, line 3 is closest in meaning to

(A) observed
(B) returned
(C) imitated
(D) indicated

GO ON TO THE NEXT PAGE

Questions 191-195 refer to the following announcement and survey.

In an effort to promote a safer and healthier work environment, we will be conducting a one-day training course on workplace safety and health management this May. The course is divided into four parts, as follows:

    I   Introduction to Safety and Health Management
    II Due Diligence and Responsibilities
    III Behavioral-based Safety and Risk Assessment
    IV Recognition, Evaluation, and Control of Hazards

Specific dates have been assigned for each department (see schedule below). Please note that all employees are required to attend the course.

May 23	Reception staff
May 24	Wait staff
May 25	Kitchen staff
May 26	Marketing staff

For further questions about the course and the schedule, you may contact the training manager's office on extension number 432.

EMPLOYEE TRAINING COURSE
Evaluation Survey

Course Title	Workplace Safety and Health Management						
Department	Reception		Wait		Kitchen	X	Marketing

Please mark the appropriate box based on level of satisfaction.
(5 being the highest and 1 being the lowest)

	1	2	3	4	5
The course materials and discussions were concise and easy to understand.					X
All my questions were answered clearly and completely.					X
It will be easy for me to apply what I have learned in the performance of my duties.					X
Overall, I am satisfied with the training I received.					X

Remarks	The part of the training about identifying and understanding dangers was especially helpful, providing us with ideas on the various preventive measures we can take against accidents and injuries within the workplace.

All data collected from this survey is anonymous and will be kept strictly confidential.
Responses will be used solely for the enhancement of future training courses.

191. What is the purpose of the course?

(A) To explain adjustments to a work schedule
(B) To discuss updates on an advertising campaign
(C) To prepare the staff for management reorganization
(D) To educate employees on workplace safety and wellness

192. What is indicated in the survey?

(A) All employees filled out a copy of the form.
(B) The names of those answering questions will be kept a secret.
(C) Completed documents must be submitted to departmental managers.
(D) The results will be discussed later by the trainees.

193. When did the survey respondent attend the course?

(A) On May 23
(B) On May 24
(C) On May 25
(D) On May 26

194. Which part of the course did the survey respondent find particularly useful?

(A) Recognition, Evaluation, and Control of Hazards
(B) Behavioral-based Safety and Risk Assessment
(C) Due Diligence and Responsibilities
(D) Introduction to Safety and Health Management

195. Who will most likely use the information indicated in the responses on the survey?

(A) The executive chef
(B) The marketing supervisor
(C) The head receptionist
(D) The training manager

GO ON TO THE NEXT PAGE

Questions 196-200 refer to the following itinerary and memo.

Bonita Cosmetics
Itinerary for: Mario Cruz

Sept. 10 Friday	10:20 A.M.	Arrival at Charles de Gaulle airport *Driver will meet you	Hotel Antoinette (Paris)
Sept. 11 Saturday	9:30 A.M.	Breakfast meeting with Isabel Trudeau, Bonita regional director	Hotel Antoinette
	11:00 A.M. - 6:00 P.M.	Visit to convention center/set up booth for trade fair	Convention center
	7:40 P.M.	Flight to Nice, Orly airport	Dauphin Hotel (Nice)
Sept. 12 Sunday		Enjoy your day off in Nice!	
	6:50 P.M.	Flight to Paris, Cote d'Azur airport	Hotel Regent (Paris)
Sept. 13 Monday	8:00 A.M.	Meeting with booth staff for the trade fair	Convention center
	10:00 A.M. - 7:00 P.M.	Trade fair opens/New product presentation	Convention center
	8:30 P.M.	Dinner with Michel Depuis, owner of Chamber Department Stores	Pomme de Terre Restaurant
Sept. 14 Tuesday	10:00 A.M. - 7:00 P.M.	Trade fair	Convention center
	10:20 P.M.	Return to Buenos Aires, Charles de Gaulle airport	

TO: Mario Cruz

FROM: Flavia Perez

SUBJECT: Your Itinerary for France

As you requested, I am sending you a copy of your itinerary and the contact information of the people you will be meeting during the trip to Paris. If you would like, I can also send you a list of phone numbers of the hotels you will be staying at, so that you can give them to your colleagues here in Buenos Aires. Let me know if you would like me to do so.

There will be a driver waiting for you in Paris, who will take care of your transportation for all appointments. All hotels have already been paid for, apart from the one in Nice, as it will be your personal expense. Also, please keep all receipts for business meals so that you can be reimbursed.

I received word from our production manager, Antonio Gutierrez, that the samples of Bonita's new line of fragrances for your presentation will be shipped today to our branch office in Paris. They will be delivered to the place you will be staying at on Friday, as you will need them for the event on Monday.

If you need anything else, or have any questions just let me know!

196. Why is Mr. Cruz traveling to Paris?

(A) To present his company's new products at a trade event
(B) To meet with retailers interested in selling Bonita merchandise
(C) To help set up a regional office for the European market
(D) To order items at a sales fair to sell in his company's store

197. What is Mr. Cruz NOT scheduled to do during his trip?

(A) Meet with the proprietor of a chain of stores
(B) Have a meal with a colleague
(C) Visit Bonita's branch office in Paris
(D) Attend an event at a convention center

198. What does Ms. Perez offer to send to Mr. Cruz?

(A) The address of a hotel
(B) A travel itinerary
(C) Some product samples
(D) Contact information

199. What is indicated about Bonita's new line of perfumes?

(A) They will be sold in Chamber Department Stores.
(B) They will be sent to Hotel Antoinette.
(C) They will not be ready in time for the event.
(D) They will be given out to potential buyers.

200. According to the memo, which expense will Mr. Cruz have to pay for?

(A) The meal with Michel Depuis
(B) The room cost at Hotel Antoinette
(C) The charge for the Dauphin Hotel
(D) The flight to Buenos Aires

Stop! This is the end of the test. If you finish before time is called, you may go back to Part 5, 6, and 7 and check your work.

COLUMN ③

TOEICの達人に聞く

50歳のおじさん
- TOEIC スコア：665点
- TOEIC 歴：1年

　某自動車メーカーに勤める「50歳のおじさん」です。ペンネームにあるとおり、私は50歳ですが、1年ほど前から、TOEIC にどっぷりはまっています。

　TOEIC を採用する企業が増える一方で、「TOEIC は使えない」という声も聞かれます。「ほんとのとこどうなんだ？」と思ってる方も多いでしょうから、いちサラリーマン学習者として、すこし意見を述べたいと思います。

●TOEIC は登竜門

　ご存じのように、日本は少子高齢化が進み、マーケットは成熟しきっています。特に私が身を置く自動車産業は、国内だけでは、拡大が非常に難しい状況です。日本メーカーが生き残るには、外に出ていくしかありません。

　その際に武器となるのが、日本独自の環境技術や、低コスト・高品質な生産技術なわけですが、それらを持っているだけでは、宝の持ち腐れです。世界にアピールをしなければいけません。そこで必要となるのが、〈英語〉です（だから、私は"50の手習い"を始めたわけです）。

　ビジネスで通用する英語を身に付けるために、TOEIC さえやっていればいいのか、と問われれば、答えはノーでしょう。しかし、何事も段階が必要です。英語を駆使する状態に駆け登るための登竜門として、私は、TOEIC は最適だろうと思っています。

●TOEIC は使える！

　なぜなら、TOEIC に出てくるビジネストピックの多くは、汎用的な内容で、初中級レベルのビジネスパーソンにとっては、ためになる表現の宝庫だからです。

　とくに、E メールの問題がたくさんでてくるのはいいですね。勉強をしながら、「あ、この依頼表現を英借文しよう」、「論理的な英文は、こう書けばいいのか」などなど、発見がたくさんあります。

　そうやって、実際に使うことを意識すれば、TOEIC は驚くほど、使える英語なのです。

　読者のなかには、学生さんも多いでしょう。とすると、TOEIC のビジネス系語彙を難しく感じるかもしれません。でも、それらは近い将来、きっと役に立ちます。私自身の経験から、これは断言できます。

　TOEIC は、上述のようにスタート地点です。少々、遅いスタートですが、私はとにかく走り始めました。50を過ぎたおじさんも悪戦苦闘しながら頑張っています。みなさんもいっしょに頑張ってみませんか。TOEIC を皮切りに一人ひとりの英語力を上げていくことが、日本の将来につながると私は感じています。英語さえ身に付けてしまえば、「もっとも大切なこと＝日本オリジナルな価値の創造」に専念できますからね。みなさんにはぜひ、日本の価値を世界中に知らしめていただきたいと思います。

　でもときには、趣味やお気に入りの内容を英語で楽しんで息抜きしてくださいね。楽しくないと、何事も続きませんから。

新 TOEIC® テスト
でる模試　600問

2012年11月 4日　初版　第1刷発行
2014年 4月14日　　　　第7刷発行

著　者	ハッカーズ語学研究所
発行者	天谷 修平
発　行	株式会社 アスク出版 〒162-8558 東京都新宿区下宮比町2-6 TEL：03-3267-6866 FAX：03-3267-6867 URL：http://www.ask-digital.co.jp/
装　幀	岡崎 裕樹
本文デザイン	コン トヨコ
DTP	株式会社 鷗来堂
印刷・製本	株式会社 光邦

ISBN 978-4-87217-808-1　　　　Printed in Japan

乱丁、落丁、CD-ROMに不具合が発生した場合はお取り替えいたします。弊社カスタマーサービス（電話：03-3267-6500　受付時間：土日祝祭日を除く平日 10:00～12:00／13:00～17:00）までご相談ください。

本書の続刊である『新TOEIC® テスト でる模試 もっと 600問』(2013年11月発売) に掲載したリーディングの解答時間を記録できるマークシートがたいへん好評でしたので、本書も**6刷目**(2014年2月) よりマークシートを更新しました。以下の使用方法を参考に、ぜひご活用ください。

「R の解答時間」ゲージの使い方

① 事前に目標時間を書き込んでおく

●マークシート下部に記載された「R の解答時間」ゲージ

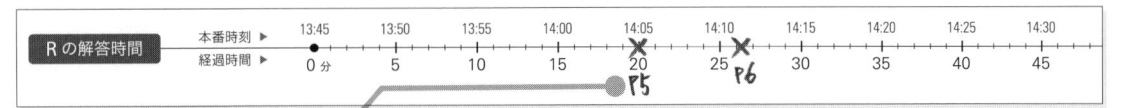

Part 5を20分、Part 6を6分というように、事前に目標時間を書き込んでおく。

　模試を開始する前に、自分が目標とする時間をマークしておきましょう。

　もっともシンプルな区切りは「Part 5／Part 6／Part 7」を終えるタイミングですが、「Part 5／Part 6／Part 7のシングルパッセージ／Part 7のダブルパッセージ」で区切ってもよいでしょうし、Part 5をより細かく10問ずつで確認するのもよいでしょう。

② 通過タイムをチェック

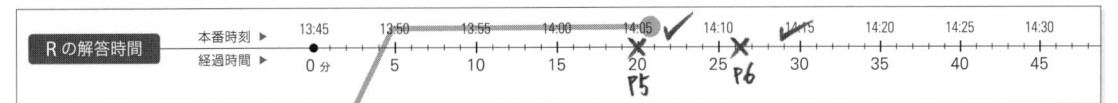

解答を始めたら、実際の所要時間にチェックマーク。

　リーディング・セクションの解答が始まったら、自分が設定した区切りごとに、通過タイムを書き込んでいきましょう。時間がもったいないので、軽くチェックをつけるだけにします。

　ちなみに、ゲージの上段は、TOEIC 公開テスト本番の時刻を示しています。リーディング・セクションは毎回、13時45分に始まり、15時に終了します。テスト本番では、時刻で進行を管理することが多いでしょうから、何時何分までに、どのパートまで進めばよいのかを、しっかり体に染み込ませておきましょう。

PDF データのダウンロード

以下のアドレスより B5 サイズの PDF データをダウンロード可能です。

http://www.ask-books.com/toeic/ms.zip/

TEST 解答用紙

学習日： 　月　　日
解答時間：　　　分

予想スコア L / R
正答数 L / R
TOTAL

LISTENING SECTION

Part 1
No.	A	B	C	D
1	A	B	C	D
2	A	B	C	D
3	A	B	C	D
4	A	B	C	D
5	A	B	C	D
6	A	B	C	D
7	A	B	C	D
8	A	B	C	D
9	A	B	C	D
10	A	B	C	D

Part 2
No.	A	B	C
11	A	B	C
12	A	B	C
13	A	B	C
14	A	B	C
15	A	B	C
16	A	B	C
17	A	B	C
18	A	B	C
19	A	B	C
20	A	B	C
21	A	B	C
22	A	B	C
23	A	B	C
24	A	B	C
25	A	B	C
26	A	B	C
27	A	B	C
28	A	B	C
29	A	B	C
30	A	B	C
31	A	B	C
32	A	B	C
33	A	B	C
34	A	B	C
35	A	B	C
36	A	B	C
37	A	B	C
38	A	B	C
39	A	B	C
40	A	B	C

Part 3
No.	A	B	C	D
41	A	B	C	D
42	A	B	C	D
43	A	B	C	D
44	A	B	C	D
45	A	B	C	D
46	A	B	C	D
47	A	B	C	D
48	A	B	C	D
49	A	B	C	D
50	A	B	C	D
51	A	B	C	D
52	A	B	C	D
53	A	B	C	D
54	A	B	C	D
55	A	B	C	D
56	A	B	C	D
57	A	B	C	D
58	A	B	C	D
59	A	B	C	D
60	A	B	C	D
61	A	B	C	D
62	A	B	C	D
63	A	B	C	D
64	A	B	C	D
65	A	B	C	D
66	A	B	C	D
67	A	B	C	D
68	A	B	C	D
69	A	B	C	D
70	A	B	C	D

Part 4
No.	A	B	C	D
71	A	B	C	D
72	A	B	C	D
73	A	B	C	D
74	A	B	C	D
75	A	B	C	D
76	A	B	C	D
77	A	B	C	D
78	A	B	C	D
79	A	B	C	D
80	A	B	C	D
81	A	B	C	D
82	A	B	C	D
83	A	B	C	D
84	A	B	C	D
85	A	B	C	D
86	A	B	C	D
87	A	B	C	D
88	A	B	C	D
89	A	B	C	D
90	A	B	C	D
91	A	B	C	D
92	A	B	C	D
93	A	B	C	D
94	A	B	C	D
95	A	B	C	D
96	A	B	C	D
97	A	B	C	D
98	A	B	C	D
99	A	B	C	D
100	A	B	C	D

READING SECTION

Part 5
No.	A	B	C	D
101	A	B	C	D
102	A	B	C	D
103	A	B	C	D
104	A	B	C	D
105	A	B	C	D
106	A	B	C	D
107	A	B	C	D
108	A	B	C	D
109	A	B	C	D
110	A	B	C	D
111	A	B	C	D
112	A	B	C	D
113	A	B	C	D
114	A	B	C	D
115	A	B	C	D
116	A	B	C	D
117	A	B	C	D
118	A	B	C	D
119	A	B	C	D
120	A	B	C	D
121	A	B	C	D
122	A	B	C	D
123	A	B	C	D
124	A	B	C	D
125	A	B	C	D
126	A	B	C	D
127	A	B	C	D
128	A	B	C	D
129	A	B	C	D
130	A	B	C	D

Part 6
No.	A	B	C	D
131	A	B	C	D
132	A	B	C	D
133	A	B	C	D
134	A	B	C	D
135	A	B	C	D
136	A	B	C	D
137	A	B	C	D
138	A	B	C	D
139	A	B	C	D
140	A	B	C	D
141	A	B	C	D
142	A	B	C	D
143	A	B	C	D
144	A	B	C	D
145	A	B	C	D
146	A	B	C	D
147	A	B	C	D
148	A	B	C	D
149	A	B	C	D
150	A	B	C	D
151	A	B	C	D
152	A	B	C	D

Part 7
No.	A	B	C	D
153	A	B	C	D
154	A	B	C	D
155	A	B	C	D
156	A	B	C	D
157	A	B	C	D
158	A	B	C	D
159	A	B	C	D
160	A	B	C	D
161	A	B	C	D
162	A	B	C	D
163	A	B	C	D
164	A	B	C	D
165	A	B	C	D
166	A	B	C	D
167	A	B	C	D
168	A	B	C	D
169	A	B	C	D
170	A	B	C	D
171	A	B	C	D
172	A	B	C	D
173	A	B	C	D
174	A	B	C	D
175	A	B	C	D
176	A	B	C	D
177	A	B	C	D
178	A	B	C	D
179	A	B	C	D
180	A	B	C	D
181	A	B	C	D
182	A	B	C	D
183	A	B	C	D
184	A	B	C	D
185	A	B	C	D
186	A	B	C	D
187	A	B	C	D
188	A	B	C	D
189	A	B	C	D
190	A	B	C	D
191	A	B	C	D
192	A	B	C	D
193	A	B	C	D
194	A	B	C	D
195	A	B	C	D
196	A	B	C	D
197	A	B	C	D
198	A	B	C	D
199	A	B	C	D
200	A	B	C	D

本番時刻： 13:45 13:50 13:55 14:00 14:05 14:10 14:15 14:20 14:25 14:30 14:35 14:40 14:45 14:50 14:55 15:00
経過時間： 0分 … 25 30 35 40 45 50 55 60 65 70 75分
Rの解答時間： … 80

TEST 解答用紙

TEST 解答用紙

LISTENING SECTION

Part 1 / **Part 2** / **Part 3** / **Part 4** (Questions 1–100)

READING SECTION

Part 5 / **Part 6** / **Part 7** (Questions 101–200)

TEST 解答用紙

TEST 解答用紙

新TOEIC®テスト
でる模試 600問

別冊 解答・解説 1

TEST 1

取り外し
可能

ゆっくり矢印のほうに
引くと外れます。
▶▶▶

新TOEIC®テスト
でる模試 600問

別冊 解答・解説 ①
TEST 1

目次・Contents

正解一覧	2
Part 1	4
Part 2	8
Part 3	18
Part 4	30
Part 5	42
Part 6	56
Part 7	64

TEST 1 ── 正解一覧

〈TEST 1〉の正解リスト。答え合せにご利用ください。また、間違った問題は、チェックボックス□にチェックをいれておきましょう（1回目は☑、2回目は☒）。復習の際、間違った問題がひと目でわかるので、便利です。

LISTENING SECTION

Part 1
1	D
2	A
3	D
4	A
5	D
6	D
7	C
8	C
9	B
10	D

Part 2
#	Answer	#	Answer	#	Answer
11	C	21	B	31	C
12	A	22	B	32	A
13	B	23	C	33	C
14	A	24	B	34	A
15	A	25	B	35	C
16	B	26	B	36	B
17	B	27	B	37	A
18	B	28	C	38	B
19	A	29	A	39	B
20	B	30	B	40	C

Part 3
#	Answer	#	Answer	#	Answer
41	D	51	C	61	A
42	C	52	B	62	D
43	A	53	A	63	C
44	D	54	C	64	A
45	D	55	C	65	B
46	A	56	A	66	B
47	C	57	C	67	D
48	C	58	A	68	C
49	C	59	B	69	A
50	B	60	C	70	D

Part 4
#	Answer	#	Answer	#	Answer
71	D	81	B	91	A
72	C	82	C	92	C
73	A	83	D	93	A
74	A	84	A	94	A
75	D	85	C	95	C
76	B	86	D	96	A
77	C	87	D	97	D
78	D	88	B	98	B
79	B	89	B	99	A
80	A	90	D	100	D

受験1回目（学習日：　　月　　日）

LISTENING				Ⓐ予想スコア
正答数				
Part 1	Part 2	Part 3	Part 4	

READING			Ⓑ予想スコア
正答数			
Part 5	Part 6	Part 7	

トータル予想スコア
Ⓐ＋Ⓑ

受験2回目（学習日：　　月　　日）

LISTENING				Ⓐ予想スコア
正答数				
Part 1	Part 2	Part 3	Part 4	

READING			Ⓑ予想スコア
正答数			
Part 5	Part 6	Part 7	

トータル予想スコア
Ⓐ＋Ⓑ

※本体のスコア換算表（p.9）をご利用ください。

READING SECTION

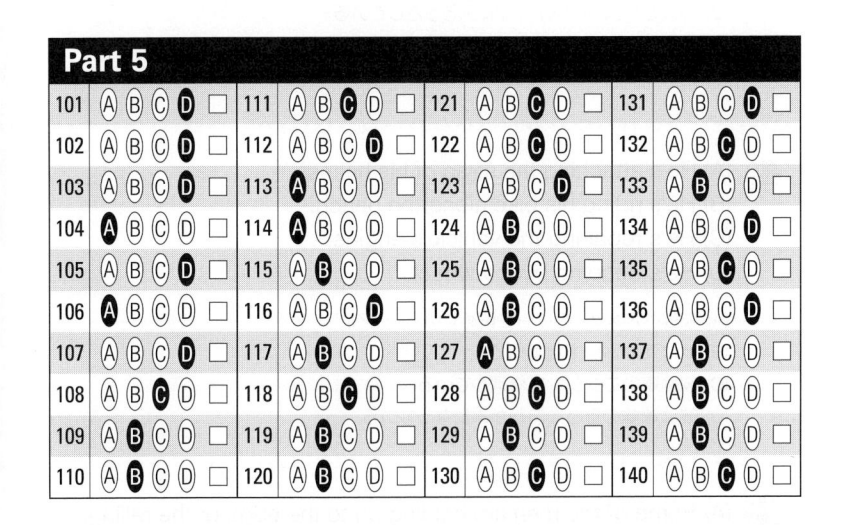

Part 5

#	Ans	#	Ans	#	Ans	#	Ans
101	C	111	C	121	C	131	D
102	D	112	D	122	C	132	C
103	D	113	A	123	B	133	A
104	A	114	A	124	A	134	A
105	D	115	B	125	A	135	C
106	A	116	D	126	D	136	D
107	D	117	B	127	A	137	B
108	C	118	D	128	C	138	B
109	B	119	C	129	A	139	B
110	B	120	B	130	C	140	C

Part 6

#	Ans
141	D
142	C
143	C
144	D
145	B
146	A
147	B
148	D
149	C
150	D

Part 7

#	Ans	#	Ans	#	Ans	#	Ans	#	Ans
151	B	161	C	171	C	181	C	191	B
152	C	162	A	172	A	182	D	192	A
153	C	163	A	173	A	183	B	193	D
154	D	164	D	174	D	184	C	194	D
155	C	165	C	175	B	185	D	195	C
156	D	166	C	176	B	186	C	196	C
157	C	167	C	177	C	187	D	197	C
158	C	168	C	178	D	188	C	198	C
159	D	169	D	179	B	189	D	199	C
160	B	170	B	180	C	190	A	200	A

TEST 1 PART 1

音声ファイル T1_P1_Q01 ▶ T1_P1_Q05

問題&訳

1.

(A) He is parking a car.
(B) He is shoveling some snow.
(C) He is digging a hole.
(D) He is opening the garage.

(A) 彼は車を駐車しようとしている。
(B) 彼は雪をショベルですくっている。
(C) 彼は穴を掘っている。
(D) 彼はガレージの戸を開けている。

2.

(A) Some people are sitting outside a café.
(B) Some people are entering a restaurant.
(C) Some people are looking at menus.
(D) Some people are taking photographs.

(A) 何人かの人がカフェの外に座っている。
(B) 何人かの人がレストランに入ろうとしている。
(C) 何人かの人がメニューを見ている。
(D) 何人かの人が写真を撮っている。

3.

(A) He's attaching the strap of his helmet.
(B) He's riding his bike along the beach.
(C) He's repairing the vehicle's engine.
(D) He's bending over a wheel.

(A) 彼はヘルメットのひもを留めているところだ。
(B) 彼は海岸沿いを自転車で走っている。
(C) 彼は車のエンジンを修理している。
(D) 彼は車輪のほうに前かがみになっている。

4.

(A) Some of the men are holding on to the edge of the railing.
(B) The tourists are resting in the shadow of a tree.
(C) A man is hiking down a mountain path.
(D) Some people are taking pictures of the scenery.

(A) 何人かの男性が手すりのへりをつかんでいる。
(B) 観光客は木陰で休憩している。
(C) 男性が山道を徒歩で下りている。
(D) 何人かの人が風景を写真に撮っている。

5.

(A) He is trimming branches from a tree.
(B) He is hiking through a forest.
(C) He is walking along a pathway.
(D) He is relaxing on a bench.

(A) 彼は木から枝を刈り取っている。
(B) 彼は森をハイキングしている。
(C) 彼は小道に沿って歩いている。
(D) 彼はベンチでくつろいでいる。

TOEIC豆知識 Part1は、意外にガテン系だ。肉体労働場面がよく登場する。次のガテン系ワード、英語で言えますか？
① 建設現場：c--- s--- ／② 重機：h--- m--- ／③ 一輪車：w---。（続く▶）

正解＆解説

間違いメモ＆単語

1. 正解 (B)　難易度：難

男性が雪かきをしている様子を **is shoveling some snow**（雪をショベルですくっている）と描写した (B) が正解。(A) の車は写っているが、すでに駐車されている。(C) の is digging a hole（穴を掘っている）は雪かきと似た動作だが、男性は穴を掘ってはいない。(D) のガレージの扉は閉じたまま。

あなたの解答　A B C D
メモ

- □ park　〜を駐車させる
- □ shovel　〜をショベルですくう
- □ dig　〜を掘る
- □ garage　ガレージ、車庫

2. 正解 (A)　難易度：難

カフェの屋外席に座っている人々を描写した (A) が正解。(B) の「レストランに入ろうとしている」人物は見当たらない。(C) の are looking at menus（メニューを見ている）という動作は、写真からは判断できない。同様に (D) の are taking photographs（写真を撮っている）という動作も確認できないので、誤り。

あなたの解答　A B C D
メモ

3. 正解 (D)　難易度：難

男性の動作をしっかり見極めたい問題。正解は is bending over a wheel（車輪のほうに身をかがめている）と描写している (D)。(A) は、ヘルメットのひもを今まさに留めている動作を描写しているが、ひもはすでに留まっている状態なので誤り。(B) は ride（〜に乗る）、beach（海岸）がともに写真と異なる。(C) は、He's repairing だけで早とちりせず、あとに続く the vehicle's engine（車のエンジン）まで聞いて判断しなければいけない。

あなたの解答　A B C D
メモ

- □ attach　〜をくっつける
- □ repair　〜を修理する　□ vehicle　車
- □ bend over 〜　〜のほうにかがむ

4. 正解 (A)　難易度：難

何人かの男性が、**the edge of the railing**（手すりのへり）をつかんでいる姿を描写した (A) が正解。男性たちは観光客だと思われるが、(B) の木陰にいるわけではない。(C) の山道はまったく写っていない。カメラは写っているが、男性たちは写真を撮っていないので (D) も誤り。

あなたの解答　A B C D
メモ

- □ hold on to 〜　〜をつかむ
- □ edge　へり　□ railing　手すり
- □ in the shadow of 〜　〜の影で
- □ path　小道　□ scenery　風景

5. 正解 (D)　難易度：難

男性がベンチに腰かけている様子を、**is relaxing on a bench**（ベンチでくつろいでいる）と描写した (D) が正解。(A) の is trimming branches（枝を刈り取っている）は、男性の動作に一致しない。男性はベンチに座っており、(B) の「ハイキングしている」、(C) の「歩いている」はすぐに誤りとわかる。

あなたの解答　A B C D
メモ

- □ trim　〜を刈り取って整える
- □ branch　枝　□ pathway　小道、歩道
- □ relax　くつろぐ

5

TEST 1 PART 1 問題&訳

音声ファイル　T1_P1_Q06 ▶ T1_P1_Q10

6.
(A) A man is reading a book in a library.
(B) There's a row of desks facing the screen.
(C) A man is erasing the blackboard.
(D) There's a clock situated near the ceiling.

(A) 男性が図書館で読書している。
(B) スクリーンに面して机が1列に並んでいる。
(C) 男性が黒板を消している。
(D) 天井の近くに時計が設置してある。

7.
(A) A woman is handing money to a clerk.
(B) Customers are putting purchases into bags.
(C) Products are displayed in cases.
(D) Merchandise is being placed onto shelves.

(A) 女性が店員にお金を手渡している。
(B) 客たちは買ったものをバッグに入れている。
(C) 商品がケースの中に陳列されている。
(D) 商品が棚に置かれようとしているところだ。

8.
(A) The musicians are practicing on the stage.
(B) A guitar is being plugged into an outlet.
(C) Posters have been put up behind the musical instruments.
(D) A live performance has started.

(A) ミュージシャンがステージで練習している。
(B) ギターのプラグがコンセントに差し込まれているところだ。
(C) ポスターが楽器の後方に貼られている。
(D) 生演奏が始まった。

9.
(A) A calendar is being removed from the wall.
(B) She is placing a book on top of the machine.
(C) A photocopier is being fixed by a repairperson.
(D) She is arranging folders on the shelf.

(A) カレンダーが壁からはがされているところだ。
(B) 彼女は機械の上に本を置いている。
(C) コピー機が修理工の手で修理されているところだ。
(D) 彼女は棚のフォルダーを整理している。

10.
(A) Glass is being installed in the windows.
(B) Some people are climbing up the flight of stairs.
(C) A metal fence encircles the lamppost.
(D) Some stairs lead up to the front door.

(A) ガラスが窓にはめられているところだ。
(B) 何人かの人がひと続きの階段を上っている。
(C) 金属のフェンスが街灯を囲んでいる。
(D) 階段は正面玄関につながっている。

TOEIC豆知識 《ガテン系ワードの答え》 ① 建設現場：construction site ／② 重機：heavy machinery ／③ 一輪車：wheelbarrow。どれも覚えておいて損はなし！

正解＆解説

6. 正解 (D) 難易度 難

天井近くに時計が設置された状態を正確に描写している (D) が正解。**situate**（〜を置く）と **ceiling**（天井）の意味を正確に捉えられるかが、ポイントとなる。男性は読書をしていると思われるが、場所が library であるかどうかは判断できないので、(A) は誤り。(B) は、screen（画面）が写っていない。(C) の is erasing（〜をぬぐい消している）は男性の動作と一致しない。

間違いメモ＆単語
あなたの解答 A B C D
メモ

☐ row 列　☐ face 〜に面する
☐ situate 〜を置く　☐ ceiling 天井

---

7. 正解 (C) 難易度 難

陳列ケースの中に商品が並んでいる様子を **are displayed in cases**（ケースの中に陳列されている）と描写した (C) が正解。(A) は真ん中の女性があやしいが、「お金を手渡している」かどうかは、はっきりしない。写真から判断できないものは正解になり得ないので、(A) は誤り。(B) の買い物客らしき人々は写っているが、ものをバッグに詰める動作はしていない。(D) は**受動態の進行形**で、商品が今まさに置かれようとしている動作を表しているが、写真ではすでに置かれた状態。

あなたの解答 A B C D
メモ

☐ hand 〜を手渡す
☐ purchase 購入品
☐ merchandise 商品

---

8. 正解 (C) 難易度 難

(C) の**受動態の現在完了形**（have been put up）は、ポスターが貼ってある状態を表しており、写真を正しく描写している。(A) は musicians が写っていない。(B) の**受動態の進行形**（is being plugged）は、ギターのプラグをコンセントにまさに差し込もうとしている**人の動作**を描写するが、写真に人は写っていない。(D) も演奏している人はいない。

あなたの解答 A B C D
メモ

☐ plug 〜を差し込む
☐ outlet コンセント
☐ musical instrument 楽器
☐ performance 演奏

---

9. 正解 (B) 難易度 難

女性が本をコピー機の上に置いている様子を表している (B) が正解。コピー機のことを **machine** と表現している。(A) は**受動態の進行形**（is being removed）で、カレンダーを今まさにはがしている**人の動作**を描写しているが、女性はカレンダーに対して何もしていない。(C) の is being fixed も同様に、女性は修理していない。加えて、女性が repairperson（修理工）であるかどうかも判断できない。(D) の is arranging folders は女性の動作に一致しない。

あなたの解答 A B C D
メモ

☐ remove 〜を取り除く　☐ place 〜を置く　☐ photocopier コピー機
☐ fix 〜を修理する
☐ arrange 〜を整理する　☐ shelf 棚

---

10. 正解 (D) 難易度 難

階段が玄関まで続いている様子を描写した (D) が正解。(A) は、**人の動作を描写する受動態の進行形**（is being installed）になっているが、写真に人物は写っていないので誤り。(B) も some people が写っていない。(C) は metal fence（金属のフェンス）は写っているが、**lamppost**（街灯）を囲んでいないので、誤り。

あなたの解答 A B C D
メモ

☐ install 〜を取付ける、設置する
☐ flight of stairs ひと続きの階段
☐ encircle 〜を囲む
☐ lamppost 街灯　☐ lead 通じる

TEST 1
PART 2

音声ファイル 🔊 T1_P2_Q11 ▶ T1_P2_Q16

問題 | **訳**

11. Who sent this package to my office?
(A) The second door on the right.
(B) I've been here for several years.
(C) It might have been Olivia.

僕のオフィスにこの荷物を送ったのは誰？
(A) 右側の2番目のドアです。
(B) 私は数年ここにいます。
(C) たぶん Olivia でしょう。

12. Where would you like me to mail this envelope?
(A) Yes, you should go now.
(B) Sit anywhere you like.
(C) To our branch office in New York.

この封筒はどこへ郵送すればいいの？
(A) そう、今行くべきだよ。
(B) 好きなところに座って。
(C) ニューヨークの支店へ。

13. This room is cozy, isn't it?
(A) Yes, it has been.
(B) It's certainly comfortable.
(C) It's in the kitchen.

この部屋は居心地がいいよね。
(A) ええ、そうだったわ。
(B) たしかに快適ね。
(C) それは台所にあるわ。

14. Weren't you in sales before this job?
(A) It starts tomorrow at 10.
(B) Only for a couple of months.
(C) Yes, I was waiting outside.

この仕事の前は、営業職に就いていたわけではないんですか。
(A) 明日の10時に始まります。
(B) 数カ月間だけですが。
(C) ええ、外で待っていました。

15. Where can I find a cash machine nearby?
(A) There's one on the corner.
(B) It's out of order.
(C) By credit card.

近くに ATM はありますか。
(A) 角にありますよ。
(B) それは壊れていますね。
(C) クレジットカードで。

16. How was the exhibit opening?
(A) We're closing in a little while.
(B) On the top floor of my building.
(C) A good number showed up.

展示会の初日はどうだった？
(A) まもなく閉店します。
(B) 私がいる建物の最上階で。
(C) かなりの数の人が来ていたわ。

| 正解&解説 | 間違いメモ&単語 |

11. 正解 (C) 難易度 難

Who 疑問文で、小包を送った〈人〉が問われている。これに、Olivia と人物名を答えている (C) が正解。(A) は場所、(B) は期間を答えており誤り。

あなたの解答 A B C
メモ

☐ package 小包

12. 正解 (C) 難易度 難

封筒を送る〈場所〉を問う Where 疑問文。branch office in New York と明解に場所を答えている (C) が正解。**疑問詞を使った疑問文に Yes/No では答えられない**ので、(A) はすぐに除外できる。(B) は、問い掛けの Where に発音が類似した anywhere を使っているのに加え、you like をくり返してひっかけをねらっている。

あなたの解答 A B C
メモ

☐ envelope 封筒
☐ branch office 支店

13. 正解 (B) 難易度 難

付加疑問文は、**通常の疑問文に置き換えるとわかりやすい**。すると、「この部屋は心地よいか」と質問されていることになるので、「たしかに快適だ」と賛同している (B) が正解。cozy を comfortable と言い換えているのがポイント。(A) は、Yes, it まではよいが、続く has been（現在完了形）が問い掛けの時制とズレている。(C) も It's まではよいが、続く in the kitchen が問い掛けの内容と一致しない。

あなたの解答 A B C
メモ

☐ cozy 居心地のいい
☐ certainly たしかに

14. 正解 (B) 難易度 難

否定疑問文に混乱する人は、**通常の疑問文に置き換えて**考えよう。すると「この仕事の前に、営業職に就いていたのか」と質問されていることになる。これに、「2、3カ月の間だけ（営業職に就いていた）」と答えて、営業職の経験を**間接的**に伝えている (B) が正解。(A) は、job から連想される始業時間を述べてひっかけをねらっている。(C) は、Yes, I was までならば正解だが、続く waiting outside が無関係。

あなたの解答 A B C
メモ

☐ in sales 営業の仕事をしている
☐ a couple of ～ 2、3の～
☐ outside 外で

15. 正解 (A) 難易度 難

Where 疑問文で、ATM の〈場所〉が問われている。これに対し、(A) の one は a cash machine を指しており、「その角にある」と ATM のありかを答えている。よって、これが正解。(B) は、cash machine から連想される out of order（故障して）でひっかけをねらっている。(C) も、cash（現金）と関連する credit card を使ったひっかけ。

あなたの解答 A B C
メモ

☐ nearby すぐそばに
☐ corner 町かど
☐ out of order 故障して

16. 正解 (C) 難易度 難

展示会初日の〈状態〉を問う How 疑問文。「かなりの数の人が来ていた」と様子を伝えている (C) が正解。(A) は opening に関連する closing で誤答を誘っている。(B) は、場所を答えているので誤り。しかし、How を Where と聞き間違えると、これを正解だと誤解することになる。Part 2 では、**疑問詞の聞き取り**がもっとも重要。

あなたの解答 A B C
メモ

☐ exhibit 展示会
☐ in a little while まもなく   ☐ floor 階
☐ show up 姿を現す

TEST 1
PART 2

音声ファイル T1_P2_Q17 ▶ T1_P2_Q22

問題 / 訳

17. Excuse me, would you mind moving your car?
(A) No, I haven't seen it.
(B) Not in the least.
(C) Everything's packed away.

すみません、車を移動していただけませんか。
(A) いいえ、私は見ていません。
(B) もちろんいいですよ。
(C) すべて荷造りしました。

18. It's all right if I leave my luggage in the lobby, isn't it?
(A) I believe it's on the left side.
(B) No, I already have one.
(C) Yes, the concierge can look after it.

ロビーに荷物を置いて行っても大丈夫ですよね?
(A) それは左側にあると思います。
(B) いいえ、私はすでに持っています。
(C) はい、コンシェルジュが管理いたします。

19. When will the board issue a press release about the acquisition?
(A) Discussions are ongoing.
(B) By unanimous vote.
(C) In a difficult position.

取締役会は買収についてのプレスリリースをいつ公表するのかしら?
(A) 話し合いが継続中なんですよ。
(B) 全会一致の採決で。
(C) 難しい立場ですよ。

20. Is someone sitting here, or can I take this chair?
(A) I've been there before.
(B) It will take about an hour.
(C) My friend is using it, I'm afraid.

このイスにどなたか座っていらっしゃいますか、私が座ってもいいですか。
(A) 私は前に、そこに行ったことがあります。
(B) だいたい1時間くらいかかるでしょう。
(C) すみません、私の友人が使っています。

21. Who is going to receive the company award this year?
(A) This evening at seven.
(B) Mr. Kenichi, most likely.
(C) No, toward the back entrance.

今年は誰が会社の賞を受け取るのかしら?
(A) 今夜7時に。
(B) たぶん、Kenichiさんかな。
(C) いや、裏口に向かってです。

22. Why didn't the office manager authorize your equipment request?
(A) I can manage it on my own.
(B) It costs too much.
(C) It's due on Friday.

なぜ部長は君の備品請求を許可しなかったのかな?
(A) 自分でなんとかできるわ。
(B) 費用が掛かりすぎるから。
(C) 期限は金曜日なのよ。

正解＆解説

17. 正解 (B) 難易度 難

車の移動を〈依頼〉されている。Would you mind doing ～? は、直訳すると「～するのを気にしますか」なので、応答の Yes は「気にする（＝依頼の拒否）」、No は「気にしない（＝依頼の承諾）」を意味する。(B) は「まったくしない」と否定しているので、ここでは「**まったく気にしない（＝もちろん移動する）**」という快諾を表す。(A) は No, I まではよいが、haven't seen it が文脈に一致しない。(C) は move から連想される「荷造り」がひっかけ。

あなたの解答 A B C
メモ

☐ pack away ～ ～をしまい込む

---

18. 正解 (C) 難易度 難

付加疑問文は、「ロビーに荷物を置いて行ってもよいか」という**通常の疑問文に置き換えて**考えよう。これに、Yes（置いて行っていい）と肯定し、「コンシェルジュがそれ（荷物）を管理する」と説明している (C) が正解。(A) は on the left side（左側に）で、luggage の置き場所について会話をしていると誤解させようとしている。(B) は all right に発音の似た already がひっかけ。

あなたの解答 A B C
メモ

☐ luggage 荷物
☐ concierge コンシェルジュ
☐ look after ～の面倒を見る

---

19. 正解 (A) 難易度 難

When 疑問文。企業買収について発表する〈時〉が問われている。具体的な日時ではなく「話し合いが継続中」と答え、発表時期がはっきりしないことを**間接的**に伝えている (A) が正解。(B) は board（取締役会）から連想される内容で誤答を誘っている。(C) は acquisition と発音の似た position がひっかけ。

あなたの解答 A B C
メモ

☐ board 取締役会　☐ issue ～を発表する
☐ acquisition 買収　☐ ongoing 進行中の
☐ unanimous vote 満場一致の議決

---

20. 正解 (C) 難易度 難

選択疑問文。イスに「すでに座っている人がいる」か「私が座ってもいい」かの〈**選択**〉が求められている。(C) は、「**友人が使っている**」と答え、座っている人がいることを伝えているので正解。(A) は here と関連する there を使ったひっかけ。(B) は問い掛けの take をくり返したひっかけ。

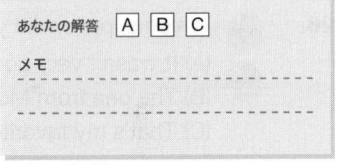

あなたの解答 A B C
メモ

☐ I'm afraid ～ すみませんが～

---

21. 正解 (B) 難易度 難

Who 疑問文で、受賞する〈人〉が問われている。これに対し、Mr. Kenichi という人物名を答えている (B) が正解。(A) は、時間を答えているので誤り。(C) は**疑問詞を使った疑問文に Yes/No で応答**しているので、すぐに除外できる。ただし、award に発音の似た toward を使ったひっかけに注意。

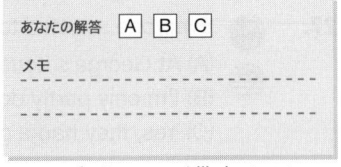

あなたの解答 A B C
メモ

☐ award 賞　☐ most likely たぶん

---

22. 正解 (B) 難易度 難

Why 疑問文で、部長が備品の請求を認めない〈理由〉が問われている。これに「費用が多く掛かる」という理由を答えている (B) が正解。このように **Why 疑問文に対して、Because を用いずに応答**することが多いことを覚えておこう。(A) は manager と発音の似た manage を使って、ひっかけをねらっている。(C) は期日を答えているので、誤り。

あなたの解答 A B C
メモ

☐ office manager 部長　☐ authorize ～を認可する　☐ equipment 備品　☐ manage ～をうまくなし遂げる　☐ on *one's* own 独力で　☐ due 期限が来て

11

TEST 1
PART 2

音声ファイル　T1_P2_Q23 ▶ T1_P2_Q28

問題 | **訳**

---

23. Did you hear the news about Henry?
(A) He's older than that.
(B) I didn't get this month's issue.
(C) No, I've been occupied all day.

Henry についてのニュースを聞いたかい？
(A) 彼はあの人より年上よ。
(B) 今月号は買わなかったわ。
(C) いいえ、1日中忙しかったの。

---

24. When do you normally go for lunch?
(A) Down to the cafeteria.
(B) I already ordered a sandwich.
(C) About half past one.

ふだんはいつランチに行くの？
(A) カフェテリアまで。
(B) もうサンドイッチを注文したよ。
(C) 1時半くらいかな。

---

25. Would you let me know when you get home?
(A) I left it at your house.
(B) Sure. I'll do that as soon as I arrive.
(C) He is staying with me.

家に着いたら連絡をくれないかな？
(A) あなたの家にそれを忘れたわ。
(B) もちろん。着いたらすぐに連絡するね。
(C) 彼は私と一緒に滞在しているの。

---

26. Which supplier did you end up choosing?
(A) It wasn't very good.
(B) The one from Mumbai.
(C) That's my favorite place.

結局、どちらの仕入先に決めたんですか。
(A) あまりよくなかったな。
(B) ムンバイの仕入先です。
(C) そこは私が大好きな場所なんですよ。

---

27. Everyone seemed to enjoy the gathering last night.
(A) At George's house in the country.
(B) I'm only partly done.
(C) Yes, they had a good time.

みんな昨夜の集まりを楽しんだようだね。
(A) 郊外の George の家で。
(B) 部分的に終えただけだわ。
(C) そうね、楽しく過ごしたみたい。

---

28. Will you be free to discuss your data this week?
(A) Yes, I'd like some more, please.
(B) I'm available tomorrow.
(C) At my desk in the office.

今週、あなたのデータについて話し合う時間があるかしら？
(A) はい、もう少しください。
(B) 明日は手があいています。
(C) オフィスの私の机で。

12

TOEIC豆知識 TOEICの住人たちは、パーティーやピクニックばかりやっているようで、実は仕事熱心。食事や映画に誘っても、仕事を理由に断られることしばしばである。

正解&解説

23. 正解 (C) 難易度 ■■□ 難

Yes/No疑問文。Henryに関するニュースを聞いたかどうかが問われている。これに、No（聞いていない）と否定したあと、「1日中忙しかった」と、その理由を説明している (C) が正解。**be occupied**（忙しい）の意味をとれるかがポイント。(A) は過去時制の問い掛けに対し、現在形で答えているうえに、内容も対応しない。(B) は news と関連する「論点、問題」といった意味もある issue で誤答を誘っている。

- issue（刊行物の）号
- be occupied 忙しくしている

24. 正解 (C) 難易度 ■■□ 難

When疑問文でランチに行く〈時〉が問われている。one（1時）を half past（半分過ぎた）、つまり「1時半くらい」と答えている (C) が正解。(A) は場所を答えている。しかし、問い掛けの When を Where と聞き間違えると、(A) を正解と誤解することになる。(B) は lunch から連想される sandwich でひっかけをねらっている。

- normally 通常は

25. 正解 (B) 難易度 ■□□ 難

Would you〜? で、家に着いたら連絡するよう〈依頼〉されている。(B) は、Sure（もちろん連絡する）に続けて「着いたらすぐに」と答えて、依頼を快諾しているので、正解。(A) は、home と同義の house でひっかけをねらっている。(C) は、He が誰を指すのか不明。home に関連する is staying with 〜（〜と一緒に滞在している）がひっかけになっている。

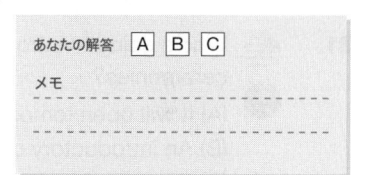

- as soon as 〜 〜するとすぐに

26. 正解 (B) 難易度 ■■□ 難

Which疑問文。〈どれ・どちら〉の仕入先にしたのかが問われている。(B) の one は supplier を指しており、「ムンバイの仕入先」という正しい返答になっている。(A) は仕入先の評価を連想させる内容だが、問い掛けに対応していない。(C) の favorite（お気に入りの、好きな）には、仕入先の選択基準だと誤解させようとするねらいがある。

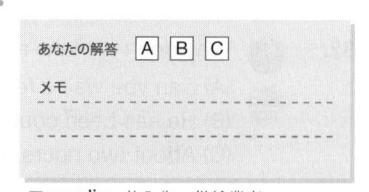

- supplier 仕入先、供給業者
- end up doing 最後には〜する

27. 正解 (C) 難易度 ■■□ 難

「みんな昨夜の集まりを楽しんだ」という意見をつぶやく平叙文。これに、Yes と答えたあと、同じことを別の表現で述べた (C) が、もっとも自然な流れになる。(A) は、**gathering**（集まり）の場所を連想させる答えだが、問い掛けにつながらない。(B) は、gathering に関連する party（パーティ）と発音が類似した **partly**（部分的に）で、ひっかけをねらっている。

- gathering 集会
- partly 部分的に

28. 正解 (B) 難易度 ■■□ 難

Yes/No疑問文で、データについて話し合う時間があるかどうかが問われている。「明日は手があいている」と答え、話し合う時間があることを**間接的**に伝えている (B) が正解。(A) は Yes/No疑問文に対し、Yes, I'd まではよいが、続く like some more 部分が問い掛けにつながらない。(C) は、データの場所（もしくは話し合う場所）を連想させる内容で、ひっかけをねらっている。

- available 手があいている

TEST 1
PART 2

音声ファイル　T1_P2_Q29 ▶ T1_P2_Q34

問題 | 訳

---

29. Would you like me to cook you some dinner?
(A) It's kind of you to offer.
(B) That was truly delicious.
(C) I don't eat out very often.

なにか夕食を作りましょうか。
(A) ご親切に、どうもありがとう。
(B) 本当においしかったよ。
(C) あまり外食はしません。

---

30. Why isn't anybody at their desk?
(A) Let's ask everybody to help.
(B) He works in public relations.
(C) They're in the conference room.

なぜ誰も席に着いていないんだい?
(A) みんなに助けを求めましょう。
(B) 彼は広報で働いているわ。
(C) 会議室にいるのよ。

---

31. Who's going to introduce the speaker at the opening ceremonies?
(A) It will open tomorrow morning.
(B) An introductory course.
(C) Rachel agreed to do it.

開会式では誰が演説者を紹介するんですか。
(A) 明日の朝開く予定です。
(B) 入門講座です。
(C) Rachelさんが引き受けてくれました。

---

32. Why don't we take a ten-minute coffee break?
(A) Can you wait a few minutes?
(B) He has been coughing all day.
(C) About two hours ago.

10分間の休憩をとろうか。
(A) ちょっと待ってもらえない?
(B) 彼は1日中咳をしているわね。
(C) 2時間ほど前よ。

---

33. Remember to bring your passport with you.
(A) There are no seats available.
(B) It's in the top drawer.
(C) I won't forget.

忘れずにパスポートをお持ちください。
(A) 空いている席はありません。
(B) いちばん上の引き出しの中にあります。
(C) 忘れません。

---

34. Haven't you already been accepted to college?
(A) To a few prestigious schools.
(B) Yes, it's been filled out.
(C) It's a popular course.

君はすでに大学に合格していなかったっけ?
(A) いくつかの名門校に。
(B) ええ、それは記入済みです。
(C) それは人気の講座です。

| 正解＆解説 | 間違いメモ＆単語 |

29. 正解 (A) 難易度 ■■□□□

夕食を作るという〈提案〉がなされている。Would you like me to do ～? は、「あなたは私に～してもらいたいですか」という意味。つまり to do ～ の動作をするのは、私（＝話し手）であることを整理しておこう。「そんな提案をしてくださるとはご親切に」と答え、提案を受け入れている (A) が正解。(B) は cook（～を料理する）から連想される delicious（おいしい）、(C) は dinner（夕食）から連想される eat out（外食する）で、それぞれひっかけをねらっている。

あなたの解答 A B C
メモ

□ truly 本当に　□ eat out 外食をする

30. 正解 (C) 難易度 ■■□□□

Why 疑問文で、誰も席に着いていない〈理由〉が問われている。これに、「彼らは会議室にいる」と答え、不在の理由を答えている (C) が正解。**Why 疑問文に対して、必ずしも Because で理由を述べるとは限らない**ことを覚えておこう。(A) は anybody と関連する everybody を使ってひっかけをねらっている。(B) は He が誰のことなのか不明。

あなたの解答 A B C
メモ

□ public relations 宣伝（広報）活動
□ conference room 会議室

31. 正解 (C) 難易度 ■□□□□

Who 疑問文。演説者を紹介する〈人〉が問われている。Rachel と人物名を答えている (C) が正解。(A) は時を答えている。(B) は、introduce の派生語 introductory を使って誤答を誘っている。

あなたの解答 A B C
メモ

□ opening ceremony 開会式
□ introductory 初歩の

32. 正解 (A) 難易度 ■■■□□

Why don't we ～? で、10分間の休憩を〈提案〉されている。これに対し、(A) は「少し待てるか」と疑問文で返している。これはつまり、「**少ししたら休憩をとる**」ということ。**間接的**に提案を受け入れているので、(A) が正解。(B) は、He が誰なのか不明。また、coffee と発音が似ている coughing を使ってひっかけをねらっている。(C) は minute と関連する hours がひっかけ。

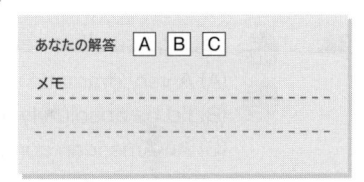

あなたの解答 A B C
メモ

□ cough 咳をする

33. 正解 (C) 難易度 ■■□□□

命令文でパスポートの持参を〈要請〉されている。これに、「忘れない（＝持参する）」と要請を承諾している (C) が正解。(A) (B) はそれぞれ、passport から連想される、飛行機の seats（座席）、しまう場所の drawer（引き出し）でひっかけをねらっている。

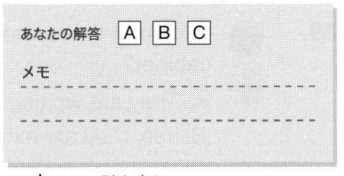

あなたの解答 A B C
メモ

□ drawer 引き出し

34. 正解 (A) 難易度 ■■■■□

否定疑問文は、**通常の疑問文に置き換えて考える**と混乱しない。ここでは「君はすでに大学に合格したのか」と問われていると考える。正解は (A) だが、「いくつかの名門校に（合格した）」と間接的に答えているのに加え、**prestigious**（一流の）という難しい単語があるので難しかったかもしれない。(B) (C) ともに、college から連想される「願書への記入」「講座」でひっかけをねらっている。

あなたの解答 A B C
メモ

□ accept ～を受け入れる、入学させる
□ prestigious 一流の
□ fill out ～ ～に記入する

TEST 1
PART 2

音声ファイル　T1_P2_Q35 ▶ T1_P2_Q40

| 問題 | 訳 |

35. Would you be interested in taking a language class every Saturday?
(A) No, I didn't take it with me.
(B) Sure, I'd like to learn something new.
(C) Three hours in the library.

毎週土曜日の語学の授業に興味はありますか。
(A) いいえ、私は持ち帰っていません。
(B) もちろん、何か新しいことを学びたくて。
(C) 図書館で3時間です。

36. Make sure you follow the detailed instructions stated in the handout.
(A) Construction will soon be over.
(B) I submitted it earlier.
(C) I think I can manage.

資料に記された詳細な指示に必ず従ってください。
(A) 建設作業はまもなく終わるでしょう。
(B) それは以前提出しました。
(C) 何とかやってみます。

37. What's the most difficult part of your job?
(A) Organizing work shifts.
(B) Each one is the same.
(C) It's hard to tell the difference.

仕事でいちばん苦労される点は何ですか。
(A) 勤務シフトを組むことです。
(B) どれも同じです。
(C) 違いを言うのは難しいですね。

38. Let's go see that new movie this weekend.
(A) A very dramatic scene.
(B) I'd be absolutely thrilled.
(C) An American comedy film.

今週末、あの新作映画を見に行きましょうよ。
(A) とても劇的なシーンだね。
(B) ワクワクするなぁ。
(C) アメリカのコメディー映画だよ。

39. Shouldn't these surveys be locked in the filing cabinet?
(A) They are waiting in your office.
(B) Yes, they are extremely confidential.
(C) I will look for the files.

この調査書は書類整理棚に鍵をかけて保管しなくてもよいのですか。
(A) 彼らはあなたのオフィスで待ってます。
(B) ええ（保管しなくてはいけません）、極秘のものなので。
(C) 私がそのファイルを探すわ。

40. Jerry, would you schedule an appointment for me with the director?
(A) Yes, let me draw you a map.
(B) Your reservation was cancelled.
(C) I'll get on it right away.

Jerry さん、あの重役と会う約束を取り付けてくれますか。
(A) はい、私が地図を描きましょう。
(B) あなたの予約はキャンセルされました。
(C) すぐにやります。

| 正解＆解説 | 間違いメモ＆単語 |

35. 正解 (B) 　難易度 ■■□ 難

Yes/No 疑問文で、語学の授業への興味の有無が問われている。これに、Sure（もちろん興味がある）と答え、「新しいことを学びたい」という理由を付け加えている (B) が正解。(A) は、問い掛けにある take をくり返したひっかけ。(C) は語学の授業から連想される、授業時間の Three hours でひっかけをねらっている。

あなたの解答 A B C
メモ

---

36. 正解 (C) 　難易度 ■■■ 難

命令文で、資料の指示に従うよう〈要請〉されている。これに対して、(C) の「何とかできると思う」が、**間接的**に要請を受け入れており、もっとも自然。(A) は instructions と発音が似ている construction、(B) は handout（配布資料）から連想される submitted（〜を提出した）で、それぞれひっかけをねらっている。

あなたの解答 A B C
メモ

□ detailed 詳細な　□ handout 配布資料　□ construction 建設
□ submit 〜を提出する

---

37. 正解 (A) 　難易度 ■■□ 難

What 疑問文。仕事でいちばんむずかしい〈こと・もの〉が問われている。これに対し、「勤務シフトを組むこと」と具体的な業務を答えている (A) が正解。(C) は difficult の類義語 hard を使ってひっかけをねらっているが、tell the difference 部分が文脈に一致しない。(B) は、part と関連する each one がひっかけになっている。

あなたの解答 A B C
メモ

□ work shift 勤務シフト

---

38. 正解 (B) 　難易度 ■■□ 難

Let's 〜で映画に行くことを〈提案〉されている。「ワクワクする」と答え、提案を**間接的**に受け入れている (B) がもっとも自然。be thrilled（ワクワクする）の意味をとれるかがポイント。(A) は movie に関連する scene を使って、(C) は movie から連想される comedy film を使ってひっかけをねらっている。

あなたの解答 A B C
メモ

□ absolutely 絶対に
□ thrilled ワクワクした

---

39. 正解 (B) 　難易度 ■■■ 難

否定疑問文は、**通常の疑問文に置き換えて**考えよう。そうすれば、応答の Yes は肯定（〜する）、No は否定（〜しない）とスムーズに理解できる。ここでは、「調査書は書類整理棚に鍵をかけて保管すべきか」と問われていると考える。すると、(B) の Yes は「保管すべき」を意味し、続けて「極秘のものだから」と理由が続いている。よって (B) が正解。(A) は surveys（調査書）や filing cabinet（書類整理棚）から連想される office でひっかけをねらっている。(C) は filing の派生語 files がひっかけ。

あなたの解答 A B C
メモ

□ survey 調査書　□ filing cabinet 書類整理棚　□ confidential 機密の
□ look for 〜 〜を探す

---

40. 正解 (C) 　難易度 ■■□ 難

Would you 〜？で重役と会う約束を取り付けるよう〈依頼〉されている。「すぐに進めます」と答えて、依頼を快諾している (C) が正解。get on 〜（（仕事など）を進める）の意味をとれるかがポイント。(B) は、appointment（人と会う約束）と意味が似ている reservation（予約）を使ってひっかけをねらっている。(A) は draw you a map で、会う場所についての会話だと誤解させようとしている。

あなたの解答 A B C
メモ

□ schedule 〜を予定する
□ director 重役　□ reservation 予約
□ get on 〜 （仕事など）を進める
□ right away すぐに

TEST 1 PART 3

41. Why is the woman going to the printing company?
(A) She wants to apply for a job.
(B) She has to deliver an order.
(C) She wants to submit an article.
(D) She has to get posters made.

42. Why is the woman concerned?
(A) She is afraid of missing a deadline.
(B) She cannot locate an office building.
(C) She may not make it to an office on time.
(D) She doesn't know how to use the printer.

43. How will the woman most likely get to the printing company?
(A) By crossing a pathway
(B) By taking the stairs
(C) By walking a few blocks
(D) By switching elevators

44. Why is the woman running late?
(A) She is stuck in traffic.
(B) She woke up late.
(C) Her car broke down.
(D) She missed her train.

45. At what time will the speakers meet?
(A) At 7 o'clock
(B) At 8 o'clock
(C) At 8:30
(D) At 10:30

46. What does the man ask the woman to do?
(A) Meet at his office
(B) Wait at the train station
(C) Call when she arrives
(D) Take an earlier train

Questions 41-43 refer to the following conversation.

W: Hi, I'm looking for the Larkin Printing Company. Isn't it located on this floor?
M: Not anymore. It moved to a bigger office in Tower 2 over a month ago.
W: Oh no. ❶I have some posters that need to be printed out by this week, and ❷I need to get there soon to place the job order before it closes in 10 minutes. Is there a quick way to get there from here?
M: Take the elevator upstairs to the fifteenth floor and ❸use the sky-bridge that connects both towers. Once you get across, the third door on your left is their new office. It should take you less than 10 minutes.

設問41から43は次の会話に関する質問です。
女：こんにちは。Larkin 印刷会社を探しているのですが。この階ではありませんでしたか。
男：もうここにはありませんよ。1カ月以上前にタワー2のより広い事務所に移転しました。
女：ええ、そんな。今週中に印刷しなければならないポスターがあって、10分後の閉店前に、発注依頼に行かなければいけないんです。近道はありませんか。
男：ここから15階までエレベーターで行き、両タワーをつなぐスカイブリッジ（高架橋）を渡ってください。渡ったら、左手の3つ目のドアが新事務所です。10分以内に着くはずです。

Questions 44-46 refer to the following conversation.

W: Hello Roger. This is Tammy calling. ❶I missed the 7 o'clock train this morning, so I'm afraid I will be late for ❷our appointment scheduled for nine.
M: No problem. When do you think you'll be able to get here?
W: Well, there's another train at eight, so I'm going to take that one. So, ❸can we meet an hour and a half later than planned?
M: Sure. Just ❹come directly up to my office when you get here.

設問44から46は次の会話に関する質問です。
女：もしもし、Roger さん。Tammy です。今朝7時の列車に乗り遅れてしまい、申し訳ないのですがお約束の9時に遅れそうです。
男：問題ありませんよ。いつこちらに来られそうですか。
女：えっと、8時に別の列車があるのでそれに乗ります。なので、予定より1時間半遅れでお会いできないでしょうか。
男：けっこうですよ。到着したら直接私のオフィスにいらしてください。

設問の訳 ☞ p.28〜29参照

TOEIC豆知識 TOEICの世界では、戦争や犯罪が話題にのぼることはない。加えて、宗教や政治などcontroversialな話題も皆無。実に、平和なのである。（続く▶）

正解＆解説

41. 正解 (D) 難易度 難

女性が印刷会社に行く理由を尋ねている。❶で女性は「今週中に**印刷しなければならないポスターがある**」と言っているので、これが理由と考えられる。従って、正解は「彼女はポスターを作らなければならない」と表現している(D)。

42. 正解 (C) 難易度 難

女性の心配事の理由を尋ねているので、女性の**ネガティブな発言に注目**する。❷で「10分後の閉店までにそこ（= Larkin Printing Company）に行かなければいけない」と言っており、**「時間内に到着できないかもしれない」**ことを心配している。よって(C)が正解。(A)のdeadlineについて、女性はひと言も述べていない。(B)はoffice building部分が×。女性はすでに建物に到着しており、見つけられずにいるのは部屋の位置。

43. 正解 (A) 難易度 難

印刷会社への移動方法を尋ねている。❸で男性は「両タワーを結ぶ**スカイブリッジを渡って行く**」ことを勧めている。話の流れから、女性はこの忠告に従うと考えられる。sky-bridgeをpathwayと言い換えて「通路を渡って」と表現した(A)が正解。(D)はswitch（〜を乗り換える）部分が会話と一致しない。

単語 □ printing company 印刷会社 □ *be* located 位置する □ place an order 発注する □ upstairs 階上へ □ sky-bridge スカイブリッジ（高架橋） □ connect 〜をつなぐ **41** □ apply for 〜 〜に応募する **42** □ *be* concerned 心配している □ deadline 締め切り □ locate 〜の所在位置を見つける □ make it to 〜 〜にうまくたどりつく □ on time 時間どおりに

44. 正解 (D) 難易度 難

女性の遅延理由を尋ねている。❶で女性は、「7時の**列車に乗れなかった**ので遅れる」と言っている。よって、正解は(D) She missed her train.（彼女は列車に乗り遅れた）。missは「〜に乗り遅れる」。乗り遅れた原因として(B)の可能性も考えられなくはないが、**会話中で言及されていない**ので、正答にはなり得ない。

45. 正解 (D) 難易度 難

話者2人が会う時刻を尋ねている。女性は、まず❷で「9時に予定していた約束」と述べ、❸で「予定より1時間半遅れで会えないか」と言っている。つまり、9時＋1時間半＝**10時半**。正解は(D)。

46. 正解 (A) 難易度 難

女性に対して、**男性が依頼**していることを尋ねているので、**男性の発言に集中**する。男性は、❹で女性に「着いたら直接、私のオフィスに来てほしい」と言っている。つまり、**「彼のオフィスで会う」**ことを頼んでいるので、(A)が正解。

単語 □ miss 〜に乗りそこなう **44** □ *be* stuck in traffic 交通渋滞で動けなくなる □ break down 故障する

TEST 1 PART 3

47. Where does the conversation most likely take place?
(A) At a performing arts center
(B) At a box office window
(C) At a dining establishment
(D) At a travel agency

48. What is the man's problem?
(A) He's late for the performance.
(B) Wrong tickets were delivered.
(C) He has not received his order.
(D) A product is missing.

49. What does the woman offer?
(A) Upgraded seats
(B) A replacement product
(C) Complimentary meals
(D) A voucher for a future visit

50. What is the problem?
(A) Some participants didn't come.
(B) Some workshop materials haven't been copied.
(C) A seminar was rescheduled.
(D) A speaker will be late for an event.

51. What does the man offer to do?
(A) Prepare the venue
(B) Contact some guests
(C) Return to the office
(D) Distribute questionnaires

52. When will the activity begin?
(A) At 8:30 A.M.
(B) At 9:00 A.M.
(C) At 2:00 P.M.
(D) At 5:00 P.M.

Questions 47-49 refer to the following conversation.

M: Pardon me, but when will our food be ready? We ordered nearly an hour ago and are still waiting!

W: I'm so sorry sir. We have several large groups this evening and are very busy. I'll check on your order right away and see what the holdup is. In the meantime, I'll bring you some complimentary appetizers.

M: I understand that, but we have tickets for the theater at 7 o'clock, and it is already 6 o'clock. The venue is across town, so we will have to eat right away, or we will be late for the show.

W: I see. I'll personally go to the kitchen and get your orders as soon as possible. And please don't worry about the bill this evening. Your meals are on the house.

設問47から49は次の会話に関する質問です。
男：すみません、いつ私たちの料理は出来上がるのですか。1時間前に注文したのにまだ待っているんですよ！
女：たいへん申し訳ございません。今夜は団体のお客さまが何組かいらしていて、とても忙しくて。すぐにご注文を確認し、何に手間取っているのか調べてまいります。その間、無料の前菜をお持ちいたします。
男：それは理解できますが、私たちは7時開演の演劇チケットを持っていて、今はすでに6時です。会場は町の反対側なので、すぐに食事しなければ、劇に遅れてしまいます。
女：わかりました。私が直接厨房に行き、できるだけ早くご注文の料理を持ってまいります。また、今夜の勘定は気になさらないでください。お客さまの食事代は当店で負担いたします。

Questions 50-52 refer to the following conversation.

W: Jim, do we have extra copies of the workshop modules? Nine participants showed up unexpectedly this morning at 8:30 for registration, and we don't have enough materials for them.

M: No, I don't have any more modules here, but I can go to the office to print out some more copies for them. It should only take five minutes.

W: Thanks, that's great! We'll be starting the first session at 9 o'clock.

設問50から52は次の会話に関する質問です。
女：Jimさん、セミナーの資料一式は余分にあるかしら。今朝8時半に予想外の参加者が9人登録にいらして、彼らの分の資料がないんです。
男：ここにはもうないけれど、事務所に行って彼らの分を印刷してきましょう。5分しかかからないでしょう。
女：ありがとう。素晴らしいわ！ 9時には最初のセッションを始めますから。

設問の訳 ☞ p.28〜29参照

TOEIC豆知識 controversialは「論争を招く、賛否両論の」という意味。しかし、その反面、頻繁に、いや必ず、飛行機と電車は遅延する。実に、時間にルーズな世界でもある。

正解＆解説

47. 正解 (C) 難易度 ■■□ 難

会話の場所を尋ねているので、場所に関連する表現に注意したい。❶「料理はいつ用意できるのか」、❸「注文を確認する」、❹「食事代は店もち」といった発言から、会話場所は**飲食店**だと推測できる。これをrestaurantやcaféではなく、抽象的な dining establishment（食事をする施設）と表現している(C)が正解。(A)は食事後に行く場所。

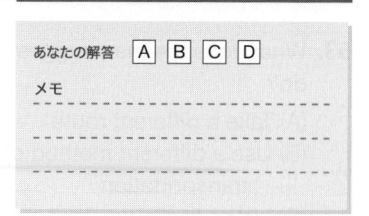

48. 正解 (C) 難易度 ■■□ 難

男性の心配事を尋ねる設問。**ネガティブな要素に注目して聞くとよい**。❷で男性が、「1時間前に注文したのに、まだ待っている」と言っている。つまり、**注文が来ていない**ことが、男性の問題なので、正解は (C) He has not received his order.（彼は注文の品を受け取っていない）。(A)の He's late は、すでに遅れてしまっていることを表す。しかし、会話の時点では、まだ演劇に遅れていないので誤り。

49. 正解 (C) 難易度 ■■■ 難

女性の提案内容を尋ねているので、**女性の発言に注目**する。❹の on the house は「店のおごりで」という意味。つまり、女性は**食事代は無料だ**と言っている。これを Complimentary meals（無料の食事）と表現している (C) が正解。**complimentary** はぜひ覚えておきたい頻出単語。

単語 ☐ holdup 停滞　☐ in the meantime その間に　☐ complimentary 無料の　☐ venue 会場　☐ personally 自ら、直接に　☐ on the house 店のおごりで　**47** ☐ performing arts 舞台芸術　☐ establishment 施設　**49** ☐ replacement 代替品　☐ voucher クーポン券、ギフト券

50. 正解 (B) 難易度 ■■□ 難

問題点を尋ねているので、**ネガティブな要素に注意**して聞く。女性が❶で「セミナー用資料一式が余分にあるか」と尋ね、❷で「十分な資料がない」とも言っているので、**研修資料が足りない**ことが問題とわかる。これを、Some workshop materials haven't been copied.（研修資料がいくつかコピーされていない）と表現した (B) が正解。会話に出てくる単語 participants につられて (A) を選ばないように。

51. 正解 (C) 難易度 ■■□ 難

男性の提案内容を尋ねているので、**男性の発言に注目**するとよい。男性は❸で「**事務所に行き、彼らの分を印刷してくる**」と提案している。このうち「事務所に行く」ことを、Return to the office（事務所に戻る）と言い換えた (C) が正解。

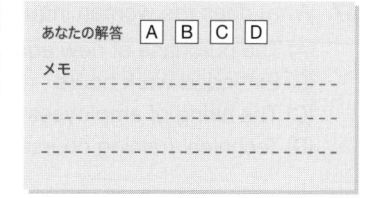

52. 正解 (B) 難易度 ■■□ 難

設問の activity はセミナー、もしくは最初のセッションのことを指している。その開始時刻を尋ねているので、**時に関連する表現**に集中する。女性が❹で「**最初のセッションが9時から始まる**」と言っている。よって、正解は (B)。(A) は、予想外の参加者がやってきた時間。

単語 ☐ module 構成単位　☐ participant 参加者　☐ unexpectedly 予想外に　☐ registration 登録　☐ material 資料　☐ session （あることをする）期間、集まり　**50** ☐ reschedule 〜の予定を変更する　**51** ☐ distribute 〜を配布する　☐ questionnaire アンケート（用紙）

TEST 1 PART 3

問題文&訳

53. What does the man suggest the woman do?
(A) Take a different route
(B) Use a different method of transportation
(C) Listen to the weather report
(D) Leave her car in the parking lot

54. What does the woman say about her apartment?
(A) It is near her workplace.
(B) It is not in the city center.
(C) It is not close to a station.
(D) It does not have parking spaces.

55. What does the man say he will do for the woman?
(A) Give her a map
(B) Drive her to the office
(C) Forward her a link
(D) Make a reservation

Questions 53-55 refer to the following conversation.

W: I can't believe ❶it took me almost two hours to drive to the office today. The traffic on the freeway was ridiculous.
M: Really? That is shocking. ❷Why don't you just take the subway? I'm sure it would be a lot faster than driving.
W: I don't know about that. ❸The nearest subway station is a 20-minute walk from my apartment. But with the rainy weather here, that's not always so convenient, and if I take my car to the subway, there's no place to park.
M: Actually, I think the 402 bus stops near your place and goes to the subway station. ❹I'll send you a link to a Web site that has all the bus routes.

設問53から55は次の会話に関する質問です。
女：きょう事務所まで車で通勤するのに約2時間もかかったなんて信じられないわ。高速道路の渋滞がひどかったのよ。
男：本当に？　それはひどいな。地下鉄を使ってみたら？　車よりずっと速いのは確かだよ。
女：そうかなぁ。最寄りの地下鉄駅は私のアパートから徒歩20分よ。ここは雨がよく降るから必ずしも便利とは言えないし、駅まで車で行くにしても駐車場がないわ。
男：実は、402番バスが君の家の近くに停まって地下鉄駅に行くと思うよ。すべてのバス路線が載っているサイトのリンクを送るよ。

56. What are the speakers mainly discussing?
(A) Project deadlines
(B) Production changes
(C) The company relocation
(D) The factory production

57. What does the woman inquire about?
(A) The purchase of new equipment
(B) Extended work hours
(C) The hiring of employees
(D) Technical training courses

58. What does the manager plan to do?
(A) Assign some tasks to workers
(B) Develop a new manufacturing manual
(C) Ask supervisors to organize an employee seminar
(D) Evaluate current operating procedures

Questions 56-58 refer to the following conversation.

W: Hi, Mr. Travis. I had to leave the office early yesterday for an appointment with a client. ❶Could you tell me what the general manager announced at the staff meeting?
M: Well, ❷he mentioned that the company is expanding operations and planning to transfer to a new location. We need a larger place in order to meet production goals.
W: That's good news, but ❸does that mean we need to work extra hours to prepare for the transfer? I still have projects to finish, so I'm not sure that I will have the time to help out.
M: No, don't worry. ❹The general manager is planning to assign some people to work on that matter. And actually, we're not moving until the end of the year.

設問56から58は次の会話に関する質問です。
女：Travisさん、私はきのう、顧客との約束で早くに会社を出なければいけなかったんです。部長が従業員会議で何を発表したのか教えてくれませんか。
男：ええと、会社の事業拡大と移転計画について話されました。生産目標を達成するためにより広い場所が必要なんです。
女：いいニュースだけど、それは、移転準備のために残業が必要という意味かしら。終わらせないといけないプロジェクトがまだあるから、協力する時間があるかしら。
男：いいや、心配無用です。部長はその件で動いてもらう人を何人か任命するみたいです。それに実際のところ、年末までは引っ越さないんです。

設問の訳 ☞ p.28〜29参照

正解＆解説

53. 正解 (B) 難易度　難

女性に対して、**男性が提案**している内容を尋ねているので、**男性の発言に注目**する。❶で女性が「車で出勤するのに2時間もかかった」と言っているのに対し、男性は❷で「(車ではなく)**地下鉄を使ったら？**」と提案している。このことを Use a different method of transportation（異なる交通手段を使う）と言い換えた (B) が正解。

54. 正解 (C) 難易度　難

自宅について、**女性が話している**内容を尋ねているので、**女性の発言に注目**。❸で女性は「地下鉄駅まで歩いて20分かかる」と言っている。あとに続く「雨がちの天候では不便」という内容から、この距離を女性は**近いとは感じていない**ことがわかるので、(C)「駅の近くにない」が正解。

55. 正解 (C) 難易度　難

女性のために、**男性がすると言っている**ことを尋ねているので、**男性の発言に集中**。❹で男性は、「バス路線が載った**サイトへのリンクを送る**」と言っている。これを「リンクを転送する」と言い換えた (C) が正解。バス路線図≒map（地図）と考えて (A) を選んだ人もいるかもしれないが、路線図そのものをあげるとは言っていないので、誤り。

単語 □ freeway 高速道路　□ ridiculous とんでもない　□ convenient 便利な　**53** □ suggest 〜を提案する　□ method 方法　□ transportation 乗り物、交通の便　□ parking lot 駐車場　**54** □ close to 〜 〜に近い

56. 正解 (C) 難易度　難

会話の主題を尋ねる設問では、**冒頭にヒントがくる**ことが多い。出だしに特に集中しよう。女性が❶で「部長の発表内容は何だったのか？」と尋ね、男性が❷で「事業拡大と**移転計画**」のふたつを答えている。以降、後者の「移転計画」についての話が続くので、正解は (C) The company relocation（会社の移転）。

57. 正解 (B) 難易度　難

女性の質問内容を尋ねているので、**女性の発言に注目**する。❸で「移転準備のために、**残業しなければいけないのか**」と質問しているので、(B) の Extended work hours（残業時間）が正解。

58. 正解 (A) 難易度　難

部長が計画していることを尋ねている。男性が❹で、「部長は that matter（＝移転準備）について、**担当者を指名する**計画だ」と説明。このことを「ある仕事を従業員に割り当てる」と表現した (A) が正解。

単語 □ general manager 本部長、事業部長　□ mention 〜に言及する　□ operation 事業　□ transfer 移る　□ meet 〜を達成する　□ production 生産　□ assign *A* to *do* A（人）に〜することを任命する　**56** □ relocation 移転　**57** □ inquire 尋ねる　□ extended 延長した　**58** □ develop 〜を開発する　□ manufacturing 製造の　□ supervisor 管理者　□ evaluate 〜を評価する

TEST 1 PART 3

59. What is the conversation mainly about?
 (A) A comedy show
 (B) A new movie
 (C) A TV program
 (D) A theater play

60. What does the man think of the plot?
 (A) It wasn't humorous enough.
 (B) It was highly entertaining.
 (C) It was not very original.
 (D) It didn't seem realistic.

61. What does the woman need to do this week?
 (A) Hand in some documents
 (B) Make a monthly presentation
 (C) Purchase a movie ticket
 (D) Attend a writing seminar

62. What most likely is the topic of the workshop?
 (A) Production techniques
 (B) International investment
 (C) Office equipment development
 (D) Marketing strategies

63. What is mentioned about Lilian Kraft?
 (A) She works for an advertising firm.
 (B) She helped organize the workshop.
 (C) She offered some useful ideas.
 (D) She will make a presentation later that day.

64. According to the woman, what will happen after today's workshop?
 (A) Ms. Kraft's book will be offered for sale.
 (B) There will be a complimentary dinner.
 (C) Attendees will receive a certificate of completion.
 (D) A short film presentation will be shown.

Questions 59-61 refer to the following conversation.

M: ❶Have you seen Greg Sheldon's latest film called *Crying for a Lost Love?* I was able to see it at the Hurles Cinema yesterday.

W: Not yet. ❷I've wanted to, but I've been working overtime a lot. Was it any good?

M: I thought ❸the plot was boring, and the story line was nothing out of the ordinary. However, the actress who played the lead character did her part quite well, especially in the dramatic scenes.

W: I see. I really want to watch it, but ❹there are some outlines for the monthly presentation I need to submit by the end of the week. I wonder if it's still showing in theaters this weekend.

設問59から61は次の会話に関する質問です。
男：Greg Sheldon の最新映画『Crying for a Lost Love』を観たかい？僕はきのう Hurles シネマで観たよ。
女：まだなの。観たいけどすごく残業があって。よかった？
男：筋書きは退屈だったし、話の流れもぱっとしなかったかな。だけど、主演女優はかなりよかったよ、特にドラマチックなシーンではね。
女：そうかぁ。とても観たいけど、月次プレゼンの概要を今週までに提出しなきゃいけなくて。今週末もまだ劇場でやっているかしら。

Questions 62-64 refer to the following conversation.

M: ❶This workshop has been great so far. I've heard a lot of new ideas about marketing products. The video on advertisements from around the world was also really interesting.

W: I think so too. Also, ❷Lilian Kraft's talk about Internet advertising was helpful. It might be a good idea to use some of her ideas in our next campaign.

M: I really wish I had recorded her talk. I think it is something our whole department should hear.

W: Well, ❸she has written a book on the topic and I was told ❹they will be selling copies at the end of today's workshop. Why don't you just buy a copy?

設問62から64は次の会話に関する質問です。
男：このワークショップは、ここまで素晴らしいね。商品販売についてたくさんの新しいアイデアを聞いたよ。世界中の広告についてのビデオもとても興味深いものだったし。
女：同感。それに、Lilian Kraft さんのネット広告についての話も役に立ったわ。うちの次のキャンペーンで、彼女のアイデアをいくつか利用するといいかもね。
男：彼女の話を録音してたらなぁ。あれは、うちの部署全員が聞くべきものだよ。
女：そうね、彼女はこのテーマで本を書いているし、きょうのワークショップ終了時にその本を販売するそうよ。1冊買ったらどうかしら。

設問の訳 ☞ p.28～29参照

正解&解説

59. 正解 (B)   難易度 ■■□□ 難

会話の主題を問う設問では、**冒頭に集中**。❶で男性が「Greg Sheldon の**最新映画**を観たか」と尋ねている。対して、女性が❷で「(観たいけど) まだ」と応じ、以降、この映画について話が進む。よって正解は、(B) A new movie (新作映画)。latest は「最新の」という意味で、選択肢では new に言い換えられている。

60. 正解 (C)   難易度 ■■□□ 難

男性の意見を尋ねているので、**男性の発言**からヒントを探す。❸から、男性は「映画の筋書きは**退屈**で、ストーリーも**平凡**だった」と考えていることがわかる。このことを not very original (独創的ではない) と表現した (C) が正解。映画が退屈だった理由として、(A) (D) の可能性もあるかもしれないが、**具体的な言及がない**ために、正解にはなり得ない。

61. 正解 (A)   難易度 ■■■□ 難

今週、女性がすべきことを尋ねている。❹で女性は「今週中にプレゼンの **outlines (概要)** を提出しなければいけない」と言っている。これを「いくつかの書類を提出」(※概要は当然、書類にまとめられると考えられる) と表現した (A) が正解。monthly presentation だけ耳に残っていると、(B) を正解と誤解してしまうが、プレゼンの実施時期は触れられていない。

単語 □ latest 最新の　□ work overtime 残業する　□ ordinary 普通の、平凡な　□ lead character 主人公　□ I wonder if ~ ~だろうかと思う　**59** □ theater play 演劇　**60** □ highly 非常に　**61** □ hand in ~ ~を提出する　□ purchase ~を購入する　□ attend ~に参加する

62. 正解 (D)   難易度 ■□□□ 難

ワークショップのテーマを尋ねている。男性が❶で「このワークショップは素晴らしい」と言ったあと、「**商品マーケティング**について、新しいアイデアをたくさん聞いた」と続けている。ということは、ワークショップは「マーケティング戦略」に関するものだと推測できるので、(D) が正解。

63. 正解 (C)   難易度 ■■□□ 難

Lilian Kraft に関する情報を尋ねている。**固有名詞 Lilian Kraft を待ち伏せながら**会話を聞こう。❷で女性が「ネット広告に関する Lilian Kraft の講演が役立った」と言い、「自社でも彼女のアイデアを活用するといい」と続けている。つまり、Lilian は「**役立つアイデアを提供した**」と考えられるので、(C) が正解。Internet advertising だけが耳に残っていると、(A) を選びたくなるが、広告会社で働いているとの言及はない。

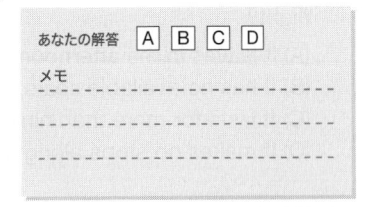

64. 正解 (A)   難易度 ■■■□ 難

ワークショップ後にあることを尋ねている。According to the woman (**女性によると**) とあるので、**女性の発言に集中**して聞くとよい。❸で「彼女 (= Lilian Kraft) は本を書いた」と述べたあと、女性は❹でワークショップ終了時に「**その本を販売する**らしい」と続けている。これを Ms. Kraft's book will be offered for sale. (Kraft さんの著書が販売される) と表現した (A) が正解。

単語 □ department (企業の) 部、課　□ copy (本などの) 1部、1冊　**62** □ investment 投資　□ strategy 戦略　**63** □ advertising firm 広告会社　**64** □ according to ~ ~によると　□ attendee 参加者　□ certificate 証明書　□ completion 完了、達成

TEST 1 PART 3

65. What is the man looking for?
(A) Some toys for his children
(B) Presents for some corporate investors
(C) Floral arrangements for an event
(D) Someone to plan a party

66. What does the man ask the woman about?
(A) The purpose of the celebration
(B) An advertisement he read in a newspaper
(C) The availability of items under a certain price
(D) Some merchandise he saw in a catalog

67. According to the woman, why is there an extra charge?
(A) The products must be wrapped in paper.
(B) There are state and national taxes.
(C) The man needs the order immediately.
(D) The purchases must be delivered.

68. Why are the speakers going to Madrid?
(A) To meet potential clients
(B) To sign a trade agreement
(C) To attend a business event
(D) To conduct a seminar

69. What does the man mention about the flight?
(A) It leaves in the afternoon.
(B) It has no available seats.
(C) It lasts for more than nine hours.
(D) It makes no stops along the way.

70. What do the speakers agree to do?
(A) Take a taxi to the airport
(B) Leave on a later date
(C) Use long-term parking
(D) Stay at the same hotel

Questions 65-67 refer to the following conversation.

M: Hello. I was told that your shop makes gift baskets. Could you tell me what types you offer?

W: Of course. We have a variety of special gift baskets for many occasions. We can fill them with fruit, chocolates, flowers, or even specialty coffees and teas. There is also a small selection of toys and household items.

M: That's exactly what I'm looking for. ❶I would like to have 10 baskets of fruit and chocolates delivered to my company's investors in celebration of our 10th anniversary. ❷Do you have any gift baskets for under $100?

W: Yes, we can arrange that for you. However, ❸we do have a fee of $10 per delivery. Now, if you'd like to look through this catalog, you can choose the specific items you want to include.

設問65から67は次の会話に関する質問です。
男：こんにちは。こちらのお店でギフトバスケットを作っているそうですね。どんな種類のものを扱っているか教えていただけますか。
女：もちろんです。さまざまな行事に応じた特別なギフトバスケットを豊富に取り揃えています。バスケットには果物やチョコレート、花、こだわりのコーヒーや紅茶といったものを詰め合わせできます。おもちゃや家庭用品などの品揃えも少しあります。
男：私が探していたものにまさにぴったりです。弊社の10周年を記念して、投資家に果物とチョコレートのバスケットを10個発送してもらいたいのです。100ドル未満のものはありますか。
女：ええ、ご用意できますが、配送ごとに10ドルかかります。このカタログをご覧いただければ、詰め合わせる具体的な品を選ぶことができます。

Questions 68-70 refer to the following conversation.

W: Carl, ❶I heard you're going to the trade fair in Madrid next month. I'm going as well and wanted to know if you've booked a flight already.

M: Yes, I did. ❷I'm leaving May 9 at 4 P.M. on Alistair Airways. You should see if there are any seats left so we can travel together.

W: I'll do that and let you know if I get a ticket. Oh, ❸I'm going to book a room at the Mendez Hotel. I stayed there before, and it's in a great location. If you haven't made a hotel reservation yet, ❹I can book you a room as well.

M: ❺Oh yes, that would be great. I was going to do that this week, but I haven't had enough time as I've been busy preparing for our booth at the fair.

設問68から70は次の会話に関する質問です。
女：Carl、あなたは来月、マドリードの見本市に行くと聞いたんだけど。私も行くから、あなたがもう飛行機の便を予約したか知りたいんだけど。
男：うん、予約したよ。Alistair航空で5月9日の午後4時に出発さ。一緒に行けるよう、座席がまだ残っているか調べてみて。
女：そうするわ。チケットが取れたら知らせるね。そうだ、私はMendezホテルの部屋を予約するつもり。以前泊まって、立地がとてもよかったから。ホテルの予約がまだなら、一緒にやっておくわよ。
男：あぁ、それはうれしいな。今週予約するつもりだったんだけど、フェアのブース準備に忙しくて時間がなかったんだ。

設問の訳 ☞ p.28〜29参照

正解＆解説

65. 正解 **(B)** 　難易度 ■■□□　難

男性が探しているものを尋ねている。ギフトバスケットを探していることは冒頭でわかるが、それだけでは正答できない。❶で「バスケットを**投資家に送ってほしい**」と言っていることから、(B)の「**企業投資家へのプレゼント**」が正解とわかる。

66. 正解 **(C)** 　難易度 ■■■□　難

女性に対して、**男性が**質問した内容を尋ねているので、**男性の発言に注目**。男性は、❷で「**100ドル未満のギフトバスケット**があるかどうか」を尋ねている。これを The availability of items under a certain price（特定の金額以下の商品の有無）と言い換えた (C) が正解。

67. 正解 **(D)** 　難易度 ■■■□　難

追加料金の理由を尋ねているが、According to the woman（**女性によると**）とあるので、**女性の発言に注目**。❸で女性は「発送ごとに10ドルの配送費がかかる」と言っている。また、❶から男性は「商品の配送を希望している」ことがわかる。つまり、**配送のために**追加料金が必要ということなので、(D) の「購入品は配送されなければならない」が正解。

単語 □ a variety of 　さまざまな～　□ occasion 行事　□ specialty 特製品　□ household 家庭の　□ investor 投資家　□ fee 料金　□ specific 具体的な　**65** □ corporate 企業の　□ floral arrangement フラワーアレンジメント　**66** □ availability（入手の）可能性　□ merchandise 商品　**67** □ tax 税　□ purchase 購入品

68. 正解 **(C)** 　難易度 ■■□□　難

2人がマドリードに行く理由を尋ねている。❶で女性が男性に「マドリードの**貿易フェア**に行くと聞いたけど、**私も行く**」と言っている。正解は、trade fair を business event と言い換えている (C) To attend a business event（ビジネスイベントに参加するため）。

69. 正解 **(A)** 　難易度 ■■■□　難

飛行機に関して、**男性が言った**ことを尋ねているので、**男性の発言に注目**。❷で「5月9日の**午後4時に出発**」と言っている。これを「**午後に出発する**」と言い換えた (A) が正解。空席については「調べてみて」と言っている。つまり、**空席の可能性がある**ということなので、(B) は誤り。

70. 正解 **(D)** 　難易度 ■■□□　難

2人が同意したことを尋ねている。❸❹で女性が「私は Mendez ホテルを予約する」けど「あなたの部屋も一緒に予約できる」と提案している。これに対して男性は、❺で「それはいい」と、**同じホテルを予約する**ことに同意している。従って、正解は (D) Stay at the same hotel（同じホテルに滞在する）。

単語 □ trade fair 貿易フェア　□ as well 同様に　□ book ～を予約する　**68** □ potential client 見込み客　□ agreement 契約　□ conduct ～を運営する　**69** □ last 続く　**70** □ long-term 長期の

TEST 1　PART 3

設問の訳

41. 女性はなぜその印刷会社に行くのか。
    - (A) 彼女は仕事に応募したい。
    - (B) 彼女は注文の品を配達しなければならない。
    - (C) 彼女は記事を提出したい。
    - (D) 彼女はポスターを作らなければならない。

42. 女性はなぜ心配しているのか。
    - (A) 彼女は締め切りに遅れることを心配している。
    - (B) 彼女は事務所のビルを見つけることができない。
    - (C) 彼女は事務所に時間通りに着けないかもしれない。
    - (D) 彼女はプリンターの使い方がわからない。

43. 女性はおそらくどうやって印刷会社に行くのか。
    - (A) 通路を渡って
    - (B) 階段を使って
    - (C) 2、3ブロック歩いて
    - (D) エレベーターを乗り換えて

44. 女性はなぜ遅れているのか。
    - (A) 彼女は渋滞につかまっている。
    - (B) 彼女は寝坊した。
    - (C) 彼女の車が故障した。
    - (D) 彼女は列車に乗り遅れた。

45. 話者たちは何時に会う予定か。
    - (A) 7時
    - (B) 8時
    - (C) 8時半
    - (D) 10時半

46. 男性は女性にどうするよう依頼しているか。
    - (A) 彼のオフィスで会う
    - (B) 列車の駅で待つ
    - (C) 彼女が到着したら電話する
    - (D) もっと早い列車に乗る

47. 会話はおそらくどこで行われているか。
    - (A) 舞台芸術センターで
    - (B) チケット売り場の窓口で
    - (C) 食事をする施設で
    - (D) 旅行代理店で

48. 男性の問題は何か。
    - (A) 彼は公演に遅れている。
    - (B) 間違ったチケットが送られてきた。
    - (C) 彼は注文の品を受け取っていない。
    - (D) 商品がなくなっている。

49. 女性は何を提案しているか。
    - (A) 座席のグレードアップ
    - (B) 代替品
    - (C) 無料の食事
    - (D) 将来の来店時の食事券

50. 何が問題なのか。
    - (A) 参加者が数人来なかった。
    - (B) 研修資料がいくつかコピーされていない。
    - (C) セミナーが予定変更された。
    - (D) 講演者が講演に遅れる。

51. 男性は何をしようと申し出ているか。
    - (A) 会場の準備をする
    - (B) 何人かのゲストに連絡する
    - (C) 事務所に戻る
    - (D) アンケートを配布する

52. その活動はいつ始まるか。
    - (A) 午前8時半
    - (B) 午前9時
    - (C) 午後2時
    - (D) 午後5時

53. 男性は女性に何をするよう提案しているか。
    - (A) 違うルートを行く
    - (B) 違う交通手段を使う
    - (C) 天気予報を聞く
    - (D) 彼女の車を駐車場に置く

54. 女性は自分のアパートについて何と言っているか。
    - (A) 彼女の職場に近い。
    - (B) 市の中心部にない。
    - (C) 駅の近くにない。
    - (D) 駐車場がない。

55. 男性は女性のために何をすると言っているか。
    - (A) 彼女に地図をあげる
    - (B) 彼女を事務所まで車で送る
    - (C) 彼女にリンクを転送する
    - (D) 予約する

設問の訳

56. 話者たちは主に何について議論しているか。
    (A) プロジェクトの締め切り
    (B) 生産の変更
    (C) 会社の移転
    (D) 工場の生産量

57. 女性は何を尋ねているか。
    (A) 新しい機材の購入
    (B) 残業時間
    (C) 従業員の雇用
    (D) 技術トレーニングのコース

58. 部長は何をする予定か。
    (A) ある仕事を従業員に割り当てる
    (B) 新しい製造マニュアルを作成する
    (C) 管理者に従業員セミナーの手配を依頼する
    (D) 現行の業務手順を評価する

59. 会話は主に何についてか。
    (A) コメディー番組
    (B) 新作映画
    (C) テレビ番組
    (D) 演劇

60. 男性は筋書きについてどう思っているか。
    (A) ユーモアが足りなかった。
    (B) 非常に面白かった。
    (C) あまり独創的ではなかった。
    (D) 現実的ではなかった。

61. 女性は今週何をしなければならないか。
    (A) 書類を提出する
    (B) 月例のプレゼンテーションを行う
    (C) 映画チケットを購入する
    (D) ライティングのセミナーに出席する

62. ワークショップの主題はおそらく何か。
    (A) 生産技術
    (B) 国際投資
    (C) オフィス設備の進歩
    (D) マーケティング戦略

63. Lilian Kraft について述べられていることは何か。
    (A) 彼女は広告会社で働いている。
    (B) 彼女はワークショップ開催を手伝った。
    (C) 彼女は役に立つアイデアを提供した。
    (D) 彼女はその日のあとのほうで発表する。

64. 女性によると、きょうのワークショップ後に何が起こるのか。
    (A) Kraft さんの著書が販売される。
    (B) 無料の夕食がある。
    (C) 参加者は修了証書を受け取る。
    (D) 短い映像による発表が上映される。

65. 男性は何を探しているか。
    (A) 彼の子供たちへのおもちゃ
    (B) 企業投資家へのプレゼント
    (C) ある行事用のフラワーアレンジメント
    (D) パーティーを計画できる人

66. 男性は女性に何について尋ねているか。
    (A) 祝賀会の目的
    (B) 彼が新聞で読んだ広告
    (C) 特定の金額以下の商品の有無
    (D) 彼がカタログで見たいくつかの商品

67. 女性によると、なぜ追加料金がかかるのか。
    (A) 商品は紙で包装されなければならない。
    (B) 州税と国税がかかる。
    (C) 男性は今すぐ注文品が必要である。
    (D) 購入品は配送されなければならない。

68. 話者たちはなぜマドリードに行くのか。
    (A) 顧客となる可能性のある人たちに会うため
    (B) 取引契約書に署名するため
    (C) ビジネスイベントに参加するため
    (D) セミナーを開催するため

69. 男性は飛行機の便について何と言っているか。
    (A) 午後に出発する。
    (B) 空席はない。
    (C) 9時間以上かかる。
    (D) ノンストップで行く。

70. 話者たちは何をすることに同意しているか。
    (A) 空港までタクシーで行く
    (B) 後日出発する
    (C) 長期駐車場を利用する
    (D) 同じホテルに滞在する

TEST 1
PART 4

音声ファイル 🔊 T1_P4_71-73 ▶ T1_P4_Q71-73 ／ T1_P4_74-76 ▶ T1_P4_Q74-76

問題文＆訳

71. Where does the speaker work?
(A) At a computer company
(B) At a department store
(C) At a market research firm
(D) At a banking establishment

72. How can the listener receive a free gift?
(A) By signing up for a credit card
(B) By answering a few questions
(C) By opening a charge account
(D) By making a purchase

73. What does Ms. Richards ask the listener to do?
(A) Return a call
(B) Fill out a survey
(C) Visit the office
(D) Pay a bill

Questions 71-73 refer to the following telephone message.

Good morning. ❶This is Melinda Richards calling from Royal Rhodes Bank. We are conducting a survey with all our corporate customers about their banking needs. ❷If you have a few minutes to answer some questions, we would be very grateful. ❸Everyone participating in the survey will receive a laptop bag courtesy of Royal Rhodes. So, ❹please call me back at 555-0123 before six this evening. Thank you for your loyalty and business. We hope to hear from you soon.

設問71から73は次の留守電メッセージに関する質問です。

おはようございます。Royal Rhodes銀行のMelinda Richardsです。当行の全法人顧客さまを対象に銀行の需要について調査しています。いくつかの質問にお答えいただける時間がございましたら、たいへんうれしく存じます。調査にご協力くださった方にはRoyal Rhodesよりノートパソコン用バッグを無料で進呈いたします。きょうの夕方6時までに555-0123まで折り返しお電話ください。弊社へのご愛顧とお取引に感謝いたします。すぐにご連絡いただけると幸いです。

74. Why is there a delay on Highway 21?
(A) There was a car accident.
(B) There is ongoing roadwork.
(C) Weather conditions are poor.
(D) Some streets are flooded.

75. What are motorists advised to do?
(A) Leave their homes early
(B) Listen to hourly reports
(C) Bring a city street map
(D) Take alternate routes

76. What will listeners most likely hear next?
(A) A business report
(B) A weather forecast
(C) Product advertisements
(D) Local news

Questions 74-76 refer to the following radio broadcast.

Good morning. You're listening to WRZ 103.9. This is Kam Chester with the latest traffic report. ❶If you're heading south on Highway 21, be prepared for delays. ❷Traffic is starting to build up due to a road construction project and two lanes have already been closed. ❸Motorists are advised to take other routes for the next three days. Traffic is moving smoothly on Denver Street leading to the city's business district. Our next traffic report will be in 30 minutes, so stay tuned. ❹Now here's Diane Brooke with the business news.

設問74から76は次のラジオ放送に関する質問です。

おはようございます。お聞きの局はWRZ 103.9です。Kam Chesterの最新交通情報です。ハイウェイ21号線を南に向かっている方は遅延に備えてください。道路工事計画による渋滞が始まり、すでに2車線が閉鎖されています。ドライバーは今後3日間別ルートの通行を勧められています。市の商業地区に続くDenver Streetでは、車はスムーズに動いています。次の交通情報は30分後にお知らせしますので、局はそのままで。次はDiane Brookeのビジネスニュースです。

設問の訳 ☞ p.40〜41参照

TOEIC豆知識 TOEICでは予定変更が日常茶飯事。ゆえにscheduleという単語が飛び交うが、この単語、実はくせ者である。なぜなら、イギリス発音では「セジュール（シェジュール）」という聞きなれない音になるからだ。（続く▶）

正解&解説

71. 正解 (D) 難易度 ■■□ 難

話し手の職場を尋ねているので、場所を想起させる表現に注意する。冒頭❶で「Royal Rhodes銀行のMelinda Richardsです」と名乗っているので、話し手は**銀行勤務**とわかる。正解は、bankを banking establishment（金融機関）と言い換えた(D)。

72. 正解 (B) 難易度 ■■□ 難

無料ギフトの入手方法を尋ねている。❷で「いくつかの質問に答える時間があれば」と述べ、続けて❸「調査への参加者全員にノートパソコン用バッグを進呈」と言っている。つまり、**無料ギフト**としてのバッグを、**質問に答える**ともらえるということ。従って、(B)の「2、3の質問に答える」が正解。

73. 正解 (A) 難易度 ■□□ 難

Richardsさん（話し手）が聞き手に依頼した内容を尋ねている。❹で「**折り返し電話してほしい**」と頼んでいる。よって、正解は(A) Return a call（折り返し電話する）。

単語 □ participate in ～に参加する　□ courtesy of ～ ～の好意で　□ loyalty 忠誠　**72** □ charge account 掛売口座　□ make a purchase 購入する　**73** □ fill out ～に記入する

---

74. 正解 (B) 難易度 ■■□ 難

ハイウェイ21号線の遅延理由を尋ねている。設問のキーである a delay on Highway 21 を意識して聞き取りを行おう。❶で「21号線を進んでいる人は遅延に備えて」と注意を喚起してから、❷で「**工事のせい**で渋滞しつつある」と理由を述べている。従って、正解は (B) There is ongoing roadwork.（進行中の工事がある）。

75. 正解 (D) 難易度 ■■□ 難

ドライバーが勧められていることを尋ねている。❸で「ドライバーは、**ほかのルートの通行**を勧められている」と言っている。正解は、other routes を alternate routes と言い換えている (D) Take alternate routes.

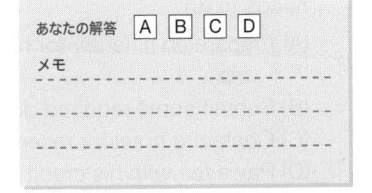

76. 正解 (A) 難易度 ■■□ 難

聞き手が次に何を聞くか、つまり、次の放送が何かを尋ねている。このように、未来のことを問う設問では、後半部分にヒントがくることが多い。**放送の終盤に注目**して聞こう。最後❹で「次は、Diane Brookeの**ビジネスニュース**」と言っている。newsをreportと言い換えた、(A) A business report が正解。

単語 □ head （～に向かって）進む　□ build up 渋滞する　□ due to ～ ～のせいで　□ district 地区　**74** □ flood ～を水浸しにする　**75** □ alternate 代わりの

TEST 1
PART 4

77. What is the announcement mainly about?
    (A) A schedule of events for a science fair
    (B) Information on exhibited photographs
    (C) Guidelines for visitors on a tour
    (D) Instructions for usage of photography equipment

78. What does the speaker ask listeners to do?
    (A) Leave their cameras at the entrance
    (B) Meet at the snack bar
    (C) Board the shuttle bus
    (D) Stay in the shuttle until told to do otherwise

79. According to the speaker, what can listeners do during the break?
    (A) Purchase something to eat
    (B) Browse through a selection of souvenirs
    (C) Fill out a registration form for a course
    (D) Participate in a wildlife presentation

80. What is the purpose of the message?
    (A) To reply to an inquiry
    (B) To promote a service
    (C) To confirm an appointment
    (D) To request some information

81. What does the speaker say Mr. Carlos needs to do?
    (A) Prepare an itinerary for his upcoming trip
    (B) Submit some required documentation
    (C) Contact a hotel for reservations
    (D) Pay a fee with his credit card

82. What service does Ms. Meyers offer?
    (A) Legal advice for a contract
    (B) Authentication of certificates
    (C) Assistance with visa applications
    (D) Booking international flights

Questions 77-79 refer to the following announcement.

Before we begin, I have a few reminders. ❶Please remember that for your own safety and the safety of the animals, food is not permitted in the wildlife preserve. Also, you are free to take photographs, but we ask that you not use a flash, as this can disturb or scare the animals. Finally, please ❷do not get off the shuttle unless you are specifically given instructions to do so. We will first be visiting the African wildlife compound. After that, ❸we will leave you at our snack bar for an hour, where you can buy a variety of items for your lunch. Lastly, we will continue to our Asian wildlife compound. Thanks for your attention and enjoy your time at Chakra Wildlife Park.

設問77から79は次のアナウンスに関する質問です。
　始める前にいくつか注意点があります。お客さまご自身の安全、そして動物の安全のためにも、野生保護地域での飲食は禁じられております。また、写真撮影は自由ですが、フラッシュは動物たちを動揺させたり怖がらせたりすることがあるので、使用しないようお願いします。最後に、特別な指示がないかぎりシャトルバスから降りないでください。私たちはまずアフリカ野生動物ゾーンを訪れます。その後、軽食堂に1時間滞在します。そこではさまざまな種類の昼食を買い求めていただけます。最後にアジア野生動物ゾーンに行きます。お聞きいただきありがとうございます。Chakra Wildlife Parkでの時間をお楽しみください。

Questions 80-82 refer to the following telephone message.

Hi, Mr. Carlos. ❶This is Samantha Meyers at Swift Travel Services. I'm calling regarding your inquiry about the requirements for passport applications. ❷You need to submit authenticated copies of your birth certificate and marriage contract. Then, you have to fill out an application form and pay a $100 processing fee. ❸We can also assist you if you wish to apply for a visa to a specific country. For more information, visit our Web site at www.swift-travel.com or call our hotline at 555-0214. Thank you and we look forward to doing business with you.

設問80から82は次の留守電メッセージに関する質問です。
　Carlosさん、こんにちは。Swift旅行社のSamantha Meyersです。パスポート申請の必要事項に関するあなたからのお問い合わせについてお電話しています。出生証明書と婚姻契約書の正本を提出していただく必要があります。それから申請書に記入し、100ドルの手数料をお支払いいただきます。特定の国のビザ申請をご希望の場合は、そのお手伝いも可能です。詳しくは、弊社ウェブサイトwww.swifttravel.comをご覧いただくか、ホットライン555-0214にお電話ください。お取引できることを楽しみにしております。

設問の訳 ☞ p.40～41参照

TOEIC豆知識 〈TEST 1〉の89-91（アメリカ発音）と92-94（イギリス発音）の説明文に schedule が含まれているので、確認してみて！

正解&解説

77. 正解 (C) 　難易度 難

この放送の主題を尋ねる設問。主題に関するヒントは冒頭にくることが多いので、**出だしを注意深く聞く**。❶で「あなたと動物の安全を守るため、動物保護区内での食事は禁止」と述べ、以降、禁止事項が続く。よって、この放送は、**動物保護区を訪ねている人への注意事項**だと考えられる。これに一致するのは、(C) Guidelines for visitors on a tour（ツアー参加者へのガイドライン）。

78. 正解 (D) 　難易度 難

聞き手への依頼内容を尋ねている。食事をしない、フラッシュの禁止など、いくつかの依頼をしているが、選択肢に該当するのは、❷の「**特別な指示がない限り、シャトルバスから降りてはいけない**」。これが (D) Stay in the shuttle until told to do otherwise（指示があるまでシャトルバスの中にいる）と一致する。

79. 正解 (A) 　難易度 難

聞き手が休憩中にできることを尋ねている。❸で「軽食堂に1時間滞在する」と言ったあと、「そこでは昼食のためにいろいろ買える」と付け加えている。1時間の休憩中に**食べ物を買える**ということなので、正解は (A) Purchase something to eat（食べ物を購入する）。

単語 □ reminder 注意　□ wildlife preserve 野生保護地域　□ disturb 〜を不安にさせる　□ scare 〜を怖がらせる　□ compound 囲いのある場所　□ lastly 最後に　77 □ usage 使用　78 □ otherwise 違ったふうに　79 □ browse（商品など）を見て回る

80. 正解 (A) 　難易度 難

留守電メッセージの目的を尋ねている。このように主題に関わる問題は、**冒頭を注意深く聞く**。❶で Samantha Meyers と名乗ったあと、「**あなたの問い合わせについて**電話した」と目的を述べている。従って、「問い合わせに回答するため」とした (A) が正解。(D) の「情報を求めている」のは、メッセージの受け手である Carlos さんの方。

81. 正解 (B) 　難易度 難

Carlos さん（メッセージの受け手）がやるべきことを尋ねている。❷で「あなた（= Carlos さん）は、**出生証明書と婚姻契約書の正本を提出する**必要がある」と言っている。これを「必要書類を提出する」と言い換えた (B) Submit some required documentation が正解。

82. 正解 (C) 　難易度 難

Meyers さん（話し手）が提案したことを尋ねている。❸で「**ビザ申請を希望なら手伝える**」と申し出ている。従って、Assistance with visa applications（ビザ申請の手伝い）の (C) が正解。

単語 □ regarding 〜に関して　□ inquiry 問い合わせ　□ requirement 必要なもの　□ application 申請　□ authenticate 〜が本物だと証明する　□ contract 契約書　□ processing fee 手数料　□ hotline ホットライン、直通電話　□ look forward to 〜 〜を楽しみにする　80 □ promote 〜を宣伝販売する　□ confirm 〜を確認する　81 □ itinerary 旅行日程　□ upcoming 今度の　82 □ assistance 手伝うこと

TEST 1 PART 4

83. Who is Justin Smith?
(A) A cross-country runner
(B) An athletic coach
(C) A radio announcer
(D) An organization leader

84. What does United Surgeons mainly do?
(A) Supply health care to those in need
(B) Establish medical clinics across the country
(C) Provide exercise programs for schools
(D) Sponsor professional sports competitions

85. What will the money raised from the fun run be used for?
(A) To pay for athletic equipment
(B) To educate children
(C) To construct a new facility
(D) To cover costs of the sporting event

86. Where does the speaker most likely work?
(A) At a reservations desk
(B) At a convention center
(C) At a real estate firm
(D) At an electronics company

87. Why have the travel plans been changed?
(A) A flight has been suddenly cancelled.
(B) Accommodations are not available.
(C) A work emergency has occurred.
(D) Staff members are too busy.

88. What are some of the listeners asked to do?
(A) Come to a joint decision
(B) Volunteer for a special project
(C) Prepare a detailed report
(D) Develop some marketing ideas

Questions 83-85 refer to the following television broadcast.

Good morning. I'm Yujin Choi with Channel 9 news. ❶Dr. Justin Smith, founder of United Surgeons, has just announced that a five-kilometer fun run will be held this coming Saturday. ❷For the past 10 years, United Surgeons has been providing medical attention to patients from low-income families. The organization has provided both regular and emergency medical care for over three hundred thousand people across the country. According to Dr. Smith, this weekend's ❸fun run aims to raise funds to finance the construction of a children's hospital for underserved communities in Kentucky. You can log on to the organization's Web site at www.usfunrun.com to register for the event or make a donation at www.unitedsurgeons.com.

設問83から85は次のテレビ放映に関する質問です。
おはようございます。Channel 9ニュースのYujin Choiです。United Surgeons創設者、Justin Smith博士は、今週土曜日に5キロの市民マラソンを開催すると発表しました。この10年間、United Surgeonsは低所得世帯の患者に治療を行ってきました。同団体は全国30万人以上の患者に定期的な、または緊急医療を施してきました。Smith博士によると、今週末の市民マラソンの目的は、ケンタッキー州の十分な医療が届かない地域での小児病院建設に出資するための資金集めです。イベント登録には同団体のウェブサイト www.usfunrun.com にてログオンしてください。または、www.unitedsurgens.com で寄付することもできます。

Questions 86-88 refer to the following talk.

Hello everyone. As you know, ❶we're scheduled to leave on Friday for next week's electronics trade fair in Las Vegas. However, ❷there has been a slight change in plans and we have to make some adjustments. Apparently, ❸the hotel cannot provide enough rooms for all 12 of us, and every other hotel in the vicinity is full. So, four of us need to stay behind. Being the CEO, I will of course be going. I'd also like all five members of the sales team to be there, as ❹we want to push our new digital music players. That leaves two more spaces for the ❺rest of you in marketing. I'd like you to discuss things amongst yourselves and choose who will stay behind. Any questions?

設問86から88は次の話に関する質問です。
みなさん、こんにちは。ご存じのように、ラスベガスで来週行われる電子機器の見本市へは金曜日に出発の予定です。しかし若干の計画変更があり、調整が必要です。どうやらホテルには私たち12人全員が泊まれる部屋がなく、周辺のどのホテルも満室です。よって、4人がここに残らなければなりません。私はCEOですので当然行きます。わが社の最新デジタル音楽プレーヤーをプッシュしたいので、販売チーム全員の5人にも現地に行ってもらいたい。そうなるとあと2人分がマーケティング部のために残っています。あなた方でこの件を話し合い、誰が残るか決めてください。質問はありますか。

設問の訳 ☞ p.40〜41参照

正解＆解説

83. 正解 **(D)** 　難易度 ■■■□ 難

Justin Smith の職業を尋ねている。この**名前を待ち伏せながら放送を聞こう**。❶で「United Surgeons の創設者である Justin Smith 博士」と言い、❷に United Surgeons が慈善団体であることの説明もある。つまり、Justin Smith は United Surgeons という「**団体のリーダー**」と考えられるので、(D) An organization leader が正解。(C) の「アナウンサー」は、話し手である Yujin Choi。

84. 正解 **(A)** 　難易度 ■■□□ 難

United Surgeons の主な業務を尋ねている。❷に「過去 10 年間、**低所得世帯の患者に治療**を施してきた」とある。これを Supply health care to those in need（必要な人に医療を提供する）と言い換えた (A) が正解。

85. 正解 **(C)** 　難易度 ■■■□ 難

市民マラソンの収益金の利用方法を尋ねている。❸で「医療サービスが不十分な地域での、**小児病院建設に出資する**ための資金を集めている」と言っている。小児病院のことを new facility（新しい施設）と言い換えている、(C) To construct a new facility（新しい施設を建設するため）が正解。

単語 ☐ founder 創設者　☐ surgeon 外科医　☐ income 所得　☐ organization 団体　☐ provide 〜を提供する　☐ raise 〜を集める　☐ funds 資金　☐ underserved （社会福祉などの）供給が十分でない　☐ register for 〜 〜に登録する　☐ donation 寄付　**84** ☐ supply 〜を供給する　☐ establish 〜を設立する　☐ competition 競技会　**85** ☐ facility 施設

86. 正解 **(D)** 　難易度 ■■□□ 難

話し手の職場を尋ねているので、場所を想起させる表現を注意深く聞く。❶「電子機器の見本市に行く」、❹「わが社の最新デジタル音楽プレーヤーを売り出したい」を考え合わせると、**電子機器メーカー**で働いていると考えられる。よって (D) At an electronics company が正解。ホテルの予約について話しているからといって、(A) を選ばないように。

87. 正解 **(B)** 　難易度 ■■□□ 難

プラン変更の理由を尋ねている。まず❷で「計画に変更がある」と述べ、❸でその原因を「12 名全員が泊まれるホテルがない。それにほかのホテルも満室だ」と説明している。つまり、「**accommodations（宿泊施設）を利用できない**」ことが理由なので、(B) Accommodations are not available. が正解。

88. 正解 **(A)** 　難易度 ■■■□ 難

聞き手（の数名）が依頼されたことを尋ねている。「12 人全員は行けない」という流れを受けて、最後❺で話し手は「あなたたち（マーケティング部）で話し合い、残る人を決めるように」と依頼している。つまり、「**話し合いで結論をだす**」ということ。これを Come to a joint decision と表現した (A) が正解。

単語 ☐ adjustment 調整　☐ apparently どうやら　☐ vicinity 周辺　☐ stay behind 居残る　☐ amongst 〜の中で　**86** ☐ convention 会議、大会、集会　☐ real estate 不動産　☐ electronics company 電子機器メーカー　**87** ☐ accommodations 宿泊施設　☐ occur 起こる　**88** ☐ joint 共同の、共通の　☐ decision 決定

TEST 1 PART 4

89. Where does the speaker most likely work?

(A) At a sports club
(B) At a publishing company
(C) At a photo studio
(D) At a textile manufacturer

90. What should Kathryn do before she leaves the office for vacation?

(A) Interview an athlete
(B) Submit a proposal
(C) Attend a workshop
(D) Organize her schedule

91. What most likely will Joanne do while Kathryn is away?

(A) Write a story for a publication
(B) Interview a subject for an article
(C) Take some pictures of a sports event
(D) Work on the layout of a magazine

92. What has Professor Montgomery done recently?

(A) Written a book
(B) Conducted a study
(C) Started a research project
(D) Made arrangements for a lecture series

93. What subject will Professor Montgomery speak about?

(A) Links between DNA and human personality
(B) Findings in the field of genetic mutation
(C) Future plans for the university
(D) The history of medical research

94. What does the speaker say will happen after the lecture?

(A) Schedules will be distributed.
(B) Copies of books will be signed.
(C) Audience questions will be answered.
(D) Refreshments will be served.

Questions 89-91 refer to the following telephone message.

Hello, Kathryn. ①This is James at the editorial office. I'd like to tell you that ②the vacation leave you recently applied for was approved. But ③you have to rearrange your schedule and ④delegate some of your writing assignments to others, since you will be out for two weeks. Before you leave on Friday, please make sure that you submit your ⑤article on extreme sports activities. Don't forget to include the photos that you plan to use. ⑥While you're on leave, Joanne will work on your next article. If you already have some materials and a list of people you'd like to interview, please discuss them with her. You may drop by my office if you have any questions. Thanks.

設問89から91は次の留守電メッセージに関する質問です。
こんにちは、Kathryn。編集部のJamesです。あなたが最近申請した休暇願が承認されたことをお知らせします。しかし、2週間の休みなので、スケジュールを再調整し、あなたの執筆分をほかの人に任せなければいけません。金曜日からの休みの前に、エクストリームスポーツの記事を必ず提出してください。使用予定の写真も忘れずに付けること。休暇中はJoanneがあなたの次の記事を担当します。すでに素材やインタビューしたい人のリストを持っていれば、それについて彼女と話し合ってください。質問があれば、私のオフィスに寄ってください。よろしくお願いします。

Questions 92-94 refer to the following introduction.

Thank you all for coming today. Welcome to our first lecture in this year's series entitled *The Future of Genetic Research*. As you all know from our schedule of events, our guest speaker today is Professor Karl Montgomery. Currently a faculty member at BIT University in Auckland, Professor Montgomery is also well-known for his research in the field of human genetic mutation. ①He is an award-winning scientist and author, and will speak to us today about his most recent study of linking personality traits to DNA. ②Following his talk, Professor Montgomery will be signing copies of his famous book, *The Final Strands*, in the reception area. So please join me in giving a warm welcome to Professor Karl Montgomery.

設問92から94は次の紹介に関する質問です。
本日はお越しいただき、ありがとうございます。『遺伝子研究の未来』と題した今年の連続講義の第1回目にようこそ。イベントスケジュールでおわかりのように、本日のゲスト講演者はKarl Montgomery教授です。現在オークランドのBIT大学職員であるMontgomery教授は人間の遺伝子変異分野の研究でも高名です。受賞歴のある科学者であり、作家でもある彼が本日、個性とDNAとの関連性の最新研究についてお話しくださいます。Montgomery教授は、講演にひき続き受付にて、著名なご著書『最後のらせん構造』にサインをしてくださいます。では、Karl Montgomery教授を温かくお迎えください。

正解＆解説

89. 正解 (B) 難易度: 難

話し手の職場を尋ねているので、**場所を想起させる表現に注意しよう**。❶「編集部の James」、❹「writing assignments（執筆担当分）をほかの人に委任する」、❺「エクストリームスポーツの記事」などの表現により、話し手は**記事を書く仕事**に関わっているとわかる。これに該当する職場は (B) At a publishing company（出版社で）。写真の話題につられて (C) を選ばないように。

90. 正解 (D) 難易度: 難

Kathryn が休暇前にすべきことを尋ねている。まず❷で「あなた（= Kathryn）の休暇申請が受理された」と述べ、❸で「あなたは日程を rearrange（～を再調整する）必要がある」と言っている。これを organize を使って、「**スケジュールを調整する**」と表現した (D) が正解。登場人物が3人いるので、それぞれの役割を把握することが大切。

91. 正解 (A) 難易度: 難

Joanne がおそらくするだろうことを尋ねている。❻で「あなた（= Kathryn）が休暇中、Joanne が**次回の記事を担当する**」と言っている。これを「publication（出版物）への記事を書く」と表現した (A) Write a story for a publication が正解。

単語 □ editorial office 編集部　□ vacation leave 休暇　□ recently 最近　□ approve ～を承認する　□ rearrange ～を再び整理する　□ delegate（責任などを）～に委任する　□ assignment 任務　□ article 記事　**89** □ publishing company 出版社　□ textile 繊維　□ manufacturer メーカー　**90** □ proposal 案、提案　**91** □ publication 出版物　□ subject 対象者

92. 正解 (B) 難易度: 難

Montgomery 教授が**最近**、行ったことを尋ねている。❶で「彼（= Montgomery 教授）は、最新研究について話す」と紹介しているので、つい最近「**研究を行った**」のだとわかる。従って、正解は (B) Conducted a study。教授は本を出してはいるが、その時期は述べられていないので (A) は誤り。また、guest speaker なので、自身で講義を手配したとも考えられない。よって (D) も誤り。

93. 正解 (A) 難易度: 難

Montgomery 教授の講義演目を尋ねている。❶で his most recent study of linking personality traits to DNA（個性と DNA との関連性の最新研究）について話をすると言っている。これを Links between DNA and human personality（DNA と人の個性の関係性）と表現した (A) が正解。(B) の genetic mutation は教授の研究分野であるが、今回の講義演目だとは述べられていない。

94. 正解 (B) 難易度: 難

講義後に何があるかを尋ねている。未来の出来事に関する質問は、**話の終盤に注目**する。❷で「講演に引き続き、教授が著名な**著書にサインする**」と言っている。これを Copies of books will be signed.（著書がサインされる）と表現した (B) が正解。

単語 □ entitle ～に（…という）題をつける　□ schedule 予定　□ currently 現在は　□ faculty（大学の）教職員　□ in the field of ～ ～の分野で　□ genetic 遺伝子の　□ mutation 変異　□ award-winning 賞を受けた　□ study 研究　□ trait 特性　□ following ～のあとで　□ reception 受付　**92** □ make an arrangement 手配をする　**93** □ subject 主題　□ finding 研究成果　**94** □ refreshment 軽食、飲み物　□ serve（食べ物）を出す

TEST 1
PART 4

音声ファイル　T1_P4_95-97　T1_P4_Q95-97 ／ T1_P4_98-100　T1_P4_Q98-100

問題文&訳

95. Who most likely is listening to the talk?
(A) Packaging experts
(B) Graphic designers
(C) Company executives
(D) Corporate accountants

96. Why have sales of Crash-Cola decreased?
(A) Customers are not familiar with the product's new packaging.
(B) There has been increased competition.
(C) They have had to raise their prices.
(D) Consumers don't like the flavors.

97. What does the speaker ask listeners to do?
(A) Test some new products
(B) Submit sales reports
(C) Redesign a logo
(D) Make some suggestions

Questions 95-97 refer to the following excerpt from a meeting.

❶I'm happy all of our departmental directors could come to our meeting this morning. Our end of year sales report has been completed and unfortunately ❷sales of our best-seller, Crash-Cola, are down nearly 10 percent. The research department has conducted some customer surveys and found that ❸the new bottle and logo of Crash-Cola may be the problem. Apparently consumers did not recognize the product. Although they did respond favorably to the new design, ❹most did not identify the new logo with our product. This week ❺I would like us to come up with some ideas on how to promote Crash-Cola so that the new bottle and logo are more identifiable with our product. ❻We will meet again on Thursday to discuss our ideas.

設問95から97は次の会議の抜粋に関する質問です。

各部署の責任者全員が今朝の会議に出席できよかったです。年度末販売報告書がまとまり、残念なことにわが社のベストセラー、Crash-Cola の売り上げが 10% 近く落ち込みました。調査部がいくつか顧客調査を行い、Crash-Cola の新ボトルとロゴマークに問題があるかもしれないことがわかりました。どうやら顧客が商品を認識していなかったようです。顧客は新デザインには好意的でしたが、ほとんどの人が新ロゴをわが社の商品と認識していませんでした。新ボトルとロゴがわが社の商品だということをより認識できるように、今週みなで Crash-Cola の宣伝方法のアイデアを考えだしてください。アイデアを議論するため木曜日にまた会いましょう。

98. Who will be giving talks during the event?
(A) Faculty members from Keller University
(B) Professionals from across the country
(C) Science writers from a journal
(D) Producers of educational programs

99. What does the speaker ask listeners to do?
(A) Refrain from using video cameras
(B) Stay in their seats until the conclusion
(C) Register by filling out forms at the entrance
(D) Take notes during the presentation

100. How can listeners learn more about other events?
(A) By calling the department of science
(B) By viewing a posted schedule
(C) By listening to a recorded message
(D) By looking at a brochure

Questions 98-100 refer to the following talk.

It is my pleasure to welcome you all to the first of Keller University's scientific lecture series. I am sure you will find all six of our planned events both educational and informative. ❶We have invited a variety of scientific experts from across the country to share with us some of their most recent studies and findings. These presenters are all well-respected in the fields of biology, chemistry, and physics. I do have a few important announcements before I introduce you all to today's guest speaker. ❷We do ask that you not use any recording devices during the lecture. This includes audio and video recording equipment. ❸Also, we request that you wait until the conclusion of the lecture to ask any questions to the lecturer. There will be a short question-and-answer period at the end of the presentation. And ❹if you are interested in our upcoming lectures, please pick up a pamphlet at the entrance to the auditorium.

設問98から100は次の話に関する質問です。

Keller 大学の連続科学講義の初回にみなさんをお迎えでき光栄です。予定される6つの講義はすべて、教育的かつ有益だと思っていただけるに違いありません。私どもは全国からさまざまな科学の専門家をお招きし、彼らの最新の研究や成果をみなで分かち合います。発表者はみなさん、生物学、化学、物理学の分野でたいへん高い評価を受けている方々です。本日のゲスト講演者を紹介する前に重要なお知らせがあります。講義中は、記録機器を使用しないようお願いします。これには音声および映像の記録機器が含まれます。講演者への質問は講義の最後までお待ちください。発表の最後に短い質疑応答の時間がございます。また、今後の講義にご興味がある場合は、講堂入り口にあるパンフレットをお持ちください。

設問の訳　☞ p.40〜41参照

> **TOEIC豆知識** 本書のPart 3〜7において、選択肢が2行にわたる場合、2行目の開始位置が2字ほど下がっているのを奇妙に感じるかもしれない。しかし、これはTOEIC本番の形式を踏襲した、こだわりポイント。ミスではないのです！

正解＆解説

95. 正解 (C) 難易度：難

この会議の出席者を尋ねている。❶で話し手が「departmental directors（部門長）が全員集まりよかった」と言っている。つまり、この会議には**重役が集まっている**と考えられるので、(C) Company executives が正解。❶を聞き逃すと、(A) や (B) も正解に思えるかもしれないが、具体的な言及がないので誤り。

96. 正解 (A) 難易度：難

Crash-Cola の売り上げ減少の理由を尋ねている。❷で「Crash-Cola の売り上げが落ちている」と報告し、以降、顧客調査の結果を説明している。❸「新ボトルとロゴが問題」、❹「ほとんどの人が、新ロゴをわが社の商品と認識していない」とあり、これを「顧客は**新しいパッケージになじみがない**」と表現した (A) が正解。

97. 正解 (D) 難易度：難

話し手が聞き手に依頼している内容を尋ねているので、依頼表現に注意して聞こう。❺で「Crash-Cola の宣伝方法についてのアイデアを考えてほしい」、❻で「木曜日にそのアイデアについて話し合う」と言っている。つまり、木曜日までに**アイデアを考え発表してほしい**、ということなので、(D) Make some suggestions（いくつかの案をだす）が正解。

単語 □ sales report 販売報告書　□ unfortunately 残念ながら　□ consumer 顧客、消費者　□ recognize 〜を認識する　□ favorably 好意的に　□ identify A with B AとBを同一視する　□ come up with 〜 〜を考案する　□ identifiable 同一と見なせる　[95] □ executive 役員、幹部　□ accountant 会計士　[96] □ packaging 包装　[97] □ suggestion 提案

98. 正解 (B) 難易度：難

このイベントで話をする人物を尋ねている。❶で「最新の研究や成果をわれわれと分かち合うために、**全国から科学の専門家を招待する**」と言っている。つまり、**科学の専門家が話をしてくれる**ということ。scientific experts を professionals に言い換えた (B) Professionals from across the country が正解。Keller 大学主催の講義だが、同大学の教授が話をするとは言っていないので (A) は誤り。

99. 正解 (A) 難易度：難

話し手が聞き手に依頼していることを尋ねているので、依頼表現に注目しよう。まず❷で「講演中、**録音・録画機器を使用しない**」ように依頼。❸では「講演が終わるまで質問を控える」よう依頼している。ふたつのうち前者を Refrain from using video cameras（ビデオカメラの使用を控える）と言い換えた (A) が正解。

100. 正解 (D) 難易度：難

この連続講義のほかのイベントについて知る方法を尋ねている。❹で「これからの講義に興味がある場合は、pamphlet（パンフレット）を持っていってほしい」と言っている。つまり、**パンフレットにほかの講義の詳細が載っている**ということ。従って、pamphlet を brochure と言い換えた (D) By looking at a brochure が正解。

単語 □ biology 生物学　□ chemistry 化学　□ physics 物理学　□ conclusion 結末　□ auditorium 講堂　[98] □ journal 定期刊行物　[99] □ refrain 控える　[100] □ brochure パンフレット

TEST 1　PART 4

設問の訳

71．話し手はどこで働いているか。
(A) コンピュータ会社
(B) 百貨店
(C) 市場調査会社
(D) 金融機関

72．聞き手はどうやって無料ギフトを手に入れるか。
(A) クレジットカードの契約をする
(B) 2、3の質問に答える
(C) 掛売口座を開く
(D) 購入する

73．Richards さんは聞き手に何を依頼しているのか。
(A) 折り返し電話する
(B) 調査票に記入する
(C) 事務所を訪ねる
(D) 請求書を支払う

74．ハイウェイ21号線でなぜ遅れがあるのか。
(A) 自動車事故があった。
(B) 進行中の工事がある。
(C) 天候がよくない。
(D) いくつかの通りが浸水している。

75．ドライバーは何をするよう勧められているか。
(A) 自宅を早めに出発する
(B) 1時間ごとの情報を聞く
(C) 市の道路地図を持っていく
(D) 別ルートを行く

76．聞き手はおそらく次に何を聞くか。
(A) ビジネス報道
(B) 天気予報
(C) 商品の宣伝
(D) 地元ニュース

77．アナウンスは主に何についてか。
(A) 科学展のイベントスケジュール
(B) 展示写真の情報
(C) ツアー参加者へのガイドライン
(D) 写真撮影機材の使用指示

78．話し手は聞き手に何を依頼しているのか。
(A) 入口でカメラを預ける
(B) 軽食堂で会う
(C) シャトルバスに乗る
(D) 指示があるまでシャトルバスの中にいる

79．話し手によると、聞き手は休憩中に何をすることができるか。
(A) 食べ物を購入する
(B) 選りすぐりの土産物を見て回る
(C) コースの登録用紙に記入する
(D) 野生動物の観察会に参加する

80．伝言の目的は何か。
(A) 問い合わせに回答すること
(B) サービスを宣伝すること
(C) 予約を確認すること
(D) 情報を要求すること

81．話し手は Carlos さんが何をする必要があると言っているか。
(A) 今回の旅行の日程表を準備する
(B) 必要書類を提出する
(C) 予約のためにホテルに連絡する
(D) 料金をクレジットカードで支払う

82．Meyers さんはどんなサービスを申し出ているか。
(A) 契約に関する法的アドバイス
(B) 証明書の認証
(C) ビザ申請の手伝い
(D) 国際線の予約

83．Justin Smith とは誰か。
(A) クロスカントリー競技者
(B) 競技コーチ
(C) ラジオアナウンサー
(D) 団体のリーダー

84．United Surgeons は主に何をするのか。
(A) 必要な人に医療を提供する
(B) 全国に病院を設立する
(C) 学校に運動プログラムを提供する
(D) プロのスポーツ競技会を主催する

85．市民マラソンの収益金は何に使われるのか。
(A) 運動用器材の代金を払うため
(B) 子供たちを教育するため
(C) 新しい施設を建設するため
(D) スポーツイベントの費用に充てるため

設問の訳

86. 話し手はおそらくどこで働いているか。
    (A) 予約窓口
    (B) コンベンションセンター
    (C) 不動産会社
    (D) 電子機器メーカー

87. 旅行プランはなぜ変更されたのか。
    (A) 飛行機の便が突然キャンセルされた。
    (B) 宿泊施設が空いていない。
    (C) 仕事上の緊急事態が起こった。
    (D) 従業員が忙しすぎる。

88. 聞き手の何人かは何をするよう求められているのか。
    (A) 話し合いで結論をだす
    (B) 特別プロジェクトに志願する
    (C) 詳細な報告書を準備する
    (D) マーケティングのアイデアを考える

89. 話し手はおそらくどこで働いているか。
    (A) スポーツクラブで
    (B) 出版社で
    (C) 写真スタジオで
    (D) 繊維メーカーで

90. 休暇で職場を空ける前に Kathryn は何をすべきか。
    (A) スポーツ選手にインタビューする
    (B) 企画案を提出する
    (C) ワークショップに出席する
    (D) スケジュールを調整する

91. Kathryn の留守中、Joanne はおそらく何をするのか。
    (A) 出版物への記事を書く
    (B) 記事の対象者にインタビューする
    (C) スポーツイベントの写真を撮る
    (D) 雑誌のレイアウトに取り組む

92. Montgomery 教授は最近何をしたのか。
    (A) 本を執筆した
    (B) 研究を行った
    (C) 調査プロジェクトを開始した
    (D) 連続講義の手配をした

93. Montgomery 教授はどんな話題を話すのか。
    (A) DNA と人の個性の関係性
    (B) 遺伝子変異の分野での成果
    (C) 大学の将来の計画
    (D) 医学研究の歴史

94. 話し手は講義後に何が起こると言っているか。
    (A) スケジュール表が配られる。
    (B) 著書がサインされる。
    (C) 聴衆の質問が回答される。
    (D) 軽い飲食物が提供される。

95. おそらく誰がこの話を聞くのか。
    (A) パッケージの専門家
    (B) グラフィックデザイナー
    (C) 会社幹部
    (D) 法人会計士

96. なぜ Crash-Cola の売り上げが減少したのか。
    (A) 顧客は商品の新パッケージになじみがない。
    (B) 競合商品が増えた。
    (C) 価格を上げなければならなかった。
    (D) 顧客がその味を好んでいない。

97. 話し手は聞き手に何をするよう求めているか。
    (A) いくつかの新商品をテストする
    (B) 販売報告書を提出する
    (C) ロゴをデザインし直す
    (D) いくつかの案をだす

98. このイベントの期間中、誰が話をするのか。
    (A) Keller 大学の教授陣
    (B) 全国の専門家
    (C) 定期刊行物の科学ライター
    (D) 教育プログラムのプロデューサー

99. 話し手は聞き手に何をするようお願いしているか。
    (A) ビデオカメラの使用を控える
    (B) 結末まで座席を離れない
    (C) 入り口で用紙に記入して登録する
    (D) 発表中はノートを取る

100. 聞き手はどうやってほかのイベントの詳細を知ることができるか。
    (A) 科学学部に電話することで
    (B) 掲示されたスケジュールを見ることで
    (C) 録音メッセージを聞くことで
    (D) パンフレットを見ることで

TEST 1 PART 5

101. The art class meets ------- every week at the community center on Vine Avenue.
(A) each
(B) one
(C) another
(D) once

芸術の授業は週に1回 Vine 街のコミュニティーセンターで開かれる。
(A) 形 めいめい
(B) 代 ひとつ
(C) 形 もうひとつの
(D) 副 1回

102. In an effort to attract more customers, Hanford Jewellers now offers ------- cleaning services for gold or silver items at any of its five branches.
(A) liberated
(B) compensated
(C) unbound
(D) complimentary

より多くの顧客を集めるために、Hanford Jewellers 社は現在5つの支店すべてで金銀製品の無料クリーニングサービスを提供している。
(A) 解放された
(B) 補償された
(C) 解き放たれた
(D) 無料の

103. Passengers are required to follow the Ministry of Transport's security policies listed on signs ------- the international terminal.
(A) among
(B) into
(C) between
(D) throughout

旅客は、国際線ターミナル各所の標識に記載されている、運輸省の安全指針に従うことを求められる。
〔選択肢訳なし〕

104. Due to financial constraints, there will be a ten-day ------- in the release of the employees' annual bonuses.
(A) delay
(B) tardy
(C) long
(D) out

財務的制約のため、従業員の年度ボーナスの支給に10日の遅延が生じる見込みだ。
(A) 名 遅れ
(B) 形 遅い
(C) 形 長い
(D) 副／前 外へ

105. Southland Manufacturing is ------- looking for a replacement for Roger Hanson, the vice president of finance, who is retiring at the end of the month.
(A) critically
(B) imperatively
(C) necessarily
(D) urgently

Southland Manufacturing 社は、今月末に退職予定の経理担当副社長 Roger Hanson の後任を至急探している。
(A) 批判的に
(B) いやおうなしに
(C) 必然的に
(D) 緊急に

106. Mr. Ing chose to fly to the conference in Los Angeles earlier than scheduled ------- he would have extra time to visit some potential clients.
(A) so that
(B) in order
(C) even if
(D) ahead of

Ing 氏は将来の顧客を訪問する時間を余分に確保するため、ロサンゼルスでの会議に予定より早く飛行機で向かうことに決めた。
(A) 〜するために
(B) 整然として
(C) たとえ〜でも
(D) 〜の前に

42

> **TOEIC豆知識** 本書には、Part 5の音声も収録。くり返し聞いて、音読すれば、語彙力強化に加え、文構造への理解も深まるので、ぜひ活用してみて！

正解＆解説

101. 正解 (D) 　難易度 ■■■□□　難

動詞 meets を修飾しながら、空所後の every week とともに「**毎週1回**」という意味になる、**副詞**の (D) once が正解。形容詞の (A) や (C)、代名詞の (B) は動詞を修飾できない。each は「めいめい」という意味で、another は「（すでに言及されているもの以外の）もうひとつの」という意味。ともに単数可算名詞の前でのみ使えることを一緒に押さえておこう。

あなたの解答 (A) B C D
メモ

102. 正解 (D) 　難易度 ■■■□□　難

選択肢には同じ品詞（形容詞的働きをする語）が並んでいるので、**文脈から答えを探る**。Hanford Jewellers now offers ------- cleaning services（Hanford Jewellers 社は、------- なクリーニングサービスを提供している）という文脈なので、選択肢のうち「**無料の**」という意味の (D) complimentary を入れると文意が通る。in an effort to *do*（〜しようと努力して）は慣用句として覚えよう。

あなたの解答 A B C D
メモ

☐ effort 努力
☐ attract 〜を引きつける

103. 正解 (D) 　難易度 ■■■□□　難

選択肢には前置詞が並んでいる。signs ------- the international terminal を「国際線ターミナル**各所にある**標識」という意味にすれば文意が通るので、(D) throughout（〜の至る所に）が正解。(A) among は「（3つ以上のものについて）〜の間に」という意味で位置を、(B) into は「〜の中に」という意味で方向を表す。(C) between は「〜の間に」という意味の位置を表す前置詞で、between *A* and *B*（A と B の間に）の形でよく使う。*be* required to *do*（〜するように求められる）は慣用句として覚えておこう。

あなたの解答 A (B) C D
メモ

☐ policy 方針　☐ list 〜を記載する

104. 正解 (A) 　難易度 ■■□□□　難

冠詞 a と前置詞 in にはさまれ、直前の**形容詞** ten-day の修飾を受けられるのは**名詞**のみ。よって、(A) delay が正解。(B) と (C) は形容詞、(D) は副詞または前置詞である。参考までに、due to 〜（〜が原因で）を慣用句として覚えておこう。

あなたの解答 A B C D
メモ

☐ constraint 制約
☐ annual 年次の、年1度の

105. 正解 (D) 　難易度 ■■■□□　難

同じ品詞（副詞）が並んでいるので、**文脈から答えを探る**。「Roger Hanson の後任者を〈どのように〉募集している」のかを考えると、「**緊急に**」という意味の (D) urgently が最適とわかる。

あなたの解答 A B C D
メモ

☐ look for 〜　〜を探す
☐ replacement 交替要員
☐ retire 退職する

106. 正解 (A) 　難易度 ■■■□□　難

空所までに**主語** Mr. Ing、**動詞** chose、**目的語** to fly が揃い、完全な文として成立している。よって空所以降は、修飾の働きをする付加的要素だと考えられる。そして、この付加的要素部分もまた、**主語** he と**動詞** would have を含む**節**なので、**節をつなぐ接続詞** (A) と (C) が候補。文脈から、「余分な時間を確保〈**するために**〉」となる (A) so that が正解。前置詞 (D) ahead of は、節を導くことはできないことも覚えておこう。

あなたの解答 A B C D
メモ

TEST 1
PART 5

107. Exhausted by her weeklong search for a suitable apartment, Ms. Stein decided to rent the one on Albright Avenue, as it was the least ------- among those she had seen.
(A) expend
(B) expenses
(C) expensively
(D) expensive

1週間にわたる部屋探しにへとへとになってしまったので、Stein さんは内見した物件の中でいちばん家賃が手頃という理由で Albright 街の部屋に決めた。
(A) 動 〜を費やす
(B) 名 費用
(C) 副 ぜいたくに
(D) 形 高価な

108. Investors are quite pleased that profits for the new hotel chain are rising steadily and will likely go ------- the company's target for this year.
(A) further
(B) ahead
(C) beyond
(D) cautiously

投資家たちはその新しいホテルチェーンの利益が順調に伸びており、今年の目標数値を超える見込みであることにたいへん満足している。
(A) さらに遠くに
(B) 前に
(C) 超えて
(D) 注意深く

109. Nurses who work in the emergency room must not only assist doctors in procedures, ------- keep patients calm during stressful situations.
(A) in addition
(B) but also
(C) let alone
(D) because of

救急処置室で働く看護師は手術の際に医師を補佐するだけでなく、緊張を強いられる状況下で患者を落ち着かせなければならない。
(A) そのうえ
(B) 〜も
(C) 〜は言うまでもなく
(D) 〜のために

110. Jack Elliot submitted his resignation to Gulliver's Café last year because he decided to establish a coffee shop of ------- own in the downtown area.
(A) him
(B) his
(C) he
(D) himself

Jack Elliot は、商業地区に自身の喫茶店を開くことを決意したため、昨年 Gulliver's Café に辞表を提出した。
(A) 彼を（目的格）
(B) 彼の（所有格）
(C) 彼は（主格）
(D) 彼自身（再帰代名詞）

111. Joanna Saunders ------- working as a ticketing agent for Starlight Travel and Tours ever since she relocated to San Francisco ten years ago.
(A) was
(B) could be
(C) has been
(D) is

Joanna Saunders は 10 年前にサンフランシスコに転居して以来、Starlight Travel and Tours 社のチケット販売員として勤務している。
(A) 〈過去形〉
(B) 〈過去形〉
(C) 〈現在完了形〉
(D) 〈現在形〉

112. All budget proposals should include ------- figures from the last fiscal year and concise spending projections for next year.
(A) obvious
(B) permanent
(C) sheer
(D) accurate

すべての予算案は、前会計年度の正確な数値と、来年度の簡潔な支出計画が含まれていなければならない。
(A) 明らかな
(B) 永続的な
(C) まったくの
(D) 正確な

正解＆解説

107. 正解 **(D)** 　難易度 ■■■□□ 難

接続詞 as（〜なので）以降が節となっている。it が主語で、空所は be 動詞 was の**補語の位置**にあたる。補語になれる**名詞** (B) と**形容詞** (D) が正解候補。文脈をみると、「それ（＝ the one on Albright Avenue）がもっとも〈高価〉ではなかった」となる (D) expensive だと文意が通る。(B) は、複数形になっていることからも it was と対応しないので、誤りとわかる。最上級の表現〈the least ＋形容詞〉（〜の度合いがもっとも少ない）を押さえておこう。

あなたの解答 A B C D
メモ

- [ ] exhausted　疲れ切った
- [ ] weeklong　1 週間にわたる
- [ ] suitable　ふさわしい

108. 正解 **(C)** 　難易度 ■■■□□ 難

まず will likely go ------- the company's target for this year が、「会社の今年の目標数値を ------- しそうだ」という文脈であることを捉える。すると、空所には直前の go とともに**「〜を超える」**という意味になる単語が入るとわかる。正解は、(C) beyond。(A) の go further は「さらに推し進める」、(B) の go ahead は「前に進む、進行する」の意。これらも一緒に覚えておこう。

あなたの解答 A B C D
メモ

- [ ] investor　投資家　　□ profit　利益
- [ ] steadily　着実に　　□ likely　おそらく
- [ ] target　目標（額）

109. 正解 **(B)** 　難易度 ■■■□□ 難

not only に気づけば、**相関接続詞** not only *A* but (also) *B*（A だけではなく B も）を作る (B) but also が正解だとすぐわかる。同じ品詞（動詞）の assist と keep をつないでいる。このように**対等な要素をつなぐ性質**があることも覚えておこう。

あなたの解答 A B C D
メモ

- [ ] emergency room　緊急救命室
- [ ] procedure　処置　　□ patient　患者
- [ ] calm　落ち着いた

110. 正解 **(B)** 　難易度 ■■■□□ 難

空所前後の of と own とともに用い、**「自分自身の」**という意味の of *one's* own を作る**所有格**の (B) his が正解。him（目的格）、he（主格）、himself（再帰代名詞）は形容詞 own とともに使えないことを覚えておこう。参考までに、by *oneself*（自ら、独力で）、for *oneself*（独力で）、of itself（ひとりでに）、in itself（それ自体では、本質的に）を一緒に押さえておこう。

あなたの解答 A B C D
メモ

- [ ] submit　〜を提出する
- [ ] resignation　辞表
- [ ] establish　〜を創設する

111. 正解 **(C)** 　難易度 ■■■□□ 難

時制を問う問題なので、時制を特定するヒントとなる**時間表現に注目**する。現在完了形とともに使われる時間表現 ever since 〜（〜以来ずっと）があるので、(C) has been が正解。(A) (B) の過去時制、(D) の現在時制は ever since とともに使うことはできない。

あなたの解答 A B C D
メモ

- [ ] ticketing agent　チケット販売員
- [ ] relocate　移住する

112. 正解 **(D)** 　難易度 ■■□□□ 難

同じ品詞（形容詞）が並んでいるので、**文脈から考える**。include ------- figures from the last fiscal year（前会計年度からの ------- な数値を含む）という意味なので、**「正確な」**という意味の (D) accurate を入れると文意が通る。

あなたの解答 A B C D
メモ

- [ ] budget　予算　　□ proposal　案
- [ ] figure　数値　　□ fiscal year　会計年度
- [ ] concise　簡潔な　　□ spending　支出
- [ ] projection　計画

45

TEST 1
PART 5

音声ファイル T1_P5_Q113 ▶ T1_P5_Q118

問題 | 訳

---

113. ------- frequent reminders about efficient energy consumption, more households are starting to buy eco-friendly appliances that use less electricity.

(A) In response to
(B) Apart from
(C) In spite of
(D) Except for

効率的なエネルギー消費を促す頻繁な注意喚起に応じ、消費電力がより少なく環境によい電化製品を購入する家庭が増え始めている。

(A) 〜に応じて
(B) 〜は別として
(C) 〜にもかかわらず
(D) 〜を除けば

---

114. Trade officials estimate that food exports ------- by 25 percent in the next three quarters because of increasing demand.

(A) will grow
(B) grow
(C) grew
(D) had grown

通商担当官は、需要の増加により食品の輸出が今後3四半期（9カ月）で25％増加すると見込んでいる。

(A) 〈未来形〉
(B) 〈原形〉
(C) 〈過去形〉
(D) 〈過去完了形〉

---

115. Invited guests were informed that the awards ceremony for the sales department will start ------- at 7 P.M. at the Ogilvy Hotel.

(A) normally
(B) promptly
(C) lately
(D) mostly

営業部の表彰式は、午後7時ちょうどにOgilvyホテルで開かれるということが招待客に告知された。

(A) ふつう
(B) きっかり
(C) 最近
(D) 主に

---

116. The president of the bank was interviewed by Melinda Carlson, a well-known ------- for an international news magazine.

(A) journalism
(B) journalistically
(C) journal
(D) journalist

その銀行頭取は、国際ニュース雑誌の有名な記者であるMelinda Carlsonのインタビューを受けた。

(A) 名 ジャーナリズム
(B) 副 ジャーナリズム的に
(C) 名 定期刊行物
(D) 名 記者

---

117. Supporters of the plan to deregulate the power industry say that ------- competition will force suppliers to better serve consumers.

(A) narrow
(B) open
(C) rolling
(D) failed

電力業界の規制緩和案の支援者によれば、自由競争によって供給企業は顧客によりよいサービスを提供するようになるとのことだ。

(A) 狭い
(B) 開かれた
(C) うねった
(D) 失敗した

---

118. An increase in the national population will ------- result in a much greater demand for social services, food, and housing.

(A) conditionally
(B) materially
(C) inevitably
(D) sparingly

国の人口増加は、必然的に福祉サービス、食糧、住宅に対するより一層の需要を生みだすだろう。

(A) 条件付きで
(B) 物質的に
(C) 必然的に
(D) 倹約して

> **TOEIC豆知識** TOEIC公開テストでは、以前出題した問題を部分的に再利用している。この点で、くり返し受験する人は、少し有利かもしれない。（続く▶）

正解＆解説 | 間違いメモ＆単語

113. 正解 (A) 難易度：難

空所のあとには名詞の固まり frequent reminders があるので、文法的にはどの選択肢も空所に入る。なので、**文脈から考えていく**。カンマまでの前半部は「効率的なエネルギー消費についての頻繁な注意喚起」、後半部は「消費電力が少なく環境によい電化製品を買う家が増えている」という内容。これらを自然につなげられるのは、「**〜に応じて**」という意味の (A) In response to。

あなたの解答 [A][B][C][D]
メモ

- □ frequent 頻繁な □ efficient 効率的な □ consumption 消費 □ appliance（家庭用の）機器 □ electricity 電力

114. 正解 (A) 難易度：難

時制を問う問題なので、時制を特定するヒントとなる**時間表現に注目**する。that 以降は、**主語 food exports と動詞（空所）**を含む節になっており、ここに**未来の時間表現 in the next three quarters**（今後3四半期）がある。従って、空所に入る動詞は未来時制が適切と判断できる。よって (A) will grow が正解。

あなたの解答 [A][B][C][D]
メモ

- □ official 担当官
- □ estimate 〜を見積もる
- □ quarter 四半期 □ demand 需要

115. 正解 (B) 難易度：難

同じ品詞（副詞）が並んでいるので、前後の**文脈から答えを探る**。「営業部の表彰式が午後7時に〈どのように〉始まる」のかを考えると、「**きっかり**」という意味の (B) promptly を入れるのがもっとも自然。参考までに、動詞 inform は inform A that 節（A に〜を知らせる）の形か、inform A of B（A に B を知らせる）の形で使われることを押さえておこう。

あなたの解答 [A][B][C][D]
メモ

- □ sales department 営業部

116. 正解 (D) 難易度：難

冠詞 a とともに用いられ、**形容詞 well-known に修飾されるのは名詞**なので、(A) (C) (D) が候補。Melinda Carlson 直後のカンマは**同格**を表し、Melinda Carlson = a well-known ------- という構文になっている。つまり「有名な ------- である Melinda Carlson」という意味なので、人を指す名詞 (D) journalist（記者）が正解。(A) journalism や (C) journal だと、それぞれ「有名なジャーナリズムである Melinda Carlson」、「有名な定期刊行物である Melinda Carlson」となり不自然。

あなたの解答 [A][B][C][D]
メモ

- □ well-known 有名な

117. 正解 (B) 難易度：難

同じ品詞（形容詞）が並んでいるので、**文脈からアプローチ**する。------- competition will force suppliers to better serve consumers（------- な競争が消費者によりよくサービスすることを供給者に強いる）という文脈なので、「**〈開かれた〉競争**」とすると自然。よって (B) open が正解。参考までに、force A to do（A に無理やり〜させる）を覚えておこう。

あなたの解答 [A][B][C][D]
メモ

- □ deregulate 〜の規制を撤廃する
- □ industry 〜産業 □ force（人）に〜を強制する □ serve 〜に尽くす

118. 正解 (C) 難易度：難

同じ品詞（副詞）が並んでいるので、**文脈から考える**。まず大意を捉えると、「人口増加は、福祉、食糧、住宅に対する一層の需要をもたらす」となる。空所は、動詞 result in 〜（〜をもたらす）を修飾する位置なので、人口増加が福祉などの需要を〈どのように〉もたらすのか考える。人口が増えれば福祉などへの需要は当然高まるので、「**必然的に**」という意味の (C) inevitably が正解。参考までに、much のように比較級を強調する副詞 even、still、far と、最上級を強調する副詞 by far、quite を一緒に押さえておこう。

あなたの解答 [A][B][C][D]
メモ

- □ result in 〜 〜に帰着する
- □ social service 社会福祉サービス
- □ housing 住宅

TEST 1 PART 5

119. The brochures released by Towler Prudential provide additional information on ------- plans offered by the insurance provider.

(A) prevailed
(B) various
(C) conquered
(D) allowing

120. It is critical during these difficult economic times for companies to ------- their most self-motivated and productive employees.

(A) attempt
(B) retain
(C) observe
(D) impress

121. The university's annual graduation ------- is slated to take place on Saturday morning at ten o'clock at the campus's main auditorium.

(A) course
(B) convention
(C) ceremony
(D) registration

122. The Department of Labor has launched a Web site designed to help companies interact with people seeking -------.

(A) employing
(B) employee
(C) employment
(D) employed

123. The family-owned company maintains a policy of promoting members to senior positions only ------- they have earned graduate degrees in business.

(A) where
(B) than
(C) whereas
(D) after

124. In addition to clothing production, KL Textiles is involved in ------- raw materials into high-quality cotton, silk, and wool cloth.

(A) packaging
(B) processing
(C) handling
(D) exchanging

TOEIC豆知識 ちなみに、こうした再利用問題のことを、TOEIC マニアは〈リサイクル問題〉、もしくは単に〈リサイクル〉と呼んでいる。

正解＆解説 ／ 間違いメモ＆単語

119. 正解 (B) 　難易度　難

同じ品詞（形容詞的働きをする語）が並んでいるので、**文脈から考える**。on -------- plans offered by the insurance provider は「保険会社が提供する -------- なプランについての」という意味で、前の additional information を修飾している。「**さまざまな、多様な**」という意味の various を入れると文意が通るので (B) が正解。

あなたの解答 A B C D
メモ

□ additional　追加の　□ insurance　保険

120. 正解 (B) 　難易度　難

同じ品詞（動詞）が並んでいるので、**文脈からアプローチ**するが、まず **It is ~ for A to do**（…することはAにとって～だ）の構文になっていることを見抜く。つまり、companies にとって critical（重要な）ことが to 以下で述べられている。その to 以下の to -------- their most self-motivated and productive employee は「やる気があり有能な社員を -------- すること」という意味なので、「**～を保有する**」という意味の (B) retain を入れると文意が通る。

あなたの解答 A B C D
メモ

□ critical　決定的に重要な
□ self-motivated　やる気のある
□ productive　生産性の高い

121. 正解 (C) 　難易度　難

同じ品詞（名詞）が並んでいるので、**文脈から答えを探る**。The university's annual graduation --------（大学の年次卒業 --------）が is slated to take place on Saturday morning（土曜日の朝に開かれる予定）という文脈なので、「**卒業〈式〉**」となる ceremony を入れると文意が通る。よって (C) が正解。

あなたの解答 A B C D
メモ

□ slate　～を予定する

122. 正解 (C) 　難易度　難

空所直前の**現在分詞** seeking の**目的語**になれるのは**名詞**。従って、(B) と (C) が正解候補。help companies interact with people seeking -------- で「企業が -------- を求める人たちと交流するのを支援する」という意味なので、文意が通るのは〈雇用〉を求める人たち」となる (C) employment。人を指す名詞 (B) employee だと、「企業が従業員を求める人たちと交流するのを支援する」となり、不自然。参考までに employee は可算名詞なので、冠詞とともに使うか、複数形で使わなければいけないことを押さえておこう。

あなたの解答 A B C D
メモ

□ launch　～を始める
□ interact with ～　～と交流する

123. 正解 (D) 　難易度　難

この文は、すでに**主語** The family-owned company、**動詞** maintains、**目的語** a policy をすべて備えている。従って、only -------- they have earned graduate in business は、修飾の付加的要素と考えられる。空所のあとは「彼らが経営学の大学院の学位を得た」という内容。これを全体の文脈に一致させるには、only とともに「**～のあとにのみ**」という意味になる (D) after を入れるとよい。(B) than は比較の対象となる節を導くときに使われる。

あなたの解答 A B C D
メモ

□ maintain　～を維持する　□ promote　～を昇進させる　□ senior position　上級職　□ earn　～を得る　□ degree　学位

124. 正解 (B) 　難易度　難

同じ品詞（動詞の動名詞形）が並んでいるので、**文脈から考える**。まず、KL Textiles is involved in（KL Textiles 社は～に従事している）なので、**空所以降は〈何〉に従事している**かを示している。-------- raw materials into high-quality cotton, silk, and wool cloth（原材料を高品質綿、絹、羊毛へと -------- すること）なので、「**～を加工する**」という意味の process の動名詞 (B) だと文意が通る。

あなたの解答 A B C D
メモ

□ clothing　衣類　□ textile　繊維
□ be involved in ～　～に携わる
□ raw material　原料

49

TEST 1 PART 5

125. In some parts of the world, sophisticated forgeries make it difficult even for experts to detect whether a product is ------- or not.
(A) factual
(B) authentic
(C) customary
(D) conclusive

世界の一部の地域では、精巧な偽造のために専門家ですら製品が本物であるかどうかを判断できない。
(A) 事実に基づいた
(B) 本物の
(C) 慣習的な
(D) 決定的な

126. Management at the new shopping center on Broad Street expects to draw large crowds on its first day, as the opening ------- with a national holiday.
(A) escorts
(B) coincides
(C) contains
(D) substitutes

Broad通りの新しいショッピングモールの経営陣は、オープン初日に多くの人出を期待している。というのも、初日は祝日だからだ。
(A) ～を護衛する
(B) 一致する
(C) ～を含む
(D) 代わりをする

127. The Hammersmith Business Association will subsidize a new ------- of lectures to promote entrepreneurship in the country.
(A) series
(B) trade
(C) ground
(D) advance

Hammersmithビジネス協会は国内での起業を促すために、新しい連続講演に補助金を出す。
(A) 連続
(B) 貿易
(C) 土地
(D) 進歩

128. We ask that all passengers please let the flight attendants know ------- you will need immigration forms or if you are just in transit.
(A) whereas
(B) than
(C) whether
(D) rather

すべてのお客さまに、入国審査用紙が必要か、あるいは乗り継ぎだけなのかを客室乗務員にお知らせくださるようお願いしています。
(A) 接 ～な反面
(B) 接／前 ～より
(C) 接 ～かどうか
(D) 副 多少、かえって

129. The manager of the restaurant is considering hiring two more waiters after receiving numerous complaints from diners ------- slow service.
(A) regarded
(B) regarding
(C) regards
(D) to regard

そのレストランの店長は、客からサービスの遅さに関してたくさんの苦情を受けて、新たに2人のウエイターを雇うことを検討中だ。
(A) 動 regardの〈過去形・過去分詞〉
(B) 前 ～に関する
(C) 動 ～を考慮する (3人称単数現在形)
(D) 動 regardの〈to不定詞〉

130. Customers are urged to read through all the ------- carefully before installing the software on their computers.
(A) confirmations
(B) schedules
(C) instructions
(D) corrections

顧客は、このソフトウェアをコンピュータにインストールする前に、すべての使用説明書をしっかり読むよう勧められている。
(A) 確認
(B) 日程
(C) 使用説明書
(D) 訂正

50

正解&解説

125. 正解 **(B)**　難易度 ■■□ 難
同じ品詞（形容詞）が並んでいるので、**文脈から考える**。sophisticated forgeries make it difficult even for experts to detect（精巧な偽造のために専門家ですら〜を判断するのが難しい）とあり、whether以降が〈何〉を判断するのが難しいのかを示している。whether a product is ------- or not（製品が-------かどうか）を判断するのが難しいということなので、「〈本物〉かどうか」となる (B) authentic が正解。

あなたの解答 A B C D
メモ

□ sophisticated 精巧な
□ forgery 偽造　□ detect 〜を見破る

126. 正解 **(B)**　難易度 ■■□ 難
同じ品詞（動詞）が並んでいるので、**文脈からアプローチ**する。カンマより前は「初日に多くの人出を期待する」という内容で、カンマ以降が as the opening ------- with a national holiday（オープン日が祝日と------- なので）という理由を示している。文意を考えると「オープン日と祝日が〈一致する〉ので」、つまり「オープン日と祝日が重なるので」となる (B) coincides が正解。coincide with 〜（〜と一致する）を慣用句として覚えよう。

あなたの解答 A B C D
メモ

□ management 経営陣
□ expect 〜を期待する、予想する
□ draw 〜を引き寄せる

127. 正解 **(A)**　難易度 ■■□ 難
空所前の a と後ろの of とともに、「一連の〜、連続の〜」という意味の **a series of 〜を作る** (A) series（連続、一連）が正解。a series of 〜はこのまま覚えておこう。

あなたの解答 A B C D
メモ

□ association 協会
□ subsidize 〜に助成する
□ entrepreneurship 起業家

128. 正解 **(C)**　難易度 ■■□ 難
目的語を取る他動詞 know の後ろに、主語と動詞を持つ節 you will need immigration forms or ... in transit がきている。ということは、この節は**目的語の役割をする名詞節**だと考えられる。従って、名詞節を導く**名詞節接続詞**の (C) whether（〜かどうか）が正解。(A) whereas、(B) than、(D) rather は名詞節を導くことができない。

あなたの解答 A B C D
メモ

□ immigration 入国審査
□ in transit 乗り継ぎの

129. 正解 **(B)**　難易度 ■■□ 難
空所のあとに名詞句 slow service があるので、**名詞を目的語に取る前置詞** (B)、または **to 不定詞** (D) が正解候補。after receiving numerous complaints from diners（客からたくさんの苦情を受けたあとで）という文脈なので、「サービスの遅さに〈関して〉」となる (B) regarding が正解。(D) の to regard だと、「サービスが遅いことを考慮するために、客からたくさんの苦情を受けたあとで」という不自然な意味になる。

あなたの解答 A B C D
メモ

□ consider 〜を検討する
□ numerous たくさんの
□ complaint 苦情　□ diner 食事客

130. 正解 **(C)**　難易度 ■■□ 難
同じ品詞（名詞）が並んでいるので、**文脈から考える**。前半部で Customers are urged to read through all the ------- carefully（顧客は ------- を注意深く読むよう勧められている）とあり、後半部で「コンピュータにソフトをインストールする前に」とある。インストール前に読むものとして、もっとも妥当なのは「**説明書**」なので (C) instructions が正解。参考までに *be* urged to *do*（〜するように勧められる）を慣用句として覚えよう。

あなたの解答 A B C D
メモ

□ urge 〜を熱心に勧める

TEST 1 PART 5

131. Claris Trading chairperson Denise Lim sent the largest ------- to the Red Crusade's dental mission in Africa.
(A) donor
(B) donating
(C) donate
(D) donation

132. Guests are entitled to a number of benefits, ------- discounted spa services and unlimited use of the resort's water sports equipment.
(A) some of
(B) as of
(C) such as
(D) similar to

133. Following the completion of their six-month study on office efficiency, Bartholomew and Associates ------- a new management system to better improve productivity in the company.
(A) was creating
(B) will create
(C) was created
(D) is created

134. Volunteers have been instructed to wear brightly colored vests so that they might be more easily ------- among the crowds of people expected to attend this weekend's parade on Main Street.
(A) shown
(B) admitted
(C) decided
(D) distinguished

135. Although the board has given the proposed service package submitted by a local firm its final -------, the parties will not enter into a contract until the price is agreed upon.
(A) achievement
(B) contemplation
(C) approval
(D) determination

136. Having reviewed the proposal, the clients indicated that they were quite satisfied with the overall plan and requested ------- major changes.
(A) lot
(B) any
(C) many
(D) few

| 正解&解説 | 間違いメモ&単語 |

131. 正解 (D) 難易度 ■■□ 難

動詞 sent の目的語の位置にきて、形容詞の最上級 largest の修飾を受けられるのは名詞なので、(A) (D) に加え、動名詞の (B) も正解候補。sent the largest ------- は「もっとも多くの ------- を送った」という文脈なので、「寄付金」という意味の (D) donation が正解。人を指す (A) donor と、動名詞 (B) donating だと、それぞれ「もっとも多くの寄贈者を送った」、「もっとも多く寄付することを送った」となり、不自然。

あなたの解答 [A] [B] [C] [D]
メモ

- chairperson 会長
- dental 歯の、歯科の
- mission 派遣団

132. 正解 (C) 難易度 ■■□ 難

文脈をみると、カンマまでの前半で「宿泊客は多くの特典を利用できる」となっている。空所以降は、その**特典内容を列記**しているので、「スパの割引やウォータースポーツ器具の無制限利用〈**などの**〉」となる (C) such as が正解。参考までに be entitled to do（〜する資格が与えられる）を押さえておこう。また、これに関連して entitle A to B（A〔人〕に B の資格、権利を与える）も一緒に押さえておこう。

あなたの解答 [A] [B] [C] [D]
メモ

- entitle A to B A に B の権利を与える
- benefit 特典 - unlimited 無制限の

133. 正解 (B) 難易度 ■■□ 難

選択肢に並んでいる create（〜を創造する）は他動詞。空所のあとに目的語 a new management system があるので、**能動態**の (A) と (B) が正解候補になる。次に Following the completion of the six-month study on office efficiency（オフィスの効率性に関する調査が**終了したら**）とあるので、新しいマネジメントシステムを作るのは未来だとわかる。従って、**未来形**の (B) will create が正解。

あなたの解答 [A] [B] [C] [D]
メモ

- efficiency 効率（性）
- productivity 生産性

134. 正解 (D) 難易度 ■■■ 難

同じ品詞（動詞の過去分詞）が並んでいるので、**文脈から考える**。Volunteers have been instructed to wear brightly colored vests（ボランティアは明るい色のベストを着るよう指示されている）とあり、その理由が so that they might be more easily -------（より簡単に ------- されるように）である。「**区別される**」となる (D) distinguished を入れると文意が通る。

あなたの解答 [A] [B] [C] [D]
メモ

- instruct 〜を指導する
- attend 〜に参加する

135. 正解 (C) 難易度 ■■■ 難

同じ品詞（名詞）が並んでいるので、**文脈からアプローチ**する。Although からカンマまでは、give A B（A に B を与える）の構文になっており、取締役会は the proposed service package submitted by a local firm（地元企業から提案されたサービスパッケージ）に、its final -------（最終 -------）を与えた、という文脈。ということは「最終〈**承認**〉を与えた」となる (C) approval が正解。参考までに enter into a contract（契約を結ぶ）を覚えておこう。

あなたの解答 [A] [B] [C] [D]
メモ

- local firm 地元企業
- party 関係者、当事者
- contract 契約

136. 正解 (D) 難易度 ■■□ 難

空所には、直後の**可算名詞 major changes を修飾する形容詞**が必要なので、(B)、(C)、(D) が正解候補。文脈をみると、the clients indicated that they were quite satisfied with the overall plan and（顧客は全体計画にとても満足したと表明し）とあるので、major changes（大きな変更）への要求は「**ほとんどない**」と考えられる。よって (D) few が正解。(B) any、(C) many だと文脈に一致しない。(A) lot は a lot of 〜の形になってはじめて、名詞を修飾できる。

あなたの解答 [A] [B] [C] [D]
メモ

- review 〜を見直す
- indicate 〜を示す

TEST 1 PART 5

137. A brief ------- from the anthology of acclaimed essayist Nigel Murphy was featured in a major daily newspaper along with a book review written by one of the paper's columnists.

(A) extractor
(B) extract
(C) extractive
(D) extracting

高い評価を受けているエッセイスト Nigel Murphy の選集からの短い引用が、ある主要日刊紙において、同紙のコラムニストによる書評とともに特集された。

(A) 名 引用者
(B) 名 引用／動 ～を引用する
(C) 形 抽出できる
(D) 動 extract の〈現在分詞・動名詞〉

138. ------- by a group of advertising professionals, Speedline Creative Concepts quickly achieved the distinction of being a leading firm in branding and logo-making.

(A) Identified
(B) Established
(C) Classified
(D) Manufactured

広告専門家グループによって設立された Speedline Creative Concepts 社は、ブランド構築とロゴ作成の一流企業として急速に抜きんでた。

(A) 識別された
(B) 設立された
(C) 分類された
(D) 製造された

139. A 20 percent discount on annual fees will be given to patrons ------- renew their gym membership before the end of the year.

(A) whose
(B) who
(C) those
(D) when

年内にジムの会員資格を更新する顧客は、年会費の20% 割引が適用される。

〔選択肢訳なし〕

140. The purpose of planning ------- is to ensure that the company can respond adequately to anticipated threats and to unforeseen opportunities.

(A) comparably
(B) redundantly
(C) strategically
(D) predictably

戦略的に計画立案することの目的は、予想される脅威や思いがけない機会に、会社が十分に対応できるようにするためだ。

(A) 比較できるくらいに
(B) 重複して
(C) 戦略的に
(D) 予想通りに

| 正解&解説 | 間違いメモ&単語 |

137. 正解 (B) 難易度 ■■■□ 難

冠詞 a とともに用いられ、**形容詞 brief の修飾を受けられるのは名詞**なので、(A) と (B) が正解候補。文脈をみると、A brief ------- from the anthology of acclaimed essayist Nigel Murphy（評価の高いエッセイストの Nigel Murphy の選集からの短い -------）となっているので、「短い〈**引用**〉」となる (B) extract が正解。人を指す名詞 (A) extractor だと、「選集からの短い引用者」となり不自然。動名詞（または分詞）の (D) extracting には冠詞は付かないので、不正解。参考までに、along with ～（～とともに）を覚えておこう。

あなたの解答 [A] [B] [C] [D]
メモ

☐ brief 短い ☐ anthology 選集
☐ acclaim ～を称賛する
☐ feature ～を特集する

138. 正解 (B) 難易度 ■■■□ 難

空所からカンマまでが、**主語 Speedline Creative Concepts に説明を加える分詞構文**になっている。つまり、------- by a group of advertising professionals（広告専門家グループによって -------）された Speedline Creative Concepts という意味なので、「**設立された**」となる establish の過去分詞形 (B) を入れると文意が通る。

あなたの解答 [A] [B] [C] [D]
メモ

☐ achieve ～を成し遂げる
☐ distinction 優秀な成績、卓越
☐ leading 主要な、先導する

139. 正解 (B) 難易度 ■■■□ 難

選択肢に**関係詞** whose／who／when が並んでいるので、**空所前の先行詞と後ろに続く節の構造**から正答を導く。まず、先行詞は patrons（客＝人）。空所以降の節に主語が見当たらないので、**主格の関係代名詞** (B) が空所にあてはまる。所有格の関係代名詞 (A) whose は、直後に修飾を受ける名詞がくる。(C) those は代名詞（または形容詞）なので節を導けない。関係副詞 (D) when は時間を表す先行詞が必要で、後ろに完全な節がくる。参考までに、those が「～な人たち」という意味で使われるとき、必ず修飾語（関係節、分詞、前置詞句）とともに使うことを押さえておこう。

あなたの解答 [A] [B] [C] [D]
メモ

☐ patron 顧客、常連
☐ renew ～を更新する

140. 正解 (C) 難易度 ■■■■ 難

同じ品詞（副詞）が並んでいるので、**文脈で考える**。The purpose of planning -------（------- に計画することの目的は）とあり、以降「会社が脅威や思いがけない機会に十分対応するためだ」となっている。「〈**戦略的に**〉計画することの目的は」とすれば文意が通るので、(C) strategically が正解。

あなたの解答 [A] [B] [C] [D]
メモ

☐ ensure ～を確実にする
☐ adequately 十分に
☐ anticipate ～を予期する
☐ threat 脅威
☐ unforeseen 思いがけない

TEST 1
PART 6

Questions 141-143 refer to the following press release.

Fireflies Set for First Concert

The Fireflies is ready to light up the Truffle Coliseum at its first major concert on June 5 at 8 P.M. The performance, which will also feature guest appearances from rock stars Lincoln Browning and Meagan Page, is ------- to be the grandest musical event of the season.

    141. (A) required
         (B) subjected
         (C) outlined
         (D) projected

Thousands of fans from all over the UK and nearby countries are expected to attend the concert. -------, VIP and general admission tickets to the show were sold out five days

    142. (A) Provided that
         (B) Instead
         (C) In fact
         (D) Nevertheless

after the event was announced on the band's Web site. The Fireflies' lead singer Alfred Morgan welcomed the public's ------- response to the announced concert.

    143. (A) persuasive
         (B) intimidated
         (C) enthusiastic
         (D) obsessed

"We are grateful for the massive support we are receiving now, and it has inspired us to work doubly hard for this upcoming show," Morgan said.

単語
- light up ～ ～を輝かせる
- appearance 出演
- admission 入場
- grateful 感謝して
- massive 極めて多い、圧倒的な
- inspire ～を刺激する、奮い立たせる

> **TOEIC豆知識**　「990点満点＝200問全問正解」と思っている人が多いが、実は、リスニングで2～4問、リーディングで0～3問ミスしても990点は取れる。

問題文の訳

設問141から143は次のプレスリリースに関する質問です。

Fireflies、初コンサートの準備整う

Firefliesは6月5日午後8時からの初メジャーコンサートで、Truffleコロシアムを光り輝かせる準備ができている。今回の公演はさらに、ロックスターのLincoln BrowningやMeagan Pageを特別出演で迎え、今シーズン最大の音楽イベントになると予想されている。

イギリス全土や近隣諸国から多くのファンがこのコンサートに参加するだろう。実際のところ、コンサートのVIPチケットや一般入場券は同バンドのウェブサイトでイベント告知された5日後に完売。FirefliesのリードボーカルAlfred Morganは、告知されたコンサートに対するファンの熱狂的な反応を歓迎している。

「僕たちが今とても大きな支持を受けていることに感謝している。間もなくはじまるこのショーに向けてますます頑張らなくてはという気にさせてもらったよ」とMorganは語っている。

選択肢の訳

141. (A) 必要とされる
     (B) 支配される
     (C) 略述される
     (D) 企てられる

142. (A) ただし～ならば
     (B) 副 代わりに
     (C) 副 実際に
     (D) 副 それにもかかわらず

143. (A) 説得力のある
     (B) おびえる
     (C) 熱狂的な
     (D)（強迫観念など）に取りつかれた（obsessの〈過去形・過去分詞〉）

正解＆解説

141. 正解 (D)　難易度 難

同じ品詞（動詞の過去形・過去分詞）が並んでいるので、**文脈から考える**。The performance ... is ------- to be the grandest musical event of the season. は、「この公演は今シーズン最大の音楽イベントだと ------- られる」という文脈なので、projectの過去分詞形 (D) をいれて「**予想される**」とすると文意が通る。

142. 正解 (C)　難易度 難

空所が**文頭に位置し**、**直後にカンマがあり**、**前後の文をつないでいる**。この条件を満たすのは、**接続副詞**の (C) と (D)。「数千人のファンがこのコンサートに来場する」という前文に対し、空所のあとは「イベントの告知5日後にチケットが完売した」という詳しい情報を付け加えている。このふたつをつなげられるのは、「**実際に**」という意味の (C) In fact。(D) Nevertheless では文意が通らない。

143. 正解 (C)　難易度 難

同じ品詞（形容詞）が並んでいるので、**文脈で考える**。空所を含む文は、「Alfred Morganはコンサートへの大衆の ------- な反応を歓迎した」という意味だが、前文に「イベントの告知5日後にチケットが完売した」とあることから、「〈**熱狂的な**〉反応」とすれば文意が通る。従って、(C) enthusiastic が正解。

TEST 1
PART 6

Questions 144-146 refer to the following article.

A New Approach to Gift Shopping

For the last four years, Alyssa Russell has helped people remember the important dates on their calendars. Her company Gift Shoppers is an online business that sells gifts for all types of events, which in ------- would make it a rather traditional company.

144. (A) it
(B) their
(C) them
(D) itself

What separates Gift Shoppers from other companies is that it automatically sends reminders to its clients about important events, including anniversaries and holidays.

"Although lots of companies sell their merchandise online, I think we ------- a novel way

145. (A) develop
(B) have developed
(C) were developed
(D) are developing

of shopping," says Russell. Members of the company's Web site mark special days on a calendar when they apply. Gift Shoppers sends messages to its members five days before each event, helping them ------- to buy a gift. The company also provides a list of

146. (A) remember
(B) record
(C) renew
(D) review

gift suggestions. "I am surprised at how successful the idea has been," explains Russell. "We have many clients who are just too busy to remember these types of things. Our service guarantees they never miss important dates again."

単語
- separate 〜を区別する
- including 〜を含めて
- novel 新しい、新鮮な
- mark 〜に印をつける
- guarantee 〜を保証する

問題文の訳

設問 144 から 146 は次の記事に関する質問です。

プレゼント購入の新たな方法

この 4 年間、Alyssa Russell は人々がカレンダー上の大切な日付を思いだす手助けをしてきた。彼女の会社 Gift Shoppers 社は、あらゆるイベント用の贈り物を販売するオンラインビジネスを行っている。それ自体は従来の企業とそう変わらないだろう。

Gift Shoppers 社がほかの会社と違うのは、記念日や祝日といった大切なイベントを通知するメッセージを顧客に自動的に送る点である。

「オンラインで商品を売る会社はたくさんありますが、私たちは今までにないショッピングのかたちを開発してきたと思います」と Russell さんは語る。同社のウェブ会員は、登録時にカレンダー上の特別な日に印をつける。Gift Shoppers 社は各イベントの 5 日前に会員へメッセージを送信し、贈り物を忘れずに購入する手助けをするのである。同社はまた、贈り物の提案リストも用意している。「このアイディアがこんなにも成功していることに驚いています」と語る Russell さん。「忙しすぎてこの手のことを思いだせないお客さまがたくさんいらっしゃるのです。私たちのサービスは、そんなお客さまが二度と大切な日を忘れないことを保証しているのです」。

選択肢の訳

144. (A) 〈主格／目的格〉
     (B) 〈所有格〉
     (C) 〈目的格〉
     (D) 〈再帰代名詞〉

145. (A) 〈原形〉
     (B) 〈現在完了形〉
     (C) 〈受動態の過去形〉
     (D) 〈現在進行形〉

146. (A) 〜を忘れない
     (B) 〜を記録する
     (C) 〜を再開する
     (D) 〜を再調査する

正解 & 解説

144. 正解 **(D)**

前置詞 in の目的語の位置にくることができるのは、目的格の (A) と (C)、再帰代名詞の (D)。カンマ以前の「Gift Shoppers 社はあらゆるイベント用の贈り物を売るオンライン企業だ」という内容について、, which 以降は関係代名詞の非制限用法で「むしろ従来通りの企業である」という補足をしている。この文脈に一致するのは、「〈本質的には〉むしろ従来通りの企業だ」となる (D) itself。**in itself**（本質的、それ自体）は、このまま覚えておこう。

145. 正解 **(B)**

空所のあとには、develop（〜を開発する）の目的語 a novel way of shopping があるので、能動態である (A) (B) (D) が候補。あとは時制で判断する。a novel way of shopping（新しいショッピングの形）とは、ここより前で言及された、「大切なイベントを忘れないために通知を送る」という Gift Shoppers 社の特徴のこと。つまり、a novel way of shopping はすでに開発され、現在も続いていることなので、現在完了形の (B) が正解。

146. 正解 **(A)**

同じ品詞（動詞）が並んでいるので、文脈から判断する。helping them ------- to buy a gift（彼らが贈り物を買うことを ------- するよう助ける）と言っているので、「買うことを〈忘れない〉よう助ける」となる (A) remember が正解。参考までに、使役動詞 help は、help A (to) do で「A（人）が〜するのを助ける」となる。to do 部分は、to 不定詞、to を省略した原形不定詞のどちらも可。

TEST 1 PART 6

Questions 147-149 refer to the following announcement.

MxGuard Released

Greyton Labs has finally made its new software, MxGuard 2.0, available on the market this week. It provides maximum ------- against malicious programs that can harm your

    147. (A) protector
          (B) protection
          (C) protectable
          (D) protective

computer system while you surf the Internet.

Features ------- identity security when banking and making online purchases, an

    148. (A) indicate
          (B) enclose
          (C) redirect
          (D) include

integrated virus and spyware scanner, an e-mail monitor for blocking unsolicited messages, and an enhanced firewall to prevent unwanted access to your system.

MxGuard 2.0 is ------- distributed by Greyton Labs and costs $55 for a one-year

    149. (A) expressively
          (B) attentively
          (C) exclusively
          (D) graciously

subscription for home users and $250 for business users. Both come with 24-hour customer support. The software is now available for download at www.greytonlabs.com/mxguard.

単語
- lab 研究所、実験室（※ laboratory の省略形）
- malicious 悪質な
- harm ～を傷つける
- feature 特徴
- integrated 統合された
- unsolicited 頼みもしないのに与えられた
- enhanced 強化された
- prevent ～を防ぐ
- subscription 会費
- come with ～ ～を備えている

問題文の訳

設問 147 から 149 は次のアナウンスに関する質問です。

MxGuard 発売

Greyton Labs 社は今週、新しいソフトウェア MxGuard2.0 の販売をついに開始しました。ネットサーフィン時に、コンピュータシステムに危害を加えかねない悪質なプログラムへの最大限の保護を提供します。

特徴として、銀行取引やオンラインショッピング時の個人情報の保護、ウイルスとスパイウェアの統合スキャナー、迷惑メールを阻止する E メールモニター、コンピュータへの不正アクセスを防ぐ強化されたファイアーウォールなどを備えています。

MxGuard2.0 は、Greyton Labs 社によって独占的に販売され、年会費は個人向けで 55 ドル、法人向けで 250 ドル。どちらも 24 時間のカスタマーサポート付き。このソフトウェアは現在、www.greytonlabs.com/mxguard. にてダウンロード可能です。

選択肢の訳

147. (A) 名 保護者
     (B) 名 保護
     (C) 形 保護できる
     (D) 名 保護物／形 保護用の

148. (A) 〜を示す
     (B) 〜を同封する
     (C) 〜を再度送る
     (D) 〜を含む

149. (A) 表情豊かに
     (B) 注意深く
     (C) 独占的に
     (D) やさしく、親切に

正解 & 解説

147. 正解 **(B)**　難易度 ■■□

空所直前の**形容詞 maximum が修飾するのは名詞**なので、(A) と (B)、もしくは形容詞としても名詞としても機能する (D) が候補。文脈をみると、「悪質なプログラムへの最高の〈**保護**〉を提供する」とすると文意が通るので、(B) protection が正解。人を指す (A) protector（保護者）は、ここではあてはまらない。(D) protective は名詞として使われる場合、「保護物」という意味。

148. 正解 **(D)**　難易度 ■■□

同じ品詞（動詞）が並んでいるので、**文脈から考える**。Features ------- identity security（特徴に個人情報保護を -------）となっているので、「**〜を含む**」という意味の (D) include だと文意が通る。(B) の enclose は、「（手紙や小包などに）具体的なものを一緒に入れる」という意味で、ここにはあてはまらない。

149. 正解 **(C)**　難易度 ■■□

同じ品詞（副詞）が並んでいるので、**文脈から考える**。「MxGuard 2.0 は Greyton Labs 社によって〈**どのように**〉配布される」のかを考えると、「〈**独占的に**〉配布される」となる (C) exclusively が正解。ほかの副詞はどれもしっくりこない。

TEST 1 PART 6

Questions 150-152 refer to the following e-mail.

TO: Ethan Reid <ethan12@geallmail.uk>
FROM: Olivia Griffith <livgriffith@nymphmail.uk>
DATE: June 8
SUBJECT: Hello

Hi Ethan,

How are you doing? I hope you're adjusting well to your new life in Birmingham. It's already been a month since you moved from Liverpool and not much has changed around here. Everybody in the office ------- you a lot.

    150. (A) was missed
          (B) missing
          (C) had missed
          (D) misses

By the way, I remember how you ------- talked about your experience as a physical education

    151. (A) very
          (B) often
          (C) fairly
          (D) apparently

teacher before you came here. I'm thinking of enrolling my seven-year-old son, Dylan, in a tennis class in the summer. I want him to engage in an activity that will help him develop his strength and coordination skills. Do you think the sport will be too ------- for him? I haven't

    152. (A) eager
          (B) crucial
          (C) strenuous
          (D) determined

played tennis myself, so I thought I'd ask your expert opinion on the matter.

I'd really appreciate your advice and look forward to hearing from you.

Regards,

Olivia

単語
- physical education 体育
- enroll ～を入会させる
- engage in ～ ～に従事する
- strength 体力、強さ
- coordination 調整
- matter 問題、事
- appreciate ～をありがたく思う

問題文の訳

設問 150 から 152 は次の E メールに関する質問です。

宛先： Ethan Reid <ethan12@geallmail.uk>
送信者： Olivia Griffith <livgriffith@nymphmail.uk>
日付： 6月8日
件名： こんにちは

こんにちは、Ethan、

お元気ですか。バーミンガムでの新しい生活にも慣れてきているころかと思います。あなたがリバプールから引っ越してもう 1 カ月が経つのですね。こちらはあまり変わりありませんよ。マンチェスター支店のみんなはあなたが**いないのをとても寂しく思っています**。

ところで、あなたがここに来る以前に体育の先生として働いていた経験を**よく**話していたのを覚えているのですが、私の 7 歳の息子 Dylan をこの夏、テニス教室に参加させようと思っています。息子の体力と調整能力を鍛える活動に参加してほしくて。このスポーツは息子には激しすぎると思いますか。私自身、テニスをしたことがないので、この件に関して専門家としてのあなたの意見を聞けたらと思ったのです。

助言していただけると大変ありがたいです。あなたからのお返事を楽しみにしております。

それでは。

Olivia

選択肢の訳

150. (A) 〈受動態の過去形〉
     (B) 〈現在分詞・動名詞〉
     (C) 〈過去完了形〉
     (D) 〈現在形〉

151. (A) たいへん
     (B) しばしば、よく
     (C) 公正に
     (D) 見たところ

152. (A) 熱心だ、真剣な
     (B) 重大な
     (C) 激しい、活発な
     (D) 決然とした

正解 & 解説

150. 正解 (D)

空所の後ろに**動詞 miss の目的語 you がある**ので、能動の (C) と (D) が正解候補。次に「あなた（= Ethan）がいなくて寂しく思う」のがいつなのか、**時制で判断**する。ここよりも前の部分で「Ethan は 1 カ月前に引っ越した」とあるが、「**今も寂しく思っている**」と考えるのが自然なので、現在形に 3 人称単数の -es が付いた (D) misses が正解。

151. 正解 (B)

同じ品詞（副詞）が並んでいるので、**文脈から判断する**。「体育教師としての経験について、どんなに〈どのように〉話していたかを覚えている」という文脈なので、「どんなに〈よく〉話していたか」となる (B) often が正解。参考までに、often は通常、一般動詞の前や、助動詞および be 動詞のあとに位置することを押さえておこう。

152. 正解 (C)

同じ品詞（形容詞）が並んでいるので、**文脈から考える**。「このスポーツ（= テニス）が、彼（= 息子）にとって ------ すぎると思うか」という流れなので、「〈激し〉すぎる」となる (C) strenuous が自然。参考までに、eager は *be* eager to *do*（〜することを熱望する）の形でよく用いられることを押さえておこう。

TEST 1 PART 7

Questions 153-154 refer to the following card.

City Explorer 3

Thank you for purchasing the City Explorer card.

This card gives you access to major attractions throughout the city for three days, and it will be activated on your first use. This card also serves as a pass to various city tours and admission to museums in different locations.

Present this card at participating restaurants and souvenir shops and get 10 percent off food and merchandise.

We hope that you enjoy your trip!
Trapezon City Travel Board

For information on major attractions, see the reverse side of the card.

---

153. What is indicated on the card?

(A) It entitles the holder to free meals.
(B) It acts as a ticket to popular destinations.
(C) It allows holders to make charges at local establishments.
(D) It gives access to public transportation for three days.

154. What information is included on the card?

(A) The locations of where it is available for purchase
(B) The admission fees for museums
(C) A list of establishments offering discounts
(D) Details about tourist sites

設問の訳

このカードについて何が述べられているか。

(A) カード保有者は無料で食事をする権利が得られる。
(B) 人気の観光スポットへの入場券となる。
(C) 保有者は当該地区の施設において、このカードで支払いができる。
(D) 3日間無料で公共交通機関を利用できる。

カードにはどのような情報が記載されているか。

(A) 買い物に利用できる場所
(B) 美術館の入場料
(C) 割引を提供している施設一覧
(D) 観光スポットの詳細説明

| TOEIC豆知識 | TOEICの世界の求人では、応募条件として前職場のletters of referenceを求められる。そんな慣習が日本になくてよかったぁ～と安心している受験者は、多いはず。（続く▶） |

問題文の訳

設問153から154は次のカードに関する質問です。

City Explorer 3

City Explorerカードのご購入ありがとうございます。

❶このカードは3日間にわたって市内各所の主な観光スポットへの入場を可能にします。初回利用日が有効期限の初日となります。また、このカードはさまざまな市内観光ツアーの参加パスとして、また各美術館への入場券としても利用が可能です。

このカードを当イベント協賛のレストランや土産物店でご提示になれば、お食事やお買い物に10%の割引が受けられます。

市内観光が楽しいものになることを願っております！
Trapezon市観光局

❷主要な観光スポットの情報については裏面をご覧ください。

単語

- attraction 見所
- activate ～を有効にする
- serve as ～ ～として役立つ
- present ～を提示する
- reverse 逆の、裏の

153
- destination 行き先、目的地
- establishment 施設

154
- admission fee 入場料
- tourist site 観光スポット

正解&解説

153. 正解 **(B)**　難易度 ■■■□□ 難

カードについて言及されていることを尋ねるTrue問題。❶に「このカードで市内の**主な観光スポットへ入場できる**」とあるので、(B)が正解。レストランで10%割引されるとはあるが、無料にはならないので(A)は誤り。3日間利用許可を得るのは、観光スポットであって、交通機関ではないので(D)も誤り。

↻ major attractions ➡ popular destinations

154. 正解 **(D)**　難易度 ■■■□□ 難

カードに記載されている情報を尋ねている。設問のキーワードinformation is included on the card（カードに記載された情報）を、❷のFor information（情報については）と結びつけられれば、答えはすぐに見つかる。❷には「**主要観光スポットの情報は、カード裏面を見て**」とある。つまり、カード裏側に「**観光スポットの詳細説明**」が記載されているということなので、(D)が正解。

↻ information on major attractions ➡ Details about tourist sites

TEST 1
PART 7

Questions 155-156 refer to the following advertisement.

EVERIDGE CERTIFIED ACCOUNTANTS
825 Burrard, Suite 19-A, Vancouver BC

Having trouble with your tax forms? Are the finances of your small business more than you can handle? Let ECA, the fastest-growing accounting firm in Canada, take care of all your accounting worries!

We offer:
- ▷ Personal income tax returns
- ▷ Setup and maintenance of a bookkeeping system
- ▷ Preparation of financial statements
- ▷ Contract assistance

For a full list of our services and accountants, visit www.everidgeacc.co.ca. To make an appointment, call us at (604) 555-8872 to speak to one of our representatives, or send an e-mail to everidgeacc@coolmail.com.

---

155. What is NOT a service offered by ECA?

(A) Assistance with income tax forms
(B) Help with creating a contract
(C) Investment consultation
(D) Developing accounting systems

156. Why would a customer visit the ECA Web site?

(A) To arrange a personal tax consultation
(B) To find out the fees for an accounting service
(C) To view online samples of business contracts
(D) To get information about ECA employees

設問の訳

ECA が提供していないサービスは何か。
(A) 所得税申告書の支援
(B) 契約書作成の支援
(C) 投資の相談
(D) 経理システムの開発

顧客はなぜ ECA のウェブサイトを訪れるのか。
(A) 個人の税金相談を予約するため
(B) 経理サービスの料金を知るため
(C) 事業契約のオンライン見本を見るため
(D) ECA の社員情報を得るため

TOEIC豆知識 letters of reference とは「推薦状」のこと。そのようなものを書いてもらえるくらい評価されているのであれば転職はしない……

問題文の訳

設問 155 から 156 は次の広告に関する質問です。

EVERIDGE 公認会計士事務所
825 Burrard、スイート 19-A、バンクーバー、ブリティッシュコロンビア

税金申告書でお困りですか。ご商売の資金管理が手に余っていませんか。カナダでもっとも急成長している会計事務所 ECA に会計の悩みはお任せください。

業務内容：
❶ ▷個人所得税の申告
❷ ▷経理システムの構築と維持
　 ▷財務諸表の準備
❸ ▷契約の支援

❹ 弊社のサービスと会計士の一覧は、ウェブサイト www.everidgeacc.co.ca をご覧ください。ご予約は (604) 555-8872 にお電話のうえ担当者とお話しいただくか、everidgeacc@coolmail.com までメールをお送りください。

単語

- certified 公認の、認証の
- tax form 納税申告書
- handle 〜に対処する
- growing 成長している
- accounting 会計
- bookkeeping 簿記
- financial statements 財務諸表
- representative 代表者
- **155** consultation 相談

正解 & 解説

155. 正解 (C) 難易度 難

ECA のサービス**ではない**ものを尋ねる Not 問題。各選択肢を、広告に記された ECA のサービスと照らし合わせ、一致しないものを選ぶ。(A) は❶「個人所得税の申告」、(B) は❸「契約支援」、(D) は❷「経理システムの構築と維持」に、それぞれ一致する。(C) の「**投資の相談**」については触れられていないので、これが正解。

⇄ income tax return → income tax forms
　 Contract assistance → Help with creating a contract
　 Setup ... of a bookkeeping system → Developing accounting systems

156. 正解 (D) 難易度 難

顧客が ECA のウェブサイトを訪問する理由を尋ねている。❹に「サービスと会計士の一覧は、www.everidgeacc.co.ca を見てほしい」とある。つまり、**サービスと会計士に関する情報を得たい顧客**が、ウェブサイトを訪れるということ。ECA は会計士事務所なので、会計士＝ ECA の社員と考えられるので、(D)「ECA の社員情報を得るため」が正解。

TEST 1
PART 7

Questions 157-159 refer to the following invitation.

The New Hampton Professionals Society
would like to invite you to attend our

12th Annual Melody for Charity Night

on Saturday, July 24, at 6:00 P.M.
at the Greenfield Theater

Six classical compositions by world-renowned composers
Johannes Linden and Vladimir Tepanor of the Salzburg Conservatory

will be performed by the
Smithson Philharmonic Orchestra

Cost per person: $80   Attire: Formal

Proceeds from the evening are set to benefit welfare institutions in the northern city of Henlin, namely St. Peter's Orphanage and the Rainbow House for Children. Please RSVP by July 1. For more information, visit www.stpetersorphanage.com and www.rainbowhouse.com.

---

157. What will take place on July 24?

(A) An organizational meeting
(B) A fundraising concert
(C) The introduction of new composers
(D) The opening of a new association

158. Who are Johannes Linden and Vladimir Tepanor?

(A) They are famous conductors of an orchestra.
(B) They are representatives of a charitable organization.
(C) They are respected artists from a music school.
(D) They are well-known producers in the entertainment industry.

159. What is NOT indicated about the event?

(A) It is sponsored by a group of professionals.
(B) Individuals are required to dress formally.
(C) It will be held on the weekend.
(D) Refreshments will be served to all guests.

設問の訳

7月24日に何が開催されるか。

(A) ある組織の会合
(B) 募金コンサート
(C) 新しい作曲家の紹介
(D) 新しい協会の設立

Johannes Linden と Vladimir Tepanor とは誰か。

(A) 交響楽団の有名な指揮者である。
(B) 慈善団体の代表である。
(C) 音楽学校の尊敬を集める音楽家である。
(D) エンターテインメント業界で名の知れたプロデューサーである。

このイベントに関して述べられていないことは何か。

(A) 専門家団体からの後援を受けている。
(B) 参加者は正装を求められている。
(C) 週末に開催される。
(D) 軽い飲食物がすべての客に提供される。

問題文の訳

設問157から159は次の招待状に関する質問です。

❶New Hampton 専門家協会からのご招待
❷**第12回チャリティー音楽祭の夕べ**

❸7月24日　❹（土）午後6時
Greenfield 劇場

❺世界に名立たる作曲家であるザルツブルグ音楽学校の Johannes Linden と Vladimir Tepanor 作曲のクラシック曲6編
Smithson フィルハーモニー管弦楽団による演奏

入場料：80ドル　　❻服装：正装

本音楽祭の売り上げは Henlin 市北部にある福祉施設 St. Peter 孤児院と Rainbow House for Children のために役立てられます。出欠のお返事は7月1日までにお願いいたします。詳細は以下のサイトをご覧ください。
www.stpetersorphanage.com
www.rainbowhouse.com

単語

- composition 楽曲
- renowned 有名な
- composer 作曲家
- conservatory 音楽学校
- attire 服装
- proceeds 収益
- benefit 〜の役に立つ、に利益を与える
- welfare 福祉
- institution 機関、団体、施設
- namely すなわち
- orphanage 孤児院
- RSVP お返事お願いいたします

157
- fundraising 募金集めの

158
- conductor 指揮者
- charitable 慈善の
- respected 尊敬を集めている

159
- sponsor 〜を後援する
- individual 個人
- refreshment 軽食、飲食物

正解 & 解説

157. 正解 (B)

7月24日に何が起きるかを尋ねている。キーワード **July 24** に注目すると、❹に記載されており、その上❷に「第12回**チャリティー音楽祭**の夕べ」とある。これを「募金コンサート」と言い換えた (B) が正解。

↪ Annual Melody for Charity Night ➡ A fundraising concert

158. 正解 (C)

Johannes Linden と Vladimir Tepanor が誰かを尋ねている。ふたりの名前が登場する❺に、「**Salzburg Conservatory（ザルツブルク音楽学校）**の世界的に**著名な作曲家**」とある。これを「音楽学校の尊敬を集める音楽家」と言い換えた (C) が正解。conservatory の意味「音楽学校」を覚えておこう。

↪ world-renowned composers ➡ respected artists
　 Conservatory ➡ a music school

159. 正解 (D)

このイベントについて、**言及されていない**ものを尋ねる Not 問題。選択肢と、招待状の情報をひとつひとつ照らし合わせ、一致しないものを選ぶ。(A) は、❶に「New Hampton 専門家協会がイベントに招待する」、つまり New Hampton 専門家協会が主催しているということなので一致。(B) は❻「服装：正装」、(C) は❸「土曜日に」とあり、これらも内容と一致する。(D) の「**飲食物**」に関する記述が見当たらないので、これが正解。

↪ Attire: formal ➡ dress formally

TEST 1
PART 7

Questions 160-162 refer to the following advertisement.

Time Out Vendors

Refresh D-02
Cold Drink Vending Machine

The all-new Refresh D-02 Vendor will give your customers wider drink selections in bottles and cans. The Refresh D-02 Vendor can now load ten types of drinks ranging from sodas and fruit juices to bottled water. This machine is an update of our D-01 model, but still includes a removable back-lighted display, which makes branding and pricing convenient. Loading drinks is also very simple with the machine's easy-loading product shelves.

Specifications	
Dimensions	Height 1.8m Width 0.8m Depth 0.8m
Weight	261kg
Number of Drink Selections	10
Standard Capacity	20 oz. Bottle (200 pieces)
Payment Mechanism	Dollar Bill Acceptor Coin Acceptor

For more details on Refresh D-02 Vendor, call 555-8591 or visit www.timeoutvendors.com.

---

160. What is indicated about Refresh D-02?

(A) It should be kept in cool areas.
(B) It is a modified version of a previous model.
(C) It is available for rent.
(D) It has a security sensor.

161. What information is NOT included in the advertisement about the machine?

(A) Specifications about its size
(B) Its storage capacity
(C) Details about rental rates
(D) A list of items that it is capable of selling

162. What is stated about the machine's payment device?

(A) It accepts paper money.
(B) It identifies foreign currency.
(C) It holds different types of containers.
(D) It does not recognize coins.

設問の訳

Refresh D-02について何が述べられているか。
(A) 涼しい場所に設置しなければならない。
(B) 以前のモデルの改良型である。
(C) レンタルできる。
(D) 防犯センサーが付いている。

この機械の広告に含まれていない情報は何か。
(A) 寸法に関する仕様
(B) 収蔵容量
(C) レンタル料金の詳細
(D) 販売可能な商品のリスト

この機械の支払装置について何が述べられているか。
(A) 紙幣を受け付ける。
(B) 外貨を認識する。
(C) 異なる種類の容器が入れられる。
(D) 硬貨は認識しない。

問題文の訳

設問 160 から 162 は次の広告に関する質問です。

Time Out 自動販売機

Refresh D-02
冷たい飲み物の自動販売機

最新の Refresh D-02 自動販売機は、お客さまにより多くの種類のボトルや缶入りの飲み物を提供します。今や Refresh D-02 自動販売機は、❶炭酸飲料やフルーツジュースからボトル入りの水まで 10 種類の飲み物を積み込むことができます。❷本機は弊社の D-01 モデルの最新型ですが、やはり取り外し可能なバックライトディスプレイがついており、ブランド構築や価格設定に便利です。本機の簡単投入製品棚で、飲み物を入れるのも簡単です。

	仕様
❸ 寸法	高さ 1.8m
	幅 0.8m
	奥行 0.8m
重さ	261kg
飲み物の種類数	10
❹ 標準容量	20 オンスボトル（200 個）
❺ 支払機構	ドル紙幣受付装置
	硬貨受付装置

Refresh D-02 自動販売機の詳細は、555-8591 にお電話いただくか www.timeoutvendors.com をご覧ください。

単語

- vendor 自動販売機
- vending machine 自動販売機
- selection 選択
- load ～を積む
- range およぶ、広がる
- removable 取り外し可能な
- specification 仕様
- dimension 寸法
- capacity 容量
- bill 紙幣
- **160** modify ～を修正する
- **161** storage 貯蔵、保管
- **162** device 装置
- currency 貨幣、通貨
- container 容器

正解 & 解説

160. 正解 (B)　難易度 難

Refresh D-02 という自動販売機について、言及されていることを尋ねる True 問題。❷に「この機械（= Refresh D-02）は D-01 の最新型だ」とある。つまり、**「以前のモデル（D-01）の改良型」**ということなので、(B) が正解。(A) (C) (D) に関する記述は見当たらない。

↻ an update → a modified version

161. 正解 (C)　難易度 難

この広告に、**含まれていない**情報を尋ねる Not 問題。(A) は、❸に Dimensions（寸法）の情報が載っている。(B) は❹「標準容量」、(D) は❶「炭酸飲料、フルーツジュースから水まで 10 種の飲料を積み込める」と、それぞれ記述がある。正解は (C)。レンタル料金に関する記述は見当たらない。

↻ Dimensions → size

162. 正解 (A)　難易度 難

この機械の支払装置について、言及されていることを尋ねる True 問題。設問の payment device（支払装置）を❺の Payment Mechanism 欄に結びつけられれば、正答できる。**Dollar Bill Acceptor**（ドル紙幣受付装置）とあるので、(A) が正解。bill と paper money はともに「**紙幣**」という意味。(C) は、自動販売機そのものに関する記述としては正しいが、支払装置には関係ない。(D) は、❺に Coin Acceptor（硬貨受付装置）とあるので、逆のことを述べている。

↻ Payment Mechanism → payment device
　Bill → paper money

TEST 1
PART 7

Questions 163-165 refer to the following notice.

The Tenth Annual Portland Holiday Gift Fair!

The City of Portland and the Willamette Convention Center are pleased to announce the opening of our Tenth Annual Holiday Gift Fair, running from November 25 to December 8. Open daily from 10 A.M. to 9 P.M. at the convention center on Naito Parkway, the fair will feature products from more than 600 vendors this year. The fair will be held in the center's largest exhibit area, Riverside Hall.

Entrance to the fair is $5 for adults and $3 for children under twelve and senior citizens. There is no admission charge for children under five years of age. Attendees can also take part in hourly draws with more than $18,000 of merchandise to be given away over the course of two weeks! Booths include holiday gifts, decorations, cards, toys, food, and so much more! Get all your holiday supplies ahead of time by visiting this amazing event.

For a list of vendors, please visit www.willamettecon.com/events. Tickets for the fair can be purchased on the Web site beginning November 10.

---

163. For whom is the notice most likely intended?

(A) City officials
(B) Senior citizens
(C) Holiday shoppers
(D) Local gift shop owners

164. What is indicated about the convention center?

(A) It was recently constructed.
(B) It has a seating capacity of 600.
(C) It sells tickets at the door.
(D) It has several exhibit halls.

165. What is NOT mentioned about the event?

(A) It will include free prizes.
(B) It will exhibit a variety of products.
(C) It is free for 10-year-old children.
(D) It is scheduled to last for two weeks.

設問の訳

この告知が対象としているのはおそらく誰か。

(A) 市の役人
(B) 高齢者
(C) 祝日の買い物客
(D) 地域のギフトショップのオーナー

コンベンションセンターについて何が述べられているか。

(A) 最近建設された。
(B) 収容人員600人である。
(C) 入場口でチケットを販売している。
(D) 複数の展示ホールがある。

このイベントについて述べられていないことは何か。

(A) 無料で商品が当たる。
(B) さまざまな商品が陳列されている。
(C) 10才の子どもは入場無料である。
(D) 2週間続く予定である。

TOEIC 豆知識 TOEIC の世界では誰かが retire するとき、かならず retirement party が計画され、サプライズのプレゼントが用意されたりもする。そのやさしさが、ちょっとうらやましい。（続く▶）

問題文の訳

問題 163 から 165 は次の告知に関する質問です。

第 10 回ポートランドホリデーギフトフェア！

ポートランド市と Willamette コンベンションセンターより❶第 10 回ホリデーギフトフェアの開催をお知らせします。開催期間は 11 月 25 日から 12 月 8 日です。当フェアは期間中毎日午前 10 時より午後 9 時まで Naito Parkway のコンベンションセンターで開催され、今年は❷600 社以上の販売会社からの商品が集まります。❸開催場所は同センター最大の展示エリアである Riverside Hall です。

❹当フェアへの入場料は大人 5 ドル、12 才未満の子どもと高齢者は 3 ドルです。❺5 才未満の子どもは入場無料です。また、2 週間の開催期間中、❻入場者は 1 時間ごとに行われる抽選に参加することができ、総額 18,000 ドル以上に相当する商品が当たります。❼各ブースではホリデーギフト、装飾品、カード類、おもちゃ、食品、そのほかさまざまな商品が販売されます。このすてきなイベントに参加して、ひと足先にホリデー用品を手に入れてみませんか。

参加販売会社の一覧は www.willamettecon.com/events で見ることができます。当フェアへの入場チケットはウェブサイトで 11 月 10 日より購入できます。

単語

- □ exhibit 展示会
- □ attendee 参加者
- □ take part in ～ ～に参加する
- □ draw くじ引き
- □ give away ～ ～を贈り物として与える
- **163** □ notice 告知
- **164** □ construct ～を建築する
- □ seating capacity 座席定員

正解＆解説

163. 正解 **(C)**

この告知の対象を尋ねている。告知全体でホリデーギフトフェアの開催情報を扱っている。(C) と (D) で迷うが、❹で、子どもの入場料に言及している点、❼で、祝日用品の購入をうながしている点などから、(C)「**祝日の買い物客**」が適切だと推測できる。(B) Senior citizens は❹に登場するが、高齢者だけを対象としているわけではない。

164. 正解 **(D)**

コンベンションセンターについて、言及されていることを尋ねている。❸に「the center's **largest** exhibit area（センターでもっとも大きい展示エリア）で開催」とある。**もっとも大きい**ということは、「**複数の展示ホールがある**」ということを示唆しているので、(D) が正解。(B) の 600 というのは、出展している企業数（❷）。入場料についての言及はあるが（❹）、入場口でチケットを販売しているとは書いてないので、(C) は誤り。

⇄ exhibit area ➡ exhibit halls

165. 正解 **(C)**

このギフトフェアについて、**言及されていない**ことを尋ねる Not 問題。(A) は❻「商品がプレゼントされる 1 時間ごとの抽選に参加できる」、(B) は❷「600 社以上の商品がある」、(D) は❶「11 月 25 日から 12 月 8 日まで開催」に、それぞれ言及あり。(C) については、❹「12 歳未満は 3 ドル」、❺「5 歳未満は無料」とある。ということは、**10 歳の子どもの入場料は 3 ドル**。従って、(C) が文書の内容と一致しておらず、正解。

⇄ products from more than 600 vendors ➡ a variety of products

TEST 1
PART 7

Questions 166-167 refer to the following e-mail.

E-mail

To:	Jude Feldstein <jfeldstein@lbm.com>
From:	Janina Winslow <customerservice@mycel.com>
Date:	December 20
Subject:	Poor reception

Dear Mr. Feldstein,

Thank you for informing us about the intermittent reception that you have been experiencing with our wireless phone service for the past few days. You wanted us to explain what the problem was and also asked for a discount on your service fee for this month.

First, we believe that this problem is due to the ongoing repair work on our cell phone towers in the Mountainview area, which were severely damaged during the recent snowstorm. Our maintenance crew is already working around the clock in order to fix the problem. Rest assured that normal service will resume at the soonest possible time.

And in regard to your second inquiry, I would first like to apologize for the inconvenience. Because you are a valued customer, we are deducting $15 from your next billing statement. We hope that this addresses the amount of trouble our service has caused you.

We hope that you continue using MyCel as your wireless service provider.

Sincerely,

Janina Winslow
MyCel Customer Service

---

166. What is the purpose of the e-mail?

(A) To inform a customer of a work date
(B) To report an Internet connection problem
(C) To respond to a customer's request
(D) To persuade a customer to renew a subscription

167. What did Ms. Winslow offer to provide Mr. Feldstein?

(A) An extended service contract
(B) A day's worth of free phone calls
(C) A revised line of credit
(D) A reduction on a monthly charge

TOEIC豆知識 retire は「退職する」／ retirement party は「退職記念パーティー」という意味。

問題文の訳

設問 166 から 167 は次の E メールに関する質問です。

宛先： Jude Feldstein <jfeldstein@lbm.com>
送信者： Janina Winslow <customerservice@mycel.com>
日付： 12月20日
件名： 受信障害

Feldstein さま

この数日間、私どもの携帯電話サービスが❶つながりにくくなっている旨をご連絡くださりありがとうございます。❷この受信障害についての説明と今月の使用料の割引をご希望とのことでした。

まず、今回の障害は Mountainview 地区で行われている中継塔の修理に起因するものと思われます。この中継塔は先日の吹雪で深刻な被害を受けたものです。弊社のメンテナンススタッフがすでに 24 時間態勢で問題の解決に当たっています。通常のサービスは可能なかぎり早く再開の予定ですのでご安心ください。

2 点目の問い合わせに関してですが、まずご不便をおかけしましたことをお詫びいたします。Feldstein さまは大切なお客さまですので、❸次回請求書から 15 ドルを差し引かせていただきます。この割引をもってご不便をおかけしたお詫びとさせていただきたく存じます。

今後も MyCel 携帯電話サービスをお使いいただければ幸いです。

敬具

Janina Winslow
MyCel お客さまサービス

単語

- □ reception 受信の状態
- □ intermittent 断続的な
- □ severely きびしく、ひどく
- □ damage 〜に被害を与える
- □ snowstorm 吹雪
- □ around the clock 24 時間通して
- □ rest assured 安心する
- □ resume 再開する
- □ deduct 〜を差し引く
- □ address 〜に対処する
- **166** □ inform 〜に知らせる
  - □ report 〜を報告する
  - □ persuade 〜を説得して（…）させる
  - □ renew 〜を更新する
- **167** □ revise 〜を改訂する
  - □ line of credit 信用限度

正解＆解説

166. 正解 **(C)** 難易度 ■■■□□ 難

E メールの目的を尋ねている。このように主題を問う設問では、文書の**冒頭部分に答えが来る**場合が多い。❶で受信障害（intermittent reception）に関する顧客の報告に対し、お礼を述べている。続けて❷で、この問題に対する説明と料金の割引を顧客が要求していることに言及し、以降、この要求に応えている。従って、(C) の**「顧客の要求に対応する」**が正解。

167. 正解 **(D)** 難易度 ■■□□□ 難

Winslow さんが、Feldstein さんに提案したことを尋ねている。❸に「次回請求から **15 ドルを差し引く**」と提案している。これを A reduction on a monthly charge（月額使用料金の割引）と言い換えた (D) が正解。

⇨ deducting $15 from your next billing statement ➡ A reduction on a monthly charge

TEST 1
PART 7

Questions 168-171 refer to the following article.

TV Station to Air New Shows

LBN Channel 5, the country's largest media corporation and most popular broadcast network, hopes to revive its flagging prime time ratings next season with the airing of two new television series, *Vanished* and *Casual Living*.

Vanished revolves around a law enforcement unit in Chicago that specializes in cases of missing persons. However, unlike other crime dramas, each episode of the program is based on real-life events. Lead character Johnny Slack (played by actor Dennis Javier) and his team of detectives struggle to solve mysterious disappearances in a short amount of time. *Vanished* will air every Thursday at 9:30 P.M.

Meanwhile, on the reality program *Casual Living*, actor and restaurant chain heir Brent Masterson gives up his privileged lifestyle and travels to a remote ranch in the small town of Banchetta. There he must take up residence with the Holsten family and learn to adjust to simple life on a farm. His experience leads him to realize that nothing is ever as easy as it looks. *Casual Living* airs every Sunday at 8:00 P.M.

168. What is the article about?

(A) A local law enforcement unit
(B) Information about a famous actor
(C) The reorganization of a media network
(D) Future television programs

169. What is indicated about *Vanished*?

(A) It will be aired at 8 P.M.
(B) It will be hosted by Brent Masterson.
(C) It is based on authentic cases.
(D) It is about life in a small town.

170. What is NOT mentioned about LBN?

(A) Its prime time ratings have been low.
(B) It produces critically acclaimed TV programs.
(C) It is a popular channel among viewers.
(D) Its media business is the biggest in the nation.

171. What does the article indicate about *Casual Living*?

(A) The first season will be filmed in Chicago.
(B) It will depict a person's real-life experiences.
(C) Each episode is about one hour long.
(D) It shows how the Holsten family run a restaurant.

設問の訳

168. この記事は何に関するものか。
　(A) ある地方の警察組織
　(B) 有名な俳優に関する情報
　(C) メディアネットワークの再編
　(D) 今後のテレビ番組

169. Vanished について何が述べられているか。
　(A) 午後8時から放送される。
　(B) Brent Masterson が司会者である。
　(C) 実際の事件に基づいている。
　(D) 小さな町での生活を描いたものである。

170. LBN について述べられていないことは何か。
　(A) ゴールデンタイムの視聴率が低調である。
　(B) 識者に評価の高い番組を製作している。
　(C) 視聴者に人気のあるチャンネルである。
　(D) メディア業界の国内最大手である。

171. この記事は Casual Living について何を述べているか。
　(A) 第1シーズンはシカゴで撮影される。
　(B) ある人物の実体験を描いている。
　(C) 各回およそ1時間である。
　(D) Holsten 家のレストラン経営ぶりが描かれる。

単語

- revive 〜を回復させる
- flagging 沈滞気味の、衰えた
- prime time ゴールデンタイム
- revolve around 〜 〜を中心に展開する
- law enforcement 警察組織
- specialize in 〜 〜を専門に扱う
- detective 刑事
- struggle 奮闘する
- disappearance 失踪
- air 放送される
- meanwhile 一方で
- heir 後継者、相続人
- privileged 特権に恵まれている
- remote 人里離れた
- ranch 農場
- take up residence 居を定める
- **169** authentic ほんとうの、本物の
- **170** critically 批評的に
- **171** depict 〜を描く

問題文の訳と解説 ☞ 次ページに続く

TEST 1 PART 7

問題文の訳

設問168から171は次の記事に関する質問です。

テレビ局の新番組

❶国内最大手のメディア企業であり、もっとも人気のある放送局LBN Channel 5は、❷低迷気味のゴールデンタイム視聴率を次のクールで回復するため、VanishedとCasual Livingという2つの新番組を放送する。

❸Vanishedは行方不明事件を専門とするシカゴの警察のいち部署を中心に展開する。しかし、ほかの刑事ドラマと異なり、❹番組内のエピソードは実在の出来事に基づいたものとなっている。主人公のJohnny Slack（Dennis Javierが演じる）と彼が指揮をとる刑事チームが謎の失踪事件の早期解決に奮闘する。❺Vanishedは毎週木曜午後9時半より放送。

一方で、❻リアリティー番組のCasual Livingでは、俳優兼レストランチェーンの跡取り息子であるBrent Mastersonが恵まれた生活を捨てて、Banchettaという小さな町の人里離れた農場に移住する。そこで彼はHolsten家と生活をともにし、農場での素朴な生活に順応していかなければならない。こうした経験を通して、何事も見た目ほどは決して簡単ではないということを彼は学ぶ。Casual Livingは毎週日曜午後8時から放送される。

正解＆解説

168. 正解 (D) 難易度 ■■□□ 難

記事のテーマを尋ねているので、**冒頭部分を重点的に確認**する。❶❷で「LBN Channel 5が **two new television series**（ふたつの新しいテレビ番組）で、次シーズンの視聴率回復を狙っている」と述べている。以降、この2番組の説明が続くので、「今後のテレビ番組」とした (D) Future television programs が正解。(A) の「ある地方の警察組織」は、新番組のひとつ Vanished の舞台。

169. 正解 (C) 難易度 ■■□□ 難

新番組の Vanished について、言及されていることを尋ねる True 問題。(A) は、❺「午後9時半から」に一致しない。(B) の Brent Masterson は、❻「Casual Living の登場人物」とある。❹で「番組内（＝ Vanished）のエピソードは**実際の出来事に基づいている**」とあるので、(C)「実際の事件に基づいている」が正解。(D) は❸で「シカゴの警察」を舞台にするとあり、誤り。

↻ real-life events ➡ authentic cases

170. 正解 (B) 難易度 ■■■□ 難

LBN について、**言及されていない**ことを尋ねる Not 問題。(A) は、❷に「低迷するゴールデンタイム視聴率の回復を期す」とある。(B) の「**識者に評価の高い番組を製作している**」については記述がないので、これが正解。(C) と (D) は、❶「国内最大手のメディア企業であり、もっとも人気のある放送局」と、それぞれ言及されている。

↻ the country's largest media corporation ➡ Its media business is the biggest in the nation

171. 正解 (B) 難易度 ■■■□ 難

Casual Living について、言及されていることを尋ねる True 問題。(A) のシカゴは Vanished のほうの舞台（❸）。(B) の「**ある人物の実体験を描いている**」は、❻の the reality program（リアリティ番組）だけでも選べるが、続く「Brent Masterson が恵まれた生活を捨て、人里離れた農場に移住する」という内容から、正解とわかる。(C) の放送時間についての記述はなし。(D) の Holsten 家の職業についても、具体的記述はない。

TEST 1
PART 7

Questions 172-175 refer to the following article.

Business Icon Tells of Journey Up the Ladder
By Ruby Wang

BEIJING—Behind the success of the Shanghai Marketing Association is a tough man of humble beginnings. President Gino Chen's valued professional advice, which has helped hundreds of businesses, did not come from books, but from his experience as an employee at a multinational firm.

Chen began his career at Keaston Corporation, a US food manufacturer. During that time, China was in the process of opening up its economy to foreign investors, and Keaston was one of the first multinational firms to expand into the mainland. Chen believed that Keaston used unconventional methods of employee training and work processes and that landing a job at the firm would give him the experience crucial to his career growth.

Chen's first job as a sales representative for Keaston had him driving a van around Beijing delivering meat products to groceries and small retailers.

"The job was difficult, but I was never disheartened. In fact, it helped me appreciate the importance of hard work as well as good communication and people skills," Chen said. "The job prepared me to handle greater responsibilities in the company."

After ten years of fieldwork, Chen was promoted to provincial sales director, managing several branches of the company. In 1998, he became the regional sales chief for East Asia, and by the time he retired, he was the general manager for South Pacific Asia with twenty-five years of experience in the retail industry.

Now the sixty-seven-year-old devotes a lot of his time to speaking to leading groups of entrepreneurs and sales executives around the globe, in an effort to enhance the marketing techniques of their businesses.

172. Why was the article written?

(A) To discuss marketing trends
(B) To give information about an executive
(C) To provide details about an association
(D) To describe award-winning companies

173. What is stated about Keaston in the article?

(A) It used management systems different from other companies.
(B) It created useful marketing strategies for new businesses.
(C) It merged with a Chinese firm.
(D) It primarily sold fresh produce.

174. What is NOT indicated about Gino Chen in the article?

(A) He started his career as a deliveryman.
(B) He has a lot of experience in the retail sector.
(C) He provides expert advice to businesses.
(D) He often gives lectures to university students.

175. The word "appreciate" in paragraph 4, line 3 is closest in meaning to

(A) upgrade
(B) understand
(C) add
(D) thank

設問の訳

172. なぜこの記事は書かれたか。
(A) マーケット動向を議論するため
(B) ある幹部に関する情報を伝えるため
(C) ある協会の詳細を述べるため
(D) 賞を受賞した企業を解説するため

173. Keaston 社について記事では何が述べられているか。
(A) ほかの企業とは異なった経営システムを用いていた。
(B) 新興企業に有益なマーケティング戦略を立てた。
(C) ある中国企業と合併した。
(D) 生鮮食品を主に販売していた。

174. Gino Chen 氏について記事で述べられていないことは何か。
(A) 配達人としてキャリアのスタートを切った。
(B) 小売部門での経験が豊富である。
(C) 企業に専門家としてのアドバイスを与えている。
(D) 大学生向けの講義を頻繁に行っている。

175. 第4段落・3行目の appreciate にもっとも近い意味の語は
(A) 〜をグレードアップする
(B) 〜を理解する
(C) 〜を加える
(D) 〜に感謝する

単語
- humble （地位が）低い、質素な
- unconventional 常識にとらわれない
- crucial 重要な
- sales representative 営業担当者
- grocery 食料雑貨店
- retailer 小売商
- dishearten 〜を落胆させる
- provincial 省（州）の、地方の
- retail 小売りの
- devote 〜をささげる
- **172** describe 〜を説明する
- **173** merge 合併する
- primarily 主に
- produce 農産物
- **174** sector 部門

TEST 1　PART 7

問題文の訳

設問172から175は次の記事に関する質問です。

ビジネス界の星が出世の道を語る
（Ruby Wang）

北京―❶上海マーケティング協会の成功の立役者は、貧しい地位から身を起こしたタフな男である。❷これまで何百もの企業を支援してきた会長Gino Chen氏の貴重な専門的アドバイスは本から得たものではなく、彼の多国籍企業の社員としての経験に裏打ちされたものである。

Chen氏の経歴は、アメリカの食品製造メーカーであるKeaston社から始まった。当時、中国は海外の投資家に門戸開放を進めており、Keaston社は初めて中国本土への進出を図った多国籍企業のひとつであった。❸Keaston社はほかと一線を画す従業員教育と作業プロセスを用いていたため、同社で働くことができれば、キャリアアップのための貴重な経験を積むことができると彼は考えた。

❹Chen氏は当初、Keaston社の営業としてライトバンに乗って北京市内を駆けまわり、食肉製品を食料雑貨店や小売商に配達して回った。

「仕事は大変なものでしたが、望みを失うことはありませんでした。事実、その仕事は上手に人と接しコミュニケーションをとる能力のほか、ハードワークの大切さも教えてくれたのです。この仕事のおかげで、私は今の会社でのより大きな責任に対処できるようになったのです。」と、Chen氏は述べている。

現場で10年働いたのち、Chen氏は省の営業部長に任ぜられ、複数の同社支店を取り仕切った。1998年には東アジア地域営業担当責任者となった。そして退職時には❺小売業で25年の経験を持つアジア南太平洋担当総責任者であった。

現在、67才のChen氏は世界中の第一線の起業家や経営者向けの講演に多くの時間を費やし、彼らの企業のマーケティング技術を向上させることに努めている。

82

| 正解＆解説 | 間違いメモ |

172. 正解 (B) 難易度 ■■□ 難

記事が書かれた理由を尋ねている。主題に関わる質問なので、**冒頭を重点的に確認**する。❶「上海マーケティング協会の成功の裏には、**タフな男性がいる**」という導入があり、以降、この男性（= Gino Chen）の情報を伝えている。President Gino Chen を an executive と言い換えて、「ある幹部に関する情報を伝えるため」と表現した (B) が正解。

あなたの解答 A B C D
メモ

173. 正解 (A) 難易度 ■■■■□ 難

Keaston 社について、言及されていることを尋ねる True 問題。❸に「Keaston 社は、**ほかと一線を画す**社員教育と業務進行を用いていた」とあるので、これを「ほかの企業とは異なった経営システムを用いていた」と言い換えた (A) が正解。(B) (C) の記述はなし。(D) の生鮮食品については、❹に「Chen 氏は食肉製品を配達した」とあるが、Keaston 社が<u>主に販売していた</u>かどうかは説明されていないので、誤り。

🔁 unconventional methods ➡ systems different from other companies
employee training and work processes ➡ management systems

あなたの解答 A B C D
メモ

174. 正解 (D) 難易度 ■■■□□ 難

Gino Chen 氏について、**述べられていない**ことを尋ねる Not 設問。(A) は❹「Chen 氏の最初の仕事はバンで北京市内を回り食肉製品を配達することだった」、(B) は❺「小売業で 25 年の経験を持つ」、(C) は❷「何百もの企業を支援してきた Gino Chen 会長の専門的アドバイス」と、それぞれ言及されている。(D) の「**大学生向けの講義を頻繁に行っている**」についてはまったく触れられていないので、これが正解。

🔁 professional advice ➡ expert advice

あなたの解答 A B C D
メモ

175. 正解 (B) 難易度 ■■■□□ 難

文書中の appreciate と似た意味の単語を問う類義語問題。文脈 it helped me appreciate the importance of hard work の主語 it は、前パラグラフの「営業担当として北京市内をバンで駆け回って配達した」ことを指している。つまり、「その仕事は、私にハードワークの重要性を〈**理解させて**〉くれた」という文脈なので、「〜を理解する」という意味の (B) understand が正解。

あなたの解答 A B C D
メモ

TEST 1
PART 7

Questions 176-180 refer to the following Web site.

Childsplay Incorporated

| NOTICE | ATTENDANCE | PERSONAL BOARD | SCHEDULE |

Training Materials

- Manuals
- Policies
- Travel Information

Holidays

Open Forum

Part of your duties at Childsplay Inc. will include attending trade fairs not only in the US, but around the world. When planning such trips and participating in these events, it is important to follow this checklist:

- ❶ Confirm with the travel and legal departments that you have all the necessary documents to attend or participate in the event. This includes visas, passports, licenses, and any other required documentation.
- ❷ Make sure to put in detailed requests for transport and hotels to our travel department at least a month in advance.
- Provide a list of contact information for the colleagues in your departments prior to departure.
- Keep all original receipts for any expenses during your travel. Without the receipts, you will not be eligible for reimbursement.
- When attending trade fairs in countries where English is not the first language, make sure at ❸ least one member of your team speaks the local language, or make arrangements to hire an interpreter. Business can be easily lost if we are unable to communicate with potential clients.
- ❹ Read up on local culture and customs. Take some time and ❺ search the Internet for information on the cuisine, history, and geography. Impress potential clients with your knowledge and respect for their culture and heritage.

Email:

Inbox: 2

Links:

- Headquarters
- Accounts
- Marketing
- Production
- Design

176. For whom was the checklist probably written?

(A) Event organizers
(B) New members of staff
(C) Potential clients
(D) Training manager

177. What are readers NOT told to research before traveling abroad?

(A) Local foods
(B) Landscape features
(C) Current governments
(D) Traditional customs

178. Why would an employee contact the legal department?

(A) To get help registering a business
(B) To receive assistance with a contract
(C) To learn about laws in foreign countries
(D) To verify necessary information

179. What is mentioned in the checklist about accommodations?

(A) It is arranged by a travel agent.
(B) It should be located near the trade fair facility.
(C) It must be requested ahead of time.
(D) It does not have to be paid for until the date of arrival.

180. What are international trade fair participants advised to do?

(A) Register at least a month in advance
(B) Make certain they speak the local language
(C) Conduct research on market trends
(D) Hire additional sales staff locally

設問の訳

176. このチェックリストはおそらく誰に向けて作成されたと考えられるか。
(A) イベントの主催者
(B) 新しいスタッフ
(C) 見込み客
(D) 研修部長

177. 海外に行く前に調べるよう指示されていないのは何か。
(A) 地元の食べ物
(B) 地形的特徴
(C) 現在の政府
(D) 伝統的な習慣

178. 従業員はなぜ法務部に連絡するのか。
(A) 会社登記の支援を得るため
(B) 契約の支援を受けるため
(C) 外国の法律について教えてもらうため
(D) 必要な情報を確認するため

179. 宿泊施設についてはチェックリストで何が述べられているか。
(A) 旅行代理店が手配する。
(B) 展示会場の近くにあるはずだ。
(C) 事前に申請しなければならない。
(D) 到着日まで支払う必要がない。

180. 国際展示会への参加者は何をするよう勧められているか。
(A) 遅くとも1カ月前には登録する
(B) 現地のことばが話せることを確認する
(C) 市場トレンドの調査を行う
(D) 現地で追加の営業担当者を雇う

単語

- duty 職務
- legal department 法務部
- put in ～ ～を提出する
- at least 少なくとも
- in advance 事前に
- prior to ～ ～より前に
- receipt 領収書
- be eligible for ～ ～について資格がある
- reimbursement 払い戻し
- interpreter 通訳
- read up on ～ ～について詳しく調べる
- cuisine 料理
- geography 地理
- heritage 伝統
- **177** landscape 地形
- **178** verify ～を確認する
- **179** facility 施設
- ahead of time 事前に
- **180** participant 参加者
- make certain 確認する
- market trend 市場動向

TEST 1 PART 7

問題文の訳

設問176から180は次のウェブサイトに関する質問です。

Childsplay 社

おしらせ | 出席 | 個人掲示板 | 日程

| 研修資料

マニュアル
方針
旅行情報

休日
フォーラム | Childsplay 社での職務には、アメリカ国内のみならず世界中の展示会に参加することが含まれます。これらのイベントに参加する出張を計画する際は、以下のチェックリストに従うことが重要です。

● ❶出張手配部と法務部に確認し、イベント参加、出展に必要な書類が揃っているか確認する。書類には、ビザ、パスポート、免許証やそのほか必要とされる文書を含む。

● ❷遅くとも1カ月前には、交通手段やホテルの詳しい希望内容を出張手配部まで提出すること。

● 連絡先の一覧を出発前に所属部の同僚に知らせること。

● 出張中は、全出費の領収証の原本を保管しておくこと。領収証がないと精算できない。

● 英語が第一言語でない国で展示会に参加する場合、❸チームの中の少なくともひとりは現地語を話す人にするか、通訳を雇う手配をすること。見込み客と意思疎通がとれなければ仕事は取れない。

● ❹現地の文化と習慣を調べること。時間をとって、❺インターネットで料理、歴史、地理について調査すること。見込み客に彼らの文化や伝統に対する理解や尊敬の念を示し印象付けること。 | E メール
受信箱：2

リンク：
本社
経理部
マーケティング部
製造部
設計部 |

TOEIC豆知識 TOEICの世界では男女平等が浸透していて、女性が上司で、男性が秘書ということも当たり前。(続く▶)

正解＆解説

176. 正解 **(B)** 難易度 ▬▬▬ 難

このチェックリストの対象者を推論させる設問。明確なヒントは見当たらないが、全体を通してChildsplay社の**社員が出張する際に守るべきポイントを指示**している。選択肢の中で、こうした情報を必要とするのは(B)の**「新しいスタッフ」**だろうと推測できる。

177. 正解 **(C)** 難易度 ▬▬▬ 難

海外に行く前に調べるよう**指示されていない**ことを尋ねるNot問題。(A)と(B)については、❺で「食事、歴史、地理についてインターネットで調査すること」と指示されている。(C)の**「現在の政府」**に関する指示はどこにも見当たらないので、これが正解。(D)は、❹「現地の文化と習慣を調べること」とある。

⇄ the cuisine ➡ foods
　geography ➡ Landscape

178. 正解 **(D)** 難易度 ▬▬▬ 難

従業員が法務部に連絡する理由を尋ねている。設問のキーであるcontact the legal departmentを手掛かりに、❶のConfirm with ... the legal departmentsを見つけられるとわかりやすい。**「必要な書類が揃っているかを出張手配部と法務部に確認する」**とあるので、documents（書類）をinformation（情報）と言い換えて表現した(D)「必要な情報を確認するため」が正解。

⇄ Confirm with the ... legal departments ➡ contact the legal department

179. 正解 **(C)** 難易度 ▬▬▬ 難

宿泊施設について、言及されていることを尋ねるTrue問題。❷の**「遅くとも1カ月前に、交通手段とホテルについての希望を出張手配部に提出すること」**を、「事前に申請しなければならない」と簡潔に表現した(C)が正解。ほかの選択肢については記述なし。

⇄ in advance ➡ ahead of time

180. 正解 **(B)** 難易度 ▬▬▬ 難

国際展示会への参加者が勧められていることを尋ねている。❸に「チームの少なくともひとりは**現地語を話せるように**」とある。よって(B)「現地のことばが話せることを確認する」が正解。ホテルや交通手段の希望提出と混同して、(A)を選ばないように。

間違いメモ

あなたの解答 A B C D
メモ

あなたの解答 A B C D
メモ

あなたの解答 A B C D
メモ

あなたの解答 A B C D
メモ

あなたの解答 A B C D
メモ

TEST 1
PART 7

Questions 181-185 refer to the following e-mail and list.

E-mail

To:	dee_stewart@highlandsmail.com
From:	custserv@fionnantiques.com
Date:	February 8
Subject:	Fionn's latest acquisitions

Dear Ms. Stewart,

We are pleased to inform you that Fionn Antiques has recently acquired some valuable items that date from the 17th through the 19th centuries. As one of our most valued clients, you have the privilege to purchase any of the items before we put them on display in our store.

Attached you will find the descriptions and prices of our newest acquisitions. Please note that the item made in France is discounted by 10 percent. As always, you can place your order either by filling out our online form or by calling us at 555-7311. Domestic delivery takes five business days, while international orders are shipped in seven to fourteen days.

We look forward to your continued patronage.

Fionn Antiques
February Acquisitions

Estrela Ceramic Vase
This exquisite work of art was handmade in Portugal in 1845. The vase has the look of a woven basket skilfully rendered by the artist. The flowers at the center are colorful and highly detailed, with flowing and overlapping petals that are very difficult to mold. Price: $420

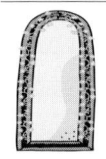

Quadri Rosewood Mirror
This deeply carved 18th-century Italian mirror has retained its warm, bleached wood tone. The sturdy rosewood edges depict luscious leaves, and the glass mirror is antiqued with fine specks. Price: $2,250

Werdenstil Oak Cabinet
This 17th-century cabinet from Austria is made of oak, with a crosshatched see-through panel at the top and a carved sun at the bottom of the door. The interior is fitted with two shelves. Price: $1,845

Anduze Crystal Candleholder
This beautifully crafted piece is considered one of the finest examples of 19th-century French glasswork. The candleholder stands 10.25 inches high and has a base of 4.75 inches in diameter. Its simple yet elegant design makes it a perfect accent piece for any room. Price: $575

181. What is the purpose of the e-mail?

(A) To promote an auction
(B) To announce a new delivery service
(C) To advertise several products
(D) To verify purchase information

182. What is indicated about Fionn Antiques?

(A) It offers a selection of contemporary furnishings.
(B) It operates several international retail outlets.
(C) It conducts some of its business on the Internet.
(D) It specializes in items from the 19th-century.

183. What is true about Ms. Stewart?

(A) She will place her order online.
(B) She is organizing an antiques auction.
(C) She has purchased from Fionn Antiques before.
(D) She recently inquired about the status of her order.

184. What is stated about the vase?

(A) It was hand-carved from rosewood.
(B) It was not easy to produce.
(C) It will require special shipping services.
(D) It was manufactured in a Portuguese factory.

185. What item is available at a reduced price?

(A) The vase
(B) The mirror
(C) The cabinet
(D) The candleholder

設問の訳

181. この E メールの目的は何か。
 (A) オークションを宣伝すること
 (B) 新しい配送サービスを告知すること
 (C) いくつかの商品を宣伝すること
 (D) 購入情報を確認すること

182. Fionn 骨董店について何が述べられているか。
 (A) 現代的な家具を取りそろえている。
 (B) 海外で小売店舗を複数経営している。
 (C) インターネット上でも営業している。
 (D) 19 世紀製の品々を専門的に取り扱っている。

183. Stewart さんについて正しいことは何か。
 (A) オンラインで注文するだろう。
 (B) アンティークのオークションを主催している。
 (C) 以前 Fionn 骨董店を利用したことがある。
 (D) 最近注文の状況を問い合わせた。

184. 花びんについて何が述べられているか。
 (A) 紫檀の手彫りである。
 (B) 制作は容易ではなかった。
 (C) 特別な配送サービスが必要である。
 (D) ポルトガルの工場で製造された。

185. 割引価格で購入できるのはどの商品か。
 (A) 花びん
 (B) 鏡
 (C) キャビネット
 (D) ろうそく立て

単語
- acquisition 入手
- acquire ～を得る
- valuable 貴重な
- privilege 特権
- on display 陳列して
- description 説明
- note ～に気をつける
- ship ～を出荷する
- patronage 愛顧
  ***
- exquisite 精巧な

- render ～を表現する
- flow 流れる
- overlap 重なり合う
- petal 花弁
- mold ～を作る
- carve ～を彫刻する
- retain ～を残す
- sturdy 頑丈な
- depict ～を描く
- luscious あでやかな
- fit ～を取り付ける

- diameter 直径
- yet それにもかかわらず
- **182** contemporary 現代的な
- furnishings 家具調度品
- operate ～を経営する
- retail outlet 小売店
- **183** status 状況
- **184** manufacture ～を製造する
- **185** reduced 減らした

問題文の訳と解説 ☞ 次ページに続く

TEST 1 PART 7

問題文の訳

設問 181 から 185 は次の E メールとリストに関する質問です。

宛先： dee_stewart@highlandsmail.com
送信者： custserv@fionnantiques.com
日付： 2月8日
件名： Fionn の最新入荷

Stewart さま

❶Fionn 骨董店にこのほど 17 世紀から 19 世紀に制作された貴重な品々を入荷いたしましたのでご連絡差し上げます。 ❷当店随一のお得意さまである Stewart さまには、新入荷商品はどれでも、店頭に並べる前にご購入いただく権利がございます。

添付のリストで、最新入荷商品の説明と価格をご覧いただけます。 ❸フランス製商品は 10% の割引となっております。 ❹これまでと同様、オンラインフォームへの記入か、555-7311 へのお電話にてご注文いただけます。国内配送には 5 営業日、国際配送には 7 日から 14 日のお時間をいただきます。

今後も変わりなきご愛顧の程をお願いいたします。

Fionn 骨董店
2月の入荷商品

❺Estrela 陶製花びん
この精巧な芸術作品は 1845 年にポルトガルで手作りで制作されました。この花びんは熟練した職人の手による手編みバスケットのような外観をしています。 ❻中心にある花は色鮮やかで凝った作りになっており、その流れるように重なりあった花弁の制作は容易なものではありません。価格：420 ドル

Quadri 紫檀枠の鏡
この手の込んだ彫刻の施された 18 世紀のイタリア製鏡は、漂白木の温かい雰囲気を残しています。頑丈な紫檀の縁取りには見事な葉形模様が施されています。ガラスの鏡面は時代がかっており、微細な斑点が見られます。価格：2,250 ドル

Werdenstil オーク材キャビネット
この 17 世紀オーストリア製のキャビネットにはオーク材が用いられています。ドアの上部には網目状透かし彫りの羽目板が使われており、下部には太陽の彫刻が施されています。内側には 2 段の棚が備え付けられています。価格：1,845 ドル

❼Anduze クリスタルろうそく立て
この丹念に美しく作り上げられた作品は 19 世紀❽フランスガラス工芸の極致といえます。このろうそく立ては高さ 10.25 インチで土台は直径 4.75 インチです。シンプルでありながら優美なその造形はどのようなお部屋のアクセントとしても最適です。価格：575 ドル

TOEIC豆知識 加えて、環境意識も非常に高い！ たとえば、ホテル建設の入札で、environmentally friendly な設計案が採用されたりする。（続く▶）

正解＆解説

181. 正解 (C) 難易度：難

Eメールの目的を尋ねている。主題に関わる設問なので、**冒頭を注意深く読む。**❶で「最近、貴重な品々が入荷したのでご連絡します」と導入し、以降、新入荷商品の購入をうながす内容が続く。このことを To advertise several products（いくつかの商品を宣伝すること）と表現した (C) が正解。

182. 正解 (C) 難易度：難

Fionn 骨董店について、述べられていることを尋ねる True 問題。❹に「**オンラインフォームへの記入**か、電話での注文ができる」とある。このことから「**インターネット上でも営業している**」ことがうかがえるので、(C) が正解。(A) は contemporary（現代の）部分が誤り。(B) に関する記述はなし。(D) は❶に続く部分で date from the 17th through the 19th centuries（17世紀から19世紀に属する）とあるので、誤り。

183. 正解 (C) 難易度：難

Stewart さんについての正しい情報を尋ねる True 問題。まず❷で「もっとも大切なお客さまのひとりとして」とあり、Stewart さんが**お得意さま**であることがうかがえる。また、❹で As always（従来どおり）と述べたあと、オンラインと電話で購入できると言っている。つまり、「**以前 Fionn 骨董店を利用したことがある**」と推測できるので、(C) が正解。(A)(B)(D) についての記述はなし。

184. 正解 (B) 難易度：難

花びんについて、述べられていることを尋ねる True 問題。まず、設問の the Vase がどの商品かを特定する。リストの商品名を見ると、花びんは❺の「Estrela 陶製花びん」しかないので、その解説を読むと、(A) は「紫檀製」という部分が誤り。❻に「流れるように重なりあう花弁の**制作は容易ではない**」とあるので、(B) の「制作は容易ではなかった」が正解。(C) についての記述はない。(D) は、「工場で作られた」が誤り。この花びんは handmade（手作りの）と書かれている。

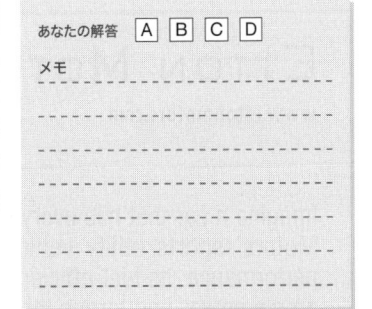

🔄 very difficult to mold ➡ not easy to produce

185. 正解 (D) 難易度：難

ふたつの文書に分散した情報を関連付けて答える**クロスリファレンス問題**。割引価格で購入できる商品を尋ねているが、まずメールの❸に「**フランス製のもの**は10％引き」とある。しかし、メールでは、フランス製の商品が何なのか触れられていない。商品リストに目を移し、フランス製のものを探すと、❽に「**フランスのガラス工芸**」とあるので、「Anduze クリスタル**ろうそく立て**」がフランス製だとわかる。これらを考え合わせて、割引されるのは (D) The candleholder。

TEST 1
PART 7

Questions 186-190 refer to the following e-mail and advertisement.

E-mail

From:	Charlie Davidson <charlie_davidson@quicksend.com>
To:	Michael Bell <mbell@ettonmotors.com>
Date:	December 1
Subject:	Car inquiry

Dear Mr. Bell,

I recently saw an advertisement for some of your vehicles in a newspaper. I am currently based in Qatar, and will be coming to London for the holidays. During my vacation, I plan to buy a new car for my family. I'm looking for one that has reliable safety features and requires little maintenance. As I live in Qatar, I also need a vehicle that can handle extreme heat and has a strong air conditioning system.

I actually tried checking your Web site to get some additional details on your sports utility vehicles, but unfortunately I was unable to download the description pages. I was wondering if you could send me information about the vehicles you carry to my e-mail, as I would like to study my options before I leave.

I will arrive on December 20 and stay in London for two weeks only. Please send me the information as soon as possible so that I may select which vehicles I would like to schedule for a test drive in advance. I would also be pleased to receive a list of requirements and options about payment terms.

Thank you and I hope to hear from you soon.

Sincerely,

Charlie Davidson
Contract Manager
Hani Rashid Corporation
Office phone: (00947) 555-2941

ETTON MOTORS
www.ettonmotors.com

Imagine a car that has everything you need for safe and convenient driving. A new addition to Etton Motors' sports utility vehicles, Nervo 200 was especially designed for outstanding off-road performance. Its fuel-efficient and low-emission 2.5-liter diesel engine has the capacity to produce ample power and torque for high-speed cruising.

Nervo 200 also boasts superior security features. The car's body has front and side impact beams that protect the interior from collisions. Rated five stars by the International Transport Safety Laboratory, the car is equipped with antilock brakes and an electronic stability control that detects and minimizes skids, preventing accidents on slippery surfaces.

Nervo 200 perfectly suits individuals with simple and practical tastes, as it includes all the features of a standard sports utility vehicle-automatic windows, a door lock system, power steering, fold-down rear seats, and a digital stereo, among others. Take a ride in a Nervo 200 at the Etton Motors dealer nearest you. To schedule a test drive, please call our customer hotline at 555-0999.

186. Why did Mr. Davidson write to Mr. Bell?
    (A) To postpone an upcoming test drive
    (B) To submit some required information
    (C) To explain what type of product he is looking for
    (D) To file a complaint about a vehicle

187. What is implied about Mr. Davidson?
    (A) He is relocating to London in two weeks.
    (B) He is paying in monthly installments.
    (C) He has insufficient funds for the Nervo 200.
    (D) He has limited time to purchase a vehicle.

188. What feature of the Nervo 200 meets Mr. Davidson's standards?
    (A) It requires little upkeep.
    (B) It consumes a small amount of fuel.
    (C) It is highly rated for safety.
    (D) It comes with a stereo system.

189. What is NOT indicated about Etton Motors?
    (A) It offers vehicle test drives to customers.
    (B) It operates several different dealerships.
    (C) It has additional product information on a Web site.
    (D) It is opening a repair and maintenance center.

190. In the advertisement, the word "boasts" in paragraph 2, line 1 is closest in meaning to
    (A) improves
    (B) possesses
    (C) widens
    (D) adds

設問の訳

186. なぜ Davidson 氏は Bell 氏に（E メールを）書いたのか。
    (A) 予定していた試乗を延期するため
    (B) 必要とされる情報を提出するため
    (C) どのようなタイプの商品を探しているのか説明するため
    (D) 自動車に関するクレームを送るため

187. Davidson 氏に関して何が示唆されているか。
    (A) 2週間後にロンドンに引っ越す。
    (B) 月賦で支払いをする。
    (C) Nervo 200 購入のための資金が不足している。
    (D) 自動車購入のための時間に余裕がない。

188. Nervo 200 のどんな特徴が Davidson 氏の要求に合致するか。
    (A) 維持費がほとんどかからない。
    (B) あまり燃料を消費しない。
    (C) 安全性能が高く評価されている。
    (D) ステレオシステムが装備されている。

189. Etton Motors 社に関して述べられていないことは何か。
    (A) 顧客に試乗サービスを提供している。
    (B) 複数の取り扱い店舗を運営している。
    (C) ウェブサイトに商品の詳細情報を掲載している。
    (D) 修理・メンテナンスセンターをオープンする予定である。

190. 広告の第2段落・1行目の boasts にもっとも近い意味の語は
    (A) 〜を改良する
    (B) 〜を所有する
    (C) 〜を広げる
    (D) 〜を加える

単語
- based 〜に拠点のある
- reliable 信頼できる
- sports utility vehicle スポーツ用多目的車
- description 説明
- option 選択肢
- term 条件
  ***
- outstanding 卓越した
- performance 性能
- emission 排気
- ample 十分な
- beam 梁、ビーム
- collision 衝突
- be equipped with 〜が備わっている
- detect 〜を感知する
- prevent 〜を防ぐ

186.
- postpone 〜を延期する
- file 〜を申し立てる

187.
- in installments 分割払いで

188.
- standard 基準
- upkeep 維持費
- consume 〜を消費する

問題文の訳と解説 ☞ 次ページに続く

TEST 1 PART 7

問題文の訳

問題186から190は次のEメールと広告に関する質問です。

送信者： Charlie Davidson <charlie_davidson@quicksend.com>
宛先： Michael Bell <mbell@ettonmotors.com>
日付： 12月1日
件名： 車に関する問い合わせ

Bell さま

先日、貴社が新聞に掲載されていた何台かの自動車の広告を拝見しました。私は現在カタールに居住しており、❶休暇でロンドンに帰る予定です。❷休暇中、家族のために新車を購入するつもりです。❸私が探しているのは信頼できる安全機能を備えていて、メンテナンスに手がかからないものです。また、カタールに住んでいるので、❹酷暑に対応でき、強力なエアコンを装備する車も探しています。

❺貴社のウェブサイトを拝見した際、販売されているSUV（スポーツ用多目的車）に関する詳細情報を手に入れようとしましたが、残念なことに商品説明のページをダウンロードできませんでした。もし販売されている自動車に関する情報をEメールで送っていただければ、出発前にどのような商品を選ぶべきか考えておくことができるのですが、よろしいでしょうか。

12月20日に❻ロンドンに到着しますが、滞在は2週間のみです。情報をできるだけ早くお送りください。そうすれば、前もって試乗の予約をしたい車を選ぶことができます。また、支払い条件に関する必要事項と選択肢の記載されたリストもお送りいただければと思います。

それではお返事お待ちしております。
敬具

Charlie Davidson
契約担当部長
Hani Rashid 社
電話：(00947)555-2941

Etton Motors
www.ettonmotors.com

安全で快適なドライブに必要なものがすべてそろった車はいかがですか。Etton Motors の SUV に新たに加わった Nervo 200は、卓越したオフロード性能を持つべく特別に設計されました。低燃費かつ低排出の2.5リッターディーゼルエンジンは高速ドライブにも十分な馬力とトルクを発揮します。

❼また、Nervo 200には優れた安全装備が充実しています。車体にはフロントとサイドにインパクトビームを備えており、衝突から車内を保護します。❽国際交通安全研究所による5つ星の評価を受けたこの車には、アンチロックブレーキシステムのほか、横滑りを感知し最小限にとどめ、滑りやすい路面での事故を防止する電子安定制御装置が備わっています。

Nervo 200はパワーウィンドウ、集中ドアロック、パワーステアリング、可倒式リアシート、デジタルオーディオシステムなど、標準的SUVの特徴をすべて兼ね備えており、シンプルで実用性を好むお客さまに完璧にマッチします。❾最寄りの Etton Motors 販売店で Nervo 200 にご試乗ください。❿試乗のご予約は、当社カスタマーセンター直通電話555-0999へご一報ください。

> **TOEIC豆知識** environmentally friendly は「環境にやさしい」。さらに、チャリティにも熱心なので、fundraising イベントがそこかしこで開催されている。なんとも健康的で、友愛に満ちた世界なのである。（続く▶）

正解＆解説

186. 正解 (C) 難易度

Davidson 氏が Bell 氏に E メールを書いた理由を尋ねている。主題に関わる設問なので、メール**冒頭を注意深く読もう**。❷❸に「家族のために車を購入したい」「信頼できる安全機能を備え、メンテナンスのいらないものを探している」とあり、以降も**どのような車を探しているのかの説明**が続く。このことを、車を product（商品）に言い換えて「どのようなタイプの商品を探しているのか説明するため」と表現した (C) が正解。

187. 正解 (D) 難易度

Davidson 氏について類推できることを尋ねている。❶「休暇でロンドンに行く」、❷「休暇中、車を購入したい」、❻「ロンドンへの滞在は2週間のみ」といった情報から推論し、(D) の**自動車購入のための時間に余裕がない**を選ぶことができる。London、two weeks という断片的な情報だけで (A)「2週間後にロンドンに引っ越す」を選ばないように。

188. 正解 (C) 難易度

クロスリファレンス問題。Davidson 氏の要求を満たす Nervo 200 の特徴を尋ねているので、まず、Davidson 氏の要求をメールから探す。すると、❸と❹で「信頼できる安全機能」「あまりメンテナンスを必要としない」「酷暑に対応」「強力なエアコン」という4点がある。これらを満たす Nervo 200 の特徴を広告から探すと、❼「優れた安全装置を備える」、❽「国際交通安全研究所による**5つ星評価**」とある。これらが、Davidson 氏の「信頼できる安全機能」という要求に合致するので、(C) の「安全性能が高く評価されている」が正解。(A) の「維持費がかからない」は、Davidson 氏の要求ではあるが、Nervo 200 の特徴としては述べられていない。

189. 正解 (D) 難易度

Etton Motors 社について、**述べられていない**ことを尋ねる Not 問題。(A) は❿「試乗の予約は、直通電話に連絡してほしい」、(B) は❾「最寄りの Etton Motors 販売店で…（※つまり販売店が複数あるということ）」、(C) は❺「詳細情報を得るためにウェブサイトを見た」と、それぞれ言及されている。一方、(D)「**修理・メンテナンスセンターをオープンする予定である**」に関する記述は見当たらないので、これが正解。

190. 正解 (B) 難易度

文書中の boasts と似た意味の単語を問う類義語問題。Nervo 200 also boasts superior security features. において、boasts は「～を持っている」という意味で使われている。従って、「**～を所有する**」という意味の (B) possesses が正解。

TEST 1
PART 7

Questions 191-195 refer to the following Web page and product brochure.

Stop and Sew
For all your dressmaking and tailoring needs

Home | About Us | Locations | **Customer's Page** | Contact Us

- Great finds at
- **Stop and Sew**
- Fabric
- Ribbons
- Laces
- Accessories
- Notions
- Find a product

Dear Stop and Sew,

Congratulations on the opening of your new store!

I have always been a fan of Stop and Sew. My three years of experience as a fashion designer wouldn't have been so successful if it weren't for the unique sewing products available at your store. Your wide selection of textiles for every taste and occasion has always allowed me to be as imaginative and creative as I want.

As always, your store is very well organized with fabrics arranged by purpose and material. On top of that, your knowledgeable salespeople are helpful and provide exceptional assistance. They made some fine recommendations recently as I was picking out textiles for my swimwear collection.

As your business thrives, more customers are bound to hear about your excellent products. I have often observed that your fabric collections quickly sell out at many of your stores. Now that the wedding season is here, many dressmakers and designers like me would be happy if you ensured that all your outlets had sufficient supplies of the fabrics we need for our production.

Thank you and I wish you continued success!

Cheers,

Jenna Palmer

Stop and Sew

Basic Fabric

Cotton
- One hundred percent natural
- Breathable and comfortable to wear
- Machine washable
- Recommended for making shirts

Merino Wool
- Made of the finest and softest wool from Merino sheep
- Breathable and insulating, this will keep people warm in the winter and cool in the summer
- Machine washable
- Recommended for making infant garments, high fashion clothing, and sportswear
- Available in different colors

Silk
- One hundred percent natural
- Lustrous, easy-to-dye fabric with exceptional flow
- Recommended for making night gowns and wedding gowns

Linen
- One hundred percent natural
- Stronger than cotton
- Recommended for making jackets and trousers as well as bed sheets, tablecloths, and curtains

Bamboo
- Made from bamboo fibers
- Environment-friendly
- Has antibacterial properties
- Recommended for making infant clothing and undergarments

Spandex
- Lightweight and highly stretchable
- Resistant to flexing, heat, sunlight, detergent, and perspiration
- Recommended for making foundation garments, swimsuits, skiwear, dance apparel, and skating costumes

191. What does Ms. Palmer like about Stop and Sew?

(A) It arranges textiles by color.
(B) It has exceptional customer service.
(C) It has a wide selection of sewing machines.
(D) It offers helpful dressmaking tutorials.

192. On the Web page, the word "taste" in paragraph 2, line 3 is closest in meaning to

(A) preference
(B) flavor
(C) decision
(D) feeling

193. What kind of textiles did Ms. Palmer buy at Stop and Sew before?

(A) Linen
(B) Bamboo
(C) Silk
(D) Spandex

194. What is indicated about Ms. Palmer?

(A) She needs samples of fabrics.
(B) She is a first-time customer of Stop and Sew.
(C) She is eligible for a bulk order rate.
(D) She may require silk for her work.

195. What is NOT mentioned about Merino wool?

(A) It can be cleaned in a washing machine.
(B) It can be used in clothing for different seasons.
(C) It has antibacterial properties.
(D) It can be used for making athletic clothing.

設問の訳

191. Palmer さんは Stop and Sew 社の何が好きか。
　(A) 布地を色別に並べている。
　(B) 顧客サービスが非常に優れている。
　(C) ミシンの品揃えが豊富である。
　(D) ドレス作りについて有益な指導を提供している。

192. ウェブページの第2段落・3行目の taste にもっとも近い意味の語は
　(A) 好み
　(B) 味
　(C) 決定
　(D) 感覚

193. Palmer さんが以前、Stop and Sew 社で買ったのはどんな布地か。
　(A) リネン
　(B) 竹
　(C) シルク
　(D) スパンデックス

194. Palmer さんについて何が述べられているか。
　(A) 布地のサンプルを必要としている。
　(B) Stop and Sew 社の初めての客である。
　(C) 大量注文割引が利用できる。
　(D) 自分の作品でシルクを必要とするかもしれない。

195. メリノウールについて述べられていないことは何か。
　(A) 洗濯機で洗える。
　(B) 異なる季節の衣料に使える。
　(C) 抗細菌性がある。
　(D) スポーツ用の服に使える。

単語
- sew 〜を縫う
- textile 布地
- fabric 布
- notion 雑貨、裁縫小物
- occasion 機会
- on top of 〜 〜に加えて
- knowledgeable 博識な、精通している
- exceptional 特別の、すぐれた
- thrive 栄える
- be bound to do 必ず〜する運命にある
- now that 〜 今や〜だから
- * * *
- breathable 通気性がよい
- insulate 〜を保温する
- garment 衣類
- environment-friendly 環境にやさしい
- antibacterial 抗菌性の
- property 特性
- undergarment 下着
- resistant 抵抗力がある
- detergent 洗剤
- perspiration 汗、発汗
- 191 tutorial 個別指導
- 194 bulk order 大量注文

問題文の訳と解説 ☞ 次ページに続く

TEST 1 PART 7

問題文の訳

設問191から195は次のウェブページと製品パンフレットに関する質問です。

Stop and Sew
あらゆるドレスと紳士服仕立てのニーズに
ホーム | 会社情報 | 店舗 | お客さまページ | お問い合わせ

掘り出し物を Stop and Sew で 布 リボン レース アクセサリー 雑貨 製品を探す	Stop and Sew さま 新店舗の開店おめでとうございます。 私は以前から Stop and Sew のファンです。私のファッションデザイナーとしての3年間は、そちらのお店で手に入る独自の裁縫用品なしでは、こんなに上手くはいかなかったでしょう。あらゆる好みや場面に対応した豊富な布地の品揃えのおかげで、いつも好きなだけ想像力と創造性を発揮することができています。 お店はいつも、生地が目的別、素材別によく整理されています。❶さらに何にも増して、知識豊富な販売員のみなさんが頼りになり、すごく助けてもらっています。最近も❷水着のコレクション用の布地を選ぶ際に、とてもよいアドバイスをくださいました。 事業が大きくなるにつれて、さらに多くのお客さんが御社の優れた製品のことを知ることになるでしょう。私は今まで、そちらの多くのお店で布地が売り切れになるのを見てきました。❸結婚シーズンが到来したので、制作に必要な布地の在庫をお店に十分確保していただけると、多くのドレスメーカーや私のようなデザイナーとしてはうれしいかぎりです。 ありがとうございます。そして、ますますのご発展をお祈りします。 では。 Jenna Palmer

Stop and Sew
基本的な布地

コットン
- 100% 天然素材
- 通気性がよく着心地もよい
- 洗濯機洗い可能
- シャツの制作におオススメ

メリノウール
- 最上級でもっとも柔らかいメリノ羊の羊毛製
- 通気性、断熱性があり❹冬は暖か、夏は涼しい
- ❺洗濯機洗い可能
- ❻幼児用衣類、高級ファッション衣料、スポーツウェアの制作にオススメ
- さまざまな色をご用意

シルク
- 100% 天然素材
- 光沢がありとてもしなやかな染めやすい布地
- ❼ナイトガウンやウェディングドレスの制作にオススメ

リネン
- 100% 天然素材
- コットンより丈夫
- ジャケット、ズボン、ベッドシーツ、テーブルクロス、カーテンの制作にオススメ

竹
- 竹繊維製
- 環境に優しい
- 抗細菌性
- 幼児服や下着の制作にオススメ

スパンデックス
- 軽量で高い伸縮性
- 屈曲、熱、太陽光、洗剤、発汗に強い
- ❽ファンデーションガーメント（体型を補正する下着）、水着、スキーウェア、ダンス衣装、スケート衣装の制作にオススメ

> TOEIC豆知識　fundraising は「募金集めの」という意味。

正解&解説

191. 正解 (B) 難易度 難

Stop and Sew 社について、Palmer さんが好む点を尋ねている。❶に「何よりも知識豊富な**販売員が頼りになり、助けてもらっている**」とある。これを「**顧客サービスが非常に優れている**」と言い換えた (B) が正解。(D) は、服作りの指導を行っているという記述はないので誤り。

🔁 exceptional assistance ➜ exceptional customer service

192. 正解 (A) 難易度 難

文書中の taste と似た意味の単語を問う類義語問題。wide selection of textiles for every taste and occasion では、「**好み**」という意味で用いられている。これと同じ意味を持つのは、(A) preference。taste には (B) flavor の「味」という意味もあるが、この文脈には合わない。

193. 正解 (D) 難易度 難

Palmer さんが以前購入した布地の種類を尋ねているが、ふたつの文書に分散した情報を関連付けて答える**クロスリファレンス問題**。ウェブサイトには、何を買ったかは述べられていない。ただ❷に「水着コレクション用の布地を選んだ」とある。製品パンフレットに各布地の用途が記されているので、「水着」を探すと、Spandex のところに❸「水着にオススメ」とある。これらを考え合わせると、購入したことがあるのは、「**スパンデックス**」と考えられるので、(D) が正解。

194. 正解 (D) 難易度 難

ひき続き**クロスリファレンス問題**。Palmer さんについて言及されていることを尋ねている。ウェブサイトの❸に「結婚シーズンなので、私のようなデザイナーやドレスメーカーにとっては、製作に必要な布地を十分に在庫してくれるとうれしい」とある。ここから、Palmer さんは結婚に関連する何かを作ろうとしていると推測できる。製品パンフレットに目を移すと、シルクの特徴に❼「ウェディングドレスにオススメ」とある。これらを考え合わせると、Palmer さんは、ドレス制作のために**シルクを必要とするだろう**と推論できる。従って、(D)「自分の作品でシルクを必要とするかもしれない」が正解。

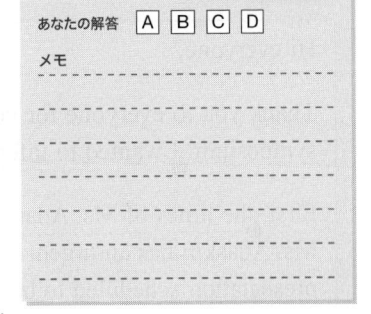

195. 正解 (C) 難易度 難

メリノウールについて、**言及されていない**ことを尋ねる Not 問題。(A) は❺「洗濯機洗い可」、(B) は❹「冬は暖かく、夏は涼しい」、(D) は❻の最後「スポーツウェアにオススメ」と、それぞれ言及されている。(C) の「**抗細菌性がある**」に関する記述が見当たらないので、これが正解（※「抗細菌性」があるのは「竹」）。

TEST 1
PART 7

Questions 196-200 refer to the following program and e-mail.

Reconstructing the Past: Traditions and Transformations
A symposium organized by the
National Consortium of Archaeologists (NCA)

Date: April 29, Wednesday
Venue: Demesne Convention Center

P R O G R A M		
8:00-8:30	Breakfast	
8:30-8:45	Opening Remarks	Saisha Gershon, President, NCA
8:45-10:15	Cultural Heritage and Awareness	Tobias Epstein
10:15-10:30	Intermission	
10:30-12:00	Artifacts and Material Culture	Dinah Adaskin
12:00-1:00	Lunch	
1:00-2:30	Indigenous Landscapes and Seascapes	Gabriel Cramer
2:30-2:45	Intermission	
2:45-4:15	Subsistence and Social Organization	Chantelle Steward
4:15-5:00	Panel Discussion	
5:00-7:00	Cocktail Party	

The deadline for registration is on the first day of April. The registration fee of $175 is inclusive of conference materials and beverages served during breaks. Meal charges for lunch and the cocktail party are not included in the fee and must be paid separately. Accepted payment methods are cash, check, and credit card.

E-mail

To: allmembers@archaeologyconsortium.org
From: frenkel@archaeologyconsortium.org
Subject: NCA Symposium
Date: March 30

Hi everyone,

Thank you to everyone for your support and assistance in organizing our upcoming symposium. I wanted to inform you all of a few changes to the program.

First, the times of Ms. Adaskin's and Mr. Cramer's presentations have been switched because Ms. Adaskin has an urgent business meeting that will run until noon that day. Second, the presentation scheduled to be given by Ms. Steward has been changed. Ms. Steward has been called to report to the Geneva Archaeological Institute to oversee a new project, so she won't be able to attend the event. Her research associate Eden Bettelheim will take her place.

Lastly, those who have not yet registered to the symposium are encouraged to do so as soon as possible. As you all know, this is the first event that our organization has ever coordinated, so we would strongly appreciate the support of all our members.

Sincerely,
Reuben Frenkel

196. What is indicated in the program?

(A) All guest speakers are members of the NCA.
(B) Attendees must pay extra for materials.
(C) Drinks will be offered to guests during intermissions.
(D) There will be a closing speech by the president.

197. What is suggested about Gabriel Cramer's presentation?

(A) It has been removed from the program.
(B) It will be given before the morning break.
(C) It has been rescheduled to an earlier time.
(D) It will be led by a research group.

198. What is the purpose of the e-mail?

(A) To give information on new consortium leaders
(B) To ask for feedback on an activity schedule
(C) To provide updates on an upcoming event
(D) To confirm attendance to a society meeting

199. What time will Ms. Bettelheim most likely start her presentation?

(A) At 8:45 A.M.
(B) At 10:30 A.M.
(C) At 1:00 P.M.
(D) At 2:45 P.M.

200. What is NOT true about the symposium?

(A) It will only charge admission to nonmembers of the consortium.
(B) It requires advance registration.
(C) It does not include a complimentary lunch.
(D) It is the first event to be hosted by the NCA.

設問の訳

196. プログラムで何が述べられているか。
　(A) ゲスト講演者はすべてNCA会員である。
　(B) 参加者は資料代を別途支払わなければならない。
　(C) 休憩中に飲み物が参加者に提供される。
　(D) 会長による閉会スピーチがある。

197. Gabriel Cramer氏の発表について何が示唆されているか。
　(A) プログラムから削除された。
　(B) 午前の休憩前に行われる。
　(C) 早い時間に変更された。
　(D) 研究グループによって進行される。

198. Eメールの目的は何か。
　(A) 新しい協会指導者を紹介すること
　(B) 活動予定への意見を募ること
　(C) 来たるイベントに関する最新情報を提供すること
　(D) 協会の会議への出席を確認すること

199. Bettelheim氏が発表を始めるのは何時と思われるか。
　(A) 午前8：45
　(B) 午前10：30
　(C) 午後1：00
　(D) 午後2：45

200. このシンポジウムについて正しくないのはどれか。
　(A) 協会の非会員のみから参加費を徴収する。
　(B) 事前の登録が必要である。
　(C) 無料の昼食は含まれない。
　(D) NCAが主催する初めてのイベントである。

単語

- reconstruct ～を再構築する
- symposium シンポジウム
- consortium 協会
- archaeologist 考古学者
- venue 会場
- opening remarks 開会のあいさつ
- intermission 休憩
- artifact 工芸品
- material culture 物質文化
- indigenous その土地固有の
- subsistence 必要最低限の生活
- inclusive of ～ ～を含めて
- accepted 容認された
- payment method 支払い方法
- switch ～を交換する
- urgent 緊急の
- institute 学会、研究機関
- oversee ～を監督する
- associate 同僚
- take one's place ～の代わりをする
- be encouraged to do ～するように奨励される
- **198** update 最新情報

TEST 1 PART 7

問題文の訳

設問 196 から 200 は次のプログラムと E メールに関する質問です。

過去を再構築：伝統と変革
シンポジウム
全国考古学者協会 (NCA) 主催

日付： ❶4月29日　水曜日
会場：Demesne コンベンションセンター

プログラム		
8:00–8:30	朝食	
8:30–8:45	開会の言葉	Saisha Gershon、NCA 会長
8:45–10:15	文化的遺産と気づき	Tobias Epstein
10:15–10:30	休憩	
❷10:30–12:00	工芸品と物質文化	Dinah Adaskin
12:00–1:00	昼食	
❸1:00–2:30	地域固有の風景と海景	Gabriel Cramer
2:30–2:45	休憩	
❹2:45–4:15	自給自足と社会組織	Chantelle Steward
4:15–5:00	パネルディスカッション	
5:00–7:00	カクテルパーティ	

❺参加登録の締め切りは4月1日です。　❻登録料の175ドルには、会議資料と❼休憩中に提供される飲み物代が含まれています。　❽昼食とカクテルパーティの食事代は料金には含まれておりませんので、別途お支払いください。可能なお支払い方法は、現金、小切手、およびクレジットカードです。

宛先：　　allmembers@archaeologyconsortium.org
送信者：　frenkel@archaeologyconsortium.org
件名：　　NCA シンポジウム
日付：　　3月30日

みなさま、
来たるシンポジウムの企画にご支援、ご助力いただきありがとうございます。　❾すべてのみなさまにいくつかのプログラム変更をお知らせしたいと思います。

まず、❿Adaskin 氏と Cramer 氏の発表時間が入れ替わりました。Adaskin 氏が当日正午まで緊急のビジネス会議があるためです。次に、⓫Steward 氏が行う予定だった発表が変更されました。Steward 氏は新たなプロジェクトを監督するためジュネーブ考古学研究所に招聘され、このイベントに参加できません。⓬彼女の研究仲間の Eden Bettelheim 氏が代行します。

最後に、まだシンポジウムに登録していない方々はできるだけ早くご登録ください。みなさまご承知の通り、⓭このイベントは当会がまとめる最初のイベントですので、全メンバーの支援をぜひともよろしくお願いします。

敬具
Reuben Frenkel

| 正解＆解説 | 間違いメモ |

196. 正解 (C)　難易度 ■■□　難

プログラムで言及されていることを尋ねる True 問題。(A) (D) に関連する記述は見当たらない。(B) は、❻「登録料は会議資料代を含む」とあるので、誤り。(C) の「休憩中に飲み物が参加者に提供される」については、❼に「休憩中に提供される飲み物」とあるので、これが正解。

↻ beverages ➡ drinks
　during breaks ➡ during intermissions

197. 正解 (C)　難易度 ■■□　難

ふたつの文書に分散した情報を関連付けて答える**クロスリファレンス問題**。Cramer 氏の発表について、示唆されていることを尋ねている。プログラムには選択肢に合致する内容は見当たらないので、E メールに目を移すと❿「Adaskin 氏と Cramer 氏の発表時間が入れ替わった」とある。プログラムに戻って発表時間❷と❸を確認すると、両氏の順番を入れ替えることで、Cramer 氏の**発表時間が早まる**とわかる。よって、(C) の「早い時間に変更された」が正解。

198. 正解 (C)　難易度 ■■□　難

E メールの目的を尋ねている。主題に関わる設問では、文書の**冒頭に注意する**とよい。メールの冒頭❾に「プログラムの変更を知らせたい」とある。これを「**来たるイベントに関する最新情報を提供すること**」と表現した (C) が正解。メール後半で、シンポジウムの事前登録をうながしているが、出欠の確認までは行っていないので、(D) の「協会の会議への出席を確認すること」は誤り。

199. 正解 (D)　難易度 ■■■　難

Bettelheim 氏の発表開始時間を尋ねているが、これもクロスリファレンス問題。プログラムには Bettelheim 氏の名前は見当たらない。メールに目を移すと、⓫「Steward 氏が行う予定だった発表が変更される」とあり、⓬で「彼女（= Steward 氏）の研究仲間 Bettelheim 氏が代行する」とある。プログラムに戻って Steward 氏の発表時間を確認すると❹「2:45 から 4:15」なので、**Bettelheim 氏の発表も 2:45 から始まる**と考えられる。よって (D)「午後 2：45」が正解。

200. 正解 (A)　難易度 ■■■　難

シンポジウムについて、**正しくない**ものを尋ねる Not 問題。(A) の参加費については、❻に「登録料は 175 ドル」とあるだけで、**会員・非会員を区別していないので**間違った情報。従って、これが正解。(B) は、❺「登録締切は 4 月 1 日」に対し、シンポジウムの開催日は❶「4 月 29 日」なので、事前登録が必要とわかる。(C) は❽「昼食とカクテルパーティ代は料金に含まれない」、(D) は⓭「当協会がとりまとめる最初のイベント」とあり、それぞれ正しい情報である。

TEST 1 重要語句 — 索引

《注意》参照先は、問題番号を示している。[Q12]は、問題 No. 12 のこと。
Part 3、4、6、7 については、会話やパッセージに含まれるものを [41-43]
と記し、設問と選択肢に含まれるものを [Q41] というように記している。

A

- a couple of～ Q14
- a variety of～ 65-67
- absolutely Q38
- accept Q34
- accepted 196-200
- acclaim Q137
- accommodations Q87
- according to～ Q64
- accountant Q95
- accounting 155-156
- achieve Q138
- acquire 181-185
- acquisition Q19, 181-185
- activate 153-154
- additional Q119
- address 166-167
- adequately Q140
- adjustment 86-88
- admission 141-143
- admission fee Q154
- advertising firm Q63
- agreement Q68
- ahead of time Q179
- air 168-171
- alternate Q75
- amongst 86-88
- ample 186-190
- annual Q104
- anthology Q137
- antibacterial 191-195
- anticipate Q140
- apparently 86-88
- appearance 141-143
- appliance Q113
- application 80-82
- apply for～ Q41
- appreciate 150-152
- approve 89-91
- archaeologist 196-200
- around the clock .. 166-167
- arrange Q9
- article 89-91
- artifact 196-200
- as soon as～ Q25
- as well 68-70
- assign A to do 56-58
- assignment 89-91
- assistance Q82
- associate 196-200
- association Q127
- at least 176-180
- attach Q3
- attend Q61
- attendee Q64
- attire 157-159
- attract Q102
- attraction 153-154

B

- auditorium 98-100
- authentic Q169
- authenticate 80-82
- authorize Q22
- availability Q66
- available Q28
- award Q21
- award-winning 92-94

B

- based 186-190
- be bound to do .. 191-195
- be concerned Q42
- be eligible for～ .. 176-180
- be encouraged to do
  196-200
- be equipped with～
  186-190
- be involved in～ Q124
- be located 41-43
- be occupied Q23
- be stuck in traffic ... Q44
- beam 186-190
- bend over～ Q3
- benefit Q132, 157-159
- bill 160-162
- biology 98-100
- board Q19
- book 68-70
- bookkeeping 155-156
- branch Q5
- branch office Q12
- break down Q44
- breathable 191-195
- brief Q137
- brochure Q100
- browse Q79
- budget Q112
- build up 74-76
- bulk order Q194

C

- calm Q109
- capacity 160-162
- carve 181-185
- ceiling Q6
- certainly Q13
- certificate Q64
- certified 155-156
- chairperson Q131
- charge account ... Q72
- charitable Q158
- chemistry 98-100
- close to～ Q54
- clothing Q124
- collision 186-190
- come up with～ ... 95-97
- come with～ 147-149

- competition Q84
- complaint Q129
- completion Q64
- complimentary ... 47-49
- composer 157-159
- composition 157-159
- compound 77-79
- concierge Q18
- concise Q112
- conclusion 98-100
- conduct Q68
- conductor Q158
- conference room .. Q30
- confidential Q39
- confirm Q80
- connect 41-43
- conservatory 157-159
- consider Q129
- consortium 196-200
- constraint Q104
- construct Q164
- construction Q36
- consultation Q155
- consume Q188
- consumer 95-97
- consumption Q113
- container Q162
- contemporary ... Q182
- contract ... 80-82, Q135
- convenient 53-55
- convention Q86
- coordination 150-152
- copy 62-64
- corner Q15
- corporate Q65
- cough Q32
- courtesy of～ 71-73
- cozy Q13
- critical Q120
- critically Q170
- crucial 172-175
- cuisine 176-180
- currency Q162
- currently 92-94

D

- damage 166-167
- deadline Q42
- decision Q88
- deduct 166-167
- degree Q123
- delegate 89-91
- demand Q114
- dental Q131
- department 62-64
- depict Q171
- deregulate Q117
- describe Q172
- description 181-185
- destination Q153
- detailed Q36
- detect Q125, 186-190
- detective 168-171

- detergent 191-195
- develop Q58
- device Q162
- devote 172-175
- diameter 181-185
- dig Q1
- dimension 160-162
- diner Q129
- director Q40
- disappearance ... 168-171
- dishearten 172-175
- distinction Q138
- distribute Q51
- district 74-76
- disturb 77-79
- donation 83-85
- draw Q126, 163-165
- drawer Q33
- due Q22
- due to～ 74-76
- duty 176-180

E

- earn Q123
- eat out Q29
- edge Q4
- editorial office ... 89-91
- efficiency Q133
- efficient Q113
- effort Q102
- electricity Q113
- electronics company .. Q86
- emergency room .. Q109
- emission 186-190
- encircle Q10
- end up doing Q26
- engage in～ ... 150-152
- enhanced 147-149
- enroll 150-152
- ensure Q140
- entitle 92-94
- entitle A to B Q132
- entrepreneurship ... Q127
- envelope Q12
- environment-friendly
  191-195
- equipment Q22
- establish Q84
- establishment Q47
- estimate Q114
- evaluate Q58
- exceptional 191-195
- executive Q95
- exhausted Q107
- exhibit Q16
- expect Q126
- exquisite 181-185
- extended Q57

F

- fabric 191-195
- face Q6
- facility Q85

104

- [ ] faculty 92-94
- [ ] favorably 95-97
- [ ] feature Q137, 147-149
- [ ] fee 65-67
- [ ] figure Q112
- [ ] file Q186
- [ ] filing cabinet Q39
- [ ] fill out~ Q34
- [ ] financial statements
  155-156
- [ ] finding Q93
- [ ] fiscal year Q112
- [ ] fit 181-185
- [ ] fix Q9
- [ ] flagging 168-171
- [ ] flight of stairs Q10
- [ ] flood Q74
- [ ] floor Q16
- [ ] floral arrangement Q65
- [ ] flow 181-185
- [ ] following 92-94
- [ ] force Q117
- [ ] forgery Q125
- [ ] founder 83-85
- [ ] freeway 53-55
- [ ] frequent Q113
- [ ] funds 83-85
- [ ] fundraising Q157
- [ ] furnishings Q182

G

- [ ] garage Q1
- [ ] garment 191-195
- [ ] gathering Q27
- [ ] general manager 56-58
- [ ] genetic 92-94
- [ ] geography 176-180
- [ ] get on~ Q40
- [ ] give away~ 163-165
- [ ] grateful 141-143
- [ ] grocery 172-175
- [ ] growing 155-156
- [ ] guarantee 144-146

H

- [ ] hand Q7
- [ ] hand in~ Q61
- [ ] handle 155-156
- [ ] handout Q36
- [ ] harm 147-149
- [ ] head 74-76
- [ ] heir 168-171
- [ ] heritage 176-180
- [ ] highly Q60
- [ ] hold on to~ Q4
- [ ] holdup 47-49
- [ ] hotline 80-82
- [ ] household 65-67
- [ ] housing Q118
- [ ] humble 172-175

I

- [ ] I wonder if~ 59-61

- [ ] identifiable 95-97
- [ ] identify A with B 95-97
- [ ] I'm afraid~ Q20
- [ ] immigration Q128
- [ ] in a little while Q16
- [ ] in advance 176-180
- [ ] in installments Q187
- [ ] in sales Q14
- [ ] in the field of~ 92-94
- [ ] in the meantime 47-49
- [ ] in the shadow of~ Q4
- [ ] in transit Q128
- [ ] including 144-146
- [ ] inclusive of~ 196-200
- [ ] income 83-85
- [ ] indicate Q136
- [ ] indigenous 196-200
- [ ] individual Q159
- [ ] industry Q117
- [ ] inform Q166
- [ ] inquire Q57
- [ ] inquiry 80-82
- [ ] inspire 141-143
- [ ] install Q10
- [ ] institute 196-200
- [ ] institution 157-159
- [ ] instruct Q134
- [ ] insulate 191-195
- [ ] insurance Q119
- [ ] integrated 147-149
- [ ] interact with~ Q122
- [ ] intermission 196-200
- [ ] intermittent 166-167
- [ ] interpreter 176-180
- [ ] introductory Q31
- [ ] investment Q62
- [ ] investor 65-67
- [ ] issue Q19, Q23
- [ ] itinerary Q81

J

- [ ] joint Q88
- [ ] journal Q98

K

- [ ] knowledgeable 191-195

L

- [ ] lab 147-149
- [ ] lamppost Q10
- [ ] landscape Q177
- [ ] last Q69
- [ ] lastly 77-79
- [ ] latest 59-61
- [ ] launch Q122
- [ ] law enforcement .. 168-171
- [ ] lead Q10
- [ ] lead character 59-61
- [ ] leading Q138
- [ ] legal department ... 176-180
- [ ] light up~ 141-143
- [ ] likely Q108
- [ ] line of credit Q167

- [ ] list Q103
- [ ] load 160-162
- [ ] local firm Q135
- [ ] locate Q42
- [ ] long-term Q70
- [ ] look after~ Q18
- [ ] look for~ Q39
- [ ] look forward to~ 80-82
- [ ] loyalty 71-73
- [ ] luggage Q18
- [ ] luscious 181-185

M

- [ ] maintain Q123
- [ ] make a purchase Q72
- [ ] make an arrangement
  .... Q92
- [ ] make certain Q180
- [ ] make it to~ Q42
- [ ] malicious 147-149
- [ ] manage Q22
- [ ] management Q126
- [ ] manufacture Q184
- [ ] manufacturer Q89
- [ ] manufacturing Q58
- [ ] mark 144-146
- [ ] market trend Q180
- [ ] massive 141-143
- [ ] material 50-52
- [ ] material culture ... 196-200
- [ ] matter 150-152
- [ ] meanwhile 168-171
- [ ] meet 56-58
- [ ] mention 56-58
- [ ] merchandise Q7
- [ ] merge Q173
- [ ] method Q53
- [ ] miss 44-46
- [ ] mission Q131
- [ ] modify Q160
- [ ] module 50-52
- [ ] mold 181-185
- [ ] most likely Q21
- [ ] musical instrument Q8
- [ ] mutation 92-94

N

- [ ] namely 157-159
- [ ] nearby Q15
- [ ] normally Q24
- [ ] note 181-185
- [ ] notice Q163
- [ ] notion 191-195
- [ ] novel 144-146
- [ ] now that~ 191-195
- [ ] numerous Q129

O

- [ ] occasion 65-67, 191-195
- [ ] occur Q87
- [ ] office manager Q22
- [ ] official Q114
- [ ] on display 181-185

- [ ] on one's own Q22
- [ ] on the house 47-49
- [ ] on time Q42
- [ ] on top of~ 191-195
- [ ] ongoing Q19
- [ ] opening ceremony Q31
- [ ] opening remarks .. 196-200
- [ ] operate Q182
- [ ] operation 56-58
- [ ] option 186-190
- [ ] ordinary 59-61
- [ ] organization 83-85
- [ ] orphanage 157-159
- [ ] otherwise Q78
- [ ] out of order Q15
- [ ] outlet Q8
- [ ] outside Q14
- [ ] outstanding 186-190
- [ ] overlap 181-185
- [ ] oversee 196-200

P

- [ ] pack away~ Q17
- [ ] package Q11
- [ ] packaging Q96
- [ ] park Q1
- [ ] parking lot Q53
- [ ] participant 50-52
- [ ] participate in~ 71-73
- [ ] partly Q27
- [ ] party Q135
- [ ] path Q4
- [ ] pathway Q5
- [ ] patient Q109
- [ ] patron Q139
- [ ] patronage 181-185
- [ ] payment method . 196-200
- [ ] performance . Q8, 186-190
- [ ] performing arts Q47
- [ ] personally 47-49
- [ ] perspiration 191-195
- [ ] persuade Q166
- [ ] petal 181-185
- [ ] photocopier Q9
- [ ] physics 98-100
- [ ] physical education
  150-152
- [ ] place Q9
- [ ] place an order 41-43
- [ ] plug Q8
- [ ] policy Q103
- [ ] postpone Q186
- [ ] potential client Q68
- [ ] present 153-154
- [ ] prestigious Q34
- [ ] prevent 147-149
- [ ] primarily Q173
- [ ] prime time 168-171
- [ ] printing company 41-43
- [ ] prior to~ 176-180
- [ ] privilege 181-185
- [ ] privileged 168-171
- [ ] procedure Q109

TEST 1　重要語句――索引

- [ ] proceeds 157-159
- [ ] processing fee 80-82
- [ ] produce Q173
- [ ] production 56-58
- [ ] productive Q120
- [ ] productivity Q133
- [ ] profit Q108
- [ ] projection Q112
- [ ] promote Q80, Q123
- [ ] property 191-195
- [ ] proposal Q90
- [ ] provide 83-85
- [ ] provincial 172-175
- [ ] public relations Q30
- [ ] publication Q91
- [ ] publishing company Q89
- [ ] purchase Q7, Q61
- [ ] put in〜 176-180

Q
- [ ] quarter Q114
- [ ] questionnaire Q51

R
- [ ] railing Q4
- [ ] raise 83-85
- [ ] ranch 168-171
- [ ] range 160-162
- [ ] raw material Q124
- [ ] read up on〜 176-180
- [ ] real estate Q86
- [ ] rearrange 89-91
- [ ] receipt 176-180
- [ ] recently 89-91
- [ ] reception 92-94, 166-167
- [ ] recognize 95-97
- [ ] reconstruct 196-200
- [ ] reduced Q185
- [ ] refrain Q99
- [ ] refreshment Q94
- [ ] regarding 80-82
- [ ] register for〜 83-85
- [ ] registration 50-52
- [ ] reimbursement 176-180
- [ ] relax Q5
- [ ] reliable 186-190
- [ ] relocate Q111
- [ ] relocation Q56
- [ ] reminder 77-79
- [ ] remote 168-171
- [ ] removable 160-162
- [ ] remove Q9
- [ ] render 181-185
- [ ] renew Q139
- [ ] renowned 157-159
- [ ] repair Q3
- [ ] replacement Q49, Q105
- [ ] report Q166
- [ ] representative 155-156
- [ ] requirement 80-82
- [ ] reschedule Q50
- [ ] reservation Q40
- [ ] resignation Q110

- [ ] resistant 191-195
- [ ] respected Q158
- [ ] rest assured 166-167
- [ ] result in〜 Q118
- [ ] resume 166-167
- [ ] retail 172-175
- [ ] retail outlet Q182
- [ ] retailer 172-175
- [ ] retain 181-185
- [ ] retire Q105
- [ ] reverse 153-154
- [ ] review Q136
- [ ] revise Q167
- [ ] revive 168-171
- [ ] revolve around〜 .. 168-171
- [ ] ridiculous 53-55
- [ ] right away Q40
- [ ] row Q6
- [ ] RSVP 157-159

S
- [ ] sales department Q115
- [ ] sales report 95-97
- [ ] sales representative
  172-175
- [ ] scare 77-79
- [ ] scenery Q4
- [ ] schedule Q40, 92-94
- [ ] seating capacity Q164
- [ ] sector Q174
- [ ] selection 160-162
- [ ] self-motivated Q120
- [ ] senior position Q123
- [ ] separate 144-146
- [ ] serve Q94, Q117
- [ ] serve as〜 153-154
- [ ] session 50-52
- [ ] severely 166-167
- [ ] sew 191-195
- [ ] shelf Q9
- [ ] ship 181-185
- [ ] shovel Q1
- [ ] show up Q16
- [ ] situate Q6
- [ ] sky-bridge 41-43
- [ ] slate Q121
- [ ] snowstorm 166-167
- [ ] social service Q118
- [ ] sophisticated Q125
- [ ] specialize in〜 168-171
- [ ] specialty 65-67
- [ ] specific 65-67
- [ ] specification 160-162
- [ ] spending Q112
- [ ] sponsor Q159
- [ ] sports utility vehicle
  186-190
- [ ] standard Q188
- [ ] status Q183
- [ ] stay behind 86-88
- [ ] steadily Q108
- [ ] storage Q161
- [ ] strategy Q62

- [ ] strength 150-152
- [ ] struggle 168-171
- [ ] study 92-94
- [ ] sturdy 181-185
- [ ] subject Q91, Q93
- [ ] submit Q36
- [ ] subscription 147-149
- [ ] subsidize Q127
- [ ] subsistence 196-200
- [ ] suggest Q53
- [ ] suggestion Q97
- [ ] suitable Q107
- [ ] supervisor Q58
- [ ] supplier Q26
- [ ] supply Q84
- [ ] surgeon 83-85
- [ ] survey Q39
- [ ] switch 196-200
- [ ] symposium 196-200

T
- [ ] take one's place .. 196-200
- [ ] take part in〜 163-165
- [ ] take up residence
  168-171
- [ ] target Q108
- [ ] tax Q67
- [ ] tax form 155-156
- [ ] term 186-190
- [ ] textile Q89, 191-195
- [ ] theater play Q59
- [ ] threat Q140
- [ ] thrilled Q38
- [ ] thrive 191-195
- [ ] ticketing agent Q111
- [ ] tourist site Q154
- [ ] trade fair 68-70
- [ ] trait 92-94
- [ ] transfer 56-58
- [ ] transportation Q53
- [ ] trim Q5
- [ ] truly Q29
- [ ] tutorial Q191

U
- [ ] unanimous vote Q19
- [ ] unconventional ... 172-175
- [ ] undergarment 191-195
- [ ] underserved 83-85
- [ ] unexpectedly 50-52
- [ ] unforeseen Q140
- [ ] unfortunately 95-97
- [ ] unlimited Q132
- [ ] unsolicited 147-149
- [ ] upcoming Q81
- [ ] update Q198
- [ ] upkeep Q188
- [ ] upstairs 41-43
- [ ] urge Q130
- [ ] urgent 196-200
- [ ] usage Q77

V
- [ ] vacation leave 89-91
- [ ] valuable 181-185
- [ ] vehicle Q3
- [ ] vending machine .. 160-162
- [ ] vendor 160-162
- [ ] venue 47-49
- [ ] verify Q178
- [ ] vicinity 86-88
- [ ] voucher Q49

W
- [ ] weeklong Q107
- [ ] welfare 157-159
- [ ] well-known Q116
- [ ] wildlife preserve ... 77-79
- [ ] work overtime 59-61
- [ ] work shift Q37

Y
- [ ] yet 181-185

新TOEIC® テスト　でる模試　600問
別冊　解答・解説 [1]　TEST 1

2012年11月 4日　　初版　第1刷発行
2014年 4月14日　　　　　第7刷発行

著　者　　ハッカーズ語学研究所
発行者　　天谷 修平
発　行　　株式会社 アスク出版
　　　　　〒162-8558
　　　　　東京都新宿区下宮比町2-6
　　　　　TEL：03-3267-6866
　　　　　FAX：03-3267-6867
　　　　　URL：http://www.ask-digital.co.jp/

ISBN 978-4-87217-808-1

新 TOEIC テスト
でる模試 600問

別冊 解答・解説 2

TEST 2

取り外し可能

ゆっくり矢印のほうに
引くと外れます。

▶ ▶ ▶

新TOEIC®テスト
でる模試 600問

別冊 解答・解説 2

TEST 2

目次・Contents

正解一覧	2
Part 1	4
Part 2	8
Part 3	18
Part 4	30
Part 5	42
Part 6	56
Part 7	64

TEST 2 — 正解一覧

〈TEST 2〉の正解リスト。答え合せにご利用ください。また、間違った問題は、チェックボックス□にチェックをいれておきましょう（1回目は☑、2回目は☒）。復習の際、間違った問題がひと目でわかるので、便利です。

LISTENING SECTION

Part 1

1	D
2	C
3	C
4	D
5	C
6	C
7	D
8	C
9	A
10	B

Part 2

No.	Answer	No.	Answer	No.	Answer
11	A	21	A	31	A
12	C	22	B	32	A
13	A	23	A	33	A
14	A	24	C	34	C
15	A	25	C	35	A
16	A	26	A	36	A
17	A	27	B	37	B
18	B	28	B	38	B
19	B	29	A	39	C
20	B	30	A	40	B

Part 3

No.	Answer	No.	Answer	No.	Answer
41	B	51	D	61	C
42	D	52	D	62	D
43	C	53	C	63	D
44	C	54	A	64	D
45	D	55	D	65	B
46	B	56	D	66	D
47	A	57	C	67	A
48	C	58	C	68	C
49	C	59	D	69	B
50	C	60	A	70	A

Part 4

No.	Answer	No.	Answer	No.	Answer
71	D	81	C	91	D
72	D	82	D	92	A
73	A	83	D	93	A
74	C	84	D	94	B
75	D	85	D	95	D
76	B	86	A	96	A
77	C	87	D	97	D
78	D	88	C	98	C
79	A	89	A	99	C
80	B	90	A	100	D

●受験1回目（学習日：　　月　　日）

LISTENING				Ⓐ予想スコア	READING			Ⓑ予想スコア	トータル予想スコア
正答数					正答数				Ⓐ＋Ⓑ
Part 1	Part 2	Part 3	Part 4		Part 5	Part 6	Part 7		

●受験2回目（学習日：　　月　　日）

LISTENING				Ⓐ予想スコア	READING			Ⓑ予想スコア	トータル予想スコア
正答数					正答数				Ⓐ＋Ⓑ
Part 1	Part 2	Part 3	Part 4		Part 5	Part 6	Part 7		

※本体のスコア換算表（p.9）をご利用ください。

READING SECTION

Part 5

#	Ans	#	Ans	#	Ans	#	Ans
101	B	111	A	121	B	131	A
102	C	112	D	122	B	132	C
103	A	113	A	123	A	133	C
104	C	114	D	124	B	134	B
105	B	115	A	125	B	135	D
106	C	116	C	126	B	136	A
107	A	117	C	127	B	137	A
108	D	118	A	128	D	138	C
109	C	119	A	129	D	139	B
110	A	120	B	130	C	140	C

Part 6

#	Ans	#	Ans
141	A	151	A
142	C	152	B
143	A	153	B
144	A	154	C
145	A	155	A
146	B	156	C
147	A	157	A
148	B	158	A
149	C	159	A
150	C	160	B

Part 7

#	Ans	#	Ans	#	Ans	#	Ans
161	C	171	D	181	B	191	B
162	C	172	C	182	A	192	D
163	C	173	D	183	C	193	D
164	C	174	A	184	C	194	C
165	D	175	D	185	D	195	A
166	B	176	D	186	B	196	D
167	D	177	C	187	D	197	C
168	A	178	B	188	A	198	B
169	D	179	D	189	C	199	C
170	A	180	A	190	B	200	D

TEST 2
PART 1

音声ファイル　T2_P1_Q1 ▶ T2_P1_Q5

問題&訳

1.

(A) He is pulling the door open.
(B) He is entering the building.
(C) He is crossing the street.
(D) He is stepping onto the bus.

(A) 彼はドアを引き開けている。
(B) 彼は建物に入ろうとしている。
(C) 彼は通りを渡っている。
(D) 彼はバスに乗り込もうとしている。

2.

(A) Some waiters are clearing the tables.
(B) A cook is preparing food in a restaurant.
(C) Some men are seated across from each other.
(D) A waiter is handing menus to the diners.

(A) 何人かのウエーターがテーブルを片付けている。
(B) レストランでコックが料理を準備している。
(C) 何人かの男性がお互いの向かいに座っている。
(D) ウエーターが食事客にメニューを手渡している。

3.

(A) He is fastening his tool belt.
(B) He is kneeling on the ground.
(C) He is removing his safety mask.
(D) He is working at a construction site.

(A) 彼は工具ベルトを締めているところだ。
(B) 彼は地面にひざまずこうとしている。
(C) 彼は安全マスクを取ろうとしている。
(D) 彼は工事現場で働いている。

4.

(A) A trash can is being emptied by a worker.
(B) Some people are waiting by the pedestal of a statue.
(C) A man is lifting the stroller onto the sidewalk.
(D) Some people are posing for a photograph.

(A) ゴミ箱は作業員によって中身を空にされているところだ。
(B) 何人かの人が像の台座のそばで待っている。
(C) 男性はベビーカーを歩道に持ち上げている。
(D) 何人かの人が写真撮影でポーズをとっている。

5.

(A) A path leads up to a waterfall.
(B) Some hikers are holding on to the railing.
(C) A stream is flowing underneath the bridge.
(D) Some stone steps have been built along the shore.

(A) 小道は滝に続いている。
(B) 何人かのハイカーは手すりをつかんでいる。
(C) 小川が橋の下を流れている。
(D) いくつかの石段が川岸に沿って作られている。

| TOEIC豆知識 | TOEICに登場するphotocopierの性能はけっしてよくない。いっつもjamってる。メイド・イン・ジャパンをhighly recommendしたくなる。（続く▶）|

正解&解説

1. 正解 (D) 難易度：難

男性がバスに乗り込もうとしている動作を、step（足を踏み出す）を使って描写した (D) が正解。(A) は、ドアをまさに開けようとしている動作を描写しているが、バスのドアはすでに開いているので誤り。(B) は the building（建物）部分が誤り。He is entering だけで早とちりせず、**最後までしっかり聞く**ことが大切。(C) の is crossing（〜を渡っている）は男性の動作と一致しない。

間違いメモ&単語
あなたの解答 [A][B][C][D]
メモ

☐ cross 〜を渡る
☐ step onto 〜 〜に乗り込む

2. 正解 (C) 難易度：難

テーブルに対面で座るふたりの男性の状態を、**are seated across from each other**（お互いの向かいに座っている）と描写した (C) が正解。(A) の Some waiters は複数形だが、写っているのはひとりだけ。(B) の料理をするコックの姿は見当たらない。(D) の is handing menus（メニューを手渡している）は、ウエーターの動作に一致しないので、誤り。

あなたの解答 [A][B][C][D]
メモ

☐ clear 〜を片付ける、きれいにする
☐ hand 〜を手渡す　☐ diner 食事客

3. 正解 (D) 難易度：難

男性が construction site（工事現場）で働いている状況を描写した (D) が正解。(A) は、ベルトを今まさに締めている動作を表現しているが、男性はすでに工具ベルトを着用済み。(B) も、今まさに進行中の動作を描写しているが、男性はすでにひざをついている。(C) の is removing（〜を脱ごうとしている）という動作は、写真に一致しない。

あなたの解答 [A][B][C][D]
メモ

☐ fasten 〜を締める
☐ kneel ひざまずく
☐ remove 〜を脱ぐ、取り去る
☐ construction site 工事現場

4. 正解 (D) 難易度：難

pose（ポーズをとる）を使って、写真撮影のために構えている3人を描写した (D) が正解。(A) は、**受動態の進行形**（is being emptied）で、ゴミ箱のゴミをまさに捨てようとしている**作業員の動作**を表現している。しかし、写真に作業員の姿は見当たらない。(B) の像の台座は写真に写ってはいるが、そばに人はいない。by は「〜のそばで」という位置を表す。(C) の **stroller**（ベビーカー）はすでに歩道上にあり、だれも動かしていないので誤り。

あなたの解答 [A][B][C][D]
メモ

☐ trash can ゴミ箱
☐ empty 〜を空にする　☐ pedestal 台座
☐ statue 彫像　☐ stroller ベビーカー
☐ sidewalk 歩道　☐ pose ポーズを取る

5. 正解 (C) 難易度：難

橋の下を小川が流れている様子を的確に描写した (C) が正解。**underneath** は「〜の真下に」という意味。(A) の waterfall（滝）、(B) の hiker（登山者）は写真に写っていないので、ともに誤り。(D) の stone steps（石段）も確認できない。**shore** は「海岸、川岸、湖畔」。

あなたの解答 [A][B][C][D]
メモ

☐ lead 通じる　☐ waterfall 滝
☐ hold on to 〜 〜をつかむ　☐ stream 小川　☐ flow 流れる　☐ underneath 〜の下に　☐ step（階段などの）段
☐ shore 海岸、川岸

TEST 2
PART 1

音声ファイル　T2_P1_Q6 ▶ T2_P1_Q10

問題&訳

6.

(A) The people are watching a performance.
(B) The computer has been switched off.
(C) A screen has been placed on the wall.
(D) The table has been cleared.

(A) 人々は演技（演奏）を見ている。
(B) コンピュータの電源がオフになっている。
(C) モニター画面が壁に設置されている。
(D) テーブルがきれいに片付けられている。

7.

(A) The table is being set up for a meeting.
(B) The curtains cover the windows.
(C) The tablecloths are being folded.
(D) The seats surrounding the table are vacant.

(A) テーブルが会議用に配置されているところだ。
(B) カーテンが窓を覆っている。
(C) テーブルクロスが折り畳まれているところだ。
(D) テーブルを囲んだイスが空席である。

8.

(A) He is pushing a cart down the sidewalk.
(B) He is driving a vehicle into a parking space.
(C) He is standing at the rear of the truck.
(D) He is delivering a package to a customer.

(A) 彼はカートを歩道で押している。
(B) 彼は車を駐車場に入れている。
(C) 彼はトラックの後方に立っている。
(D) 彼は顧客に荷物を配達している。

9.

(A) Artwork is displayed inside a store window.
(B) The glass on the door is being cleaned.
(C) A woman is painting the store's exterior.
(D) Customers are waiting in a line near a gallery.

(A) 美術品は店のショーウィンドウ内に飾られている。
(B) ドアのガラスが磨かれているところだ。
(C) 女性は店の外装にペンキを塗っている。
(D) 顧客はギャラリー付近で1列に並んで待っている。

10.

(A) The lane is crowded with people.
(B) Some trees line the edge of the road.
(C) A group of people is jogging across a footbridge.
(D) A bicycle is being parked along the street.

(A) 車道は人で混雑している。
(B) 何本かの木が道路の端に並んでいる。
(C) 人の集団がジョギングで歩道橋を渡っている。
(D) 自転車が通り沿いに駐輪されようとしている。

TOEIC豆知識 photocopier は「コピー機」／jam は「(機械が) 動かなくなる」／highly recommend は「〜を強くオススメする」という意味。

正解＆解説

6. 正解 **(C)** 　難易度：難

モニター画面が左手の壁に設置されている状態を、**受動態の現在完了形**（has been placed）で描写した (C) が正解。画面に映っているのは、テレビ会議の相手のようだがはっきりしない。演技や演奏が映っているかどうかも判断できないので、(A) は誤り。(B) のコンピュータは、写真では電源が入った状態。テーブルの上には、いろいろなものが置かれているので (D) も誤り。

間違いメモ＆単語

あなたの解答 [A] [B] [C] [D]
メモ

- □ performance 演技、演奏、公演
- □ screen 画面、スクリーン
- □ place 〜を設置する

7. 正解 **(D)** 　難易度：難

イスに誰も座っていない状態を、**vacant**（あいている、使用されていない）を使って描写した (D) が正解。(A) は、**人の動作**を表す**受動態の進行形**（is being set up）だが、写真に人の姿は見当たらない。写真に写っているのはブラインドであって、(B) の curtains（カーテン）ではない。(C) も (A) と同様、受動態の進行形（are being folded）なので、誤り。

あなたの解答 [A] [B] [C] [D]
メモ

- □ set up 〜 〜を配置する
- □ cover 〜を覆う　□ fold 〜を折り畳む
- □ surround 〜を囲む
- □ vacant 空いている、使われていない

8. 正解 **(C)** 　難易度：難

男性がトラックの後方に立っている状況を描写した (C) がもっとも適切。**cart**（カート）らしきものは写っているが、男性はそれを押しているわけではないので、(A) は誤り。(B) の is driving（〜を運転している）は男性の動作と一致しない。(D) は、1人の人物写真にも関わらず、he（彼）と a customer（客）の2人の人物に言及しているので、誤り。

あなたの解答 [A] [B] [C] [D]
メモ

- □ cart カート、手押し車
- □ vehicle 車、乗り物　□ rear 後部、後ろ　□ deliver 〜を配達する
- □ package 小包

9. 正解 **(A)** 　難易度：難

店のショーウィンドウ内に美術品が飾られている様子を描写した (A) が正解。(B) は**受動態の進行形**（is being cleaned）で、ドアのガラスを磨いている**人物の動作**を描写している。しかし、写真の女性はそのような動きをしていない。(C) の is painting（〜をペンキで塗っている）も女性の動作と無関係。ひとりの人物写真で、customers と複数の人に言及しているので、(D) も誤り。

あなたの解答 [A] [B] [C] [D]
メモ

- □ artwork 美術品　□ display 〜を展示する　□ exterior 外装
- □ wait in a line 1列に並んで待つ
- □ gallery 美術館、画廊

10. 正解 **(B)** 　難易度：難

木が道路沿いに並んで植えられている様子を描写した (B) が正解。**line** には「並ぶ、整列する」という動詞の意味もある。(A) 写真の道は、人で混み合っているとは言えない。(C) の footbridge（歩道橋）は写っていない。(D) は、**受動態の進行形**（is being parked）を使って、自転車をまさに駐輪しようとしている**人の動作**を表現している。しかし、そのような動作をしている人物は見当たらない。手前の自転車はすでに置かれてある。

あなたの解答 [A] [B] [C] [D]
メモ

- □ lane 通り、車線
- □ line 〜に沿って並ぶ
- □ footbridge 歩道橋
- □ park 〜を駐車（輪）する

TEST 2
PART 2

11. Have you stayed at this hotel before?
 (A) Not that I remember.
 (B) I'll be staying for five days.
 (C) A double room, please.

このホテルに以前ご宿泊されたことはありますか。
(A) 覚えている限りでは、ないですね。
(B) 5日間滞在します。
(C) ダブルルームをお願いします。

12. Will you be coming to the networking seminar?
 (A) Yes, it was conducted just last week.
 (B) We have quite a large network.
 (C) I'm planning on attending.

ネットワークセミナーにいらっしゃいますか。
(A) ええ、ちょうど先週行われました。
(B) 私たちはとても大きなネットワークを持っているんです。
(C) 出席する予定です。

13. I can leave the contract with your receptionist.
 (A) That would be appreciated.
 (B) I haven't made contact yet.
 (C) Please sign on the dotted line.

契約書を受付に預けておきましょう。
(A) そうしてもらえるとありがたいです。
(B) まだ連絡を取っていません。
(C) この点線の上に署名をお願いします。

14. What should I bring to the company picnic?
 (A) Paper plates would be nice.
 (B) The drinks are over there.
 (C) It gets boring sometimes.

会社のピクニックに何を持って行けばいい?
(A) 紙皿がいいね。
(B) 飲み物はあそこだよ。
(C) 時々つまらなくなるなぁ。

15. Is the office open on Saturdays?
 (A) Not normally.
 (B) Here are your keys.
 (C) Wait for me there.

事務所は土曜日に開いていますか。
(A) 通常は開いていません。
(B) あなたの鍵をどうぞ。
(C) そこで私を待っていてください。

16. Where's the research manager?
 (A) Have you checked the lab?
 (B) I'll reserve a table right away.
 (C) Management is planning to.

研究管理者はどこかしら。
(A) 実験室は見た?
(B) すぐに席を予約するよ。
(C) 経営陣が計画しているよ。

TOEIC豆知識 故障しやすいだけでなく、TOEICの世界のコピー機とプリンターは、頻繁に紙切れを起こす。なのに、用紙の保管場所を知らない人ばかりで、すぐ人に聞いてくる。

正解&解説 | 間違いメモ&単語

11. 正解 (A) 　難易度：難

Yes/No 疑問文。ホテルへの宿泊経験を尋ねられている。「覚えている限りない」、つまり No と答えている (A) が正解。(B) は、問い掛けの stay を staying の形でくり返し、混同をねらっている。(C) は、ホテルから連想される double room がひっかけ。

あなたの解答 A B C
メモ

12. 正解 (C) 　難易度：難

未来時制の Yes/No 疑問文。セミナーへの出席の有無を問われている。これに「出席する予定だ」と答える (C) が正解。(A) は、未来のことを問われているのに、過去時制（was）で答えているので誤り。(B) は networking と network という類似した単語で混同をねらっている。

あなたの解答 A B C
メモ

□ conduct 〜を実施する　□ quite かなり、なかなか　□ plan on 〜 〜するつもりである　□ attend 出席する

13. 正解 (A) 　難易度：難

平叙文で、契約書を受付に預けておくことを〈提案〉されている。これに対して、「そうしてもらえるとありがたい」と提案を受け入れている (A) が正解。問い掛けの contract（契約書）に対して、(B) は発音が類似した contact、(C) は意味から連想される sign（署名する）を使って、誤答を誘っている。

あなたの解答 A B C
メモ

□ contract 契約（書）　□ receptionist 受付係　□ appreciate 〜を感謝する　□ make contact 連絡を取る

14. 正解 (A) 　難易度：難

ピクニックに持っていく〈もの・こと〉を問う What 疑問文。「紙皿がいい」つまり「**紙皿を持ってきて**」と答えている (A) が正解。(B) は、picnic から連想される drinks（飲み物）で混同をねらっている。(C) は、bring に発音が類似した boring がひっかけ。

あなたの解答 A B C
メモ

□ boring 退屈させるような、つまらない

15. 正解 (A) 　難易度：難

Yes/No 疑問文。土曜日に事務所が開いているかどうかが問われている。これに「通常は開いていない」と答える (A) が正解。(B) は、open（〜を開く）から連想される keys（鍵）がひっかけ。(C) は、office で待ち合わせをしているという誤解を誘っている。**on Saturdays** のように、曜日を複数形にすると「**毎週土曜日に**」という意味になることを覚えておこう。

あなたの解答 A B C
メモ

□ normally 通常は

16. 正解 (A) 　難易度：難

Where 疑問文で〈場所〉が問われているのに対し、「実験室を確認したか」と場所を尋ね返している (A) がもっとも自然。このように**疑問文で返すケース**もあるので覚えておこう。(B) は research に対して reserve、(C) は manager に対して management というように、それぞれ発音の類似した単語で誤答を誘っている。

あなたの解答 A B C
メモ

□ lab 研究所、実験室　□ reserve 〜を予約する　□ right away すぐに　□ management 経営、経営陣

9

TEST 2
PART 2

音声ファイル 🔊 T2_P2_Q17 ▶ T2_P2_Q22

問題	訳

17. What time should we expect you at the reception?
(A) I'm not sure. I'll let you know.
(B) Just a 15-minute walk.
(C) To the downtown office.

何時に受付で待っていればよいですか。
(A) わからない。あとで知らせるわ。
(B) 徒歩でたったの15分よ。
(C) ダウンタウンの事務所へ。

---

18. How long is the drive from here to Catalina?
(A) Only by sea.
(B) About half a day.
(C) It gets good mileage.

ここから Catalina まで車でどれくらいかかるかな。
(A) 海路のみなのよ。
(B) 約半日かしら。
(C) それは燃費がいいわよ。

---

19. Would you like to present your proposal tomorrow, or are you still working on it?
(A) That's a generous offer.
(B) I need some more time.
(C) At a computer firm.

企画提案は明日発表したいですか、それともまだ作業中ですか。
(A) それは寛大な提案ですね。
(B) もう少し時間が必要です。
(C) コンピュータ会社で。

---

20. I'll contact you when I close the deal with the investor.
(A) I'm considering it.
(B) Thanks. Call me on my mobile.
(C) We met at the seminar in Seattle.

投資家と契約を結んだら連絡するわ。
(A) 検討中です。
(B) ありがとう。携帯電話に連絡して。
(C) 私たちはシアトルの会議で会いました。

---

21. Why don't you consult someone from technical assistance?
(A) I probably should.
(B) No, I don't see him.
(C) It's technically wrong.

技術支援の誰かに相談したら?
(A) たぶんそうすべきだな。
(B) いいえ、彼には会わないよ。
(C) それは厳密に言えば間違いです。

---

22. We'll need boxes to store those decorations.
(A) He needs help today.
(B) No, in the storage closet.
(C) There are some in the garage.

これらの飾りつけを保管する箱が必要だな。
(A) 彼はきょう助けを必要としているわ。
(B) いいえ、保管庫の中よ。
(C) 車庫にいくつかあるわ。

正解＆解説

17. 正解 (A)　難易度：難

What time ～？で〈時〉が問われている。I'm not sure.（わからない）と応じている (A) は、時間を答えていないが**自然に会話がつながる**ので、正解。「わからない、知らない」は、**どのような問い掛けに対しても正解**となり得る。(B) には、15-minute（15分の）という時間表現があるが、自然な応答にならない。(C) は場所を答えているので、誤り。

- expect ～を期待する、予想する
- reception 受付

18. 正解 (B)　難易度：難

How long ～？は〈期間〉を問う疑問文。Catalinaまでの所要時間が問われているので、「約半日」と答えている (B) が正解。(A) は、手段を答えているので誤り。(C) は、drive（車での旅）から連想される mileage（燃費）でひっかけをねらっている。

- mileage 燃費

19. 正解 (B)　難易度：難

選択疑問文で、A or B の〈選択〉が求められている。「明日発表する」か「まだ作業中」かに対して、「もう少し時間がほしい」と答えている (B) が正解。これは「**まだ作業中**」ということを**間接的**に伝えている。(A) は、proposal（提案）の同意語 offer（提案）で混同を誘っている。(C) は選択を無視して場所を答えているので、誤り。選択疑問文に対して、**選択をしない応答もあり得る**ことを覚えておこう。

- present ～を提示する
- proposal 提案
- still まだ
- work on ～ ～に取り組む
- generous 寛大な
- firm 会社

20. 正解 (B)　難易度：難

契約したら連絡するという〈提案〉の平叙文。これに対して、Thanks. で提案を受け入れたあと、「私の携帯に電話して」と依頼している (B) が正解。(A) は「契約を結ぶ」という内容から連想される consider（～を検討する）、(C) は contact（～に連絡する）と意味が似た met（会った）で、それぞれ誤答を誘っている。

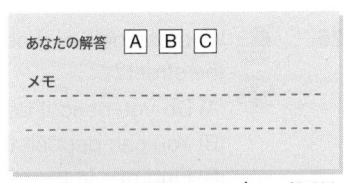

- contact ～に連絡する
- close（取引など）をまとめる
- deal 契約
- investor 投資家
- consider ～を検討する

21. 正解 (A)　難易度：難

Why don't you ～？で、技術支援の人への相談を〈提案〉されている。「そうすべきだろう」と提案を受け入れている (A) が正解。(A) は I probably should (consult someone from technical assistance). の省略形である。(B) は、Why don't you ～？に対して、No で答えたまではよいが、以降の内容が文脈にあわない。(C) は、technical の派生語 technically で誤答を誘っている。

- consult ～に相談する
- technical 技術上の
- assistance 援助、助力

22. 正解 (C)　難易度：難

飾りつけを保管する箱が必要という事実を伝える平叙文。「車庫に少しある」という新情報を伝える (C) だと、**自然に会話がつながる**。(A) は、he が誰を指すのか不明。また、問い掛けの need をくり返すことで誤答を誘っている。(B) は、store の派生語 storage がひっかけになっている。

- store ～を保管する
- decoration 装飾、飾りつけ
- garage 車庫

TEST 2
PART 2

音声ファイル T2_P2_Q23 ▶ T2_P2_Q28

| 問題 | 訳 |

23. Why are all the trains to Bern running behind schedule?
(A) It will be delivered today, though.
(B) There's a problem on the tracks.
(C) We should leave at once.

Bern 行きの列車がすべて予定より遅れているのはなぜなの?
(A) それはきょう配達されますが。
(B) 線路に問題があるんです。
(C) 私たちはすぐに出発すべきです。

24. How do I register for the art contest?
(A) Let's try again tomorrow.
(B) Mr. Cooper painted it.
(C) Have you checked the brochure?

その芸術コンクールにどうやって登録するのかな?
(A) 明日もう一度やってみましょう。
(B) Cooper 氏がそれを描いたのよ。
(C) 小冊子は確認したの?

25. You haven't seen my notebook around here, have you?
(A) He writes excellent reports.
(B) You haven't been around lately.
(C) The one with the yellow binding?

このへんで私のノートを見かけてないわよね。
(A) 彼は優れた報告書を書くんだ。
(B) 最近あなたを見かけないね。
(C) 黄色い装丁のやつ?

26. Who can deliver these packets to the bank across the street?
(A) Do you need it done right away?
(B) You can deposit those there.
(C) Find one in the directory.

これらの小包を通りの向こうの銀行へ誰が運んでくれるんだい?
(A) すぐに終わらせる必要がある?
(B) それらをそこに預け入れられるわよ。
(C) この名簿で見つけて。

27. Should I post the schedule of activities or do you want to look over it first?
(A) No, she isn't coming.
(B) Actually, can you forward it to Ms. Cole?
(C) A marketing workshop.

活動予定表を掲示しましょうか、それとも先に目を通されますか。
(A) いいや、彼女は来ない。
(B) 実は、Cole さんに転送してくれるかい?
(C) マーケティングの研修会だ。

28. Isn't Mr. McAvoy going to join us for dinner?
(A) His meeting still hasn't ended.
(B) The plans are over there.
(C) During the last session.

McAvoy 氏はわれわれと夕食をご一緒されないのですか。
(A) 彼は会議がまだ終わってないのよ。
(B) その計画案はあそこにあるわ。
(C) 以前の開催期間中に。

TOEIC豆知識 TOEIC人は非常に仕事熱心だが、それは、convention や trade fair、conference がしょっちゅう開かれていることからも、うかがい知ることができる。（続く▶）

正解＆解説

23. 正解 (B) 難易度 難
Why 疑問文で、列車遅延の〈理由〉が問われている。正解は「線路に問題がある」という理由を答えている (B)。(A) は、理由の問いに対して日時を答えている。(C) は、**behind schedule**（予定より遅れて）から連想される leave at once（すぐに出発する）で混同をねらっている。

☐ run 運行する
☐ behind schedule 予定より遅れて
☐ track 鉄道線路　☐ at once すぐに

24. 正解 (C) 難易度 難
How 疑問文で、コンクールへの登録〈方法・手段〉が問われている。これに対して、(C) は「小冊子を確認したか」と聞き返すことで、暗に**「登録方法が小冊子に載っていること」**を伝えている。会話が成立するので、これが正解。(A) は登録期限についての会話だと誤解してしまうと、tomorrow がひっかけになる。(B) は、art（芸術）から連想される painted（〜を描いた）で誤答を誘っている。

☐ register for 〜 〜に登録する
☐ brochure 小冊子、パンフレット

25. 正解 (C) 難易度 難
現在完了時制の付加疑問文。付加疑問文は混乱しがちだが、「ノートを見かけたか」という**通常の疑問文に置き換えて**考えよう。これに対して、(C) の one は notebook を指しており、「黄色い装丁のノートか」という確認になる。自然な応答なので、これが正解。(A) は he が誰なのか不明。また、notebook から連想される write（〜を書く）がひっかけ。(B) は問い掛けの You haven't と around をくり返して誤答を誘っている。

☐ lately 最近、近ごろ
☐ binding 表紙、装丁

26. 正解 (A) 難易度 難
小包を銀行に運んでくれる〈人〉を尋ねる Who 疑問文。(A) は直接的な応答ではないが、「すぐに運ばなければいけないのか」と聞き返すことで**自然な会話**になっている。(B) は、bank（銀行）から連想される deposit（〜を預金する）でひっかけをねらっている。(C) は「directory（名簿）から見つけて」という人に関わる応答だが、常識的に考えて「荷物を運ぶ人を名簿から見つける」というのは不自然なので誤り。

☐ packet 小包
☐ deposit 〜を預け入れる
☐ directory 名簿

27. 正解 (B) 難易度 難
「予定表を掲示する」か「その前に確認する」かの〈選択〉が求められている。しかし、**どちらも選択せずに**「Cole さんへの転送」を依頼している (B) が正解。(A) は、she が誰なのか不明で会話が成立しない。(C) も文脈に一致しない。

☐ post 〜を掲示する
☐ look over 〜 〜に目を通す
☐ forward 〜を転送する

28. 正解 (A) 難易度 難
否定疑問文が苦手な人は、「McAvoy 氏は夕食を一緒に食べるのか」という**通常の疑問文に置き換えて**考えよう。正解は「会議がまだ終わっていない」、つまり「夕食を一緒に食べない」と**間接的**に伝える (A)。(B) は「McAvoy 氏が夕食に行くこと」を plans（計画）だと誤解させようとしている。(C) は、時の表現 last session（先の開催期間）で、夕食時間を答えていると誤解させようとしている。

13

TEST 2
PART 2

音声ファイル 🔊 T2_P2_Q29 ▶ T2_P2_Q34

問題 | **訳**

---

29. Does your store offer refunds and exchanges?
(A) Only under certain circumstances.
(B) It sells electronic equipment.
(C) I exchanged some dollars this morning.

あなたの店では払い戻しや交換を受け付けてらっしゃいますか。
(A) 特定の状況下のみで、ですが。
(B) 電子機器を販売しています。
(C) 今朝数ドルを両替しました。

---

30. We're extremely pleased with your work on this project.
(A) Thank you. I'm quite proud of it myself.
(B) I no longer work there.
(C) That's an excellent suggestion.

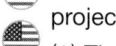

このプロジェクトでのあなたの功績にたいへん満足しています。
(A) ありがとうございます。私自身も誇りに思っています。
(B) 私はもうそこでは働きません。
(C) それは素晴らしい提案です。

---

31. I'll install those shelves in the garage this weekend.
(A) It's about time.
(B) It's very close to home.
(C) Choose a parking stall.

今週末に、それらの棚を車庫に取り付けるのよ。
(A) ようやくだね。
(B) それは家にとても近いんだ。
(C) 駐車スペースを選んでね。

---

32. Can you send me a copy of the sales invoice?
(A) Twenty cents each.
(B) In the bottom drawer.
(C) Check your in-box.

販売請求書の写しを私に送ってくれますか。
(A) それぞれ20セントだわ。
(B) いちばん下の引き出しの中よ。
(C) 受信トレイを確認して。

---

33. Our new ad should start appearing on TV this month.
(A) How often will it be on?
(B) No, it's an old one.
(C) I'll make an appearance.

われわれの新しい広告は今月からテレビに出始めるはずです。
(A) どれくらいの頻度で出るんだい?
(B) いいや、それは古いものだよ。
(C) 私が出演するんだ。

---

34. You've been to these parts before, haven't you?
(A) We depart this evening.
(B) No, let's do it after.
(C) On several occasions, actually.

これらの地域に行ったことがあるよね。
(A) 私たちは今晩出発するわ。
(B) いいえ、あとでやりましょう。
(C) 実は、何度かね。

TOEIC豆知識 convention は「大会、会議」／trade fair は「見本市、展示会」／conference は「会議」。これらが出題されない回はない！ そう言い切れるほど、超頻出。

正解＆解説

29. 正解 (A) 難易度 ■■□ 難

Yes/No 疑問文。お店で、払い戻しと商品交換の可否が問われているのに対し、正解は (A)。「特定の状況下では（受け付けている）」という応答で、**間接的に**払い戻しと交換が可能だと伝えている。(B) は store（お店）から連想される sells electronic equipment（電子機器を売る）、(C) は exchanges（交換）に対する exchanged（～を両替した）で、それぞれひっかけをねらっている。

間違いメモ＆単語

あなたの解答 A B C

メモ

☐ refund 払い戻し ☐ exchange 交換
☐ under ～のもとで ☐ certain ある、特定の ☐ circumstance 状況

30. 正解 (A) 難易度 ■■□ 難

相手の功績に満足しているという意見を伝える平叙文に対し、もっとも**自然な流れ**になるのは (A)。Thank you. と感謝したあと、自分の意見を付け加えている。(B) は、問い掛けの work（功績）を動詞（働く）としてくり返して、誤答を誘っている。(C) は project から連想される suggestion（提案）がひっかけ。

あなたの解答 A B C

メモ

☐ extremely とても、たいへん
☐ no longer もはや～ない
☐ suggestion 提案

31. 正解 (A) 難易度 ■■■ 難

平叙文で、車庫に棚を付ける計画を述べている。これに「そろそろ、そうする時期だ」と賛同を示している (A) が正解。(B) は garage（車庫）から連想される home（家）、(C) は install と類似した発音の stall で誤答を誘っている。

あなたの解答 A B C

メモ

☐ install ～を取り付ける、設置する
☐ shelf 棚
☐ stall（駐車場などの）区画

32. 正解 (C) 難易度 ■■■ 難

Can you ～？の形で、請求書の送付を〈**依頼**〉されている。これに「（もう送ったので）受信トレイを確認して」と答えた (C) が正解。**送付済みであることを間接的に伝えている**。(A) は、invoice（請求書）から連想される金額で誤答を誘っている。(B) は、「送ってほしい」という依頼に対して、場所を答えるだけでは不自然。

あなたの解答 A B C

メモ

☐ a copy of ～ ～の写し
☐ invoice 請求書 ☐ drawer 引き出し
☐ in-box 受信トレイ

33. 正解 (A) 難易度 ■■□ 難

新しい広告の放送が始まるという情報を、平叙文で伝えている。これに対し、放送の頻度を尋ね返す (A) だと自然な会話になる。(B) の「いや、それは古いもの（広告）だ」は、ぎこちないやりとり。(C) は、appearing の派生語 appearance でひっかけをねらっている。

あなたの解答 A B C

メモ

☐ ad 広告（※ advertisement の省略形）
☐ appear 出現する
☐ make an appearance 登場する

34. 正解 (C) 難易度 ■■□ 難

現在完了時制の付加疑問文。**通常の疑問文に置き換えて**「これらの地域に行ったことがあるか」と問われていると考えよう。正解は、「実は、何度か（行ったことがある）」と答え、肯定をしている (C)。(A) は、these parts と depart という発音の類似した語句で、(B) は、before の反意語 after で、誤答を誘っている。

あなたの解答 A B C

メモ

☐ part 地方、地域
☐ depart 出発する
☐ on several occasions 何度か

TEST 2
PART 2

音声ファイル 🔊 T2_P2_Q35 ▶ T2_P2_Q40
問題 / 訳

35. Am I supposed to lock up the building before I leave?
(A) The custodian takes care of that.
(B) We can look for it later.
(C) It's never too late.

建物を出る前に鍵をかけなければいけないの?
(A) それは管理人が対処してくれるよ。
(B) あとで探せるさ。
(C) けっして遅すぎるということはないよ。

36. Why did you buy so many stacks of paper?
(A) There was a sale at the store.
(B) The printer is stuck again.
(C) I forgot to stop by.

どうしてそんなに山ほど紙を買ったの?
(A) その店で特売をしてたんだ。
(B) またプリンターが動かなくなったよ。
(C) 立ち寄るのを忘れてしまってね。

37. Should we color the illustrations on the computer?
(A) Yes, he's the illustrator doing the project.
(B) That is probably the easiest way.
(C) It's quite colorful.

コンピュータ上でその絵に色を付けるべきかな。
(A) ええ、彼がこの計画に取り組んでいるイラストレーターよ。
(B) たぶんそれがいちばん簡単ね。
(C) それはとても色鮮やかよ。

38. Who should we hire to cater the event?
(A) At noon in the main dining hall.
(B) I've got a list on my computer.
(C) Later this evening.

このイベントの仕出しを誰に頼むべきかしら。
(A) 正午に大食堂で。
(B) 僕のコンピュータにリストがあるよ。
(C) 今晩遅くに。

39. The department supervisor changed the job assignments, didn't he?
(A) No, in the newspaper.
(B) He took some notes.
(C) Yes. Have you seen them?

部門長は仕事の割り当てを変えたんだよね。
(A) いいえ、新聞です。
(B) 彼はメモを取りました。
(C) ええ。それらを見ました?

40. It's not the best time for employees to go on holiday.
(A) Yes, I just took a week off.
(B) You're right. A lot of orders are coming in.
(C) I'll mark my calendar.

従業員が休暇に出かけるのに最適な時期ではないわ。
(A) ええ、ちょうど1週間の休みを取ったところです。
(B) そうですね。たくさんの注文が来ていますから。
(C) カレンダーに印を付けます。

正解＆解説

35. 正解 (A) 難易度 難

Yes/No 疑問文で、施錠すべきかどうかが問われている。これに「管理人が対処する」と答え、**「施錠しなくてよい」**ことを**間接的**に伝えている (A) が正解。(B) は later（後で）、(C) は late（遅い）が、それぞれ before（〜する前に）から連想されるひっかけになっている。

あなたの解答 A B C
メモ

☐ *be* supposed to *do* 〜することになっている ☐ custodian 管理人 ☐ take care of 〜 〜を責任をもって引き受ける

36. 正解 (A) 難易度 難

Why 疑問文で、紙をたくさん買った〈理由〉が問われている。「店で特売があった」という理由を答えた (A) が正解。Part 2 では、このように **Because なしで、理由を答えるケース**が多いことを覚えておこう。(B) は、paper（紙）から連想される printer（プリンター）に加え、stacks と stuck という発音の類似した単語で誤答を誘っている。buy に対する (C) の by もひっかけ。

あなたの解答 A B C
メモ

☐ stacks of 〜 多量（数）の〜
☐ stuck 動かない

37. 正解 (B) 難易度 難

コンピュータで色をつけるべきかどうかが問われている。正解は「それがいちばん簡単だ」と答えている (B)。**間接的**に「パソコンで色をつけるべき」ということを伝えている。(A) は he が何を指すか不明。また、illustrations の派生語 illustrator でひっかけをねらっている。(C) も color の派生語 colorful がひっかけ。

あなたの解答 A B C
メモ

☐ color 〜に色を付ける

38. 正解 (B) 難易度 難

Who 疑問文で、仕出しを頼む〈人〉が問われている。正解は「コンピュータにリストがある」と答えた (B)。これは**間接的**に「仕出しを頼める候補者リストを渡す」と伝えている。(A) は時間と場所を答えているので、誤り。また cater（〜に料理を提供する）から連想される dining hall（食堂）がひっかけ。(C) は、時間を答えている。

あなたの解答 A B C
メモ

☐ cater 〜の料理をまかなう、〜に仕出しをする

39. 正解 (C) 難易度 難

付加疑問文は**通常の疑問文に置き換える**とわかりやすい。「部門長は仕事の割り当てを変えたのか」と問われていると考える。これに Yes（＝変えた）と答えたあと、「それを見たか」と尋ね返している (C) が正解。(A) は No で答えたのはよいが、続く in the newspaper（新聞で）が質問に対応しない。(B) は、assignments（割り当て）の別の意味「宿題」から連想される「ノートを取る」という内容で誤答を誘っている。

あなたの解答 A B C
メモ

☐ department （企業の）部、課
☐ job assignment 職務分担

40. 正解 (B) 難易度 難

平叙文で「従業員が休暇を取るのにいい時期ではない」と意見を述べている。これに対して、You're right. と同意したあと、「注文がたくさん来ている」という理由を付け加えた (B) が正解。(A) は Yes まではよいが、以降の内容が問い掛けに対応しない。(C) は、holiday（休暇）から連想される calendar（カレンダー）が誤答を誘っている。

あなたの解答 A B C
メモ

☐ go on holiday 休暇に出かける
☐ mark 〜に印をつける

TEST 2 PART 3 問題文＆訳

41. What is the man working on?
   (A) A budget report
   (B) An analysis of production
   (C) An agenda for a meeting
   (D) A manufacturing schedule

42. What does the man say he will do?
   (A) Contact the board chairman
   (B) Make copies of a report
   (C) Calculate production costs
   (D) Update the woman on his work progress

43. What does the woman ask the man to do?
   (A) Meet for lunch
   (B) Schedule an appointment
   (C) Forward some documents
   (D) Speak to a client

Questions 41-43 refer to the following conversation.

W: Hi Warren. ❶Could I have a look at your production analysis before you present it to the board tomorrow morning?

M: Actually, ❷I'm not quite finished working on it. I should be done by noon. ❸I will call you when it's completed and show you what I've accomplished.

W: That sounds fine. Also, ❹could you send me a copy of the reports you plan to hand out to the board members? I just want to have a look at some of the figures you've calculated.

設問41から43は次の会話に関する質問です。

女：こんにちは、Warrenさん。明朝の取締役会での発表前に、あなたの生産分析を見せてもらえますか。

男：実は、まだ終わってなくて。昼までには終わらせます。完成したら電話して、できたものをお見せします。

女：それでいいです。それと取締役に配布する報告書のコピーも送ってくれますか。算出した数値のいくつかに目を通しておきたいので。

---

44. Where most likely are the speakers?
   (A) At a repair shop
   (B) In a factory
   (C) In a store
   (D) In an office

45. What does the woman say about the new products?
   (A) They are imported.
   (B) They are colorful.
   (C) They are discounted.
   (D) They are comfortable.

46. What problem does the man mention?
   (A) An item has been sold out.
   (B) He is suffering from a medical problem.
   (C) The color he wants is not available.
   (D) He doesn't have enough support staff.

Questions 44-46 refer to the following conversation.

M: Hi. I'm looking for a computer chair with a comfortable backrest to use at the office. ❶I was told this shop carries a wide selection of office chairs.

W: We have a selection of ❷new chairs especially designed to provide good back support. They come in blue and black, and have adjustable features. Would you like to check them out?

M: Yes, please. ❸My current chair has been giving me chronic back pains, so I really need to buy a new one as soon as possible.

設問44から46は次の会話に関する質問です。

男：こんにちは。会社用に、心地よい背もたれのついたコンピュータ・チェアを探しているんです。このお店では事務用のイスを幅広く取り扱っていると聞いたんですが。

女：私どもは、背中をしっかりサポートするよう特別にデザインされた新しいイスを取り揃えております。青と黒があり、調節機能がついています。ご覧になりますか。

男：ええ、ぜひ。今の私のイスだと、慢性的な腰痛になるので、できるだけ早く新しいものを買いたいんですよ。

設問の訳 ☞ p.28〜29参照

TOEIC豆知識 TOEICに登場する電話番号は、市外局番がほぼ間違いなく「555」である。ただ、細かい番号を聞き分けるような問題は出題されないので、まったく気にする必要はないんだけど。

正解＆解説

41. 正解 (B) 難易度■■□□ 難

男性が取り組んでいる仕事が何かを尋ねている。❶で女性が「**production analysis**（生産分析）を見せてほしい」と依頼し、❷で男性が「まだ終わっていない」と答えている。つまり、今、男性は生産分析に取り組んでいるということ。従って、(B) が正解。

42. 正解 (D) 難易度■■■□ 難

これから何をすると、**男性が言っている**かを尋ねているので、**男性の発言に注目**。❸で「それ（= production analysis）が完成したら電話して、お見せする」と言っている。これを「仕事の進み具合を女性に知らせる」と言い換えた (D) が正解。**update** は「〜に最新情報を伝える」の意。

43. 正解 (C) 難易度■■□□ 難

女性が依頼した内容を尋ねているので、**女性の発言に注目**。女性は❹で「報告書の写しを送ってほしい」と依頼している。これを Forward some documents（書類を転送する）と言い換えた (C) が正解。Could you 〜 ? は典型的な依頼表現なので覚えておこう。

単語 □ production 生産 □ analysis 分析 □ board 取締役会 □ accomplish 〜を成し遂げる □ hand out 〜を配布する □ figure 数値 □ calculate 〜を算出する [41] □ budget 予算 □ agenda 議題 □ manufacturing 製造の [42] □ chairman 会長、議長 □ update 〜に最新情報を伝える [43] □ schedule 〜を予定する

44. 正解 (C) 難易度■□□□ 難

会話の場所を尋ねる、全体的な設問。❶に「この店には**事務用のイス**がたくさんあると聞いた」とあるので、ここが**家具店**だろうとわかる。これに一致するのは、幅広く「店舗に」としている (C)。

45. 正解 (D) 難易度■■■□ 難

新製品について、**女性が言っている**ことを尋ねているので、**女性の発言に注目**。❷の new chairs が設問の new products（新製品）のこと。「新しいイスは背中をサポートするようデザインされている」と言っている。このことは「**（座り）心地がよい**」と言い換えることもできるので (D) が正解。They come in blue and black（青と黒がある）としか言っていないので、(B) は誤り。

46. 正解 (B) 難易度■■□□ 難

男性が言及している問題点を尋ねているので、**男性のネガティブな発言要素に注目**する。❸で「今のイスのせいで**慢性的な腰痛**だ」と言っている。この問題点を「健康上の問題に苦しんでいる」と言い換えた (B) が正解。

単語 □ backrest 背もたれ □ carry 〜を（商品として）置いている、取り扱っている □ a wide selection of 〜 〜の豊富な品ぞろえ □ provide 〜を提供する □ feature 特徴、機能 □ check out 〜を調べる、試す □ current 現在の □ chronic 慢性的な [44] □ repair 修理 [46] □ suffer from 〜 （病気など）〜に苦しむ、悩む

TEST 2 — PART 3

47. What are the speakers discussing?
(A) A university class
(B) A language course
(C) A travel package
(D) A work schedule

48. What does the woman mention about the hotel?
(A) It will raise its charges.
(B) It is located in South America.
(C) It often accommodates foreign guests.
(D) It provides student rates.

49. When will the classes most likely start?
(A) On Monday
(B) On Tuesday
(C) Next Wednesday
(D) Next Friday

Questions 47-49 refer to the following conversation.

M: Hi Arlene. Have you heard that ❶we will be having Spanish classes starting next week?
W: Oh really? ❷That's good. The hotel's had many South American visitors over the years, so I'm sure learning a new language will help us improve our customer service. Do you know the schedule?
M: Yeah. I think classes will be held every Wednesday and Friday at 5 P.M. The same class is offered twice each week, so you can choose to go either on Wednesdays or on Fridays.
W: Thanks. ❸I'll probably attend the first class on Friday.

設問47から49は次の会話に関する質問です。
男：やあ、Arlene。来週から始まるスペイン語のクラスがあるって聞いた？
女：ええ、本当？　いいわね。ここ数年ホテルには南米からのお客さまがたくさんいるから、新しいことばを学べばカスタマーサービス向上に役立つわ。日程は知ってる？
男：うん。毎水曜日と金曜日の午後5時からだよ。同じクラスが週2回あるから、水曜か金曜のどちらかを選ぶことができるよ。
女：ありがとう。たぶん金曜の最初のクラスに出席するわ。

50. What type of business do the speakers work for?
(A) A recruitment company
(B) A public relations firm
(C) A legal office
(D) A banking institution

51. What does the woman require for an assistant?
(A) College education
(B) Willingness to relocate
(C) Flexible schedule
(D) Relevant experience

52. What does the man say about Sam Washington?
(A) He currently works in Baltimore.
(B) He has an educational background in law.
(C) He resides near the office.
(D) He recently relocated.

Questions 50-52 refer to the following conversation.

M: Hey Natasha, ❶have you managed to find a personal assistant yet?
W: ❷No. I interviewed six applicants last week, but none of them had any experience working at a law office. Sandra Chen said she found an assistant through a recruitment company, so I may contact them, but I really don't want to have to pay a recruitment fee.
M: Well, I was asking because my neighbor ❸Sam Washington just moved here from Baltimore. He was a ❹legal aid there and is looking for work here in Philadelphia. He sent me a copy of his résumé and references, and seems quite professional. I can forward them to you if you want.

設問50から52は次の会話に関する質問です。
男：やあ、Natasha、もう個人秘書を見つけることができたかい。
女：いいえ。先週6人の候補者を面接したけど、誰も法律事務所で働いた経験がないの。Sandra Chen さんは、人材紹介会社を通じて秘書を見つけたと言っていたから、私も連絡するかも。けど、どうしても人材紹介料を払いたくないの。
男：僕の近所の Sam Washington さんが、ボルティモアから引っ越してきたばかりなので聞いてみたんだけど。彼は向こうで法律支援をやっていて、ここフィラデルフィアで仕事を探しているんだ。履歴書と推薦状のコピーを送ってくれたけど、かなり専門的なようだよ。よかったらコピーを転送するよ。

設問の訳 ☞ p.28〜29参照

正解＆解説

47. 正解 (B)　難易度：難

会話の主題を問う設問なので、**冒頭に注目**。❶の男性の発言「スペイン語のクラスが来週から始まる」に対し、❷で女性は「ホテルには南米からの宿泊客がくるから、カスタマーサービスの向上につながる」と答え、以降もこのクラスについての話が続く。これらのことから、この**授業はホテルの語学研修**だと考えられるので、(A)「大学の授業」ではなく、(B)「語学コース」が正解。

48. 正解 (C)　難易度：難

ホテルについて、**女性が触れている**ことを尋ねているので、**女性の発言に注目**。❷で「ここ数年、**ホテルには南米から宿泊客がくる**」と言っているのを、「ホテルは外国客をよくもてなしている」と言い換えた (C) が正解。South American につられて、(B) を選ばないように。

49. 正解 (D)　難易度：難

スペイン語のクラスがいつ始まるかを尋ねている。❶から「来週始まること」がわかり、❸から「金曜日が最初の授業」とわかる。従って、**来週の金曜日**から授業が始まると考えられるので、正解は (D)。

単語 □ hold ～を開催する　**48** □ raise ～を引き上げる　□ charge 料金　□ be located 位置する　□ accommodate ～を宿泊させる　□ rate 料金、値段

50. 正解 (C)　難易度：難

話者2人の職種を尋ねている。❶で男性が「秘書は見つかったか」と尋ね、❷で女性が「いいえ、6人面接したが、誰も law office（法律事務所）での勤務経験がない」と応じている。このやりとりから、2人が**法律事務所で働いている**とわかる。正解は legal office と言い換えた (C)。

51. 正解 (D)　難易度：難

女性が秘書に求めていることを尋ねている。❷から女性は、any experience working at a law office（法律事務所での勤務経験）のある人を探しているとわかる。これを Relevant experience（関連した経験）と言い換えた (D) が正解。

52. 正解 (D)　難易度：難

Sam Washington について、**男性が語った**内容を尋ねているので、**男性の発言に注目**する。❸で「ボルティモアからここに just moved（ちょうど引っ越してきた）」と言っている。これを recently relocated（最近引っ越した）と言い換えている (D) が正解。❹で legal aid をやっていたと言っているが、学歴については言及していないので (B) は誤り。

単語 □ manage to do なんとか～する　□ personal assistant 個人秘書　□ interview ～を面接する　□ applicant 応募者　□ law office 法律事務所　□ recruitment 採用　□ fee 料金　□ legal aid 法律に関する援助者　□ résumé 履歴書　□ reference 推薦状　**50** □ public relations 宣伝（広報）活動　□ institution 機関、団体　**51** □ willingness 意欲　□ relocate 移住（移転）する　□ relevant 関係のある　**52** □ background 経歴　□ reside 住む

TEST 2 PART 3

53. Who does the woman say she just spoke to?
 (A) A trade fair representative
 (B) A clerk from a rental agency
 (C) An employee from a printing business
 (D) A layout designer

54. What does Mr. Fredrick recommend the woman do?
 (A) Ask a colleague to accompany her
 (B) Contact the print shop
 (C) Attend the trade fair
 (D) Distribute some catalogs

55. What does the woman offer to do?
 (A) Send a billing statement
 (B) Check for errors in a catalog
 (C) Arrange a meeting with Mohinder
 (D) Deliver a payment to the printer

56. Where most likely do the speakers work?
 (A) At a convention center
 (B) At a travel agency
 (C) At a financial firm
 (D) At a hotel

57. Why is Greystone Financial calling?
 (A) To schedule a conference
 (B) To ask about ticket availability
 (C) To inquire about vacancies
 (D) To request a deposit payment

58. What will the woman probably do next?
 (A) Call Greystone Financial
 (B) Reschedule a conference event
 (C) Contact another department
 (D) Fill out a reservation form

Questions 53-55 refer to the following conversation.

W: ❶Mr. Fredrick, ❷someone from the print shop just called and said the catalogs we ordered for the trade fair are ready.

M: Excellent. Could you drop by the shop after lunch and pick them up? You can take one of the company cars. ❸You may want to ask Mohinder to go with you if you think you'll need some extra help.

W: No problem. Actually, ❹I can also pay our bill while I'm there.

M: That's a good idea. First, have a look through the catalogs and make sure there aren't any problems or errors. Then you can give them a check.

設問53から55は次の会話に関する質問です。

女：Fredrickさん、印刷店の人から電話があり、見本市のために注文したカタログが出来あがったとのことです。
男：素晴らしい。昼食後、印刷店に寄って取って来てくれますか。社用車を使ってください。人手が必要なら、Mohinderさんに同行を頼んでもいいですよ。
女：大丈夫です。それだけじゃなく、そのときに代金を支払うこともできますが。
男：それはいい考えですね。まず、カタログに目を通して、問題や間違いがないことを確かめるように。そうしてから、小切手を切ってください。

Questions 56-58 refer to the following conversation.

M: Danielle, it's Greystone Financial on the phone. ❶They want to know if we have any vacancies for seven single rooms from June fourth through the sixth.

W: Let me check. Yes, it looks like we can ❷make the booking for them. But they should book the rooms as soon as possible, as there will be another convention in town.

M: Great. They also want to know if we have a conference room they could use on the morning of the fifth from 9 A.M. until noon.

W: ❸I don't have that information right here. I'll have to call the business center and find out. Tell them I will call them back in about 15 minutes.

設問56から58は次の会話に関する質問です。

男：Danielleさん、Greystone Financial社から電話です。6月4日から6日でシングルが7部屋空いているか知りたいそうです。
女：確認します。はい、予約できると思います。でも町で別のコンベンションがあるので、できるだけ早く部屋を予約していただかなければいけないですね。
男：よかった。5日の午前9時から正午まで使用できる会議室があるかどうかも知りたいようです。
女：その情報は今ここにはないんです。ビジネスセンターに電話して確認しなければいけません。15分ほどで折り返し電話すると伝えてください。

設問の訳 ☞ p.28〜29参照

TOEIC豆知識 TOEICに登場する病院は、土日も開業していて親切である。が、平日とはビミョーに開業時間が違っていて、問題を解くうえでは、その親切があだとなる。

正解＆解説

53. 正解 (C) 難易度 難
誰と話したと女性が言っているかを尋ねているので、女性の発言に注目。❷で「someone from the print shop（印刷店の人）から電話があり〜と言った」と話している。つまり、印刷店の店員と話したということなので、これを An employee from a printing business（印刷業者の社員）と言い換えた (C) が正解。(A) は会話に登場する trade fair を使ったひっかけ。

54. 正解 (A) 難易度 難
Fredrick さんが女性に勧めていることを尋ねている。まず❶で女性が Mr. Fredrick と呼びかけていることから、男性＝ Fredrick さんということを把握。その男性が❸で「人手が必要なら Mohinder さんに頼んで一緒に行ってもらうといい」と勧めている。これを「同僚に同行を頼む」と言い換えた (A) が正解。

55. 正解 (D) 難易度 難
女性の提案内容を尋ねているので、女性の発言に注目。❹で「そこで代金の支払いもできる」と提案している。これを Deliver a payment to the printer（印刷業者に代金を届ける）と言い換えた (D) が正解。

単語 □ trade fair 見本市、展示会　□ drop by 〜 〜に立ち寄る　□ pick up 〜 〜を取って来る　□ bill 請求金額、請求書　□ check 小切手　**53** □ representative 担当者　**54** □ recommend （人に）〜を勧める　□ colleague 同僚　□ accompany 〜に付いて行く　□ distribute 〜を配布する　**55** □ billing statement 請求書　□ arrange 〜の手はずを整える

56. 正解 (D) 難易度 難
話者2人の職場を尋ねている。❶「シングルが7部屋空いているか知りたがっている」、❷「予約する」などの表現から、2人がホテルに勤めているだろうと推測できる。(D) が正解。❶で if we have any vacancies（私たちに空室があるか）と言っているので、(B) の「旅行代理店」は不適切と判断できる。

57. 正解 (C) 難易度 難
Greystone Financial 社が電話している理由を尋ねている。❶で「彼ら（＝ Greystone Financial 社）は、空室があるかどうかを知りたがっている」と言っているので、目的は To inquire about vacancies（空室を問い合わせるため）だと明らか。(C) が正解。

58. 正解 (C) 難易度 難
女性の次の行動を尋ねている。このように会話後に何をするかを問う設問では、会話の終盤にヒントがあることが多い。❸で「その情報は、今ここにない」と言ったあと、「ビジネスセンターに電話して確認する」と言っている。正解は、ビジネスセンター、つまり「別の部署に連絡する」となっている (C)。

単語 □ vacancy 空室　□ convention 集会、大会　□ conference room 会議室　**56** □ travel agency 旅行代理店　□ financial 金融上の　**57** □ availability （入手の）可能性　□ inquire 尋ねる　□ deposit 手付金　**58** □ fill out 〜 〜に記入する　□ reservation 予約　□ form 用紙、書式

TEST 2 PART 3

音声ファイル T2_P3_59-61 ▶ T2_P3_Q59-61 / T2_P3_62-64 ▶ T2_P3_Q62-64

問題文＆訳

59. What type of business do the speakers probably work at?
(A) A local newspaper
(B) A supermarket
(C) A culinary school
(D) A restaurant

60. What did the critic mention in the review?
(A) Items are reasonably priced.
(B) A book will soon be available.
(C) Service was excellent.
(D) A product will help business owners.

61. What does the man say he will do?
(A) Advertise a job position
(B) Try a new product
(C) Post an article
(D) Write to a publication

Questions 59-61 refer to the following conversation. W M

W: Brian, did you see the review in yesterday's paper? The critic gave us four stars and wrote a very positive article.
M: Wonderful! Positive reviews like that should really help our business. ❶Did the critic mention anything specifically about our menu?
W: ❷He said he was pleased someone finally opened a place that serves Greek dishes, as there is no other establishment which has that type of food in this area. And ❸he also said that the food was delicious and our prices are reasonable.
M: That's great! I think ❹I'll get a copy of the review and put it up on the wall.

設問59から61は次の会話に関する質問です。

女：Brian、きのうの新聞のレビュー見た？ 批評家が私たちに4つ星をつけて、とても好意的な記事を書いていたわよ。
男：素晴らしい！ そういう好意的なレビューは私たちの仕事を本当に助けてくれるんだ。批評家はメニューについて特に何か言っていなかった？
女：ギリシャ料理を出す店がついにオープンしたと喜んでいたわ。この地域にその類の料理を出す店がほかにないから。それに、おいしくて価格は良心的だとも言ってたわね。
男：それはすごい！ そのレビューをコピーして壁に貼ろう。

62. Who is Ellen Grey?
(A) A security officer
(B) A personal assistant
(C) A workshop instructor
(D) A new employee

63. Why is the woman meeting Mr. Chambers?
(A) She is interviewing for a job.
(B) She needs to get a security pass.
(C) She is scheduled to receive training.
(D) She wants to discuss a building project.

64. According to James Walsh, what is the security pass for?
(A) Going through the main office entrance
(B) Usage of the elevators
(C) Accessing a parking facility
(D) Entering a private office

Questions 62-64 refer to the following conversation. W M

W: Hello. My name is Ellen Grey and ❶I'm looking for Mr. Chambers. He is supposed to do my orientation this morning.
M: Oh yes. I'm James Walsh, his assistant. Mr. Chambers hasn't arrived yet but should be here shortly. ❷Why don't I show you to your office and get you a security pass?
W: That sounds good. ❸Is the pass to enter the building?
M: No, ❹it's for your personal office. Doors to the building and our main entrance remain open during regular business hours. If you'll just follow me, I'll take you to your office.

設問62から64は次の会話に関する質問です。

女：こんにちは。Ellen Greyと申しますが、Chambersさんを探しています。今朝、彼がオリエンテーションをしてくださることになっているんです。
男：ああ、なるほど。私はJames Walshと申しまして、彼の秘書です。Chambersさんはまだ出社していないのですが、まもなく来ます。あなたのオフィスへご案内して、セキュリティパスを取ってきましょう。
女：それはいいですね。そのパスは建物に入るためのものですか。
男：いいえ、あなた個人のオフィス用です。建物のドアと正面玄関は通常の勤務時間内は開いたままになっています。一緒に来ていただければ、あなたのオフィスまでお連れします。

設問の訳 ☞ p.28〜29参照

正解＆解説　　　　　　　　　　　　　　　　　　　間違いメモ

59. 正解 **(D)**　難易度 ■■■□ 難

話者2人の職種を尋ねている。❶で「メニューについて、批評家は何か言っていたか」と質問している。また❷「ギリシャ料理」、❸「料理がおいしい」といった表現から、2人は**飲食店で働いている**と推測できる。従って、(D) A restaurant が正解。料理に関連した (C) A **culinary** school（料理学校）はひっかけ。

あなたの解答　A B C D
メモ

60. 正解 **(A)**　難易度 ■■■□ 難

批評家が言及した内容を尋ねている。批評家の言及内容に触れているのは、❷「ギリシャ料理の店がついにオープンした」、❸「料理がおいしい」「**価格が手頃**」の3点。これに一致するのは (A) の Items are reasonably priced.（料理は手頃な価格である）。

あなたの解答　A B C D
メモ

61. 正解 **(C)**　難易度 ■■■□ 難

男性がこれからすることを尋ねている。未来の行動を問う設問では、会話の**終盤部分に注目**。❹で「レビューのコピーを手に入れて、**壁に貼ろう**」と言っている。この行動を Post an article（記事を貼る）と言い換えた (C) が正解。

あなたの解答　A B C D
メモ

単語 □ article 記事　□ review レビュー、批評　□ critic 批評家　□ mention ～に言及する　□ specifically 特に、具体的に　□ serve （食べ物）を出す　□ dish 料理　□ establishment 施設　59 □ culinary 料理の　61 □ job position 職、勤め口　□ publication 出版物

---

62. 正解 **(D)**　難易度 ■■■□ 難

Ellen Grey、つまり女性が誰かを尋ねている。女性の❶「彼（= Chambers さん）が私のオリエンテーションをしてくれる予定」、男性の❷「あなたのオフィスに案内しよう」「セキュリティパスを取ってこよう」といった表現から、女性は**新しい従業員**だと推測できる。よって (D) が正解。(B) の A personal assistant（個人秘書）は男性（James Walsh）のこと。

あなたの解答　A B C D
メモ

63. 正解 **(C)**　難易度 ■■■□ 難

女性が Chambers さんに会う理由を尋ねている。女性は❶で「Chambers さんを探している」と言ったあと、「彼が私のオリエンテーションをしてくれる予定」と続けている。つまり、**オリエンテーションのため**に会おうとしていることがわかる。orientation を training と言い換えた (C)「彼女は訓練を受ける予定だ」が正解。

あなたの解答　A B C D
メモ

64. 正解 **(D)**　難易度 ■■■□ 難

セキュリティパスの用途を尋ねている。According to James Walsh（James Walsh に**よれば**）とあるので、**男性の発言に注目**。女性の❸「このパスは建物に入るためのものか」という質問に対し、男性は❹「**個人オフィス用**」という用途を答えている。これを Entering a private office（個人オフィスへの入室）と表現した (D) が正解。

あなたの解答　A B C D
メモ

単語 □ orientation オリエンテーション、（職業や進路の）指導　□ shortly まもなく　□ business hour 営業時間、勤務時間　64 □ according to ～ ～によれば　□ usage 使用　□ access ～に接近する、入る　□ facility 施設

25

TEST 2
PART 3

音声ファイル 🔊 T2_P3_65-67 ▶ T2_P3_Q65-67 / T2_P3_68-70 ▶ T2_P3_Q68-70

問題文&訳

65. Where most likely does the woman work?
(A) At a food factory
(B) At a newspaper company
(C) At a consultancy firm
(D) At an advertising agency

66. According to the man, why was the merger delayed?
(A) Employees are refusing to follow some policies.
(B) Production equipment had to be improved.
(C) Executives are still working on the contract.
(D) Financial issues had to be settled.

67. What does the man say will happen on May 1?
(A) The companies will announce some information.
(B) The current contracts will expire.
(C) An official offer will be made.
(D) A corporate purchase will be completed.

68. What are the speakers talking about?
(A) A shipment of supplies
(B) Bill payment options
(C) Changes to a purchase
(D) Home renovation plans

69. What does the woman offer to do for the man?
(A) Send his purchase through expedited delivery
(B) Give him a price reduction on some products
(C) Mail him a catalog of merchandise
(D) Provide him with a full refund

70. What does the man ask the woman to do?
(A) Use the same method of payment
(B) Forward a price list
(C) Send him a bill
(D) Exchange an item

Questions 65-67 refer to the following conversation.

W: Mr. Lowell, ❶I'm writing a business report for *Norwood Chronicles*. You recently mentioned that ❷there will be a merger between Pristine Corporation and Yokona Foods, but ❸there seems to be a delay. Are there any changes in the plan?

M: No, we are still pushing through with it. Actually, ❹directors from both companies are finalizing the details. We want to make sure that everything is clear in the agreement.

W: Oh, I see. So, ❺when will you officially announce the merger?

M: ❻We intend to do it by May 1 and hope to settle new company operations by the second week of the month.

設問65から67は次の会話に関する質問です。

女：Lowellさん、私はNorwood Chronicles紙にビジネスレポートを書いております。あなたは最近Pristine Corporation社とYokona食品は合併するとおっしゃっていましたが、遅れがみえます。計画に変更はございませんか。

男：ありません。われわれはまだその件を押し進めています。実際のところ、両社の幹部で詳細を詰めているところです。契約に関してあらゆることを明確にしておきたいのです。

女：なるほど。では、合併の正式発表はいつになりますか。

男：5月1日までに、と考えており、5月の第2週までには新会社の業務を軌道に乗せたいと思っています。

Questions 68-70 refer to the following conversation.

W: Good morning. This is Tracey Champlain calling from Devinyl Furniture. ❶I received an e-mail from you regarding your recent order. You mentioned there was a change you wanted to make.

M: Yes, there is. ❷I ordered six chairs with the dining table and want to increase the number to eight. Could you tell me how much extra that would cost?

W: Well, I will first have to check if we have any more in stock. Let's see ... yes, you are in luck. They will cost an additional $120 a piece. But, as you've already purchased a full set, ❸I can give you a 20 percent discount.

M: That sounds perfect. Go ahead and add them to my order then. ❹You can charge the extra amount to the same credit card I used before. Thanks so much for your assistance.

設問68から70は次の会話に関する質問です。

女：おはようございます。Devinyl家具店のTracey Champlainです。最近のご注文に関して、Eメールを頂戴しました。変更したいことがあるとのことでしたが。

男：ええ、そうなんです。イス6脚をダイニングテーブルと一緒に注文したのですが、それを8脚に増やしたいんです。いくら追加になりますか。

女：まず、在庫を確認しなければ。ええと…、ああ、運がいいですね（在庫があります）。1脚120ドルの追加です。が、すでにフルセットをご購入済みなので、20パーセント割引いたします。

男：完璧です。それでは注文に追加してください。追加額は以前使用したのと同じクレジットカードに請求してください。お手伝いくださり、ありがとうございます。

設問の訳 ☞ p.28～29参照

26

| 正解＆解説 | 間違いメモ |

65. 正解 (B) 難易度 ■■□ 難

女性の職場を尋ねている。女性は❶で「Norwood Chronicles 紙にビジネスレポートを書いている」と言っているので、**新聞社**で働いていると推測できる。よって (B) が正解。chronicle は「（新聞紙名に続けて）〜新聞」という意味。

あなたの解答 A B C D
メモ

66. 正解 (C) 難易度 ■■□ 難

合併遅延の理由を尋ねている。According to the man（**男性によると**）とあるので、**男性の発言に注目**。女性の❷「合併がある」、❸「遅れが見えるが、計画に変更があるのか」という発言を受けて、男性は❹で「役員が**詳細を詰めている**」と答えている。これが遅延の理由と考えられるので、この内容を「役員がまだ契約に取り組んでいる」と言い換えた (C) が正解。

あなたの解答 A B C D
メモ

67. 正解 (A) 難易度 ■■■ 難

5月1日に何があるかを尋ねている。設問のキーワード May 1 に注目して会話を聞こう。女性の❺「合併を公式に発表するのはいつか」という質問に、男性は❻で「5月1日に予定」と答えている。つまり、5月1日に 2社 (Pristine Corporation 社と Yokona 食品) が正式に**合併を発表する**ということ。合併を some information と言い換えた (A)「2社がある情報を発表する」が正解。

あなたの解答 A B C D
メモ

単語 □ merger 合併　□ delay 遅れ　□ push through with 〜　〜をやり通す　□ director 重役　□ finalize 〜を仕上げる　□ agreement 合意　□ intend to do 〜するつもりである　□ settle 〜を確定する、解決する　□ operation 業務　**65** □ consultancy コンサルタント業　**66** □ follow 〜に従う　□ policy 方針　□ executive 役員、幹部　□ issue 問題　**67** □ purchase 買い入れ

68. 正解 (C) 難易度 ■■□ 難

会話の主題を尋ねているので、**冒頭に意識を集中して**聞こう。❶で女性が「（男性から）注文を変更したいとのEメールを受け取った」と述べたのに対し、❷で男性が「イスを6脚から8脚に増やしたい」という具体的な**変更内容**を伝えている。従って、正解は (C) Changes to a purchase（購入の変更）。

あなたの解答 A B C D
メモ

69. 正解 (B) 難易度 ■■□ 難

男性に対して、**女性が提案**していることを尋ねているので、**女性の発言に注目**。❸で「（追加の2脚について）各120ドル必要だが、フルセット購入済みなので、**20パーセント割引する**」と提案している。従って正解は、(B) Give him a price reduction on some products（いくつかの商品で割引をする）。

あなたの解答 A B C D
メモ

70. 正解 (A) 難易度 ■■■ 難

女性に対して、**男性が依頼**している内容を尋ねているので、**男性の発言に注目**。男性は❹で「追加料金は**以前使ったのと同じクレジットカードに請求してほしい**」と頼んでいる。これを Use the same method of payment（同じ支払い方法を使う）と表現した (A) が正解。

あなたの解答 A B C D
メモ

単語 □ regarding 〜に関して　□ stock 在庫　□ luck 幸運　□ additional 追加の　□ charge 〜を請求する　**68** □ supply（通常 -ies で）供給品　□ option オプション、選択肢　□ renovation 改築　**69** □ expedite 〜を迅速に遂行する、急送する　□ reduction 割引、値下げ　□ merchandise 商品、製品　**70** □ method 手段、方法

TEST 2 PART 3

設問の訳

41. 男性は何に取り組んでいるか。
    (A) 予算報告書
    (B) 生産分析
    (C) 会議の議題
    (D) 製造日程

42. 男性は何をすると言っているか。
    (A) 取締役会長に連絡する
    (B) 報告書のコピーを取る
    (C) 生産コストを計算する
    (D) 仕事の進み具合の最新情報を女性に伝える

43. 女性は男性に何をするよう依頼しているか。
    (A) 昼食で会う
    (B) 面会の予定を決める
    (C) 書類を転送する
    (D) 顧客と話す

44. 話者たちはおそらくどこにいるか。
    (A) 修理店に
    (B) 工場に
    (C) 店舗に
    (D) 会社に

45. 女性は新製品について何と言っているか。
    (A) 輸入品である。
    (B) 色とりどりである。
    (C) 割引されている。
    (D) 心地よい。

46. 男性は何が問題だと言っているか。
    (A) 商品が売り切れている。
    (B) 彼は健康上の問題に苦しんでいる。
    (C) 好みの色がない。
    (D) 彼には十分な助手がいない。

47. 話者たちは何を話しているか。
    (A) 大学の授業
    (B) 語学コース
    (C) パッケージ旅行
    (D) 仕事の日程

48. 女性はホテルについて何と言っているか。
    (A) 値段が上がる。
    (B) 南米にある。
    (C) 外国客がよく宿泊する。
    (D) 学生価格を提供する。

49. クラスはおそらくいつ始まるか。
    (A) 月曜日
    (B) 火曜日
    (C) 来週の水曜日
    (D) 来週の金曜日

50. 話者たちはどんな職種で働いているか。
    (A) 人材紹介会社
    (B) PR 会社
    (C) 法律事務所
    (D) 金融機関

51. 女性は秘書に何を求めているか。
    (A) 大学教育
    (B) 引っ越す意志
    (C) 融通が利くスケジュール
    (D) 関連した経験

52. 男性は Sam Washington について何と言っているか。
    (A) 彼は現在ボルティモアで働いている。
    (B) 彼は法律に関する学歴がある。
    (C) 彼は会社の近くに住んでいる。
    (D) 彼は最近引っ越した。

53. 女性はちょうど誰と話したと言っているか。
    (A) 見本市の担当者
    (B) レンタル会社の店員
    (C) 印刷会社の社員
    (D) レイアウトデザイナー

54. Fredrick さんは女性に何をするよう勧めたか。
    (A) 同僚に彼女への同行を頼む
    (B) 印刷店に連絡する
    (C) 見本市に出席する
    (D) カタログを配布する

55. 女性は何をすると申し出ているか。
    (A) 請求書を送る
    (B) カタログの間違いを確認する
    (C) Mohinder さんとの会議を設定する
    (D) 印刷店に代金を届ける

設問の訳

56. 話者たちはおそらくどこで働いているか。
    (A) コンベンションセンター
    (B) 旅行代理店
    (C) 金融会社
    (D) ホテル

57. なぜ Greystone Financial 社は電話しているのか。
    (A) 会議の日程を決めるため
    (B) チケットが手に入るか尋ねるため
    (C) 空室を問い合わせるため
    (D) 前払いを要請するため

58. 女性はおそらく次に何をするか。
    (A) Greystone Financial 社に電話する
    (B) 会議のイベント日程を再調整する
    (C) 別の部署に連絡する
    (D) 予約用紙に記入する

59. おそらく話者たちはどんな職種で働いているか。
    (A) 地元新聞社
    (B) スーパーマーケット
    (C) 料理学校
    (D) レストラン

60. 批評家はレビューで何と述べていたか。
    (A) 料理は手頃な価格である。
    (B) 本がまもなく入手できる。
    (C) サービスが素晴らしかった。
    (D) 製品が経営者の役に立つ。

61. 男性は何をすると言っているか。
    (A) 仕事の募集広告を出す
    (B) 新しい製品を試す
    (C) 記事を貼る
    (D) 出版物に手紙を書く

62. Ellen Grey とは誰か。
    (A) 警備員
    (B) 個人秘書
    (C) ワークショップインストラクター
    (D) 新入社員

63. 女性はなぜ Chambers さんに会うのか。
    (A) 彼女は仕事の面接を受けている。
    (B) 彼女はセキュリティパスを入手する必要がある。
    (C) 彼女は訓練を受ける予定だ。
    (D) 彼女は建設プロジェクトについて話し合いたい。

64. James Walsh によると、セキュリティパスは何のためのものか。
    (A) 本社入り口を通り抜けること
    (B) エレベーターの使用
    (C) 駐車場にアクセスすること
    (D) 個人オフィスへの入室

65. 女性はおそらくどこで働いているか。
    (A) 食品工場
    (B) 新聞社
    (C) コンサルティング会社
    (D) 広告代理店

66. 男性によると、なぜ合併が遅れたのか。
    (A) 社員がいくつかの方針に従うのを拒んでいる。
    (B) 製造設備が改善されなければならなかった。
    (C) 役員がまだ契約に取り組んでいる。
    (D) 財政上の問題が解決されなければならなかった。

67. 男性は5月1日に何が起こると言っているか。
    (A) 2社がある情報を発表する。
    (B) 現在の契約が失効する。
    (C) 正式な申し入れがなされる。
    (D) 企業買収が完了する。

68. 話者たちは何について話しているか。
    (A) 補給品の発送
    (B) 代金の支払方法
    (C) 購入の変更
    (D) 家の改築プラン

69. 女性は男性のために何をすると申し出ているか。
    (A) 優先配送で購入品を送る
    (B) いくつかの商品で割引をする
    (C) 製品カタログを郵送する
    (D) 全額返金をする

70. 男性は女性に何をするよう依頼しているか。
    (A) 同じ支払い方法を使う
    (B) 価格リストを転送する
    (C) 彼に請求書を送る
    (D) 商品を交換する

TEST 2
PART 4

71. What is the organization raising money for?
    (A) An association of teachers
    (B) A planned renovation
    (C) Regional parks
    (D) School libraries

72. What type of event will the association hold?
    (A) A benefit concert
    (B) An athletic competition
    (C) A family picnic
    (D) A seasonal celebration

73. What does the speaker ask listeners to do?
    (A) Volunteer to work with a committee
    (B) Donate books to the school
    (C) Help clean up city parks
    (D) Sell tickets for an event

Questions 71-73 refer to the following announcement.

Thank you all for attending this meeting for the Riverton Parent's Association. This year we plan to host several fundraising events to raise money for our local schools. ❶The first event will be our Spring Festival to be held in City Park. We will need volunteers to help with promotions and planning. ❷The money raised from the festival will go to help purchase new books for the schools' libraries. I am going to pass around a sign-up sheet and ❸hope that you will all volunteer to work in one of the committees that are listed.

設問71から73は次のアナウンスに関する質問です。
　Riverton保護者協会の集会にお集まりいただき、ありがとうございます。今年は、当地域にある学校への寄付を募る募金イベントをいくつか主催予定です。最初のイベントは、City公園で開催されるスプリング・フェスティバルです。広報宣伝や計画のお手伝いをしてくれるボランティアが必要です。このお祭で集められたお金は、学校図書館のための新しい本の購入に役立てられます。登録用紙を回しますので、みなさんが、記載されているいずれかの委員会に志願して働いてくださることを期待しています。

---

74. What is the purpose of the message?
    (A) To offer a discounted subscription plan
    (B) To announce a regular maintenance schedule
    (C) To assist customers outside of office hours
    (D) To promote a new selection of products

75. What should listeners do if they have Internet problems?
    (A) Scan their computers
    (B) Reset their machines
    (C) Visit a repair center
    (D) Call another number

76. Who would most likely leave a message?
    (A) A subscriber experiencing slow connectivity
    (B) A customer questioning some charges
    (C) A field technician submitting a report
    (D) A business client making a proposal

Questions 74-76 refer to the following recorded message.

❶Thank you for calling Connecters Broadband customer service. ❷For information about our products and services, or to speak to a sales representative, please call back during our regular business hours from 9 A.M. to 6 P.M. Mondays to Saturdays. ❸However, if you are currently experiencing problems with your Internet connection, please contact our 24-hour technical support department at 555-4231. ❹For billing inquiries, please leave your contact information after the tone and someone from our office will return your call on the next business day. Thank you.

設問74から76は次の録音メッセージに関する質問です。
　Connecters Broadband社お客様サービスにお電話いただき、ありがとうございます。当社商品やサービスに関する情報をお求めの場合、または販売員とお話しになりたい場合は、通常営業時間、月曜から金曜の午前9時から午後6時までの間におかけ直しください。しかし、いま現在、インターネット接続に問題がある場合は、24時間対応の技術サポート窓口、555-4231までご連絡ください。請求に関するお問い合わせは、発信音のあとにお客様のご連絡先を残していただければ、翌営業日に当社スタッフが折り返し連絡いたします。ありがとうございます。

設問の訳 ☞ p.40〜41参照

TOEIC 豆知識 TOEICの世界は請求ミスや、発送ミスだらけでうんざりするが、必ず料金の減額や無料クーポンが提供される。事後対応はなかなかよいのである。

正解&解説　　　　　　　　　　　　　　　　　　　間違いメモ

71. 正解 (D)　難易度

何のために寄付を募るのか、目的を尋ねている。❷で「集められたお金は、**学校図書館のため**の本の購入に役立てられる」と言っている。従って (D) School libraries が正解。

72. 正解 (D)　難易度

団体が主催するイベントの種類を尋ねている。❶で「最初のイベントは**スプリング・フェスティバル**」と言っているので、これを A seasonal celebration（季節のお祭）と言い換えた (D) が正解。

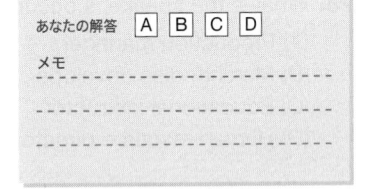

73. 正解 (A)　難易度

話し手の聞き手に対する依頼内容を尋ねている。❸で「みなが volunteer to work in ... the committees（**志願して委員会で働く**）ことを望む」と言っているので、正解は (A) Volunteer to work with a committee（委員会でボランティアとして働く）。

単語 □ association 協会　□ host ～を主催する　□ fundraising 募金集めの　□ raise（寄付金）を集める　□ promotion 広報宣伝　□ pass around ～を回す　□ committee 委員会　□ list（一覧表に）～を載せる　**71** □ organization 組織　□ regional 地域の　**72** □ benefit 慈善　□ competition 競技会、試合　□ seasonal 季節の　**73** □ donate ～を寄贈する、寄付する

74. 正解 (C)　難易度

この録音メッセージの目的を尋ねている。このように主題に関わる設問は、**冒頭に注目しよう**。まず❶から、企業に電話をした際のメッセージだとわかる。続けて、❷で「通常の営業時間内にかけ直してほしい」と言っているので、**営業時間外に電話してきた人**に向けたメッセージだとわかる。これを To assist customers outside of office hours（営業時間外に顧客を援助すること）と表現した (C) が正解。

75. 正解 (D)　難易度

インターネット接続に問題がある場合にすべきことを尋ねている。❸で「接続に問題があれば、**技術サポート窓口、555-4231 に連絡**してほしい」と言っている。電話番号を伝えていることから、(D) Call another number（別の番号に電話する）が正解。

76. 正解 (B)　難易度

どのような人が留守電メッセージを残すのかを尋ねている。❹で「For billing inquiries（請求に関する問い合せ）は、連絡先を残してほしい」と言っている。ここから、**料金について質問したい人**が留守電を残す、とわかるので、正解は (B) A customer questioning some charges（料金に疑問を抱く顧客）。

単語 □ sales representative 販売員、営業担当者　□ inquiry 質問　**74** □ subscription 会費、購読料　□ office hour 営業時間　□ promote ～を宣伝販売する　**76** □ subscriber 加入者　□ connectivity 相互通信能力、接続（可能）性　□ field（作業が行われる）現場　□ submit ～を提出する

TEST 2
PART 4

音声ファイル 🔊 T2_P4_77-79 ▶ T2_P4_Q77-79 / T2_P4_80-82 ▶ T2_P4_Q80-82
問題文&訳

77. Why is the speaker contacting Ms. Lee?
    (A) To ask for an application form
    (B) To inform her of a company event
    (C) To arrange a job interview
    (D) To request a deadline extension

78. What is the speaker's occupation?
    (A) Production manager
    (B) Merchandise developer
    (C) Educational instructor
    (D) Human resource director

79. What is Ms. Lee asked to do?
    (A) Bring copies of documents
    (B) Mail a registration form
    (C) Submit a production report
    (D) Attend an employee meeting

Questions 77-79 refer to the following telephone message.

Hello, this is Sara Barnaby from Equinox Manufacturing calling for Sun Young Lee. ❶I'm the head of human resources and just received your online application for the product development position. ❷I would be very interested in meeting you for an interview sometime next week. ❸Please call me back and let me know what day is best for you. I am free to conduct interviews between 11 A.M. and 4 P.M. ❹You will also need to bring a copy of your résumé, two letters of reference, and copies of any educational certificates that are applicable. My number is 555-0093. Thank you.

設問77から79は次の電話メッセージに関する質問です。
　こんにちは、Equinox 製造の Sara Barnaby と申します、Sun Young Lee さんにお電話しております。私は人事部長をしており、当社商品開発部門へのあなたからのオンライン申請をたったいま受け取りました。ぜひ来週のどこかでお会いして、面接の機会を設けたいと存じます。折り返しお電話いただき、ご都合のよい日をお教えください。私は午前11時から午後4時の間は面接を行う時間を取れます。また、履歴書の写しを1部、推薦状を2通、適用可能な任意の教育修了証明書の写しをお持ちください。私の電話番号は、555-0093です。ありがとうございます。

80. Why was the announcement made?
    (A) To inform passengers of a change in schedule
    (B) To announce a train's delayed departure
    (C) To ask listeners to submit travel documents
    (D) To recommend places of interest to visitors

81. What does the speaker recommend?
    (A) Waiting at Port Edgerton
    (B) Taking a taxi into Manhattan
    (C) Boarding a bus to River Road
    (D) Catching a train at Midtown

82. What should listeners do if they want more information?
    (A) Check a schedule posted on the wall
    (B) View a monitor in the waiting area
    (C) Telephone a ticket counter at the station
    (D) Speak to a company representative

Questions 80-82 refer to the following announcement.

❶Attention all passengers bound for Manhattan Midtown on the 10:30 A.M. commuter ferry. ❷We apologize for the inconvenience, but a forty-minute delay is being reported at this time due to a mechanical failure on one of our boats. If you do not want to wait, you may refund your tickets at counter 1. ❸Passengers are further advised to take advantage of free shuttle transit to the River Road train station from the bus stop across the terminal. Once again, the 10:30 A.M. ferry to Manhattan Midtown is delayed. ❹For more information, please consult any Port Edgerton ferry employee. Thank you.

設問80から82は次のアナウンスに関する質問です。
　午前10時30分発マンハッタン・ミッドタウン行きの通勤用フェリーにご乗船のお客さまにお知らせいたします。ご不便をおかけし申し訳ございませんが、当社の船の1隻に技術的な問題が発生したため現在40分の遅れが報告されております。お待ちいただけない場合は、1番カウンターにてチケットの払い戻しが可能です。さらに、ターミナル向かいのバス停から River Road 鉄道駅までの無料シャトルバスのご利用をお勧めいたします。再度お知らせいたします、午前10時30分発マンハッタン・ミッドタウン行きフェリーが遅れております。詳細は、Edgerton 港フェリーの従業員までお尋ねください。ありがとうございます。

設問の訳 ☞ p.40~41参照

正解＆解説

77. 正解 (C) 　難易度 ■■□□□ 難

話し手が Lee さんに連絡している理由を尋ねている。❷で「面接のために会いたい」と言い、❸では「都合のよい日を知らせてほしい」とも言っている。つまり、**Lee さんとの面接日程を決める**ことが目的とわかるので、正解は (C) To arrange a job interview（就職面接を設定するため）。

78. 正解 (D) 　難易度 ■■■■□ 難

話者の職種を尋ねている。❶で「**人事部長**」とはっきり名乗っている。よって、head を director と言い換えた (D) が正解。(A) と (B) は、Lee さんが応募している product development position と類似した単語を含めて、ひっかけをねらっている。

79. 正解 (A) 　難易度 ■■□□□ 難

Lee さんが依頼されていることを尋ねている。❹で a copy of your résumé（**履歴書の写し** 1部）、two letters of reference（推薦状2通）、copies of any educational certificates（**教育修了証の写し**）の3つを持参するよう依頼している。ひとつ目と3つ目を指して、「copies of documents（書類の写し）を持参する」と表現した (A) が正解。

単語 ▶ □ human resource 人材　□ application 申請、応募　□ interview 面接　□ certificate 証明書　□ applicable 適用できる、適切な　**77** ▶ □ inform 〜に知らせる　□ deadline 締め切り　□ extension 延期、延長　**78** ▶ □ occupation 職業、仕事　**79** ▶ □ registration 登録

80. 正解 (A) 　難易度 ■■■■□ 難

このアナウンスの目的を尋ねている。主題に関わる設問なので、**冒頭に意識を集中**させよう。❶で乗客の注意を喚起し、❷で「（フェリーの）40分の遅延」を伝えている。これらから「乗客に**スケジュールの変更を知らせるため**」のアナウンスとわかるので、(A) が正解。

81. 正解 (C) 　難易度 ■■■□□ 難

話し手が勧めていることを尋ねている。❸で「**River Road 鉄道駅への無料シャトルバスの利用を勧める**」と言っているので、正解は (C) Boarding a bus to River Road（River Road 行きのバスに乗ること）。Midtown はフェリーの行き先であり、列車の駅の場所ではないので (D) は誤り。

82. 正解 (D) 　難易度 ■■■□□ 難

さらに情報を得るために、乗客がすべきことを尋ねている。❹で「詳細は、Edgerton 港フェリーの**従業員に問い合わせ**てほしい」と言っている。consult を speak to、any Port Edgerton ferry employee を a company representative と言い換えた、(D)「会社のスタッフに話しかける」が正解。

単語 ▶ □ bound for 〜 〜行きの　□ commuter 通勤者　□ inconvenience 不便　□ due to 〜のせいで　□ failure 故障　□ take advantage of 〜 〜を利用する　□ transit 輸送　**80** ▶ □ departure 出発　□ place of interest 観光地　**81** ▶ □ catch （列車など）に間に合う

TEST 2 PART 4

83. What type of products are being tested?
(A) Freshly baked goods
(B) Fast-food sandwiches
(C) Dietary supplements
(D) Instant meals

84. What does the speaker ask listeners to provide?
(A) Identification cards
(B) Reactions to a product design
(C) Personal details
(D) A list of qualifications

85. What can listeners expect to receive?
(A) Discounts on merchandise
(B) Monetary compensation
(C) A free ticket to an event
(D) A complimentary gift basket

86. Where most likely does the speaker work?
(A) At an academic institution
(B) At a research facility
(C) In a science laboratory
(D) In the admissions office

87. What problem does the speaker mention?
(A) A lack of faculty members
(B) Increased enrollment
(C) Shortage of classrooms
(D) Expensive tuition fees

88. What will most likely happen next semester?
(A) Professors will get a salary raise.
(B) The science club will accept more members.
(C) Some students can choose to study at night.
(D) Some classes may be cancelled due to overcrowding.

設問の訳 ☞ p.40～41参照

Questions 83-85 refer to the following announcement.

I'd like to welcome you all to our market research group this morning. ❶The first thing we will do is fill out some forms with your personal information. This data will help us determine our target market, and will be kept entirely confidential. After that, ❷you will have the chance to sample Dolly's newest line of frozen microwaveable dishes. After trying each item, please record your reactions and comments on the questionnaires provided. We ask that you be honest about your opinions, as this will help us decide which products will be released. Once you have finished sampling all the items, please leave your questionnaires at the front of the room. ❸Each participant will receive a $100 check for their services and a $50 gift certificate for Dolly's products. Thank you for your participation.

設問83から85は次のアナウンスに関する質問です。

みなさん、今朝はわれわれ市場調査グループにようこそお越しくださいました。まず私たちがすることは、みなさんの個人情報を用紙に記入していただくことです。この情報は、私たちがターゲット市場を決定する助けとしますが、完全部外秘といたします。その後、Dolly 社の電子レンジ加熱対応の最新冷凍食品群をみなさんに試食していただきます。各商品の試食後、配布したアンケート用紙にご感想とご意見を記入してください。これに基づいて発売商品が決定されますので、ご自身の意見については正直にご記入くださいますようお願いいたします。すべての商品を試し終えたら、アンケート用紙を部屋の前方に置いて行ってください。参加者はそれぞれ、ご協力に対し 100 ドルの小切手と Dolly 社製品にお使いいただける 50 ドル分の商品券をお受け取りください。ご参加ありがとうございます。

Questions 86-88 refer to the following short talk.

I know that you're all busy ❶preparing for your classes, so I promise to make this meeting short. First, I'd like to introduce Mr. Zachary Kline, a new ❷faculty member from Ramsey Hill who will be ❸teaching advanced courses in information technology ❹this school year. He'll also serve as a coordinator for ❺our university's computer science club. I hope that you'll all make him feel welcome. Another thing I'd like to mention is the ❻increased number of students currently registered here at our campus. ❼Next semester, the school management will be adding night classes to avoid overcrowded classes during the daytime. If you'd like to add a night class to your schedule, please e-mail the administrator to let him know.

設問86から88は次の短い話に関する質問です。

みなさん授業の準備に忙しいでしょうから、この会議を手短にすると約束します。まず、Ramsey Hill から来た新しい教職員、Zachary Kline 氏を紹介したいと思います。彼は今年度、情報技術の上級課程を担当します。また、当大学のコンピュータ科学クラブのコーディネーターも務めていただきます。みなさんどうぞ温かく迎えてください。もうひとつお伝えしたいのは、現在、当大学への登録学生数が増加していることについてです。来学期、昼間の授業の混雑を避けるため、学校運営当局は夜間クラスを追加予定です。もしご自身の日程に夜間クラスを追加したい場合は、管理者にEメールを送ってお知らせください。

TOEIC豆知識 TOEICの世界では、明らかに客側のミスであっても、レシートさえあれば、たいがい返品を受け付けてくれる。良心的なお店が多いのである。

正解＆解説

83. 正解 (D) 難易度

どのような商品がテストされるのかを尋ねている。❷に「電子レンジ用の**冷凍食品を試食**してもらう」とあるが、ここでは設問のtestをsample（〜を試食する）と言い換えている。正解は、冷凍食品をInstant meals（インスタント食品）と言い換えた(D)。

84. 正解 (C) 難易度

話し手が聞き手に提供を求めていることを尋ねている。❶で「まず**個人情報**を記入する」と言っていることから、(C) Personal details（個人情報）が正解。求めているのは情報だけで、身分証そのものは必要としていないので(A)は誤り。(B)も、商品への感想は求めているが、デザインに限定しているわけではないので、誤り。

85. 正解 (B) 難易度

聞き手の報酬が何かを尋ねている。❸に各参加者が得るものとして「**100ドルの小切手**」と「**50ドル分の商品券**」が挙げられている。これらをMonetary compensation（金銭的報酬）と表現した(B)が正解。割引でも、無料の贈り物でもないので(A)(D)は誤り。

単語 □ target 対象　□ entirely 完全に　□ confidential 秘密の　□ sample 〜を試食する　□ microwaveable 電子レンジに使える　□ reaction 反応　□ questionnaire アンケート（用紙）　□ participant 参加者　**83** □ dietary supplement 栄養補助食品　**84** □ qualification 資格　**85** □ monetary 金銭的な　□ compensation 報酬　□ complimentary 無料の

86. 正解 (A) 難易度

話し手の職場を尋ねている。❶「授業の準備をしている」、❷「教職員」、❸「教えている」、❹「今年度」、❺「当大学」などの表現より、これは**大学での話**だとわかる。大学を抽象的に言い換えた(A) At an academic institution（学術機関）が正解。

87. 正解 (B) 難易度

話し手が指摘している問題点を尋ねている。**ネガティブな要素に集中**して聞き取ろう。❻で「登録学生数が増加している」と述べ、❼で「授業の混雑回避のため、夜間クラスを追加する」と言っている。**登録学生数の増加**が問題につながっているので、正解は(B) Increased enrollment（入学者数の増加）。授業数が足りないのであって、教員や教室の不足については言及されていないので、(A)(C)は誤り。

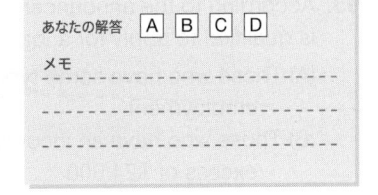

88. 正解 (C) 難易度

来学期に起こると予測されることを尋ねている。❼で「来学期から、授業の混雑回避のため、**夜間クラスを追加**する」と言っている。これをSome students can choose to study at night.（夜間学習を選択できる学生がいる）と表現した、(C)が正解。

単語 □ faculty member 教職員　□ serve as 〜 〜を務める　**86** □ laboratory 研究所、実験室　□ admission 入場、入学　**87** □ enrollment 入学、入学者数　□ tuition fees 授業料　**88** □ salary 給料　□ accept 〜を受け入れる

TEST 2 PART 4

音声ファイル 🔊 T2_P4_89-91 ▶ T2_P4_Q89-91 / T2_P4_92-94 ▶ T2_P4_Q92-94
問題文＆訳

89. Where most likely did Ms. Kim meet Ms. Santino?

(A) At a fashion event
(B) At a trade fair
(C) At a business conference
(D) At a human resources office

90. Why did Ms. Santino leave the message?

(A) To ask about some products
(B) To inquire about a job position
(C) To schedule an interview
(D) To provide information on an event

91. What will Ms. Santino probably do this morning?

(A) Return from a trip
(B) Call again later
(C) Complete a design sample
(D) Send some documents

Questions 89-91 refer to the following telephone message.

Good morning. ❶This message is for So Ra Kim. This is Penelope Santino and ❷we met briefly during fashion week in Paris last month. ❸You mentioned to me that your company was looking for a new designer for your accessories collection. I'm inquiring whether or not the position is still available. I am very interested in the job and the possibility of moving to Italy. I have had extensive experience working with reputable designers in New York, including Sasha Coen and Bradley Dean. ❹I will send you my résumé and a copy of my portfolio this morning. If you need anything else, please feel free to call me at 082-555-0788. I look forward to hearing from you soon.

設問89から91は次の留守電メッセージに関する質問です。

おはようございます。So Ra Kinさんあての伝言です。私はPenelope Santinoと申します。先月パリでのファッション・ウィーク期間中に短時間ですが、あなたにお会いしました。御社は、アクセサリー・コレクション部門の新しいデザイナーを探しているとのことでした。そのポジションがまだ空いているかどうかをお尋ねしたく存じます。その仕事とイタリア移住の可能性にたいへん興味を持っています。私には、ニューヨークでSasha CoenやBradley Deanをはじめとする一流デザイナーとともに仕事をした豊富な経験があります。本日午前中に履歴書と作品集のコピーをお送りします。ほかに必要なものがあれば、どうぞお気軽に082-555-0788までお電話ください。早急なご連絡をお待ちしております。

92. What is the main purpose of the announcement?

(A) To inform listeners about a service
(B) To report changes in public policy
(C) To promote the services of a bank
(D) To remind citizens to pay their taxes

93. According to the announcement, who is qualified to apply for a loan?

(A) Those who have some type of employment
(B) Those who have an income in excess of $24,000
(C) Those who reside within the state
(D) Those who have no outstanding debt

94. According to the speaker, what can be found on a Web site?

(A) A list of pension benefits
(B) The complete details of a program
(C) An application form for housing relief
(D) The terms and conditions of a contract

Questions 92-94 refer to the following radio announcement.

❶This message is brought to you by the National Welfare Administration. In relation to recent economic events, ❷the government has announced the launching of its Housing Relief Plan. Under the plan, short-term financial credit will be made available to ❸individuals and households whose combined income does not exceed $24,000 a year. ❹Qualified applicants must be citizens of the country and be fully or partially employed. These loans may be used to cover monthly mortgage payments up to $4,000. To apply, please call the local representative from your nearest welfare office. ❺You may also visit the NWA Web site at www.nwa.gov to view the full text of the government's Housing Relief Plan.

設問92から94は次のラジオアナウンスに関する質問です。

このメッセージは全国福祉庁がお送りいたします。昨今の経済事象を踏まえ、政府は住宅支援措置の開始を発表しました。この措置により、年間所得合計額が24,000ドル以下の個人や世帯への短期融資が提供可能になります。応募資格者は本国国民であり、常勤もしくは非常勤の仕事についていなければいけません。これらの貸付金は最大4,000ドルまで、月々の住宅ローン支払いに充てることができます。応募は、最寄りの福祉事務局の地域担当までお電話ください。またNWA（全国福祉庁）のウェブサイトwww.nwa.govにアクセスすると、政府の住宅支援措置の全文を閲覧可能です。

設問の訳 ☞ p.40〜41参照

正解 & 解説

89. 正解 (A) 難易度 ■■■□ 難

Santino さん（話し手）が Kim さんに会った場所を尋ねている。まず、❶で So Ra Kim がメッセージの受け手、Penelope Santino が話し手であることを把握。続けて❷で「パリの**ファッション・ウィーク**で会った」と言っているので、(A) At a fashion event（ファッション・イベントで）が正解。

90. 正解 (B) 難易度 ■■■□ 難

Santino さんがメッセージを残した理由を尋ねている。主題に関わる設問なので、**冒頭に集中**して聞き取ろう。❸に「あなた（= Kim さん）は、新デザイナーを探していると言っていたが、そのポジションがまだ空いているかを問い合わせたい」とある。つまり「**求人について問い合わせる**」のが目的なので、(B) To inquire about a job position が正解。まだ面接まで話は進んでいないので、(C) は誤り。

91. 正解 (D) 難易度 ■■■■ 難

Santino さんが、このメッセージを残した午前中にすることを尋ねている。設問のキーワード this morning を意識しながら聞き取ろう。❹に「this morning（午前中）に**履歴書と作品集の写しを送る**」と言っている。これを Send some documents（書類を送る）と言い換えた (D) が正解。

単語 □ briefly 少しの間、短く　□ possibility 可能性　□ extensive 広範囲にわたる　□ reputable 評判のよい、尊敬すべき　□ including 〜を含めて　□ portfolio （代表作品の）選集

---

92. 正解 (A) 難易度 ■■■□ 難

このラジオ放送の目的を尋ねている。主題に関わる設問なので、**冒頭に注目**。まず❶で行政機関（全国福祉庁）からのメッセージだとわかる。続けて❷で「政府は住宅支援計画の開始を発表した」と言っている。これらから、**新しい政策の告知**が目的とわかるので、「聞き手にサービスについて知らせること」と表現した (A) が正解。新しい政策の開始であって、変更ではないので (B) は誤り。

93. 正解 (A) 難易度 ■■■□ 難

ローンへの応募資格者を尋ねている。応募資格は、❸「年間所得 24,000 ドル以下の個人および世帯」、❹「本国国民」「**常勤もしくは非常勤の仕事**についている」と言っている。3つ目に一致する (A) Those who have some type of employment（ある種の職がある者）が正解。州内ではなく、国内なので (C) は誤り。

94. 正解 (B) 難易度 ■■■□ 難

ウェブサイトに記載されている情報を尋ねている。❺で「NWA のサイトでは**住宅支援計画の全文**を見られる」と言っている。これを The complete details of a program（プログラムの完全な詳細）と言い換えた (B) が正解。

単語 □ welfare 福祉　□ in relation to 〜 〜に関係して　□ launching 開始　□ relief 救済　□ credit 貸与金　□ combined 合わせた　□ income 所得　□ exceed 〜を上回る　□ qualified 資格のある　□ partially 部分的に　□ mortgage 住宅ローン　□ apply 応募する　**92** □ public policy 公共政策　**93** □ excess 超過　□ outstanding 未払いの　□ debt 負債　**94** □ pension 年金　□ complete 完全な　□ terms and conditions （諸）条件

TEST 2
PART 4

95. What does the message mainly concern?
    (A) A travel itinerary
    (B) Payment options
    (C) Requested information
    (D) A lease agreement

96. According to the message, what will Ms. Forbes need to do?
    (A) Transmit a photocopied document
    (B) Send her credit card information
    (C) Apply to renew her passport
    (D) Fill out an application form

97. What is mentioned about Brent Stewart?
    (A) He works out of the Hong Kong branch.
    (B) He will address Ms. Forbes's further concerns.
    (C) He will be arriving at the airport on August 4.
    (D) He received the payment for a deposit.

98. What is the report about?
    (A) A health beverage
    (B) A restaurant chain
    (C) A business merger
    (D) A marketing project

99. What may Hagley-Weldon be planning to do in the future?
    (A) Develop new items to sell
    (B) Expand its operations into North America
    (C) Form a partnership with Gridleys Corporation
    (D) Hire a new board chairman

100. According to the report, why was Hagley-Weldon formed?
    (A) To decrease the cost of manufacturing
    (B) To broaden operations internationally
    (C) To increase the amount of production
    (D) To deal with a competitor in the market

Questions 95-97 refer to the following telephone message.

❶This message is for Michelle Forbes. This is Kira Farrell calling from Midas Car Rentals. ❷I just wanted to confirm your rental request which we received this morning. You asked for a two-door sedan in Hong Kong from August fourth through the seventh. I have gone ahead and charged a deposit to your credit card. When you arrive in Hong Kong, simply go to the Midas desk in the arrivals area and show them your passport. However, ❸we will need a copy of your current driver's license before you leave on your trip. ❹Please fax a copy to (509) 555-9307. ❺Address the fax to Brent Stewart, as he will be handling your request from now on. Thank you for using Midas Car Rentals.

設問95から97は次の留守電メッセージに関する質問です。

このメッセージはMichelle Forbesさんあてです。私はMidasレンタカーのKira Farrellと申します。今朝受け取りましたレンタル申込の確認をさせていただきたく、お電話いたしました。8月4日から7日まで、香港にて2ドアセダンとのご依頼でした。手配を進め、保証金をあなたのクレジットカードに請求いたしました。香港に到着されましたら、到着エリアにあるMidasデスクまで進み、パスポートをお見せいただくだけで結構です。しかしながら、ご旅行出発前に現在の運転免許証の写しが必要です。写しを(509)555-9307までファックスでお送りください。Brent Stewartが今後あなたのご依頼に対応しますので、ファックスは彼あてでお願いします。Midasレンタカーのご利用、ありがとうございます。

Questions 98-100 refer to the following news report.

Good evening. I'm Sharon Warner, and this is Business Central. Earlier today, ❶Hagley Foods and Weldon Juice Company closed the deal to integrate their operations in the United States and Canada. Now called Hagley-Weldon, they will be the second biggest producer of health food and beverages in North America. According to an interview with Greg Valence, the chairman of Hagley-Weldon, ❷the unified company hopes to create more innovative products and services that will drive profitable growth in the years to come. ❸This joint venture is also aimed at competing against Gridleys Corporation, which dominates almost half of the region's food market. Reporter Harold Ritter now joins us to tell us more.

設問98から100は次のニュース報道に関する質問です。

こんばんは。Sharon WarnerがBusiness Centralをお届けします。本日、Hagley食品とWeldon飲料がアメリカ合衆国とカナダにおける経営を統合する契約を締結しました。これによりHagley-Weldon社となり、北米の健康食品飲料市場で2番目に大きな生産者となります。Hagley-Weldon社の取締役会長、Greg Valenceはインタビューにて、統合会社では数年のうちに、収益を拡大する革新的商品とサービスを創造していきたいと述べました。この共同事業はまた、当該地域の食品市場のおよそ半分を占めるGridleys社に対抗するねらいもあります。ではHarold Ritterレポーターが詳細をお伝えします。

設問の訳 ☞ p.40～41参照

正解＆解説

95. 正解 (D)
この留守電メッセージの主題を尋ねているので、**冒頭に注目**。❶から、Midas レンタカーの Farrell さんが、Forbes さんにあてたメッセージだとわかる。続いて❷で、「あなた（= Forbes さん）の**レンタル申込**について確認したい」と主旨を伝え、以降は詳細を説明している。従って、レンタカーを借りることが主題なので、A lease agreement（リース契約）と言い換えた (D) が正解。

96. 正解 (A)
Forbes さん（メッセージの受け手）がすべきことを尋ねている。❸で「**免許証の写し**が必要」と言い、続けて❹で「その写しを**ファックス**してほしい」と Forbes さんに依頼している。これを Transmit a photocopied document（コピーした資料を送信する）と言い換えた (A) が正解。

97. 正解 (B)
第三者の Brent Stewart について尋ねている。❺で「**あなたの依頼に対応する**ので、ファックスを Brent Stewart あてにしてほしい」と言っている。従って、(B)「彼は Forbes さんの今後の問題を対処する」が正解。車を借りるのは香港だが、Stewart さんが香港支店に勤めているとは言っていないので、(A) は誤り。**address** が説明文と選択肢で異なる意味で用いられている点に注目。

単語 □ confirm ～を確認する　□ handle ～に対処する　**95** ▶ □ itinerary 旅程、旅行計画　□ lease リース、賃貸借　**96** ▶ □ transmit ～を送信する　□ photocopy ～をコピーする　**97** ▶ □ branch 支店、支社　□ address ～に対処する、～を処理する　□ concern 心配、懸念

98. 正解 (C)
この報道の主題を尋ねているので、**冒頭を注意深く**聞こう。❶で「Hagley 食品と Weldon 飲料が経営を統合する契約を結んだ」と言っている。以降もこの**経営統合**の詳細が続くので、正解は (C) A business merger（企業合併）。

99. 正解 (A)
Hagley-Weldon 社（合併後の企業名）の計画を尋ねている。❷で「the unified company（= Hagley-Weldon 社）は**革新的商品**とサービスを創造したい」と言っている。これを「新たな商品を開発する」と表現した (A) が正解。Hagley-Weldon 社はすでに北米で事業展開しているので、(B) は誤り。Gridleys 社は競合するライバル企業なので、(C) も誤り。

100. 正解 (D)
Hagley-Weldon 社の結成理由を尋ねている。❸で「This joint venture（= 2社の統合）には Gridleys 社に対抗するねらいもある」と言っている。つまり合併は「**競合企業に対処するため**」なので、(D) To deal with a competitor in the market が正解。(A) (B) (C) の意図もあるかもしれないが、具体的な言及が見当たらないので、正解にはなり得ない。

単語 □ integrate ～をひとつにする　□ producer 生産者　□ beverage 飲料　□ unify ～を統合する　□ innovative 革新的な　□ drive ～を推進する　□ profitable 利益をもたらす　□ joint 共同の　□ venture 冒険的事業　□ aim at ～ ～をねらう、目指す　□ dominate ～を支配する　□ region 地域　**99** ▶ □ develop ～を開発する　□ form ～を形成する　**100** ▶ □ broaden ～を拡大する　□ deal with ～ ～に対処する　□ competitor 競争相手

TEST 2 PART 4

設問の訳

71. この組織は何のために寄付を募るのか。
    - (A) 教師協会
    - (B) 改築計画
    - (C) 地域の公園
    - (D) 学校図書館

72. この団体はどんなイベントを開催するのか。
    - (A) 慈善コンサート
    - (B) 運動競技会
    - (C) 家族遠足
    - (D) 季節のお祭

73. 話し手は聞き手に何をするよう依頼しているか。
    - (A) 委員会でボランティアとして働く
    - (B) 学校に本を寄贈する
    - (C) 街の公園の清掃を手伝う
    - (D) イベントのチケットを販売する

74. このメッセージの目的は何か。
    - (A) 割引の会員料金プランを勧めること
    - (B) 定期的な保守計画を案内すること
    - (C) 営業時間外に顧客を援助すること
    - (D) 新たな商品群を販促すること

75. 聞き手はインターネットに問題がある場合、何をすべきか。
    - (A) コンピュータをスキャンする
    - (B) 機械を初期化する
    - (C) 修理センターに行く
    - (D) 別の番号に電話する

76. おそらく誰がメッセージを残すだろうか。
    - (A) 接続が遅くなっている加入者
    - (B) 料金に疑問を抱く顧客
    - (C) 報告書を提出する現場技術者
    - (D) 提案を行う取引先

77. 話し手はなぜ Lee さんに連絡しているのか。
    - (A) 申込用紙を請求するため
    - (B) 彼女に会社のイベントを知らせるため
    - (C) 就職面接を設定するため
    - (D) 締め切りの延長を依頼するため

78. 話し手の職種は何か。
    - (A) 生産部長
    - (B) 商品開発者
    - (C) 教育指導者
    - (D) 人事部長

79. Lee さんは何をするよう求められているか。
    - (A) 書類の写しを持参する
    - (B) 登録用紙を郵送する
    - (C) 生産高報告書を提出する
    - (D) 従業員会議に出席する

80. なぜこのアナウンスは行われたのか。
    - (A) 乗客にスケジュール変更を知らせるため
    - (B) 列車の出発遅延を案内するため
    - (C) 聞き手に旅券の提出を求めるため
    - (D) 訪問者に観光名所を勧めるため

81. 話し手は何を勧めているか。
    - (A) Edgerton 港で待つこと
    - (B) マンハッタン行きのタクシーに乗ること
    - (C) River Road 行きのバスに乗ること
    - (D) ミッドタウンで列車に乗ること

82. 詳細を知りたい場合、聞き手は何をすべきか。
    - (A) 壁に掲示されたスケジュールを確認する
    - (B) 待合所でモニターを見る
    - (C) 駅でチケットカウンターに電話する
    - (D) 会社のスタッフに話しかける

83. テストされている製品の種類は何か。
    - (A) 焼きたての食品
    - (B) ファストフードのサンドウィッチ
    - (C) 栄養補助食品
    - (D) インスタント食品

84. 話し手は聞き手に何を提供するよう依頼しているか。
    - (A) 身分証明書
    - (B) 製品デザインへの感想
    - (C) 個人情報
    - (D) 資格の一覧表

85. 聞き手は何を受け取ると考えられるか。
    - (A) 商品の割引
    - (B) 金銭的報酬
    - (C) イベントへの無料チケット
    - (D) 無料の贈り物詰め合わせ

設問の訳

86. 話し手はおそらくどこで働いているか。
    (A) 学術機関で
    (B) 研究調査施設で
    (C) 科学研究所で
    (D) 入学事務局で

87. 話し手が述べている問題は何か。
    (A) 教職員不足
    (B) 入学者数の増加
    (C) 教室不足
    (D) 高額な授業料

88. 来学期におそらく起こりそうなことは何か。
    (A) 教授が昇給を受ける。
    (B) 科学クラブがより多くの会員を受け入れる。
    (C) 夜間学習を選択できる学生がいる。
    (D) 混雑のために中止される授業があるかもしれない。

89. KimさんとSantinoさんはおそらくどこで会ったのか。
    (A) ファッション・イベントで
    (B) 見本市で
    (C) ビジネス会議で
    (D) 人材会社で

90. Santinoさんはなぜメッセージを残したのか。
    (A) 製品について尋ねるため
    (B) 求人について問い合わせるため
    (C) 面接の予定を立てるため
    (D) イベントについての情報を提供するため

91. Santinoさんは午前中におそらく何をするか。
    (A) 旅行から戻る
    (B) あとで再度電話をかける
    (C) デザイン見本を仕上げる
    (D) 書類を送る

92. このアナウンスの主な目的は何か。
    (A) 聞き手にサービスについて知らせること
    (B) 公共政策の変更を報告すること
    (C) 銀行サービスの利用を促進すること
    (D) 市民に税の支払いを促すこと

93. このアナウンスによると、貸付への応募資格があるのは誰か。
    (A) ある種の雇用がある者
    (B) 24,000ドルを超える収入のある者
    (C) その州内に住む者
    (D) 未払負債がない者

94. 話し手によると、ウェブサイトで見つけられるものは何か。
    (A) 給付年金の一覧表
    (B) プログラムの完全な詳細
    (C) 住宅支援措置の申込用紙
    (D) 契約条件

95. このメッセージは主に何に関するものか。
    (A) 旅行日程
    (B) 支払方法
    (C) 要請された情報
    (D) リース契約

96. メッセージによると、Forbesさんは何をする必要があるか。
    (A) コピーした資料を送信する
    (B) クレジットカード情報を送る
    (C) パスポートの更新を申請する
    (D) 申込用紙に記入する

97. Brent Stewartについて述べられていることは何か。
    (A) 彼は香港支店で仕事をしている。
    (B) 彼はForbesさんの今後の問題に対処する。
    (C) 彼は8月4日、空港に到着する。
    (D) 彼は保証金の支払いを受け取る。

98. この報道は何に関するものか。
    (A) 健康飲料
    (B) レストラン・チェーン
    (C) 企業合併
    (D) マーケティング・プロジェクト

99. Hagley-Weldon社は将来何を行う計画があるか。
    (A) 新たな商品を開発する
    (B) 北米に事業を拡大する
    (C) Gridleys社と提携する
    (D) 新しい取締役会長を雇う

100. この報道によると、Hagley-Weldon社はなぜ結成されたのか。
    (A) 製造コストを削減するため
    (B) 経営を国際的に広げるため
    (C) 生産量を増やすため
    (D) 市場の競合企業に対処するため

TEST 2 PART 5

問題

101. Please call me once Mr. Bates confirms our appointment with ------- regarding preparations for the art exhibit.
(A) he
(B) him
(C) his
(D) himself

102. The new kitchen appliances from Eaton Electronics are ------- easy to use and affordable.
(A) every
(B) both
(C) while
(D) such

103. Avion Air ------- the right to add a fuel surcharge to any tickets purchased up to 24 hours before the scheduled time of departure.
(A) reserves
(B) relates
(C) collects
(D) allows

104. The studio must quickly find a ------- for the director before production begins next month.
(A) member
(B) predecessor
(C) equivalent
(D) replacement

105. To enter the literary contest, write a one-page essay about a travel destination and send it ------- the specified envelope.
(A) of
(B) in
(C) at
(D) by

106. Environmental groups campaigned ------- against the construction of a cement factory near the national park.
(A) persistence
(B) persistent
(C) persistently
(D) persisting

訳

美術展の準備に関して、Bates さんがわれわれとのアポを確認したら、お電話いただきたい。
(A) 彼は（主格）
(B) 彼に（目的格）
(C) 彼の（所有格）
(D) 彼自身（再帰代名詞）

Eaton Electronics 社の新しい台所用品は、使いやすくかつ値段も手頃だ。
(A) すべての
(B) 両方とも
(C) 〜する間
(D) そのような

Avion 航空は、出発予定時刻の24時間前までに購入されたすべての航空券に対し、燃料サーチャージ費用を加える権利を有する。
(A) 〜を保有する
(B) 〜を関連づける
(C) 〜を集める
(D) 〜を許可する

そのスタジオは、来月製作が始まる前に早急に後任監督を見つけなければならない。
(A) 会員
(B) 前任者
(C) 同等物
(D) 後任

その文学コンクールにエントリーするには、旅行先に関する1ページのエッセイを書き、指定の封筒に入れて送ってください。
〔選択肢訳なし〕

環境団体は、国立公園近くのセメント工場建設に粘り強く反対運動をした。
(A) 名 粘り強さ
(B) 形 粘り強い
(C) 副 粘り強く
(D) 動 persist（持続する）の〈現在分詞・動名詞〉

TOEIC豆知識 Part 1～4のディレクション中に Part 5 を解く、という受験テクニックが有名だが、このテクニックで半分（20問！）を解き終えてしまうツワモノもいるのだとか。しかし…（続く▶）

正解＆解説

101. 正解 **(B)**　難易度 ■■□□ 難

選択肢には人称代名詞が並んでいる。**前置詞 with の目的語になるのは目的格**の (B) と、**再帰代名詞**の (D)。Mr. Bates confirms our appointment with -------（Bates さんが ------- とのわれわれのアポを確認する）という文脈なので、「彼とのわれわれのアポ」となる (B) him が正解。himself だと「彼自身とのわれわれのアポ」となり不自然。参考までに、once は「いったん～すれば」という意味の接続詞として使われていることを押さえておこう。

間違いメモ＆単語
あなたの解答 A B C D
メモ

☐ preparation 準備
☐ exhibit 展覧会

102. 正解 **(B)**　難易度 ■■□□ 難

and とともに、**相関接続詞 both A and B**（A と B の両方）を作る (B) both が正解。easy to use（使いやすい）と affordable（価格が手頃な）という対等な要素（ともに補語）を結んでいることを押さえておこう。(A) every（すべての）は単数名詞の前、(C) while は接続詞なので完全な節の前、形容詞の (D) such は名詞の前にくる。

あなたの解答 A B C D
メモ

☐ appliance （家庭用の）機器
☐ affordable （値段が）手頃な、購入しやすい

103. 正解 **(A)**　難易度 ■■■□ 難

同じ品詞（動詞）が並んでいるので、**文脈から考えてみよう**。Avion Air ------- the right to add a fuel surcharge to any tickets（Avion 航空はすべての航空券に燃料サーチャージを加える権利を ------- する）という文脈なので、「権利を〈保有する〉」という意味になる (A) reserves が正解。reserve the right to do（～する権利を有する）という慣用句として覚えておこう。

あなたの解答 A B C D
メモ

☐ fuel 燃料
☐ surcharge 追加料金
☐ up to ～ ～まで

104. 正解 **(D)**　難易度 ■■□□ 難

同じ品詞（名詞）が並んでいるので、**文脈からアプローチ**。find a ------- for the director（監督の ------- を見つける）なので、「後任者」という意味の (D) replacement を空所に入れると文意が通る。

あなたの解答 A B C D
メモ

105. 正解 **(B)**　難易度 ■■□□ 難

空所前後は「それ（= a one-page essay）を指定された封筒〈の中に入れて〉送る」という文脈だと考えるのが自然。従って、何かの**中に入っていることを表す前置詞**の (B) in が正解。(A) of は「～の」という意味で、所有や同格の関係を表す。(C) at は「～に、～で」という意味で、時や場所を表す。(D) by は「～までに」という意味で時を、「～によって」という意味で行為者や手段、方法などを表す。

あなたの解答 A B C D
メモ

☐ literary 文学の　☐ destination 行き先、目的地　☐ specify ～を指定する
☐ envelope 封筒

106. 正解 **(C)**　難易度 ■□□□ 難

空所には直前の**動詞 campaigned を修飾する副詞**がはいる。よって (C) persistently（粘り強く）が正解。campaign は「運動を起こす」という意味の自動詞なので、直接目的語を取ることはできない。また参考までに、前置詞の against はここでの「～に反して」という意味に加えて、「～によりかかって」という状態を表すことも押さえておこう（Part 1 に頻出する）。

あなたの解答 A B C D
メモ

☐ environmental 環境の
☐ campaign 運動を起こす
☐ construction 建設

TEST 2 PART 5

107. All office employees were asked to make sure to turn ------- all the lights in the office before leaving for the day.
(A) over
(B) off
(C) around
(D) along

オフィスの全社員は退社前に、必ずオフィス内のすべての電気を消すよう求められた。
〔選択肢訳なし〕

108. Mr. Lynch asked to see several samples of products before ------- to sign the contract with the supply company.
(A) agreement
(B) agreed
(C) agrees
(D) agreeing

Lynch 氏は納入企業との契約書に合意する前に、製品サンプルをいくつか見ることを依頼した。
(A) 名 合意
(B) 動 agree (〜に同意する) の〈過去形・過去分詞〉
(C) 動 agree の〈現在形〉
(D) 動 agree の〈現在分詞・動名詞〉

109. The vintage paintings to be auctioned off by the Heritage Foundation are kept ------- in a well-ventilated location.
(A) certain
(B) realistic
(C) secure
(D) confident

Heritage 財団がオークションにかける年代物の絵画は、通気のよい場所で安全に保管されている。
(A) 確かな
(B) 現実的な
(C) 安全な
(D) 自信がある

110. Mr. Wilkins would like some ------- setting up the audio-visual equipment in the conference room before the seminar on Thursday.
(A) assisted
(B) assistance
(C) assist
(D) assisting

Wilkins 氏は、木曜日のセミナー前に会議室の AV 機器の設置を手伝ってほしい。
(A) 動 assist の〈過去形・過去分詞〉
(B) 名 手助け
(C) 動 〜を助ける
(D) 動 assist の〈現在分詞・動名詞〉

111. Every $200 purchase of Billow Swimwear entitles shoppers to receive ------- a towel or a pair of slippers.
(A) also
(B) either
(C) until
(D) neither

Billow 水着社の商品を200ドル分買うごとに、タオルかスリッパのどちらかを受け取ることができる。
(A) 〜もまた
(B) どちらか
(C) 〜までずっと
(D) どちらも〜ない

112. If the building owner ------- the proposed lobby renovation tomorrow, work will begin as soon as next week.
(A) approval
(B) approving
(C) will approve
(D) approves

明日、ビルの所有者がロビー改修の提案を承認すれば、作業は早ければ来週にも始まる。
(A) 名 承認
(B) 動 approve (〜を承認する) の〈現在分詞・動名詞〉
(C) 動 approve の〈未来形〉
(D) 動 approve の〈現在形〉

TOEIC豆知識 しかし、2012年9月のテストから「リスニング中にリーディングの問題を見る行為、リーディング中にリスニングの問題を見る行為」が禁止項目として受験票に明示されるようになり、このテクニックは使えなくなった。

正解&解説

107. 正解 (B) 難易度

turn ------- all the light in the office before leaving for the day（退社前にオフィスのすべての電気を -------する）という文脈なので、「電気を〈消す〉」とするのが自然。よって turn off ～で「(照明、TV など) を消す」という意味になる (B) が正解。(A) だと turn over（転覆する、～をひっくり返す）、(C) だと turn around（回転させる、後ろを向く）となり、文脈に合わない。(D) along は「～に沿って、～にしたがって」という意味。along with（～とともに）の形でよく使われることを押さえておこう。

あなたの解答 A B C D
メモ

108. 正解 (D) 難易度

この文には、すでに主語 Mr. Lynch と動詞 asked が揃っているので、before 以降は修飾の働きをする付加的要素。この before は前置詞「～の前に」として機能しており、後ろには名詞か動名詞が続く。従って、(A) と (D) が正解候補だが、空所のあとに目をやると、to 不定詞の to sign the contract（契約書にサインすること）がある。これは、空所の目的語だと考えられるので、動詞としての機能を併せ持つ動名詞の (D) agreeing が正解。名詞は目的語をとることはできないので、(A) は誤り。

あなたの解答 A B C D
メモ

☐ supply 供給

109. 正解 (C) 難易度

選択肢には同じ品詞（形容詞）が並んでいるので、文脈から答えを見つける。主語が The vintage paintings（年代物の絵画）で、それが are kept ------- in a well-ventilated location（換気のよい場所で -------な状態に置かれている）という意味になっている。選択肢のうち、この文脈に一致するのは「安全な」という意味の (C) secure。

あなたの解答 A B C D
メモ

☐ auction off ～ ～を競売する
☐ well-ventilated 通気のよい

110. 正解 (B) 難易度

空所直前に形容詞 some がある。形容詞に修飾されるのは名詞なので、(B) assistance が正解。動詞、分詞、動名詞は some の修飾を受けることはできないので、(A) (C) (D) は誤り。

あなたの解答 A B C D
メモ

☐ audio-visual AV の、視聴覚の

111. 正解 (B) 難易度

or とともに、相関接続詞 either A or B（A かそれとも B）を作る (B) either が正解。ここでは、a towel と a pair of slippers（ともに名詞）をつないでいる。このように対等な要素をつなぐ性質があることを押さえておこう。(A) also は「～もまた」という意味の副詞。(C) until は「～までずっと」という意味の前置詞や接続詞として用いられる。(D) は、nor とともに相関接続詞 neither A nor B（A でも B でもない）の形で頻出。

あなたの解答 A B C D
メモ

☐ entitle A to B A (人) に B の権利・資格を与える

112. 正解 (D) 難易度

冒頭の If からカンマまでが条件の副詞節になっているが、動詞が見当たらない。従って、動詞 (C) と (D) が正解候補となる。この節には未来を表す tomorrow があるので、時制は未来である。しかし〈条件の副詞節では、現在時制で未来を表す〉というルールがあるため、approve（～を承認する）の3人称単数現在形である (D) approves が正解。

あなたの解答 A B C D
メモ

☐ propose ～を提案する

TEST 2
PART 5

113. ------- of purchases made on our Web site will be sent to customers' e-mail accounts within one day of the transactions.

(A) Confirmation
(B) Observation
(C) Delegation
(D) Admission

114. The renowned author ------- his award-winning autobiography with a short quote from a Japanese poet which summarized the theme of the book.

(A) conclude
(B) was concluded
(C) to conclude
(D) concluded

115. Ms. Desi has been operating ------- fast food franchise for the past ten years and is hoping to open another branch in the near future.

(A) her own
(B) hers
(C) she
(D) herself

116. Sullivan Properties has requested an official ------- from a licensed realtor to find out the current value of its commercial building in Portland.

(A) level
(B) total
(C) appraisal
(D) capital

117. Arayat Tours is offering summer cruise packages to customers ------- in exploring the Caribbean Islands.

(A) interesting
(B) interest
(C) interested
(D) interestingly

118. Since the donation contained perishable food items, volunteers were concerned it might ------- have expired when it reached its final destination.

(A) never
(B) already
(C) more
(D) occasionally

正解＆解説

113. 正解 **(A)**　難易度 ■■□　難

同じ品詞（名詞）が並んでいるので、**文脈から答えを探る**。made on our Web site が purchases を後ろから修飾しているので、------- of purchases made on our Web site は「当社ウェブサイトでなされた買い物の -------」という意味。この文脈に合うのは「買い物の〈確認〉」となる (A) Confirmation。

あなたの解答　A B C D
メモ

☐ transaction 取引

---

114. 正解 **(D)**　難易度 ■■□　難

主語と動詞の一致を問う問題。主語は**3人称単数**の The renowned author（高名な作家）で、選択肢に並ぶ conclude は「〜を終える、結論づける」という意味の他動詞。**空所のあとに目的語** his award-winning autobiography（賞を獲得した自伝）があるので、「作家は自伝を締めくくった」という**能動**の意味になる。従って、能動態の過去形である (D) が正解。原形の (A) は、主語と数が一致しない。(B) は受動態なので誤り。to 不定詞の (C) はそもそも動詞の位置にくることはできない。

あなたの解答　A B C D
メモ

☐ renowned 有名な
☐ autobiography 自伝　☐ quote 引用
☐ summarize 〜を要約する

---

115. 正解 **(A)**　難易度 ■■□　難

空所の後ろには、名詞の固まり fast food franchise（ファストフードフランチャイズ店）がきている。これを**前から形容詞のように修飾**できるのは、**所有格**の (A) her own。「彼女自身のファストフードフランチャイズ店」という意味になる。own は、主に所有格のあとに用いられ、所有の意味を強調する。補足として、形容詞 another は「もうひとつの」という意味で、次に単数名詞（ここでは branch）がくることを押さえておこう。

あなたの解答　A B C D
メモ

☐ operate 〜を経営する

---

116. 正解 **(C)**　難易度 ■■■　難

同じ品詞（名詞）が並んでいるので、**文脈から考えよう**。has requested an official ------- from a licensed realtor（認可不動産業者からの公式な ------- を依頼した）とあり、その目的が to find out 以下で「商業ビルの価値を知るために」と述べられている。appraisal を入れて「ビルの価値を知るために、公式な〈評価〉を依頼した」とすると文意が通るので、(C) が正解。

あなたの解答　A B C D
メモ

☐ licensed 免許を持つ
☐ realtor 不動産業者　☐ value 価値
☐ commercial 商業の

---

117. 正解 **(C)**　難易度 ■■■　難

すでに、主語と動詞、目的語が揃っているので、空所以降は名詞 customers を修飾する付加的要素。**名詞を後ろから修飾できる分詞** (A) と (C) が正解候補となる。それぞれ感情を表す他動詞 interest（〜に興味を持たせる）の現在分詞と過去分詞だが、修飾の対象が興味を**持たせる**のか、**持たされる**のかを見極める。customers は「興味を〈持たされる〉」ほうなので、**受動**の意味を持つ過去分詞 (C) が正解。現在分詞の interesting は、能動を表し「(物や人が) 興味深い」という意味。

あなたの解答　A B C D
メモ

☐ explore 〜を探検する

---

118. 正解 **(B)**　難易度 ■■■　難

同じ品詞（副詞）が並んでいるので、**文脈から答えを探る**。まず、冒頭の Since からカンマまでは「寄付は傷みやすい食品を含むので」という意味。そして it might ------- have expired について「〈どのように〉賞味期限が過ぎているかもしれない」のかを考える。「**すでに**」という意味の already を入れると文意が通るので、(B) が正解。参考までに、ここの since は「〜なので」という理由を表す接続詞として使われていることを押さえておこう。

あなたの解答　A B C D
メモ

☐ donation 寄付　☐ contain 〜を含む
☐ perishable 傷みやすい
☐ expire 賞味期限が過ぎる

TEST 2 — PART 5

119. Young painters are encouraged to attend workshops ------- to learn new techniques that will improve their skills.
(A) frequented
(B) frequently
(C) frequency
(D) frequenting

120. The report ------- mentioned an upcoming merger between a textile company in the United States and a prominent fashion boutique in France.
(A) intensely
(B) briefly
(C) rarely
(D) anymore

121. Business class passengers on Trans-Con Air receive several benefits ------- access to the lounge, larger seats, and gourmet meals.
(A) inclusive
(B) including
(C) inclusively
(D) included

122. To promote its ecologically friendly technology, Kazka Motors will ------- a hybrid car model by the end of the year.
(A) store
(B) spend
(C) submit
(D) launch

123. The financial consultant ------- Ms. Broderick to downsize the staff at the Denver branch to lower operational expenses.
(A) suggested
(B) advised
(C) commented
(D) argued

124. ------- intense competition in the market, HiMobile continues to be the top cellular phone manufacturer in Asia.
(A) Concerning
(B) Except
(C) Around
(D) Despite

TOEIC豆知識
TOEICの受験料がもっと安くなればいいのに、と思っている人は多いだろうが、以前は6,615円もした。5,565円でも安くなったと感じているオールドTOEICファンは多い。もちろん、もっと値下げしてほしいけど。

正解&解説 | 間違いメモ&単語

119. 正解 (B) 　難易度 ■■■□ 難

空所は直前の動詞 attend を修飾していると考えられるので、**副詞** (B) frequently（頻繁に）が正解。

あなたの解答 [A][B][C][D]
メモ

□ painter 画家
□ encourage 〜を勧める

---

120. 正解 (B) 　難易度 ■■■□ 難

同じ品詞（副詞）が並んでいるので、**文脈からアプローチ**しよう。The report ------- mentioned an upcoming merger（その報道は〈どのように〉間もなく行われる合併に言及した）のかを考えると、「〈**簡潔に**〉言及した」となる briefly が自然。従って、(B) が正解。

あなたの解答 [A][B][C][D]
メモ

□ upcoming 今度の、来たる
□ textile 繊維　□ prominent 有名な
□ boutique ブティック

---

121. 正解 (B) 　難易度 ■■■□ 難

主語 Business class passengers、**動詞** receive、**目的語** several benefits がすでに揃っているので、文として成立している。従って、空所以降は**名詞 benefits を修飾**する付加的要素である。**名詞を後ろから修飾できるのは分詞**なので、現在分詞 (B) と過去分詞 (D) が正解候補。現在分詞は「〜している」という**能動**の意味を、過去分詞は「〜される（た）」という**受動**の意味を持つ。修飾される benefits は、ラウンジ利用や広い座席などを〈**含む**〉と考えられるので、能動を表す現在分詞 (B) が正解。

あなたの解答 [A][B][C][D]
メモ

□ benefit 特典
□ gourmet meal 美食家向けの食事

---

122. 正解 (D) 　難易度 ■■■□ 難

選択肢には同じ品詞（動詞）が並んでいるので、**文脈から考えよう**。Kazka Motors will ------- a hybrid car model（Kazka 自動車はハイブリッド車を -------する）なので、「ハイブリッド車を〈**売り出す**〉」となる (D) launch が正解。

あなたの解答 [A][B][C][D]
メモ

□ ecologically friendly 環境に優しい

---

123. 正解 (B) 　難易度 ■■■■ 難

「コンサルタントが Broderick さんに人員削減をさせようとしている」という文脈だと推測できるが、どの選択肢も正解に思える。なので、文の構造を考えると、主語 The financial consultant、動詞（空所）、目的語 Ms. Broderick に加え、目的格補語 to downsize the staff ... がある**第5文型**だとわかる。選択肢のうち、目的格補語を取ることができる動詞は、**advise**（〜に助言する）のみなので、(B) が正解。ほかはすべて、他動詞として用いる場合、第3文型になる。

あなたの解答 [A][B][C][D]
メモ

□ consultant コンサルタント、顧問
□ downsize 〜を削減する

---

124. 正解 (D) 　難易度 ■■■□ 難

前置詞の問題。カンマまでが「熾烈な市場競争」、カンマ以降が「HiMobile 社はアジアトップの携帯電話メーカーであり続けている」という流れなので、「熾烈な競争〈**にもかかわらず**〉、トップであり続けている」という意味になる (D) Despite が正解。参考までに、despite と同じ意味の群前置詞 **in spite of 〜**も一緒に押さえておこう。

あなたの解答 [A][B][C][D]
メモ

□ intense 激しい、強烈な
□ cellular phone 携帯電話

49

TEST 2 PART 5

125. ------- are nearly finished for Oakville's centennial anniversary parade to be held along Main Street this coming Sunday.
(A) Preparers
(B) Preparations
(C) Prepared
(D) Preparing

126. Scientists have been saying for years that solar energy has incredible ------- to become the world's leading power source in place of fossil fuels.
(A) insight
(B) potential
(C) relevance
(D) suggestion

127. Somerset Airlines provides special boarding services at the departure gates for ------- requiring extra help or traveling with small children.
(A) that
(B) whose
(C) those
(D) they

128. Because of her new position as financial vice president at the company's European headquarters, Marina Latke ------- to London in October.
(A) relocate
(B) relocating
(C) is relocated
(D) will relocate

129. Chemical materials such as detergents and other cleaning agents should be kept in locked locations which are not ------- to small children.
(A) access
(B) accessing
(C) accessed
(D) accessible

130. At a meeting of finance ministers in June, Mr. Yao Jie Bin will give a brief ------- on the benefits of China's efforts to control its currency.
(A) situation
(B) revelation
(C) presentation
(D) perception

| 正解&解説 | 間違いメモ&単語 |

125. 正解 **(B)** 　難易度 ■■■■□ 難

問題文には主語が欠けているので、空所には主語として機能する**名詞**（もしくは名詞の働きをする語句）が入る。つまり (A) と (B)、動名詞の (D) が正解候補。文脈をみると「Oakville の 100 周年記念パレードのための ------- は、ほぼ終わった」となっているので、「**準備**」という意味の (B) Preparations が正解。(A) Preparers だと「パレードの準備者はほぼ終わった」となり不自然。動名詞の (D) Preparing は後ろに目的語を必要とするが、空所の直後は動詞 are なので、誤り。

あなたの解答 A B C D
メモ

☐ centennial　100周年の

126. 正解 **(B)** 　難易度 ■■■■□ 難

選択肢に同じ品詞（名詞）が並んでいるので、**文脈から答えを探ろう**。solar energy has incredible -------（太陽エネルギーには驚くべき ------- がある）、または ------- to become the world's leading power source（世界をリードする電力源になる -------）となっている。「**可能性**」という意味の potential を入れると文意が通るので、(B) が正解。

あなたの解答 A B C D
メモ

☐ incredible　信じられないほど素晴らしい
☐ leading　重要な、先導する
☐ in place of ～　～の代わりに

127. 正解 **(C)** 　難易度 ■■■■□ 難

前置詞 for の目的語となり、かつ、**現在分詞 requiring の修飾を受けられる**のは (C) those（人々）のみ。「人々」という意味で用いられる場合、those のあとには、必ず関係詞節、分詞、または前置詞句がくることを押さえておこう。(A) that は「それ」という意味の指示代名詞として用いられるが、those と異なり、修飾を受けることはできない。関係代名詞の (B) whose と、主格の人称代名詞 (D) they は、前置詞の目的語にはなれない。

あなたの解答 A B C D
メモ

☐ boarding　搭乗
☐ departure gate　出発ゲート

128. 正解 **(D)** 　難易度 ■■■□□ 難

この文には、主語 Marina Latke はあるが、動詞がないので (A) (C) (D) が正解候補。**時制**と**態**、**主述の一致**を見極めながら答えを探る。まず、主語が 3 人称単数なので、それに一致しない原形の (A) を除外。次に時制を見ていくと、in October（10 月に）という時の表現があるので、「**10 月にロンドンに引っ越すだろう**」となる未来時制の (D) will relocate が正解とわかる。relocate には自動詞「移転する、移住する」と他動詞「～を移転させる、移住させる」、両方の用法があることを覚えておこう。

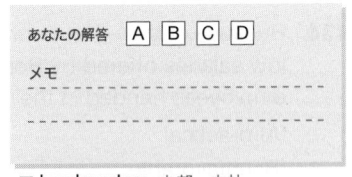

あなたの解答 A B C D
メモ

☐ headquarters　本部、本社

129. 正解 **(D)** 　難易度 ■■■□□ 難

be 動詞 are の後ろは、名詞／現在分詞／過去分詞／形容詞のいずれも可。従って、**文脈から考える**。locked locations which are not ------- to small children（小さな子供に ------- ない鍵のかかった場所）なので、「（場所が）**届きやすい**」という意味の (D) accessible が正解。accessible to ～（～に届きやすい）として覚えておこう。(B) だと、locked locations が「子供に接近していない」となり、不自然。(C) だと、受動態になり、後ろに行為の主体を表す前置詞 by が必要。

あなたの解答 A B C D
メモ

☐ chemical　化学的な
☐ material　物質　☐ detergent　洗剤
☐ agent　薬剤

130. 正解 **(C)** 　難易度 ■■■□□ 難

同じ品詞（名詞）が並んでいるので、**文脈から答えを探ろう**。Mr. Yao Jie Bin will give a brief -------（Yao Jie Bin 氏は短い ------- を与えるだろう）となっているので、「短い**〈発表〉**をするだろう」となる (C) presentation が正解。give a presentation（発表をする）を慣用句として覚えておこう。参考までに、空所直後の前置詞 on は「～について」という意味で使われており、同じ意味の前置詞 about、over、as to、concerning、regarding も一緒に押さえておきたい。

あなたの解答 A B C D
メモ

☐ brief　手短な、簡潔な
☐ effort　努力
☐ currency　通貨、貨幣

TEST 2 PART 5

問題

131. For this year's annual company conference, the planning committee is putting together an ------- trip to Hawaii that will last for three days.
(A) exciting
(B) excited
(C) excites
(D) excitement

132. Please note that all publications on sale at the West-End Book Store are categorized and arranged on shelves ------- subject and genre.
(A) in order to
(B) permitting
(C) according to
(D) alike

133. For train passengers with excess baggage, FineTrak Railways will impose a fee of $13 for every ------- bag.
(A) promising
(B) supplementary
(C) additional
(D) unprepared

134. Because of the ------- working conditions and the low salaries offered by Benton Manufacturing, many employees handed in their resignations.
(A) practical
(B) unfavorable
(C) combined
(D) functional

135. Refunds or exchanges for any of Dunway Electronics' products may be requested at all ------- dealers.
(A) authorization
(B) authority
(C) authorize
(D) authorized

136. The company judiciously added a popular item to an existing product bundle with the expectation that sales of the new combination would ------- the targeted goal for the quarter.
(A) exceed
(B) react
(C) declare
(D) apprise

訳

今年の年次会議のために、準備委員会はわくわくするような3日間のハワイ旅行をまとめている。
(A) 形 興奮させる
(B) 形 興奮した
(C) 動 ～を興奮させる
(D) 名 興奮

West-End書店で販売中の全出版物はテーマとジャンルによって分類され、棚に並べられていることに留意のこと。
(A) ～するために
(B) ～を許す
(C) ～に従って
(D) 形 同様に／副 同様に

手荷物の重量制限を超過している乗客に対し、FineTrak鉄道は追加の手荷物ひとつにつき13ドルの料金を課す。
(A) 前途有望な
(B) 補足の
(C) 追加の
(D) 準備できていない

Benton Manufacturing社の好ましくない労働条件と低賃金のせいで、多くの労働者が辞表を提出した。
(A) 実用的な
(B) 好ましくない
(C) 組み合わせた
(D) 機能の

Dunway電子の全製品の返金・交換は、すべての認定販売店で依頼できる。
(A) 名 権限付与
(B) 名 権威
(C) 動 ～を認定する
(D) 形 認定された

同社は賢明にも既存の製品セットに人気商品を加え、その新しい組み合わせの売上が四半期の目標を超えることを期待している。
(A) ～を超える
(B) 反応する
(C) ～を宣言する
(D) ～を知らせる

正解＆解説

131. 正解 **(A)**　難易度　難

冠詞 an と名詞 trip に挟まれているので、空所には **trip を修飾する形容詞**が入る。形容詞（または形容詞として機能する分詞）は (A) exciting（興奮させる）と (B) excited（興奮した）のふたつ。修飾の対象である trip（旅行）は「**興奮させる**」ほうなので (A) が正解。excited trip とすると trip が「興奮した」という意味になり不自然。

間違いメモ＆単語
あなたの解答 A B C D
メモ

☐ annual　年次の、年1度の
☐ put together　（考えなど）をまとめる
☐ last　続く

---

132. 正解 **(C)**　難易度　難

all publications ... are categorized and arranged on shelves（すべての出版物は分類され、棚に並べられている）とある。従って、空所には subject and genre とともに「テーマとジャンル〈**によって**〉」となる、(C) according to を入れると文意が通る。(A) は、後ろに動詞の原形がくる。(B) だと、shelves を修飾して「テーマとジャンルを許す棚」となり、不自然。(D) は形容詞としては be 動詞の補語、副詞としては old and young alike（老いも若きも一様に）のように、用いる。

あなたの解答 A B C D
メモ

☐ note　～に気をつける
☐ categorize　～を分類する
☐ subject　主題　☐ genre　ジャンル

---

133. 正解 **(C)**　難易度　難

同じ品詞（形容詞）が並んでいるので、**文脈からアプローチ**しよう。impose a fee of $13 for every ------- bag（------- の手荷物ごとに13ドルの料金を課す）という文脈なので、(C) additional を入れて「〈**追加の**〉手荷物ごとに」とすれば文意が通る。

あなたの解答 A B C D
メモ

☐ excess　超過した
☐ baggage　手荷物
☐ impose　～を課す

---

134. 正解 **(B)**　難易度　難

同じ品詞（形容詞）が並んでいるので、**文脈から答えを探す**。Because of the ------- working conditions（------- な労働環境のせいで）、多くの従業員が辞表を提出した、という文脈になっている。従って、「**好ましくない**」という意味の (B) unfavorable だと文意が通る。

あなたの解答 A B C D
メモ

☐ salary　給料
☐ hand in ～　～を提出する
☐ resignation　辞表

---

135. 正解 **(D)**　難易度　難

空所に入るのは、直後の**名詞 dealers を修飾する形容詞**。よって (D) authorized（認定された）が正解。参考までに、all は可算名詞の複数形だけでなく、不可算名詞とも一緒に使えることを押さえておこう。

あなたの解答 A B C D
メモ

☐ dealer　販売業者

---

136. 正解 **(A)**　難易度　難

同じ品詞（動詞）が並んでいるので、**文脈から考える**。sales of the new combination would ------- the targeted goal（新しいセット商品の売上が、目標を ------- するだろう）という文脈なので、「**～を越える、突破する**」という意味の (A) exceed を入れると文意が通る。

あなたの解答 A B C D
メモ

☐ judiciously　賢明に
☐ bundle　セット、束
☐ expectation　期待　☐ goal　目標

TEST 2 PART 5

137. ------- the author satisfies the publishing company's requirements for a new edition of the book Art Through the Ages, publication will have to be postponed.

(A) Unless
(B) Rather than
(C) Whenever
(D) As long as

138. Staff members attending the picnic should bring ------- food they would like to share with the group, apart from burgers and beverages, which will be provided by the company.

(A) whenever
(B) whomever
(C) whatever
(D) wherever

139. The tour leader is making arrangements to accommodate a group of visitors who have requested an ------- to a small island near their location.

(A) itinerary
(B) excursion
(C) option
(D) approach

140. In ------- with the health department's stipulations, restaurant owners must conduct sessions with kitchen service operators to familiarize them with food safety regulations.

(A) participating
(B) pursuing
(C) according
(D) keeping

著者が Art Through the Ages の新版に関する出版社の要求を満たさないかぎり、出版は延期せざるを得ない。

(A) 〜しない限り
(B) 〜よりむしろ
(C) 〜するときはいつも
(D) 〜するかぎり

ピクニックに参加するスタッフは会社が提供するハンバーガーと飲み物以外で、ほかのメンバーと分けあいたい食べ物ならなんでも持参すべきだ。

(A) いつでも
(B) 誰にでも
(C) どんな〜でも
(D) どこでも

ツアーリーダーは、近くの小島への小旅行を要望した来訪者一行の希望に沿うよう調整を行っている。

(A) 旅程
(B) 小旅行
(C) 選択
(D) 接近

保健省の規定を踏まえて、レストランオーナーたちはキッチンの担当者に食品安全規則を周知させるための会合を実施しなければならない。

〔選択肢訳なし〕

正解&解説

137. 正解 (A)　難易度：難

この文にはすでに、**主語** publication と**動詞** will have to be postponed が揃っている。従って、------- the author satisfies ... Ages 部分は修飾の働きをする付加的要素。この付加的要素部分も**主語** the author と**動詞** satisfies を備えた**節**になっているので、空所には節動詞をつなぐ**接続詞** (A) (C) (D) が入る。カンマまでの前半部が「著者が出版社の要求を満たす」、後半部が「出版は延期される」となっているので、自然につなげられるのは「**～しない限り**」という意味の (A) Unless。

間違いメモ&単語

あなたの解答　A B C D
メモ

□ satisfy　～を満たす　□ publishing company　出版社　□ requirement　要求されること　□ postpone　～を延期する

---

138. 正解 (C)　難易度：難

空所は、**名詞 food を修飾しつつ、動詞 bring の目的語となる節**（------- food they ... group）を導いている。このような働きをするのは、**複合関係形容詞**の (C) whatever（どんな～でも）。複合関係形容詞には、ほかに whichever がある。複合関係副詞の (A) whenever と (D) wherever は副詞節を導くので、主語と動詞を持つ完全な節があとに続く。複合関係代名詞 (B) whomever は、名詞を修飾することができない。

あなたの解答　A B C D
メモ

□ apart from ～　～のほかに、～を除いて

---

139. 正解 (B)　難易度：難

同じ品詞（**名詞**）が並んでいるので、**文脈からアプローチ**。a group of visitors who have requested an ------- to a small island（小島への ------- を依頼した観光客の一行）とあるので、「小島への〈**何**〉を希望した」のかを考える。文意が通るのは「小島への〈**小旅行**〉」となる (B) excursion。

あなたの解答　A B C D
メモ

□ arrangement　手配
□ accommodate　～の世話をする

---

140. 正解 (D)　難易度：難

カンマまでの前半部分を「the health department's stipulations（保健省の規程）に〈**従って**〉」という意味にできれば、後半に自然につながる。正解は、**in keeping with ～**で「～に従って、～と一致して」という意味になる (D) keeping。(C) は accordance であれば、in accordance with ～（～に合致して、～にしたがって）となり、正解。参考までに、safety regulations（安全規定）は、〈**名詞＋名詞**〉の形で、前の名詞が後ろの名詞を修飾している。これを《**複合名詞**》と言うが、ほかにも safety precautions（安全予防策）、safety measures（安全措置）などを覚えておこう。

あなたの解答　A B C D
メモ

□ stipulation　規定
□ familiarize　(人を)～に精通させる
□ regulation　規則

TEST 2
PART 6

Questions 141-143 refer to the following article.

Napping is Healthy, Not a Sign of Laziness!

Young children often get away with taking naps in the afternoon, but any adult who tries to do the same will usually be called "lazy". -------, new studies show that such brief

141. (A) However
(B) Since
(C) Besides
(D) Otherwise

afternoon naps, or "power naps", may actually be good for health, regardless of age.

Naps lasting between 20 and 60 minutes in the afternoon have numerous -------,

142. (A) evidence
(B) attempts
(C) benefits
(D) improvements

including stress reduction and heightening learning abilities and reaction times. In addition, naps can even help with people's vision and upgrade their work performance.

Studies show that 20 minutes of sleep in the second half of the day is actually more helpful to our bodies than 20 minutes of extra sleep in the morning. People who take naps wake up feeling more ------- and motivated than those who sleep in during the

143. (A) energize
(B) energetically
(C) energy
(D) energetic

morning. So the next time your boss catches you napping on the job, just say, "I'm only having a nap because it will help me be more productive," and see if the excuse works!

単語
- nap 昼寝
- laziness 怠惰
- get away with ~ ~を許される、~の罰を受けない
- study 研究
- regardless of ~ ~に関係なく
- numerous たくさんの
- reduction 減少、縮小
- heighten ~を高める
- reaction time 反応時間
- in addition さらに、加えて
- performance 仕事ぶり、業績
- motivated やる気のある
- catch ~を見つける
- productive 生産性の高い
- excuse 言い訳

TOEIC豆知識 TOEICは、2006年に大改訂が行われたのだが、Part 6は改訂当初、4つの空所がある長文が3題出題される形式だった。

問題文の訳

設問141から143は次の記事に関する質問です。

昼寝は健康によく、怠け者の証ではない！

幼児は午後に昼寝をしても許されるが、大人が同じく昼寝をしようとすると、たいていは「怠け者」と呼ばれるだろう。しかし、このような短い昼寝、すなわち「パワーナップ」は、年齢に関係なく実は健康によいということを新研究が示している。

午後に20分から60分間の昼寝をすると、ストレスの軽減、学習能力や反応時間の向上など非常に多くの利点がある。加えて、昼寝は人の洞察力を高め、仕事の効率を向上させることも可能なのである。

数々の研究から、午後の20分間の睡眠は、朝20分余計に寝るよりも、実際は私たちの身体に有益なことが明らかになっている。昼寝をする人は目覚めたときに、朝遅くまで寝ている人よりも、多くの活力とやる気を感じる。という訳で、今度あなたが仕事中にうたた寝をしているところを上司に見つかったときは、「生産性が高まるので、昼寝をしているだけです」と言って、この言い訳が通用するか確かめてみよう！

選択肢の訳

141. (A) 副 しかしながら
　　　(B) 接 ～なので
　　　(C) 副 さらに、その上
　　　(D) 副 さもなければ

142. (A) 証拠
　　　(B) 試み
　　　(C) 利点
　　　(D) 改良、進歩

143. (A) 副 ～を元気づける
　　　(B) 副 はりきって
　　　(C) 名 元気、活力
　　　(D) 形 元気な

正解&解説

141. 正解 (A)　難易度：難

選択肢には、前後の文をつなげる単語が並んでいる。空所の位置が**文頭で直後にカンマがある**ので、**接続副詞**の (A) (C) (D) が候補。あとは文脈から答えを探す。空所前が「昼寝する成人は『なまけもの』と呼ばれる」で、空所以降が「新研究は、昼寝が健康によいことを示している」という**逆の内容**になっている。これらを自然につなげられるのは、「しかしながら」という意味の (A) However。(B) Since は接続詞なので、直後にはカンマなしで、主語と動詞を含む節が続く。

142. 正解 (C)　難易度：難

同じ品詞（名詞）が並んでいるので、前後の**文脈から答えを探ろう**。「ストレス軽減、学習能力と反応時間の向上など、たくさんの ------- がある」という文脈になっている。「ストレス軽減」「学習能力と反応時間の向上」はいずれもよいことなので、**benefit（利点、恩恵）**の複数形 (C) benefits だと文意が通る。

143. 正解 (D)　難易度：難

空所前後をよくみると、feeling の補語として、**空所と形容詞 motivated（やる気がある）が and で並列されている**ことがわかる。**等位接続詞 and は等しいものを並べる**ので、空所にも形容詞がはいる。よって、形容詞 (D) energetic（元気な）が正解。参考までに、動詞 feel は形容詞を補語として取る動詞である。また、and、or、but、yet のような等位接続詞は、単語と単語、句と句、節と節のように等しいものをつなげることを押さえておこう。

TEST 2
PART 6

Questions 144-146 refer to the following letter.

Tina Louis
1877 Birchwood Street
Summerland, BC, Canada

Dear Ms. Louis,

It is my pleasure on behalf of the company to ------- offer you a summer internship at HBC-

144. (A) honorably
(B) exceptionally
(C) temporally
(D) officially

TV. The internship will begin on June 2 and end on August 31. You will work together with our reporters, producers, and technical staff during this period to learn about the operations and production of a TV news program.

As was explained at your interview, all interns work on a ------- basis for the first two weeks.

145. (A) provisional
(B) undecided
(C) permanent
(D) persistent

At this point, the staff you work with will evaluate your performance. Following that, a decision ------- about which particular department would be best suited for you. And though

146. (A) has been making
(B) was made
(C) will be made
(D) is making

we do not offer salaries for any intern positions, we do provide a modest allowance of $100 per week to cover the cost of your meals and transportation.

I hope you will find the internship useful and educational. Please let me know by Friday, May 25, whether you are interested.

Sincerely,

Robert Denver
Programming Director, HBC-TV

単語
- on behalf of 〜 〜を代表して
- on a 〜 basis 〜制で（〜勤務で）
- evaluate 〜を評価する
- particular 特定の
- suited 〜に適した、ふさわしい
- modest 控えめな、質素な
- allowance 手当
- transportation 交通手段、乗り物

問題文の訳

設問144から146は次の手紙に関する質問です。

Tina Louis
1877 Birchwood Street
Summerland, ブリティッシュ・コロンビア州, カナダ

Louis さま

HBC-TV を代表し、貴殿に当局での夏季インターンシップを<u>正式に</u>オファーいたします。インターンシップは6月2日から始まり、8月31日に終わります。貴殿はこの期間、当局のレポーター、プロデューサー、技術スタッフと連携し、テレビのニュース番組の業務や制作について学んでいただきます。

面接時に説明した通り、インターンのみなさんには最初の2週間は<u>仮採用扱い</u>で勤務していただきます。その時点で、いっしょに働いたスタッフが貴殿の能力を評価いたします。そののち、どの部門が貴殿にもっとも適しているかの<u>決定がなされます</u>。インターンのみなさんに給与はお支払いしませんが、食事代と交通費として、週100ドルの手当てを心ばかりではありますが支給いたします。

貴殿にとってこのインターンシップが有益でためになるものになれば幸いです。ご関心の有無を5月25日金曜日までにお知らせください。

敬具

Robert Denver
番組制作ディレクター、HBC-TV

選択肢の訳

144. (A) 立派に
　　 (B) 例外的に
　　 (C) 一時的に
　　 (D) 公式に

145. (A) 仮の、暫定的な
　　 (B) 決まっていない
　　 (C) 永久的な
　　 (D) 粘り強い

146. (A) 〈現在完了進行形〉
　　 (B) 〈受動態の過去形〉
　　 (C) 〈受動態の未来形〉
　　 (D) 〈現在進行形〉

正解＆解説

144. 正解 (D)

同じ品詞（副詞）が並んでいるので、**前後の文脈からアプローチ**する。空所以降に offer you a summer internship（夏季インターンシップをオファーする）とあるので、「〈どのように〉オファー」したのかを考える。この手紙では全体を通して、インターンの仕事内容を詳しく説明していることから、「〈正式に〉オファー」していると考えられるので、(D) officially が正解。

145. 正解 (A)

同じ品詞（形容詞）が並んでいるので、空所を含む文だけでなく、**全体の文脈から考えよう**。空所前後は「はじめの2週間は ------- ベースで働く」という意味。そして、あとに続く2文で「その時点（＝2週間経った時点）で、能力を評価し、適した部署を決める」と述べられていることから、(A) provisional（仮の、暫定的な）を入れて「〈暫定的に〉働く」とすると文意が通る。

146. 正解 (C)

動詞 make の変化形が並んでいるので、前後の流れから適切な**時制**と**態**を考える。ひとつ前の文が未来時制で will evaluate（〜を評価する）と述べたあとに、空所を含む文が Following that（そのあとに）で始まっている。ということは、空所を含む文も未来時制だと考えられる。また、主語 a decision（決定）は**なされる**ものなので、受動態の未来形 (C) が正解。

TEST 2
PART 6

Questions 147-149 refer to the following letter.

Dear Editor,

I am writing in response to an article that appeared in your June 16 issue, entitled "The Real Cost of Business," in which you assert that Leyton Teas CEO Dana Brubeck is being pushed out of the company by management. That statement is simply false. In fact, our company ------- involved in merger negotiations with a competitor and Mr. Brubeck will most likely be

147. (A) has been
(B) have had
(C) will have been
(D) will have

serving on the board of directors.

While it is ------- that Leyton Teas has suffered decreasing profitability under Mr. Brubeck,

148. (A) inevitable
(B) true
(C) particular
(D) complex

this is not a reflection of his leadership abilities and we feel any suggestions to that effect are damaging to his reputation. Therefore, we ask that you print a ------- of the article in an

149. (A) version
(B) definition
(C) retraction
(D) caption

appropriate and timely manner.

In the future, should you need any further information about our affairs, I will be happy to assist you. Please feel free to contact me at lizbyron@leyton.com.

Thank you.

Elizabeth Byron
Public Relations
Leyton Teas

単語
- in response to ～ ～に応えて
- issue（刊行物の）号
- entitle ～に（…という）題をつける
- assert ～を断言する
- be pushed out of ～ ～から締め出される
- be involved in ～ ～に携わる、従事する
- board of directors 取締役会
- profitability 収益性
- reflection 反映、影響
- suggestion 示唆
- to that effect その趣旨での
- reputation 名声、信望
- appropriate 適切な
- in a timely manner 時機を逸せずに
- affair 業務

問題文の訳

設問147から149は次の手紙に関する質問です。

編集者殿

貴誌6月16日号に掲載された「ビジネスの本当の費用」と題する記事についてお手紙差し上げます。その記事には、Leyton Teas 社の最高経営責任者 Dana Brubeck が経営陣により会社から追放されると書かれていました。この記事は完全に間違っています。実際には、当社は競合他社との合併交渉を進めているところで、Brubeck 氏は取締役会の一員を務める可能性がもっとも高いのです。

Brubeck 氏の下で Leyton Teas 社が減益に陥っていることは事実ですが、彼の統率力の影響によるものではありませんし、そういった趣旨の示唆は、彼の名誉を傷つけるものと私どもは感じております。そのため、適切かつ適時に、この記事の撤回記事を掲載するようお願い申し上げます。

今後、当社の業務に関する情報が必要であれば、喜んでお手伝いいたします。どうぞお気軽に私のアドレス lizbyron@leyton.com までご連絡ください。

よろしくお願い申し上げます。

Elizabeth Byron
広報部
Leyton Teas 社

選択肢の訳

147. (A)〈受動態の現在完了形〉
     (B)〈現在完了形〉
     (C)〈受動態の未来完了形〉
     (D)〈未来完了形〉

148. (A) 必然的な
     (B) 真実の
     (C) 特有の
     (D) 複雑な

149. (A) バージョン、版
     (B) 定義
     (C) 撤回、取り消し
     (D) 説明文

正解＆解説

147. 正解 **(A)**

動詞の変化形が並んでいるので、前後の流れから適切な**態**と**時制**を探る。空所直後の他動詞 involve（〜を含む）の後ろには、〈何〉を含むのかを示す**目的語**がない。よって involved とともに**受動態を作れる** (A) と (C) が候補。次に時制だが、いつ merger negotiations（合併交渉）するのかを考えると、前後の文脈から**すでに始まって今も続いている**ことがわかる。よって受動態の現在完了形となる (A) が正解。

148. 正解 **(B)**

While からカンマまでの内容「Brubeck 氏の下で減益に苦しんでいるのは -------- だが」と、カンマの後ろの「彼のリーダーシップのせいではない」を考え合わせる。**「真実の」**という意味の (B) true を入れると、「苦しんでいるのは〈**真実**〉だが、彼のリーダーシップのせいではない」となり、文意が通る。

149. 正解 **(C)**

同じ品詞（名詞）が並んでいるので、**全体の文脈から答えを探ろう**。ここまでに、Brubeck 氏は追放されるだろうという記事がでたこと、そして、それを否定する主張が述べられている。従って、we ask that you print a ------- of the article は「この記事の〈**撤回記事**〉を掲載して欲しい」という文脈にするのが自然。(C) retraction が正解。参考までに、提案、要請、義務を表す動詞 ask、suggest、recommend や、形容詞 essential、necessary などが主節に用いられる場合、従属節には動詞の原形がくることを押さえておこう。

TEST 2
PART 6

Questions 150-152 refer to the following e-mail.

From: Laura Masterson <lauram@bizpeople.org>
To: Zachary Wilson <zwilson@cybermail.net>
Date: July 7
Subject: Schedule

Dear Mr. Wilson,

You have registered to participate in Biz People's leadership skills course.

Because of the sudden increase in ------- this year, our organization has decided to

    150. (A) enlistment
        (B) attention
        (C) enrollment
        (D) occupancy

divide the course into two separate sessions. Instead of just Wednesdays from 9:00 A.M. to 11:00 A.M., we will now offer the same course on Fridays, which will meet from 7:00 P.M. to 9:00 P.M. Both sessions will be taught by Ms. Christina Lopez, a former chief executive officer ------- over 30 years of experience in corporate management.

    151. (A) plus
        (B) with
        (C) about
        (D) from

Due to the change, we are asking all those who have already signed up to register again by visiting our Web site at http://www.bizpeople.com/seminars.

We are sorry for the inconvenience and for more information, kindly respond to this e-mail or call our office at (809) 555-9238 during ------- business hours.

    152. (A) frequent
        (B) normal
        (C) opened
        (D) average

Truly yours,

Laura Masterson
Biz People Career Development Services

単語
- participate in ～ ～に参加する
- sudden 突然の
- divide ～を分ける
- separate 別個の
- chief executive officer 最高経営責任者
- corporate management 企業経営
- kindly すみませんが、どうか～
- career キャリア、経歴

問題文の訳

設問150から152は次のEメールに関する質問です。

送信者： Laura Masterson <lauram@bizpeople.org>
宛先： Zachary Wilson <zwilson@cybermail.net>
日付： 7月7日
件名： スケジュール

Wilson さま

貴殿は Biz People のリーダーシップスキルコースへの参加をご登録されました。

今年は、登録者数の急増により、当機関はこのコースをふたつのセッションに分けることを決定いたしました。毎週水曜午前9時から午前11時の開催だけでしたが、毎週金曜にも同じコースを設け、こちらは午後7時から午後9時までとなります。両コースともに30年以上の企業経営経験を持つ前最高経営責任者 Christina Lopez 氏が担当いたします。

この変更により、すでにご登録済みのみなさまには、当機関のウェブサイト http://www.bizpeople.com/seminars にアクセスし、再度ご登録くださいますようお願いしております。

ご不便をおかけし申し訳ありません。詳細につきましては、このEメールにご返信いただくか、もしくは通常の業務時間内に当事務所（809) 555-9238 までお電話いただきますようお願い申し上げます。

敬具

Laura Masterson
Biz People　キャリア開発サービス

選択肢の訳

150. (A) 入隊
 (B) 注意
 (C) 登録、登録者数
 (D) 占有

151. (A) 〜に加えて
 (B) 〜がある
 (C) 〜について
 (D) 〜から

152. (A) 頻繁な
 (B) 通常の
 (C) 開かれた
 (D) 平均の

正解 & 解説

150. 正解 (C)
同じ品詞（名詞）が並んでいるので、**文脈から答えを探る**。Because of the sudden increase in ------- this year（今年は ------- の急激な増加のせいで）となっているので、「〈何〉が増加した」のかをみていく。our organization 以降で「コースをふたつに分けた」とあることから、「〈登録者数〉が増加した」とすると文意が通る。(C) enrollment が正解。

151. 正解 (B)
空所前後をみると、a former chief executive officer（前 CEO）と over 30 years of experience in corporate management（30年以上の企業経営経験）となっているので、「**〜がある**」という意味の with をいれて、「30年以上の経験〈がある〉前 CEO」とすると、文意が通る。よって、(B) が正解。

152. 正解 (B)
同じ品詞（形容詞）が並んでいるので、**文脈からアプローチ**する。call our office ... during ------- business hours（------- な営業時間内に電話して欲しい）となっていることから、normal を入れて「〈通常の〉営業時間内に電話して欲しい」とすると文意が通る。よって (B) が正解。

TEST 2
PART 7

Questions 153-154 refer to the following notice.

Milton Furnishings

To our valued customers,

Beginning September 1, you will be required to present a valid identification card every time you make a credit card purchase at Milton Furnishings. This is in connection with the increasing incidence of credit card fraud at retail stores across the country. Please show any of the following proofs of identification at the checkout counter:

Passport
Driver's license
Voter's ID
Company ID

Thank you for your cooperation.

Management

---

153. Why was the notice written?

(A) To announce the closure of a business
(B) To inform clients of a new store policy
(C) To recommend a payment option
(D) To publicize a sale

154. What will the store do to protect itself from fraud?

(A) Limit the number of accepted credit cards
(B) Call banks before accepting credit payments
(C) Ask customers to show personal documents
(D) Request shoppers to make purchases with cash

TOEIC豆知識

Part 7に登場する文書を読んでいると、小さく書かれた注釈部分（よく＊が付いている）で、大切なことを述べている場合が多い。悪徳業者の契約書みたいだが、みなさんアスタリスクに注意です！

問題文の訳

設問153から154は次の告知に関する質問です。

Milton 家具店

お得意さま

❶9月1日より、❷Milton 家具店でクレジットカードによるお買い物の際に、毎回、有効な身分証明書をご提示いただく必要があります。❸これは、全国の小売店におけるカード詐欺の増加に関連するものです。以下の身分証明書のいずれかを精算カウンターでご提示ください。

パスポート
運転免許証
有権者証
社員証

ご協力をお願いいたします。

店主

単語

- furnishings 備え付け家具
- valued 貴重な
- valid 有効な
- in connection with ～ ～に関連して
- incidence 発生
- fraud 詐欺
- retail 小売の
- following 以下の
- proof 証拠品
- checkout counter 精算カウンター、レジ
- cooperation 協力

153
- closure 閉鎖
- publicize ～を宣伝する

154
- limit ～を制限する
- document 文書
- make a purchase 購入する
- cash 現金

正解＆解説

153. 正解 (B)

告知が書かれた理由を尋ねている。このように主題を問う設問では、文書の**冒頭部分に注目**する。❶❷で「9月1日から、クレジットカード払いには、身分証の提示を求める」という**新方針を打ち出している**。以降も、この方針の説明が続くので、(B)「顧客に店の新方針を知らせるため」が正解。

154. 正解 (C)

詐欺から身を守るために、店が何をするのかを尋ねている。設問のキーワード **fraud**（詐欺）に注意していくと、❸で「This（これ）はクレジットカード詐欺に関連している」と書かれている。この This が指しているのは、前文❷の「身分証の提示を求める」という内容。これを「顧客に個人に関する文書の提示を求める」と言い換えた (C) が正解。

↻ present a valid identification card ➡ show personal documents

TEST 2
PART 7

Questions 155-157 refer to the following e-mail.

E-mail

To:	All bank staff
From:	Donald Manzo
Subject:	Welcome reception
Date:	August 5

We are holding a reception to welcome our new regional vice president, Gertrude Crowley. Ms. Crowley previously worked as branch manager of Knightland Bank's affiliate in Charleston. After five years there, she led our branch in Atlanta for two years and then transferred to New Orleans, where she has been since working as their district manager. She will now head the southeast district from our regional office here in Nashville.

The reception will be held at the Bluegrass Hotel on Friday, Aug. 9, at 7:30 P.M. If you plan on coming, please notify my secretary at extension #44. Also, please let him know if you will be bringing a guest.

Thank you.

---

155. What is the main purpose of the e-mail?

(A) To invite employees to an event
(B) To inform staff of a work schedule
(C) To request attendance to a branch meeting
(D) To ask for help setting up a reception

156. Where has Ms. Crowley NOT previously worked?

(A) Charleston
(B) Atlanta
(C) New Orleans
(D) Nashville

157. How can employees confirm their attendance?

(A) By sending a reply e-mail
(B) By contacting Mr. Manzo's assistant
(C) By calling the hotel
(D) By speaking to Mr. Manzo

問題文の訳

設問155から157は次のEメールに関する質問です。

宛先： 全行員
送信者： Donald Manzo
件名： 歓迎会
日付： 8月5日

Gertrude Crowley 新地区担当副社長の❶歓迎会を行います。❷Crowley 副社長は以前、チャールストンにある Knightland 銀行の支店長を務められていました。そこでの5年ののち、❸当行のアトランタ支店を2年間率い、ニューオリンズに異動。それ以降はそこで地区責任者として勤務されました。❹今回、ここナッシュビルの地区オフィスにて南東部地区を率いることになります。

歓迎会は Bluegrass ホテルで8月9日（金）の午後7：30から行われます。❺参加される場合は内線44番で私の秘書に知らせてください。また、ゲストを連れてくる場合も彼に知らせてください。

よろしくお願いします。

単語

- reception 歓迎会
- previously 以前に
- affiliate 支社、支店
- transfer 異動する
- district 地区
- head 〜を率いる
- plan on *doing* 〜する計画だ
- notify 〜に知らせる
- secretary 秘書
- extension 内線
- **155** attendance 出席

正解&解説

155. 正解 (A)

Eメールの目的を尋ねている。主題を問う設問なので、文書の**冒頭部分に注目**しよう。まず、❶で「歓迎会を開く」と述べ、以降は歓迎会の詳細が続く。そして、最後❺で「出欠確認」していることから、正解は「**従業員をイベントに誘う**」という内容の (A)。準備の手伝いを依頼しているわけではないので、(D) は誤り。

⇄ a reception ➡ an event

156. 正解 (D)

Ms. Crowley が、これまで**勤めたことのない**場所を尋ねる Not 問題。(A) は、❷に「チャールストンにある Knightland 銀行の支店長として勤務」とある。(B) と (C) は、❸に「当行のアトランタ支店を率いたあと、ニューオリンズに異動し、今現在働いている」とある。(D) は、❹に She will now head ... とあるので、**これからナッシュビルに勤める**のだとわかる。従って、(D) Nashville が勤めたことのない場所として正しい。

157. 正解 (B)

社員が出欠連絡をする手段を尋ねている。設問の confirm their attendance（参加を確認する）を、Eメールの❺If you plan on coming（出席予定なら）に結び付けられるかがカギとなる。❺に「出席予定なら、私（= Mr. Manzo）の**秘書まで extension #44 に知らせてほしい**」とある。これを「Manzo 氏のアシスタントに連絡して」と言い換えた (B) が正解。extension は「内線」という意味。

⇄ notify my secretary at extension #44 ➡ contacting Mr. Manzo's assistant

TEST 2
PART 7

Questions 158-159 refer to the following information.

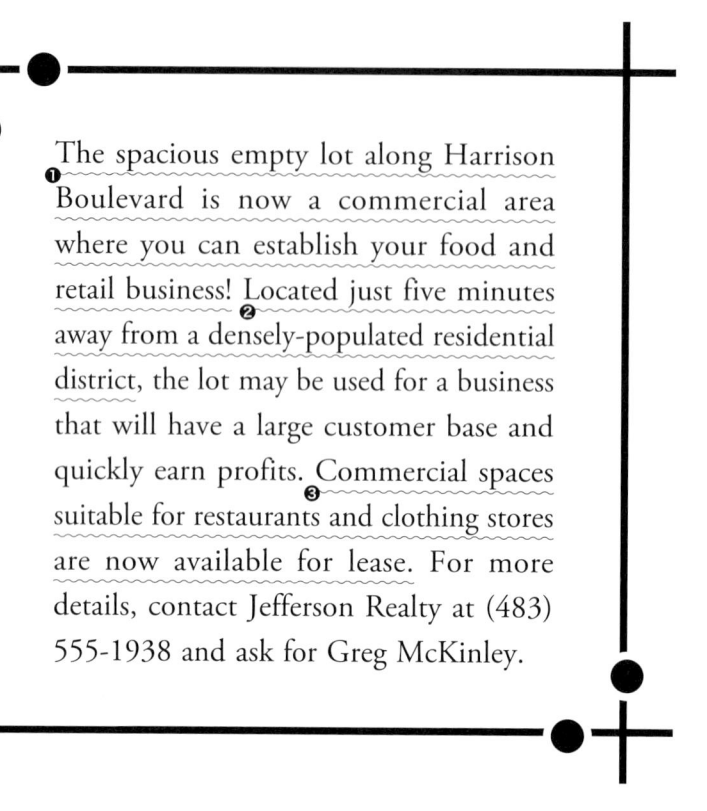

The spacious empty lot along Harrison Boulevard is now a commercial area where you can establish your food and retail business! Located just five minutes away from a densely-populated residential district, the lot may be used for a business that will have a large customer base and quickly earn profits. Commercial spaces suitable for restaurants and clothing stores are now available for lease. For more details, contact Jefferson Realty at (483) 555-1938 and ask for Greg McKinley.

158. For whom is the information most likely intended?

(A) Prospective tenants
(B) Real estate agents
(C) Residents near the commercial area
(D) Retailing experts

159. What is stated about the commercial spaces?

(A) They are located near an area inhabited by many people.
(B) They are five minutes away from Harrison Boulevard.
(C) They are available for residential use.
(D) They are suitable for food establishments only.

| TOEIC豆知識 | メールや電話で買い物する際、「この前のクレジットカードに請求しといて」という支払い方法が登場する。日本ではなじみのない方法なので、「そんなのアリ？」と面喰らってしまう。 |

問題文の訳

設問 158 から 159 は次のお知らせに関する質問です。

❶Harrison 大通り沿いの広い空き区画が商業区域となり、外食事業や小売業を始めることができます！ ❷多くの人が住んでいる住宅地からわずか徒歩 5 分の距離なので、この区画は、大きな顧客基盤を有し、素早く利益を得られるビジネスに活用できるでしょう。❸レストランや衣料品店に適した商業スペースが現在リース可能です。詳細は Jefferson 不動産あてに (483) 555 1938 までお電話のうえ、Greg McKinley とお話しください。

単語

- □ spacious 広々とした
- □ establish ～を創設する
- □ densely-populated 人口密度の高い
- □ residential 居住の
- □ earn （利益）を生む
- □ profit 利益
- □ suitable 適している
- □ lease リース、賃貸借

158
- □ prospective 将来の、見込みのある
- □ real estate agent 不動産代理店
- □ resident 住民
- □ retailing 小売り業

159
- □ inhabit ～に住む

正解 & 解説

158. 正解 **(A)**　難易度 ■■■□ 難

このお知らせの対象者を尋ねている。このように主題に関わる設問は、**冒頭に注目**しよう。❶で「Harrison 大通り沿いの空き地が、外食事業や小売業用の商業区域になった」述べられ、商業用地の紹介をしている。また❸に「商業スペースがリース可能」とあることを考え合わせると、**土地を借りたいと考えている人に対して、土地の宣伝をしている**とわかる。よって (A)「見込みの借主」が正解。(B) はむしろ、この文書の書き手。(D) は「小売り」に限定している点が誤り。

159. 正解 **(A)**　難易度 ■■□□ 難

商業スペースについて述べられていることを尋ねる True 問題。(A) は、❷に「a densely-populated residential district（人口の密集した住宅地）から**わずか 5 分**」とあるので、お知らせの内容に一致している。これが正解。(B) は、❶で「Harrison 大通り沿い」と述べられているので誤り。(C) と (D) は、❸に「飲食店と衣料品店に適した」とあるので、お知らせに一致しないとわかる。

↻ a densely-populated residential district ➡ an area inhabited by many people
　restaurants ➡ food establishments

間違いメモ

あなたの解答 [A] [B] [C] [D]
メモ

あなたの解答 [A] [B] [C] [D]
メモ

TEST 2
PART 7

Questions 160-161 refer to the following information.

Ace Venture Systems

Home   Products   News   Contact Us

Accounting Software Version 1

Ace Venture Systems brings you new business accounting software for small and medium enterprises. Accounting Software Version 1 is a FREE software package that includes standard accounting functions essential to small business operations. Like other customized software, it has features that allow users to manage inventories, purchase orders, and sales data. It can also be used to organize financial reports and bank account information. Discover what Accounting Software Version 1 can do for your business by clicking the button below:

Download
Accounting Software Version 1

Ace Venture Systems is a promoter of open source software. It develops reliable business applications for more than 200,000 users free of charge. For comments and suggestions on Accounting Software Version 1, please complete our user feedback sheet by clicking here.

---

160. Why was the information published?

(A) To introduce accounting methods
(B) To promote a computer program
(C) To form a network of small companies
(D) To gather suggestions for a new project

161. What is NOT true about Ace Venture Systems?

(A) It supports the use of open source computer programs.
(B) It asks for clients to give them feedback.
(C) It offers software on a trial basis.
(D) It provides direct downloads on its Web site.

設問の訳

このお知らせはなぜ発表されたのか。
(A) 会計処理方法を紹介するため
(B) コンピュータプログラムを宣伝するため
(C) 中小企業のネットワークを構築するため
(D) 新しいプロジェクトに関する提案を集めるため

Ace Venture Systems 社について正しくないのはどれか。
(A) オープンソースプログラムの利用を支援している。
(B) 顧客にフィードバックをお願いしている。
(C) 試験的にソフトを提供している。
(D) ウェブサイトから直接ダウンロードできるようにしている。

問題文の訳

設問160から161は次のお知らせに関する質問です。

Ace Venture Systems

　　　　　　　　ホーム　　製品　　最新情報　　お問い合わせ

Accounting Software バージョン1

❶Ace Venture Systems 社は、中小企業様向けの新しい企業会計ソフトをお届けします。Accounting Software バージョン1は、無料のパッケージソフトで、中小企業の運営に不可欠な標準的会計機能を備えています。ほかのカスタマイズされたソフト同様、在庫、注文書、売り上げデータの管理が可能です。また財務報告書や銀行口座情報の整理にも使えます。Accounting Software バージョン1で何ができるか、❷下のボタンをクリックしてお確かめください。

　　　　　　　❸Accounting Software バージョン1を
　　　　　　　　　　　　ダウンロード

❹Ace Venture Systems 社はオープンソースソフトウェアの推奨者です。信頼できる企業用アプリケーションを無料で20万人以上のユーザーのために開発しています。❺Accounting Software バージョン1に関する意見や提案は、ここをクリックしてユーザーフィードバックシートにご入力ください。

単語

- accounting　会計、経理
- enterprise　企業
- function　機能
- essential　不可欠な
- inventory　在庫
- sales data　売り上げデータ
- account　口座
- promoter　促進者、推奨者
- reliable　信頼できる

160 □ publish　〜を発表する
　　　 □ gather　〜を集める

161 □ trial　試み、試し

正解&解説

160. 正解 (B)　難易度 ■■□□□ 難

このお知らせが発行された目的を尋ねる主題探しの設問なので、**冒頭部分を集中的に確認**しよう。❶で「中小企業向け会計ソフトウェアを提供する」と述べ、その後も**ソフトウェアの機能紹介、宣伝**が続くので、(B)「コンピュータプログラムを宣伝するため」が正解。「会計ソフト」を「コンピュータプログラム」と抽象的に言い換えている点に注意。

⇄ business accounting software ➡ a computer program

161. 正解 (C)　難易度 ■■■□□ 難

Ace Venture Systems 社について、**正しくない**ものを選ぶ Not 問題。(A) は、❹に a promoter of open source software（オープンソースソフトの推奨者）とあるので、お知らせの内容に一致。(B) は、❺に「意見や提案は、フィードバックシートに記入してほしい」とあるので、一致。(C) の「**試験的にソフトを提供している**」については、関連する記述が見当たらない。従って、(C) が正解。(D) は❷に案内、❸にダウンロードボタンがあり、内容に一致している。

⇄ a promoter ➡ supports the use
　　comments and suggestions ➡ feedback

TEST 2
PART 7

Questions 162-164 refer to the following article.

CEO of Nature's Wonders Pens Insightful Autobiography

Anna Broderick decided it was time for a change. After working for over fifteen years in the cosmetics industry, she handed in her resignation at Landon Cosmetics and embarked on forming her own beauty product empire. Ten years later, Nature's Wonders is now one of the most prominent cosmetics companies on the globe. With stores in more than 30 countries, Broderick credits her success to creating products that are natural, affordable, and environmentally friendly.

In her autobiography released this week entitled *The Search for the Fountain of Youth,* Broderick tells her story. She proves herself to be not only a brilliant businesswoman, but also a talented writer. She describes her struggle to create a company that focuses more on social issues rather than profit. The book is already number eight on the best-seller list and is a great read for struggling entrepreneurs or those looking for inspiration in the often brutal world of business.

162. In what type of publication would this article most likely appear?

(A) A company manual
(B) A travel guide
(C) A business journal
(D) A product brochure

163. Why did Ms. Broderick quit her job at Landon Cosmetics?

(A) A competitor offered her a better position.
(B) She wanted to pursue a graduate degree.
(C) There wasn't enough opportunity for advancement.
(D) She decided to open her own business.

164. What is indicated about *The Search for the Fountain of Youth*?

(A) It hasn't yet been released.
(B) It has sold many copies.
(C) It won an award.
(D) It is part of a series.

設問の訳

この記事はおそらくどのような出版物に掲載されるか。

(A) 会社のマニュアル
(B) 旅行ガイド
(C) ビジネス誌
(D) 製品パンフレット

Broderick 氏はなぜ Landon Cosmetics 社を辞めたのか。

(A) ライバル社がよりよいポストを用意してくれた。
(B) 大学院の学位を取りたかった。
(C) 昇進の機会が十分でなかった。
(D) 自分の会社を立ち上げると決めた。

『若さの泉を求めて』について何が述べられているか。

(A) まだ発売されていない。
(B) よく売れている。
(C) 賞を受賞した。
(D) シリーズの中の1冊である。

TOEIC豆知識 〈TEST 2〉の176-180に登場するSanjay Raghavanのように、読みがサッパリわからない人名が頻繁に登場して、混乱させられる。そんな問題に出会うたび、意地悪そうな出題者の顔が頭に浮かぶ。(続く▶)

問題文の訳

設問162から164は次の記事に関する質問です。

❶ **Nature's Wonders社CEO、洞察に満ちた自伝を執筆**

Anna Broderickは変革のときだと決意したのだった。15年以上化粧品業界で働いたのち、❷Landon Cosmetics社を退職し、自身による美容化粧品の帝国作りに着手。10年後の現在、Nature's Wonders社は世界でもっとも有力な化粧品会社のひとつだ。30カ国以上に店舗を構え、Broderick氏は自身の成功は、無添加で手頃な価格、そして環境に優しい製品を作ったおかげだと考えている。

❸今週発売された彼女の自伝『若さの泉を求めて』の中で、Broderick氏は自身について述べている。彼女は、有能なビジネスウーマンであるだけでなく、優れた書き手であることも証明してみせた。彼女は利益よりもむしろ社会問題に焦点を当てた会社を作る苦労を描いている。❹同書はすでにベストセラーの8位で、奮闘中の起業家や往々にして残酷なビジネスの世界でひらめきを求めている人たちにとって素晴らしい読み物である。

単語

- □ industry ～産業
- □ embark on ～ ～を開始する、～に乗り出す
- □ empire 帝国
- □ credit A to B Aの功績がBにあると認める
- □ environmentally friendly 環境に優しい
- □ prove ～を証明する
- □ brilliant きわめて優秀な
- □ talented 才能のある、優れた
- □ describe ～を描写する、記述する
- □ struggle 苦労、努力
- □ focus on ～ ～に焦点を当てる
- □ social issue 社会問題
- □ entrepreneur 起業家
- □ inspiration ひらめき、突然の着想
- □ brutal 残酷な、厳しい
- 162 □ journal 定期刊行物
- 163 □ pursue ～を追求する
  - □ graduate degree 大学院の学位
  - □ opportunity 機会
  - □ advancement 昇進

正解＆解説

162. 正解 (C) 難易度 ■■□ 難

この記事が掲載されるだろう出版物の種類を尋ねている。まず**記事のタイトル❶**に注目すると、「企業の最高経営責任者の自叙伝」に関する記事だとわかる。また記事本文においても、Anna Broderickというビジネスパーソンの紹介、起業の経緯についての説明が続く。こうした内容が掲載されるのは、「**ビジネス誌**」と推測できるので(C)が正解。journalは「雑誌」の意。

---

163. 正解 (D) 難易度 ■■■ 難

Broderick氏がLandon Cosmetics社を辞めた理由を尋ねている。設問のquit her job（仕事を辞める）を、記事の❷handed in her resignation（辞表を提出した）に結び付けられるかがカギ。❷で、その理由として「her own beauty product empire（自身の美容化粧品の帝国）形成に着手した」と述べられている。この「美容化粧品の帝国」という表現は、**自分自身の化粧品会社**を意味している。よって(D)が正解。

⇄ handed in her resignation ➡ quit her job
  forming her own beauty product empire ➡ open her own business

---

164. 正解 (B) 難易度 ■■□ 難

The search for the Fountain of Youthについて、述べられていることを尋ねるTrue問題。(A)は❸にIn her autobiography released this week ... とあり、すでに発売されていることがわかるので誤り。(B)については、❹にある「ベストセラーランクの8位」という記述から、「**よく売れている**」と推測でき、内容が一致する。よって(B)が正解。(C)(D)に関する記述は見当たらない。

TEST 2
PART 7

Questions 165-167 refer to the following Web site.

The Knowledge Encyclopedia
Seek. Read. Discover.

About us | Daily Trivia | Site Map | Contact Us

Today's Trivia
Did you know that the traffic light was originally invented for railways?

In the nineteenth century, railroad engineers invented the traffic light to prevent train collisions and, most importantly, pedestrian accidents. However, it took much trial and error before the first railway traffic light was formally used. Railroad engineers had a problem selecting colors that would effectively communicate warnings to people. In the 1830s, they tried using red for "stop" and green for "caution". For "go", they used a white light that signaled "all clear". This combination of lights did not work since the green light was often mistaken for "go". Because of this, they settled on green for "go" and introduced a yellow light to signal "caution".

The device was used for road traffic as early as 1868 in London, England. Outside the Parliament building stood a gas-powered traffic light that was manually controlled to shift from red to green. It was intended to facilitate steam automobiles and wagon traffic.

The first electric traffic light was created by James Hoge of Ohio in 1918. Two years later, a Detroit policeman named William Potts came up with the three-colored traffic light we use today. The device evolved as it spread across the world, with varying functions depending on the needs of specific locations.

Go
Search

The Knowledge Encyclopedia
©Copyright 2010
All rights reserved

---

165. Why was the traffic light invented?

(A) To increase the speed of train travel
(B) To protect people traveling on foot
(C) To allow cars to cross railway tracks safely
(D) To replace gas-powered lamps

166. What is mentioned about the traffic light made by railway engineers?

(A) It could not be modified for road use.
(B) It could not be seen from far distances.
(C) It had confusing colors.
(D) It was operated manually.

167. According to the information, when was the modern traffic light first put into use?

(A) In 1830
(B) In 1868
(C) In 1918
(D) In 1920

TOEIC豆知識

人名に関して言うと、文書にはフルネームで登場するくせに、設問では Mr. ●● というようにラストネームだけになっていることがある。焦っていると、誰のことかわからず、かなり混乱させられる。

問題文の訳

設問165から167は次のウェブサイトに関する質問です。

知識百科事典
探す。読む。見つける。
私たちについて ｜ 日々のトリビア ｜ サイトマップ ｜ お問い合わせ

探す
検索

きょうのトリビア
信号機はもともと鉄道用だったのをご存知ですか？

19世紀に❶鉄道技師が列車の衝突や、もっとも重要なことですが、歩行者との事故を防ぐために信号機を発明しました。しかし、鉄道の信号機が正式に使われるようになるまでには数々の試行錯誤が必要でした。鉄道技師は人々に効果的に危険を知らせる色を選ぶのに苦労しました。1830年代には、❷「止まれ」に赤、「注意」に緑色を使ってみました。「進め」には、「危険なし」を意味する白を使いました。この色の組み合わせは、うまく行きませんでした。というのも緑色が「進め」と間違われることが多かったからです。このため、緑を「進め」にすることで落ち着き、「注意」には黄色を導入しました。

❸この仕組みは、早くも1868年にイギリスのロンドンで道路に用いられました。議会の建物の外に、ガス式の信号機が立ち、手動で赤から緑へ変えられていました。これは、蒸気自動車や荷馬車の交通を助けるためでした。

❹最初の電気信号機はオハイオ州の James Hoge によって1918年に作られました。2年後、デトロイトの警察官 William Potts が今日使われている3色の信号機を考案しました。信号機は世界中に広がるとともに進化し、地域ごとのニーズに合わせてさまざまな機能を持つようになりました。

知識百科事典
ⓒ Copyright 2010
禁無断複写、転載

単語

- encyclopedia 百科事典
- trivia トリビア、雑学
- invent 〜を発明する
- prevent 〜を防ぐ
- collision 衝突
- pedestrian 歩行者
- trial and error 試行錯誤
- formally 正式に
- effectively 効果的に
- caution 注意
- settle on 〜 〜に決める
- device 装置
- parliament 議会
- manually 手動で
- facilitate 〜を容易にする
- name 〜に名前をつける
- come up with 〜 〜を思いつく
- evolve 進化する
- vary 〜を変える、多様にする
- specific 特定の

165
- on foot 徒歩で

166
- modify 〜を変更する、修正する
- distance 距離
- confusing まごつかせる、混乱させる

正解＆解説

165. 正解 (B) 難易度 難

信号機が発明された理由を尋ねている。❶に「**列車の衝突と、もっとも重要なことだが、歩行者の事故を防ぐため**」とある。このふたつの理由のうち、より重要な後者にフォーカスした (B) の「徒歩で移動している人を守るため」が正解。

🔁 pedestrian ➡ people traveling on foot

166. 正解 (C) 難易度 難

鉄道技師が作った信号機について、言及されていることを尋ねる True 問題。(A) は、❸に「この装置（＝鉄道技師が作った信号機）が1868年にロンドンで道路交通に使われた」とあり、誤り。(B) に関する記述はない。(C) については、❷に「〈注意〉を示す緑が、しばしば〈進め〉に勘違いされた」とあるので、「**紛らわしい色を使っていた**」のだとわかる。よってこれが正解。(D) の「手動式だった」のは、1868年にロンドンで用いられた道路用の信号。

167. 正解 (D) 難易度 難

現代の信号機が、初めて使用された時を尋ねている。設問の the modern traffic light を、ウェブサイトの❹ the three-colored traffic light we use today に結び付けられるかがカギ。❹の1文目にまず「**1918年に初の電気信号機が製作**」とあり、2文目に **Two years later**（2年後に）「デトロイトの警察官が、今日の3色信号機を考案」とある。つまり、1918年の2年後である (D)「**1920年**」に、初めて使用されたことになる。

Questions 168-171 refer to the following flyer.

The Night
A concert

①On December 5, French balladeers Roy Easton and Melissa Amber will be at the Maroon Theatre for their second concert in Los Angeles, California. The event will also feature French pianist Amanda Ewell as well as ②American soul singers Andy Red and Cindy Dawson, who will accompany Mr. Easton and Ms. Amber during their performance. During the concert, ③Ms. Amber will also be introducing her inspirational album, *Crossroads*, which was launched in Paris last week.

Witness an extraordinary fusion of French and American artists. ④Buy three tickets and get a backstage pass absolutely free. This promotion is good until November 20 and is not valid for general admission ticket purchases. Tickets are available at any Gatewing outlet nationwide. They may also be purchased online at www.gatewing.com. A flat rate shipping fee of $8 applies. ⑤Recordings from both Mr. Easton and Ms. Amber will be available for purchase.

GATEWING
555-2541

168. Why was the flyer written?

(A) To introduce a new artist
(B) To promote an event
(C) To advertise an upcoming album
(D) To launch a Web site

169. In paragraph 2, line 4 the word "flat" is closest in meaning to

(A) bland
(B) marginal
(C) smooth
(D) fixed

170. What is suggested about the general admission tickets?

(A) They will be given free to French nationals.
(B) They do not come with backstage passes.
(C) They will be sold at a discount.
(D) They cannot be purchased in other states.

171. What is NOT mentioned about the concert?

(A) Several singers will perform with Mr. Easton and Ms. Amber.
(B) Items will be available for sale.
(C) A new recording will be promoted.
(D) Performers will sign autographs.

設問の訳

168. なぜこのチラシは書かれたか。
　(A) 新人アーティストを紹介するため
　(B) イベントを販促するため
　(C) 発売予定のアルバムを宣伝するため
　(D) ウェブサイトを立ち上げるため

169. 第2段落・4行目の flat にもっとも近い意味の語は
　(A) 穏やかな
　(B) 周辺部の
　(C) 円滑な
　(D) 一定の

170. 一般の入場券について何が示唆されているか。
　(A) フランス国民には無料で提供される。
　(B) バックステージパスはついていない。
　(C) 割引価格で販売される。
　(D) ほかの州では購入できない。

171. このコンサートについて述べられていていないことは何か。
　(A) 数名の歌手が Easton と Amber と一緒に演奏する。
　(B) 物品販売が行われる。
　(C) 新譜が宣伝される。
　(D) 歌手がサインする。

単語
- balladeer バラード歌手
- feature ～を出演させる
- accompany ～に伴奏する
- witness ～を目撃する
- extraordinary 非凡な、途方もない
- fusion 融合
- absolutely 完全に
- outlet 直販店
- nationwide 全国的に
- shipping 配送
- recording 録音したもの、レコード
- **170** suggest ～を示唆する
- **171** performer 演奏者
- autograph サイン

問題文の訳と解説 ☞ 次ページに続く

TEST 2 PART 7

問題文の訳

設問168から171は次のチラシに関する質問です。

The Night
コンサート

❶12月5日にフランスのバラード歌手 Roy Easton と Melissa Amber が Maroon 劇場にて、カリフォルニア州ロサンゼルスで2度目のコンサートを開きます。このイベントにはフランス人ピアニスト Amanda Ewell と❷アメリカ人ソウル歌手 Andy Red、Cindy Dawson も登場し、Easton、Amber と一緒に演奏します。コンサート中に❸Amber は、先週パリで発売された彼女の心をゆさぶるアルバム『Crossroads』を紹介します。

フランスと、アメリカのアーティストの驚くべき融合を目撃してください。❹チケット3枚を購入すれば、バックステージパスが完全無料で手に入ります。このプロモーションは11月20日までで、一般入場券の購入では得られません。チケットは全国の Gatewing 店で発売中です。www.gatewing.com でのオンライン購入も可能。一律8ドルの送料がかかります。❺Easton と Amber のアルバムも販売いたします。

GATEWING
555-2541

正解 & 解説

168. 正解 (B) 難易度 ■■□□□

チラシが書かれた理由、つまり目的を尋ねている。このように主題に関わる設問は、**冒頭に着目**。❶に「12月5日に、Roy Easton と Melissa Amber の2回目のコンサートがある」とあり、以降、コンサートの詳細説明が続く。従って、**コンサートの宣伝**が目的とわかるが、これを「**イベントを販促するため**」と言い換えた (B) が正解。

↻ a concert ➡ an event

169. 正解 (D) 難易度 ■■□□□

文書中の flat と似た意味を持つ単語を尋ねる類義語問題。A flat rate shipping fee of $8 applies において、flat は「**均一の**」、つまり「**一定の**」という意味で使われている。従って、同じ意味を持つ (D) fixed が正解。

170. 正解 (B) 難易度 ■■□□□

一般の入場券について、示唆されていることを尋ねている。❹に「3枚同時購入で、バックステージパスが無料でつく」とあり、続けて「このプロモーションは、一般の入場券購入には有効ではない」とある。つまり、一般の入場券には「**バックステージパスがついていない**」ということ。よって、(B) が正解。

171. 正解 (D) 難易度 ■■■□□

コンサートについて、**述べられていない**ことを尋ねる Not 問題。(A) については、❷に「アメリカのソウル歌手が、一緒に出演」とある。(B) は、❺に「Easton と Amber のアルバムを販売する」とあるので、物品の販売があると考えられる。(C) については、❸に「Amber が先週発売されたアルバムを紹介するだろう」とある。(D) の「**歌手がサインする**」については、まったく触れられていないので、これが正解。

↻ Recordings ... will be available for purchase ➡ Items will be available for sale
introducing ... album ➡ recording will be promoted

Questions 172-175 refer to the following advertisement.

Carlton Motors CLEARANCE SALE ON NOW!

Prices on all cars, trucks, and minivans have been slashed at Carlton Motors at 219 Birch Avenue! In preparation for our move to a new location, all current stock must go. Take advantage of incredible savings of up to 40 percent on vehicles from Carson, Miyaki Automotive, DMC, and Ridgemont Motors! We also carry a full range of scooters and motorbikes. We are sure to have the perfect vehicle for all of your needs!

Carlton Motors ensures the reliability of its vehicles by offering full warranties, biannual car tune-ups, and comprehensive repair services. All vehicles sold come with a full one-year warranty, with reasonable rates offered for additional coverage. Also, we will change your oil every four months for two years, free of charge!

So come on down to Carlton Motors for a test drive of one of our many quality vehicles today! But hurry, as this sale lasts only until January 2! Our showroom is open from 10 A.M. to 8 P.M. For further information, call us at 555-7798, or visit our Web site at www.carltonmotors.co.au for descriptions of the vehicles we have on offer.

172. Why is Carlton Motors having a sale?
(A) It is closing one of its stores.
(B) It needs to make space for new stock.
(C) It is relocating the showroom to another area.
(D) It did not meet its sales target for the year.

173. What is indicated about Carlton Motors?
(A) It stocks a wide range of car accessories.
(B) It is open seven days a week.
(C) It also sells used automobiles.
(D) It has several brands of vehicles available.

174. According to the advertisement, what does the business encourage people to do?
(A) Try out any of their vehicles
(B) Sign up for car insurance
(C) Pay for vehicles in installments
(D) Compare their prices with competitors'

175. What service is NOT mentioned in the advertisement?
(A) Vehicular repairs
(B) Complete warranties
(C) Oil change
(D) Car registration

設問の訳

172. なぜ Carlton Motors はセールをしているのか。
　(A) 販売店のひとつを閉鎖する。
　(B) 新しい在庫のためのスペースが必要である。
　(C) ショールームを別の地域に移転する。
　(D) 今年の売上目標を達成できなかった。

173. Carlton Motors について何が述べられているか。
　(A) カーアクセサリーの品揃えが豊富である。
　(B) 週7日営業している。
　(C) 中古車も販売している。
　(D) いくつかのメーカーの車を扱っている。

174. 広告によると、この会社は人々に何をするよう促しているか。
　(A) 車を試乗する
　(B) 自動車保険に申し込む
　(C) 車の代金を分割払いで支払う
　(D) 価格を同業他社と比較する

175. 広告で述べられていないサービスは何か。
　(A) 車の修理
　(B) 完全保証
　(C) オイル交換
　(D) 車両登録

単語
- slash（予算、価格など）を大幅に切り下げる
- in preparation for ～　～の準備のために
- saving　値引き、節約
- ensure　～を保証する
- reliability　信頼性
- warranty　保証
- biannual　年2回の
- comprehensive　あらゆる、包括的な
- coverage　（保険の）補償、適用範囲
- description　説明

172 meet　～を達成する
173 stock（商品）を置く、仕入れる
174 insurance　保険
- in installments　分割払いで
- compare　～を比較する
175 vehicular　車の

問題文の訳と解説 ☞ 次ページに続く

TEST 2 PART 7

問題文の訳

設問172から175は次の広告に関する質問です。

Carlton Motors クリアランスセール開催中！

Birch 通り219の Carlton Motors では、乗用車、トラック、ミニバンのすべてが大幅値下げ！ ❶新店舗への移転準備のため、在庫全品売り尽くし。❷Carson、Miyaki Automotive、DMC、Ridgemnt Motors の車が驚きの最大40％割引となるこの機会をぜひご利用ください。当店ではスクーターやバイクも幅広く取り扱っています。お客さまのニーズにぴったりの乗り物がきっと見つかります。

Carlton Motors では、❸完全保証、年2回の整備、あらゆる修理サービスに対応し、車の信頼性を保証します。販売しているすべての車は1年間の保証付きで、お手頃価格の追加保証もございます。また、❹2年間は無料で4カ月ごとにオイル交換いたします！

今すぐ、❺Carlton Motors にご来店のうえ、高品質な車にご試乗ください。このセールは1月2日までですので、お急ぎください！ ❻弊社ショールームは午前10時から午後8時までオープンしています。詳しくは555-7798までお電話いただくか、ウェブサイト www.carltonmotors.co.au で取り扱い車種の詳細をご覧ください。

正解＆解説

172. 正解 **(C)** 　難易度 ■■■□ 難

Carlton Motors がセールをする理由を尋ねている。❶に「**新店舗への移転準備のため、現在庫はすべて売り切る**」とあるので、これを「**ショールームを別の地域に移転する**」と言い換えた (C) が正解。店を閉めるのではなく、あくまで移転なので、(A) の「販売店のひとつを閉鎖する」は誤り。

🔁 move to a new location ➡ relocating the showroom to another area

173. 正解 **(D)** 　難易度 ■■■□ 難

Carlton Motors について、述べられていることを問う True 問題。(A) (C) に関する記述はない。(B) については、❻に営業時間の記述はあるが、営業日については述べられていない。(D) は、❷に「Carson、Miyaki Automotive、DMC、Ridgemnt Motors の車が最大 40% 割引」とあり、「**いくつかのメーカーの車を扱っている**」ことがわかるので、これが正解。

🔁 vehicles ➡ automobiles

174. 正解 **(A)** 　難易度 ■■■□ 難

この会社が、人々に勧めていることを尋ねている。❺に「**試乗するために Carlton Motors に足を運んでほしい**」とあるので、「**車を試乗する**」ことを勧めているとわかる。従って (A) が正解。

🔁 a test drive ➡ Try out any of their vehicles

175. 正解 **(D)** 　難易度 ■■■■ 難

広告で**触れられていない**サービスを問う Not 問題。(A) と (B) については、❸に full warranties（完全保証）と a comprehensive repair services（あらゆる修理サービス）として言及あり。(C) については、❹に we will change your oil every four months（4カ月ごとにオイル交換）とある。(D) の「**車両登録**」に関する記述は見当たらないので、これが正解。

🔁 full warranties ➡ Complete warranties

TEST 2
PART 7

Questions 176-180 refer to the following newsletter.

August Highlights Union of Nations
Sanjay Raghavan

Sanjay Raghavan has been working for the Union of Nations for twelve years. He began working as a volunteer at the children's welfare division in our South Asia headquarters in Calcutta, India. Since then, he has participated in numerous missions to help carry out development goals of the organization in developing countries. He also worked as one of our fundraising officers in London and director for relief operations in Haiti. A year ago, he transferred to our main headquarters in New York, where he is now the executive director at the World Children's Fund.

Mr. Raghavan has always given priority to helping the world's children, for he believes that they hold the key to improving the future. He believes that children should be nurtured and encouraged to obtain an education to become successful later in their lives. He recalls meeting a peacekeeper when he was just ten years old, who helped evacuate his family after a tsunami wiped out their makeshift home in Chennai. "Since that day, I've always wanted to make a difference by helping others, and that's what inspired me to follow this career path."

Christa Ramstein, a current member of Mr. Raghavan's staff, describes him as a responsive person who is always ready to provide assistance to those in need. "He has even set up his own foundation to give scholarships to underprivileged children in his hometown."

Prior to becoming a volunteer for the Union of Nations, Mr. Raghavan earned his bachelor's degree in development studies from Cochin State College and his master's degree in international affairs at the University of East Calcutta.

176. What is the purpose of the article?

(A) To give information about outreach programs
(B) To outline the achievements of an employee
(C) To announce a yearly fundraising event
(D) To describe living conditions in foreign countries

177. Where did Mr. Raghavan start his career?

(A) Chennai
(B) New York
(C) Calcutta
(D) London

178. The word "responsive" in paragraph 3, line 2 is closest in meaning to

(A) adventurous
(B) communicative
(C) persuadable
(D) grateful

179. What is suggested about Ms. Ramstein?

(A) She began her own foundation.
(B) She participated in relief operations.
(C) She is giving away scholarships.
(D) She is working in New York.

180. What is NOT mentioned about Mr. Raghavan?

(A) He donated money to charity institutions.
(B) He experienced hardship at a young age.
(C) He worked in different parts of the world.
(D) He obtained his education in India.

設問の訳

176. この記事の目的は何か。
 (A) 支援活動の情報を提供すること
 (B) 従業員の業績の概要を述べること
 (C) 年に1度の資金集めのイベントを発表すること
 (D) 外国での生活環境について説明すること

177. Raghavan 氏が働き始めたのはどこか。
 (A) チェンナイ
 (B) ニューヨーク
 (C) カルカッタ
 (D) ロンドン

178. 第3段落・2行目の responsive にもっとも近い意味の語は
 (A) 大胆な
 (B) 話し好きな
 (C) 説得できる
 (D) 感謝している

179. Ramstein 氏について何が示唆されているか。
 (A) 自身の財団を設立した。
 (B) 救援活動に参加した。
 (C) 奨学金を提供している。
 (D) ニューヨークで働いている。

180. Raghavan 氏について述べられていないことは何か。
 (A) 慈善団体にお金を寄付した。
 (B) 若いころに苦労した。
 (C) 世界のさまざまな地域で働いた。
 (D) インドで教育を受けた。

単語
- carry out 〜を実行する
- developing country 発展途上国
- relief operation 救援活動
- priority 優先権
- nurture 〜を養育する
- obtain 〜を獲得する
- recall 〜を思い出す
- peacekeeper 平和維持軍兵士
- evacuate 〜を避難させる
- makeshift 仮設の
- inspire 〜を動機付ける
- in need 困っている
- foundation 財団、基金
- underprivileged 恵まれない
- prior to 〜 〜より前に
- earn 〜を得る
- bachelor's degree 学士号
- master's degree 修士号

176 outreach 支援活動
outline 〜の概要を述べる
achievement 業績
179 give away 〜 〜を授与する
180 hardship 困難、苦難

TEST 2 PART 7

問題文の訳

設問176から180は次のニュースレターに関する質問です。

❶ **国家連合　8月の注目点**
Sanjay Raghavan

❷Sanjay Raghavanは国家連合で12年間働いている。❸彼はインド、カルカッタの南アジア本部の児童福祉部でボランティアとして働き始めた。以来、彼は多数のミッションに参加し、発展途上国における国家連合の開発目標の実行を支援してきた。❹彼はまた、ロンドンで国家連合の資金調達担当やハイチでの救援活動の管理者としても働いた。1年前に❺彼はニューヨーク本部に異動となり、現在そこで世界子供基金の常任理事を務めている。

Raghavan氏は常に世界の子供たちを助けることを優先してきた。というのも彼は、子供が未来をよくする鍵を握っていると信じているからだ。彼は、子供たちがのちの人生で成功するために教育が受けられるよう育まれ、後押しされるべきだと信じている。❻彼はわずか10歳のとき、チェンナイの仮設住宅が津波で流されたあと、家族を避難させてくれた平和維持軍兵士に会ったことを思いだす。「あの日以来、私は人を助けることで影響を及ぼしたいと思い続けてきた。それがこのキャリアを進むきっかけだった」

❼現在、Raghavan氏の下で働いているChrista Ramsteinは、彼のことを困っている人をいつでも喜んで助けようとする敏感な人だと評する。「❽彼は、故郷の恵まれない子供たちに奨学金を供与するみずからの財団も設立しているんです」。

国家連合でボランティアをする前、Raghavan氏はCochin州立大学で開発学の学士号を取得し、❾東カルカッタ大学では国際関係学の修士号を取得している。

TOEIC豆知識　TOEICの世界で流通している通貨は、① $ ／② € ／③ £。それぞれ、何の通貨記号がわかりますか？　（続く▶）

正解＆解説

176. 正解 **(B)**　難易度 ■■□□難

記事の目的を問う主題探しの設問なので、**冒頭に注目**。❶のタイトルに「国家連合の8月の注目点」として、Sanjay Raghavan の名が挙がっているので、この人物についての記事だろうとわかる。また❷に「Sanjay Raghavan は国家連合で12年間働いている」とあり、Raghavan 氏が**国家連合の職員**だとわかる。以降、彼の業績説明が続くので、「従業員の業績の概要を述べること」となっている (B) が正解。

177. 正解 **(C)**　難易度 ■■□□難

Raghavan 氏が働き始めた場所を尋ねている。設問の start his career（働き始める）と、文書中の❸ began working を結び付けられるかがカギ。❸には「彼は、**カルカッタでボランティアとして働き始めた**」とあるので、(C) Calcutta が正解。

⇄ began working ➡ start his career

178. 正解 **(B)**　難易度 ■■■□難

文書中の responsive と似た意味の単語を問う類義語問題。文脈 a responsive person who is always ready to provide assistance to those in need では、responsive が「共鳴しやすい、敏感な」、つまり「交感しやすい」という意味で使われている。これに類似しているのは「話し好きな、意思疎通がしやすい」という意味を持つ (B) communicative。

179. 正解 **(D)**　難易度 ■■■□難

Ramstein 氏について、示唆されていることを尋ねている。まず❼に Ramstein 氏は「Raghavan 氏の現スタッフ」という記述がある。そして、その Raghavan 氏は、❺に「現在、ニューヨークで常任理事を務めている」とある。これらを考え合わせると、Ramstein 氏は、**ニューヨークで Raghavan 氏のスタッフとして働いている**と考えられるので、(D) She is working in New York. が正解。

180. 正解 **(A)**　難易度 ■■■□難

Raghavan 氏について、**述べられていない**ことを問う Not 問題。Raghavan 氏は、多くの慈善活動に関わっているのに加え、「自身の基金を設立」(❽) ともある。しかし、**お金を寄付しているわけではない**ので、(A) の「慈善団体にお金を寄付した」が文書の内容と一致しない。従って、これが正解。(B) については❻で言及。(C) については、❸❹❺にカルカッタ、ロンドン、ハイチ、ニューヨークで働いたとの記述がある。(D) については、❾に「東カルカッタ大学で修士号を取得」とある。

TEST 2
PART 7

Questions 181-185 refer to the following e-mails.

E-mail

From:	Lou Northman <l.northman@petrolcorp.com>
To:	Staff <staff@petrolcorp.com>
Date:	July 16
Subject:	Programs for employees

Dear All,

With the success of the recent technical skills training, management has decided to launch personality development programs to help employees become better team players. Our human resources consultant, Mr. Christian Olsen, will be conducting a series of classes next month. The sessions will primarily be about stress management and interpersonal skills enhancement. Classes in interpersonal skills enhancement will be held on Thursdays from 6 P.M. to 8 P.M., while stress management classes will be conducted on Fridays, at the same time slot. Since the conference room can accommodate up to fifty persons only, the classes will be filled on a first-come-first-served basis.

If you are interested, please e-mail Mr. Olsen (c.olsen@corpway.com) with your chosen program. He and his team are finalizing the training, and they wish to know which departments most of the participants will come from. In addition, we have attached Mr. Olsen's new e-book, *The Game of Work*, which was launched last week. This free e-book about the benefits of efficient communication at work is exclusive to employees of the company. We hope that the book will be useful to all of you.

Please respond to acknowledge receipt of this e-mail. We will be happy to address your questions regarding the program. Thank you.

Lou Northman
Assistant Director
Human Resources Department

E-mail

From:	Ashley Gibson <a.gibson@petrolcorp.com>
To:	Christian Olsen <c.olsen@corpway.com>
Date:	July 23
Subject:	Personality Development Programs

Dear Mr. Olsen,

I was pleased when I received an e-mail from the human resources department, saying that you would be offering personality development programs for the staff. I want to sign up for your Friday class. I've learned a lot from reading your books on career enhancement and leadership, and I believe attending the program will improve my efficiency at work.

Thank you very much, and I look forward to meeting you in person.

Sincerely,

Ashley Gibson
Junior Accountant
Finance Department

181. Why was the first e-mail written?

(A) To recommend a book about work productivity
(B) To announce upcoming company activities
(C) To gather feedback on a recently offered program
(D) To provide teamwork enhancement tips

182. What did Mr. Northman mention about Mr. Olsen?

(A) He will hold classes for the staff.
(B) He organized the technical skills training.
(C) He works as a professor in a business school.
(D) He leads the human resources department.

183. What is indicated about the book?

(A) It is a known reference material.
(B) It is a revised edition.
(C) It was written by a psychologist.
(D) It was recently published.

184. What program will Ms. Gibson attend?

(A) Interpersonal skills enrichment
(B) Leadership skills development
(C) Stress management
(D) Career enhancement

185. What is indicated about Ms. Gibson?

(A) She has met Mr. Olsen before.
(B) She wants to read some of Mr. Olsen's published work.
(C) She works in a managerial position.
(D) She received a message from another department.

設問の訳

181. ひとつ目のEメールはなぜ書かれたか。
   (A) 仕事の生産性についての本を推薦するため
   (B) 今後の会社のアクティビティを発表するため
   (C) 最近提供されたプログラムの反響を集めるため
   (D) チームワークを高めるコツを提供するため

182. Northman氏はOlsen氏について何を述べているか。
   (A) 社員向けのクラスを実施する。
   (B) 技術研修を企画した。
   (C) 経営学大学院で教授として働いている。
   (D) 人事部を率いている。

183. 本については何が述べられているか。
   (A) 有名な参考書である。
   (B) 改訂版である。
   (C) 心理学者が書いた。
   (D) 最近出版された。

184. Gibsonさんはどのプログラムに参加するか。
   (A) 対人能力強化
   (B) リーダーシップ能力の開発
   (C) ストレス管理
   (D) キャリアアップ

185. Gibsonさんについて何が述べられているか。
   (A) 以前、Olsen氏に会ったことがある。
   (B) Olsen氏が出版した本を読みたい。
   (C) 管理職として働いている。
   (D) 別の部署からメッセージを受け取った。

単語

- personality 個性、人格
- primarily 主に、第一に
- interpersonal 対人関係の
- enhancement 増進、強化
- on a first-come-first-served basis 先着順で
- efficient 効率的な
- exclusive 独占的な
- acknowledge ～を受け取ったことを知らせる、認める
- receipt 受領
- address ～に対処する
- human resources department 人事部
- ***
- efficiency 効率
- in person じかに、本人が直接に
- finance department 財務部
- **181** productivity 生産性
- tip コツ、秘訣
- **182** lead ～を率いる
- **183** reference 参考、参考書
- material 資料
- revised edition 改訂版
- psychologist 心理学者
- **184** enrichment 強化、豊かにすること
- **185** managerial 管理上の、経営上の

問題文の訳と解説 ☞ 次ページに続く

TEST 2　PART 7

問題文の訳

設問181から185は次のEメールに関する質問です。

送信者： Lou Northman <l.northman@petrolcorp.com>
宛先： スタッフ <staff@petrolcorp.com>
日付： 7月16日
件名： 従業員向けプログラム

社員のみなさん、

先の技術研修の成功を受け、❶経営陣は従業員がよりよいチームプレーヤーになるのを支援する人柄向上プログラムを立ち上げることを決定しました。❷当社の人材コンサルタント、Christian Olsen 氏が、来月、一連のクラスを行います。クラスは主にストレス管理と対人能力の向上に関するものです。対人能力向上のクラスは毎週木曜日の午後6時から8時まで、❸ストレス管理のクラスは毎週金曜日に同じ時間帯で行います。会議室に最大50名しか入れないために、先着順での受付になります。

ご興味がある場合は、選んだプログラムを書いて Olsen さん（c.olsen@corpway.com）あてにEメールを送ってください。彼と彼のチームが研修をまとめていて、どの部署からもっとも多くの参加者があるのか知りたがっています。さらに、❹先週発表された Olsen さんの新しい電子書籍、『仕事ゲーム』を添付しています。職場での効果的なコミュニケーションの恩恵に関するこの無料の電子書籍は当社社員専用です。この本がみなさん全員にとって役に立つことを願っています。

このEメールを受け取ったことをお知らせください。このプログラムに関する質問に喜んでお答えします。ありがとうございます。

Lou Northman
次長
人事部

送信者： Ashley Gibson<a.gibson@petrolcorp.com>
宛先： Christian Olsen<c.olsen@corpway.com>
日付： 7月23日
件名： 個性向上プログラム

Olsen さま、

貴殿が社員向けに個性向上プログラムをご提供くださるとの❺メールを、人事部よりもらい喜んでいます。❻金曜日のクラスに申し込みたいと思います。私はあなたのキャリアアップとリーダーシップに関する❼著作を読んで多くのことを学びました。このプログラムに参加すれば仕事の効率を高めてくれると信じています。

ありがとうございます。直接お会いできるのを楽しみにしております。

敬具

Ashley Gibson
❽経理補佐
❾財務部

TOEIC豆知識　《通貨記号の答え》　① $ ＝ドル／② € ＝ユーロ／③ £ ＝ポンド

正解＆解説

181. 正解 (B)　難易度 ■■□□□ 難

ひとつ目のEメールの目的を尋ねている。主題に関わる設問では、**冒頭に着目**。❶で「従業員がチームプレーヤーになるための**研修プログラムを経営陣が立ち上げた**」と述べ、以降、その詳細を発表している。従って、正解は、研修プログラムのことを「会社のアクティビティ」と言い換えた (B)「これからの会社のアクティビティを発表するため」。このメールで tips（コツ）を伝えているわけではないので、(D) は誤り。

182. 正解 (A)　難易度 ■■□□□ 難

Northman 氏が、Olsen 氏について述べたことを問う True 問題。From（送信者）欄から Northman 氏が書き手だとわかるので、ひとつ目のメールをみていく。すると❷に「Christian Olsen 氏が**一連の講義を行う**」とあるので、(A)「社員向けのクラスを実施する」が正解。(B) (C) の記述はない。(D) の「人事部を率いている」は、❷に Our human resources consultant, Mr. Christian Olsen（当社の人材コンサルタント、Olsen 氏）とあり、誤り。

183. 正解 (D)　難易度 ■■■□□ 難

本について述べられた内容を問う True 問題。本について言及しているのは❹部分。ここに「**先週発表された** Olsen 氏の新しい電子書籍」とある。(A) (B) は無関係。(C) は、Olsen 氏は心理学者ではないので誤り。(D) の「最近出版された」は、**先週発表された**という部分に一致するので、これが正解。

184. 正解 (C)　難易度 ■■■■□ 難

ふたつの文書に散らばった情報を関連付けて答える**クロスリファレンス問題**。Gibosn さんが参加するプログラムを尋ねている。Gibson さんはふたつ目のメールの差出人なので、そちらを中心にみていくと、❻に「金曜のクラスに参加したい」とある。金曜のクラスについての情報はふたつ目のメールにはないので、ひとつ目に目を移すと、❸に「ストレス管理のクラスは金曜日に実施」とある。これらを総合すると、Gibson さんが参加するのは (C) の「**ストレス管理**」だとわかる。ちなみに (A) は、木曜日に実施。

185. 正解 (D)　難易度 ■■■■■ 難

Gibson さんについて、言及されていることを問う True 問題。Gibosn さんが書いたふたつ目のメールを中心にみていくと、(A) についての記述はなし。(B) は、❼に「Olsen 氏の本を読んで勉強になった」とはあるが、これから読みたいとの記述はない。(C) は❽の「経理補佐」という役職と、一致しない。(D) については、❺に「人事部よりメールを受け取った」とあり、❾に自身の部署を「財務部」と記している。つまり、ひとつ目のメールは**異なる部署からのもの**とわかるので、(D)「別の部署からメッセージを受け取った」が正解。

TEST 2
PART 7

Questions **186-190** refer to the following advertisement and e-mail.

Rajasiha Travels
Thailand's Premier Travel Agency

810 Maruek Blvd. Pomprab, Bangkok 10100
(662) 555-9174
www.rajasihatravels.th

Day Tours
Hiking Trips
Luxury Cruises
Safari Adventures

Log on to our Web site to learn more about our affordable tour packages!
*Special rates are available to groups of five people or more.

For inquiries, please contact our sales manager,
Sunee Mookjai, at mookjai@rajasihatravels.th.

E-mail

To:	mookjai@rajasihatravels.th
From:	eddy.dakila@yphmail.com
Date:	December 18
Subject:	Safari adventure

Dear Ms. Mookjai,

Your agency was highly recommended by my colleague, Anita Bayani, who went on your Phuket Luxury Cruise last October. She said that your tour packages were reasonably priced and that your agents were very friendly and accommodating. So I visited your Web site to check out your packages and I have to say that the Kanchanaburi Safari Adventure is exactly what my friends and I are looking for. I plan on booking the tour for our group of eight, but I have a few questions that I hope you can answer.

First, I want to know whether you accept payments through bank transfer. Also, I am wondering whether you charge a fee for making changes to a reservation, like if I need to reschedule the tour dates. Lastly, will there be a tour guide to accompany us when we explore the local scenery and wildlife in Kanchanaburi?

I would appreciate it if you could call me on my mobile number, 555-2583, to address these inquiries. I will book the tour at that time and pay by bank transfer, if it is acceptable. Otherwise, I will pay by money order. Thank you and I hope to hear from you soon.

Eduardo Dakila

186. What is NOT mentioned in the advertisement about Rajasiha Travels?

(A) The rates of its packages
(B) The location of its office
(C) The address of its Web site
(D) The name of its sales manager

187. What is indicated about Rajasiha Travels?

(A) It has job openings in sales.
(B) It prefers cash payments.
(C) It upgraded its Web site last October.
(D) It has been used by Ms. Bayani in the past.

188. What does Mr. Dakila NOT ask about?

(A) Whether any free services are included with the package
(B) Whether a tour guide will be present
(C) Whether he can pay by wiring money through a bank
(D) Whether making booking changes is free

189. How does Mr. Dakila intend to make his reservation?

(A) By e-mail
(B) In person
(C) On the phone
(D) On the Rajasiha Web site

190. What can be inferred about Mr. Dakila?

(A) He will travel to Thailand with Ms. Bayani.
(B) He is eligible for a discount on his booking.
(C) He is a long-time client of Rajasiha Travels.
(D) He will reserve more than one tour package.

設問の訳

186. Rajasiha 旅行社についての広告で述べられていないことは何か。
　(A) パッケージツアーの料金
　(B) オフィスの場所
　(C) ウェブサイトのアドレス
　(D) 販売部長の名前

187. Rajasiha 旅行社について何が述べられているか。
　(A) 営業職に欠員がある。
　(B) 現金払いを好む。
　(C) 昨年 10 月にウェブサイトを改善した。
　(D) 以前、Bayani さんが利用したことがある。

188. Dakila さんが質問していないことは何か。
　(A) パッケージツアーに無料サービスが含まれているかどうか
　(B) ツアーガイドが付くかどうか
　(C) お金を銀行経由で電信送金できるかどうか
　(D) 予約の変更が無料かどうか

189. Dakila さんはどうやって予約をするつもりか。
　(A) E メールで
　(B) 対面で直接
　(C) 電話で
　(D) Rajasiha のウェブサイト上で

190. Dakila さんについて何が推測できるか。
　(A) Bayani さんと一緒にタイ旅行に行く。
　(B) 予約の際、割引が利用できる。
　(C) Rajasiha 旅行社の長年の顧客である。
　(D) ふたつ以上のパッケージツアーを予約する。

単語
- accommodating 親切な、世話好きの
- bank transfer 銀行振込
- wonder 〜かどうかと思う
- scenery 風景
- otherwise もしそうでなければ
- money order 郵便為替
- **187** prefer 〜を好む
- **188** wire 〜を電信で送る
- **190** infer 〜を推測する
- eligible 資格のある

問題文の訳と解説 ☞ 次ページに続く

TEST 2　PART 7

問題文の訳

設問186から190は次の広告とEメールに関する質問です。

Rajasiha 旅行社
タイで1番の旅行会社

❶810 Maruek 大通り、Pomprab、バンコク 10100
(662) 555-9174
❷www.rajasihatravels.th

日帰りツアー
ハイキング旅行
豪華クルーズ
サファリ探検

当社ウェブサイトにログオンして、お手頃なパッケージツアーをご覧ください。
❸＊5人以上のグループには特別割引料金がございます。
お問い合わせは、❹弊社販売部長の Sunee Mookjai まで、mookjai@rajasihatravels.th にご連絡を。

宛先：　mookjai@rajasihatravels.th
送信者：eddy.dakila@yphmail.com
日付：　12月18日
件名：　サファリ探検

Mookjai さま、

❺昨年10月に、「豪華プーケットクルーズ」に参加した同僚の Anita Bayani から貴社を強く勧められました。彼女によると、御社のパッケージツアーは値段も安く、ガイドの方も親しみやすく気が利いていたとのことです。そこで、貴社サイトでパッケージツアーの内容を見たところ、Kanchanburi サファリ探検がまさに私と友人が探しているものでした。❻8人分の予約をしたいと思っていますが、いくつかお答えいただきたい質問がございます。

まず、❼銀行振込による支払いは可能でしょうか。また❽予約の変更には手数料が掛かりますか。例えば、ツアーの日程を変更しなければならない場合などです。最後に、Kanchanburi の景色と野生生物を見て回るときに、❾ツアーガイドは同行してくださいますか。

❿私の携帯電話、555-2583にお電話で回答いただければ幸いです。⓫その際に予約をし、可能なら銀行振込にてお支払いします。可能でなければ、郵便為替で支払います。ご連絡をお待ちしています。

Eduardo Dakila

正解＆解説

186. 正解 (A) 難易度

広告で**述べられていない**ことを問う Not 問題。(A) の「パッケージツアーの料金」については、記述が見当たらない。❸で特別割引に触れているが、**具体的な金額は述べていないので** (A) が正解。(B) は❶に住所が、(C) は❷にサイトアドレスが記されている。(D) は❹に氏名が明記されている。

187. 正解 (D) 難易度

Rajasiha 旅行社について、言及されていることを問う True 問題。広告には選択肢に一致する記述がないので、E メールに目を移すと、❺に「Anita Bayani が昨年10月に貴社（= Rajasiha 旅行社）のプーケット豪華クルーズ旅行に行った」とある。これを「**以前、Bayani さんが利用したことがある**」と表現した (D) が正解。(A) (B) (C) についての記述はない。

188. 正解 (A) 難易度

Dakila さんが**問い合わせていない**ことを問う Not 問題。ふたつ目の E メールが、Dakila さんの問い合せメールなので、そちらを中心にみていくと、(A) の「**無料サービス**」に関する質問が見当たらないので、これが正解。(B) は❾で質問。(C) の wiring money は「電信送金」のことだが、❼の「口座振込」と同じことを指す。(D) は❽で質問している。

⇄ will there be a tour guide ➡ whether a tour guide will be present
　payments through bank transfer ➡ pay by wiring money through a bank
　making changes to a reservation ➡ making booking changes

189. 正解 (C) 難易度

Dakila さんが予約する手段を尋ねている。Dakila さんが書いた E メールをみると、⓫に「そのときに予約する」とある。これは前文❿の「私（= Dakila さん）の携帯電話に電話してくれると嬉しい」を受けての記述なので、「そのとき」とは「電話してくれたとき」ということ。従って、**電話で予約する**ということなので、(C)「電話で」が正解。

190. 正解 (B) 難易度

ふたつの文書に散らばった情報を関連付けて答える**クロスリファレンス問題**。Dakila さんについて推測できることを尋ねている。Dakila さんのメール❻に「8人の団体の予約をしたい」とあるが、これに関連しているのが広告の❸。「5人以上のグループには特別料金あり」ということなので、Dakila さんは**特別料金の対象になる**。従って、(B)「予約の際、割引が利用できる」が正解。

⇄ Special rates are available ➡ is eligible for a discount

TEST 2
PART 7

Questions 191-195 refer to the following memo and e-mail.

MEMORANDUM

FROM: Meena Rajpur, public relations associate director, Cassa Bank
TO: Gianna Vinti, regional manager, Cassa Bank
DATE: Oct. 5
SUBJECT: Requested menu changes

Dear Ms. Vinti,

I received the requested menu changes you sent me for our awards dinner on Oct. 12. I contacted the hotel and worked out a few things. First, we have added a bar and cocktail service at the beginning of the evening. Below is the revised menu. The only things that are unchanged are items that will be served during speeches and presentations.

Cocktail hour	6:00-7:00 P.M.	Cocktails, hors d'oeuvres
Dinner	7:00-8:30 P.M.	Cream of asparagus soup
Fresh tomato and mozzarella salad
Roasted rack of lamb
OR
Tortellini with spinach and ricotta (vegetarian option)
Grilled pepper and zucchini
Bread rolls and butter
Speeches and presentations	8:30-9:30 P.M.	Assorted desserts
Coffee and tea

I also want to mention that the dining hall is ours to use until 11:00 P.M. However, we may want to inform everyone that valet service will not be available after 10:30 P.M.

I hope these changes will suit your requirements. Please contact me to confirm.

E-mail

To:	Meena Rajpur <mraj@cassabank.com>
From:	Andrew Norton <Norton@nirvanahotel.net>
Subject:	Confirmation of reservation and menu
Date:	Oct. 4

Dear Ms. Rajpur,

This e-mail is confirmation for the reservation of our Ruby Dining Hall for your company's awards ceremony on Oct. 12, from 6:00-11:00 P.M. We are also pleased to provide a coat check room on the second floor of the hotel, near the stairs leading to the Ruby Dining Hall.

I can also confirm that all the changes you requested to the menu will be made. You also asked if our hotel can provide flower arrangements for the tables. We would be more than happy to arrange this for you. You can contact our flower shop at 555-9887 ext. 18, or visit our florist personally at the hotel. Her name is Veronica Darby, and the shop is located on the same floor as the coat check.

If I can be of any further service, please don't hesitate to contact me.

Sincerely yours,

Andrew Norton, Nirvana Hotel event coordinator

191. What is the main purpose of Ms. Rajpur's memo?

(A) To request a menu
(B) To confirm some changes
(C) To provide an invitation
(D) To ask for a guest list

192. What item on the menu has not been changed?

(A) Soup
(B) Cocktails
(C) Salad
(D) Dessert

193. When will the guests have to leave the facility?

(A) By 8:30 P.M.
(B) By 9:30 P.M.
(C) By 10:30 P.M.
(D) By 11:00 P.M.

194. What is NOT provided by the hotel?

(A) Bar service
(B) Coat check
(C) Internet access
(D) Valet service

195. What is indicated about floral arrangements?

(A) They have already been paid for.
(B) They can be provided by an establishment in the hotel.
(C) They will be ordered by the event coordinator.
(D) They can be delivered for an additional charge.

設問の訳

191. Rajpur さんのメモの主な目的は何か。
   (A) メニューを要求するため
   (B) 変更を確認するため
   (C) 招待状を送るため
   (D) 来客リストを求めるため

192. メニューのどの料理が変更されていないか。
   (A) スープ
   (B) カクテル
   (C) サラダ
   (D) デザート

193. 客はいつ施設をあとにしなければならないか。
   (A) 午後8:30までに
   (B) 午後9:30までに
   (C) 午後10:30までに
   (D) 午後11:00までに

194. ホテルが提供しないものは何か。
   (A) バーのサービス
   (B) クローク
   (C) インターネット接続
   (D) 駐車サービス

195. フラワーアレンジメントについて何が述べられているか。
   (A) すでに料金は支払われている。
   (B) ホテル内のお店が用意する。
   (C) イベントコーディネーターが注文する。
   (D) 追加料金を払えば配達してもらえる。

単語
- associate 準〜、副〜、次席の
- work out 〜 〜を解決する
- assorted 盛り合わせの
- valet service 駐車サービス
- confirmation 確認
- coat check 手荷物預り所、クローク
- ext. 内線（※ extension の省略形）
- florist 花屋
- hesitate ためらう
- **191** invitation 招待状

TEST 2 PART 7

問題文の訳

設問191から195は次のメモとEメールに関する質問です。

メモ

差出人： Meena Rajpur、広報次長、Cassa銀行
宛先： Gianna Vinti、地域担当マネージャー、Cassa銀行
日付： 10月5日
件名： ご依頼いただいたメニューの変更

Vintiさま、
10月12日にお送りいただいた、❶表彰晩餐会のメニュー変更依頼を受け取りました。ホテルに連絡し、いくつか調整をしました。まず、当日は最初に、❷バーとカクテルのサービスを追加しました。以下が改訂されたメニューです。❸以前のままなのは、スピーチと発表の際に出す料理だけです。

カクテルアワー 午後6:00 – 7:00	カクテル、オードブル
ディナー 午後7:00 – 8:30	アスパラガスのクリームスープ 新鮮なトマトとモッツァレラチーズのサラダ 子羊のローストラック あるいは ほうれん草とリコッタのトルテッリーニ（ベジタリアン向け） 焼きピーマンとズッキーニ ロールパンとバター
❹スピーチと発表 午後8:30 – 9:30	デザート盛り合わせ コーヒーと紅茶

❺ダイニングホールは、午後11時まで使用できることも申し添えたいと思います。しかし、❻駐車サービスは午後10時30分以降、利用できないこともみなに知らせておきたいと思います。

以上の変更でご要望にお応えできたと思います。❼確認のご連絡をいただけますか。

宛先： Meena Rajpur<mraj@cassabank.com>
送信者： Andrew Norton<Norton@nirvanahotel.net>
件名： ご予約とメニューの確認
日付： 10月4日

Rajpurさま、
このEメールは10月12日の午後6時から11時まで、貴社の表彰式のためにRubyダイニングホールをご予約いただいていることを確認するものです。ホテル2階、Rubyダイニングホールへ続く階段近くに❽クロークもご用意いたします。

また、ご依頼いただいたメニューの変更はすべて実施することをお約束します。各テーブルにフラワーアレンジメントを用意できるかというご質問もいただいておりましたが、喜んでご用意いたします。❾当ホテルの花屋に555-9887の内線18でご連絡いただくか、あるいは直接ホテルの花屋にお話しにいらしてください。担当者はVeronica Darbyで、❿お店はクロークと同じ階にございます。

ほかに何かお役に立てることがございましたら、ご遠慮なくお申し付けください。

敬具
Andrew Norton、Nirvanaホテル イベントコーディネーター

正解＆解説

191. 正解 (B) 難易度：難

社内メモの目的を尋ねている。主題に関わる設問は、**冒頭に注目**しよう。❶に「表彰晩餐会のメニュー変更の要望を受け取った」とあり、以降、変更内容の説明が続く。そして、最後の❼に「確認の連絡がほしい」とある。これらを「**変更を確認するため**」と表現した (B) が正解。メニューを要求してはいないので、(A) は誤り。

192. 正解 (D) 難易度：難

メニューで**変更されていない**ものを尋ねている。❸に「変更していないのは、スピーチと発表の間に出すものだけ」とある。そこで、スケジュール部分の❹「スピーチと発表」欄を確認すると、「**デザートとコーヒー、紅茶**」とある。従って、この3つが変更されないとわかるが、正解はひとつ目の「デザート」を指した (D)。

193. 正解 (D) 難易度：難

客が施設を退出しなければいけない時間を尋ねている。スケジュールが記載されている社内メモをみていくと、❺に「ダイニングホールは**午後11時まで利用可**」とある。従って、正解は (D)「午後11:00までに」。

194. 正解 (C) 難易度：難

ホテルが**提供しない**ものを問う Not 問題。(A) は❷に「バーを追加」とあり、(B) は❽に「クロークを用意」とある。(C) についての記述が、どちらの文書にもないので、これが正解。(D) の「**駐車サービス**」については、❻に「**valet service**（駐車サービス）は午後10時半まで」とあるので、提供されるとわかる。

195. 正解 (B) 難易度：難

フラワーアレンジメントについて、言及されていることを問う True 問題。関連する記述が集中している E メールに目を向けると、❾に「ホテルの花屋に電話するか、直接出向くこともできる」とあるので、**ホテル内の花屋**がフラワーアレンジメントを手配するとわかる。従って、(B)「ホテル内のお店が用意する」が正解。(A) (C) (D) に関連する記述は見当たらない。

TEST 2
PART 7

Questions 196-200 refer to the following review and e-mail.

Midsummer Bed and Breakfast
Clopton Bridge, Stratford-on-Avon
CV37 7HP, United Kingdom

Located in the historic town of Stratford-on-Avon, Midsummer Bed and Breakfast is in a fascinating location and is surrounded by incredible scenery. The renovated farmhouse is just a five-minute walk from the village center, where visitors can explore numerous shops, attend performances at the Royal Shakespeare Theatre, and tour numerous museums and tourist sites. Only 20 miles from Birmingham, Midsummer Bed and Breakfast is easily reached by rental car. A bus service also runs between Stratford, Birmingham, and Warwick. Midsummer provides a full buffet breakfast and lunch, private suites, parking, telephone and Internet access, and can even arrange tours of Stratford for its guests. Members of the Allied Frequent Flier Plan receive a discounted room rate. For further information or to inquire about reservations, visit www.alliedfliers/UKhotels.co.uk.

E-mail

To:	Kenji Watanabe <wantken@yippee.co.jp>
From:	Ann Reeves <reservations@alliedfliers.co.uk>
Subject:	Confirmation of reservation
Date:	June 24

Dear Mr. Watanabe,

Thank you for your reservation request for the Midsummer Bed and Breakfast located in Stratford-on-Avon. Your booking has been confirmed for the following dates:

Check-in	August 10
Check-out	August 14
Number of guests	2
Reservation number	PC-549613
Cost per night	£45
Allied Frequent Flier number	KW-22872

The following policies apply to your reservation:

1. Cancellations can be made up to 48 hours prior to the date of stay. Cancellations made after 48 hours are subject to a £50 cancellation fee.
2. Guests may check in after 11 A.M. and check out at the same time on their day of departure. There is a charge of £10 for each additional hour after check-out.
3. Credit cards will be charged for half the total amount on the day of check-in. The balance will be paid along with any additional room charges when checking out.

Should you require any further information, or have any questions about your reservation, feel free to send me an e-mail.

Ann Reeves
Allied Fliers Reservations UK

196. What feature of Midsummer Bed and Breakfast is NOT mentioned in the review?
 (A) It is located near several tourist attractions.
 (B) It provides parking facilities for guests.
 (C) It is within walking distance of public transportation.
 (D) It serves two meals every day.

197. Where is Midsummer located?
 (A) Next door to a museum
 (B) A short walk from Warwick
 (C) In a scenic area
 (D) By the entrance of a historic site

198. What is the main purpose of the e-mail?
 (A) To request payment
 (B) To ask for credit card information
 (C) To provide details of a reservation
 (D) To inform customers of a policy change

199. When will Mr. Watanabe probably arrive at Midsummer?
 (A) June 10
 (B) June 24
 (C) August 10
 (D) August 14

200. What can be inferred about Mr. Watanabe?
 (A) He has stayed at Midsummer before.
 (B) He is traveling with his wife.
 (C) He will first travel to Birmingham.
 (D) He received a discounted rate.

設問の訳

196. レビューで述べられていない Midsummer Bed and Breakfast の特徴は何か。
 (A) いくつかの観光地の近くにある。
 (B) 宿泊客用の駐車施設がある。
 (C) 公共交通機関から徒歩圏内にある。
 (D) 毎日2食提供している。

197. Midsummer はどこに位置しているか。
 (A) 美術館の隣
 (B) Warwick から歩いてすぐ
 (C) 景色のよい地域
 (D) 旧跡の入り口近く

198. Eメールの主な目的は何か。
 (A) 支払いを依頼すること
 (B) クレジットカードの情報を求めること
 (C) 予約の詳細を提供すること
 (D) 規定の変更を顧客に知らせること

199. Watanabe さんはおそらくいつ Midsummer に到着するか。
 (A) 6月10日
 (B) 6月24日
 (C) 8月10日
 (D) 8月14日

200. Watanabe さんに関して何が推測できるか。
 (A) 以前 Midsummer に宿泊したことがある。
 (B) 妻と一緒に旅行する。
 (C) 初めて Birmingham に旅行する。
 (D) 割引を受けた。

単語
- bed and breakfast 朝食付きホテル
- fascinating 魅惑的な
- performance 公演
- suite スイートルーム
- frequent flier plan マイレージサービス

***
- be subject to ~ ~を必要とする
- balance 残高
- along with ~ ~とともに

196
- attraction 人を引きつける場所・もの
- distance 隔たり、距離

197
- scenic 景色のよい

問題文の訳と解説 ☞ 次ページに続く

TEST 2　PART 7

> 問題文の訳

設問196から200は次のレビューとEメールに関する質問です。

Midsummer Bed and Breakfast
Clopton Bridge、Stratford-on-Avon
CV37 7HP、イギリス

歴史のある町、Stratford-on-Avonに位置する❶Midsummer Bed and Breakfastは魅力的な立地で、信じられないほど素晴らしい景色に囲まれている。❷農家の家屋を改装した施設は、村の中心からわずか徒歩5分の距離にあり、村の中心では多くのお店を探索したり、王立シェイクスピア劇場で公演を観たり、多くの美術館や観光地を回ることも可能。Birminghamからわずか20マイルの距離なので、Midsummer Bed and Breakfastへはレンタカーで簡単に行くことができる。❸バスもStratford、Birmingham、Warwickの間を運行している。❹Midsummerでは、本格的なビュッフェ形式の朝食と昼食、プライベート用のスイートルーム、駐車場、電話とインターネット接続を提供しており、宿泊客にStratfordのツアーも手配する。❺共同マイレージサービスの会員には室料の割引も。詳しい情報や予約の問い合わせはwww.alliedfliers/UKhotels.co.ukまで。

宛先：　Kenji Watanabe<wantken@yippee.co.jp>
送信者：　Ann Reeves<reservations@alliedfliers.co.uk>
件名：　ご予約の確認
日付：　6月24日

Watanabeさま、
Stratford-on-AvonのMidsummer Bed and Breakfastへの予約依頼ありがとうございます。❻以下の日程でご予約が確認されました。

❼チェックイン	8月10日
チェックアウト	8月14日
❽お客さまの人数	2名
予約番号	PC-549613
1泊あたりの料金	45ポンド
❾共同マイレージサービス番号	KW-22872

以下の規定がお客さまのご予約に適用されます：

1. キャンセルはご宿泊日の48時間前まで可能です。48時間前を過ぎてのキャンセルになりますと、50ポンドのキャンセル料がかかります。
2. チェックインは午前11時から、チェックアウトは出発日の同じ時刻に可能です。チェックアウト時間を1時間過ぎるごとに10ポンドの追加料金がかかります。
3. チェックイン日に、宿泊費の半額がクレジットカードに請求されます。残額は追加の宿泊費とともにチェックアウト時の精算となります。

もしさらに詳しい情報が必要、あるいはご予約に関してご質問がございましたら、私あてに遠慮なくメールをお送りください。

Ann Reeves
Allied Fliers Reservations　イギリス

TOEIC豆知識 TOEICに登場する本や映画、演劇の批評記事は、基本ベタ褒め。さぞかし名作ぞろいなのだろう。

正解＆解説

196. 正解 (C)　難易度■■■□ 難

レビューでMidsummer Bed and Breakfastの特徴として**述べられていない**ことを問うNot問題。(A)は、❷に「お店や劇場、美術館が集まる市の中心部から5分」とある。(B)と(D)は、❹に「朝食と昼食」「駐車場」を提供との記述あり。(C)の「公共交通機関から徒歩圏内にある」については、❸に「Stratfordとほかの町を結ぶバスがある」との記述はある。しかし、**そのバス停がMidsummer B&Bから徒歩圏内にある**とは述べられていないので、これがレビュー内容に一致せず、正解。

🔄 tourist sites ➡ tourist attraction
　a full buffet breakfast and lunch ➡ two meals

197. 正解 (C)　難易度■■■□ 難

Midsummer B&Bの位置を尋ねている。❶に「Midsummer B&Bは**素晴らしい景色に囲まれている**」とある。「景色のよい地域」と言い換えた(C)が正解。

🔄 surrounded by incredible scenery ➡ located in a scenic area

198. 正解 (C)　難易度■■■□ 難

Eメールの目的を尋ねている。このように主題を問う設問では、その文書の**冒頭に注目**。❻に「予約が確認された」とあり、続けてチェックイン日など、**予約の詳細**が続く。従って(C)の「予約の詳細を提供すること」が正解。メールには規程も記されているが、変更を伝えているわけではないので(D)の「規定の変更を顧客に知らせること」は誤り。

199. 正解 (C)　難易度■■■□ 難

Watanabeさんが、Midsummer B&Bにいつ到着するのかを尋ねている。到着日は**チェックイン日**と考えられるので、予約詳細を記したEメールを確認。❼のチェックインの項目に「8月10日」とあるので、(C)が正解。

200. 正解 (D)　難易度■■■■ 難

ふたつの文書に分散した情報を関連付けて答える**クロスリファレンス問題**。Eメールをみていくと、❾に「共同マイレージサービス番号」とあり、Watanabeさんはマイレージサービスの会員だとわかる。レビューに目を移すと❺に「共同マイレージサービス会員には割引あり」とある。このふたつから、**Watanabeさんは割引を受けた**と考えられるので、(D)「割引を受けた」が正解。❽のお客さまの人数欄に「2名」とあるが、もうひとりが誰かは明記されていないので(B)「妻と一緒に旅行する」は誤り。

TEST 2 重要語句 — 索引

《注意》参照先は、問題番号を示している。[Q12]は、問題 No. 12 のこと。
Part 3、4、6、7については、会話やパッセージに含まれるものを [41-43]
と記し、設問と選択肢に含まれるものを [Q41] というように記している。

A

- a copy of〜 ... Q32
- a wide selection of〜 ... 44-46
- absolutely ... 168-171
- accept ... Q88
- access ... Q64
- accommodate ... Q48, Q139
- accommodating ... 186-190
- accompany ... Q54, 168-171
- accomplish ... 41-43
- according to〜 ... Q64
- account ... 160-161
- accounting ... 160-161
- achievement ... Q176
- acknowledge ... 181-185
- ad ... Q33
- additional ... 68-70
- address ... Q97
- admission ... Q86
- advancement ... Q163
- affair ... 147-149
- affiliate ... 155-157
- affordable ... Q102
- agenda ... Q41
- agent ... Q129
- agreement ... 65-67
- aim at〜 ... 98-100
- allowance ... 144-146
- along with〜 ... 196-200
- analysis ... 41-43
- annual ... Q131
- apart from〜 ... Q138
- appear ... Q33
- appliance ... Q102
- applicable ... 77-79
- applicant ... 50-52
- application ... 77-79
- apply ... 92-94
- appreciate ... Q13
- appropriate ... 147-149
- arrange ... Q55
- arrangement ... Q139
- article ... 59-61
- artwork ... Q9
- assert ... 147-149
- assistance ... Q21
- associate ... 191-195
- association ... 71-73
- assorted ... 191-195
- at once ... Q23
- attend ... Q12
- attendance ... Q155
- attraction ... Q196
- auction off〜 ... Q109
- audio-visual ... Q110
- autobiography ... Q114
- autograph ... Q171

B

- availability ... Q57
- bachelor's degree ... 176-180
- background ... Q52
- backrest ... 44-46
- baggage ... Q133
- balance ... 196-200
- balladeer ... 168-171
- bank transfer ... 186-190
- be involved in〜 ... 147-149
- be located ... Q48
- be pushed out of〜 ... 147-149
- be subject to〜 ... 196-200
- be supposed to do ... Q35
- bed and breakfast ... 196-200
- behind schedule ... Q23
- benefit ... Q72, Q121
- beverage ... 98-100
- biannual ... 172-175
- bill ... 53-55
- billing statement ... Q55
- binding ... Q25
- board ... 41-43
- board of directors ... 147-149
- boarding ... Q127
- boring ... Q14
- bound for〜 ... 80-82
- boutique ... Q120
- branch ... Q97
- brief ... Q130
- briefly ... 89-91
- brilliant ... 162-164
- broaden ... Q100
- brochure ... Q24
- brutal ... 162-164
- budget ... Q41
- bundle ... Q136
- business hour ... 62-64

C

- calculate ... 41-43
- campaign ... Q106
- career ... 150-152
- carry ... 44-46
- carry out〜 ... 176-180
- cart ... Q8
- cash ... Q154
- catch ... Q81, 141-143
- categorize ... Q132
- cater ... Q38
- caution ... 165-167
- cellular phone ... Q124
- centennial ... Q125
- certain ... Q29
- certificate ... 77-79
- chairman ... Q42
- charge ... Q48, 68-70
- check ... 53-55
- check out〜 ... 44-46
- checkout counter ... 153-154
- chemical ... Q129
- chief executive officer ... 150-152
- chronic ... 44-46
- circumstance ... Q29
- clear ... Q2
- close ... Q20
- closure ... Q153
- coat check ... 191-195
- colleague ... Q54
- collision ... 165-167
- color ... Q37
- combined ... 92-94
- come up with〜 ... 165-167
- commercial ... Q116
- committee ... 71-73
- commuter ... 80-82
- compare ... Q174
- compensation ... Q85
- competition ... Q72
- competitor ... Q100
- complete ... Q94
- complimentary ... Q85
- comprehensive ... 172-175
- concern ... Q97
- conduct ... Q12
- conference room ... 56-58
- confidential ... 83-85
- confirm ... 95-97
- confirmation ... 191-195
- confusing ... Q166
- connectivity ... Q76
- consider ... Q20
- construction ... Q106
- construction site ... Q3
- consult ... Q21
- consultancy ... Q65
- consultant ... Q123
- contact ... Q20
- contain ... Q118
- contract ... Q13
- convention ... 56-58
- cooperation ... 153-154
- corporate management ... 150-152
- cover ... Q7
- coverage ... 172-175
- credit ... 92-94
- credit A to B ... 162-164
- critic ... 59-61
- cross ... Q1
- culinary ... Q59
- currency ... Q130
- current ... 44-46
- custodian ... Q35

D

- deadline ... Q77
- deal ... Q20
- deal with〜 ... Q100
- dealer ... Q135
- debt ... Q93
- decoration ... Q22
- delay ... 65-67
- deliver ... Q8
- densely-populated ... 158-159
- depart ... Q34
- department ... Q39
- departure ... Q80
- departure gate ... Q127
- deposit ... Q26, Q57
- describe ... 162-164
- description ... 172-175
- destination ... Q105
- detergent ... Q129
- develop ... Q99
- developing country ... 176-180
- device ... 165-167
- dietary supplement ... Q83
- diner ... Q2
- director ... 65-67
- directory ... Q26
- dish ... 59-61
- display ... Q9
- distance ... Q166, Q196
- distribute ... Q54
- district ... 155-157
- divide ... 150-152
- document ... Q154
- dominate ... 98-100
- donate ... Q73
- donation ... Q118
- downsize ... Q123
- drawer ... Q32
- drive ... 98-100
- drop by〜 ... 53-55
- due to〜 ... 80-82

E

- earn ... 158-159, 176-180
- ecologically friendly ... Q122
- effectively ... 165-167
- efficiency ... 181-185
- efficient ... 181-185
- effort ... Q130
- eligible ... Q190
- embark on〜 ... 162-164
- empire ... 162-164
- empty ... Q4
- encourage ... Q119
- encyclopedia ... 165-167
- enhancement ... 181-185
- enrichment ... Q184
- enrollment ... Q87
- ensure ... 172-175
- enterprise ... 160-161
- entirely ... 83-85

- ☐ entitle 147-149
- ☐ entitle A to B Q111
- ☐ entrepreneur 162-164
- ☐ envelope Q105
- ☐ environmental Q106
- ☐ environmentally friendly
  162-164
- ☐ essential 160-161
- ☐ establish 158-159
- ☐ establishment 59-61
- ☐ evacuate 176-180
- ☐ evaluate 144-146
- ☐ evolve 165-167
- ☐ exceed 92-94
- ☐ excess Q93, Q133
- ☐ exchange Q29
- ☐ exclusive 181-185
- ☐ excuse 141-143
- ☐ executive Q66
- ☐ exhibit Q101
- ☐ expect Q17
- ☐ expectation Q136
- ☐ expedite Q69
- ☐ expire Q118
- ☐ explore Q117
- ☐ ext. 191-195
- ☐ extension Q77, 155-157
- ☐ extensive 89-91
- ☐ exterior Q9
- ☐ extraordinary 168-171
- ☐ extremely Q30

F

- ☐ facilitate 165-167
- ☐ facility Q64
- ☐ faculty member 86-88
- ☐ failure 80-82
- ☐ familiarize Q140
- ☐ fascinating 196-200
- ☐ fasten Q3
- ☐ feature 44-46, 168-171
- ☐ fee 50-52
- ☐ field Q76
- ☐ figure 41-43
- ☐ fill out~ Q58
- ☐ finalize 65-67
- ☐ finance department
  181-185
- ☐ financial Q56
- ☐ firm Q19
- ☐ florist 191-195
- ☐ flow Q5
- ☐ focus on~ 162-164
- ☐ fold Q7
- ☐ follow Q66
- ☐ following 153-154
- ☐ footbridge Q10
- ☐ form Q58, Q99
- ☐ formally 165-167
- ☐ forward Q27
- ☐ foundation 176-180
- ☐ fraud 153-154
- ☐ frequent flier plan .. 196-200

- ☐ fuel Q103
- ☐ function 160-161
- ☐ fundraising 71-73
- ☐ furnishing 153-154
- ☐ fusion 168-171

G

- ☐ gallery Q9
- ☐ garage Q22
- ☐ gather Q160
- ☐ generous Q19
- ☐ genre Q132
- ☐ get away with~ 141-143
- ☐ give away~ Q179
- ☐ go on holiday Q40
- ☐ goal Q136
- ☐ gourmet meal Q121
- ☐ graduate degree Q163

H

- ☐ hand Q2
- ☐ hand in~ Q134
- ☐ hand out~ 41-43
- ☐ handle 95-97
- ☐ hardship Q180
- ☐ head 155-157
- ☐ headquarters Q128
- ☐ heighten 141-143
- ☐ hesitate 191-195
- ☐ hold 47-49
- ☐ hold onto~ Q5
- ☐ host 71-73
- ☐ human resource 77-79
- ☐ human resources
  department 181-185

I

- ☐ impose Q133
- ☐ in a timely manner
  147-149
- ☐ in addition 141-143
- ☐ in connection with~
  153-154
- ☐ in installments Q174
- ☐ in need 176-180
- ☐ in person 181-185
- ☐ in place of~ Q126
- ☐ in preparation for~
  172-175
- ☐ in relation to~ 92-94
- ☐ in response to~ 147-149
- ☐ in-box Q32
- ☐ incidence 153-154
- ☐ including 89-91
- ☐ income 92-94
- ☐ inconvenience 80-82
- ☐ incredible Q126
- ☐ industry 162-164
- ☐ infer Q190
- ☐ inform Q77
- ☐ inhabit Q159
- ☐ innovative 98-100
- ☐ inquire Q57

- ☐ inquiry 74-76
- ☐ inspiration 162-164
- ☐ inspire 176-180
- ☐ install Q31
- ☐ institution Q50
- ☐ insurance Q174
- ☐ integrate 98-100
- ☐ intend to do 65-67
- ☐ intense Q124
- ☐ interpersonal 181-185
- ☐ interview 50-52, 77-79
- ☐ invent 165-167
- ☐ inventory 160-161
- ☐ investor Q20
- ☐ invitation Q191
- ☐ invoice Q32
- ☐ issue Q66, 147-149
- ☐ itinerary Q95

J

- ☐ job assignment Q39
- ☐ job position Q61
- ☐ joint 98-100
- ☐ journal Q162
- ☐ judiciously Q136

K

- ☐ kindly 150-152
- ☐ kneel Q3

L

- ☐ lab Q16
- ☐ laboratory Q86
- ☐ lane Q10
- ☐ last Q131
- ☐ lately Q25
- ☐ launching 92-94
- ☐ law office 50-52
- ☐ laziness 141-143
- ☐ lead Q5, Q182
- ☐ leading Q126
- ☐ lease Q95
- ☐ legal aid 50-52
- ☐ licensed Q116
- ☐ limit Q154
- ☐ line Q10
- ☐ list 71-73
- ☐ literary Q105
- ☐ look over~ Q27
- ☐ luck 68-70

M

- ☐ make a purchase Q154
- ☐ make an appearance Q33
- ☐ make contact Q13
- ☐ makeshift 176-180
- ☐ manage to do 50-52
- ☐ management Q16
- ☐ managerial Q185
- ☐ manually 165-167
- ☐ manufacturing Q41
- ☐ mark Q40
- ☐ master's degree 176-180

- ☐ material Q129, Q183
- ☐ meet Q172
- ☐ mention 59-61
- ☐ merchandise Q69
- ☐ merger 65-67
- ☐ method Q70
- ☐ microwaveable 83-85
- ☐ mileage Q18
- ☐ modest 144-146
- ☐ modify Q166
- ☐ monetary Q85
- ☐ money order 186-190
- ☐ mortgage 92-94
- ☐ motivated 141-143

N

- ☐ name 165-167
- ☐ nap 141-143
- ☐ nationwide 168-171
- ☐ no longer Q30
- ☐ normally Q15
- ☐ note Q132
- ☐ notify 155-157
- ☐ numerous 141-143
- ☐ nurture 176-180

O

- ☐ obtain 176-180
- ☐ occupation Q78
- ☐ office hour Q74
- ☐ on a ~ basis 144-146
- ☐ on a first-come-first-
  served basis 181-185
- ☐ on behalf of~ 144-146
- ☐ on foot Q165
- ☐ on several occasions ... Q34
- ☐ operate Q115
- ☐ operation 65-67
- ☐ opportunity Q163
- ☐ option Q68
- ☐ organization Q71
- ☐ orientation 62-64
- ☐ otherwise 186-190
- ☐ outlet 168-171
- ☐ outline Q176
- ☐ outreach Q176
- ☐ outstanding Q93

P

- ☐ package Q8
- ☐ packet Q26
- ☐ painter Q119
- ☐ park Q10
- ☐ parliament 165-167
- ☐ part Q34
- ☐ partially 92-94
- ☐ participant 83-85
- ☐ participate in~ 150-152
- ☐ particular 144-146
- ☐ pass around~ 71-73
- ☐ peacekeeper 176-180
- ☐ pedestal Q4
- ☐ pedestrian 165-167

105

TEST 2　重要語句──索引

- [ ] pension Q94
- [ ] performance Q6, 141-143
- [ ] performer Q171
- [ ] perishable Q118
- [ ] personal assistant 50-52
- [ ] personality 181-185
- [ ] photocopy Q96
- [ ] pick up〜 53-55
- [ ] place Q6
- [ ] place of interest Q80
- [ ] plan on doing 155-157
- [ ] plan on〜 Q12
- [ ] policy Q66
- [ ] portfolio 89-91
- [ ] pose Q4
- [ ] possibility 89-91
- [ ] post Q27
- [ ] postpone Q137
- [ ] prefer Q187
- [ ] preparation Q101
- [ ] present Q19
- [ ] prevent 165-167
- [ ] previously 155-157
- [ ] primarily 181-185
- [ ] prior to〜 176-180
- [ ] priority 176-180
- [ ] producer 98-100
- [ ] production 41-43
- [ ] productive 141-143
- [ ] productivity Q181
- [ ] profit 158-159
- [ ] profitability 147-149
- [ ] profitable 98-100
- [ ] prominent Q120
- [ ] promote Q74
- [ ] promoter 160-161
- [ ] promotion 71-73
- [ ] proof 153-154
- [ ] proposal Q19
- [ ] propose Q112
- [ ] prospective Q158
- [ ] prove 162-164
- [ ] provide 44-46
- [ ] psychologist Q183
- [ ] public policy Q92
- [ ] public relations Q50
- [ ] publication Q61
- [ ] publicize Q153
- [ ] publish Q160
- [ ] publishing company ... Q137
- [ ] purchase Q67
- [ ] pursue Q163
- [ ] push through with〜
  65-67
- [ ] put together〜 Q131

Q

- [ ] qualification Q84
- [ ] qualified 92-94
- [ ] questionnaire 83-85
- [ ] quite Q12
- [ ] quote Q114

R

- [ ] raise Q48, 71-73
- [ ] rate Q48
- [ ] reaction 83-85
- [ ] reaction time 141-143
- [ ] real estate agent Q158
- [ ] realtor Q116
- [ ] rear Q8
- [ ] recall 176-180
- [ ] receipt 181-185
- [ ] reception Q17, 155-157
- [ ] receptionist Q13
- [ ] recommend Q54
- [ ] recording 168-171
- [ ] recruitment 50-52
- [ ] reduction Q69, 141-143
- [ ] reference 50-52, Q183
- [ ] reflection 147-149
- [ ] refund Q29
- [ ] regarding 68-70
- [ ] regardless of〜 ... 141-143
- [ ] region 98-100
- [ ] regional Q71
- [ ] register for〜 Q24
- [ ] registration Q79
- [ ] regulation Q140
- [ ] relevant Q51
- [ ] reliability 172-175
- [ ] reliable 160-161
- [ ] relief 92-94
- [ ] relief operation 176-180
- [ ] relocate Q51
- [ ] remove Q3
- [ ] renovation Q68
- [ ] renowned Q114
- [ ] repair Q44
- [ ] representative Q53
- [ ] reputable 89-91
- [ ] reputation 147-149
- [ ] requirement Q137
- [ ] reservation Q58
- [ ] reserve Q16
- [ ] reside Q52
- [ ] resident Q158
- [ ] residential 158-159
- [ ] resignation Q134
- [ ] résumé 50-52
- [ ] retail 153-154
- [ ] retailing Q158
- [ ] review 59-61
- [ ] revised edition Q183
- [ ] right away Q16
- [ ] run Q23

S

- [ ] salary Q88
- [ ] sales data 160-161
- [ ] sales representative
  74-76
- [ ] sample 83-85
- [ ] satisfy Q137
- [ ] saving 172-175
- [ ] scenery 186-190
- [ ] scenic Q197
- [ ] schedule Q43
- [ ] screen Q6
- [ ] seasonal Q72
- [ ] secretary 155-157
- [ ] separate 150-152
- [ ] serve 59-61
- [ ] serve as〜 86-88
- [ ] set up〜 Q7
- [ ] settle 65-67
- [ ] settle on〜 165-167
- [ ] shelf Q31
- [ ] shipping 168-171
- [ ] shore Q5
- [ ] shortly 62-64
- [ ] sidewalk Q4
- [ ] slash 172-175
- [ ] social issue 162-164
- [ ] spacious 158-159
- [ ] specific 165-167
- [ ] specifically 59-61
- [ ] specify Q105
- [ ] stacks of〜 Q36
- [ ] stall Q31
- [ ] statue Q4
- [ ] step Q5
- [ ] step onto〜 Q1
- [ ] still Q19
- [ ] stipulation Q140
- [ ] stock 68-70, Q173
- [ ] store Q22
- [ ] stream Q5
- [ ] stroller Q4
- [ ] struggle 162-164
- [ ] stuck Q36
- [ ] study 141-143
- [ ] subject Q132
- [ ] submit Q76
- [ ] subscriber Q76
- [ ] subscription Q74
- [ ] sudden 150-152
- [ ] suffer from〜 Q46
- [ ] suggest Q170
- [ ] suggestion ... Q30, 147-149
- [ ] suitable 158-159
- [ ] suite 196-200
- [ ] suited 144-146
- [ ] summarize Q114
- [ ] supply Q68, Q108
- [ ] surcharge Q103
- [ ] surround Q7

T

- [ ] take advantage of〜
  80-82
- [ ] take care of〜 Q35
- [ ] talented 162-164
- [ ] target 83-85
- [ ] technical Q21
- [ ] terms and conditions .. Q94
- [ ] textile Q120
- [ ] tip Q181
- [ ] to that effect 147-149

- [ ] track Q23
- [ ] trade fair 53-55
- [ ] transaction Q113
- [ ] transfer 155-157
- [ ] transit 80-82
- [ ] transmit Q96
- [ ] transportation 144-146
- [ ] trash can Q4
- [ ] travel agency Q56
- [ ] trial Q161
- [ ] trial and error 165-167
- [ ] trivia 165-167
- [ ] tuition fees Q87

U

- [ ] under Q29
- [ ] underneath Q5
- [ ] underprivileged ... 176-180
- [ ] unify 98-100
- [ ] up to〜 Q103
- [ ] upcoming Q120
- [ ] update Q42
- [ ] usage Q64

V

- [ ] vacancy 56-58
- [ ] vacant Q7
- [ ] valet service 191-195
- [ ] valid 153-154
- [ ] value Q116
- [ ] valued 153-154
- [ ] vary 165-167
- [ ] vehicle Q8
- [ ] vehicular Q175
- [ ] venture 98-100

W

- [ ] wait in a line Q9
- [ ] warranty 172-175
- [ ] waterfall Q5
- [ ] welfare 92-94
- [ ] well-ventilated Q109
- [ ] willingness Q51
- [ ] wire Q188
- [ ] witness 168-171
- [ ] wonder 186-190
- [ ] work on〜 Q19
- [ ] work out〜 191-195

新TOEIC® テスト でる模試 600問
別冊 解答・解説 [2] TEST 2

2012年11月 4日　初版　第1刷発行
2014年 4月14日　　　 第7刷発行

著　者　　ハッカーズ語学研究所

発行者　　天谷 修平

発　行　　株式会社 アスク出版
　　　　　〒162-8558
　　　　　東京都新宿区下宮比町2-6
　　　　　TEL：03-3267-6866
　　　　　FAX：03-3267-6867
　　　　　URL：http://www.ask-digital.co.jp/

ISBN 978-4-87217-808-1

新TOEIC® テスト
でる模試 600問

別冊 解答・解説 3

TEST 3

取り外し可能

ゆっくり矢印のほうに
引くと外れます。
▶▶▶

新TOEIC®テスト
でる模試 600問

別冊 解答・解説 3

TEST 3

目次 • Contents

正解一覧	2
Part 1	4
Part 2	8
Part 3	18
Part 4	30
Part 5	42
Part 6	56
Part 7	64

TEST 3 ——正解一覧

〈TEST 3〉の正解リスト。答え合わせにご利用ください。また、間違った問題は、チェックボックス□にチェックをいれておきましょう（1回目は☑、2回目は☒）。復習の際、間違った問題がひと目でわかるので、便利です。

LISTENING SECTION

Part 1
#	Ans
1	B
2	A
3	A
4	A
5	A
6	B
7	C
8	B
9	A
10	A

Part 2
#	Ans
11	B
12	A
13	C
14	B
15	A
16	B
17	B
18	B
19	C
20	A

#	Ans
21	C
22	B
23	C
24	A
25	C
26	B
27	C
28	B
29	A
30	A

#	Ans
31	A
32	A
33	C
34	A
35	B
36	B
37	A
38	C
39	B
40	A

Part 3
#	Ans
41	C
42	B
43	A
44	D
45	C
46	A
47	D
48	B
49	A
50	C

#	Ans
51	B
52	B
53	B
54	A
55	B
56	C
57	C
58	A
59	B
60	C

#	Ans
61	A
62	D
63	D
64	B
65	C
66	C
67	A
68	C
69	D
70	D

Part 4
#	Ans
71	D
72	D
73	C
74	D
75	D
76	A
77	C
78	B
79	C
80	A

#	Ans
81	C
82	B
83	B
84	C
85	A
86	B
87	B
88	B
89	C
90	C

#	Ans
91	D
92	B
93	D
94	B
95	B
96	C
97	D
98	C
99	D
100	A

●受験1回目（学習日：　　月　　日）

LISTENING				Ⓐ予想スコア
正答数　　　　62				310
Part 1	Part 2	Part 3	Part 4	
9	17	20	16	

READING			Ⓑ予想スコア
正答数			
Part 5	Part 6	Part 7	

トータル予想スコア
Ⓐ＋Ⓑ

●受験2回目（学習日：　　月　　日）　26　46　62

LISTENING				Ⓐ予想スコア
正答数				
Part 1	Part 2	Part 3	Part 4	

READING			Ⓑ予想スコア
正答数			
Part 5	Part 6	Part 7	

トータル予想スコア
Ⓐ＋Ⓑ

※本体のスコア換算表（p.9）をご利用ください。

READING SECTION

Part 5

#	Ans	#	Ans	#	Ans	#	Ans
101	A	111	B	121	A	131	C
102	D	112	C	122	C	132	B
103	B	113	B	123	D	133	D
104	D	114	D	124	A	134	C
105	B	115	C	125	B	135	D
106	C	116	B	126	C	136	A
107	B	117	B	127	B	137	B
108	C	118	B	128	B	138	C
109	B	119	D	129	D	139	A
110	B	120	A	130	A	140	B

Part 6

#	Ans
141	C
142	C
143	D
144	C
145	D
146	C
147	B
148	C
149	A
150	D

#	Ans
151	A
152	D
153	C
154	B
155	B
156	B
157	C
158	D
159	A
160	B

Part 7

#	Ans	#	Ans	#	Ans	#	Ans	#	Ans
161	B	171	C	181	C	191	D
162	C	172	C	182	C	192	B
163	D	173	D	183	A	193	C
164	A	174	B	184	C	194	A
165	C	175	B	185	C	195	D
166	B	176	B	186	C	196	A
167	B	177	A	187	D	197	C
168	B	178	D	188	D	198	C
169	B	179	D	189	B	199	D
170	B	180	B	190	D	200	C

TEST 3
PART 1

音声ファイル T3_P1_Q1 ▶ T3_P1_Q5

問題&訳

1.
(A) He's arranging a window display.
(B) He's standing on a ladder.
(C) He's measuring the size of a sign.
(D) He's putting away some paint brushes.

(A) 彼はショーウィンドウの展示を整えている。
(B) 彼ははしごの上に立っている。
(C) 彼は看板のサイズを測っている。
(D) 彼はペンキブラシを片付けている。

2.
(A) The man is riding a bicycle.
(B) The man is fixing a tire.
(C) The man is walking down a path.
(D) The man is crossing his legs.

(A) 男性は自転車に乗っている。
(B) 男性はタイヤを修理している。
(C) 男性は小道を歩いている。
(D) 男性は脚を組んでいる。

3.
(A) They are seated in an auditorium.
(B) They are browsing through some books.
(C) They are removing items from some shelves.
(D) They are gathered around a table.

(A) 彼らは講堂に座っている。
(B) 彼らはいくつかの本に目を通している。
(C) 彼らはいくつかの棚から品物を取り除いている。
(D) 彼らはテーブルの周りに集まっている。

4.
(A) Folders are being stacked on the shelves.
(B) An assortment of items is being placed in the drawer.
(C) Photographs are lying on top of the desk.
(D) A clock is hanging on the wall.

(A) フォルダーが棚に積み重ねられているところだ。
(B) さまざまな物が引き出しに入れられているところだ。
(C) 写真が机の上に置いてある。
(D) 時計が壁に掛かっている。

5.
(A) Passengers are boarding a train.
(B) Lines are painted on the edge of the platform.
(C) Some people are viewing the screens.
(D) Travelers are holding their suitcases down the hallway.

(A) 乗客が列車に乗り込んでいる。
(B) 線がホームの端に引かれてある。
(C) 何人かの人が画面を見ている。
(D) 旅行者が通路でスーツケースを運んでいる。

TOEIC豆知識 以前、男性が自転車にまたがりながら、本を読んでいて、しかもショーウィンドウ前に止まっている、という、注目ポイント満載の写真が出題されたことがある。案の定、間違った人が多かったらしい。

正解＆解説 | 間違いメモ＆単語

1. 正解 (B) 難易度：難

男性が **ladder**（はしご）の上に立っている姿を描写した (B) が正解。(A) の is arranging（〜を整えている）、(C) の is measuring（〜を測っている）、(D) の is putting away（〜を片付けている）は、どれも男性の動作に一致しない。しかし、それぞれ window display、sign、paint brushes など、写真中の要素を含んでいるので、それらにつられて選ばないように注意が必要。

あなたの解答 A B C D
メモ

- arrange 〜を整理する、配列する
- ladder はしご
- measure 〜を測る
- put away 〜 〜を片付ける、しまう

2. 正解 (D) 難易度：難

男性が脚を組んでいる様子を **is crossing his legs** と描写した (D) が正解。(A) の is riding a bicycle（自転車に乗っている）、(B) の is fixing a tire（タイヤを修理する）、(C) の is walking（歩いている）は、いずれも男性の動作に一致しない。

あなたの解答 A B C D
メモ

- fix 〜を修理する
- path 小道、通り道
- cross *one's* legs 脚を組む

3. 正解 (D) 難易度：難

テーブルを囲んで席に着いている人々の様子を、**are gathered around a table**（テーブルの周りに集まっている）と描写した (D) が正解。写真の場所が auditorium（講堂）かどうかは判断できないので、(A) は誤り。(B) の are browsing through some books（いくつかの本に目を通している）は、人々の動作に一致しない。(C) の are removing items（品物を取り除いている）も同様。

あなたの解答 A B C D
メモ

- auditorium 講堂、ホール
- browse through 〜 〜にざっと目を通すす
- remove 〜を取り除く、移動させる
- gather 〜を集める

4. 正解 (D) 難易度：難

机の右手の壁に、時計が掛かっている。これを **is hanging on the wall**（壁に掛かっている）と描写した (D) が正解。このように**目立たない**要素を描写した選択肢が正解になることもあるので、細部にまで注意を払いたい。(A) の**受動態の進行形**（are being stacked）は、主語はモノだが**人の動作**を表す。しかし、写真に人物は写っていないので、誤り。(B) も (A) と同じく受動態の進行形（is being placed）なので、誤り。(C) は、壁に貼られている写真のことを「机の上に置いてある」と描写している。

あなたの解答 A B C D
メモ

- stack 〜を積み重ねる、束にする
- shelf 棚 assortment いろいろ取り合わせたもの drawer 引き出し
- lie 置かれている、ある

5. 正解 (B) 難易度：難

鉄道駅のホームの端に線が描かれている。この状態を受動態で **Lines are painted**（線が描かれている）と表現した (B) が正解。このように**目立たない要素にも注意**が必要。写真には乗客は写っているが、電車に乗り込んではいないので (A) は誤り。(C) の are viewing the screens（画面を見ている）は写真の人物の動作に一致しない。(D) の are holding their suitcases（スーツケースを持っている）という動作をしている人は見当たらない。

あなたの解答 A B C D
メモ

- passenger 乗客 board 〜に乗る
- paint 〜を描く edge 端、へり
- platform プラットホーム

TEST 3 PART 1

音声ファイル 🔊 T3_P1_Q6 ▶ T3_P1_Q10

問題&訳

6.

(A) They're putting helmets on their heads.
(B) They're having a conversation.
(C) They're stopped at a traffic light.
(D) They're riding a motorcycle across the intersection.

(A) 彼らはヘルメットをかぶっているところだ。
(B) 彼らは会話をしている。
(C) 彼らは信号で止まっている。
(D) 彼らはバイクで交差点を渡っている。

7.

(A) There are clouds floating in the sky.
(B) Parasols are being opened up at a beach.
(C) There are some trees standing in a row.
(D) Some birds are landing on a curved wall.

(A) 空に雲が浮かんでいる。
(B) 浜辺でパラソルが開かれているところだ。
(C) 木が何本か1列に並んでいる。
(D) 鳥が何羽か曲線状の壁に止まろうとしている。

8.

(A) Shoppers are paying for their groceries.
(B) Products have been placed on a counter.
(C) A cart has been left near an entrance.
(D) A clerk is putting money into the cash register.

(A) 買い物客が食料品の代金を払っている。
(B) 商品がカウンターの上に置かれている。
(C) カートが入り口近くに置きっぱなしになっている。
(D) 店員がお金をレジに入れている。

9.

(A) The man is opening the rear door of a van.
(B) The man is standing on the back end of a truck.
(C) The man is loading boxes onto a cart.
(D) The man is lifting some crates off of the ground.

(A) 男性はバンの後部ドアを開けているところだ。
(B) 男性がトラック後部の端に立っている。
(C) 男性はカートに箱を積み込んでいる。
(D) 男性は木箱を地面から持ち上げている。

10.

(A) A cabinet has been placed inside the room.
(B) The walls are decorated with paintings.
(C) Blinds have been pulled down in front of the windows.
(D) The armchairs have been arranged next to the doorway.

(A) 部屋の中に戸棚が置かれている。
(B) 壁は絵画で飾られている。
(C) 窓のブラインドが下げてある。
(D) 肘掛け椅子が出入り口の隣に並べられている。

TOEIC豆知識 Part 1は、海辺・湖畔・川岸と、とにかく水辺が大好き。毎回、必ずと言っていいほど登場する。

正解＆解説

6. 正解 (B) 難易度 難

写真の2人は向かい合って、会話しているように見える。この様子を **are having a conversation**（会話をしている）と描写した (B) が正解。(A) の英文は、今まさにヘルメットをかぶろうとしている動作を表す。しかし、2人はすでにヘルメットをかぶった状態なので、誤り。(C) の traffic light（信号機）が写真には見当たらない。(D) は主語が「彼らは」なので、2人ともにバイクに乗っていることになるが、女性は道に立っている。加えて、写真からは intersection（交差点）を確認できない。

□ put on ～ ～を身につける
□ have a conversation 会話をする
□ traffic light 信号機
□ intersection 交差点

7. 正解 (C) 難易度 難

木が3〜4本、並んで立っているのが見える。これを **some trees standing in a row**（1列に並んだ木々）があると表現した (C) がもっとも適切。写真からは空に浮かぶ雲を確認できないので、(A) は誤り。(B) は**受動態の進行形**（are being opened）を使って、パラソルを今まさに開こうとしている**人の動作**を表す。しかし、写真のパラソルはすでに開いた状態にあるので、誤り。(D) の birds（鳥）は、見当たらない。

□ parasol 日傘、パラソル
□ in a row 1列に
□ curved 曲がっている、曲線状の

8. 正解 (B) 難易度 難

レジカウンター上に商品が置かれている状態を、**受動態の現在完了形**（have been placed）で描写した (B) が正解。お金を払っている人は見当たらないので、(A) の are paying（代金を払う）は写真に一致しない。(C) の cart（カート）は、奥の男性が使用中で、入り口近くに置かれてはいない。店員がレジにお金を入れているかどうかは、写真からは判断できないので、(D) も誤り。

□ groceries 食料雑貨類
□ cart（ショッピング）カート
□ entrance 入り口
□ cash register レジ

9. 正解 (B) 難易度 難

男性がトラック後部で、立って作業している様子を描写した (B) がもっとも適切。(A) は後部ドアを今まさに開けようとしている動作を表すが、写真ではすでに開いている。(C) の is loading boxes onto a cart（カートに箱を積み込んでいる）は、男性の動作に一致しない。しかし、**cart** を car と聞き間違うと、正解だと勘違いしてしまう。この cart と car の混同をねらったひっかけは頻出なので要注意。(D) の **crates**（木箱）を地面から持ち上げてはいない。crate も Part 1 によくでるので覚えておこう。

□ rear 後ろの、後部の
□ load ～を載せる、積み込む
□ cart カート、手押し車　□ lift ～を持ち上げる　□ crate 木箱、梱包用の箱

10. 正解 (A) 難易度 難

写真奥に戸棚が設置されている。この状態を**受動態の現在完了形**を使って、A cabinet has been placed と描写した (A) が正解。壁には、paintings（絵画）は見当たらないので、(B) は誤り。(C) は、ブラインドが窓を覆っている状態を描写しているが、写真のブラインドは、どれも完全に窓を覆ってはいない。(D) は、肘掛け椅子が食卓の周りに並べてあるのを、next to the doorway（出入り口の隣に）と描写しているので、誤り。

□ cabinet 飾り棚、戸棚　□ place ～を設置する　□ decorate ～を飾る
□ painting 絵画　□ blinds ブラインド
□ doorway 戸口、出入り口

TEST 3
PART 2

音声ファイル　T3_P2_Q11 ▶ T3_P2_Q16

問題　　　　　　　　　　　　　　　　　　　　　　　　　**訳**

11. Why was the equipment delivery delayed?
(A) For the new manufacturing plant.
(B) Some products were out of stock.
(C) Everything arrived in perfect condition.

なぜ備品の配送は遅れたんだい?
(A) 新しい製造工場用です。
(B) 在庫切れの商品があったからです。
(C) すべて完全な状態で届きました。

12. Could you tell me where we keep the printer paper?
(A) There's some in that cabinet.
(B) I will tell them about it.
(C) It needs a new cartridge.

プリンター用紙をどこに保管しているか教えてくれませんか。
(A) あの戸棚の中にいくらかあるよ。
(B) それについて私が話しましょう。
(C) 新しいカートリッジが必要だね。

13. When is the board meeting?
(A) I thought it was really boring.
(B) We need to get there early.
(C) It's scheduled for Monday morning.

取締役会議はいつなの?
(A) それは本当に退屈だったよ。
(B) 私たちは早くそこに着く必要がある。
(C) 月曜の朝の予定だよ。

14. Which candidate did you choose to hire?
(A) A position in the technical department.
(B) The one who has a college degree.
(C) No, the interview is tomorrow.

どっちの候補者を採用するか決めましたか?
(A) 技術部のポジションです。
(B) 大学の学位を持っているほうだな。
(C) いや、面接は明日だよ。

15. Where are you thinking of doing your graduate studies?
(A) In business administration.
(B) I've applied to a school in London.
(C) They're introducing a new course.

君はどこで大学院研究をしようと考えているんだい?
(A) 企業経営学よ。
(B) ロンドンにある学校に出願しているの。
(C) そこでは新しい課程を導入しているのよ。

16. Who organizes the meetings for our association?
(A) Yes, it's only for management staff.
(B) At the beginning of each month.
(C) The woman over there in the gray dress.

私たちの協会の会議を組織しているのは誰かしら。
(A) ええ、管理スタッフに対してのみです。
(B) 毎月の初めです。
(C) あそこの灰色のドレスを着た女性です。

TOEIC 豆知識 Part 1 が好きなモノ。① 手すり：r-----／②（梱包用の）木箱：c-----／③ はしご：l-----。
3つとも英語で言えますか？

正解＆解説

11. 正解 (B)　難易度 ■■□□□ 難

Why 疑問文で、備品の配達が遅れた〈理由〉が問われている。これに、いくつかの商品が **out of stock**（在庫切れ）だったという理由を答えている (B) が正解。(A) は、理由を表す前置詞 for（〜のために）があるが、内容が問い掛けに対応していない。(C) は、delivery（配送）から連想される arrived（到着した）で、ひっかけをねらっている。

間違いメモ＆単語
あなたの解答 A B C
メモ
☐ equipment 備品、機器
☐ manufacturing 製造の
☐ out of stock 在庫切れの

12. 正解 (A)　難易度 ■■□□□ 難

Could you 〜？で、プリンター用紙の保管場所を教えてほしいと〈依頼〉されている。「戸棚の中に」と場所を答えている (A) が正解。(B) は、them が誰を指すか不明。問い掛けにある tell をくり返すことで、ひっかけをねらっている。(C) は、プリンターと関連するインクの cartridge（カートリッジ）がひっかけ。

☐ cartridge カートリッジ

13. 正解 (C)　難易度 ■■□□□ 難

取締役会議を開催する〈時〉を問う When 疑問文。(C) が、**Monday morning** と時をはっきりと答えており、正解。(A) は、meeting（会議）から連想される、boring（退屈な）で誤答を誘っているが、時制が過去であることからも間違いなのは明らか。(B) は、時に関連する表現 early を使って、ひっかけをねらっている。

☐ board meeting 取締役会議
☐ schedule 〜を予定する

14. 正解 (B)　難易度 ■■■□□ 難

Which 疑問文で、〈どれ・どちら〉の候補者を採用するのかが問われている。(B) は、one が問い掛けの candidate（候補者）を指しており、「**大学の学位を持っている候補者（のほうを採用する）**」という意味。これが正解。(A) の position は「職位、勤め口」という意味。雇用に関連した内容で誤答を誘っているが、問い掛けにつながらない。(C) は、Which 疑問文に対して No と答えているので、すぐに誤りとわかる。

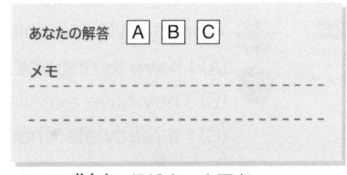

☐ candidate 候補者、志願者
☐ position 地位、職　☐ college degree 学位　☐ interview 面接

15. 正解 (B)　難易度 ■■■■□ 難

Where 疑問文で、大学院研究の〈場所〉を問われている。これに対し、**a school in London**（ロンドンにある学校）に出願している、つまり**そこで研究する予定**と答えている (B) が正解。(A) は graduate studies（大学院研究）から連想される、専攻科目 business administration（企業経営学）で誤答を誘っている。(C) も同じように、関連した course（課程）がひっかけになっている。

☐ graduate study 大学院での研究
☐ business administration 企業経営学
☐ apply to 〜 〜に出願する

16. 正解 (C)　難易度 ■■■□□ 難

Who 疑問文で、会議を組織している〈人〉が問われている。「あそこの女性」と人物を示している (C) が正解。(A) は、Who 疑問文に Yes で答えているので、すぐに除外できる。(B) は時を答えているので、誤り。**疑問詞を使った疑問文に Yes/No では答えられない**、ということを覚えておこう。

☐ organize 〜を組織する、準備する
☐ association 協会
☐ management 経営、管理

TEST 3
PART 2

音声ファイル 🔊 T3_P2_Q17 ▶ T3_P2_Q22

問題 | 訳

---

17. When did we receive the bill from the Internet provider?
(A) Yes, the Internet has been slow lately.
(B) You can make an online payment.
(C) Sometime last week.

インターネット・プロバイダーからいつ請求書を受け取ったんだい。
(A) そうです、インターネットが最近遅いのよ。
(B) オンラインで支払いができますよ。
(C) 先週のいつだったかな。

---

18. Do you have enough time to revise the articles?
(A) He's the company vice president.
(B) If I finish my work early.
(C) When did you arrive?

この記事を修正するのに時間を取れるかしら。
(A) 彼がこの会社の副社長なんだ。
(B) 私の仕事が早く終わればね。
(C) いつ着いたんだい?

---

19. Have you mailed those registration forms out yet?
(A) Here's the list of addresses.
(B) No, I haven't received your letter.
(C) They were sent days ago.

その登録用紙をもう郵送した?
(A) これが住所録よ。
(B) いいえ、あなたの手紙を受け取ってないわ。
(C) 数日前に送ったわ。

---

20. What are you planning to serve for lunch?
(A) I have to discuss that with my caterer.
(B) They have excellent service.
(C) I already ate, thanks.

昼食には何を出すつもりなの?
(A) その件で仕出し業者と話し合わないといけないんだ。
(B) 彼らのサービスは素晴らしいよ。
(C) もう食べたんだ、ありがとう。

---

21. Where should I leave these packages?
(A) I left them at the front desk.
(B) From the moving company.
(C) Just give them to my secretary.

これらの小包をどこに置きましょうか。
(A) 私はそれを受付に置きました。
(B) 引越業者からです。
(C) 私の秘書に渡してください。

---

22. Why don't you request a raise from your boss?
(A) The rate went up this quarter.
(B) You're right, I should do that.
(C) No, I don't have any more.

上司に昇給を要求すれば?
(A) この四半期にその割合が上がったのよ。
(B) そうですよね、そうするべきね。
(C) いいえ、これ以上持ってないわ。

TOEIC豆知識 《Part 1が好きなモノの答え》 ①手すり：railing／②（梱包用の）木箱：crate／③はしご：ladder。

正解＆解説

17. 正解 (C) 難易度 ■■□ 難
請求書を受け取った〈時〉を問うWhen疑問文。これに、正確な日時ではなく、「**先週のいつか**」というおおまかな時期を答えている(C)が正解。(A)は、When疑問文にYesで答えているので、すぐに誤りとわかる。ただ、問い掛けのInternetをくり返したひっかけがあるので、注意したい。(B)はbill（請求書）から連想される、on-line payment（オンライン支払い）が誤答を誘っている。

間違いメモ＆単語
あなたの解答 A B C
メモ
☐ bill 請求金額、請求書
☐ make payment 支払いをする

18. 正解 (B) 難易度 ■■■ 難
Yes/No疑問文。記事を修正する時間があるかどうかが問われている。(B)は「**自分の仕事が早く終われば（記事を修正する時間を取れる）**」という意味。**間接的に**問い掛けに答えており、これが正解。(A)は代名詞Heが誰を指すのか不明。ただ、reviseに発音の似たviceを使ったひっかけに注意。(C)はtime（時間）に関連するWhen疑問文で誤答を誘っている。**Yes/No疑問文に、YesとNoで答えるとは限らない**ことを覚えておこう。

あなたの解答 A B C
メモ
☐ revise 〜を修正する、見直す
☐ article 記事

19. 正解 (C) 難易度 ■■■ 難
現在完了形のYes/No疑問文。登録用紙をすでに送ったかどうかが問われている。(C)のTheyはregistration formsを指しており、「**登録用紙は数日前に送られた**」という意味。つまり、Yesという答えであり、会話が成立するので、これが正解。(A)はmailed（〜を郵送した）に関連するaddresses（住所）がひっかけ。(B)は、No, I haven'tまではよいが、続くreceived your letter（あなたの手紙を受け取った）が問い掛けに対応していない。

あなたの解答 A B C
メモ
☐ registration 登録
☐ form 用紙、書式

20. 正解 (A) 難易度 ■■■ 難
昼食に出す〈こと・もの〉を問うWhat疑問文。何かのイベントの昼食について会話していると考えられる。「**caterer（仕出し業者）と相談しなければ**」と答えている(A)が正解。何を出すのか答えていないが、メニューがまだ決まっていないことを間接的に伝えており、会話が成立している。(B)は代名詞Theyが何を指すか不明。serveの派生語serviceがひっかけになっている。(C)は、昼食から連想される内容で誤答を誘っている。

あなたの解答 A B C
メモ
☐ caterer 仕出し業者

21. 正解 (C) 難易度 ■■■ 難
Where疑問文。小包を置く〈場所〉が問われている。これに対し、「**secretary（秘書）に渡してくれ**」と答えた(C)が正解。このように、場所を問うWhere疑問文に、人物を答えることもできると覚えておこう。(A)は、at the front desk（受付に）にひっかからないようにしたい。(B)はpackages（小包）から連想される、moving company（引越業者）を使ったひっかけ。

あなたの解答 A B C
メモ
☐ package 小包、小荷物
☐ moving company 引越業者
☐ secretary 秘書

22. 正解 (B) 難易度 ■■■ 難
Why don't you〜?で、昇給を要求することを〈提案〉している。You're rightで提案に同意し、さらに自分の意見を添えている(B)が正解。(A)はraise（昇給）に関連する、went up（上がった）がひっかけになっている。(C)は、Noで答えたまでは正しいが、続くI don't have any more（これ以上は持っていない）が、文脈に一致しない。

あなたの解答 A B C
メモ
☐ raise （賃金の）値上げ、昇給
☐ rate 割合、相場
☐ quarter 4分の1、四半期

TEST 3
PART 2

音声ファイル　T3_P2_Q23 ▶ T3_P2_Q28
問題 / 訳

23. Do you need some help carrying these boxes?
(A) I need three boxes please.
(B) Of course I can help you with that.
(C) Thanks. That's very kind of you.

これらの箱を運ぶのを手伝いましょうか。
(A) 3箱頂けますか。
(B) もちろん、手伝うよ。
(C) ご親切に、どうもありがとう。

24. Don't you need a credit card to place an order?
(A) No, I can make the payment later.
(B) I'm not ready to order yet.
(C) Yes, I put them in the shopping cart.

注文するのにクレジットカードは必要ないのかい。
(A) いえ、支払いはあとにしてもよいから。
(B) まだ注文が決まってないの。
(C) ええ、ショッピングカートに入れたわ。

25. Who runs the branch office in Budapest?
(A) No, it won't open until next year.
(B) I believe Mr. Ivanovich does.
(C) We have several branches across Europe.

ブダペスト支店は誰が運営していますか。
(A) いいえ、来年まで開店しません。
(B) Ivanovichさんだと思います。
(C) ヨーロッパ各地に支店があります。

26. Isn't the financial planning meeting supposed to be finished by now?
(A) Yes, we've met several times.
(B) I felt that it was a good plan.
(C) It probably won't be over for another hour.

財政計画会議は、今ごろもう終わっているはずではないんですか?
(A) ええ、数回会ったことがあります。
(B) 優れた計画だと感じました。
(C) おそらく、あと1時間は終わらないでしょう。

27. Could you give me a hand with this research?
(A) I searched for a solution.
(B) No, I haven't handed them out.
(C) Later, after I complete this report.

この調査に手を貸してくれませんか。
(A) 解決策を探しました。
(B) いいえ、それらを配ってはいません。
(C) あとで、この報告書を書き終えたら。

28. Is the subject of next week's workshop about marketing or public relations?
(A) It will last for three days.
(B) Neither. It's about advertising trends.
(C) Yes, in the main auditorium.

来週の勉強会のテーマはマーケティングでしたっけ、それとも広報活動だったかしら。
(A) 3日間続くよ。
(B) どちらでもないな。広告の動向についてだよ。
(C) ええ、大ホールで。

正解＆解説

23. 正解 (C)　難易度 ■■□ 難
Yes/No 疑問文で、手助けが必要かどうかが問われている。これに、Thanks と お礼を述べたあと、**「ご親切にどうも」**と、さらに感謝を強調している (C) が正解。(A) は、問い掛けにある単語 need、boxes をくり返して、ひっかけをねらっている。(B) は、**手助けを依頼された**場合の応答。

24. 正解 (A)　難易度 ■■□ 難
否定疑問文は、**通常の疑問文に置き換えて**考えよう。そうすれば、応答の Yes は肯定（〜する）、No は否定（〜しない）とスムーズに理解できる。ここでは「クレジットカードが必要か」と問われていると考える。すると、(A) の No は「**必要ない**」を意味し、あとにその理由が続いている。会話が成立するので、これが正解。一方、(C) の Yes は「**カードが必要**」を意味するが、あとに続く内容が対応していないので、誤り。(B) は、注文に関連した内容でひっかけをねらっている。

□ place an order 注文する

25. 正解 (B)　難易度 ■■□ 難
Who 疑問文で、ブダペスト支店を運営している〈人〉が問われている。**Mr. Ivanovich does** と人物名を答えている (B) が正解。この does は、問い掛けの runs the branch office in Budapest を意味している。(A) は、Who 疑問文に No で答えているので誤答。(C) は、問い掛けの branch を branches と複数形でくり返し、混同をねらっている。

□ run 〜を経営する、運営する
□ branch office 支店、支社

26. 正解 (C)　難易度 ■■■ 難
否定疑問文は、**通常の疑問文に置き換えて**考えよう（☞ Q24の解説も参照）。ここでは「財務計画会議はそろそろ終わりでは」と問われていると考える。これに、「**another hour（さらに1時間）は終わらない**」と状況を説明している (C) が正解。(A) は Yes で答えたまではよいが、あとの内容が問い掛けに対応していない。(B) は、問い掛けの planning を plan の形でくり返し、ひっかけをねらっている。

□ financial 財政の、金融の
□ be supposed to do 〜することになっている

27. 正解 (C)　難易度 ■■■ 難
Could you 〜? で、調査への協力を〈依頼〉されている。(C) は、「**報告書を書き終えたあとで（協力する）**」という意味で、間接的に依頼を受諾している。よって、これが正解。(A) は、research に発音が類似した searched でひっかけをねらっている。(B) は、問い掛け中の名詞 hand を動詞としてくり返し、ひっかけをねらっている。

□ give a hand 手を貸す、協力する
□ solution 解答、解決策
□ complete 〜を仕上げる、終える

28. 正解 (B)　難易度 ■■■ 難
選択疑問文。勉強会のテーマが「マーケティング」なのか「広報活動」なのかが問われている。(B) は、まず Neither で「マーケティングでも広報でもない」と両方を否定。そのあとに「**広告の動向に関してだ**」と正しいテーマを伝えており、会話が成立している。(A) は workshop から連想される、開催期間 for three days（3日間）を述べて、誤答を誘っている。(C) は、A or B の選択を問う選択疑問文に Yes/No では答えられないので、誤り。

□ subject 主題　□ public relations 宣伝（広報）活動　□ trend 傾向、動向
□ auditorium 講堂

TEST 3
PART 2

音声ファイル 🔊 T3_P2_Q29 ▶ T3_P2_Q34

問題

訳

---

29. How many people have signed up for the aerobics class?
(A) Yes, I've tried it many times before.
(B) There are 30 people in my department.
(C) Not as many as I was expecting.

エアロビクスのクラスに何名登録してるんだい?
(A) ええ、以前何度もやってみたの。
(B) 私の部署には30名いるの。
(C) 期待していたほど多くはないわね。

---

30. Marian used to be Mr. Granger's assistant, didn't she?
(A) She doesn't use it very much.
(B) I'm the assistant manager.
(C) Yes, until she got a promotion.

Marianは以前Grangerさんの助手だったわよね。
(A) 彼女はそれをあまり使わないな。
(B) 私は部長補佐です。
(C) ええ、昇格するまでは。

---

31. How do I switch off the photocopier?
(A) Press the red button on that panel.
(B) Yes, he's an excellent photographer.
(C) We need about 20 copies of the report.

コピー機の電源はどうやって切るんだっけ?
(A) そのパネルの赤いボタンを押すのよ。
(B) そう、彼は素晴らしい写真家だわ。
(C) その報告書が20部ほど必要なの。

---

32. Does the bank open at nine on Saturdays?
(A) No, it is closed on the weekend.
(B) You don't have to deposit it.
(C) It closes soon.

あの銀行は、土曜日は9時に開くんだっけ?
(A) いいえ、週末は閉まっているわ。
(B) 預金する必要はないわ。
(C) すぐに閉まるわよ。

---

33. I will make the flight reservations later today.
(A) Sorry, but I can't make it.
(B) We need to arrive at the airport early.
(C) Do you think you could do it now?

きょうこのあと、飛行機の予約をしますね。
(A) ごめん、私にはできないわ。
(B) 空港には早めに着かないと。
(C) 今できないかしら。

---

34. Would you prefer the paper or the cloth napkins?
(A) They only sell clothing.
(B) The cloth ones seem more attractive.
(C) For the main dining area.

紙と布のナプキンのどちらがよろしいですか。
(A) 彼らは服を販売しているだけだ。
(B) 布の方がいいかな。
(C) 大食堂用に。

正解 & 解説 / 間違いメモ & 単語

29. 正解 (C) 難易度：難

How many ~? で、エアロビクスのクラスに登録した人の〈数〉が問われている。(C) は、明確な数を答えてはいないが、「**期待したほど多くない**」と間接的に応答することで会話を成立させている。Part 2では、このように**自然な会話が成り立つかどうかという視点**を常に持つようにしよう。(A) は How 疑問文に Yes で答えているので、誤り。問い掛けの many をくり返してひっかけをねらっている。(B) は 30 people (30人) と数を答えているので迷うが、答えているのは部署の人数であり、不自然。

あなたの解答 A B C
メモ
- department （企業の）部、課
- expect ～を期待する、予想する

---

30. 正解 (C) 難易度：難

付加疑問文は、**通常の疑問文に置き換えて**考えよう。ここでは「Marian は Granger さんの助手だったのか」と問われていると考える。すると、Yes で肯定し、「**昇進するまでは（Granger さんの助手だった）**」と補足をしている (C) が正解とわかる。(A) は、問い掛けの used を use の形でくり返し、誤答を誘っている。(B) は、主語が異なる。assistant をくり返したひっかけに注意。

あなたの解答 A B C
メモ
- promotion 昇進、進級

---

31. 正解 (A) 難易度：難

How 疑問文で、コピー機の電源を切る〈方法・手段〉が問われている。これに対し、Press the red button（赤いボタンを押す）と方法を明確に答えている (A) が正解。(B) は、How 疑問文に Yes で応答しているので、誤り。photocopier と発音の似た photographer を使ったひっかけに注意。(C) は photocopier（コピー機）から連想される 20 copies（20部）がひっかけ。

あなたの解答 A B C
メモ
- switch off ～ ～のスイッチを切る、電源を切る
- photocopier コピー機

---

32. 正解 (A) 難易度：難

Yes/No 疑問文で、銀行が土曜日の9時に開くかどうかが問われている。(A) は、まず No で否定。それから、Saturdays を weekend に言い換えて「**週末は閉まっている**」と説明を加えている。自然な流れになっているので、これが正解。(B) は bank（銀行）から連想される、deposit（～を預金する）でひっかけをねらっている。(C) は closes（閉まる）で誤答を誘っているが、soon（まもなく）部分が問い掛けに対応していない。

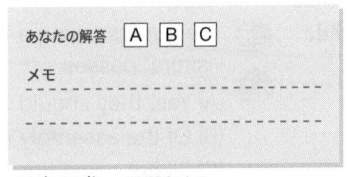

あなたの解答 A B C
メモ
- deposit ～を預金する

---

33. 正解 (C) 難易度：難

平叙文。あとで飛行機の予約をする、と予定を伝えている。これに対し、自然なやりとりになる応答を選ぶ。「あとで」と言っているのに対し、「**今、そうする（予約する）ことができないか**」と依頼をしている (C) だと、自然な会話になる。(A) は、問い掛けの make をくり返して、ひっかけをねらっている。(B) は、「飛行機の予約」に関連した、airport（空港）がひっかけ。

あなたの解答 A B C
メモ
- reservation 予約
- make it 成功する、うまくやる

---

34. 正解 (B) 難易度：難

選択疑問文で、「**紙ナプキン**」か「**布ナプキン**」の選択を問われている。(B) の ones は napkins を指しており、cloth ones（布ナプキン）のほうがより attractive（魅力的な）と言っている。つまり、**布ナプキンのほうを選択**しており、(B) が正解。(A) は、cloth の派生語 clothing でひっかけをねらっている。(C) は、napkin を使う場所として連想される、dining area（食堂）で誤答を誘っている。

あなたの解答 A B C
メモ
- prefer ～が好きである、好む
- cloth 布　clothing 衣料品、衣類
- attractive 魅力的な

TEST 3
PART 2

音声ファイル T3_P2_Q35 ▶ T3_P2_Q40

問題 | 訳

35. Gretchen will discuss that issue with the client, won't she?
(A) Yes, it was a fascinating discussion.
(B) She said there are still tickets available.
(C) I think she's planning to speak with him on Monday.

Gretchen さんがその問題について顧客と話すのですね。
(A) ええ、興味深い議論でした。
(B) チケットはまだあると彼女は言っていました。
(C) 彼女は彼と月曜に話す予定だと思います。

36. Would you like a room with a view of the sea or the courtyard?
(A) I need a double room please.
(B) It would be nice to see the ocean.
(C) We really liked that hotel.

海が見える部屋と中庭が見える部屋のどちらになさいますか。
(A) ダブルベッドの部屋をお願い。
(B) 海が見えるといいですね。
(C) あのホテルはとっても気に入ったわ。

37. We need you to do some research for the marketing team's presentation.
(A) That sounds like a challenging job.
(B) About the new advertising promotion.
(C) Mainly stock market trends.

マーケティングチームのプレゼンのために、調査をしてほしいのですが。
(A) やりがいのある仕事のようですね。
(B) 新しい広告宣伝についてです。
(C) 主に株式市場の動向です。

38. The guests taking a tour of the factory will need visitors' passes.
(A) Yes, they should begin at the main plant.
(B) Of the assembly line and warehouse.
(C) I'll get some from the security department right away.

工場見学参加者は入館許可証が必要です。
(A) そうね、彼らはメイン工場から始めた方がいいわ。
(B) 組立ラインと倉庫のです。
(C) すぐに警備部門から持ってきます。

39. Wasn't there an announcement about the staff work schedule the other day?
(A) It's supposed to be on Monday or Tuesday.
(B) I haven't heard anything about that.
(C) Because of the upcoming holiday.

この前、従業員の勤務予定についての案内がなかったっけ？
(A) 月曜か火曜の予定だよ。
(B) 何も聞いてないなぁ。
(C) 今度の休暇のせいだね。

40. Isn't Ms. Tang making the arrangements for the real estate fair?
(A) No, they purchased a different building.
(B) That's why she has been out of the office so much.
(C) Yes, I thought the offer was fair.

Tang さんが不動産フェアの準備をしているのではないんですか？
(A) いえ、彼らは別の建物を購入しました。
(B) だから彼女は事務所を離れていることが多いんです。
(C) ええ、その申し出は公平だと思います。

| 正解＆解説 | 間違いメモ＆単語 |

35. 正解 (C) 難易度 ■■■□ 難

未来形の付加疑問文。「Gretchen さんは、顧客とその問題について話すのか」という**通常の疑問文に置き換えて**考えよう。これに「彼女（= Gretchen さん）は、月曜日に彼（=顧客）と話す予定だ」と、**話す日時を答えることで、肯定をしている** (C) が正解。(A) は、未来形の問い掛けに対し、過去時制になっており不自然。(B) は、issue（問題）の動詞としての意味「〜を発行する」から連想される tickets（チケット）で、誤答を誘っている。

あなたの解答 A B C
メモ

- [ ] issue 問題、論争点
- [ ] fascinating 興味をそそる、魅惑的な

36. 正解 (B) 難易度 ■■■□ 難

選択疑問文で、「海が見える」客室か「中庭が見える」客室かの選択を求められており、ホテルのフロントでの会話だろうと推測できる。これに「ocean（海）が見えるといい」と答えることで、**間接的に海が見える客室**を選択した (B) が正解。(A) (C) ともに、ホテルに関連した内容で誤答を誘っている。

あなたの解答 A B C
メモ

- [ ] view 眺め、風景　　[ ] courtyard 中庭

37. 正解 (A) 難易度 ■■■□ 難

プレゼンテーションのための調査を要請する平叙文。これに対し、もっとも自然な流れになる応答を選ぶ。「それ（=調査をすること）は、やりがいのある仕事だ」と答え、**間接的に要請を受け入れている** (A) が正解。(B) は、marketing（マーケティング）から連想される advertising promotion（広告プロモーション）でひっかけをねらっている。(C) は、marketing の派生語 market がひっかけ。

あなたの解答 A B C
メモ

- [ ] challenging やりがいのある
- [ ] promotion 広報宣伝　[ ] mainly 主に
- [ ] stock market 株式市場

38. 正解 (C) 難易度 ■■■■ 難

平叙文で、工場見学参加者は入館許可書が必要という情報を伝えている。(C) の some は、some visitors' passes を意味し、「**すぐに（入館許可証を）何枚か持ってくる**」という応答になる。自然なやりとりなので、これが正解。(A) (B) ともに、問い掛けの factory（工場）に関連する、main plant（メイン工場）、assembly line（組立ライン）、warehouse（倉庫）を使って、誤答を誘っている。

あなたの解答 A B C
メモ

- [ ] plant 工場　[ ] assembly（機械などの）組立　[ ] warehouse 倉庫　[ ] right away すぐに

39. 正解 (B) 難易度 ■■■■ 難

過去形の否定疑問文。否定疑問文は、**通常の疑問文に置き換える**とよいので（☞Q24 の解説も参照）、「勤務予定についての案内があったか」と問われていると考える。(B) は「**それについては何も聞いてない**」と答え、案内がなかったことを間接的に伝えており、正解。(A) は、schedule（日程）に関連する表現 Monday or Tuesday でひっかけをねらっている。(C) は、理由を表す Because of 〜（〜という理由で）を使って応答しており、不自然。

あなたの解答 A B C
メモ

- [ ] announcement 発表、案内
- [ ] the other day 先日は
- [ ] upcoming 今度の、来たる

40. 正解 (B) 難易度 ■■■■ 難

否定疑問文は、**通常の疑問文に置き換えて**考えよう。ここでは「Tang さんが不動産フェアの準備をしているのか」と問われていると考える。これに「だから彼女は頻繁に事務所を空けていた」と答えて、**Yes ということを間接的に伝えている** (B) が正解。(A) は、不動産に関連した内容で誤答を誘っているが、They が誰を指すのか不明。(C) は、問い掛けの fair（展示会）を「公平な」という意味でくり返し、ひっかけをねらっている。

あなたの解答 A B C
メモ

- [ ] make arrangement for 〜 〜の準備をする　[ ] real estate 不動産
- [ ] purchase 〜を購入する

TEST 3
PART 3

41. What most likely is the woman's job?
(A) A travel agent
(B) A restaurant employee
(C) A hotel receptionist
(D) A tour guide

42. What is the problem?
(A) Tickets are sold out.
(B) A facility is fully booked.
(C) There are no free tables.
(D) A tour has been cancelled.

43. What does the woman suggest?
(A) Trying another establishment
(B) Making a booking for Monday
(C) Delaying a trip
(D) Reserving a room in advance

44. Why is the man calling?
(A) He has to register for a convention.
(B) He has to cancel an appointment.
(C) He wants to get a prescription.
(D) He needs to see a doctor.

45. What does the woman suggest the man do?
(A) Visit a nearby pharmacy
(B) Fill out an application form
(C) Come back on another day
(D) Check his schedule

46. What will the man probably do?
(A) Sign up for insurance
(B) Meet with a different physician
(C) Attend a hospital meeting
(D) Purchase medicines at a pharmacy

Questions 41-43 refer to the following conversation.

M: ①Excuse me, are there any rooms available for this evening?
W: ②Sorry sir, but we are fully booked for this weekend. There are several conferences in town, so ③there is nothing free until Monday.
M: I see. Do you happen to know if there are any vacancies in ④other hotels in town?
W: ⑤Why don't you try the Courtland Hotel? It's just across the street and I believe they still have a few vacancies.

設問41から43は次の会話に関する質問です。
男：すみませんが、今晩、空室はありますか。
女：申し訳ございません。今週末は満室になっております。町で会議がいくつかあり、月曜日まで空きがないのです。
男：なるほど。町のほかのホテルに空室があるかどうかご存じじゃありませんか。
女：Courtland ホテルをあたってみてはいかがでしょうか。ちょうど通りの向かい側で、まだ数室の空きがあると思います。

Questions 44-46 refer to the following conversation.

M: Hi. ①I'd like to schedule an appointment with Dr. Elton. I've been experiencing chronic back pain lately and ②I really want it checked out.
W: ③I'm sorry, but Dr. Elton is out of the country this week. He's attending a convention and won't be back until Saturday evening. ④Can you make it on Monday at 9 A.M.?
M: ⑤No, I don't think I can wait until then. Are there any other doctors available?
W: ⑥Certainly. Dr. Johnson will be here tomorrow. If you want, I can schedule you to see her at 1 P.M.

設問44から46は次の会話に関する質問です。
男：こんにちは。Elton 先生の予約を取りたいのですが。最近、慢性の背中痛があるので、ぜひ診てもらいたいのです。
女：恐れ入りますが、Elton 医師は今週国外にいます。会議に出席していて土曜日の夕方まで戻りません。月曜日の午前9時でもよろしいでしょうか。
男：いいえ、それまで待てません。ほかの先生のご都合はどうですか。
女：かしこまりました。Johnson 医師なら明日参ります。よろしければ、午後1時に面会の予約をお取りすることができます。

設問の訳 ☞ p.28～29参照

TOEIC豆知識 TOEICの世界では、裁判が盛んらしく、legal office が頻繁に登場する。しかし、そのわりに、具体的な訴訟内容が話題にのぼることはない。（続く▶）

正解＆解説

41. 正解 (C)　難易度■■□　難

女性の職業を尋ねている。男性が❶で「rooms available（空室）があるか」と尋ね、女性は❷で「fully booked（予約でいっぱい）だ」と答えている。ほかにも❹の other hotels（ほかのホテル）といった表現から、女性はホテルのフロントで仕事をしていると推測できる。よって、(C) A hotel receptionist（ホテルのフロント係）が正解。

42. 正解 (B)　難易度■■□　難

会話中の問題点を尋ねている。**ネガティブな要素に注目して会話を聞こう。**❷で女性は「今週末は fully booked（予約でいっぱい）だ」といい、「月曜まで空きがない」（❸）とも言っている。つまり、**ホテルの空き室がない**ことが問題だとわかる。従って、ホテルを「施設」と言い換えた (B) A facility is fully booked.（施設は予約でいっぱいだ）が正解。

43. 正解 (A)　難易度■■□　難

女性が提案していることを尋ねているので、**女性の発言に注目。**❺で「Courtland ホテルをあたってみたらどうか」と、別のホテルを薦めている。これを、another establishment（別の施設）をあたる、と言い換えた (A) が正解。Why don't you ～？は、典型的な提案の表現なので覚えておこう。

単語　□ available 利用できる、入手できる　□ fully 完全に、十分に　□ book ～を予約する　□ conference 会議　□ happen to do たまたま～する　□ vacancy 空室　**41**　□ most likely 多分、おそらく　□ receptionist 受付係　**42**　□ facility 施設　**43**　□ suggest ～を提案する　□ establishment 施設　□ delay ～を延期する、遅らせる

44. 正解 (D)　難易度■■■　難

男性が電話をした目的を尋ねている。このように**主題に関わる設問では、多くの場合、冒頭にヒントがくる。**会話の出だしに注目しよう。❶で男性は「Elton 先生の予約を取りたい」と目的を述べ、その理由として❷で「it（＝ chronic back pain）を診てほしい」と言っている。このことを「彼は医師に診てもらう必要がある」と表現した (D) が正解。

45. 正解 (C)　難易度■■□　難

男性に対して、**女性が提案**したことを尋ねているので、**女性の発言に注目**しよう。女性は❸で Elton 医師の不在を伝えたあと、❹「月曜日の9時はどうか」と提案をしている。これを「別の日に来る」と言い換えた (C) Come back on another day が正解。

46. 正解 (B)　難易度■■■　難

会話のあと、男性がとるだろう行動を尋ねている。**未来の行動を問う設問では、会話の終盤部分にヒントがくる**ことが多い。ここでも、男性が❺で「それ（＝月曜の9時）まで待てない」ので、ほかの先生の都合を尋ねている。それに対し、女性は❻で「明日の Johnson 医師の診察予約が可能」と答えている。これらのことから、男性は明日「different physician（別の医者）に会う」だろうと推測できるので、(B) が正解。

単語　□ chronic 慢性的な　□ back pain 背中の痛み　□ attend ～に出席する　□ convention 会議　□ certainly（質問への返答）かしこまりました　□ see ～に診てもらう　**44**　□ register for ～ ～に登録する　□ prescription 処方箋　**45**　□ pharmacy 薬局　□ application form 申込用紙　**46**　□ insurance 保険　□ physician 内科医、医者

TEST 3 PART 3

47. Where is Ms. Garner?
(A) At a client meeting
(B) At an accounting seminar
(C) On vacation
(D) On her lunch break

48. Why does the man want to see Ms. Garner?
(A) To discuss his taxes
(B) To give her some documents
(C) To inquire about a billing statement
(D) To talk about his work schedule

49. What does the woman offer to do?
(A) Deliver a message
(B) Copy the papers
(C) Order lunch for Ms. Garner
(D) Schedule a meeting

Questions 47-49 refer to the following conversation.

M: Hello, my name is Walter Jennings and I need to speak with Ms. Garner. I'm a client of hers.
W: Unfortunately ❶Ms. Garner is out for lunch at the moment. If it is urgent, I can call her.
M: Don't worry about it. ❷I just needed to leave these documents she requested for my tax claims.
W: Oh, well ❸you can leave those with me and write her a note, and I'll make sure she gets them.

設問47から49は次の会話に関する質問です。
男：こんにちは。Walter Jenningsと申しますが、Garnerさんにお話があります。私は彼女の顧客なんですが。
女：申し訳ございませんが、Garnerは今、昼食に出ています。お急ぎなら彼女に電話しますが。
男：大丈夫です。彼女から依頼された、私の納税請求用の書類を届けに来ただけだったので。
女：あら、それでは彼女へのメモを書いて、書類と一緒に私にお渡しください。彼女にちゃんと渡しておきます。

50. Why is the man going to Montreal?
(A) To attend a conference
(B) To meet an investor
(C) To visit relatives
(D) To purchase merchandise

51. What does the man say will happen while he is away?
(A) An advertising campaign will be launched.
(B) A colleague will take care of his work.
(C) The company directors will meet.
(D) An order of products will arrive.

52. What type of company do the speakers most likely work for?
(A) Product development
(B) Event planning
(C) An advertising agency
(D) An airline

Questions 50-52 refer to the following conversation.

W: Warren, I heard you won't be in the firm next week. Where are you going?
M: Yes, all the company directors are going to the merchandising conference in Toronto on Monday and Tuesday. After that ❶I plan to visit my grandparents in Montreal for a few days. I haven't seen them for quite some time, so it will be nice to see them again.
W: That sounds great. ❷Who is going to be handling your clients while you're away?
M: ❸My assistant Leanne is going to take care of them. ❹She's worked with most of them on different advertising campaigns before, so I'm not worried about it.

設問50から52は次の会話に関する質問です。
女：Warren、あなたは来週出社しないと聞いたけど、どこに行くの？
男：あぁ、会社重役はみな、月曜日と火曜日にトロントの販売計画会議に行くんだ。そのあとで、私はモントリオールの祖父母を2、3日訪ねる予定でね。彼らにはしばらく会ってないから、また会えるといいなと思って。
女：それはいいわね。あなたが留守の間、誰が顧客対応するの？
男：アシスタントのLeanneが対応するよ。彼女は以前別の広告キャンペーンで顧客のほとんどと仕事をしているから、心配してないんだ。

設問の訳 ☞ p.28〜29参照

> **TOEIC豆知識** legal office は「法律事務所」のこと。law office、legal firm、legal office ともいう。

正解＆解説

47. 正解 (D) 難易度 難

Garner さんの居場所を尋ねている。キーワードである **Ms. Garner** に注意をしていると、❶に「Garner は今、昼食に出ている」とある。つまり **lunch break**（昼休み）中ということなので、(D) が正解。

48. 正解 (B) 難易度 難

男性が Garner さんに会いに来た理由を尋ねている。❷で男性は「彼女（＝ Garner さん）に**頼まれた書類を届けに来た**だけだ」と、来訪の目的を告げている。従って (B) To give her some documents（彼女に書類を渡すため）が正解。

49. 正解 (A) 難易度 難

女性が申し出ていることを尋ねているので、**女性の発言に注目**するとよい。女性は❸で「書類を私に預けて、**write her a note**（彼女にメモを書いて）。そうすれば、**彼女に必ず渡しておく**」と提案している。このことを Deliver a message（伝言を伝える）と表現した (A) が正解。

単語 □ unfortunately 残念ながら、あいにく □ at the moment ちょうど今 □ urgent 緊急の □ tax 税金、税 □ claim 要求、請求 **47** □ accounting 会計、経理 **48** □ document 文書、書類 □ inquire 尋ねる □ billing statement 請求書 **49** □ deliver ～を伝える、届ける

50. 正解 (C) 難易度 難

男性がモントリオールに行く理由を尋ねている。キーワード **Montreal** に意識を集中する。男性は❶で「**my grandparents in Montreal**（モントリオールの祖父母）を訪ねる」と言っている。これを「親戚を訪ねるため」と言い換えた (C) が正解。ただし、❶のまえに「重役はみなトロントの物品販売会議に行く」という発言もある。設問の内容を正確にとらえていないと、これにつられて (A) を選ぶことになるので要注意。

51. 正解 (B) 難易度 難

自分の留守中に何があると、**男性が言っている**のかを尋ねているので、**男性の発言に注目**。❷の女性の問い「留守中、誰があなたの顧客に対応するのか」に対し、男性は❸で「**アシスタントの Leanne が対応する**」と答えている。アシスタントの Leanne を colleague（同僚）と言い換えた (B) A colleague will take care of his work.（同僚が彼の仕事の対応をする）が正解。

52. 正解 (C) 難易度 難

話者2人の会社の種類を尋ねている。❹で男性が「彼女（＝ Leanne）は、**different advertising campaigns**（ほかの広告キャンペーン）で私の顧客と仕事をしたことがある」と述べている。選択肢のうち、「広告キャンペーンについて顧客と仕事をする」という仕事内容に合致する職種は、(C) の An advertising agency（広告代理店）。

単語 □ firm 会社 □ director 重役 □ merchandising 販売計画、販売促進戦略 □ quite かなり、なかなか □ handle ～に対処する □ take care of ～ ～を責任もって引き受ける **50** □ investor 投資家 □ relative 親戚 **51** □ launch ～を始める **52** □ development 開発、発達 □ advertising agency 広告代理店

TEST 3
PART 3

音声ファイル T3_P3_53-55 ▶ T3_P3_Q53-55 / T3_P3_56-58 ▶ T3_P3_Q56-58

問題文&訳

53. What does the woman want?
(A) Directions to a convention center
(B) Some new furniture
(C) Information about reservations
(D) Some flowers for an event

54. What does the man suggest?
(A) Creating the same kind of arrangements as before
(B) Checking out the event location
(C) Viewing the products at the shop
(D) Placing a larger order

55. What does the man offer to send the woman?
(A) A price quotation
(B) A coupon for a discount
(C) A schedule of events
(D) A list of items

56. What event does the man mention?
(A) A feedback session
(B) A conflict resolution meeting
(C) A workshop for personnel department staff
(D) A seminar for departmental directors

57. What does the man say will be discussed next week?
(A) Executive coaching
(B) Developing teamwork
(C) Evaluating workers
(D) Work productivity

58. What does the woman mention about the skills to be taught at the workshop?
(A) They are needed for building work relationships.
(B) They are helpful in improving customer service.
(C) They are important for solving personnel issues.
(D) They are required for employee promotions.

設問の訳 ☞ p.28〜29参照

Questions 53-55 refer to the following conversation.

W: Good morning. This is Patricia Cummings calling from Adelaide Convention Center. We are hosting a company banquet on November 16. ❶We would like to order some floral arrangements for the event.

M: That shouldn't be a problem. We've done this type of work for your company before. ❷Why don't we do the same types of centerpieces for the tables?

W: Yes, that would work. However, I would also like a large arrangement for the stage. How much will that cost?

M: It will depend on the size of the arrangement and types of flowers you request. ❸Why don't I e-mail you a list of our products and you can let me know what works best for you?

設問53から55は次の会話に関する質問です。
女：おはようございます。アデレード・コンベンションセンターのPatricia Cummings です。11月16日に会社の宴会を催すことになっています。その宴会用にフラワー・アレンジメントをいくつか注文したいのですが。
男：問題ございません。以前、御社向けにこのての仕事をしたことがあります。テーブルの中心に、以前と同じ花飾りを置くのはいかがでしょうか。
女：ええ、それでいいのですが、ステージにも大きなアレンジメントが欲しいですね。おいくらですか。
男：ご希望のアレンジメントの大きさと花の種類によります。弊社の製品リストをEメールでお送りするので、いちばん希望に合うものをご連絡いただく、というのはどうでしょうか。

Questions 56-58 refer to the following conversation.

M: Hi. I just came from the personnel manager's office and she told me that ❶there will be a workshop on effective communication for team leaders and department heads next week.

W: Really? That sounds very interesting. Do you know ❷what specific topics will be discussed?

M: She mentioned something about ❸understanding behavior, giving feedback, and relating well with employees. I think the invited speaker will also talk about ❹conflict resolution and facilitating teamwork.

W: Great! ❺We really need to develop those skills to interact and work effectively with our staff.

設問56から58は次の会話に関する質問です。
男：やあ、人事部長のオフィスから戻ったところだけど、来週チームリーダーと部門長のために、効果的コミュニケーションに関するワークショップがあると言っていたよ。
女：本当？ とてもおもしろそうね。具体的にどんな題目が議論されるか知ってる？
男：行動理解やフィードバックの与え方、従業員との関係強化などについてだと言っていたよ。ゲストスピーカーが問題解決やチームワーク促進についても話すみたい。
女：素晴らしい！ スタッフと効果的に付き合い、働くためには、確かにそうしたスキルを養う必要があるもの。

正解 & 解説

53. 正解 (D) 難易度：難
女性が望んでいるものを尋ねているので、**女性の発言内容に注目**。❶で「宴会用に floral arrangements（フラワー・アレンジメント）を注文したい」と要望を述べている。従って正解は、floral arrangements を flowers と言い換えた (D) Some flowers for an event（イベント用の花）。会話中に登場する convention center につられて、(A) を選ばないように。

54. 正解 (A) 難易度：難
男性が提案していることを尋ねているので、**男性の発言に注目**。男性は❷で「以前と同種の花飾りを置く」ことを提案している。このことを別の言葉で表現した (A) Creating the same kind of arrangements as before（以前と同種のアレンジメントを作る）が正解。提案の表現 Why don't we ～? を覚えておこう。

55. 正解 (D) 難易度：難
女性に対して、**男性が送ると申し出**ているものを尋ねている。**男性の発言に注目**。❸で男性は「list of our products（製品リスト）をメールしましょう」と申し出ている。従って、正解は (D) A list of items（商品のリスト）。

単語 □ host ～を主催する □ banquet 宴会、祝宴 □ floral arrangement フラワーアレンジメント □ centerpiece（テーブルの）中央に置く装飾品 □ work うまくいく □ depend on ～ ～によって決まる
53 □ direction 行き方、道順 **54** □ create ～を創造する、創作する **55** □ quotation 見積もり（額）

56. 正解 (D) 難易度：難
男性が話題にしているイベントについて尋ねているので、**男性の発言に注目**。❶に「team leaders（チームリーダー）と department heads（部門長）のための workshop（ワークショップ）がある」とある。workshop を seminar（セミナー）と言い換え、対象者を departmental directors（部門責任者）と表現した (D) が正解。workshop だけで (C) を選ばないこと。「人事部スタッフのための」が発言に一致していない。

57. 正解 (B) 難易度：難
男性が言っていることを尋ねているので、**男性の発言に注目**。来週のワークショップ（❶）について、女性が❷で「どのようなテーマが議論されるのか」と質問。答えとして男性は❸「行動理解」「フィードバックの与え方」「従業員との関係強化」、❹「問題解決」「チームワーク促進」を挙げている。このうち relating well with employees（従業員との関係強化）、facilitating teamwork（チームワーク促進）から、(B) が適切だとわかる。

58. 正解 (A) 難易度：難
ワークショップで学ぶスキルについて、**女性の言及内容を尋ねているので、女性の発言に集中**。❺で女性は「従業員と効果的に interact（交流する）と work（働く）ために、そうしたスキルが必要」と言っている。これを building work relationships（仕事上の関係を築く）ために必要と表現した (A) が正解。(B)「顧客サービス」、(C)「人事問題」、(D)「従業員の昇進」については、女性は何も言っていない。

単語 □ personnel 人事の □ effective 効果的な □ head（部局などの）長 □ specific 具体的な □ mention ～に言及する □ behavior 行動、態度 □ relate with ～ ～と関わる □ conflict 争い、紛争 □ resolution 解決 □ facilitate ～を促進する □ interact ～と交流する **56** □ departmental 部門の **57** □ evaluate ～を評価する □ productivity 生産性

TEST 3 PART 3

59. What does the woman want to do?
(A) Schedule an appointment
(B) Have landscaping work done
(C) Pick up a cost estimate
(D) Visit a project site

60. What is the problem?
(A) A landscape project is incomplete.
(B) The man is unable to locate the work site.
(C) An employee is currently unavailable.
(D) The woman is late for an appointment.

61. Why can't the woman return in half an hour?
(A) She has another engagement.
(B) She is late for a meeting.
(C) She is leaving town.
(D) She has to return to her office.

62. What are the speakers discussing?
(A) A computer factory
(B) A renovated office building
(C) A convention center
(D) A storage facility

63. According to the man, what is convenient about the building's location?
(A) It is in the country.
(B) It is near the subway station.
(C) It is by an industrial area.
(D) It is situated near the office.

64. Why is the man pleased?
(A) He won't have to travel so far to work.
(B) He will be able to place orders online.
(C) He will save time at work.
(D) He won't have to take public transportation.

Questions 59-61 refer to the following conversation.

W: Good morning. A friend of mine recommended your company for landscaping. I just moved into a new house and I'm interested in making a few changes to my yard.

M: I see. Unfortunately, our manager Austin Stevenson is meeting another client right now. He is the person that usually takes care of designs and price estimates. But if you come back in about 30 minutes, I'm sure he would be more than happy to sit down with you.

W: Thanks, but I have an appointment at that time. Will he be in after three?

M: Actually, he'll be out checking on one of our projects at Renton Park. Why don't you leave your name and number and I'll make sure he gets back to you sometime today?

設問59から61は次の会話に関する質問です。
女：おはようございます。友人が造園に関して御社を紹介してくれました。新居に引っ越したばかりで、庭に少し手を加えたいと思っているんです。
男：わかりました。申し訳ございませんが、部長のAustin Stevensonが今、ほかのお客さまと打ち合せ中です。通常、彼がデザインや費用見積もりを担当していまして。30分後にもう一度お越しいただければ、喜んでお話しさせていただきます。
女：ありがとうございます。ですが、その時間には約束があります。彼は3時以降はこちらにいらっしゃいますか。
男：実は、Renton公園でのプロジェクトを確認するため、外出していると思います。お名前と電話番号をお聞かせいただけませんか。そしたら、本日中に彼から連絡させます。

Questions 62-64 refer to the following conversation.

W: Have you been over to Silver Creek Road to see the company's new warehouse? I was there this afternoon, and it looks really great!

M: Yes, I heard that they had finished construction on it. I will have to go over there and check it out for myself. It's going to be much more convenient having it so close to the main office.

W: Absolutely. It's also located near the freeway, which makes transport of our merchandise a lot faster. And they've added a computerized inventory system which will help a lot.

M: I hadn't heard about that. That is good news as it will save us a lot of time here in the accounting department.

設問62から64は次の会話に関する質問です。
女：Silver Creek Roadまで、会社の新倉庫を見に行きましたか？ きょうの午後行ってきたけど、すごく立派だったわ。
男：うん、建設が完了したとは聞いていたよ。自分で行って、確かめなくちゃね。本社に近くなったから、ずいぶん便利になるだろうね。
女：ほんとそうね。高速道路にも近いから製品をより速く輸送できるし。それに、コンピュータ化した在庫システムを導入したからとても助かるね。
男：それは聞いてなかったな。この経理部にとっては、多くの時間節約になるだろうからよい知らせだね。

設問の訳 ☞ p.28〜29参照

TOEIC豆知識 TOEICの世界では、オフィスのrelocationやrenovationがしょっちゅう行われている。案外、せっかちな性格の人が多いらしい。（続く▶）

正解＆解説

59. 正解 (B) 難易度 ■■□ 難

女性が望んでいることが何なのかを尋ねている。❶に「庭に手を加えたいと思っている」とあるので、正解は (B) Have landscaping work done（造園作業をしてもらう）。〈have A ＋過去分詞〉の形で「Aを～してもらう」という意味。

60. 正解 (C) 難易度 ■■□ 難

会話中の問題点を尋ねている。**ネガティブな内容を集中的に**聞き取ろう。❷で男性が「残念ながら、部長が今、接客中だ」と述べ、**女性に対応する従業員の手が空いていない**ことを伝えている。従って、(C) An employee is currently unavailable. が正解。女性は、appointment（約束）があるとは言っているが、それに遅れているとは言っていないので (D) は誤り。

61. 正解 (A) 難易度 ■■■ 難

女性が30分後に戻って来られない理由を尋ねている。まず、男性が❸で「30 minutes（30分）後に戻って来れば」、部長が対応できると提案をしている。これに対し、女性は❹で「その時間には、appointment（約束）がある」と理由を述べて、戻って来られない旨を伝えている。従って正解は (A) She has another engagement.（彼女は別の予定がある）。appointment を engagement と言い換えている。

単語 □ recommend ～を推薦する □ landscape 造園する □ yard 家の庭、裏庭 □ estimate 見積もり（額） □ sit down with ～ ～とじっくり話し合う □ get back to ～ ～にあとで連絡する **60** □ incomplete 未完成の □ locate（場所）を突き止める □ site 場所、現場 □ currently 現在は □ unavailable 手がふさがっている **61** □ engagement 約束、用事

62. 正解 (D) 難易度 ■■□ 難

会話のテーマを尋ねている。主題に関わる設問は、**冒頭を注意深く**聞こう。❶で女性が「会社の new warehouse（新倉庫）に行ったことがあるか」と尋ね、以降、この**倉庫**についての話が続いていく。従って、正解は「倉庫」を別の言葉に言い換えた (D) A storage facility が正解。

63. 正解 (D) 難易度 ■■■ 難

建物（＝新倉庫）の立地の利点を尋ねている。According to the man（男性によると）とあるので、**男性の発言に注目**する。❷で男性は「**それ（＝新倉庫）が本社の近くにあって、便利になるだろう**」と言っている。これを It is situated near the office.（会社の近くにある）と表現した (D) が正解。

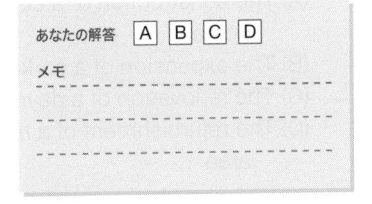

64. 正解 (C) 難易度 ■■■ 難

男性が喜んでいる理由を尋ねている。男性は❸でまず、That is good news（よい知らせだ）と喜びを示し、あとに「**経理部にとって時間節約になるから**」と理由を続けている。ポイントは here in the accounting department 部分。here があることで「この経理部」、つまり「**男性が所属する経理部**」という意味になり、**男性にとっても時間を節約できる**ことになる。従って、(C)「彼は仕事で時間を節約する」が正解。

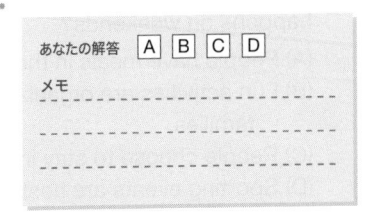

単語 □ construction 建設 □ for oneself 独力で、自分で □ convenient 便利な □ absolutely（返事として）そうだとも、まったくその通り □ transport 輸送 □ inventory 在庫 **62** □ renovate ～を改装する □ storage 保管、格納 **63** □ industrial 産業の、工業の □ situate ～を置く、位置づける

25

TEST 3 PART 3

65. Where does the man most likely work?
 (A) At a gift shop
 (B) At a recording studio
 (C) At a music store
 (D) At a print shop

66. What is the woman looking for?
 (A) A book for a friend
 (B) Some tickets to a concert
 (C) A gift for her daughter
 (D) Some information about a performer

67. What does the man offer to do for the woman?
 (A) Contact her when an item is available
 (B) Call another branch
 (C) Make a copy
 (D) Show other merchandise

68. What is the main subject of the show?
 (A) The new leader of an organization
 (B) The achievements of a local group
 (C) The launch of an association
 (D) The plans for a restoration project

69. What project has the woman recently worked on?
 (A) The construction of a community center
 (B) The expansion of a parking site
 (C) The renovation of a daycare center
 (D) The refurbishment of a recreational area

70. According to Ms. Fontana, what happens on weekends?
 (A) People have meals in the park.
 (B) Fun activities are organized for families.
 (C) People choose to stay indoors.
 (D) Sporting events are hosted by the association.

Questions 65-67 refer to the following conversation.

W: Excuse me, ❶I'm looking for a CD that one of my friends recommended. ❷I want to buy it for my daughter's graduation next weekend. It's a female singer who is very popular these days, but I cannot remember her name!

M: Do you happen to know the title of the album?

W: Sorry, I don't. The only thing I can remember is that she sings a song called "A Romantic Feeling".

M: Ah, yes. That would be Christina Lambert. She is very popular these days. But actually, ❸we sold out of all the copies of her newest CD just yesterday. However, we're expecting more to arrive tomorrow. ❹If you'd like, I can reserve a copy for you and call you when it arrives.

設問65から67は次の会話に関する質問です。
女：すみません、友人の1人が薦めてくれたCDを探しています。来週の娘の卒業祝いに買いたいのです。最近人気の女性歌手なんですが、名前を思い出せなくて。
男：アルバムタイトルはご存じじゃありませんか
女：すみません、わからなくて。覚えているのは、A Romantic Feelingという歌をうたっているということだけです。
男：ああ、わかりました。Christina Lambertでしょう。彼女は最近とても人気がありますから。しかし、実はきのうちょうど最新CDが完売したところなんです。ただ明日さらに入荷予定です。よろしければ、1枚予約をしておき、入荷したらお電話します。

Questions 68-70 refer to the following conversation.

M: Thank you for joining us here at the People Show today, Ms. Fontana. ❶Your association has done a great job in restoring the children's playground in our community. What inspired you to do this project?

W: As a child, I always went to the playground. I did many fun things such as riding the swings or playing sports. Nowadays, children spend too much time in front of the TV or the computer. I thought of rebuilding the playground in a way that was attractive to children so that they would want to play more outside.

M: Well, it looks like parents were really happy about this development. Now they don't have to worry about their children spending too much time indoors.

W: Yes, ever since we restored the playground, ❷a lot of families hold picnics there every weekend. We also put tables and installed portable restrooms for their convenience.

設問68から70は次の会話に関する質問です。
男：Fontanaさん、きょうはPeople Showにお越しいただきありがとうございます。あなたの団体は、私たちの地域の児童公園を修復するのにたいへん貢献されていますね。この計画を行うのにどんな動機があったのですか。
女：私は子供のころ、いつも公園へ行っていました。ブランコに乗ったり、スポーツをしたり、たくさん楽しみました。最近の子供たちは、テレビやコンピュータの前であまりに多くの時間を過ごします。だから、彼らがもっと外で遊びたくなるように、子供にとって魅力的な公園に造り直そうと考えたんです。
男：この開発に親御さんたちはたいへん喜んでいるようですよ。これで、子供たちが屋内で長時間過ごすことを心配せずに済むんですから。
女：ええ、公園を修復して以来、毎週末、多くの家族がピクニックにやって来ます。私たちはさらに、彼らの利便性のために、テーブルを置き、簡易トイレも設置しました。

設問の訳 ☞ p.28～29参照

TOEIC豆知識 relocation は「移転、移住」／ renovation は「改築、リフォーム」という意味。

正解＆解説

65. 正解 (C) 難易度 ■■■□□ 難

男性の職場を尋ねている。❶で女性が男性に「**CDを探している**」と言っていることから、あたりをつけられる。加えて、❸で男性が「彼女の最新CDが売り切れた」と言っていることからも、(C) At a music store（音楽ストアで）が正解とわかる。

66. 正解 (C) 難易度 ■■■□□ 難

女性が探しているものを尋ねている。女性は❶で「CDを探している」と言ったあと、❷で「**娘の卒業祝いのために買いたい**」と続けている。よって、正解は A gift for her daughter（娘への贈り物）の (C)。

67. 正解 (A) 難易度 ■■■□□ 難

女性のために、**男性が申し出**ていることを尋ねているので、**男性の発言に意識を集中**しよう。❹で「予約をしておき、**入荷したら電話しましょう**」と、男性は提案している。これを Contact her when an item is available（商品が入荷したら彼女に連絡する）と表現した (A) が正解。

単語 □ graduation 卒業　□ female 女性の　□ sell out of ～ ～を売り切ってしまう　□ copy（本、レコードなどの）1部、1冊
66 □ performer 演奏者　**67** □ contact ～に連絡する

68. 正解 (B) 難易度 ■■■■□ 難

このショーのテーマを尋ねている。主題に関わる設問なので、**冒頭を集中的に聞き取ろう**。男性は番組名を紹介したあと、❶で「Your association（あなたの団体）は our community（私たちの地域）の児童公園修復に貢献している」と述べ、以降、この話題が続く。これを「地域団体の功績」と表現した (B) The achievements of a local group が正解。

69. 正解 (D) 難易度 ■■■■□ 難

女性が行った仕事内容を尋ねている。❶で男性が女性に対し「あなたの団体は、**restoring the children's playground**（児童公園の修復）に貢献している」と言っている。これを The refurbishment of a recreational area（レクリエーションエリアの修復）と言い換えた (D) が正解。

70. 正解 (A) 難易度 ■■■■□ 難

週末に起こることを尋ねている。According to Ms. Fontana（Fontana さんによると）とあるので、**女性の発言を集中的に聞き取る**。女性は❷で「**毎週末、多くの家族がそこで（＝児童公園で）ピクニックをしている**」と発言。従って、ピクニックを「ご飯を食べる」と言い換えた (A) People have meals in the park.（人々は公園でご飯を食べる）が正解。

単語 □ restore ～を修復する　□ playground 遊び場、運動場　□ inspire ～を動機付ける　□ nowadays 近ごろは　□ rebuild ～を再建する　□ install ～を取り付ける、設置する　**68** □ achievement 業績、功績　□ restoration 修復
69 □ expansion 拡張　□ renovation 改装、修復　□ refurbishment 改修

TEST 3 PART 3

設問の訳

41. 女性の仕事はおそらく何か。
    - (A) 旅行代理店員
    - (B) レストランの従業員
    - (C) ホテルのフロント係
    - (D) ツアーガイド

42. 何が問題なのか。
    - (A) チケットが売り切れている。
    - (B) 施設は予約でいっぱいだ。
    - (C) 空いているテーブルがない。
    - (D) ツアーがキャンセルになった。

43. 女性は何を提案しているのか。
    - (A) 別の施設をあたってみること
    - (B) 月曜日の予約をすること
    - (C) 旅行を遅らせること
    - (D) 事前に部屋を予約すること

44. 男性はなぜ電話しているのか。
    - (A) 彼は会議に登録しなければならない。
    - (B) 彼は予約を取り消さなければならない。
    - (C) 彼は処方箋をもらいたい。
    - (D) 彼は医師に診てもらう必要がある。

45. 女性は男性に何をすることを提案しているか。
    - (A) 近所の薬局を訪れる
    - (B) 申込用紙に記入する
    - (C) 別の日に来る
    - (D) 彼のスケジュールを確認する

46. 男性はおそらく何をするのか。
    - (A) 保険の契約をする
    - (B) 別の医者に会う
    - (C) 病院での会議に出席する
    - (D) 薬局で薬を買う

47. Garnerさんはどこにいるか。
    - (A) 顧客との会議
    - (B) 会計セミナー
    - (C) 休暇中
    - (D) 昼休み中

48. 男性はなぜGarnerさんに会いたいのか。
    - (A) 納税について話し合うため
    - (B) 彼女に書類を渡すため
    - (C) 請求書について問い合わせるため
    - (D) 仕事の予定について話すため

49. 女性は何をしようと申し出ているか。
    - (A) 伝言を伝える
    - (B) 書類をコピーする
    - (C) Garnerさんの昼食を注文する
    - (D) 会議の予定を決める

50. 男性はなぜモントリオールに行くのか。
    - (A) 会議に出席するため
    - (B) 投資家に会うため
    - (C) 親戚を訪ねるため
    - (D) 商品を購入するため

51. 男性は留守中、何があると言っているか。
    - (A) 広告キャンペーンが始まる。
    - (B) 同僚が彼の仕事の対応をする。
    - (C) 会社重役が集まる。
    - (D) 注文の品が届く。

52. 話者たちはおそらくどんな種類の会社で働いているか。
    - (A) 商品開発
    - (B) イベント企画
    - (C) 広告代理店
    - (D) 航空会社

53. 女性は何を望んでいるのか。
    - (A) コンベンションセンターへの行き方
    - (B) 新しい家具
    - (C) 予約情報
    - (D) イベント用の花

54. 男性は何を提案しているか。
    - (A) 以前と同種のアレンジメントを作る
    - (B) イベントの場所を確認する
    - (C) 店で商品を見る
    - (D) 大口注文をする

55. 男性は女性に何を送ると申し出ているか。
    - (A) 価格見積もり
    - (B) 割引クーポン
    - (C) イベントの日程
    - (D) 商品のリスト

設問の訳

56. 男性はどんな行事について言及しているか。
    - (A) 意見交換の集まり
    - (B) 問題解決の会議
    - (C) 人事部スタッフのためのワークショップ
    - (D) 部門責任者のためのセミナー

57. 男性は来週何が議論されると言っているか。
    - (A) 重役向けのコーチング
    - (B) チームワークの育成
    - (C) 従業員の評価
    - (D) 作業生産性

58. 女性はワークショップで教わるスキルについて何と述べているか。
    - (A) 仕事上の関係を築くために必要である。
    - (B) 顧客サービスの改善に役立つ。
    - (C) 人事問題の解決に重要である。
    - (D) 従業員の昇進に必須である。

59. 女性は何をしたいのか。
    - (A) 予約を入れる
    - (B) 造園作業をしてもらう
    - (C) 費用見積もりを受け取る
    - (D) 計画用地を訪れる

60. 何が問題なのか。
    - (A) 造園計画が未完成である。
    - (B) 男性は作業現場を見つけられない。
    - (C) 従業員が現在、手が空いていない。
    - (D) 女性は約束に遅れている。

61. 女性はなぜ30分後に戻って来られないのか。
    - (A) 彼女は別の予定がある。
    - (B) 彼女は会議に遅れる。
    - (C) 彼女は町を出る。
    - (D) 彼女は自分の会社に戻らなければならない。

62. 話者たちは何を話し合っているか。
    - (A) コンピュータ工場
    - (B) 改築された社屋
    - (C) コンベンションセンター
    - (D) 倉庫

63. 男性によると、建物の場所について何が便利か。
    - (A) 田舎にある。
    - (B) 地下鉄駅に近い。
    - (C) 工業地帯のそばにある。
    - (D) 会社の近くにある。

64. なぜ男性は喜んでいるのか。
    - (A) 彼は仕事で遠くに行く必要がない。
    - (B) 彼はオンラインで発注できる。
    - (C) 彼は仕事で時間を節約する。
    - (D) 彼は公共交通機関を使わなくてよい。

65. 男性はおそらくどこで働いているか。
    - (A) お土産店で
    - (B) 録音スタジオで
    - (C) 音楽ストアで
    - (D) 印刷所で

66. 女性は何を探しているか。
    - (A) 友人への本
    - (B) コンサートチケット
    - (C) 娘への贈り物
    - (D) 演奏者の情報

67. 男性は女性のために何をすると申し出ているか。
    - (A) 商品が入荷したら彼女に連絡する
    - (B) 別の支店に電話する
    - (C) コピーする
    - (D) ほかの商品を見せる

68. このショーの主題は何か。
    - (A) 組織の新リーダー
    - (B) 地域団体の功績
    - (C) 協会の設立
    - (D) 修復プロジェクトの計画

69. 女性は最近どんなプロジェクトを手がけたか。
    - (A) 地域センターの建設
    - (B) 駐車場の拡張
    - (C) 託児所の改修
    - (D) レクリエーションエリアの修復

70. Fontanaさんによると、週末に何が起こるのか。
    - (A) 人々は公園でご飯を食べる。
    - (B) 楽しい活動が家族のために計画される。
    - (C) 人々は屋内にいることを選ぶ。
    - (D) スポーツイベントが団体によって催される。

TEST 3 PART 4

71. What is the purpose of the announcement?
 (A) To give information about airport services
 (B) To notify people about a departure change
 (C) To direct passengers to another gate
 (D) To advise travelers to be careful

72. What problem is mentioned?
 (A) The airport in Madrid has not yet reopened.
 (B) The city has bad weather conditions.
 (C) The area has heavy air traffic.
 (D) The aircraft has mechanical problems.

73. What are passengers asked to do?
 (A) Call a travel agent
 (B) Wait at the terminal
 (C) Take other flights
 (D) Request a refund

74. Where does the caller work?
 (A) At an island resort
 (B) In a bridal store
 (C) In a party supply company
 (D) At a flower shop

75. According to the speaker, what is the problem?
 (A) A product is unavailable.
 (B) A price quote is incorrect.
 (C) A shipment has been delayed.
 (D) A purchase was damaged.

76. What does the speaker want to know from Ms. Johnson?
 (A) Which type of product she prefers
 (B) How much she'd like to pay for shipping
 (C) Where to deliver an item
 (D) What her credit card number is

Questions 71-73 refer to the following announcement.

Attention all passengers bound for Madrid, Spain. TurboAir flight OG 809, which was scheduled to depart at 9:15 tonight, has been cancelled due to some engine trouble. We therefore advise passengers to please proceed to the airline's customer service desk near the boarding gate to make arrangements for a later flight. We are sorry for the inconvenience. Once again, TurboAir flight OG 809 to Madrid has been cancelled.

設問71から73は次のアナウンスに関する質問です。

スペイン、マドリード行きのお客さまにご案内いたします。TurboAir OG809便は今夜9時15分に出発の予定でしたが、エンジントラブルにより欠航になりました。これにより、当便をご利用のお客さまは、搭乗口近くの当航空会社のお客さまサービスデスクまでお進みになり、後発便の手続きをお願い申し上げます。ご不便をおかけし、たいへん申し訳ございません。くり返しご案内いたします、マドリード行き TurboAir OG809便は欠航になりました。

Questions 74-76 refer to the following telephone message.

Good afternoon. This is Leila Kamalo from Waikiki Florists calling for Linda Johnson. I wanted to speak to you about the items you requested for your company reception scheduled for Thursday. You asked for two large arrangements of yellow roses. Unfortunately, my supplier just called and informed me that the cost of yellow roses is much higher than I quoted, as they have to be sent by air. The price per bouquet would be $270 and not the $180 I previously quoted. If the cost is too high, I would suggest using yellow orchids, as they are much cheaper. Please contact me as soon as possible and let me know what you would like to do. Thanks!

設問74から76は次の留守電メッセージに関する質問です。

こんにちは。私は Waikiki 花店の Leila Kamalo と申しますが、Linda Johnson さんにお電話しております。木曜に予定されている御社の祝賀会用にご要望いただきました品について、お話ししたかったのです。黄色いバラのアレンジメントの大をふたつご希望でした。申し訳ございませんが、供給業者からたった今電話があり、航空便で配達しなければならないため、黄色のバラの価格は、私の見積もり額よりもずっと高額になると知らされました。ブーケの価格はひとつにつき、私が以前お伝えした180ドルではなく、270ドルになります。もしこの価格が高すぎるようであれば、黄色のランがより安価なのでお勧めいたします。できるだけ早くご連絡いただき、ご希望をお知らせください。ありがとうございます。

設問の訳 ☞ p.40〜41参照

TOEIC豆知識 TOEICには「著名な」人物や企業や、なんやかやが登場するが、この「著名な、有名な」を表す単語はバリエーション豊か。もっとも有名なのはfamousだが、ほかにも思いつくものを挙げてみる。(続く▶)

正解＆解説

71. 正解 (B) 難易度■■□□□ 難

このアナウンスの目的を尋ねている。このように**主題に関わる設問では、ヒントは冒頭にくる**ことが多い。出だしに意識を集中しよう。❶で、スペイン、マドリード行きの乗客の注意を喚起。続けて❷で「9時15分出発予定の便が、エンジントラブルにより欠航になった」と言っている。このことから**「出発の変更を人々に知らせる」**アナウンスだとわかるので、(B) To notify people about a departure change が正解。

72. 正解 (D) 難易度■■□□□ 難

アナウンスで触れられる問題点を尋ねている。**ネガティブな要素を重点的に聞き取ろう**。❷で「**engine trouble**（エンジントラブル）のせいで欠航になった」という問題を伝えている。engine trouble を mechanical problems（機械的な問題）と言い換えている (D) The aircraft has mechanical problems.（飛行機に機械的な問題がある）が正解。

73. 正解 (C) 難易度■■■□□ 難

アナウンスが乗客に求めている行動を尋ねている。❸の We therefore advise passengers to ... make arrangements for a later flight. 部分で、**後発便への振り替え手続**を勧めている。これを「別の便に乗る」と言い換えた (C) Take other flights が正解。make arrangements for ～は「～の手配をする」という意味。

単語 □ bound for ～　～行きの　□ depart 出発する　□ due to ～　～のせいで　□ proceed 進む、向かう　□ boarding gate 搭乗口　□ inconvenience 不便、迷惑　**71** □ notify ～に知らせる　□ direct ～に道を教える　**72** □ aircraft 飛行機　**73** □ refund 払い戻し

74. 正解 (D) 難易度■□□□□ 難

話者の職場を尋ねている。❶で This is Leila Kamalo **from Waikiki Florists**（ワイキキ花店の Leila Kamalo です）と、名乗っていることから、女性は**「花屋」**で働いているとわかる。よって、(D) At a flower shop が正解。ただ、ここを聞き逃しても、以降、花の注文に関する内容が続くので、答えを導き出すことは可能。

75. 正解 (B) 難易度■■□□□ 難

メッセージ中で触れられる問題点を尋ねているので、**ネガティブな要素に注目する**。❷で「黄色いバラの価格が、**見積もった額よりもかなり高くなってしまう**」と問題点を伝えている。これを「見積価格が間違っている」と表現した (B) A price quote is incorrect. が正解。❷が、Unfortunately（残念ながら）で始まっている点に気づきたい。これは、ネガティブな内容を導く表現なので、問題点を尋ねる設問のヒントになる。

76. 正解 (A) 難易度■■■□□ 難

話し手が Johnson さんに求めていることを尋ねている。まず❶で、このメッセージが Linda Johnson 向けであることを把握。❷で黄色いバラが見積りより高くなることを伝え、❸で代替として、安価な黄色いランを提案している。そして最後、❹で Johnson さんに「何を使いたいか知らせてほしい」と依頼している。つまり、バラとラン**「どちらの商品を好むか」**を知りたい、ということなので (A) が正解。

単語 □ reception 宴会、祝賀会　□ supplier 仕入れ先、供給業者　□ inform ～に知らせる　□ quote ～を見積もる　□ by air 航空便で　□ bouquet ブーケ、(手に持つ)花束　□ orchid ラン　**74** □ supply 供給(品)　**75** □ shipment 配送、輸送

TEST 3 PART 4

77. Who is Ellen Rossi?
    (A) A graphic designer
    (B) A professional artist
    (C) A language instructor
    (D) A software developer

78. What does the speaker say about the computer program?
    (A) It has features that are difficult to use.
    (B) It will be useful for professional designers.
    (C) It is recently developed software.
    (D) It is available for purchase on a Web site.

79. What will the listeners do this afternoon?
    (A) View a brief demonstration
    (B) Learn how to manage their time
    (C) Experience a product first-hand
    (D) Submit samples of their work

80. When is the report being broadcast?
    (A) In the morning
    (B) At noon
    (C) In the afternoon
    (D) At night

81. What is causing the traffic problems?
    (A) A bridge has been closed for repairs.
    (B) A construction crew is occupying several lanes.
    (C) Some vehicles are slowing down the flow of traffic.
    (D) A snowstorm has severely restricted visibility.

82. What will listeners hear next?
    (A) A weather forecast
    (B) An advertisement
    (C) A talk show
    (D) A news report

Questions 77-79 refer to the following talk.

Thanks for coming this morning to our workshop. ❶My name is Ellen Rossi and I will be your trainer. ❷I am one of the creators of Teepee Illustrator, the software we will be learning about today. Throughout the development of this program, we worked closely with ❸visual designers like you, so we have come to understand the work challenges you face on a daily basis and are confident ❹you will find this program extremely easy and helpful to use. This morning we will explore all of the features and functions of Teepee Illustrator. ❺Then, this afternoon, each of you will have the opportunity for some hands-on training in the computer lab. If you have questions, please feel free to ask me at any time.

設問77から79は次の話に関する質問です。

今朝は私たちのワークショップにお越しいただき、ありがとうございます。私はEllen Rossiと言いまして、みなさんのトレーナーを務めます。私はTeepee Illustrator、つまり、本日みなさんが学習するソフトウェアの開発者の1人です。このプログラムの開発期間を通して、みなさんのようなビジュアル・デザイナーの方々と密接に連携しました。そのため、みなさんが日々直面している業務上の課題がわかり、この新しいプログラムを非常に簡単で便利だと感じていただけると確信しています。午前中は、Teepee Illustratorの特徴と機能のすべてを探っていきます。それから午後は、コンピュータ室において、各自が実際に操作しながら学ぶ機会を設けます。質問がございましたら、遠慮なくいつでもお尋ねください。

Questions 80-82 refer to the following radio broadcast.

❶This is W-NOW radio with your morning traffic report. Winter is officially here with more than 25 centimeters of snow falling overnight. ❷Plows from the transport authority are busy trying to clear the city's main roads, which is causing some delays in the downtown area. Commuters are urged to slow down to 30 kilometers per hour when passing the plows and work crews. Also, please be reminded that Loughton Bridge will be closed for repair for the rest of this month. ❸Stay tuned for regional news with Sylvia Miller, coming up next.

設問80から82は次のラジオ放送に関する質問です。

W-NOWラジオが朝の交通情報をお届けします。ひと晩で雪が25センチ以上積もり、冬が本格的に到来しました。交通局の除雪車が街の主要道路の除雪作業に追われているため、中心部では遅延も起きています。通勤される方には、除雪車と除雪作業員を追い越す際に時速30キロの速度規制が課せられます。また、Loughton橋は補修のため今月いっぱい閉鎖されていることも気に留めておいてください。次はSylvia Millerの地域ニュースです、チャンネルはそのままで。

設問の訳 ☞ p.40~41参照

TOEIC豆知識 《「著名な、有名な」のバリエーション》 renowned / well-known / prominent / acclaimed などがある。

正解＆解説

77. 正解 (D) 難易度
Ellen Rossi の職業を尋ねている。まず❶で「話者＝Ellen Rossi」であることを把握。❷で「私は Teepee Illustrator というソフトウェアの creators（創作者）の1人」と言っている。つまり「**ソフトウェアの開発者**」ということなので、(D) A software developer が正解。❶のあとに「トレーナーを務める」とも言っているが、これはあくまでこのワークショップにおける役割であり、本職ではない。

78. 正解 (B) 難易度
話し手が Teepee Illustrator について言っていることを尋ねている。❸に「みなさんのようなビジュアル・デザイナー」とあるので、聞き手がデザイナーだとまずわかる。次に❹で「みなさん（＝デザイナー）は、このプログラムを簡単で便利だと感じるだろう」と言っている。つまり、「**プロのデザイナーにとって便利である**」ということで、正解は (B)。

79. 正解 (C) 難易度
聞き手が午後にすることを尋ねている。設問にある時の表現 this afternoon を待ち伏せながら、音声を聞こう。すると❺に「this afternoon に、**hands-on training（実地訓練）の機会がある**」とある。実地訓練とは、ここではソフトウェアを実際に操作しながら学ぶことを指すので、Experience a product first-hand（製品をじかに体験する）と言い換えた (C) が正解。

単語 □ closely 密接に、綿密に　□ face（問題など）に直面する　□ on a daily basis 日々、日常的に　□ confident 自信がある　□ extremely たいへん　□ feature 特徴、機能　□ hands-on 実際的な、実地の　**77** □ developer 開発者　**78** □ recently 最近は　**79** □ brief 簡潔な　□ first-hand じかに　□ submit 〜を提出する

80. 正解 (A) 難易度
この交通情報がいつ放送されるのかを尋ねている。❶で morning traffic report とはっきり言っているので、(A) が正解。

81. 正解 (C) 難易度
交通問題の要因を尋ねている。❷で「**Plows が除雪を行っており、遅延を引き起こしている**」と言っている。これを「交通の流れを遅らせている車両がある」と言い換えた (C) が正解。plows の意味（除雪車）を知っているだけでなく、vehicles と言い換えられていることにも気づく必要がある。

82. 正解 (D) 難易度
この放送のあとに続く番組を尋ねている。未来のことを尋ねる設問では、**放送の終盤部分に注目しよう**。そこにヒントがくるケースが非常に多い。ここでも、最後の❸で「**次は regional news（地域ニュース）だ**」と言っている。従って、正解は (D) A news report（ニュース報道）。

単語 □ plow 除雪機、すき　□ authority 当局、公共事業機関　□ commuter 通勤者　□ be urged to do 〜するよう強く促される　□ pass 〜を追い越す　□ remind 〜に気付かせる、念を押す　□ regional 地域の　**81** □ occupy 〜を占める、ふさぐ　□ vehicle 車、乗り物　□ flow 流れ　□ severely きびしく、ひどく　□ restrict 〜を制限する、限定する

TEST 3 PART 4

83. What field does Ms. Stevens work in?
 (A) Interior decoration
 (B) Construction management
 (C) Event planning
 (D) Landscaping design

84. What does Ms. Stevens recommend?
 (A) Including a seating area
 (B) Holding the event in a park
 (C) Adding a walkway to the plan
 (D) Installing a water fountain

85. What does Ms. Stevens ask Mr. Carranza to do?
 (A) Return a phone call
 (B) Decide on a meeting place
 (C) Look over a planned budget
 (D) Start working on a project

Questions 83-85 refer to the following telephone message.

Good Afternoon. ❶This is Gwendolyn Stevens from Horizon Landscaping calling for Paul Carranza. We've come up with several proposals for the design of your building's courtyard. I am considering using a Japanese-inspired design that will include a man-made stream. ❷I also suggest including a pathway that leads to the existing picnic tables and seating areas. I have some sketches of different designs that my office has put together. ❸Could you call me back and let me know what would be a good time for us to meet and go through the proposals? Thank you for this opportunity, and I look forward to getting started.

設問83から85は次の留守電メッセージに関する質問です。
　こんにちは。Horizon造園のGwendolyn StevensですがPaul Carranzaさんにお電話しています。御社屋の中庭デザインについて、提案をいくつか用意しました。人工の小川を備えた、日本風デザインの採用を考えています。また、既存のピクニックテーブルと座席エリアに続く小道も設けてはいかがでしょうか。当事務所がまとめた異なるデザインラフが数点ございます。折り返しご連絡いただき、この提案について、会って検討するのに都合のよいお時間をお知らせください。このような機会をくださり、ありがとうございます。着工できるのを楽しみにしております。

86. Why has there been a change?
 (A) A speaker has announced his resignation.
 (B) A discussion has been extended.
 (C) A lecturer has fallen ill.
 (D) A holiday has been declared.

87. What will Ms. Armstrong speak about?
 (A) Developing economies
 (B) World trade agreements
 (C) Global recession
 (D) Departmental news

88. When will Mr. Cornelius most likely give his talk?
 (A) In a few minutes
 (B) Later that afternoon
 (C) The following morning
 (D) At the next seminar

Questions 86-88 refer to the following announcement.

Good morning everyone. My name is Sandra Park, dean of the school of business here at Langdon University. I hope you've found our conference useful and informative so far. I have a few announcements regarding today's schedule. ❶Robert Cornelius, who was scheduled to speak on developing economies this afternoon, called in sick and will not be able to make his presentation at 2 o'clock as expected. So ❷Sara Armstrong, professor of economics here at the university, will speak about world trade agreements instead. ❸Mr. Cornelius hopes he will feel well enough to make his presentation tomorrow at 11 A.M. We will keep you updated. In a few minutes, at 9 o'clock, we can begin with our scheduled panel discussion on global recession.

設問86から88は次のアナウンスに関する質問です。
　みなさん、おはようございます。私はここLangdon大学経営学部の学部長、Sandra Parkです。ここまでで、当会議が有益で参考になるものだと感じていただければ幸いです。本日の日程に関してご案内します。きょうの午後に発展途上経済について講演予定だったRobert Cornelius氏から病欠との連絡があり、予定されていた2時の講演を行なえなくなりました。ですので、代わりに当大学の経済学部教授、Sara Armstrongが世界の通商協定についてお話します。Cornelius氏は、明日の午前11時には発表できるくらいには回復するだろうとのことです。最新情報は随時お知らせします。数分後の9時から、予定されております世界不況についてのパネルディスカッションを開始します。

設問の訳 ☞ p.40～41参照

83. 正解 (D)

Stevens さんの仕事の分野を尋ねている。❶で「Horizon 造園の Gwendolyn Stevens です」と名乗っていることから、「Stevens さん＝話し手」であることを把握。つまり、設問は話し手の仕事を尋ねているわけだが、「Horizon 造園」という社名から、(D) の「造園デザイン」が正解とわかる。

84. 正解 (C)

Stevens さん（＝話し手）の提案内容を尋ねている。❷で「既存のピクニックテーブルと座席エリアへの **pathway（小道）を含める**」ことを提案。pathway を walkway と言い換えた (C)「設計に小道を追加すること」が正解。(A) の「座席エリア」は、❷に existing（既存）とあるので、いま現在すでに存在しているもの。提案は、そこに続く小道を造ろうということで、座席エリアを設けようとは言っていない。

85. 正解 (A)

Stevens さんの Carranza 氏に対する依頼内容を尋ねている。まず❶で「Stevens さん＝話し手」、「Carranza 氏＝聞き手」という関係を把握。Stevens さんは、❸で「**折り返し電話してほしい**」と依頼しているので、(A) が正解。

単語 □ come up with ～ ～を思い付く　□ proposal 案、提案　□ consider ～を検討する　□ put together ～をまとめる　□ go through ～ ～をくまなく調べる　□ opportunity 機会　□ get started 始める　**83** □ work in ～ ～で働く　**84** □ hold ～を開催する　□ water fountain 噴水　**85** □ look over ～ ～に目を通す　□ budget 予算

86. 正解 (C)

変更があった理由を尋ねている。❶で「**Cornelius 氏が called in sick（病欠の連絡をした）**」という理由で、「2時の講演を行なえなくなった」という変更を伝えている。従って、変更の理由としては、(C) A lecturer has fallen ill.（講演者が体調を崩した）が正解。

87. 正解 (B)

Armstrong さんの講演テーマを尋ねている。❷で「代わりに、Sara Armstrong が **world trade agreements（世界の通商協定）について話す**」と言っている。正解は、そのままの選択肢 (B)。

88. 正解 (C)

Cornelius 氏が講演するだろう日時を尋ねている。本日の講演を病気でキャンセルした Cornelius 氏だが、❸で「**明日の午前11時には、発表できるくらいに回復することを見込んでいる**」と言っている。ここから、(C) The following morning（次の日の午前）に講演するだろうと推測できる。

単語 □ dean 学部長　□ informative 有益な　□ so far これまでは　□ regarding ～に関して　□ call in sick 病気で休むと電話する　□ economics 経済学　□ trade agreement 通商協定　□ update ～に最新情報を伝える　□ recession 不況　**86** □ resignation 辞職　□ lecturer 講演者　□ declare ～を宣言する

TEST 3
PART 4

89. What is the main purpose of the talk?
    (A) To introduce a new replacement
    (B) To provide updates about a program
    (C) To ensure the continuity of projects
    (D) To motivate underperforming staff

90. What recently happened at the business?
    (A) A key employee has resigned.
    (B) An office building was damaged.
    (C) A product launch was delayed.
    (D) A team leader was reassigned.

91. What are listeners asked to expect?
    (A) Stricter employee evaluations
    (B) A heavier work load
    (C) Larger performance bonuses
    (D) A flexible schedule

92. Who most likely are the listeners?
    (A) Market analysts
    (B) Restaurant staff
    (C) Sales representatives
    (D) Consulting firm specialists

93. According to the speaker, why are French Bistro's sales low?
    (A) It is located on the outskirts of the city.
    (B) Their products are too expensive.
    (C) The quality of service has deteriorated.
    (D) They are losing business to competitors.

94. What does the speaker suggest?
    (A) Providing food samples
    (B) Increasing the amount of advertising
    (C) Reducing the number of menu items
    (D) Extending operating hours

設問の訳 ☞ p.40〜41参照

Questions 89-91 refer to the following speech.

❶I've called this emergency meeting to inform you of some developments. You may have heard by now that ❷Ms. Linda Goodwin has left the company. Her departure is not a reflection of poor performance. She merely has important personal matters to take care of. But her exit comes at a critical time for us. In just four months, we are scheduled to release our latest line of video games. ❸Without Ms. Goodwin, a number of projects are in danger of falling behind. Therefore, ❹I'll be asking each one of you to fill in for her by assuming greater responsibilities. We have no plans to find a permanent replacement for Ms. Goodwin until early September.

設問89から91は次のスピーチに関する質問です。

この緊急会議を招集したのは、みなさんにあることを知らせるためです。もうすでに聞いているかもしれませんが、Linda Goodwin さんが退職されました。彼女の退職は能力不足によるものではありません。彼女にはただ、対処すべき重要な個人的事情があるのです。しかし、彼女の離職は、われわれの重要な時期と重なります。わずか4カ月後には、テレビゲームの最新ラインナップを発売予定です。Goodwin さんがいなくては、多くのプロジェクトに遅れが発生する危険があります。従って、みなさんひとりひとりがより責任を持ち、彼女の穴を埋めるようお願いします。Goodwin さんの後任となる正社員の採用予定は9月初旬までありません。

Questions 92-94 refer to the following excerpt from a meeting.

I've just finished looking over the sales report for ❶French Bistro and noticed that ❷the volume of diners has decreased steadily since April. ❸This is most likely due to the number of new restaurants that have opened in the area over the past year. So, ❹in order to recover lost ground, I propose that we create a series of small sampler plates to entice people into the restaurant. Without sacrificing taste or quality, we can offer a set of lower-priced menu items that showcase the range of our cooking. If you have any other suggestions, please feel free to share them and we can discuss them as a group.

設問92から94は次の会議の抜粋に関する質問です。

French Bistro の売上報告にちょうど目を通し終えたところですが、4月以降、食事客数が徐々に減少していることに気づきました。この1年、当該地域に新しいレストランが数多く開店していることが原因でしょう。それで、巻き返しを図るため、少量ずつ試食できる小皿を作って、客を店に呼び込んでみてはどうでしょうか。味や質を落とすことなく、われわれの料理の幅広さを紹介できる低価格メニューをひとまとめにセットとして提供することができます。もしほかに提案があれば、遠慮なくおっしゃってください。そうすればグループで議論もできます。

正解&解説

89. 正解 (C)　難易度 ■■■□ 難

この話の目的を尋ねている。主題に関わる設問は、冒頭に注目するのが定石だが、ここでは❶に「あることを知らせるため」とあるだけ。これだけでは正答できない。話の流れを追うと、❷「Goodwinさんが退職した」、❸「それにより、プロジェクトが遅れる危険性がある」と続き、❹に「みなさんがより責任を持ち、彼女の穴を埋めてほしい」とある。これらから、話の目的としては (C)「プロジェクトの継続を確認すること」が適切。

90. 正解 (A)　難易度 ■□□□ 難

最近起こった出来事を尋ねている。❷で「**Goodwinさんが退職した**」という出来事が述べられている。加えて、❸に「Goodwinさんなしだと、**多くのプロジェクトで遅れが発生する危険性がある**」とあることから、**彼女は重要な社員だった**と推測できる。従って、(A) A key employee has resigned.（重要な社員が退職した）が正解。

91. 正解 (B)　難易度 ■■■□ 難

聞き手が見込んでおかなければならないことを尋ねている。聞き手は、❹で「みなさんがより責任を持ち、彼女（= Goodwinさん）の穴を埋めてほしい」と依頼されている。またこのあとに、「正社員の補充は9月までない」との発言もある。ということは、当然**これまでよりも仕事量が増える**と予想されるので、正解は (B)。

単語 □ development 進展、新事態　□ reflection 反映、影響　□ merely 単に、ただ　□ matter 問題、事情　□ critical 決定的に重要な　□ latest 最新の　□ in danger of ~　~の危険がある　□ fill in for ~　~の代わりをする　□ assume（責任など）を引き受ける　□ replacement 代わりの人　**89** □ ensure ~を保証する、確実にする　□ continuity 継続　**90** □ resign 退職する　□ reassign ~を再び割り当てる　**91** □ strict 厳格な　□ evaluation 評価　□ work load 仕事量

92. 正解 (B)　難易度 ■■□□ 難

この会議抜粋の聞き手を尋ねている。❶の French Bistro という店名から**レストランの売上について議論している**のだとわかる。加えて、❹で「レストランに客を呼び込むために、試食用の小皿を作ろう」と、we を主語にして提案している。つまり、話し手も聞き手も「**レストランの従業員**」だと考えられるので、正解は (B)。

93. 正解 (D)　難易度 ■■■□ 難

French Bistro の売上が減少している理由を尋ねている。❷で「4月以降、食事客数が徐々に減少」という状況を伝え、続けて❸で「**この地域に新しいレストランが数多く開店しているせいだ**」と原因を述べている。他店のことを competitors（競争相手）と言い換えている (D)「競合店に客を奪われている」が正解。原因を導く表現 **due to ~**（~のせいで）を覚えておこう。

94. 正解 (A)　難易度 ■■□□ 難

話し手の提案内容を尋ねている。❹で話者は「**small sampler plates（試食用の小皿）を作ることを提案する**」と言っている。これを、「食品のサンプルを提供すること」と表現した (A) Providing food samples が正解。

単語 □ diner 食事客　□ steadily 着実に　□ recover lost ground 巻き返しを図る　□ entice ~を誘う、おびきよせる　□ sacrifice ~を犠牲にする　□ showcase ~を紹介する　□ range 幅、範囲　**92** □ analyst 分析者　□ sales representative 販売員　□ consulting firm コンサルティング会社　**93** □ outskirts 町はずれ、郊外　□ deteriorate 悪化する、低下する　□ competitor 競争相手　**94** □ extend ~を延長する

TEST 3 PART 4

95. Who is Tommy Holmes?
    (A) A school principal
    (B) A pediatrician
    (C) A psychologist
    (D) A college professor

96. What will be discussed in the program?
    (A) A survey about parenting
    (B) A new medical breakthrough
    (C) The effects of insufficient sleep
    (D) The diseases affecting children

97. What did Dr. Holmes do recently?
    (A) He wrote a best-selling book about the brain.
    (B) He developed a partial cure for insomnia.
    (C) He hosted an educational program on TV.
    (D) He published his medical findings.

98. Who most likely is the talk intended for?
    (A) Company shareholders
    (B) Publication editors
    (C) Web site designers
    (D) Security officers

99. What have customers complained about?
    (A) High subscription rates
    (B) Low level of security
    (C) Incorrect billing figures
    (D) Complicated payment process

100. How does the company intend to address the problem?
    (A) By redesigning a Web site
    (B) By hiring a marketing expert
    (C) By sending out a mass e-mail
    (D) By launching an advertising campaign

Questions 95-97 refer to the following radio broadcast.

This is Cathy Bentham, host of Health Watch here on WSXF radio. ❶Today's program will feature an interesting study conducted by Dr. Tommy Holmes, a resident pediatrician at Mt. Kingsley County Hospital. ❷He'll be talking to us about the effects of lack of sleep in the brain development of children. I know it's hard to put our children to bed at night, but it is very important that they get enough sleep. ❸Dr. Holmes's recently published study indicates that watching too much television, playing video games, and surfing the Internet interfere with the children's normal sleeping habits. Do you want to know how these activities can affect them? Join us after the break when he shares with us the results of his research.

設問95から97は次のラジオ放送に関する質問です。
WSXFラジオのHealth Watchの司会を務めるCathy Benthamです。本日は、Mt. Kingsley County病院の小児科研修医、Tommy Holmes医師が行っている興味深い研究を特集。子供の脳の発達過程で、睡眠不足がおよぼす影響について、先生がお話しくださいます。夜、子供を寝かしつけるのはたいへんですね。でも、十分な睡眠は子供にとって非常に大切です。Holmes医師が最近公表した研究では、テレビの見すぎやゲーム、インターネットのしすぎが子供の正常な睡眠習慣を妨げていることが指摘されています。これらの活動が子供にどのような影響を与え得るか知りたいですか。では中断のあと、先生が研究結果をお話しくださるので、一緒に聞きましょう。

Questions 98-100 refer to the following talk.

This morning ❶I want to give you an update on the performance of our new Web site. The good news is that the number of customers ordering our products online has been consistently increasing. We've sold more than 800 magazine subscriptions since the Web site became operational in June. However, we have received ❷some feedback from customers that the payment system is quite difficult to navigate. Many potential clients have been unable to subscribe to our publications because they couldn't figure out how to use the secure payment system. Because of this, ❸we are going to start work on redesigning the payment process on the site. ❹I'd like all of you on the Web design team to meet this week and come up with some ideas for simplifying the system.

設問98から100は次の話に関する質問です。
今朝は、われわれの新しいウェブサイトの実績について、最新情報をお伝えします。よい知らせとして、オンラインで商品を注文する顧客数が着実に増えています。6月にサイトが運用開始されてから、800件以上の雑誌定期購読契約を獲得しました。しかし、決済システムの操作がとても難しいという意見もお客さまからいただいています。安全な決済システムの利用方法がわからないために、出版物を定期購読できない潜在的顧客が多数いるのです。このため、サイトの支払い処理の再設計に取り掛かります。ウェブザインチームのみなさんには、今週会議をし、システムを簡略化するアイデアを考えだしてほしいのです。

設問の訳 ☞ p.40〜41参照

正解＆解説

95. 正解 (B) 難易度: 難

Tommy Holmes の職業を尋ねている。❶で話者が、**Dr. Tommy Holmes, a resident pediatrician** at Mt. Kingsley County Hospital（Mt. Kingsley County 病院の小児科研修医、Tommy Holmes 医師）と紹介しているが、**pediatrician（小児科医）**を聞き取れるかどうかがポイント。正解は (B)。

96. 正解 (C) 難易度: 難

番組で議論されるテーマを尋ねている。❷に「(Holmes 医師が) 脳の発達過程における、**lack of sleep（睡眠不足）の影響について話す**」とある。lack of sleep を insufficient sleep と言い換えた (C) The effects of insufficient sleep が正解。(A) の parenting（子育て）も関連した内容ではあるが、正答に比べると漠然としすぎている。

97. 正解 (D) 難易度: 難

Holmes 医師が最近行ったことを尋ねている。**recently（最近）という時の表現に注目**しながら聞き取ろう。❸ Dr. Holmes's recently published study（Holmes 医師は最近、研究を発表した）とある。study を medical findings と言い換えた (D) He published his medical findings.（彼は医学的発見を公表した）が正解。

単語 □ study 研究　□ conduct 〜を行う　□ resident 研修医　□ pediatrician 小児科医　□ interfere with A A を妨げる　□ affect 〜に影響を与える　□ share 〜を話す　**95** □ principal 長、校長　□ psychologist 精神分析医　**96** □ survey 調査　□ parenting 育児　□ breakthrough 躍進　□ insufficient 不十分な　□ disease 病気　**97** □ partial 部分的な　□ cure 治療薬　□ insomnia 不眠症

---

98. 正解 (C) 難易度: 難

この話の聞き手を尋ねている。❶で「新しいウェブサイトの最新情報」を聞き手に伝えているとわかる。そして、最後❹で「**all of you on the Web design team（ウェブデザインチームのみなさん）に、今週会議をしてもらいたい**」と言っている。ウェブデザインチームに所属しているのは、当然「**ウェブサイトのデザイナー**」なので、正解は (C)。

99. 正解 (D) 難易度: 難

顧客の苦情内容を尋ねている。❷に「**payment system（決済システム）の操作がとても難しい**という顧客の意見」とある。この苦情内容を、「**複雑な支払処理**」と言い換えた (D) Complicated payment process が正解。

100. 正解 (A) 難易度: 難

問題点の対処方法を尋ねている。まず❷で「決済システムが使いにくい」という問題点があることを把握。その問題点への対処方法として、❸で「**サイトの支払い処理の再設計に取り掛かる**」と述べているので、(A) By redesigning a Web site（ウェブサイトを再設計する）が正解。

単語 □ consistently 絶えず、いつも　□ subscription 定期購読　□ operational 使用可能な、運行可能な　□ publication 出版物　□ figure out 〜 〜を見つけ出す　□ secure 安全な　**98** □ intend for 〜 〜を意図する　□ shareholder 株主　□ editor 編集者　**99** □ figure 数字、数値　□ complicated 複雑な　**100** □ address 〜に対処する

TEST 3　PART 4

設問の訳

71. このアナウンスの目的は何か。
    (A) 空港のサービスに関する情報を提供すること
    (B) 出発の変更について人々に知らせること
    (C) 別の搭乗口に乗客を誘導すること
    (D) 旅行者に用心をすすめること

72. 述べられている問題は何か。
    (A) マドリードの空港がまだ再開していない。
    (B) その街が悪天候である。
    (C) その地域の航空交通量が多い。
    (D) 飛行機に機械的な問題がある。

73. 乗客は何をするよう求められているか。
    (A) 旅行代理店に電話する
    (B) ターミナルで待つ
    (C) 別の便に乗る
    (D) 払い戻しを要求する

74. 電話の発信者はどこで働いているか。
    (A) 島のリゾート地
    (B) 婚礼用品店
    (C) パーティー用品会社
    (D) 花屋

75. 話し手によると、問題は何か。
    (A) 商品が入手不可能である。
    (B) 見積価格が間違っている。
    (C) 配送が遅れている。
    (D) 購入品が壊れていた。

76. 話し手がJohnsonさんから知りたいことは何か。
    (A) どちらの商品を彼女が好むか
    (B) 配送に支払える価格
    (C) 商品の配達場所
    (D) 彼女のクレジットカード番号

77. Ellen Rossiは誰か。
    (A) グラフィック・デザイナー
    (B) プロの芸術家
    (C) 言語講師
    (D) ソフトウェア開発者

78. 話し手がコンピュータ・プログラムについて言っていることは何か。
    (A) 使用が難しい機能がある。
    (B) プロのデザイナーにとって便利である。
    (C) 最近開発されたソフトウェアである。
    (D) ウェブサイトで購入可能である。

79. 聞き手が午後にすることは何か。
    (A) 簡単な実演を見る
    (B) 時間の管理法を学ぶ
    (C) 製品をじかに体験する
    (D) 自身の作品見本を提出する

80. このレポートはいつ放送されるか。
    (A) 朝に
    (B) 正午に
    (C) 午後に
    (D) 夜に

81. 交通問題を引き起こしているのは何か。
    (A) 橋が補修のために閉鎖されている。
    (B) 建設作業員が数車線をふさいでいる。
    (C) 交通の流れを遅らせている車両がある。
    (D) 吹雪が視界をひどくせばめている。

82. 聞き手は次に何を聞くか。
    (A) 天気予報
    (B) 広告
    (C) トークショー
    (D) ニュース報道

83. Stevensさんが働いている分野は何か。
    (A) 室内装飾
    (B) 建築管理
    (C) イベント企画
    (D) 造園デザイン

84. Stevensさんは何を勧めているか。
    (A) 座席エリアを取り入れること
    (B) 公園でイベントを開催すること
    (C) 設計に小道を追加すること
    (D) 噴水を導入すること

85. StevensさんはCarranza氏に何をするよう依頼しているか。
    (A) 折り返し電話する
    (B) 会合場所を決める
    (C) 計画予算に目を通す
    (D) プロジェクトに着手する

設問の訳

86. なぜ変更があったのか。
    - (A) 講演者が辞任を表明した。
    - (B) 議論が延長された。
    - (C) 講演者が体調を崩した。
    - (D) 休日が宣言された。

87. Armstrong さんは何について話すのか。
    - (A) 発展途上経済
    - (B) 世界の通商協定
    - (C) 世界不況
    - (D) 学部ニュース

88. Cornelius 氏が講演をするのはおそらくいつか。
    - (A) 数分後に
    - (B) その日の午後遅く
    - (C) 次の日の午前
    - (D) 次のセミナーで

89. この話の主な目的は何か。
    - (A) 新たな後任を紹介すること
    - (B) プログラムについての最新情報を伝えること
    - (C) プロジェクトの継続を確認すること
    - (D) 働きの悪い従業員にやる気を起こさせること

90. この会社で最近、何が起こったのか。
    - (A) 重要な社員が退職した。
    - (B) 社屋が損壊した。
    - (C) 商品の発売が遅れた。
    - (D) チームリーダーが転任させられた。

91. 聞き手は何を見込むよう求められているか。
    - (A) 人事考課の強化
    - (B) 仕事量の増加
    - (C) 業績手当の拡大
    - (D) 融通の利くスケジュール

92. 聞き手は誰だと考えられるか。
    - (A) 市場分析者
    - (B) レストランの従業員
    - (C) 販売員
    - (D) コンサルティング会社の専門家

93. 話し手によると、French Bistro の売上が低いのはなぜか。
    - (A) 町の外れにある。
    - (B) 彼らの製品は高すぎる。
    - (C) サービスの質が劣化している。
    - (D) 競合店に客を奪われている。

94. 話し手は何を提案しているか。
    - (A) 食品のサンプルを提供すること
    - (B) 広告量を増やすこと
    - (C) メニューの品目数を減らすこと
    - (D) 営業時間を延ばすこと

95. Tommy Holmes は誰か。
    - (A) 校長
    - (B) 小児科医
    - (C) 精神分析医
    - (D) 大学教授

96. この番組で何が議論されるのか。
    - (A) 子育てに関する調査
    - (B) 医学の新たな飛躍的進歩
    - (C) 睡眠不足の影響
    - (D) 子供が罹患する病気

97. Holmes 医師は最近何を行ったのか。
    - (A) 彼は脳に関するベストセラー本を書いた。
    - (B) 彼は不眠症の部分的治療薬を開発した。
    - (C) 彼はテレビの教育番組で司会を務めた。
    - (D) 彼は医学的発見を公表した。

98. この話は誰に対するものだと考えられるか。
    - (A) 会社の株主
    - (B) 出版編集者
    - (C) ウェブサイトのデザイナー
    - (D) 警備員

99. 顧客は何について苦情を言ったのか。
    - (A) 高い定期購読料
    - (B) 低レベルのセキュリティー
    - (C) 間違った請求金額
    - (D) 複雑な支払処理

100. 会社はこの問題にどうやって対処するつもりか。
    - (A) ウェブサイトを再設計する
    - (B) マーケティング専門家を雇用する
    - (C) 大量の一斉メールを送る
    - (D) 広告キャンペーンを立ち上げる

TEST 3
PART 5

101. Ms. Jackson just called to ask that ------- meeting be moved to Thursday rather than Friday as scheduled.
(A) her
(B) she
(C) hers
(D) herself

102. Ambassador Carl Ferrer was ------- the six diplomats who sponsored a medical mission to several countries in Latin America.
(A) late
(B) chosen
(C) apart
(D) among

103. Customers can upsize beverages at ------- extra expense by presenting their Coffee Tree loyalty cards.
(A) none
(B) no
(C) not
(D) nor

104. The number of customers requesting refunds or exchanges at the electronics store has decreased ------- since last quarter.
(A) noticing
(B) notices
(C) noticeable
(D) noticeably

105. The company wanted to build its headquarters in the financial district ------- near the city center.
(A) so
(B) or
(C) to
(D) either

106. Fairview Hotels has six ------- on the North American mainland and two resorts in Hawaii, and has plans to build one more hotel in Alaska next year.
(A) amenities
(B) supplements
(C) locations
(D) categories

TOEIC豆知識 TOEIC学習者のブログを読んでいると、よく「塗り絵しちゃった～」という表現にでくわす。〈塗り絵〉とは、時間が足りなくて、適当にマークシートを塗りつぶすことを意味するマニア用語である。

正解＆解説

101. 正解 (A) 難易度■□□ 難

人称代名詞の格を問う問題。that 以降が節になっており、------- meeting が主語、be moved が動詞である。従って、空所には名詞 meeting を形容詞のように修飾できる**所有格**が入る。(A) her が正解。主格、所有格、再帰代名詞はいずれも名詞を修飾できない。参考までに、that 節の動詞が原形（be moved）なのは、主節の動詞が ask のように提案、要請、義務を表す場合には、従属節の動詞は原形になるため。このような動詞は、ほかに suggest、propose、recommend など。

間違いメモ＆単語
あなたの解答 A B C D
メモ

□ rather than ～ ～よりむしろ

102. 正解 (D) 難易度■■■ 難

空所の後ろに名詞句 the six diplomats（6人の外交官）があるので、**名詞を導く前置詞**(D) among が正解。「6人の外交官の1人」という意味になる。参考までに、among は一般的に3つ以上の人やものについて、「**～の間で、～のなかに**」という意味を表す。動詞の過去分詞形である (B) chosen は、空所前の was とともに受動態になるので、目的語（the six diplomats）を取ることができない。(C) の apart は副詞であり、名詞を導くことはできない。apart from ～（～は別として）の形でよく用いられる。

あなたの解答 A B C D
メモ

□ ambassador 大使
□ diplomat 外交官
□ sponsor ～を後援する

103. 正解 (B) 難易度■■□ 難

選択肢には否定をする単語が並んでいるので、at ------- extra expense を「**追加料金なしで**」という意味にすればよいとわかる。extra expense（追加料金）は名詞句なので、空所には**名詞を修飾できる形容詞**が必要。よって (B) no（少しの～もない）が正解。(A) none は「誰も～しない」という意味の代名詞で、単独で名詞の位置にくる。(C) not は「～ではない、～しない」という意味の副詞。接続詞および副詞の (D) nor は neither とともに、相関接続詞 neither *A* nor *B*（A でも B でもない）を作る。

あなたの解答 A B C D
メモ

□ upsize ～を大型化する
□ present ～を提示する

104. 正解 (D) 難易度■□□ 難

この文にはすでに、主語 The number of customers（顧客の数）と動詞（※自動詞）has decreased（減少している）が揃っているので、動詞直後の空所には「〈**どのように**〉減少している」のかを示す**副詞**が入る。従って、(D) noticeably（著しく）が正解。

あなたの解答 A B C D
メモ

□ exchange 交換
□ quarter 4分の1、四半期

105. 正解 (B) 難易度■■□ 難

選択肢に前後の内容をつなぐ単語が並んでいるので、空所が前後をどのようにつなげているのかを考える。空所前後には、in the financial district（金融街に）と near the city center（都心近くに）という、ふたつの前置詞句が対等に並んでいる。**対等な要素をつなぐ等位接続詞**で、「金融街か都心近くに」という意味になる (B) or が正解。(A) は文脈に一致しないのに加え、節しかつなげられない。(C) は方向を表す前置詞。(D) either は or とともに相関接続詞 either *A* or *B*（A または B のどちらか）を作るので、誤り。

あなたの解答 A B C D
メモ

□ headquarters 本部、本社
□ district 地区

106. 正解 (C) 難易度■□□ 難

選択肢には同じ品詞（名詞）が並んでいるので、**文脈からアプローチ**する。Fairview ホテルが、six ------- on the North American mainland（北米本土に6つの -------）を持っている、という文脈なので「**所在地、店舗**」という意味の location の複数形 (C) を入れると文意が通る。

あなたの解答 A B C D
メモ

TEST 3 PART 5

107. A team of psychologists conducted an ------- study about the negative effects of video games on the thought processes of young children.
(A) extent
(B) extensive
(C) extensively
(D) extents

108. As ------- as the visiting guests arrive, staff from the personnel office will give them a tour of the factory, then take them to the auditorium for the presentation.
(A) fast
(B) long
(C) soon
(D) lately

109. There was such high demand for the new mobile phones ------- customers had to sign up on a waiting list.
(A) before
(B) that
(C) unless
(D) still

110. Please be reminded that proper business attire must be worn in the office at ------- times.
(A) much
(B) all
(C) every
(D) almost

111. As a special promotion, customers who sign up for a one-year ------- to Emerald Cable TV by the end of the week can enjoy a month of free service.
(A) contribution
(B) subscription
(C) dealership
(D) partnership

112. During her time working as an editor at the publishing company, Natasha worked quite ------- with most of the staff writers.
(A) closing
(B) close
(C) closely
(D) closed

正解 & 解説

107. 正解 **(B)** 難易度 ■■■□

冠詞 an と名詞 study に挟まれた空所には、**名詞を修飾する形容詞**しか入らない。従って、形容詞 (B) extensive（広範囲な）が正解。

あなたの解答 A B C D
メモ

☐ thought 思考　☐ process 過程

---

108. 正解 **(C)** 難易度 ■■■■

同じ品詞（副詞）が並んでいるので、**文脈から考える**。最初のカンマまでの「訪問客が到着する」と、以降の「スタッフが彼らを工場見学ツアーに案内する」が、As -------- as でつながれている。**as soon as ～**で「**～するとすぐに**」という接続詞になる (C) soon だと、文意が通る。(B) も as long as ～で「～するかぎり」という接続詞になるが、文脈に一致しない。(A) (D) の as fast as ～（～くらい速く）と as lately as ～（～くらい最近）は原級の比較表現であって、接続詞としては機能しない。

あなたの解答 A B C D
メモ

☐ personnel office 人事課（部）

---

109. 正解 **(B)** 難易度 ■■■□

空所の前と後ろは、それぞれ主語と動詞を備えた節になっている。空所にはふたつの節をつなぐ接続詞が入るが、ヒントは3語目の **such**。**such ～ that…の構文**で「とても～なので…」という意味になる that を空所に入れると、「とても需要が高かったので、顧客は順番待ちリストに登録しなければならなかった」となり、文意が通る。従って、(B) が正解。類似した so ～ that…構文（あまりに～なので…する）も一緒に押さえておこう。(A) (C) も接続詞だが、文脈に一致しない。(D) は副詞。

あなたの解答 A B C D
メモ

☐ demand 需要
☐ waiting list 順番待ちリスト

---

110. 正解 **(B)** 難易度 ■■■□

選択肢に数や量の多さを示す単語が並んでいることや、文脈から at ------- times で「**あらゆるときに、常に**」という意味になるだろうと考えられる。正解は、at all times となる (B)。「常に」という意味の慣用句として、このまま覚えておこう。ほかの選択肢も似たような意味なので迷うが、(A) の much のあとには**不可算名詞**が、(C) の every のあとには**可算名詞の単数形**がこなければいけない。(D) almost は副詞であり、名詞 times を修飾できない。

あなたの解答 A B C D
メモ

☐ proper 適切な、ふさわしい
☐ attire 服装

---

111. 正解 **(B)** 難易度 ■■■□

同じ品詞（名詞）が並んでいるので、**文脈から考えていこう**。a one-year ------- to Emerald Cable TV で「Emerald ケーブルテレビとの1年間の -------」となっているので、「**定期購読、定期会員**」という意味の subscription だと文意が通る。よって、(B) が正解。

あなたの解答 A B C D
メモ

---

112. 正解 **(C)** 難易度 ■■□□

空所は副詞 quite の修飾を受けつつ、動詞 worked を修飾している。そのような働きをするのは**副詞**なので、(C) closely（緊密に）が正解。

あなたの解答 A B C D
メモ

☐ publishing company 出版社

TEST 3 PART 5

113. The flowers planted in front of the building did not survive because they do not ------- well in the direct sunlight.
(A) discover
(B) grow
(C) behave
(D) accept

114. Dalton Insurance Company now gives clients more ------- in regard to payments, permitting them to purchase policies in installments.
(A) credibility
(B) research
(C) acceptance
(D) flexibility

115. The local amusement park offers residents a far less ------- option for spending their holidays than traveling overseas.
(A) assumed
(B) remote
(C) expensive
(D) reduced

116. Because the restaurant appliances were damaged during shipment, Mr. Morgan ------- them to the supplier and requested that they be replaced as quickly as possible.
(A) adjusted
(B) returned
(C) refunded
(D) prohibited

117. The construction crew closed Sunset Avenue for several days so they could install a new water pipe system ------- street level.
(A) by
(B) below
(C) near
(D) beside

118. It is advisable to have a dental checkup ------- because only a dentist can identify potential teeth problems before they worsen.
(A) regularize
(B) regularly
(C) regulars
(D) regularization

TOEIC豆知識　〈アビメ〉という表現もよく見かけるが、これは「公式認定証」に記載されている Abilities Measured（アビリティーズメジャード）を縮めたマニア用語。（続く▶）

正解 & 解説 | 間違いメモ & 単語

113. 正解 (B)　難易度：難

選択肢には同じ品詞（動詞）が並んでいるので、**文脈からアプローチ**。because よりも前が「花は枯れた」という内容。because 以降が、「それらは、直射日光ではうまく ------- しない」という内容。「直射日光ではうまく〈育た〉ないので、花は枯れた」とすれば文意が通るので、正解は「育つ」という意味の (B) grow。

□ survive　生き残る

114. 正解 (D)　難易度：難

同じ品詞（名詞）が並んでいるので、**文脈から考えよう**。Dalton 保険会社が支払い方法に関して、gives clients more -------（顧客にいっそうの ------- を与える）という文脈になっている。flexibility を入れると、「顧客にいっそうの〈柔軟性〉を与える」、つまり支払い方法に関して、より多くの選択肢を提供するという意味になり、文意が通る。(D) が正解。permit *A* to *do* は「A（人）が〜するのを許す」という意味。また、in regard to 〜は「〜に関して、について」という意味。ともに重要表現。

□ in regard to 〜　〜に関して
□ permit　〜を許す　□ policy　保険契約（証券）　□ in installments　分割払いで

115. 正解 (C)　難易度：難

同じ品詞（形容詞）が並んでいるので、**文脈から考える**。遊園地が住民に、a far less ------- option for spending their holiday（はるかに ------- でない休日の過ごし方）を提供する、となっている。expensive を入れると、海外旅行より「はるかに〈高価〉ではない休日の過ごし方」となり、文意が通る。(C) が正解。一方がもう一方よりも程度が低いことを表す比較表現〈less + 原級 + than 〜〉を押さえておこう。また、比較級を強調するものとしては、far 以外にも **much**、**even**、**still**、**a lot**、**by far** がある。

□ amusement park　遊園地
□ resident　住民　□ option　選択肢

116. 正解 (B)　難易度：難

同じ品詞（動詞）が並んでいるので、**文脈からアプローチ**する。冒頭の Because からカンマまでが、「レストラン用器具が破損していたので」という内容。それを受けて、Mr. Morgan ------- them to the supplier（Morgan 氏はそれらを業者に ------- した）ということなので、「**返送した**」という意味の (B) returned を入れると、文意が通る。

□ appliance　（家庭用の）機器、器具
□ shipment　配送、輸送

117. 正解 (B)　難易度：難

位置関係を表す前置詞が並んでいるので、install a new water pipe system ------- street level は、道路の高さに対して〈どの位置〉に、水道管を設置しようとしているのかを考える。常識的に考えて、地下、つまり道路の下に設置すると考えられるので、(B) below（〜の下に）が正解。(A) by は「〜のそばに」、(C) near は「〜の近くに」、(D) beside は「〜の横に」という意味。参考までに、near は形容詞「近い」、副詞「近くに」という意味にも用いられることを押さえておこう。

□ crew　（作業の）一団、チーム

118. 正解 (B)　難易度：難

まず問題文は、It が仮主語で、to have a dental checkup ------- が真主語となっていることを見抜く。この真主語部分を見ると、空所には「歯科検診を〈どのように〉受ける」のか、**動詞 have を修飾する副詞**が入るとわかる。従って、(B) regularly（定期的に）が正解。

□ advisable　望ましい　□ checkup　検診
□ dentist　歯科医　□ identify　〜を確認（特定）する　□ worsen　悪化する

47

TEST 3
PART 5

119. ------- the safety of both drivers and passengers, the Department of Transportation urges everyone not to keep flammable substances in the trunks of vehicles.
(A) Around
(B) About
(C) With
(D) For

運転手と歩行者双方の安全のために、運輸局は自動車のトランクの中に可燃物を置いておかないよう要請している。
(A) 〜のまわりに
(B) 〜について
(C) 〜で、〜を使って
(D) 〜のために

120. Mrs. Nordstrom seemed very pleased with the planned ------- to the main entrance of her firm's main office, and gave her approval to go ahead with construction.
(A) permissions
(B) adaptations
(C) modifications
(D) regulations

Nordstromさんは彼女の会社の本社正門の改修プランにたいへん満足したようで、工事の着工を承認した。
(A) 許可
(B) 適応
(C) 修正
(D) 規則、規制

121. The mechanic said he can fix Ms. Ang's car, but that it will soon be ------- for her to replace the engine.
(A) necessary
(B) permissible
(C) prohibited
(D) considerable

整備士は、Angさんの車を修理することは可能だが、すぐにエンジンを交換する必要が生じるだろうと言った。
(A) 必要な
(B) 許された
(C) 禁止された
(D) 相当な、重要な

122. Clients are required to sign the shipping order that ------- their merchandise to confirm receipt of their purchases.
(A) accompanying
(B) accompanies
(C) accompany
(D) accompaniment

顧客は購入品の受け取り確認のため、商品に付いてくる配送指示書にサインする必要がある。
(A) 〈現在分詞・動名詞〉
(B) 〈現在形〉
(C) 〈原形〉
(D) 名 付属物

123. Ms. Bana ------- for Richmond Bank for 15 years by the time she was promoted to financial vice president.
(A) has worked
(B) will have worked
(C) is working
(D) had worked

BanaさんはRichmond銀行の財務担当副社長に昇進したとき、勤続15年であった。
(A) 〈現在完了形〉
(B) 〈未来完了形〉
(C) 〈現在進行形〉
(D) 〈過去完了形〉

124. After opening the protective cover of the photocopier, remove the empty ink cartridge by pressing the green tabs and ------- lifting it from the machine.
(A) carefully
(B) internally
(C) automatically
(D) vaguely

コピー機の保護カバーを開けてから、緑色のタブを押し、本体から慎重に持ち上げることで、空のインクカートリッジを取り外してください。
(A) 慎重に
(B) 内部に
(C) 自動的に
(D) 漠然と

TOEIC豆知識 ちなみに、アビメ（Abilities Measured）とは、リスニングで4つ、リーディングで5つの項目別正答率のこと。得意分野・苦手分野を知ることができる。

正解＆解説

119. 正解 (D)　難易度　難

前置詞の問題。カンマまでの前半が「運転手と歩行者双方の安全」、後半が「運輸局はトランクに可燃物を置かないよう要請する」という内容で、空所に入る前置詞がこのふたつをつないでいる。目的を表す For を入れて、「運転手と歩行者双方の安全の〈ために〉」とすれば、文意が通るので (D) が正解。参考までに、相関接続詞 both A and B（A も B も）を押さえておこう。

間違いメモ＆単語
あなたの解答 A B C D
メモ

☐ urge ～に（…するよう）うながす
☐ flammable 可燃性の　☐ substance 物質、物　☐ trunk トランク

120. 正解 (C)　難易度　難

同じ品詞（名詞）が並んでいるので、**文脈から考えよう**。カンマまでが、the planned ------- to the main entrance（正門の予定された -------）に Nordstrom さんが満足した、という内容。これだけだとはっきりしないが、カンマ以降の「工事の着工を承認した」と考え合わせると、「正門の予定された〈改修〉」とすれば文意が通るとわかるので、(C) modifications（修正）が正解。

あなたの解答 A B C D
メモ

☐ approval 承認
☐ go ahead with ～　～を進める、推進する

121. 正解 (A)　難易度　難

同じ品詞（形容詞）が並んでいるので、**文脈から考える**。it will soon be ------- for her to replace the engine は、it is ～ to do の構文になっており、「エンジンを交換することがすぐに ------- だろう」という意味。(A) の necessary を入れると、「エンジン交換がすぐに〈必要になる〉だろう」となり、文意が通るので、これが正解。ちなみに、ここの for her は、to 不定詞（to replace）の意味上の主語、つまり「彼女が～を交換する」という意味になっている。

あなたの解答 A B C D
メモ

☐ fix ～を修理する
☐ replace ～を取り替える

122. 正解 (B)　難易度　難

まず文の構造を見極めよう。that 以降が、先行詞 the shipping order を修飾する関係代名詞節になっている。しかし、節に動詞が見当たらないので、空所に入るものとして動詞の (B) と (C) が正解候補になる。先行詞の the shipping order が **3人称単数**であることから、関係代名詞節の動詞もこれに対応する必要がある。よって、**3人称単数現在形**の (B) accompanies が正解。(C) は動詞の原形。(A) は形容詞または分詞、(D) は名詞なので誤り。

あなたの解答 A B C D
メモ

☐ shipping order 配送指示書
☐ confirm ～を確認する
☐ receipt 受領

123. 正解 (D)　難易度　難

時制を問う問題では、**時の表現**を探そう。ここではまず、完了形とともに用いる **for 15 years**（15年間）があることから、(A) と (D) に候補をしぼることができる。さらに、**by the time**（～するときまでに）に導かれる副詞節が続いている。その中が過去時制 was promoted（昇進した）になっていて、過去の特定時点より以前の期間を示している。ということは空所の動詞は、**過去完了形**を用いて「彼女は昇進したときまでに、15年間働いていた」という意味にしなければならない。よって、(D) が正解。

あなたの解答 A B C D
メモ

☐ promote ～を昇進させる

124. 正解 (A)　難易度　難

同じ品詞（副詞）が並んでいるので、**文脈から答えを探る**。まず、前置詞 by の目的語として、pressing the green tabs（緑色のタブを押す）と ------- lifting it from the machine が and で並べられていることを見抜く。つまり、by ------- lifting it from the machine ということなので、「機械から〈どのように〉それを持ち上げることで」インクカートリッジを取り外すのかを考える。文意が通るのは「〈慎重に〉持ち上げる」となる (A) carefully。

あなたの解答 A B C D
メモ

☐ protective 保護用の
☐ machine 機械

TEST 3 PART 5

125. Wentworth TV studios is currently developing a production schedule of upcoming projects for its recently ------- documentary film department.
(A) creating
(B) creator
(C) creates
(D) created

126. Mai-Thai Resort in Phuket ------- right beside the beach and just a 10-minute drive from the international airport.
(A) situates
(B) has situated
(C) is situated
(D) situating

127. The work on the new subway station is ------- complete and the line should be fully operational in less than a month's time.
(A) rapidly
(B) usually
(C) nearly
(D) possibly

128. Only applicants who meet the requirements for the design position will be contacted to arrange ------- for interviews.
(A) methods
(B) appointments
(C) developments
(D) services

129. ------- the problems with the new assembly line equipment have been repaired, the factory's new production schedule will be put into effect.
(A) Meantime
(B) Despite
(C) Moreover
(D) Once

130. Recent reports show that Southeast Asian countries have decreased their ------- on fossil fuels by using alternative energy sources.
(A) reliance
(B) relies
(C) reliable
(D) reliability

125. 正解 (D)

空所は、副詞 recently と名詞句 documentary film department にはさまれている。副詞の修飾を受けつつ、名詞を修飾できるのは、**形容詞（もしくは形容詞的働きをする分詞）**なので、分詞 (A) と (D) が候補。修飾対象の documentary film department と分詞の関係をみると、「**創設された**ドキュメンタリー映像部門」という**受動の関係**になるので、create の過去分詞 (D) created が正解。現在分詞の (A) だと、**能動の意味**（創設するドキュメンタリー映像部門）になり、不自然。

- production 生産、制作
- documentary film ドキュメンタリー映像

126. 正解 (C)

選択肢に動詞 situate の変化形が並んでいるので、空所は situate の正しい形を求めているとわかる。ポイントは、situate が「~を置く、~を位置づける」という意味の**他動詞で、後ろに目的語をとる**点。しかし、空所の後ろに「〈何〉を置くのか、位置づけるのか」を示す目的語がない。よって、受動態にして「Mai-Thai リゾートは**位置づけられている**（=位置している）」とすべきだとわかる。正解は**受動態の現在形** (C) is situated。(A) と (B) は能動態。(D) は、そもそも動詞の位置にくることができない。

- drive （自動車の）道のり、ドライブ

127. 正解 (C)

同じ品詞（副詞）が並んでいるので、**文脈からアプローチ**する。The work ... is ------- complete は「仕事が〈**どのように**〉完了している」かを示している。あとに続く「1 カ月以内に全線通常運行が可能」という内容を考え合わせると、「〈**ほとんど**〉完了している」となる (C) nearly だと文意が通る。参考までに always、usually、often、hard のような頻度を表す副詞は通常、一般動詞の前、あるいは助動詞や be 動詞の後ろで用いられることを覚えておこう。

- line 線、路線

128. 正解 (B)

同じ品詞（名詞）が並んでいるので、**文脈から答えを探る**。to arrange ------- for interviews で「面接のための ------- を調整するために」という内容。この文脈に一致するのは、「(面会の)**約束**」という意味の (B) appointments。

- applicant 志願者、応募者
- meet ~を満たす
- requirement 必要条件、資格

129. 正解 (D)

この問題文はすでに、**主語** the factory's new production schedule と**動詞** will be put into effect を備え、文として成立している。従って、冒頭の空所からカンマまでは、修飾の働きをする付加的要素である。さらに、この付加的要素にも**主語** the problems と**動詞** have been があり、節になっている。**節を導けるのは、接続詞**なので (D) Once（~するやいなや）が正解。(A) Meantime と (C) Moreover は、ともに接続副詞で、文頭に位置するときは必ず直後にカンマがくる。(B) Despite は前置詞。

- put into effect ~を実行する

130. 正解 (A)

that 以降の節の中で、**主語** Southeast Asian countries、**動詞** have decreased に対して、**their ------- は目的語の位置**にきている。their の修飾を受けつつ、**目的語になれるのは、名詞**なので (A) と (D) が正解候補。次に、文脈をみていくと「代替エネルギーの使用により、化石燃料への彼らの ------- を減らしてきた」となっている。これに一致するのは、「**依存**」という意味の (A) reliance。(D) の reliability（信頼性）だと不自然。動詞 (B) と形容詞 (C) は、目的語の位置にくることはできない。

- recent 最近の
- fossil fuel （石炭、石油など）化石燃料
- alternative 代替の
- source 源、源泉

TEST 3 PART 5

131. During the opening remarks, the speaker announced that the first lecture at the workshop was cancelled due to the ------- illness of the guest speaker.
(A) treated
(B) stringent
(C) unexpected
(D) comprehensive

開式の辞の中で、ゲストスピーカーの予期せぬ体調不良により、ワークショップの最初の講演がキャンセルになったとの告知があった。
(A) 治療された
(B) 厳格な
(C) 予想外の
(D) 包括的な

132. The company president told the union representative that he would increase pay by 2 percent in an ------- to appease the striking workers.
(A) obligation
(B) effort
(C) option
(D) indication

会社社長は、ストライキ中の労働者をなだめる努力として、賃金を2％引き上げると労働組合代表に伝えた。
(A) 義務
(B) 努力
(C) 選択
(D) 指示

133. Many of the newspaper's readers wrote in to praise Sunday's short but ------- article explaining everything there is to know about the healthcare debate.
(A) adversary
(B) reminding
(C) compound
(D) informative

ヘルスケア関連の論争について、知っておくべき点を網羅的に説明した、日曜日の短いながらもためになる記事に対して、多くの新聞読者が投書によって賞賛の意を表した。
(A) 敵の
(B) 思いださせている
(C) 複合の
(D) 有益な

134. The executive officer's memorandum cited the investors' ------- about using investment funds for research into alternative energy sources.
(A) limitations
(B) combinations
(C) reservations
(D) contractions

その取締役の備忘録は、代替エネルギー源の研究に投資資金を使用することに対する投資家の留保に言及していた。
(A) 限界、制限
(B) 組み合わせ
(C) 留保
(D) 収縮

135. Museum caretakers have blocked off a section opposite the abstract art exhibit to prevent visitors from wandering into the area where a damaged oil pastel painting -------.
(A) is restoring
(B) having been restored
(C) had restored
(D) is being restored

美術館の管理人は、抽象画展示エリアの向かい側の区画を立入禁止にし、損傷したオイルパステル画の修復が行われている場所に入館者が入ってくることのないようにした。
(A) 〈現在進行形〉
(B) 〈現在分詞〉
(C) 〈過去完了形〉
(D) 〈受動態の現在進行形〉

136. If one of Tottenham Department Store's products is ------- out of stock, a sales assistant can request an order from another branch for a customer.
(A) temporarily
(B) promptly
(C) normally
(D) extremely

Tottenham デパートの商品が一時的に品切れした場合、販売員が顧客のために、ほかの支店に注文を依頼できる。
(A) 一時的に
(B) 即座に
(C) 通常は
(D) 極端に

TOEIC豆知識　TOEICのインターネット申込には〈楽天あんしん支払いサービス〉という支払い方法がある。これを利用すれば楽天スーパーポイントで受験料を支払えるうえに、ポイントも貯まる。楽天会員にとって、お得なサービスだ。

正解＆解説

131. 正解 **(C)**　難易度 難

同じ品詞（形容詞）が並んでいるので、**文脈から考えよう**。due to the ------- illness of the guest speaker で「ゲストスピーカーの ------- な病気のせいで」という意味。ここの前の「ワークショップの最初の講演がキャンセルされた」という内容とも考え合わせると、「〈予期せぬ〉病気のせいで」とすれば、文意が通る。従って、正解は (C) unexpected（予想外の）。参考までに、**opening remarks**（開会の辞）は慣用句として覚えておこう。

間違いメモ＆単語
あなたの解答　A B C D
メモ

☐ opening remark　開式の辞、開会の挨拶

132. 正解 **(B)**　難易度 難

空所前後の意味をとらえると、「社長は労働組合代表に賃金引き上げを伝えた」、「ストライキの労働者をなだめる」となっている。このふたつをつなげるためには、**in an effort to** *do* で「〜するための努力として」という意味になる (B) effort が正解。ちなみに、to *do* は不定詞なので、動詞は原形になることに注意。

あなたの解答　A B C D
メモ

☐ union representative　労働組合代表
☐ pay　賃金　　☐ appease　〜をなだめる
☐ strike　ストライキを行う

133. 正解 **(D)**　難易度 難

同じ品詞（形容詞）が並んでいるので、**文脈から答えを探ろう**。to praise Sunday's short but ------- article で「日曜日の短いが ------- な記事を賞賛するために」という内容。「短いが〈有益な〉記事」とすれば、文意が通るので、正解は (D) informative。

あなたの解答　A B C D
メモ

☐ write in　投書する　☐ praise　〜を賞賛する　☐ healthcare　ヘルスケア、健康管理　☐ debate　議論、論争

134. 正解 **(C)**　難易度 難

同じ品詞（名詞）が並んでいるので、**文脈から考える**。the investors' ------- about using investment funds は「投資資金の使用に関する投資家の -------」という意味。あとに続いている「代替エネルギー源の研究のための」という内容とも考え合わせると、**「留保」**という意味の (C) reservations がもっとも適切とわかる。**reservation** は「予約」だけでなく、この「留保、差し控え」という意味も覚えておこう。

あなたの解答　A B C D
メモ

☐ executive officer　取締役
☐ memorandum　備忘録、メモ　☐ cite　〜に言及する　☐ fund　基金、資金

135. 正解 **(D)**　難易度 難

まず、where a damaged oil pastel painting ------- が、関係副詞 where に導かれた関係副詞節になっていることを見抜く（※先行詞は the area）。この節には主語 a damaged oil pastel painting（損傷したオイルパステル画）しかないうえに、選択肢に動詞 restore の変化形が並んでいるので、空所には動詞の正しい形が必要。restore は**後ろに目的語を取る他動詞**だが、空所の後ろに目的語がないので、**目的語を主語の位置に持ってくる受動態**にしなければならない。従って、正解は (D)。

あなたの解答　A B C D
メモ

☐ caretaker　管理人　☐ block off　〜を閉鎖する　☐ abstract art　抽象芸術
☐ prevent *A* from *doing*　A が〜するのを妨げる　☐ wander　歩き回る

136. 正解 **(A)**　難易度 難

「デパートの商品のひとつが品切れになれば、ほかの支店に注文を依頼できる」という文脈なので、(A) **temporarily（一時的に）**が正解。(B) promptly は「すぐに、滞りなく」、normally は「普通に、普段は」、(D) extremely は「極端に」という意味。

あなたの解答　A B C D
メモ

☐ sales assistant　販売員

TEST 3 PART 5

137. ------- the exercise routine conducted during the morning workout session is tedious, it has proven quite beneficial for reducing excess weight.
(A) Whenever
(B) Although
(C) However
(D) After

朝の運動時間に行われるお決まりの体操は退屈だが、余分な体重を落とすのにとても有益であることが明らかになってきた。
(A) ～するときはいつでも
(B) ～ではあるが
(C) しかしながら
(D) ～のあと

138. ------- donating a sum of money to an area damaged by the flood, the RADG Company has decided that contributing needed services and goods would be more helpful.
(A) Aside from
(B) Because of
(C) Instead of
(D) In addition

RADG 社は、洪水で被害を受けた地域に金銭を寄付する代わりに、必要とされるサービスや物品を寄付するほうがより役立つと考えた。
(A) ～はさておき
(B) ～のために
(C) ～の代わりに
(D) さらに

139. Customers who request express delivery of their orders from BookEnd's Web site will have to pay a(n) ------- fee of eight dollars per publication.
(A) additional
(B) contrary
(C) exaggerated
(D) promotional

BookEnd 社のウェブサイトから注文した商品の速達配送を希望する顧客は、刊行物あたり8ドルの追加料金を支払う必要がある。
(A) 追加の
(B) 反対の
(C) 誇張された
(D) 販促の

140. Peerless Travel has formulated ------- plans to ensure that all travelers who enroll in a tour package have a safe journey.
(A) immigration
(B) contingency
(C) survival
(D) indication

Peerless Travel 社は、パッケージツアー参加者全員の旅行中の安全を保証する、緊急事態対策計画を考案した。
(A) 移住
(B) 不測の事態、偶発事件
(C) 生存
(D) 指示

正解＆解説

137. 正解 (B) 難易度：難

この問題文はすでに、カンマ以降に主語 it、動詞 has proven、補語 beneficial を備えており、文として成立している。従って、冒頭からカンマまでは修飾の働きをする付加的要素。その付加的要素にも主語 the exercise routine と動詞 is があり、節になっているので、空所には節と節をつなぐ接続詞が入る。次に、文脈をみると、各節が「お決まりの体操は退屈だ」、「それは体重を減らすのに有益だ」という内容になっている。このふたつを論理的につなげられるのは、「体操は退屈〈だが〉、体重を減らすのに有益だ」となる (B) Although。(C) However は、接続副詞なので節を導くことはできず、文頭に位置する場合は直後に必ずカンマが続く。

- routine 決まってすること、日課
- workout 運動   tedious 退屈な
- beneficial 有益な
- excess 超過した、余分の

138. 正解 (C) 難易度：難

この問題文はすでに、主語 the RADG Company、動詞 has decided、目的語 that 以下を備えており、文として成立している。よって、冒頭からカンマまでは、修飾の働きをする付加的要素。この付加的要素は「洪水被害地域に金銭を寄付すること」という名詞句になっている。これを、主節の「必要なサービスや物品を寄付するほうが役立つと考えた」という内容と論理的につなげられるのは、「金銭を寄付することの〈代わりに〉」となる (C) Instead of。(D) In addition は「その上」という意味の接続副詞で、名詞句を導くことはできない。

- donate ～を寄付する
- contribute（金、援助）を与える、寄付する

139. 正解 (A) 難易度：難

同じ品詞（形容詞）が並んでいるので、文脈から答えを探ろう。pay a(n) ------- fee of eight dollars で「8ドルの ------- な料金を支払う」という意味。これより前にある「速達配送を希望する顧客は」という内容も考え合わせると、「追加の」という意味の additional を入れると文意が通る。従って、(A) が正解。参考までに、各種手数料およびサービス料を意味する fee と、交通費を表す fare を区別できるようにしておこう。

140. 正解 (B) 難易度：難

同じ品詞（名詞）が並んでいるので、文脈から考える。------- plans は動詞 has formulated（～を考案した）の目的語となっている。また、to 以下が ------- plans を修飾して、どのような計画かを示しているので、意味をみていくと、「ツアー参加者全員が安全な旅ができることを保証する ------- 計画」となっている。「〈不測の事態への〉計画」となる (B) contingency だと、文意が通るので、これが正解。contingency plans は〈名詞＋名詞〉の形で、前の名詞が後ろの名詞を修飾する複合名詞であることを覚えておこう。

- formulate（考えなど）を練り上げる
- enroll in～ ～に加入する、登録する

TEST 3
PART 6

Questions 141-143 refer to the following letter.

Barbara Underwood
602 Infinity Lane
Houston, TX 77014

Dear Ms. Underwood,

I am pleased to inform you that we have received your application for the bachelor's program in chemistry for this coming school year. Your ID number is #1209241. Please keep this number for future -------. The school will always try to notify you when a

141. (A) promotion
(B) resource
(C) reference
(D) consideration

change in your application occurs. However, in the event that you do not receive a notification, it remains your responsibility to ensure you are up-to-date with all application requirements. Therefore, you are encouraged to log on to our Web site at www.hamilton.edu/newapps, using the ID number to gain access and ------- your admission status.

142. (A) trail
(B) stalk
(C) solve
(D) track

Once logged in, your status page will indicate which documents have been received and which ones still need to be submitted. If you have been approved for admission, several links will appear to pages ------- further details on financial aid and other student services.

143. (A) provide
(B) provides
(C) provided
(D) providing

Thank you for your interest in Hamilton University and we wish you all the best!

Sincerely,

Jenna Hoffman
Admissions Officer

単語
- bachelor 学士
- chemistry 化学
- occur 起こる、生じる
- notification 通知、告知
- remain ～のままである
- responsibility 責任
- be encouraged to do ～するよう奨励される
- gain ～を得る
- status 状態、状況
- indicate ～を表示する
- approve ～を承認する
- admission 入学、入場
- appear 現われる、載る
- detail 詳細

TOEIC豆知識 他パートと比べて存在感の薄いPart 6だが、2006年の改訂前は、短い英文に含まれた文法的誤りを見つけ出す、という最難関パートだった。

問題文の訳

設問141から143は次の手紙に関する質問です。

Barbara Underwood
602 Infinity Lane
テキサス州ヒューストン、77014

Underwoodさま

来学年度の化学の学士課程に対する貴殿の申請書を受領したことをご連絡いたします。貴殿のID番号は1209241です。この番号はあとで参照できるよう保管しておいてください。申請に変更が生じた際は、当校から貴殿へ常にお知らせするよう努めてまいります。しかし、万一通知がない場合にも、申込要件に関する最新情報を把握しておくことは貴殿の責任になります。そのため、当校のウェブサイト、www.hamilton.edu/newappsにログオンすることをお勧めいたします。このサイトへはID番号を使ってアクセスし、申請状況を追跡することができます。

一度ログインされると、貴殿の状況を確認できるページに、受領済書類と未提出書類が表示されます。入学が承認されますと、学資援助やそのほかの学生サービスに関する詳細情報を提供するページへのリンクが表示されます。

Hamilton大学に関心をお寄せいただき、ありがとうございます。私ども一同、貴殿のご多幸をお祈り申し上げます。

敬具

Jenna Hoffman
入学事務局責任者

選択肢の訳

141. (A) 昇進
    (B) 資源
    (C) 参考
    (D) 考慮

142. (A) ～の跡を追う
    (B) ～に忍び寄る
    (C) ～を解明する
    (D) ～を追跡する

143. (A) 〈原形〉
    (B) 〈現在形〉
    (C) 〈過去形・過去分詞〉
    (D) 〈現在分詞・動名詞〉

正解&解説

141. 正解 (C)　難易度：難

選択肢に同じ品詞（名詞）が並んでいるので、**全体の文脈から答えを探る**。空所を含む文は「将来の------のために**この数字**を保管しておくこと」だが、「この数字」とは、前文の**ID番号**のこと。また、以降に「学校のサイトにログオンする際に、**ID番号を使う**」とあることから、空所には「参照、参考」という意味のreferenceを入れて、「将来の〈参照〉のために保管しておく」とすれば、文脈に一致する。よって(C)が正解。

142. 正解 (D)　難易度：難

同じ品詞（動詞）が並んでいるので、**文脈を意識**。using the ID number to gain access and ------- your admission status で「ID番号を使ってアクセスし、入学申請状況を------- するために」という意味。「入学申請状況を〈**追跡す る**〉ために」となる(D) trackを入れると、文意が通る。

143. 正解 (D)　難易度：難

空所を含む文には、すでに主語several linksと動詞will appearが揃っており、文として成立している。従って、to pages以降は修飾の働きをする付加的要素である。-------以下がpagesを修飾しているので、**名詞を後ろから修飾できる分詞**(C)と(D)が正解候補。修飾の対象であるpagesと分詞の関係をみると「further details（詳細）を**提供するページ**」という**能動関係**なので、現在分詞(D) providingが正解。過去分詞だと受動の関係になる。

TEST 3
PART 6

Questions 144-146 refer to the following memo.

To: All Interested Individuals
From: Natasha Zimmerman
Date: February 20
Subject: Baking Classes

Bake the best cakes and pastries with Chef Phil Lassopo!

Next month, the Culinary Institute of Bourdain (CIB) will be offering baking classes with Chef Phil Lassopo, host of the Cuisine Channel's *The Sweetest Things*. Learn how to make ------- baked goods from cupcakes to éclairs and other signature confections. Listen to

144. (A) inedible
    (B) profound
    (C) quality
    (D) imported

informative lectures and demonstrations made by none other than Chef Phil Lassopo himself! Beginners and professionals in the food industry are welcome.

------- classes will be held on Saturdays from 1:00 P.M. to 3:00 P.M. at the CIB campus in

145. (A) Much
    (B) Every
    (C) Each
    (D) All

Baltimore.

For more information, please contact the institute's registration office at 555-3832.

We are looking forward to ------- you there!

    146. (A) joining
        (B) viewing
        (C) having
        (D) getting

単語
- pastry ペストリー（パイ、タルトなどの菓子）
- culinary 料理の
- institute 協会、機関
- cuisine 料理
- signature 特徴的な、代表的な
- confection 菓子類
- industry 〜産業

問題文の訳

設問 144 から 146 は次のメモに関する質問です。

宛先： 関係者各位
差出人： Natasha Zimmerman
日付： 2月20日
件名： 焼き菓子教室

Phil Lassopo シェフと一緒に最高のケーキとパイを焼こう！

来月、Bourdain 料理協会（CIB）は、料理チャンネルにおいて「The Sweetest Things」の司会を務める Phil Lassopo シェフによる焼き菓子教室を開講いたします。カップケーキからエクレア、またそのほかの代表的なお菓子まで、上質な焼き菓子の作り方を学びましょう。ほかならぬ Phil Lassopo シェフ自身による参考になる講義と実演が受けられます！ 初心者の方から食品産業の専門家の方まで歓迎いたします。

教室はすべて、毎週土曜の午後1時から3時まで、ボルチモアの CIB キャンパスで催されます。

詳細は、当機関の登録事務所、555-3832 までご連絡ください。

みなさんをお迎えできるのを楽しみにしています。

選択肢の訳

144. (A) 食用に不適な
    (B) 深い、大規模な
    (C) 上質の
    (D) 輸入された

145. (A) たくさんの
    (B) あらゆる
    (C) めいめいの
    (D) すべての、全部の

146. (A) 〜に参加する
    (B) 〜を見る
    (C) 〜を迎える、招待する
    (D) 〜を手に入れる

正解 & 解説

144. 正解 (C)
同じ品詞（形容詞）が並んでいるので、**全体の文脈から答えを探ろう**。Learn how to make ------- baked goods は「------- な焼き菓子の作り方を学ぼう」という意味。前後の文脈から、この文書は、お菓子教室の案内だとわかるので、空所には (C) の quality を入れて「〈**上質な**〉焼き菓子」とするのがもっとも自然。

145. 正解 (D)
選択肢には「あらゆる、たくさん」といった意味の単語が並んでいる。ポイントは、**修飾を受ける名詞の種類と数**。空所後の classes は**可算名詞の複数形**だが、これを修飾できるのは (D) All のみ。(A) Much は、**不可算名詞を修飾**。(B) Every と (C) Each はともに、可算名詞の単数形を修飾する。それぞれの対応に加え、all は可算名詞と不可算名詞の両方を修飾できることを覚えておこう。

146. 正解 (C)
同じ品詞（動名詞）が並んでいるので、**全体の文脈からアプローチ**。この文書は、読み手をお菓子教室に誘う流れになっている。従って、空所には「〜を迎える、招待する」という意味のある have を入れて、「あなたを〈**お迎えすること**〉を楽しみにしている」とすれば、文脈に一致する。**look forward to 〜**（〜を楽しみにする）を慣用句として覚えておきたいが、to のあとには、名詞または動名詞がくることに要注意。

TEST 3
PART 6

Questions 147-149 refer to the following e-mail.

TO: Aldo Hernandez [hernal@dmail.com]
FROM: Heather Heaton [heatheat@service.mtelectric.com]
SUBJECT: Repair update
DATE: May 12

Dear Mr. Hernandez,

Our technician has found the problem with your mobile phone, which you left at the MT Electric service center on May 10. The speaker ------- is damaged, which can happen when

147. (A) invention
(B) element
(C) substance
(D) matter

a phone is dropped or exposed to water.

Unfortunately, I also noticed that your warranty on this particular phone -------. You can

148. (A) expires
(B) expire
(C) has expired
(D) expiring

purchase an additional year of warranty, or we can go ahead with the repairs if you wish. The cost of repair will be $48.50, including labor and replacement parts.

Please let us know if you would like us to proceed. Your phone can be ready by tomorrow at noon. Credit card or cash payments are -------, but we do not take personal checks.

149. (A) acceptable
(B) negotiable
(C) capable
(D) deferred

Thank you, and I hope to hear from you soon.

単語
- expose ～をさらす
- warranty 保証
- particular 特定の
- additional 追加の
- including ～を含めて
- labor 労働、作業
- personal check 個人小切手

問題文の訳

設問147から149は次のEメールに関する質問です。

宛先： Aldo Hernandez [hernal@dmail.com]
送信者： Heather Heaton [heatheat@service.mtelectric.com]
件名： 修理の最新情報
日付： 5月12日

Hernandezさま、

5月10日にMTエレクトリック・サービス・センターにお預けになりました携帯電話に問題があることを当社技術スタッフが突き止めました。スピーカーの構成部品が損傷していまして、これは携帯電話を落としたり、水にさらされたりしたときに起こり得るものです。

あいにくですが、この携帯電話の保証期限も切れているようです。1年の追加保証をご購入いただくこともできますし、もしくはご希望であれば修理を続けることも可能です。修理費用は、作業費と交換部品費を含めて、48ドル50セントになります。

修理開始をご希望であれば、お知らせください。明日の正午までには貴殿の携帯電話をご用意できます。クレジットカード、もしくは現金でのお支払いを受け付けておりますが、個人小切手は受け付けておりません。

ありがとうございます、お返事をお待ち申し上げます。

選択肢の訳

147. (A) 発明
     (B) 構成要素
     (C) 物質
     (D) 問題、物質

148. (A) 〈現在形〉
     (B) 〈原形〉
     (C) 〈現在完了形〉
     (D) 〈現在分詞・動名詞〉

149. (A) 受諾できる、容認できる
     (B) 交渉の余地がある
     (C) 有能な
     (D) 延期された

正解&解説

147. 正解 **(B)**
同じ品詞（名詞）が並んでいるので、**文脈から考える**。The speaker ------- is damaged は「スピーカーの ------- が損傷している」という意味なので、「構成要素」という意味のelementを入れて、「スピーカーの〈**構成部品**〉が損傷している」とすれば、文意が通る。従って、(B)が正解。

148. 正解 **(C)**
空所を含む文の構造は、主語I、動詞noticed、そして接続詞that以下が目的語。接続詞thatは、節を導くので、ここにも主語と動詞が必要だが、主語your warrantyしか見当たらない。従って、空所には動詞expireの正しい形が入る。この文の動詞noticedが過去形なので、that節も過去または過去完了時制となるべきだが、「**保証期限が切れている**」という今も続く状態を表す文なので、**現在完了形**の(C)が適切。

149. 正解 **(A)**
同じ品詞（形容詞）が並んでいるので、**文脈から答えを探ろう**。空所を含む文は「クレジットカードや現金は ------- だ、しかし、小切手は受け付けない」という内容。小切手を受け付けないことを「しかし」で結んでいることから、クレジットカードと現金は「**受け付ける**」ということがわかる。従って、(A) acceptable（受諾できる、容認できる）が正解。

TEST 3
PART 6

Questions 150-152 refer to the following announcement.

Southwestern Residences
IMPORTANT ANNOUNCEMENT

The building management ------- maintenance checks on the condominium's electrical

150. (A) has performed
(B) was performing
(C) to perform
(D) will be performing

circuits and switch boxes on Monday, between 10 A.M. and 1 P.M. This is in accordance with the city government's Fire Protection Policy. During the activity, power supply throughout the condominium will be unavailable. If there is no urgent repair work to be done, electricity will be restored immediately following the inspection. -------, the power

151. (A) Otherwise
(B) Above all
(C) Consequently
(D) On the contrary

interruption will last for a few more hours.

For details ------- this and other related matters, please contact the building

152. (A) attending
(B) considering
(C) persisting
(D) regarding

superintendent, Ms. Jena Gordon, at 555-2124, ext. 21.

Thank you for your patience and understanding.

単語
- residence 邸宅、住宅
- condominium 分譲マンション
- electrical circuit 電気回路
- switch box 配電箱
- in accordance with ~ ~に従って、一致して
- power supply 電力供給
- immediately ただちに
- inspection 点検、検査
- interruption 妨害、中断
- superintendent 監督者、管理人
- patience 忍耐、しんぼう強さ

問題文の訳

設問 150 から 152 は次のお知らせに関する質問です。

Southwestern Residences
重要なお知らせ

月曜の午前10時から午後1時にかけて、ビル管理部門は当マンションの電気回路と配電箱の保守点検を行います。これは市役所の防火方針に従ったものです。この点検の間、当マンション全体の電力供給は停止します。緊急を要する修理作業が行われない場合は、点検後すぐに電力は復旧いたします。そうでない場合は、停電はもう2～3時間続く見込みです。

この件と、そのほか関連事項に関する詳細は、当建物の管理人である Jena Gordon さん、555-2124 の内線21へお問い合わせください。

ご辛抱とご理解を賜りますようお願い申し上げます。

選択肢の訳

150. (A) 〈現在完了形〉
     (B) 〈過去進行形〉
     (C) 〈to 不定詞〉
     (D) 〈未来進行形〉

151. (A) さもなければ
     (B) 何よりも
     (C) その結果として
     (D) それどころか

152. (A) 形 主治医である
     (B) 前 ～を考慮すれば
     (C) 動 persist（持続する）の〈現在分詞・動名詞〉
     (D) 前 ～に関して

正解＆解説

150. 正解 (D)
選択肢には動詞 perform（～を実行する）のさまざまな形が並んでいるので、**時制・態・数**を見極めながら、正しい形を選ぼう。ここでは、maintenance checks（保守点検）をいつ実行するのか、時制が不明。読み進めると、During the activity 以降で、「点検中は、電力供給ができないだろう」と**未来形**で述べられている。つまり、**保守点検は未来に行われる**とわかるので、**未来進行形**の (D) が適切と判断できる。

151. 正解 (A)
空所は、文頭にあり、直後にカンマ、そして前後の文の流れをつないでいる。この条件に合致するのは、**接続副詞**だが、選択肢がすべて接続副詞なので、文脈からアプローチする。前文に「緊急の修理がなければ、電力はすぐに復旧」とあり、空所を含む文が「電力の停止はもう数時間続くだろう」となっている。これらを論理的につなげられるのは、(A) Otherwise（さもなければ）。「さもなければ（＝緊急の修理が必要になれば）、電力の停止がもう数時間続く」という文脈になる。

152. 正解 (D)
名詞 details の後ろで、名詞句 this and other related matters を取ることができるのは**前置詞**なので、(B) と (D) が正解候補。次に文脈を考えると、「～に関して」という意味の regarding であれば、「これとそのほか関連事項〈**に関する**〉詳細」となり文意が通る。よって (D) が正解。(B) considering（～を考慮すれば）だと不自然な文脈になる。

TEST 3 PART 7

Questions 153-154 refer to the following memo.

MEMORANDUM

TO: All staff

We have come to the end of another successful year and would like to thank all our staff members for their hard work. As we do each year, we are organizing a special holiday evening for you all. This year it will be held at the Mansfield Hotel on Lakeview Avenue on Dec. 22 at 7:00 P.M. Staff are free to bring their husbands, wives, or partners.

Reservations need to be made in advance, so please RSVP Lionel Grimm of the personnel department at ligrimm@austel.com and let him know how many guests you will be bringing.

Thank you!

---

153. What is the memo mainly about?
    (A) Work schedules for the upcoming year
    (B) Taking time off for holidays
    (C) An annual company event
    (D) An awards ceremony for hardworking staff

154. What are staff members asked to do?
    (A) Come to a company meeting
    (B) Send an e-mail to a colleague
    (C) Inform the company of vacation plans
    (D) Confirm a reservation

TOEIC豆知識 TOEICの試験官は、意外に親切。常識的な要望であれば、臨機応変に対応してくれる。以前、咳がひどいときに、試験中、のど飴をなめることを許可してくれたことがある。

問題文の訳

設問153から154は次のメモに関する質問です。

メモ

対象：全従業員

今年も成功裏に年の瀬を迎えることができました。従業員のみなさんのご尽力に感謝いたします。さて、❶例年通り、私たちはみなさんのために謝恩パーティーを計画しています。本年度は12月22日午後7時より、Lakeview街のMansfieldホテルでの開催を予定しています。従業員のみなさんはご伴侶、あるいはパートナーの方をご自由にお連れください。

前もっての予約が必要なので、❷人事課のLionel Grimm、ligrimm@austel.comまでご連絡いただき、ゲストを何人同伴されるかお伝えください。

ありがとうございました。

単語

- partner つれあい、パートナー
- in advance 前もって
- RSVP お返事をお願いします
- guest （招待された）客
- **153** take time off for ～ ～のために休みを取る
- hardworking 勤勉な
- **154** colleague 同僚

正解＆解説

153. 正解 (C)

このメモの主題を問う設問。**主題に関わる設問へのヒントは冒頭にくる**ことが多い。ここでも従業員に1年間の感謝を述べたあと、❶で「例年通り、**謝恩パーティーを計画している**」と告知をしている。以降もこのイベントの場所や日時など、詳細説明が続いていることから、このイベントが主要テーマだとわかる。また、「**例年通り**」から、このイベントが毎年開催されていることがうかがえるので、正解は(C)「企業の毎年恒例のイベント」。

154. 正解 (B)

従業員が依頼されていることを尋ねている。依頼表現の **please** に気づけるかがポイント。❷で「人事課の **Lionel Grimm に、ligrimm@austel.com まで連絡**してほしい」と依頼している。アドレスが載っているので、Eメールで連絡しなければならないとわかる。また、Lionel Grimm は同僚なので、(B)「**同僚にEメールを送る**」が正解。**RSVP** は、フランス語の répondez s'il vous plaît の省略形で「**ご返事ください**」という意味。

TEST 3
PART 7

Questions 155-156 refer to the following notice.

NOTICE:
Residents of Mayfair Towers

Starting next week on June 5, the main parking garage will be closed for renovations. We apologize for the inconvenience this will cause, but hope that the renovations will be worth it. All surfaces will be repaved and the walls will be painted. Work is expected to take two weeks. In the meantime, provisional parking will be provided for residents across the street in the Orleans Parkade. Please pick up a parking pass for the facility at the administrative office. Parking will also be permitted at the tower's outdoor parking lot and at the rear of the building as well. If you have any questions, please call us at 555-9988.

Thank you for your cooperation in this matter.

155. What is the main purpose of the notice?

(A) To provide information on parking passes
(B) To inform tenants of temporary changes
(C) To announce upcoming roadwork
(D) To ask for volunteers for a project

156. What is NOT an area where residents can park their vehicles?

(A) The back of the tower
(B) The Mayfair garage
(C) The Orleans Parkade
(D) The outdoor parking area

設問の訳

この告知の主な目的は何か。

(A) 駐車許可証に関する情報を伝えること
(B) 住人に一時的な変更を伝えること
(C) 今度の道路工事を知らせること
(D) ある計画にボランティアを募集すること

居住者が車を止める場所ではないのはどれか。

(A) タワーマンションの裏手
(B) Mayfair 駐車場
(C) Orleans 駐車場ビル
(D) 屋外駐車場

問題文の訳

設問155から156は次の告知に関する質問です。

❶告知：Mayfair Towers 居住者のみなさま

❷来週6月5日より、第1駐車場が改修工事のため閉鎖されます。ご不便をおかけして申し訳ありませんが、この改修はそれに見合うものになると思います。路面全体を再舗装、そして壁面は塗装が施されます。工事期間は2週間の予定です。期間中、❸居住者のみなさまは道路を挟んだ向かい側のOrleans駐車場ビルを臨時の駐車場として利用することができます。駐車場の利用許可証は管理人室で受け取れます。また、❹当タワーマンションの屋外駐車場、あるいは建物の裏手に駐車することもできます。何か質問がございましたら、555-9988までお電話ください。

ご協力ありがとうございます。

単語

- garage ガレージ、車庫
- renovation 改装、修復
- apologize for ～ ～を謝罪する
- worth it それだけの価値がある
- surface 表面
- repave ～を再舗装する
- in the meantime その間に
- provisional 一時の、暫定的な
- parkade 駐車場ビル
- administrative 管理の、運営の
- permit ～を許可する
- cooperation 協力

155
- tenant 賃借人、借家人
- temporary 一時的な、仮の
- roadwork 道路工事
- volunteer ボランティア

正解＆解説

155. 正解 (B)　難易度 ■■■□ 難

告知の目的を尋ねている。主題に関わる設問では、**冒頭を集中的に確認**。**タイトルがある場合は、そこにも注目**したい。ここでも❶のタイトルから、住民向けの告知であることを把握できる。そして❷で「**改装のため駐車場が閉鎖される**」と述べ、以降も、**改装が2週間続く**ことなどを住民に伝えている。正解は、この改装による駐車場の閉鎖を「**一時的な変更**」と表現した (B) To inform tenants of temporary changes。

156. 正解 (B)　難易度 ■■■□ 難

住人が**駐車できない**場所を尋ねるNot問題。各選択肢を文書の内容と照らし合わせ、答えを探す。(A)と(D)は、❹に駐車が許可される場所として「当タワーの屋外駐車場」と「建物の裏手」が挙げられている。(B)の「Mayfair 駐車場」は、Mayfair Towersの駐車場のことだと考えられるが、❶で「**改装のため閉鎖**」とあり駐車できない。従って、これが正解。(C)については、❸に「Orleans 駐車場ビルを臨時の駐車場として利用できる」とある。

⟲ the rear of the building ➡ The back of the tower

Questions 157-158 refer to the following e-mail.

E-mail

To: Madeleine Poirot <madpoi@dmail.fr>
From: Harold Penwright <harpen@greygardens.net>
Subject: Moving

Dear Ms. Poirot,

I have truly enjoyed working for you as your gardener and landscaper. However, I must inform you that I will be retiring from Grey Gardens Landscaping at the end of this month and moving with my wife to Orlando. I just want to thank you for all your kindness and generosity over the past five years.

When I leave, my assistant Geraldine Smith will be taking over my duties. She has worked with you on numerous occasions, so you are probably aware of her professionalism. She will contact you shortly to find out if you would like to continue having Grey Gardens conduct your regular weekly service. I am sure you will be pleased with her quality of work. Thanks once again for your patronage.

Sincerely,

Harold Penwright

---

157. What is the main purpose of the e-mail?

(A) To request payment for services
(B) To show appreciation to a customer
(C) To inform a customer of a staff change
(D) To recommend a new company

158. What is mentioned about Ms. Smith?

(A) She owns the gardening service company.
(B) She is a long-term customer.
(C) She has been employed by Grey Gardens for a long time.
(D) She has worked for Ms. Poirot before.

問題文の訳

設問157から158は次のEメールに関する質問です。

宛先： Madeleine Poirot <madpoi@dmail.fr>
送信者： Harold Penwright <harpen@greygardens.net>
件名： 引越し

Poirotさま

これまでPoirotさまの庭師、また造園師として本当に楽しくお仕事をさせていただいておりましたが、❶私は今月末でGrey Gardens Landscapingを退社し、妻とともにOrlandoに移り住むこととなりました。過去5年間にわたるご厚意とご寛容に感謝いたします。

私の退職後、❷助手を務めておりましたGeraldine Smithが後任となる予定です。❸Smithは幾度もPoirotさまのお仕事をさせていただいているので、そのプロ意識はおそらくご承知のことと思います。まもなくSmithより連絡があり、Grey Gardensの週1回のレギュラーサービスを継続されるかどうかの確認があるかと思います。Smithのていねいな仕事にはきっとご満足いただけると確信しております。Poirotさまのご愛顧にあらためて感謝いたします。

敬具

Harold Penwright

単語

- truly 本当に、心から
- gardener 庭師
- landscaper 造園家
- retire 退職する、引退する
- generosity 寛容
- take over〜 〜を引き継ぐ
- duty 義務、職務
- on numerous occasions 何度も
- be aware of〜 〜に気付いている
- professionalism プロ意識、専門家気質
- shortly まもなく
- patronage ひいき、愛顧

157
- appreciation 感謝、正しい評価

正解＆解説

157. 正解 (C)　難易度 ■■■□ 難

Eメールの目的を尋ねている。主題に関わる設問なので、冒頭に注目すると、❶に「引退することを伝えなければならない」とあるが、これだけでは正答できない。読み進むと❷に「助手のGeraldine Smithが仕事を引き継ぐ」とあり、以降もSmithの説明が続く。これらから、このメールは**顧客に人員交代を伝える**ためのものと判断できるので、(C)「顧客に社員の変更を伝えること」が適切。感謝を述べる部分もあるので、(B) と迷うが、言及個所の多さからも、重点を置いているのは (C) だと判断できる。

158. 正解 (D)　難易度 ■■■□ 難

Smithさんについて言及されていることを尋ねるTrue問題。Not問題と同じく、各選択肢と文書の内容をひとつひとつ照らし合わせていく。(A) は、まったく触れられていない。(B) は❷に「私（＝ Harold Penwright）の助手のGeraldine Smith」とあるので、一致しない。Smithさんは、文脈からGrey Gardensの従業員だと考えられるが、「長年勤務している」との記述はないので (C) は誤り。(D) の「以前Poirotさんのために作業をしたことがある」は、❸の「**Poirotさんの仕事を何度もしたことがある**」という内容に一致するので、これが正解。

⟲ has worked with ... on numerous occasions ➡ has worked for ... before

TEST 3
PART 7

Questions 159-161 refer to the following notice.

Ocean Breeze Resort
Shipwon Islands, Seychelles

Welcome to Ocean Breeze Resort!

The Shipwon Islands are known for their rich marine life and unique tourist attractions. To enjoy the best of the islands, we recommend that you try these activities:

Island Hopping
Hop onto one of our boats for a day tour among Shipwon's many mangroves and jungles, lagoons, limestone cliffs, and white sand beaches. Snorkeling gear is provided for those who want to explore Shipwon's extensive coral reefs, which are home to thousands of underwater creatures.

Miligan Tour
Located south of Shipwon is Miligan, a wildlife sanctuary where you can interact with monkeys and exotic birds in their natural environment. Miligan is a 30-minute boat ride from Ocean Breeze Resort.

Trekking
Join a guided tour of Mt. Amitan and enjoy splendid views of Engle Bay. Our tour guides and mountaineers will accompany you on this adventure.

To book an activity, please coordinate with the receptionists at the front desk. Discounts will be given to groups of ten or more.

---

159. What is the purpose of the notice?
(A) To describe activities
(B) To provide a travel schedule
(C) To promote special discounts
(D) To explain animal conservation

160. What is indicated in the notice?
(A) All tours will include a guide.
(B) Boats will be used on some tours.
(C) Tourists must pay in advance.
(D) Reduced rates are not available.

161. What will NOT be seen during an Island Hopping trip?
(A) Tropical forests
(B) Underwater wildlife
(C) An animal park
(D) Sandy shores

設問の訳

この告知の目的は何か。
(A) 活動の説明をすること
(B) 旅程を伝えること
(C) 特別割引の宣伝をすること
(D) 動物保護について説明すること

この告知では何が述べられているか。
(A) すべてのツアーにガイドが同行する。
(B) いくつかのツアーでボートを利用する
(C) 旅行者は前払いしなければならない。
(D) 割引価格は利用できない。

アイランドホッピングツアーで見ることのできないものは何か。
(A) 熱帯林
(B) 野生の水中生物
(C) 動物公園
(D) 砂浜

TOEIC豆知識

TOEIC公開テストは、全会場、統一問題を使っているわけではない。毎回、問題の異なるいくつかの〈フォーム〉が確認されている。2012年10月現在、各回2種類が一般的だが、3種類の回もあり。（続く▶）

問題文の訳

設問159から161は次の告知に関する質問です。

Ocean Breeze Resort
セイシェル共和国 Shipwon 諸島

Ocean Breeze Resortへようこそ！
Shipwon諸島は豊富な海洋生物と旅行者向けの珍しいアトラクションで知られています。❶Shipwon諸島を満喫していただくために、これらの活動を試すことをお勧めします。

アイランドホッピング
❷❸ボートに乗ってShipwonの豊かなマングローブとジャングル、ラグーン、白亜の絶壁、そして白い砂浜をめぐる1日のツアーに出かけましょう。❹何千もの水生生物が生息するShipwonの広大なサンゴ礁の探検をご希望の方には、シュノーケリング用の装備もご用意しております。

Miliganツアー
MiliganはShipwonの南に位置しており、自然のままのサルや珍しい鳥たちと触れ合うことのできる野生生物の自然保護区です。❺MiliganへはOcean Breeze Resortよりボートで30分です。

トレッキング
Amitan山への❻ガイド付きツアーに参加してEngle湾の素晴らしい眺めをお楽しみください。この冒険には、ツアーガイドと山岳ガイドがあなたのお供をします。

ご予約はフロントの受付係にお申し付けください。❼10名以上のグループのお客さまには割引があります。

単語

- □ *be* known for ~ ～で知られている
- □ unique 類のない、独特の
- □ tourist attraction 観光名所
- □ hop onto ~ ～にとび乗る
- □ mangrove マングローブ
- □ lagoon ラグーン、礁湖
- □ limestone 石灰岩
- □ cliff 絶壁、がけ
- □ extensive 広大な
- □ coral reef サンゴ礁
- □ creature 生物
- □ sanctuary 鳥獣保護区、聖域
- □ interact ～と交流する、ふれ合う
- □ environment 環境
- □ guided tour ガイド付きツアー
- □ splendid 素晴らしい
- □ mountaineer 登山家
- □ accompany ～に付いて行く
- □ coordinate 調整する
- 159 □ describe ～を述べる、説明する
  - □ promote ～を宣伝販売する
  - □ conservation 保護
- 160 □ reduced 減らされた
- 161 □ shore 岸、海岸

正解＆解説

159. 正解 (A)　難易度 難

告知の目的を尋ねている。主題に関わる設問なので、**冒頭に注目**しよう。❶で「この諸島を楽しむために、これらの**活動を勧める**」と述べ、以降、3つの活動内容を説明している。従って、正解は (A) To describe activities（活動の説明をすること）。

160. 正解 (B)　難易度 難

告知で述べられていることを尋ねるTrue問題。各選択肢を文書の内容と照らし合わせていこう。(A) のガイドに関しては、Trekkingの説明に❻「ガイド付きツアー」とあるだけなので、誤り。(B) の「ボート利用」については、❷に「ボートに飛び乗って1日ツアーに出かける」、❺に「Miliganへはボートで30分」とあり、**ふたつのツアーで利用する**ことがわかるので、これが正解。(C) についてはまったく触れられていない。(D) は❼に「10人以上の団体には割引あり」とあるので、誤り。

161. 正解 (C)　難易度 難

アイランドホッピングで**見ることができない**ものを尋ねるNot問題。各選択肢と文書の内容をひとつひとつ照らし合わせていこう。(A) と (D) は、❸に「マングローブとジャングル」、「白い砂浜」とあるので、見ることができる。(B) は❹に「水生生物の生息地を探検したい方には、シュノーケリングの装備を用意」とあるので、誤り。(C) の**動物公園**に関する記述はどこにもないので、これを見ることができないと判断できる。よって (C) が正解。

🔁 Mangroves and jungles ➡ Tropical forests
　 white sand beaches ➡ Sandy shores

TEST 3
PART 7

Questions 162-164 refer to the following advertisement.

BTC 12
An Entertainment Network

Advertise With Us

Make your products and services known by advertising on the prime time shows of the BTC Channel. As the No. 1 entertainment channel in the country, the network reaches more than ten million viewers every day, according to the latest report of MediaLine-UK Survey. Our award-winning shows attract a wide range of viewers, so marketing your product or service on our channel will reach thousands of consumers.

Prime time Package

- One-to-two-minute airtime for advertising spots on all prime time shows
- A button advertisement on the BTC Web site
- Inclusion of your company logo in SMS promotions flashed after the end of each show

For more details about the package, please contact the BTC 12 Advertising Services Department at 555-8888 and ask for an account executive.

Learn more about our ongoing and upcoming prime time shows on www.BTC12.com.

---

162. What is mentioned about BTC 12?

(A) It is the most profitable TV network in the country.
(B) It is the country's top entertainment network.
(C) It offers only nighttime programming.
(D) It has affiliates around the world.

163. What is NOT included in the Prime time Package?

(A) An online advertisement
(B) Broadcast commercial spots
(C) SMS advertising
(D) A product presentation on a show

164. How can clients find out about the cost of the package?

(A) By calling a network representative
(B) By visiting a Web site
(C) By writing an e-mail
(D) By sending a text message

設問の訳

BTC 12について何が述べられているか。

(A) 国内でもっとも高収益なテレビ放送網である。
(B) 国内トップのエンターテインメント放送網である。
(C) 夜間帯にのみ放送している。
(D) 世界中に系列局がある。

ゴールデンタイムパッケージプランに含まれていないものは何か。

(A) オンライン広告
(B) スポットCMの放送
(C) ショートメッセージ広告
(D) 番組内での商品の紹介

パッケージプランの料金を顧客が知るにはどうすればよいか。

(A) 局の担当者に電話する
(B) ウェブサイトを見る
(C) Eメールを書く
(D) 携帯メールを送る

> **TOEIC豆知識** 各〈フォーム〉は、すべての問題が異なるわけではなく、共通問題も織り交ぜながら構成されている。（続く▶）

問題文の訳

設問 162 から 164 は次の広告に関する質問です。

BTC 12
エンターテインメント放送網

当社で広告をだしませんか

BTC Channel のゴールデンタイムの番組で貴社の商品やサービスを宣伝し、知名度を高めませんか。MediaLine-UK 調査会社の最新報告によれば、❶国内 No. 1 のエンターテインメントチャンネルである当社放送網の視聴者数は毎日 1000 万人以上に達します。私どもの受賞歴のある番組の視聴者は広範囲に及ぶので、私どものチャンネルで貴社の商品やサービスを宣伝すれば、何千もの消費者の目に触れることになります。

ゴールデンタイムパッケージプラン

❷・すべてのゴールデンタイム番組での 1~2 分のスポット CM 放送
❸・BTC のウェブサイト上でのボタン広告
❹・各番組後に提示されるショートメッセージ広告での貴社のロゴ表示

❺パッケージプランの詳細につきましては、BTC 12 広告サービス部（電話番号 555-8888）にご連絡いただき、顧客主任にお問い合わせください。

ゴールデンタイムに放送中、または今後放送予定の番組については www.BTC12.com をご覧ください。

単語

- □ prime time （テレビ、ラジオの）ゴールデンタイム
- □ reach ～に達する、届く
- □ according to ～ ～によれば
- □ consumer 消費者
- □ airtime 放送時間
- □ inclusion 含めること、包含
- □ flash ～をぱっと見せる
- □ account executive 顧客担当主任、営業部長
- □ ongoing 進行している、実施中の

162 □ profitable 利益をもたらす、もうかる
□ affiliate 支店、系列会社

163 □ broadcast 放送の

164 □ find out about ～ ～について知る、情報を得る
□ representative 代表者
□ text message 携帯電話のメール

正解＆解説

162. 正解 **(B)**　難易度 ■■□難

BTC 12 について言及されていることを尋ねている。❶に「<u>the No. 1 entertainment channel in the country</u>（国内 No. 1 のエンターテインメントチャンネル）として」とある。これを、<u>the country's top entertainment network</u>（国内トップのエンターテインメント放送網）と言い換えた (B) が正解。

⇄ the No. 1 entertainment channel in the country ➡ the country's top entertainment network

163. 正解 **(D)**　難易度 ■■□難

ゴールデンタイムパッケージに**含まれていない**ものを尋ねる Not 問題。選択肢をひとつひとつ文書の内容と照らし合わせて、答えを見つけよう。(A) の「オンライン広告」については❸に、(B) の「CM 放送」については❷に、(C) の「ショートメッセージ広告」については❹にそれぞれ記述がある。(D) の**「番組内での商品の紹介」**についてだけ、記述が見当たらないので、これが正解。

164. 正解 **(A)**　難易度 ■■■難

料金について知る方法を尋ねている。しかし、この広告は料金についていっさい触れていない。ポイントは、❺の **For more details about the package**（パッケージの詳細については）に、料金に関することも含まれると気づけるかどうか。❺では、詳細を知る方法として「広告サービス部、**555-8888 まで連絡して、顧客主任に問い合わせてほしい**」と指示をしている。これを「局の担当者に電話する」と表現した (A) が正解。

TEST 3 PART 7

Questions 165-167 refer to the following e-mail.

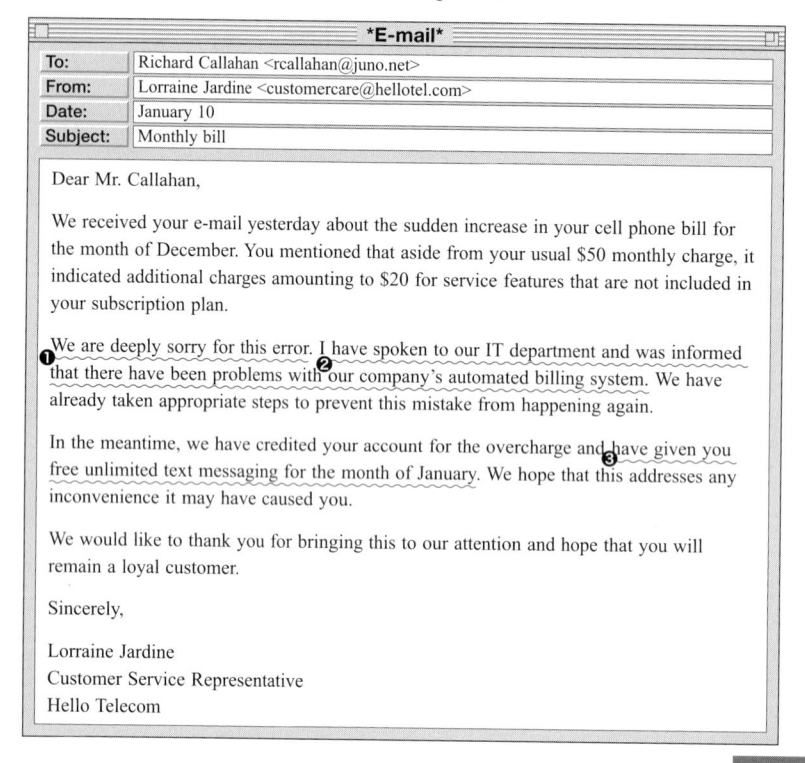

E-mail

To:	Richard Callahan <rcallahan@juno.net>
From:	Lorraine Jardine <customercare@hellotel.com>
Date:	January 10
Subject:	Monthly bill

Dear Mr. Callahan,

We received your e-mail yesterday about the sudden increase in your cell phone bill for the month of December. You mentioned that aside from your usual $50 monthly charge, it indicated additional charges amounting to $20 for service features that are not included in your subscription plan.

❶ We are deeply sorry for this error. I have spoken to our IT department and was informed that there have been problems with ❷ our company's automated billing system. We have already taken appropriate steps to prevent this mistake from happening again.

In the meantime, we have credited your account for the overcharge and ❸ have given you free unlimited text messaging for the month of January. We hope that this addresses any inconvenience it may have caused you.

We would like to thank you for bringing this to our attention and hope that you will remain a loyal customer.

Sincerely,

Lorraine Jardine
Customer Service Representative
Hello Telecom

---

165. What is the main purpose of the e-mail?

(A) To request additional payment
(B) To cancel a subscription
(C) To apologize for a problem
(D) To report an error

166. What is the reason for the increase in Mr. Callahan's bill?

(A) He signed up for an extra service.
(B) He forgot to make a payment.
(C) There was a computer problem.
(D) There were hidden charges.

167. What does Ms. Jardine offer Mr. Callahan?

(A) A free service for a limited time
(B) A refund check
(C) An updated billing statement
(D) New product discounts

> **TOEIC豆知識** 〈フォーム〉の違いは、問題冊子の表紙右肩にある「Form 4IIC22」といった表記から判断できる。今度受験するときに確認してみよう。（続く▶）

問題文の訳

設問 165 から 167 は次の E メールに関する質問です。

宛先： Richard Callahan <rcallahan@juno.net>
送信者： Lorraine Jardine <customercare@hellotel.com>
日付： 1月10日
件名： 月額料金

Callahan さま
12 月分の携帯電話利用料金が急上昇したとのメールをきのういただきました。基本料金の月額 50 ドルのほかに、ご契約プランに含まれていないサービスについての余分な請求が 20 ドルにのぼるとのことでした。

❶このたびの手違いについて、深くお詫びいたします。❷IT 課に確認したところ、当社の自動料金請求システムに問題が発生したとのことでした。このような誤りが二度と起こることのないよう、すでに適切な措置は講じられております。

一方、過剰請求分につきましては、Callahan さまのお口座に払い戻しいたしました。また、❸1 月分の携帯メールのご利用を無料で無制限とさせていただきます。これが今回お掛けしたご迷惑の埋め合わせになればと思います。

今回の件をお知らせくださいましてありがとうございました。今後とも変わらぬご愛顧をお願い申し上げます。

敬具
Lorraine Jardine
お客さまサービス担当
Hello Telecom

単語

- □ sudden 突然の
- □ aside from ～ ～のほかに
- □ amount to ～ ～に達する、のぼる
- □ subscription 定期購読、会費
- □ automated 自動の
- □ billing 請求書作成
- □ take steps 対策を講じる
- □ appropriate 適切な
- □ credit （お金を）口座に入れる
- □ overcharge 過剰請求
- □ address ～に対処する
- □ remain ～のままでいる
- □ loyal customer お得意さま、ひいきの顧客

166 □ hidden 隠された、秘密の

正解 & 解説

165. 正解 **(C)** 難易度 ■■■□ 難

E メールの目的を尋ねている。このように主題に関わる設問のヒントは、冒頭にくることが多いが、ここでは**中盤**の❶にある。このようなケースもあることを心に留めておこう。❶で「このたびの**手違いについてお詫びする**」と謝罪し、以降も、手違いへの対応、補償について説明しているので、目的は「問題の謝罪をすること」だと判断できる。従って、(C) が正解。

↻ sorry for ... error ➡ apologize for a problem

166. 正解 **(C)** 難易度 ■■■□ 難

Callahan 氏の請求金額が増えた理由を尋ねている。20 ドルの余計な請求が発生した理由について、❷で「IT 課に確認したところ、**自動料金請求システムに問題があった**」と述べている。これを「コンピュータの問題があった」と抽象的に表現した (C) が正解。

167. 正解 **(A)** 難易度 ■■■□ 難

Jardine さんが、Callahan 氏に提供を申し出たことを尋ねている。❸に「あなた（= Callahan 氏）に **1 月の間、無料で無制限の携帯メールサービス**を提供」とある。これは、1 月の間だけの「期間限定の無料サービス」なので、(A) A free service for a limited time が正解。

↻ free ... for the month of January ➡ free ... for a limited time

間違いメモ

165. あなたの解答 A B C D
メモ

166. あなたの解答 A B C D
メモ

167. あなたの解答 A B C D
メモ

TEST 3
PART 7

Questions 168-171 refer to the following memo.

TO: Sharon Littleton, branch manager
FROM: Shawn Bell, regional accounting director
SUBJECT: Expense reports
DATE: Sept. 5

Hi Sharon,

I received your quarterly expense report last week and have had some time to look over it. I wanted to write you and say how happy I am that you are managing to follow the budget in the Portland branch, as the expenditures have been quite moderate. I did want to mention that my associate, Brenda Russell, has been doing some research to find out if we can find a better Internet provider for you. You mentioned that your current provider, Oregon-Com has recently raised their rates, and that you haven't been pleased with their service, as the Internet is often down and the staff haven't been helpful. She is looking to see if there's a better package deal for businesses which supplies Internet and a telephone connection together. This might help lower your expenses even further. I will let you know what we find out, and you can also contact me if you have any ideas or preferences.

EXPENSE REPORT: PORTLAND BRANCH

Expenditures	May	June	July	August
Utilities	$489.34	$547.87	$532.29	$496.52
Office supplies	$113.67	$87.54	$76.38	$122.57
Telephone	$429.92	$321.76	$214.96	$378.45
Internet	$280	$280	$280	$280
TOTAL	$1312.93	$1237.17	$1103.63	$1277.54

168. What is the main purpose of the memo?

(A) To inform Ms. Littleton of budget cuts
(B) To request figures on office expenditures
(C) To give feedback on a financial report
(D) To suggest a new Internet service

169. The word "moderate" in paragraph 1, line 3 is closest in meaning to

(A) unimportant
(B) average
(C) negotiable
(D) timid

170. What does the memo indicate about the Internet provider currently used in Portland?

(A) It offers discounted package rates.
(B) Ms. Littleton has been unsatisfied with its service.
(C) It recently contacted Ms. Russell.
(D) Its staff always provides assistance when needed.

171. According to the memo, what is Ms. Russell currently doing?

(A) Creating a budget for the next financial quarter
(B) Sending payments to creditors
(C) Working on a deal with Oregon-Com
(D) Looking for better offers

設問の訳

168. このメモの主な目的は何か。
　(A) Littleton さんに予算の削減を伝えるため
　(B) オフィス関連の出費の数値を求めるため
　(C) 財務報告に意見を述べるため
　(D) 新しいインターネットサービスを提案するため

169. 第1段落・3行目の moderate にもっとも近い意味の語は
　(A) 重要でない
　(B) 平均的な、並の
　(C) 交渉可能な
　(D) 臆病な

170. 現在ポートランドで利用されているインターネットプロバイダについて、このメモは何を述べているか。
　(A) パッケージ料金の割引を行っている。
　(B) Littleton さんはサービスに不満である。
　(C) 最近 Russell さんに連絡してきた。
　(D) 必要なときにはいつでもスタッフが手助けしてくれる。

171. このメモによると、Russell さんは現在何をしているか。
　(A) 次の会計四半期の予算を作成している
　(B) 債権者への支払いを行っている
　(C) Oregon-Com との契約作業に取り組んでいる
　(D) よりよいオファーを探している

単語
- quarterly　4分の1の、四半期の
- manage to do　なんとか〜する、〜できる
- expenditure　経費、支出額
- associate　仲間、同僚
- deal　契約
- supply　〜を提供する、供給する
- lower　〜を減らす
- preference　好み
- utilities　光熱費、公共料金
- office supply　オフィス用品
- **168** cut　削減
- **171** financial quarter　会計四半期
- creditor　債権者、貸し主

TEST 3　PART 7

> 問題文の訳

設問168から171は次のメモに関する質問です。

宛先： 　Sharon Littleton 支店長
差出人：　Shawn Bell 地域経理担当局長
件名： 　支出報告
日付： 　9月5日

Sharon さん

❶四半期支出報告を先週受け取り、目を通しました。ポートランド支店では支出がそれほど大きくならず、予算内でことが運べていることを非常にうれしく思い、このたびメールを差し上げました。そのほかにお伝えしたいことは、目下私の同僚の❷Brenda Russell が、Sharon さんのためによりよいインターネットプロバイダを見つけるべく調査しているということです。現在ご利用中のプロバイダの Oregon-Com は近ごろ料金を値上げし、また❸インターネットがしばしば利用不可能になったり、担当者の対応がよくなかったりと、サービスが満足できるものではないとのことでしたね。Brenda はインターネットと電話サービスをセットで提供する企業向けのよりよいパッケージプランがあるか探しています。これによって支出をより一層抑えることができるのではないかと思います。詳細が判明次第ご連絡いたします。また、ご意見やご希望があればお伝えください。

支出報告：ポートランド支店

支出	5月	6月	7月	8月
光熱費	489.34 ドル	547.87 ドル	532.29 ドル	496.52 ドル
オフィス用品	113.67 ドル	87.54 ドル	76.38 ドル	122.57 ドル
電話	429.92 ドル	321.76 ドル	214.96 ドル	378.45 ドル
インターネット	280 ドル	280 ドル	280 ドル	280 ドル
合計	1312.93 ドル	1237.17 ドル	1103.63 ドル	1277.54 ドル

TOEIC豆知識 〈フォーム〉の識別は、マークシートA面（氏名やアンケートを記入する側）の色でも可能。〈フォーム〉が2種類の場合は、ピンクと緑色の2パターンのマークシートが確認されている。B面（解答する側）は共通のうす茶色。

正解 & 解説

168. 正解 **(C)**　難易度 ■■■□□ 難

メモの目的を尋ねている。主題に関わる設問なので、**冒頭に注目**しよう。❶で「四半期**支出報告を受け取り、目を通した**」と用件を切りだし、以降、この支出報告書に対する評価やアドバイスが続く。従って、expense report を financial report（財務報告）と言い換えている (C) To give feedback on a financial report（財務報告に意見を述べるため）が正解。

🔄 expense report ➡ financial report

169. 正解 **(B)**　難易度 ■■■□□ 難

メモで用いられている moderate と似た意味を持つ単語を尋ねる類義語問題。文脈 as the expenditures have been quite moderate（支出がとても適度である）の中で、moderate は「**適度の、並の**」という意味で用いられている。これに類似するのは「**平均の、並の**」という意味の (B) average。

170. 正解 **(B)**　難易度 ■■■□□ 難

ポートランドで利用しているプロバイダについて、述べられていることを尋ねる True 問題。各選択肢の内容をメモと照らし合わせていく。(A) の「割引」をしているとの記述はない。(B) の「Littleton さん」は、このメモの受け手であり、メモ中の you にあたる。❸に「あなたは、**彼ら（＝現在のプロバイダ）のサービスに満足していない**」とあり、(B) の内容に一致するので、これが正解。(C) については触れられていない。(D) については❸の後半でまったく反対のことが述べられている。

🔄 haven't been pleased with ➡ has been unsatisfied with

171. 正解 **(D)**　難易度 ■■■□□ 難

Russell さんが今、行っていることを尋ねている。設問のキーワードである、固有名詞の **Ms. Russell** に注目しながらメモをみていくと、❷に Brenda Russell があり、彼女は「**よりよいインターネットプロバイダを見つけるべく調査している**」とある。このことを「よりよいオファーを探している」と表現した (D) Looking for better offers が正解。

TEST 3
PART 7

Questions 172-175 refer to the following e-mail.

E-mail

From:	Leonard Irvin <l.irvin@ecca.com>
To:	Violet Curtis <v_curtis@bestmail.com>
Subject:	Admission to Empress Center for Culinary Arts
Date:	July 30

Dear Ms. Curtis,

We are pleased to inform you that you have passed the written entrance exam for the Culinary Arts and Technology Management Course at the Empress Center for Culinary Arts (ECCA).

As a standard school policy, we require applicants of academic programs to take our 12-hour Kitchen Discovery Training in order to assess their cooking skills. Training begins on September 2 and will be conducted on every successive Friday of the month from 1 P.M. to 4 P.M. Top ECCA alumni will facilitate classes in Italian pasta, French cuisine, and basic baking. Taster magazine editor in chief Pedro de Luca will hold the Italian pasta class on the first Friday, while Chef's Delight host Allan Spears will be in charge of the French cuisine class on the following Friday. Pastry chef Noreen Baltimore of Oregon Hotel will give baking classes on the last two Fridays of the month. The training fee is $300. Payment includes cooking ingredients, a culinary knife set, and copies of featured recipes.

If you are interested in pursuing the application, please register for training before August 25. For inquiries, reply to this e-mail or call our office hotline at 555-9687.

Thank you.

Sincerely,

Leonard Irvin
Director
Student Admissions Office

172. What is mentioned about Kitchen Discovery Training?
(A) It is a requirement for a job application.
(B) It is offered to professional chefs.
(C) It is a prerequisite to a culinary arts course.
(D) It is organized by ECCA students.

173. What is implied about Ms. Curtis?
(A) She is interested in baking.
(B) She wants to take up an academic program.
(C) She works for a food magazine.
(D) She is applying for a position in the ECCA.

174. Who will NOT teach one of the courses?
(A) Allan Spears
(B) Noreen Baltimore
(C) Pedro de Luca
(D) Leonard Irvin

175. On which Friday of September will the French cuisine class be held?
(A) The first
(B) The second
(C) The third
(D) The fourth

設問の訳

172. キッチンディスカバリー研修について何が述べられているか。
(A) 求職の申し込みの際に必要である。
(B) プロのシェフのために開講される。
(C) 料理法クラス受講のために必須である。
(D) ECCA の学生によって運営されている。

173. Curtis さんについて何が示唆されているか
(A) ベーキングに興味を持っている。
(B) 教育プログラムの受講を希望している。
(C) 食品関連の雑誌で仕事をしている。
(D) ECCA の求人に応募している。

174. クラスを担当しないのは誰か。
(A) Allan Spears
(B) Noreen Baltimore
(C) Pedro de Luca
(D) Leonard Irvin

175. フランス料理のクラスが開かれるのは9月のどの金曜日か。
(A) 第1金曜
(B) 第2金曜
(C) 第3金曜
(D) 第4金曜

単語
- entrance exam 入学試験
- assess 〜を評価する
- successive 連続する
- alumni alumnus（（男の）卒業生）の複数形 ※ただし、alumni で男女を含めた「卒業生」を意味することも。
- facilitate 〜を容易にする、手助けする
- editor in chief 編集長
- in charge of 〜 〜を担当して
- ingredient （料理の）材料
- recipe 調理法、レシピ
- pursue 〜を実行する、遂行する
- inquiry 質問
- **172** prerequisite 必須条件
- **173** imply 〜を暗に意味する、ほのめかす
- take up 〜 〜に取りかかる、〜を始める

問題文の訳と解説 ☞ 次ページに続く

TEST 3 PART 7

問題文の訳

設問172から175は次のEメールに関する質問です。

送信者： Leonard Irvin <l.irvin@ecca.com>
宛先： Violet Curtis <v_curtis@bestmail.com>
件名： Empress料理法センターへの入学許可
日付： 7月30日

Curtisさま

❶貴殿がEmpress料理法センター(ECCA)の料理法・テクノロジー管理コースへの筆記試験に合格されたことをお伝えします。

当校の一般方針に基づき、❷教育プログラムの志望者は、調理技術の評価を受けるため、12時間のキッチンディスカバリー研修を受講する必要があります。❸研修は9月2日にはじまり、同月の毎週金曜日午後1時から4時まで実施されます。成績優秀であったECCAの卒業生たちがイタリアンパスタ、フランス料理、そしてベーキング基礎の各クラスの授業補助を行います。Taster誌編集長の❹Pedro de Luca氏が第1金曜日にイタリアンパスタクラスを担当し、Chef's Delight司会の❺Allan Spears氏が翌週金曜のフランス料理クラスを受け持ちます。そして❻Oregonホテルの焼き菓子シェフであるNoreen Baltimore氏が最後ふたつの金曜にベーキングクラスを開きます。研修クラス受講料は300ドル。支払金額には料理材料、調理用ナイフセット、そしてクラスで使用するレシピ冊子が含まれています。

応募に興味をお持ちでしたら、8月25日までに研修クラスに登録してください。ご質問は、このメールに返信されるか、当校の専用電話555-9687にお電話ください。

ありがとうございました。

敬具

❼Leonard Irvin
局長
入学事務局

正解＆解説

172. 正解 **(C)**　難易度　難

キッチンディスカバリー研修について、言及されていることを尋ねる True 問題。❷で「**教育プログラムの志望者は、キッチンディスカバリー研修を受講する必要がある**」と述べている。ここでは料理学校の授業が話題なので、「教育プログラム」とは料理に関する教育プログラムのこと。その受講を希望する人はまず、キッチンディスカバリー研修を受けなければいけないと言っている。このことを **prerequisite**（必要条件）と表現した (C) It is a prerequisite to a culinary arts course.（料理法クラス受講のために必須である）が正解。

173. 正解 **(B)**　難易度　難

Curtis さんについて、示唆されていることを尋ねている。まず、Curtis さんがメールの受け手であることを把握。❶で「**あなた（＝ Curtis さん）は料理法・テクノロジー管理コースの筆記試験に合格した**」と述べられている。ここから、この「**教育プログラムの受講を希望している**」と推測できる。従って、(B) She wants to take up an academic program. が正解。(A) の「ベーキングに興味を持っている」は、ベーキングに限定してしまっている点が誤り。

174. 正解 **(D)**　難易度　難

授業を**担当しない**人を尋ねる Not 問題。選択肢をひとつひとつ、E メールの内容と照らし合わせていこう。(A) の Allan Spears は、❺に「フランス料理クラス」担当とあり、(B) の Noreen Baltimore は、❻に「ベーキングクラス」担当とある。(C) の Pedro de Luca は、❹で「イタリアンパスタクラス」担当と述べられている。(D) の Leonard Irvin については、**担当クラスが示されていない**のに加え、❼に「**入学事務局　局長**」とあることから、授業を担当しないとわかる。従って、(D) が正解。

175. 正解 **(B)**　難易度　難

フランス料理クラスが、9月のどの金曜日に実施されるかが問われている。まず❸でトレーニングが9月2日に始まることを把握。次に、❹でイタリアンパスタの授業が「最初の金曜日（＝9月2日）」に開催されることを押さえる。そして最後、❺でフランス料理のクラスは「その次の金曜日」と述べられていることから、「**第2金曜日**」に開催されると判断できる。よって (B) The second が正解。

PART 7

Questions 176-180 refer to the following article.

New Museum to Open in the Spring

At a press conference held yesterday, Minister of Antiquity, Fatima Hawas said that the deadline for the completion of the Royal National Museum of History has been delayed until the spring.

Originally scheduled to open in November of this year, the new museum and its facilities will now open on March 1 next year. Hawas said the delay was due to the unexpected challenges of moving the nation's treasures from across the country to the new museum in a safe manner. "We did not expect that the transfer of some larger artifacts and sculptures would be so difficult. But we don't want to rush the process and risk damage to any of our nation's treasures."

Construction of the new museum, located on the outskirts of the capital city, started five years ago. In addition to the public exhibition areas, the facility boasts large warehouses for artifacts not on display, a 500-seat auditorium for special events, an educational center for visiting archaeologists and professors, and dining and shopping establishments.

Mohammad Sharrif was appointed to head up the project by Hawas six years ago. Sharrif said, "This is probably the most challenging project I have ever worked on, but also the most rewarding." Sharrif claims that the current museum facilities in the capital city are in terrible condition and lack the necessary security systems. "My main goal was to make a home for our nation's treasures where they can be kept safely for generations to come. In addition, we hope that the Royal National Museum will benefit the tourism industry. We are predicting a 20 percent increase in tourists next year due primarily to the grand opening of this new facility."

176. What is the purpose of the article?

(A) To announce an upcoming renovation project
(B) To give an update on a facility construction
(C) To promote a museum exhibition
(D) To provide details of a grand opening

177. According to the article, why was the opening rescheduled?

(A) There were problems relocating some items.
(B) There were insufficient funds to complete the building.
(C) There was a problem caused by government policy.
(D) There was a security system malfunction.

178. Who is Mohammad Sharrif?

(A) A government representative
(B) A university professor
(C) A local archaeologist
(D) A leader for a project

179. What is NOT mentioned as being a part of the new facility?

(A) Display spaces
(B) Storage areas
(C) Eating facilities
(D) Library archives

180. What did Mr. Sharrif indicate about the project?

(A) It is costing more than expected.
(B) It will attract more visitors to the country.
(C) It is being promoted internationally.
(D) It was not as difficult as he had expected it to be.

設問の訳

176. この記事の目的は何か。
 (A) きたるべき改修プロジェクトを公表すること
 (B) 施設建設の最新情報を伝えること
 (C) 博物館の展示を宣伝すること
 (D) グランドオープンの詳細を説明すること

177. 記事によれば、開館予定が変更されたのはなぜか。
 (A) 物品の移動に問題が生じた。
 (B) 建物の完成には資金が足りなかった。
 (C) 政府の政策によって問題が生じた。
 (D) セキュリティーシステムに障害があった。

178. Mohammad Sharrif とは誰か。
 (A) 政府代表
 (B) 大学教授
 (C) 地元の考古学者
 (D) 計画のリーダー

179. 新しい施設の一部として述べられていないのは何か。
 (A) 展示スペース
 (B) 保管エリア
 (C) 飲食施設
 (D) 図書館資料室

180. Sharrif 氏は計画について何を述べたか。
 (A) 予想より費用が掛かっている。
 (B) より多くの観光客を国内に呼び込む。
 (C) 国際的に宣伝されている。
 (D) 予想ほど困難ではなかった。

単語
- press conference 記者会見
- completion 完成
- unexpected 予期しない
- treasure 貴重品、宝物
- manner 方法
- artifact 工芸品、美術品
- sculpture 彫刻品、彫像
- rush 急いで～をする
- risk ～の危険を冒す
- boast （施設など）を持っている
- on display 展示中の
- archaeologist 考古学者
- appoint ～を指名する、任命する
- head up ～ ～を指揮する
- rewarding 価値のある、やりがいのある
- claim ～と主張する
- terrible ひどい
- lack ～を欠いている
- generation 世代
- benefit ～の利益になる
- predict ～を予測する
- primarily 主に、第一に
- **177** relocate ～を移転させる
- insufficient 不十分な
- government 政府
- malfunction 故障、不調
- **179** archive 記録保管所

問題文の訳と解説 ☞ 次ページに続く

TEST 3 PART 7

> 問題文の訳

設問176から180は次の記事に関する質問です。

春に新しい博物館が開館

きのう開かれた記者会見で、考古大臣の Fatima Hawas は❶ロイヤル・ナショナル歴史博物館の完成期限が来春まで延期されると述べた。

当初今年11月の開館予定だったが、新博物館とその関連施設は、現在は来年3月1日にオープンすることになっている。❷Hawas 大臣によると、この遅延は、国宝を国中から新博物館へと安全に輸送することが予想外に困難であったためと話した。「複数の大型工芸品と彫刻品の輸送がこれほど困難だとは考えてもいませんでした。しかし、作業を急ぐことによって、わが国の国宝に損害を与える危険を冒すことはできません」と大臣は述べている。

新博物館の建設は、首都の近郊で5年前に始まった。❸一般展示エリアのほか、展示されていない美術品のための大型倉庫、特別イベントのための500名収容の講堂、そして客員考古学者・教授のための教育施設、さらに飲食とショッピングのための施設が併設されている。

❹Mohammad Sharrif 氏は6年前 Hawas 大臣によってこの計画を指揮するよう任命された。「これはおそらく私がこれまで関わったプロジェクトの中で、もっとも困難なものですが、同時にもっともやりがいがあります」と Sharrif 氏は述べている。氏によれば、首都にある博物館施設の現在の状態はひどいものであり、必須のセキュリティーシステムすら備えていないのだという。「私の主たる目標は、私たちの国宝を今後何世代にもわたって安全に保管できる場所を作ることです。また、ロイヤル・ナショナル博物館は観光産業に寄与できるとも考えています。❺私たちはこの新しい施設の開館を主な理由として、来年観光客数が20%増加すると見込んでいます」と Sharrif 氏は述べている。

正解＆解説

176. 正解 (B) 難易度：難

記事の目的を尋ねている。主題に関わる設問では、**冒頭に注意**しよう。❶で「**歴史博物館の完成期限が春まで延期された**」という**新情報を伝え**、以降もこの博物館の建設工事に関する情報が続く。よって、正解は (B) To give an update on a facility construction（施設建設の最新情報を伝えること）。(D) の「グランドオープンの詳細を説明すること」は、開館は延期されたと述べられているので誤り。

⇄ completion of Royal National Museum of History ➡ a facility construction

177. 正解 (A) 難易度：難

開館スケジュールが調整された理由を尋ねている。❷で「この遅延は、**国宝を安全に移動させることが予想外に困難であったため**」と遅れの理由を説明している。これを「**物品の移動に問題が生じた**」と言い換えた (A) There were problems relocating some items. が正解。

⇄ moving the nation's treasures ➡ relocating some items

178. 正解 (D) 難易度：難

Mohammad Sharrif が誰かを尋ねている。この**固有名詞に注目**すると、❹に登場する。「**Mohammad Sharrif はこの計画を指揮するよう任命された**」と述べられているので、このことを「計画のリーダー」と表現した (D) A leader for a project が正解。

179. 正解 (D) 難易度：難

新しい施設について**言及されていない**ことを尋ねる Not 問題。各選択肢を記事の内容と照らし合わせて、答えを探る。新しい施設（＝歴史博物館）の特徴は、❸でまとめて述べられている。言及されているのは **public exhibition areas**（一般展示エリア）、**large warehouses**（大型倉庫）、auditorium（講堂）、educational center（教育施設）、**dining and shopping establishments**（飲食とショッピングのための施設）。この 5 つのなかに、(A)「展示スペース」、(B)「保管エリア」、(C)「飲食施設」は含まれている。言及がないのは、(D) Library archives（図書館書庫）。よって、これが正解。

⇄ exhibition areas ➡ Display spaces
　warehouses ➡ Storage areas
　dining establishments ➡ Eating facilities

180. 正解 (B) 難易度：難

Sharrif 氏が、この計画について述べていることを尋ねる True 問題。(A) の費用についての言及は見当たらない。(B) の「より多くの観光客を国内に呼び込む」は、❺の「新しい施設の開館により、**観光客が 20 パーセント増加する**」という内容に一致するので、これが正解。(C) (D) に関連した記述はない。

⇄ increase in tourists ➡ attract more visitors

TEST 3
PART 7

Questions 181-185 refer to the following list and e-mail.

Red Lantern Tours

See the ancient wonders of Beijing with Red Lantern Tours! We can provide you with tour guides who are fluent in English, French, Japanese, or Spanish. They are government-licensed guides that will help make your trip to Beijing both exciting and memorable. Included in all tours are transportation, entrance fees to all sites, and brochures and maps for places of interest. Red Lantern Tours offers the following four packages:

Morning Tour 9:00 A.M.-12:30 P.M. $65	Pickup from hotel Tour of Forbidden City Snack and beverage Return to hotel	Day Tour 9:00 A.M.-6:00 P.M. $120	Pickup from hotel Tour of Forbidden City Lunch Buffet Tour of Olympic Village Visit to National Museum of China Return to hotel
Day and Evening Tour 9:00 A.M.-9:00 P.M. $180	Pickup from hotel Tour of Forbidden City Lunch Buffet Visit to Palace Museum Tour of Olympic Village Dinner Buffet Visit to Tiananmen Square Visit to Night Market Return to hotel	Two Day Tour $240	Day one same as Day and Evening Tour Day two Pickup from hotel Tour of Great Wall of China Lunch Buffet Visit to tourist market Tour of Ming Dynasty Tombs Return to hotel

If you have questions, or would like to make a reservation, send us an e-mail at reservations@redlanterntours.net or visit our Web site at www.beijingredlantours.com.

***Groups of four or more visitors are eligible for a 20 percent discount.

E-mail

To:	reservations@redlanterntours.net
From:	Judie Bond <jbond@spemail.com>
Subject:	Change to reservations

I booked a tour of Beijing through your company for four colleagues and myself. I was recently informed that our company has given us an additional day in the city to do some sightseeing. So I would like to change our reservations from the Day Tour to the one that includes a visit to the Great Wall of China. You may charge the additional fee to the credit card number I gave you before.

Also, some of my colleagues and I are vegetarian and I was wondering if there are options for us in the meals you provide. Please let me know. In addition, we will be staying at the Ching Hotel, so please inform me at what time we should be ready for pickup.

Thank you for your patience, and I hope these changes will not be too much trouble.

Sincerely,

Judie Bond

181. What is NOT included in the price of the tours?
  (A) A tour guide
  (B) Admission charges
  (C) Airport transportation
  (D) Maps and pamphlets

182. Which tour does Ms. Bond want to go on?
  (A) Morning Tour
  (B) Day Tour
  (C) Day and Evening Tour
  (D) Two Day Tour

183. What is suggested about the tours?
  (A) Some food and drinks are provided.
  (B) They are highly recommended.
  (C) They are operated by the government.
  (D) Refunds are not provided for cancellations.

184. What can be inferred about Ms. Bond's reservation?
  (A) It hasn't been made.
  (B) It was discounted.
  (C) It is only for one day.
  (D) It was paid for by the company.

185. What is mentioned about Ms. Bond's colleagues in the e-mail?
  (A) They are visiting a branch in Beijing.
  (B) Some of them do not eat meat.
  (C) They are staying at different hotels.
  (D) Some of them are unable to come on the trip.

設問の訳

181. ツアーの料金に含まれていないのは何か。
  (A) ツアーガイド
  (B) 入場料
  (C) 空港への交通手段
  (D) 地図とパンフレット

182. Bond さんが参加したいのはどのツアーか。
  (A) モーニングツアー
  (B) デイツアー
  (C) デイ・イブニングツアー
  (D) ツーデイツアー

183. ツアーについて何が示唆されているか。
  (A) 食事と飲みものがだされる。
  (B) 非常におすすめできる。
  (C) 政府によって運営されている。
  (D) キャンセルしても返金されない。

184. Bond さんの予約について何がわかるか。
  (A) まだ完了していない。
  (B) 割引を受けた。
  (C) 1日用のものである。
  (D) 会社負担である。

185. メールの中で、Bond さんの同僚について何が述べられているか。
  (A) 北京支社を訪問予定である。
  (B) 肉類を食べない人がいる。
  (C) 別々のホテルに滞在する。
  (D) 何名かは旅行に参加できない。

単語
- wonder 不思議なもの、出来事
- fluent 流暢な
- memorable 記憶に残る
- pickup 乗客を乗せること
- Forbidden City 紫禁城
- buffet バイキング式の食事、ビュッフェ
- Palace Museum 故宮博物館
- Tiananmen Square 天安門広場
- Great Wall of China 万里の長城
- Ming Dynasty Tombs 明の十三陵
- eligible 資格のある
- 181 pamphlet パンフレット
- 183 highly 非常に、大いに
- 184 infer 〜を推測する

問題文の訳と解説 ☞ 次ページに続く

TEST 3 PART 7

問題文の訳

設問181から185は次のリストとEメールに関する質問です。

Red Lantern ツアー

Red Lantern ツアーで北京の往古の不思議を体験しませんか。私たちは英語、フランス語、日本語、またはスペイン語に堪能な❶ツアーガイドをご用意できます。ツアーガイドは政府の認可を受けており、北京への旅行を刺激的で忘れがたいものにしてくれるはずです。❷すべてのツアーには交通手段、施設への入場料、そして観光名所のパンフレットと地図が含まれています。Red Lantern Tours では以下の4つのパッケージプランをご用意しています。

モーニングツアー 午前9時～午後0時30分 65ドル	ホテルにお出迎え 紫禁城見学 ❸軽食とお飲み物 ホテルに到着	デイツアー 午前9時～午後6時 120ドル	ホテルにお出迎え 紫禁城見学 ❹バイキング形式の昼食 北京オリンピック村見学 中国国家博物館訪問 ホテルに到着
デイ・イブニングツアー 午前9時～午後9時 180ドル	ホテルにお出迎え 紫禁城見学 ❺バイキング形式の昼食 故宮博物館訪問 北京オリンピック村見学 ❻バイキング形式の夕食 天安門広場訪問 夜市訪問 ホテルへ到着	ツーデイツアー 240ドル	1日目 デイ・イブニングツアーと同様 2日目 ホテルへお出迎え ❼万里の長城見学 ❽バイキング形式の昼食 旅行者向け市場訪問 明の十三陵見学 ホテルへ到着

ご質問、ご予約はEメールを reservations@redlanterntours.net にお送りいただくか、弊社ウェブサイト www.beijingredlanterntours.com にお越しください。
❾***4名さま以上のグループには、20%の割引が適用されます。

宛先： reservations@redlanterntours.net
送信者： Judie Bond <jbond@spemail.com>
件名： 予約の変更

❿私と4名の同僚で北京ツアーを貴社にて予約したものです。つい先日会社から、観光のため市内での休暇をもう1日もらえることになりました。そこで、⓫予約していましたデイツアーを万里の長城訪問を含むツアーに変更したいと考えています。追加分の費用は先日お伝えしたクレジットカード番号にご請求ください。

また、⓬私と同僚数名はベジタリアンですので、おだしいただける食事の内容を選択することは可能でしょうか。ご連絡お願いします。加えて、⓭私たちは Ching Hotel に滞在予定なのですが、何時にお迎えに来ていただけるのかもお伝え願います。

ご寛容に感謝いたします。この変更が多大なご面倒をお掛けすることがなければよいのですが。

敬具

Judie Bond

| 正解＆解説 |

181. 正解 **(C)** 難易度 ■■■■□ 難

ツアー料金に**含まれていない**ものを尋ねる Not 問題。(A) の「ツアーガイド」は、❶に「用意できる」とある。(B) (C) (D) については、❷の内容と対比する。❷で述べられているのは「交通手段」「入場料」「観光名所のパンフレットと地図」の3つ。(B) と (D) はふたつ目と3つ目に一致する。(C) の「空港への交通手段」はひとつ目の「交通手段」に一致するように思われるが、❷で述べられているのは**ツアー中の移動手段**のことであり、**空港への送迎は含まれていない**。従って、(C) がツアーに含まれないものとして正しい。

↻ entrance fees ➡ Admission charges
　brochures ➡ pamphlets

182. 正解 **(D)** 難易度 ■■■■□ 難

ふたつの文書に分散した情報を関連付けて答える**クロスリファレンス問題**。Bond さんが希望するツアーを尋ねているので、まず Bond さんの E メールに目を通す。すると⓫に「デイツアーの予約を、**万里の長城訪問を含むものに変更したい**」とある。しかし、万里の長城を含むツアーがどれかは、メールには記されていないのでリストに目を移す。4種類のツアーの構成内容を調べていくと、❼に Tour of Great Wall of China とあるので、この「**ツーデイツアー**」が Bond さんが参加したいツアーだと判断できる。よって (D) Two day tour が正解。

183. 正解 **(A)** 難易度 ■■■■□ 難

ツアーについて、示唆されていることを尋ねている。リストにあるツアー内容を確認すると❸❹❺❻❽に Snack and beverage、Lunch Buffet、Dinner Buffet とある。つまり、**すべてのツアーに軽食か昼食、もしくは夕食が含まれている**ということ。これを「食事と飲みものがだされる」と表現した (A) Some food and drinks are provided. が正解。

184. 正解 **(B)** 難易度 ■■■■□ 難

これも**クロスリファレンス問題**。Bond さんの予約について、推論できることを尋ねている。まず Bond さんのメールから確認していくと、❿に「私と同僚4名の北京ツアーを予約した」とある。つまり、**5名の団体**で予約したということ。人数に関連する記述が、リストの❾に「4名以上のグループには20% の割引あり」とあることと考え合わせると、**Bond さんの予約は割引対象**だと判断できる。よって、(B) It was discounted.（割引を受けた）が正解。

↻ are eligible for a ... discount ➡ was discounted

185. 正解 **(B)** 難易度 ■■■■□ 難

Bond さんの同僚について言及されていることを尋ねる True 問題。各選択肢を文書の内容と照らし合わせて、答えを探る。(A) の「北京支社訪問」という内容は見当たらない。(B) の「**肉類を食べない人がいる**」は、⓬に「同僚数人と私は**ベジタリアン**だ」とあるので、これが正解。(C) の「別のホテルに滞在する」は⓭で反対のことが述べられている。(D) の「何名かが参加しない」という内容は見当たらない。

↻ vegetarian ➡ do not eat meat

TEST 3
PART 7

Questions 186-190 refer to the following e-mails.

E-mail

To:	Lalaine Bryant <l.bryant@fastmail.com>
From:	Touch Shopping <orders@touchshopping.com>
Subject:	Order confirmation
Date:	July 13

Dear Ms. Bryant,

Thank you for purchasing products from Touch Shopping. The details of your order are as follows:

Customer name: Lalaine Bryant
Billing and shipping address: Unit 501 Baritone Gardens, 95 Belair Court, Matawan, NJ 07747

Product #	Description	Unit	Price
KP2053	Baker's Choice loaf pan: Nonstick metal	2	$29.98
KP5125	Childe mixing bowl: Three-piece set of stainless steel mixing bowls	1	$13.25
KP0245	Socorro measuring cups: Four-piece set of dry plastic measuring cups	1	$14.50
KP4800	Feighton pizza wheel: Stainless steel	1	$10.99
Delivery charge			$0
Total			$68.72
Mode of payment: Galaxy Credit Card Card number: 6677 5369 3140 4500			

*All products are inclusive of tax. Free delivery applies to areas within New Jersey only.

Please allow three days for the shipment of your order. Merchandise may be returned within two weeks following delivery. For questions and other concerns, please send an e-mail to orders@touchshopping.com. Visit www.touchshopping.com to learn more about our new products and promotions.

We hope to serve you again.

Respectfully yours,

Touch Shopping

E-mail

To:	Touch Shopping <orders@touchshopping.com>
From:	Lalaine Bryant <l.bryant@fastmail.com>
Subject:	Product order
Date:	July 19

Dear Touch Shopping,

I received the merchandise I bought from your store yesterday. Although the products were in good condition, I noticed that you sent me the wrong loaf pans. I ordered nonstick metal pans, but you delivered ceramic ones. Since I needed extra pans for baking today, I had no choice but to use the ones you sent me. One thing I liked about the ceramic pans was that I was able to use them for both baking and serving cake. However, I still find it easier to bake using the metal pans as they conduct heat more quickly and evenly. In addition, they are durable and their nonstick surface makes them easy to clean.

Nevertheless, I've decided not to return the ceramic pans. But I do request that you coordinate with my bank and make the necessary deductions to my credit card bill because the ceramic pans are cheaper than the ones I originally ordered. I expect to see the changes reflected in my next billing statement.

I look forward to your immediate action on this matter.

Sincerely,

Lalaine Bryant

186. What information is included in the first e-mail?

(A) A delivery date
(B) A company address
(C) Client details
(D) Product discounts

187. What is implied about Touch Shopping?

(A) It publishes baking recipes.
(B) It operates a shipping firm.
(C) It is located in Matawan.
(D) It sells cooking equipment.

188. What is NOT stated about product KP2053?

(A) It is easy to clean.
(B) It is good for serving cakes.
(C) It is long lasting.
(D) It is designed to distribute heat evenly.

189. What did Ms. Bryant ask Touch Shopping to do?

(A) Deliver new products
(B) Correct the charge to her account
(C) Provide her with a replacement
(D) Send her an order form

190. In the second e-mail, the word "reflected" in paragraph 2, line 3 is closest in meaning to

(A) observed
(B) returned
(C) imitated
(D) indicated

設問の訳

186. ひとつ目の E メールにはどんな情報が含まれているか。
(A) 配送日
(B) 企業の住所
(C) 顧客の詳細情報
(D) 商品の割引

187. Touch Shopping について何がわかるか。
(A) ケーキ作りのレシピを発行している。
(B) 運送会社を経営している。
(C) Matawan が所在地である。
(D) 調理器具を販売している。

188. 製品 KP2053 について述べられていないのはどれか。
(A) 手入れが容易である。
(B) ケーキを（テーブルに）だすのに向いている。
(C) 長持ちする。
(D) 熱が均等に伝わるよう設計されている。

189. Bryant さんは Touch Shopping に何をするよう依頼したか。
(A) 新商品を配達する
(B) 請求金額を訂正する
(C) 商品の交換に応じる
(D) 注文用紙を送る

190. ふたつ目の E メールの第 2 段落・3 行目の reflected にもっとも近い意味の語は
(A) 観察された
(B) 返送された
(C) 模倣された
(D) 示された

単語

- as follows 以下の通りで
- loaf pan パン焼き用鍋
- nonstick こげつかない
- mode of payment 支払い方法
- inclusive 含めて、勘定に入れて
- apply to 〜 〜にあてはまる、適用される
- Respectfully yours （ていねいな手紙の結び）敬具

＊＊＊

- ceramic 陶磁器の
- conduct 〜を伝導する
- evenly 均等に
- durable 耐久力のある
- nevertheless それにもかかわらず
- coordinate 調整する
- deduction 差し引き、控除
- originally もともと、当初は
- immediate 迅速な
- **188** lasting 長持ちする
- **189** correct 〜を訂正する

問題文の訳と解説 ☞ 次ページに続く

TEST 3　PART 7

問題文の訳

設問186から190は次のふたつのEメールに関する質問です。

宛先： Lalaine Bryant <l.bryant@fastmail.com>
送信者： Touch Shopping <orders@touchshopping.com>
件名： ご注文内容の確認
日付： 7月13日

Bryantさま
Touch Shoppingで商品をお買い上げいただきありがとうございました。ご注文の詳細は以下の通りです。

❶お客さま氏名：Lalaine Bryant
請求・商品配送先住所：Unit 501 Baritone Gardens, 95 Belair Court, Matawan, ニュージャージー 07747

製品番号	詳細	数量	価格
❷KP2053	❸Baker's Choice パン焼き用鍋：こびりつき防止金属製	2	29.98ドル
KP5125	Childe 混ぜ鉢：ステンレススチール製混ぜ鉢3点セット	1	13.25ドル
KP0245	Socorro 計量カップ：ドライプラスチック製計量カップ4点セット	1	14.50ドル
KP4800	Feighton ピザカッター：ステンレススチール製	1	10.99ドル
配送料			0ドル
合計			68.72ドル
お支払い方法：Galaxy クレジットカード			
カード番号：6677 5369 3140 4500			

＊すべての商品は税込価格です。無料配送エリアはニュージャージー州内のみとなります。

注文品の配達には3日を要します。商品は配達から2週間以内であれば返品可。ご質問や気になる点がございましたら、orders@touchshopping.com までEメールをお送りください。新商品や販促について、さらにお知りになりたければwww.touchshopping.com をご覧ください。

またのご利用をお待ちしております。

よろしくお願い申し上げます。
Touch Shopping

宛先： Touch Shopping <orders@touchshopping.com>
送信者： Lalaine Bryant <l.bryant@fastmail.com>
件名： 商品の注文
日付： 7月19日

Touch Shoppingさま
きのうそちらで購入した商品が届きました。商品の状態は問題なかったのですが、注文したものとは異なったパン焼き用鍋が送られてきました。私はこびりつき防止金属製のものを注文したのですが、セラミック製のものが届きました。本日のケーキ作りのために必要だったため、やむを得ず届いた商品を使わなければなりませんでした。セラミック製鍋のよいところは、ケーキを焼くこととテーブルにだすことの両方に使える点です。ですが、❹やはり熱を素早くかつ均等に伝導する金属製のほうがケーキを焼くのには使いやすいと思います。それに、❺金属製のほうが耐久性に優れており、こびりつき防止加工はお手入れが楽ということもあります。

ですが、このセラミック製の鍋は返品しないでおこうと思いますので、❻私の銀行と調整してクレジットカードの請求額からしかるべき金額を差し引いてください。セラミック製鍋のほうが、私のもともと注文したものより値段が安いためです。来月の請求明細でこの変更の確認ができれば幸いです。

迅速な対応をよろしくお願いします。

敬具
Lalaine Bryant

正解&解説

186. 正解 **(C)**　難易度 ■■■□□ 難

ひとつ目のEメールに含まれる情報を尋ねるTrue問題。選択肢とEメールの内容を照らし合わせて、一致するものを見つけよう。(A) の「配送日」については、「配達に3日かかる」との記述はあるが、具体的な日にちを述べていないので、誤り。(B) の「企業の住所」は、❶に記載されているBryantさんの住所と混同しないようにしなければいけない。(C) の「**顧客の詳細情報**」は、この❶の内容に一致するので、これが正解。(D) の「商品の割引」に関する情報は見当たらない。

187. 正解 **(D)**　難易度 ■■■■□ 難

Touch Shopping社について示唆されていることを尋ねている。❸の列を見ると、Bryantさんが購入した商品として、「パン焼き用鍋」「混ぜ鉢」「計量カップ」「ピザカッター」が記載されている。これらはすべて、**料理道具**なので、Touch Shopping社は「調理器具を販売している」と推測ができる。よって、(D) It sells cooking equipment. が正解。

188. 正解 **(B)**　難易度 ■■■■■ 難

ふたつの文書に分散した情報を関連付けて答える**クロスリファレンス問題**。製品KP2053について**述べられていない**ことを尋ねている。まず、ひとつ目のEメールの❷の行から、KP2053が「**パン焼き鍋**」であり、「**こびりつき防止の金属製**」であることを確認。ひとつ目のメールには、それ以上の情報はないので、次のメールに目を移すと、❹に金属製の特徴として「**熱を素早く、均等に伝える**」とある。加えて、❺に「**耐久性があり、こびりつき防止加工は手入れが楽**」ともある。(A) (C) (D) は、これらの内容に一致するが、(B) It is good for serving cakes.（ケーキをだすのに向いている）については触れられていないので、これが正解。この特徴は、セラミック製の鍋のもの。

⇄ durable ➡ long lasting
conduct heat ➡ distribute heat

189. 正解 **(B)**　難易度 ■■■■□ 難

Bryantさんが、Touch Shopping社に依頼したことを尋ねている。Bryantさんが出したふたつ目のEメールを見ていくと、❻に **I do request ...** という依頼表現がある。依頼内容は「銀行と調整してクレジットカードの**請求額から、しかるべき額を差し引いてほしい**」というもの。これを「請求金額を訂正する」と表現した (B) Correct the charge to her account が正解。

⇄ make the necessary deductions to ... credit card bill ➡ Correct the charge to ... account

190. 正解 **(D)**　難易度 ■■■□□ 難

ふたつ目のEメールで用いられているreflectedと似た意味の単語を尋ねる類義語問題。I expect to see the changes reflected in my next billing statement. は、「次回請求明細でこの修正が〈**反映されている**〉のを確認したい」という意味。この文脈中の「**反映された、示された**」という意味にもっとも近いのは、(D) indicated。

TEST 3
PART 7

Questions 191-195 refer to the following announcement and survey.

In an effort to promote a safer and healthier work environment, we will be conducting a one-day training course on workplace safety and health management this May. The course is divided into four parts, as follows:

    I   Introduction to Safety and Health Management
    II Due Diligence and Responsibilities
    III Behavioral-based Safety and Risk Assessment
    IV Recognition, Evaluation, and Control of Hazards

Specific dates have been assigned for each department (see schedule below). Please note that all employees are required to attend the course.

Date	Department
May 23	Reception staff
May 24	Wait staff
May 25	Kitchen staff
May 26	Marketing staff

For further questions about the course and the schedule, you may contact the training manager's office on extension number 432.

EMPLOYEE TRAINING COURSE
Evaluation Survey

Course Title	Workplace Safety and Health Management						
Department	Reception		Wait		Kitchen	X	Marketing	

Please mark the appropriate box based on level of satisfaction.
(5 being the highest and 1 being the lowest)

	1	2	3	4	5
The course materials and discussions were concise and easy to understand.					X
All my questions were answered clearly and completely.					X
It will be easy for me to apply what I have learned in the performance of my duties.					X
Overall, I am satisfied with the training I received.					X

Remarks   The part of the training about identifying and understanding dangers was especially helpful, providing us with ideas on the various preventive measures we can take against accidents and injuries within the workplace.

All data collected from this survey is anonymous and will be kept strictly confidential.
Responses will be used solely for the enhancement of future training courses.

191. What is the purpose of the course?
 (A) To explain adjustments to a work schedule
 (B) To discuss updates on an advertising campaign
 (C) To prepare the staff for management reorganization
 (D) To educate employees on workplace safety and wellness

192. What is indicated in the survey?
 (A) All employees filled out a copy of the form.
 (B) The names of those answering questions will be kept a secret.
 (C) Completed documents must be submitted to departmental managers.
 (D) The results will be discussed later by the trainees.

193. When did the survey respondent attend the course?
 (A) On May 23
 (B) On May 24
 (C) On May 25
 (D) On May 26

194. Which part of the course did the survey respondent find particularly useful?
 (A) Recognition, Evaluation, and Control of Hazards
 (B) Behavioral-based Safety and Risk Assessment
 (C) Due Diligence and Responsibilities
 (D) Introduction to Safety and Health Management

195. Who will most likely use the information indicated in the responses on the survey?
 (A) The executive chef
 (B) The marketing supervisor
 (C) The head receptionist
 (D) The training manager

設問の訳

191. この講座の目的は何か。
 (A) 作業スケジュールの変更を説明するため
 (B) 宣伝キャンペーンの最新情報を話し合うため
 (C) 経営陣の再編についてスタッフに前もって準備させるため
 (D) 職場の安全と健康について従業員を教育するため

192. 調査票について何が述べられているか。
 (A) 全従業員が用紙に記入した。
 (B) 質問回答者の氏名は秘密にされる。
 (C) 記入済み書類は各部門長に提出しなければならない。
 (D) 調査結果はのちに研修受講者によって議論される。

193. 調査票の回答者がコースに出席したのはいつか。
 (A) 5月23日
 (B) 5月24日
 (C) 5月25日
 (D) 5月26日

194. 調査票の回答者は講座のどの部分を特に有益だと感じたか。
 (A) 危険性の認識・評価・コントロール
 (B) 行動に基づく安全性と危険性の評価
 (C) 適正評価と責任
 (D) 安全と健康管理入門

195. 調査票の回答から得られる情報を利用すると考えられるのは誰か。
 (A) 主任シェフ
 (B) マーケティング監督者
 (C) 受付主任
 (D) トレーニングマネージャー

単語
- workplace 職場
- divide ～を分割する
- due diligence 適正評価
- behavioral 行動に関する
- assessment 査定、評価
- recognition 認識、承認
- evaluation 評価
- hazard 危険、危険要素
- assign ～を割り当てる
- reception 受付
- extension 内線

***

- appropriate 適切な、ふさわしい
- satisfaction 満足
- concise 簡潔な
- overall 全体としては
- remark 所見、感想
- preventive 予防の
- measures 対策、手段
- injury けが
- anonymous 匿名の
- strictly 厳しく
- confidential 秘密の、他言無用の
- solely ただ～だけで
- enhancement 増進、強化
- **191** adjustment 調整、調節
- reorganization 再組織、再編
- wellness 健康
- **193** respondent 回答者
- **194** particularly 特に

問題文の訳と解説 ☞ 次ページに続く

TEST 3 PART 7

> 問題文の訳

設問191から195は次のお知らせと調査票に関する質問です。

❶職場環境をより安全で健康的なものとするために、今年5月に職場の安全と健康管理について学ぶ1日研修講座を開講いたします。講座は以下の4つのパートに分けられています。

    I   安全と健康管理入門
    II 適正評価と責任
    III 行動に基づく安全性と危険性の評価
    IV 危険性の認識・評価・コントロール

日程は部署別になっています（下表をご覧ください）。すべての従業員が講座に出席しなければなりません。

5月23日	受付スタッフ
❷5月25日	調理スタッフ
5月24日	給仕スタッフ
5月26日	営業スタッフ

講座やスケジュールに関する質問は、研修管理者のオフィス（内線432）までご連絡ください。

従業員研修講座
評価調査票

講座名	職場での安全と健康管理						
部局	受付		給仕		❸調理	X	マーケティング

満足度に応じて該当するボックスにマークしてください。
（5が最高で1が最低です）

	1	2	3	4	5
コース教材とその内容は簡潔でわかりやすかった。					X
すべての疑問に対して明確で十分な回答が得られた。					X
今回学習した内容を職務の遂行に生かすのは容易だと思う。					X
全体的に見て、受講した研修に満足している。					X
コメント	❹研修の中では、危険性の発見と理解に関する部分が特に役に立ちました。と言うのは、職場内での事故やけがに対して私たちが講じることのできるさまざまな予防策を知ることができたからです。					

❺この調査で集められたすべてのデータは匿名化され、極秘扱いとなります。
❻回答は今後の研修講座をよりよくするためにのみ使用されます。

正解＆解説

191. 正解 **(D)**　難易度 ■■□ 難

研修の目的を尋ねている。研修内容を知らせる案内のほうを確認していくと、冒頭❶で「**職場環境を安全で健康的なものにするため、研修講座を実施する**」と目的が述べられている。これに一致するのは (D) To educate employees on workplace safety and wellness（職場の安全と健康について従業員を教育するため）。

---

192. 正解 **(B)**　難易度 ■■□ 難

調査票について述べられていることを尋ねる True 問題。各選択肢をひとつひとつ文書と照らし合わせ、内容が一致するものを選ぶ。調査票を見ていくと、(A) (C) (D) に関する記述は見当たらない。(B) の「質問回答者の氏名は秘密にされる」は、❺の「すべてのデータは anonymous（匿名）であり、**strictly confidential**（極秘として）扱われる」という内容に一致する。従って、(B) が正解。

⇄ be kept ... confidential ➡ be kept a secret

---

193. 正解 **(C)**　難易度 ■■□ 難

ふたつの文書に分散した情報を関連付けて答える**クロスリファレンス問題**。調査票の回答者が講座に出席した日を尋ねている。日付に関して触れているのは、案内の中ほど。部署別に受講日を指示している。調査票に目をやると❸で、回答者が「**調理部**」に所属するとわかる。❷から、調理部の受講日は「**5月25日**」とわかるので、正解は (C) On May 25。

---

194. 正解 **(A)**　難易度 ■■■ 難

調査票の回答者が、特に有益だと感じている部分を尋ねている。調査票を確認していくと、❹のコメント欄に「**identifying and understanding dangers**（危険性の発見と理解）に関する部分が特に役立った」とある。これが講座のどの部分を指しているかを考えると、IV Recognition, Evaluation, and Control of Hazards のなかでも、特に **Recognition ... of Hazards**（危険の認知）という部分に一致するとわかる。従って、正解は (A)。

⇄ identifying and understanding dangers ➡ Recognition ... of Hazards

---

195. 正解 **(D)**　難易度 ■■□ 難

調査票の情報を利用する人を推論する問題。この調査票が、**従業員研修**に関するものであることに加え、❻に「回答は今後の**研修講座の強化**にのみ用いられる」とある。ということは、調査票の情報は「**研修管理者**」が利用するだろうと判断できるので、正解は (D) The training manager。

TEST 3
PART 7

Questions 196-200 refer to the following itinerary and memo.

Bonita Cosmetics
Itinerary for: Mario Cruz

Sept. 10 Friday	10:20 A.M.	Arrival at Charles de Gaulle airport *Driver will meet you	Hotel Antoinette (Paris)
Sept. 11 Saturday	9:30 A.M.	Breakfast meeting with Isabel Trudeau, Bonita regional director	Hotel Antoinette
	11:00 A.M. - 6:00 P.M.	Visit to convention center/set up booth for trade fair	Convention center
	7:40 P.M.	Flight to Nice, Orly airport	Dauphin Hotel (Nice)
Sept. 12 Sunday		Enjoy your day off in Nice!	
	6:50 P.M.	Flight to Paris, Cote d'Azur airport	Hotel Regent (Paris)
Sept. 13 Monday	8:00 A.M.	Meeting with booth staff for the trade fair	Convention center
	10:00 A.M. - 7:00 P.M.	Trade fair opens/New product presentation	Convention center
	8:30 P.M.	Dinner with Michel Depuis, owner of Chamber Department Stores	Pomme de Terre Restaurant
Sept. 14 Tuesday	10:00 A.M. - 7:00 P.M.	Trade fair	Convention center
	10:20 P.M.	Return to Buenos Aires, Charles de Gaulle airport	

TO: Mario Cruz

FROM: Flavia Perez

SUBJECT: Your Itinerary for France

As you requested, I am sending you a copy of your itinerary and the contact information of the people you will be meeting during the trip to Paris. If you would like, I can also send you a list of phone numbers of the hotels you will be staying at, so that you can give them to your colleagues here in Buenos Aires. Let me know if you would like me to do so.

There will be a driver waiting for you in Paris, who will take care of your transportation for all appointments. All hotels have already been paid for, apart from the one in Nice, as it will be your personal expense. Also, please keep all receipts for business meals so that you can be reimbursed.

I received word from our production manager, Antonio Gutierrez, that the samples of Bonita's new line of fragrances for your presentation will be shipped today to our branch office in Paris. They will be delivered to the place you will be staying at on Friday, as you will need them for the event on Monday.

If you need anything else, or have any questions just let me know!

100

196. Why is Mr. Cruz traveling to Paris?
(A) To present his company's new products at a trade event
(B) To meet with retailers interested in selling Bonita merchandise
(C) To help set up a regional office for the European market
(D) To order items at a sales fair to sell in his company's store

197. What is Mr. Cruz NOT scheduled to do during his trip?
(A) Meet with the proprietor of a chain of stores
(B) Have a meal with a colleague
(C) Visit Bonita's branch office in Paris
(D) Attend an event at a convention center

198. What does Ms. Perez offer to send to Mr. Cruz?
(A) The address of a hotel
(B) A travel itinerary
(C) Some product samples
(D) Contact information

199. What is indicated about Bonita's new line of perfumes?
(A) They will be sold in Chamber Department Stores.
(B) They will be sent to Hotel Antoinette.
(C) They will not be ready in time for the event.
(D) They will be given out to potential buyers.

200. According to the memo, which expense will Mr. Cruz have to pay for?
(A) The meal with Michel Depuis
(B) The room cost at Hotel Antoinette
(C) The charge for the Dauphin Hotel
(D) The flight to Buenos Aires

設問の訳

196. Cruz 氏はなぜパリへ出張するのか。
(A) 見本市で自社の新商品を発表するため
(B) Bonita 社の商品の販売に関心を持っている小売業者に会うため
(C) ヨーロッパ市場のための地方支社の設立を手助けするため
(D) 自社の店で販売する商品を販売フェアで注文するため

197. 出張中に Cruz 氏の予定に入っていないのは何か。
(A) チェーン店のオーナーと会う
(B) 同僚と会食する
(C) Bonita 社のパリ支店を訪問する
(D) コンベンションセンターでのイベントに参加する

198. Perez さんは何を Cruz 氏に送ると申し出ているか。
(A) ホテルの住所
(B) 旅程表
(C) 商品サンプル数点
(D) 連絡先情報

199. Bonita 社の新作香水について何が述べられているか。
(A) Chamber デパートで販売される。
(B) Antoinette ホテルに送られる。
(C) イベントには間に合わない見込みだ。
(D) 見込客に配られる。

200. メモによれば、Cruz 氏が支払わなければならないのはどの費用か。
(A) Michel Depuis 氏との会食代
(B) Antoinette ホテルの部屋代
(C) Dauphin ホテルの料金
(D) ブエノスアイレスへの航空運賃

単語
- itinerary 旅程、旅行計画
- trade fair 見本市、展示会

***
- apart from ～ ～は別として、～のほかに
- receipt レシート、領収書
- reimburse （経費など）を返済する
- word 知らせ、ことづて
- fragrance 香水、よい香り

196 retailer 小売業者
197 proprietor 所有者
199 perfume 香水、芳香
- in time for ～ ～に間に合って
- give out ～ ～を配る

問題文の訳と解説 ☞ 次ページに続く

TEST 3 PART 7

問題文の訳

設問 196 から 200 は次の旅程表とメモに関する質問です。

Bonita Cosmetics

旅程表：Mario Cruz さま

9月10日 (金)	午前10時20分	シャルルドゴール空港到着 ※ドライバーが出迎え	❶Antoinette ホテル（パリ）
9月11日 (土)	午前9時30分	❷Bonita 社地域主任 Isabel Trudeau と朝食会	Antoinette ホテル
	午前11時～午後6時	コンベンションセンター訪問／見本市のブース設営	コンベンションセンター
	午後7時40分	空路ニースへ。オルリー空港発	❸Dauphin ホテル（ニース）
9月12日 (日)		ニースでの休日をお楽しみください。	
	午後6時50分	❹空路パリへ　コートダジュール空港発	Regent ホテル（パリ）
9月13日 (月)	午前8時	見本市のブーススタッフと会合	コンベンションセンター
	午前10時～午後7時	❺見本市開幕／新商品の発表	❻コンベンションセンター
	午後8時30分	❼Chamber デパートオーナー Michel Depuis 氏と夕食	レストラン Pomme de Terre
9月14日 (火)	午前10時～午後7時	見本市	コンベンションセンター
	午後10時20分	ブエノスアイレスへ帰還　シャルルドゴール空港発	

宛先：　 Mario Cruz
差出人：Flavia Perez
件名：　 フランスでの旅程表

ご要望通り、旅程表とパリ出張中に会合予定の方の連絡先をお送りします。お望みでしたら、ブエノスアイレスの同僚に伝えられるよう、❽滞在するホテルの電話番号リストもお送りできます。ご希望でしたらお伝えください。

パリではドライバーが待機しており、すべての面会のための移動の世話をしてくれます。❾ホテルはすべて支払い済みですが、個人的出費であるニースのホテルは除きます。また、業務上の食事については、レシートを保存しておいていただければ、払い戻しを受けることができます。

生産責任者の Antonio Gutierrez より連絡があり、❿あなたの発表のために Bonita の新作香水のサンプルが本日パリ支社に発送されるということです。⓫そのサンプルは、月曜のイベントで必要でしょうから、金曜日に滞在予定のホテルに届けられます。

そのほかご入用のもの、またはご質問などがありましたらご連絡ください。

TOEIC豆知識 毎試験後、ツイッターやフェイスブックなどの SNS 上で、テストの感想が盛んにやりとりされている。こうした情報交換も、TOEIC を受験する楽しみのひとつ。あなたも参加してみては？

正解＆解説

196. 正解 (A) 難易度：難

ふたつの文書に分散した情報を関連付けて答える**クロスリファレンス問題**。Cruz 氏がパリへ出張する理由を尋ねている。まず、旅程表に目を向けると❹に「パリ行きフライト」とあり、**9月12日にパリに向かう**ことがわかる。その翌日9月13日の❺に「見本市開催／新製品の発表」とある。しかし、これだけでは Cruz 氏が、具体的に何をするのかはっきりしない。次のメモまで読み進めていくと、❿に「**あなた（＝ Cruz 氏）の発表のために、Bonita の新作香水のサンプルが発送される**」とある。ここではじめて、Cruz 氏の出張目的が「見本市で自社の新商品（＝新作香水）を発表するため」と判断できる。正解は (A) To present his company's new products at a trade event.

197. 正解 (C) 難易度：難

Cruz 氏が出張中に**行わない**だろうことを尋ねる Not 問題。(A) の「チェーン店のオーナーと会う」は、❼「Chamber Department Stores のオーナーと夕食」で予定されている。Stores と複数形になっていることから、この Chamber Department には複数の店舗がある、つまりチェーン店だということがわかる。(B) は、❷の「Bonita 社の地域主任と朝食会議」という予定に一致。(C) の「**Bonita 社のパリ支店を訪問する**」という予定はどこにも記載されていないので、これが正解。(D) については、❺と❻から、見本市がコンベンションセンターで開催されるとわかるので、誤り。

🔁 owner of Chamber Department Stores ➡ proprietor of a chain of stores
Trade fair ➡ an event

198. 正解 (D) 難易度：難

Perez さんが、何を送ると提案しているのかを尋ねている。Perez さんのメモを確認すると、❽で「ご希望なら、滞在する**ホテルの電話番号リストを送る**」と提案している。電話番号を「連絡先情報」と言い換えた (D) Contact information が正解。「住所リストを送る」と勘違いして (A) を選ばないように。また、(C) についても、❿の内容につられて選びたくなるが、新作香水のサンプルを発送するのは、Antonio Gutierrez である。

🔁 a list of phone numbers ➡ Contact information

199. 正解 (B) 難易度：難

Bonita 社の新しい香水について述べられていることを尋ねる True 問題であると同時に、**クロスリファレンス問題**でもある。まず、新作香水に言及しているメモから確認していくと、❿⓫に「新作香水のサンプルはパリ支社に発送され、**金曜日にあなた（＝ Cruz 氏）が滞在するホテルに届けられる**」とある。金曜日のホテルを旅程表で確認すると、❶に **Hotel Antoinette** とあるので、(B)「Antoinette ホテルに送られる」が正解。(A) と (D) に関する記述は見当たらない。(C) の「イベントには間に合わない」は、⓫「月曜日のイベントに必要だろうから、金曜日に届ける」という内容に一致しない。

🔁 perfumes ➡ fragrances

200. 正解 (C) 難易度：難

ふたつの文書に分散した情報を関連付けて答える**クロスリファレンス問題**。Cruz 氏が負担すべき費用を尋ねている。「メモによれば」とあるので、まずメモから見ていくと、❾に「**個人的出費であるニースのホテルを除いて**、ホテル代はすべて支払い済み」とある。つまり、ニースのホテル代を Cruz 氏は負担しなければならない。旅程表に移動して、ニースのホテルを確認すると❸に **Dauphin Hotel** とある。よって Cruz 氏が負担するのは、(C)「Dauphin ホテルの料金」。

TEST 3
重要語句——索引

《注意》参照先は、問題番号を示している。[Q12]は、問題No.12のこと。
Part 3、4、6、7については、会話やパッセージに含まれるものを[41-43]と記し、設問と選択肢に含まれるものを[Q41]というように記している。

A

- absolutely 62-64
- abstract art Q135
- accompany 159-161
- according to～ 162-164
- account executive 162-164
- accounting Q47
- achievement Q68
- additional 147-149
- address Q100
- adjustment Q191
- administrative 155-156
- admission 141-143
- advertising agency Q52
- advisable Q118
- affect 95-97
- affiliate Q162
- aircraft Q72
- airtime 162-164
- alternative Q130
- alumni 172-175
- ambassador Q102
- amount to～ 165-167
- amusement park Q115
- analyst Q92
- announcement Q39
- anonymous 191-195
- apart from～ 196-200
- apologize for～ 155-156
- appear 141-143
- appease Q132
- appliance Q116
- applicant Q128
- application form Q45
- apply to～ Q15, 186-190
- appoint 176-180
- appreciation Q157
- appropriate 165-167
- approval Q120
- approve 141-143
- archaeologist 176-180
- archive Q179
- arrange Q1
- article Q18
- artifact 176-180
- as follows 186-190
- aside from～ 165-167
- assembly Q38
- assess 172-175
- assessment 191-195
- assign 191-195
- associate 168-171
- association Q16
- assortment Q4
- assume 89-91
- at the moment 47-49
- attend 44-46

B

- attire Q110
- attractive Q34
- auditorium Q3
- authority 80-82
- automated 165-167
- available 41-43

- bachelor 141-143
- back pain 44-46
- banquet 53-55
- be aware of～ 157-158
- be encouraged to do 141-143
- be known for～ 159-161
- be supposed to do Q26
- be urged to do 80-82
- behavior 56-58
- behavioral 191-195
- beneficial Q137
- benefit 176-180
- bill Q17
- billing 165-167
- billing statement Q48
- blinds Q10
- block off～ Q135
- board Q5
- board meeting Q13
- boarding gate 71-73
- boast 176-180
- book 41-43
- bound for～ 71-73
- bouquet 74-76
- branch office Q25
- breakthrough Q96
- brief Q79
- broadcast Q163
- browse through～ Q3
- budget Q85
- buffet 181-185
- business administration Q15
- by air 74-76

C

- cabinet Q10
- call in sick 86-88
- candidate Q14
- caretaker Q135
- cart Q8
- cartridge Q12
- cash register Q8
- caterer Q20
- centerpiece 53-55
- ceramic 186-190
- certainly 44-46
- challenging Q37
- checkup Q118
- chemistry 141-143
- chronic 44-46
- cite Q134
- claim 47-49, 176-180
- cliff 159-161
- closely 77-79
- cloth Q34
- clothing Q34
- colleague Q154
- college degree Q14
- come up with～ 83-85
- commuter 80-82
- competitor Q93
- complete Q27
- completion 176-180
- complicated Q99
- concise 191-195
- condominium 150-152
- conduct 95-97, 186-190
- confection 144-146
- conference 41-43
- confident 77-79
- confidential 191-195
- confirm Q122
- conflict 56-58
- conservation Q159
- consider 83-85
- consistently 98-100
- construction 62-64
- consulting firm Q92
- consumer 162-164
- contact Q67
- continuity Q89
- contribute Q138
- convenient 62-64
- convention 44-46
- cooperation 155-156
- coordinate 159-161
- copy 65-67
- coral reef 159-161
- correct Q189
- courtyard Q36
- crate Q9
- create Q54
- creature 159-161
- credit 165-167
- creditor Q171
- crew Q117
- critical 89-91
- cross one's legs Q2
- cuisine 144-146
- culinary 144-146
- cure Q97
- currently Q60
- curved Q7
- cut Q168

D

- deal 168-171
- dean 86-88
- debate Q133
- declare Q86
- decorate Q10

- deduction 186-190
- delay Q43
- deliver Q49
- demand Q109
- dentist Q118
- depart 71-73
- department Q29
- departmental Q56
- depend on～ 53-55
- deposit Q32
- describe Q159
- detail 141-143
- deteriorate Q93
- developer Q77
- development Q52, 89-91
- diner 92-94
- diplomat Q102
- direct Q71
- direction Q53
- director 50-52
- disease Q96
- district Q105
- divide 191-195
- document Q48
- documentary film Q125
- donate Q138
- doorway Q10
- drawer Q4
- drive Q126
- due diligence 191-195
- due to～ 71-73
- durable 186-190
- duty 157-158

E

- economics 86-88
- edge Q5
- editor Q98
- editor in chief 172-175
- effective 56-58
- electrical circuit 150-152
- eligible 181-185
- engagement Q61
- enhancement 191-195
- enroll in～ Q140
- ensure Q89
- entice 92-94
- entrance Q8
- entrance exam 172-175
- environment 159-161
- equipment Q11
- establishment Q43
- estimate 59-61
- evaluate Q57
- evaluation Q91
- evenly 186-190
- excess Q137
- exchange Q104
- executive officer Q134
- expansion Q69
- expect Q29
- expenditure 168-171
- expose 147-149

- [ ] extend ... Q94
- [ ] extension ... 191-195
- [ ] extensive ... 159-161
- [ ] extremely ... 77-79

F
- [ ] face ... 77-79
- [ ] facilitate ... 56-58, 172-175
- [ ] facility ... Q42
- [ ] fascinating ... Q35
- [ ] feature ... 77-79
- [ ] female ... 65-67
- [ ] figure ... Q99
- [ ] figure out~ ... 98-100
- [ ] fill in for~ ... 89-91
- [ ] financial ... Q26
- [ ] financial quarter ... Q171
- [ ] find out about~ ... Q164
- [ ] firm ... 50-52
- [ ] first-hand ... Q79
- [ ] fix ... Q2
- [ ] flammable ... Q119
- [ ] flash ... 162-164
- [ ] floral arrangement ... 53-55
- [ ] flow ... Q81
- [ ] fluent ... 181-185
- [ ] for oneself ... 62-64
- [ ] form ... Q19
- [ ] formulate ... Q140
- [ ] fossil fuel ... Q130
- [ ] fragrance ... 196-200
- [ ] fully ... 41-43
- [ ] fund ... Q134

G
- [ ] gain ... 141-143
- [ ] garage ... 155-156
- [ ] gardener ... 157-158
- [ ] gather ... Q3
- [ ] generation ... 176-180
- [ ] generosity ... 157-158
- [ ] get back to~ ... 59-61
- [ ] get started ... 83-85
- [ ] give a hand ... Q27
- [ ] give out~ ... Q199
- [ ] go ahead with~ ... Q120
- [ ] go through~ ... 83-85
- [ ] government ... Q177
- [ ] graduate study ... Q15
- [ ] graduation ... 65-67
- [ ] groceries ... Q8
- [ ] guest ... 153-154
- [ ] guided tour ... 159-161

H
- [ ] handle ... 50-52
- [ ] hands-on ... 77-79
- [ ] happen to do ... 41-43
- [ ] hardworking ... Q153
- [ ] have a conversation ... Q6
- [ ] hazard ... 191-195
- [ ] head ... 56-58
- [ ] head up~ ... 176-180

- [ ] headquarters ... Q105
- [ ] healthcare ... Q133
- [ ] hidden ... Q166
- [ ] highly ... Q183
- [ ] hold ... Q84
- [ ] hop onto~ ... 159-161
- [ ] host ... 53-55

I
- [ ] identify ... Q118
- [ ] immediate ... 186-190
- [ ] immediately ... 150-152
- [ ] imply ... Q173
- [ ] in a row ... Q7
- [ ] in accordance with~ ... 150-152
- [ ] in advance ... 153-154
- [ ] in charge of~ ... 172-175
- [ ] in danger of~ ... 89-91
- [ ] in installments ... Q114
- [ ] in regard to~ ... Q114
- [ ] in the meantime ... 155-156
- [ ] in time for~ ... Q199
- [ ] including ... 147-149
- [ ] inclusion ... 162-164
- [ ] inclusive ... 186-190
- [ ] incomplete ... Q60
- [ ] inconvenience ... 71-73
- [ ] indicate ... 141-143
- [ ] industrial ... Q63
- [ ] industry ... 144-146
- [ ] infer ... Q184
- [ ] inform ... 74-76
- [ ] informative ... 86-88
- [ ] ingredient ... 172-175
- [ ] injury ... 191-195
- [ ] inquire ... Q48
- [ ] inquiry ... 172-175
- [ ] insomnia ... Q97
- [ ] inspection ... 150-152
- [ ] inspire ... 68-70
- [ ] install ... 68-70
- [ ] institute ... 144-146
- [ ] insufficient ... Q96
- [ ] insurance ... Q46
- [ ] intend for~ ... Q98
- [ ] interact ... 56-58
- [ ] interfere with A ... 95-97
- [ ] interruption ... 150-152
- [ ] intersection ... Q6
- [ ] interview ... Q14
- [ ] inventory ... 62-64
- [ ] investor ... Q50
- [ ] issue ... Q35
- [ ] itinerary ... 196-200

L
- [ ] labor ... 147-149
- [ ] lack ... 176-180
- [ ] ladder ... Q1
- [ ] lagoon ... 159-161
- [ ] landscape ... 59-61
- [ ] landscaper ... 157-158

- [ ] lasting ... Q188
- [ ] latest ... 89-91
- [ ] launch ... Q51
- [ ] lecturer ... Q86
- [ ] lie ... Q4
- [ ] lift ... Q9
- [ ] limestone ... 159-161
- [ ] line ... Q127
- [ ] load ... Q9
- [ ] loaf pan ... 186-190
- [ ] locate ... Q60
- [ ] look over~ ... Q85
- [ ] lower ... 168-171
- [ ] loyal customer ... 165-167

M
- [ ] machine ... Q124
- [ ] mainly ... Q37
- [ ] make arrangements for~ ... Q40
- [ ] make it ... Q33
- [ ] make payment ... Q17
- [ ] malfunction ... Q177
- [ ] manage to do ... 168-171
- [ ] management ... Q16
- [ ] mangrove ... 159-161
- [ ] manner ... 176-180
- [ ] manufacturing ... Q11
- [ ] matter ... 89-91
- [ ] measure ... Q1
- [ ] measures ... 191-195
- [ ] meet ... Q128
- [ ] memorable ... 181-185
- [ ] memorandum ... Q134
- [ ] mention ... 56-58
- [ ] merchandise ... Q8
- [ ] merchandising ... 50-52
- [ ] merely ... 89-91
- [ ] mode of payment ... 186-190
- [ ] most likely ... Q41
- [ ] mountaineer ... 159-161
- [ ] moving company ... Q21

N
- [ ] nevertheless ... 186-190
- [ ] nonstick ... 186-190
- [ ] notification ... 141-143
- [ ] notify ... Q71
- [ ] nowadays ... 68-70

O
- [ ] occupy ... Q81
- [ ] occur ... 141-143
- [ ] office supply ... 168-171
- [ ] on a daily basis ... 77-79
- [ ] on display ... 176-180
- [ ] on numerous occasions ... 157-158
- [ ] ongoing ... 162-164
- [ ] opening remark ... Q131
- [ ] operational ... 98-100
- [ ] opportunity ... 83-85

- [ ] option ... Q115
- [ ] orchid ... 74-76
- [ ] organize ... Q16
- [ ] originally ... 186-190
- [ ] out of stock ... Q11
- [ ] outskirts ... Q93
- [ ] overall ... 191-195
- [ ] overcharge ... 165-167

P
- [ ] package ... Q21
- [ ] paint ... Q5
- [ ] painting ... Q10
- [ ] pamphlet ... Q181
- [ ] parasol ... Q7
- [ ] parenting ... Q96
- [ ] parkade ... 155-156
- [ ] partial ... Q97
- [ ] particular ... 147-149
- [ ] particularly ... Q194
- [ ] partner ... 153-154
- [ ] pass ... 80-82
- [ ] passenger ... Q5
- [ ] pastry ... 144-146
- [ ] path ... Q2
- [ ] patience ... 150-152
- [ ] patronage ... 157-158
- [ ] pay ... Q132
- [ ] pediatrician ... 95-97
- [ ] performer ... Q66
- [ ] perfume ... Q199
- [ ] permit ... Q114
- [ ] personal check ... 147-149
- [ ] personnel ... 56-58
- [ ] personnel office ... Q108
- [ ] pharmacy ... Q45
- [ ] photocopier ... Q31
- [ ] physician ... Q46
- [ ] pickup ... 181-185
- [ ] place ... Q10
- [ ] place an order ... Q24
- [ ] plant ... Q38
- [ ] platform ... Q5
- [ ] playground ... 68-70
- [ ] plow ... 80-82
- [ ] policy ... Q114
- [ ] position ... Q14
- [ ] power supply ... 150-152
- [ ] praise ... Q133
- [ ] predict ... 176-180
- [ ] prefer ... Q34
- [ ] preference ... 168-171
- [ ] prerequisite ... Q172
- [ ] prescription ... Q44
- [ ] present ... Q103
- [ ] press conference ... 176-180
- [ ] prevent A from doing ... Q135
- [ ] preventive ... 191-195
- [ ] primarily ... 176-180
- [ ] prime time ... 162-164
- [ ] principal ... Q95

TEST 3 重要語句——索引

☐ proceed 71-73	☐ remain 141-143	☐ solely 191-195	☐ unique 159-161
☐ process Q107	☐ remark 191-195	☐ solution Q27	☐ upcoming Q39
☐ production Q125	☐ remind 80-82	☐ source Q130	☐ update 86-88
☐ productivity Q57	☐ remove Q3	☐ specific 56-58	☐ upsize Q103
☐ professionalism 157-158	☐ renovate Q62	☐ splendid 159-161	☐ urge Q119
☐ profitable Q162	☐ renovation Q69	☐ sponsor Q102	☐ urgent 47-49
☐ promote Q123, Q159	☐ reorganization Q191	☐ stack Q4	☐ utilities 168-171
☐ promotion Q30, Q37	☐ repave 155-156	☐ status 141-143	**V**
☐ proper Q110	☐ replace Q121	☐ steadily 92-94	☐ vacancy 41-43
☐ proposal 83-85	☐ replacement 89-91	☐ stock market Q37	☐ vehicle Q81
☐ proprietor Q197	☐ representative Q164	☐ storage Q62	☐ view Q36
☐ protective Q124	☐ requirement Q128	☐ store Q8	☐ volunteer Q155
☐ provisional 155-156	☐ reservation Q33	☐ strict Q91	**W**
☐ psychologist Q95	☐ residence 150-152	☐ strictly 191-195	☐ waiting list Q109
☐ public relations Q28	☐ resident 95-97, Q115	☐ strike Q132	☐ wander Q135
☐ publication 98-100	☐ resign Q90	☐ study Q8, 95-97	☐ warehouse Q38
☐ publishing company Q112	☐ resignation Q86	☐ subject Q28	☐ warranty 147-149
☐ purchase Q40	☐ resolution 56-58	☐ submit Q79	☐ water fountain Q84
☐ pursue 172-175	☐ Respectfully yours 186-190	☐ subscription 98-100, 165-167	☐ wellness Q191
☐ put away～ Q1	☐ respondent Q193	☐ substance Q119	☐ wonder 181-185
☐ put into effect Q129	☐ responsibility 141-143	☐ successive 172-175	☐ word 196-200
☐ put on～ Q6	☐ restoration Q68	☐ sudden 165-167	☐ work 53-55
☐ put together～ 83-85	☐ restore 68-70	☐ suggest Q43	☐ work in～ Q83
Q	☐ restrict Q81	☐ superintendent 150-152	☐ work load Q91
☐ quarter Q22, Q104	☐ retailer Q196	☐ supplier 74-76	☐ workout Q137
☐ quarterly 168-171	☐ retire 157-158	☐ supply Q74, 168-171	☐ workplace 191-195
☐ quite 50-52	☐ revise Q18	☐ surface 155-156	☐ worsen Q118
☐ quotation Q55	☐ rewarding 176-180	☐ survey Q96	☐ worth it 155-156
☐ quote 74-76	☐ right away Q38	☐ survive Q113	☐ write in Q133
R	☐ risk 176-180	☐ switch box 150-152	**Y**
☐ raise Q22	☐ roadwork Q155	☐ switch off～ Q31	☐ yard 59-61
☐ range 92-94	☐ routine Q137	**T**	
☐ rate Q22	☐ RSVP 153-154	☐ take care of～ 50-52	
☐ rather than～ Q101	☐ run Q25	☐ take over～ 157-158	
☐ reach 162-164	☐ rush 176-180	☐ take steps 165-167	
☐ real estate Q40	**S**	☐ take time off for～ Q153	
☐ rear Q9	☐ sacrifice 92-94	☐ take up～ Q173	
☐ reassign Q90	☐ sales assistant Q136	☐ tax 47-49	
☐ rebuild 68-70	☐ sales representative Q92	☐ tedious Q137	
☐ receipt Q122, 196-200	☐ sanctuary 159-161	☐ temporary Q155	
☐ recent Q130	☐ satisfaction 191-195	☐ tenant Q155	
☐ recently Q78	☐ schedule Q13	☐ terrible 176-180	
☐ reception 74-76, 191-195	☐ sculpture 176-180	☐ text message Q164	
☐ receptionist Q41	☐ secretary Q21	☐ the other day Q39	
☐ recession 86-88	☐ secure 98-100	☐ thought Q107	
☐ recipe 172-175	☐ see 44-46	☐ tourist attraction 159-161	
☐ recognition 191-195	☐ sell out of～ 65-67	☐ trade agreement 86-88	
☐ recommend 59-61	☐ severely Q81	☐ trade fair 196-200	
☐ recover lost ground 92-94	☐ share 95-97	☐ traffic light Q6	
☐ reduced Q160	☐ shareholder Q98	☐ transport 62-64	
☐ reflection 89-91	☐ shelf Q4	☐ treasure 176-180	
☐ refund Q73	☐ shipment Q75	☐ trend Q28	
☐ refurbishment Q69	☐ shipping order Q122	☐ truly 157-158	
☐ regarding 86-88	☐ shore Q161	☐ trunk Q119	
☐ regional 80-82	☐ shortly 157-158	**U**	
☐ register for～ Q44	☐ showcase 92-94	☐ unavailable Q60	
☐ registration Q19	☐ signature 144-146	☐ unexpected 176-180	
☐ reimburse 196-200	☐ sit down with～ 59-61	☐ unfortunately 47-49	
☐ relate with～ 56-58	☐ site Q60	☐ union representative Q132	
☐ relative Q50	☐ situate Q63		
☐ relocate Q177	☐ so far 86-88		

新TOEIC® テスト でる模試 600問
別冊 解答・解説 [3] TEST 3

2012年11月 4日　初版　第1刷発行
2014年 4月14日　　　　第7刷発行

著　者　ハッカーズ語学研究所

発行者　天谷 修平

発　行　株式会社 アスク出版
　　　　〒162-8558
　　　　東京都新宿区下宮比町2-6
　　　　TEL：03-3267-6866
　　　　FAX：03-3267-6867
　　　　URL：http://www.ask-digital.co.jp/

ISBN 978-4-87217-808-1